Applied Business Correspondence

APPLIED BUSINESS CORRESPONDENCE

BY
HERBERT WATSON

A. W. SHAW COMPANY
CHICAGO   NEW YORK
LONDON

HF 5726
W25

COPYRIGHT, 1922, BY
A W SHAW COMPANY

©28780

PRINTED IN THE UNITED STATES OF AMERICA

PREFACE

COMPLETELY to cover theory, routine and individual application in a book is of course ordinarily prohibitively expensive. It was possible in the case of this book because the Course in Business Correspondence prepared by Mr. Watson for the A. W. Shaw Company could be drawn on to any extent desired

In the Course Mr. Watson brought together the results of many years of experience of the correspondence experts of the Shaw organization and several years of work which had been undertaken preparatory to publishing a course in business correspondence which would adequately reflect this experience. To this unique background he added the lessons crystallized during the years he had himself specialized in selling and business correspondence. Mr. Watson was formerly in charge of the mail sales departments of the A. W. Shaw Company, has been similarly connected with other concerns, and has for a number of years maintained, in New York, offices as an advertising and sales specialist.

The Course in Business Correspondence amply justified the expectations which this unusual background warranted. Its success uncovered a demand for a similarly comprehensive treatment of the subject, but without consultation privileges and some of the detailed developments only possible in an extended course. The publishers decided to supply this demand by drawing together into this book the necessary text from the Course itself.

To the reader not interested in undertaking a supervised course in business correspondence, this book therefore supplies several of those distinctive characteristics of a course of study ordinarily not to be expected of a book. It contains complete machinery for the application, step by step, of its exposition. The division in the treatment is in fact so marked that the portion of the text providing specific application can be skipped, and the exposition alone—in itself a complete book on business correspondence in the usual sense of the expression—read for purposes of review or coverage of the subject in the usual way.

In connection with the provisions for application, each section is followed by problems. These problems are obviously specific assignments of work intended merely to make clear the application of the principles discussed in the text. They are in no way to be confused with the fundamental and illustrative type of problem characteristic of the case method of instruction used in the group of books now being written by members of the faculty of the Harvard Graduate School of Business Administration and published by the A. W. Shaw Company. The headings of the letters reproduced illustratively have been in the majority of instances informally set up without any attempt to indicate the actual 'letterheads involved. In many cases they for obvious reasons contain fictitious names. The final application section was written by W. S. Zimmerman, formerly Director of the Educational Division of the A. W Shaw Company.

CONTENTS

PREFACE   v

PART I

SIZING UP THE WORK YOUR LETTER MUST DO   1

    Getting the right start for the study of letter writing —The importance of mastering each point as it comes up.—Knowing before you start what purpose you want to accomplish —How to size up the complete "load" which your letter must carry —Gaging the "self-interest" of the man you are writing to.—Turning ideas into words —How to overcome the indifference or opposition of the reader to your idea.—What to avoid using in your letter —Determining your prospect's attitude to your proposition —The method of approach.—When it is necessary to inspire enthusiasm —The creation of self-interest —Why a successful letter writer must carefully analyze and lay out his problem before starting.—Combining the theory and practise of letter writing.

PART II

EXPRESSING FEELING OR IDEAS IN WORDS   51

    The fundamentals of the art of good letter writing —Making your prospect visualize your product —The negative effect of unsupported statements —The underlying principle of good letters —How to establish the "big idea" of your letter.—Picking the "features" of your letter —Connecting the "features" with the "big idea."—How atmosphere is secured. —Why some letters grasp your attention —The reason one letter failed —Changing a poor letter into a good one —An example in picking "features."—Simple language as a strong point in letter writing —How to avoid jarring the thought of your letter out of the reader's mind—Applying these principles to other letters —Points to be considered when writing a complaint letter.—How to build up a feeling of satisfaction —A good collection letter and how it was written —A plan for overcoming indifference —The indirect approach and how to build it up

BUSINESS CORRESPONDENCE

PART III

OVERCOMING INDIFFERENCE OR OPPOSITION   107

How to overcome the weakness of the buyer —Two great orations, Abraham Lincoln's Gettysburg address and Ingersoll's nominating speech for Blaine· how they help the letter writer —The consideration given to the attitude of the audience —A comparison of the orations with two successful business letters —The negative argument in letter writing — A practical test of a negative argument.—Examples which show how to meet the reader's attitude.—Two letters which failed, and why —Consideration of the "willing" and "unwilling" types of reader —The "big idea" and "features" in a visionary appeal —Analyzing the construction of the negative idea — Its use in a good collection letter —How to win over an indifferent reader.—Underlying methods of a glove dealer's successful letter —Breaking down dealers' indifference.—An exception which proves the rule —Using the visionary idea in a successful dealer's letter, a result-pulling sales letter, and a subtle collection letter —A sales series, and how it can best be handled —An analysis of the first four letters of a collection series

PART IV

HOW TO MAKE YOUR MEANING CLEAR   179

Why the reader will not translate a jumble of words into ideas. —How to avoid "waste-basket editions" in letter writing — The importance of using the right word —Arranging and stacking your ideas logically —Herbert Spencer on "The Philosophy of Style "—How to express the idea so that it will live in the reader's mind.—An analysis of Victor Hugo's greatest description.—Utilizing Hugo's "arrangement of features" in a successful sales letter.—The principle of piling small ideas on big ones in letter writing —Victor Hugo's idea applied to a matter-of-fact letter —Working your |prospect up to an appreciation of your proposition —How to group ideas for easy reading —Holding the reader's attention by saving his mental energy —A collection letter which builds up a powerful picture by suggestion.—An example where wide gaps between the "features" ruined the letter —Avoiding short letters which leave too much mental work for the reader — Lincoln's statement that a man's legs should be "long enough to reach the ground" applied to letter writing —Being sure that the letter actually carries the complete "load," as a principle for determining length —Choosing the right

CONTENTS

words.—Why the language of a letter should be determined by what you are writing about and to whom you are writing.—What Spencer has to say regarding the choice of words —Learning from Edgar Allan Poe how to select words —Acquiring style through a self-compiled dictionary of your business trade terms —How to build such a word file.—Where to find the words —An easy method for sorting your ideas.—How to use the word file with the least effort

PART V

How to Make Your Letter Sincere 243

Why readers often fail to believe the truth when it is written.—Reasons why some people find it easy to win the confidence of others.—Creating friendliness in a letter —How the point of contact helps letter writers —Bookish theory boiled down to practical business principles —What the letter writer can learn from the salesman —How to put over the impression of a strong, sincere, winning personality —Analyzing the typical complaint letter —A successful answer to this letter —How to arrive at a basis of mutual understanding —A sales letter which attracts attention in the first paragraph —An example of a letter which beams with frankness and sincerity.—Personality as a personal quality, how to develop and use it in your letters.—How successful letter writers make their personality felt.—Why the "you" in letters sometimes is a mixed blessing.—The fault with "you" in many letters —Turning the "you" in a letter to your own use —Sizing up the "load" of the typical "you" letter problem.—Making "your interest and mine" the connecting link —A successful appeal to human nature —How dividing the Big Idea into "features" makes interests mutual —Why sizing up the "load" is helpful —Why a human appeal gets results —A letter that won a good job in spite of strong competition.—The importance of understanding the prospect's doubts.—Copy which pulled 36% returns, and the reason behind it —The thought behind it.—The thought behind Mr. Root's appeal to the Russian people —The same thought applied to a simple business letter.—Applying this principle in the letter to "Smith"—Putting mutual understanding and sympathy in the very first line —Getting "Smith" in a receptive mood for your thought —Clinching the thought of your sincerity in "Smith's" mind.—Building a credit man's letter on the same idea —A garage man's letter which reflects a keen personality —Putting both dignity and good fellowship in letters.—The knack of sincerity, and how anyone can cultivate it.

BUSINESS CORRESPONDENCE

PART VI

How to Make Your Letter Persuasive   291

How to start the motive power which makes a prospect act — Human actions and the influences which prompt them — Using persuasion to arouse a *motive* for action — The difference between motives and ideas — A sales letter, and why it failed. — Turning the love motive to business uses — The six motives from which all human action springs love, gain, duty, pride, self-indulgence, self-preservation — Determining whether a letter carries persuasion or not — Using curiosity as a motive — Billy Sunday's use of the six prime motives. — Sunday's methods applied to an everyday business problem — How to find "fuel" which will arouse a motive for acting. — The effect of mixing "fuel" with the "features" — Using imagination as "fuel" in a collection letter — Mystery, and how it may be worked up to get results — How the Self-Indulgence motive can be used — Why a classification of motives helps to write a letter — A system built upon the same principle — Determining the quantity of motive "fuel" a persuasive letter requires — A successful sales letter and why only a little "fuel" was used — How to write collection letters that get results — Applying the "motive" principle to a sales letter series — How to select the best motive for a letter — Why the Self-Preservation motive is the most difficult to arouse — The best method for attracting the slow-pay customer — Distinguishing between the idea that the reader is to be sold on, and the motive that persuades him to sign the order

PART VII

How to Make Your Letter Get Action   349

Impulse and the part it plays in making people act — How salesmen make use of the old circus idea for securing action — How to determine whether or not the close of a letter is effective — How suggestion generated action in one sales letter — Why one collection letter pulled in the money — An unsuccessful close which made it possible for the reader to side-step the issue — Why a "let-down" at the close spoils a letter — How a purchasing letter put its idea across — Making it hard for a reader to decline the action desired — Closing a sales letter — How the reader was made to act — A slight change in a collection letter which increased results by 80% — A letter which won a good job for an advertising man — Building up a close for a successful sales letter. — How the reader's fear of

CONTENTS

losing a good opportunity was aroused.—How to analyze your proposition.—The final action desired, the motive, the preliminary job, the easy connecting path —How to use this analysis in everyday work.—A letter worked out on this principle that secured women sales agents by the score — Using the idea to secure dealer cooperation.—How to insure that your reply blanks come back to you —Why the enclosure should be given as careful consideration as the letter —A good plan to follow when specifications are part of the order.—How to make legal requirements simple—Other ways of putting a punch at the close of your letter

PART VIII

How to Make Your Letter Grip Attention   397

The importance of the beginning of a business letter —How to attract and hold the reader's attention in your form letters —A follow-up letter which gripped the attention of its reader —Insuring that the busy man reads your letters by putting yourself in his place —The two elements to be considered when planning attention-grippers: the receiver's attention, the idea to which his attention must be led —How the busy reader may be led to pick out your letter —Gaging the attention-rays, of your reader —The second step in building up grippers selecting the "feature" of your letter which can most easily be built up to constitute a stopper —A stopper which drew the attention of women readers.—Two letters and two stoppers compared: why one was a success and the other a failure.—The four principles of getting attention.—A practical test of these principles —Linking up a stopper to the Big Idea of a sales letter —How a good opener overcame a weak close.—How to choose an attention-ray.—One "don't" to keep in mind as you work up an opener: never attract attention merely for the sake of attracting attention.—The idea behind an opener that lined up book lovers —Gripping the attention before the prospect begins to read.—Adapting the idea of the stopper to the envelop —Why unique and original schemes are not always necessary or best —An example of how the "features" of a letter may be used as openers —How an appeal to women was based on a feature —The importance of limiting your appeal so as to attract the essential attention-ray of your letter.—A useful idea on hunting the possible attention-rays of readers.—How "fuel" for the motive may also be used —Bringing your appeal into prominence at the very start of your letter.—A final suggestion regarding the building of attention-stoppers

BUSINESS CORRESPONDENCE
PART IX

PLANNING LETTERHEADS, ENVELOPS AND ENCLOSURES   451

The mechanics of the letter: new ideas on enclosures —The purpose of the letterhead —How it developed —A first consideration are your letterheads and envelops safe, efficient vehicles for carrying the "loads" of your letters?—A simple letterhead how, when and where to use it —Considering the letterhead and envelop from your own viewpoint —Establishing confidence by our letterhead and envelop —Building up or protecting reputation —When a decorative effect is desirable —How to specify the work of designing correspondence forms —Charting the work your letterheads ought to do —A practical test in laying out a sales letterhead —Questions to ask yourself when you face this problem —An answer to the question "Should officers' names have a place on the letterhead?"—How to make type and paper reflect your personality. —Facts which are often needed on a letterhead —The science of efficient stationery applied —Simplicity, as an ideal to be striven for, when working out a letterhead —Special letters which require an out-of-the-ordinary make-up —The rule to apply as you design the card for an envelop.—The cover to use for circular letters and special mailings —When varying the character of the stationery pays.—How to decide on the size and shape of letters and envelops —The three types of enclosures missionary, reenforcement and selling —Missionary circulars and the purpose they serve.—Reenforcing a letter by the use of a special circular.—Selling enclosures and how they may be put to work —Viewing your business as a whole when enclosures are planned —Increasing sales through using a series of circulars —New ways to reenforce a selling letter — Why many enclosures stuffed in letters fail to get results — When enclosures will fail in their purpose —Booklets which will increase the returns on a sales letter —A chart which helps analyze the needs of a sales letter —A chart which helps analyze the needs of a letter —How to use the chart —A fundamental to base the plan of the circular on —Giving the Big Idea first consideration —Selecting "features" that will reenforce the sales letter —How to figure the costs on an enclosure —A plan which helps when cutting costs is necessary — Mechanical layout: the first steps in making a dummy.—How to meet the mental process of the reader —Making it easy for the reader to get the idea of your copy.—How to route the attention of the indifferent prospect —Prices and other ways of reenforcing the text.—Meeting the natural question of the prospect.—How to get an artistic balance —When it will pay

CONTENTS

to disregard the rules of the artist —What the layout man can learn from his salesman.—The value of putting the Big Idea squarely up to your reader —Contrast, and how it should be used to get the best effect —The use of colors from a business point of view

PART X

Organizing Correspondence Work and Testing Letters   501

The first principles of producing a letter and its enclosures —Using with greater effectiveness the letters you write —The first steps in organizing the letters used in a business —Increasing your letter-writing facilities as the business grows and develops.—A one-man-business organization chart for handling letters —How a form paragraph system is gradually developed.—Organizing the routine for easy handling of letters to carry the same "features"—Putting a word file to use —A simple index which lightens the work of the dictator —The simplest method of using a system of form paragraphs —Some plans of indexing to be avoided —An outline of a thoroughly successful indexing scheme —Where and how to begin organizing a form-paragraph system —Why a study of old letters will suggest Big Ideas on which to build —Your next step picking "features" and visualizing them —Getting the right "openers" for your form letters —How to find the reader's mental attitude and the approach to it —Fundamental types and why it pays to hunt for them —How to work over and standardize paragraphs for form letters —Methods of indexing which may be adapted to your system —When a system of paragraphs will save money —How to reduce letter writing to automatic routine —Using forms in smaller businesses as an aid to dictation —Dictating from forms to speed up production of routine letters —Form-letter systems and how they help to meet standard needs —How to handle complaints, inquiries and collections with letter forms —Building the routine for circular-letter systems —The first step to take in testing a letter for pulling power —Little errors which testing will help to disclose —How the test will increase profits or stop losses —How practical ideas are brought to light —What a series of tests on a list of bankers disclosed —How a local selling campaign indicates the trend of the market —A way prices and policies may be tried out —How to profit by the facts that a test brings to light —Analyzing results and checking up on the mailing

BUSINESS CORRESPONDENCE

PART XI

MATERIALS FOR LETTERS AND USES FOR THEM   543

How to find new uses for your letters and material for them — The conditions which determine mailings of business letters — A simple principle. why a letter which will accomplish some definite benefit greater than its cost should be the controlling factor in deciding on a mailing.—The real reason why some circulars fail to get results —One way of making letters to the trade bring in orders —An Idea Record, and how it can be used in any business —How live ideas may be merchandised within the business —A chart which shows how letters can help your business.—Seven generic types which include all business letters.—Analyzing to find new uses for your circular matter —Final touches that make the chart a help to the advertising man.—How the chart of ideas can be put to permanent, practical use —How an Idea Record is used by an automobile distributor.—Classifying the field for circulars and for advertising copy —How an Idea Record will suggest new plans for publicity —Suggestions for using old ideas in new ways.—How an Idea Record turned failure into success for one firm.—Putting the Record to work: where the ideas come from —How the store owner may profit by using the chart — An answer to the question, "What Shall I Write About?"—A banker's experience in making letters bring in new depositors. —Where to get ideas for the letter you have to write —A "scout letter" which helped to bring in new ideas —How a laundry secured new ideas for letters —How to build up and maintain representative mailing lists.—The sources of lists for any going business directories, lists compiled by houses in allied but non-competing lines, lists sold by regular list houses —How references to permanent lists may be made easily —The importance of retaining the identity of individual lists —Keeping the mailing lists weeded out and up to date.—How to apply the "clean-up" mailing idea to your list.

INDEX   595

PART I

SIZING UP THE WORK YOUR LETTER MUST DO

CHAPTER I

SIZING UP THE WORK YOUR LETTER MUST DO

THERE is but one good place to begin a study of the writing and the use of business letters, and that is at the very beginning.

Probably most of us could write a pretty fair letter right now for almost any purpose. Doubtless many of us could write a masterpiece for some purposes. But there is something that all of us aren't so well versed in as we want to be or we wouldn't be studying. There is something that *every last one of us lacks* or we would be supermen at writing. So we shall begin at the very beginning of good letter writing and *master each point as it comes up,* just as if we knew nothing at all about it now. In that way we shall be sure not to skip one thing or fifty things that each of us needs.

We shall begin as far down on the ladder as, let us say, the first step a retailer must take when he wants to write a letter to his jobber ordering a single barrel of sugar—about as simple a matter as we can conceive of for a letter. And then we shall go on to the time when the same grocer wants to order 20 barrels, some to be shipped on one date, some on another, and the balance to be held for orders—not quite so simple.

We shall see what he must do when he wants to write a letter that will get his order for 100 barrels filled after the jobber's credit man has cut him down to smaller purchases because of his credit. We shall see what he must do when instead of writing letters to order goods—which are letters anyone is glad to get and attend to—he wants to write *letters that will sell goods,* and those are letters people are not so eager to get and read.

BUSINESS CORRESPONDENCE

And so we shall go from the letters of a retailer to those of wholesaler, banker, real estate man, manufacturer or any other business man; from letters which sell or collect to letters which satisfy complaints; from letters which inspire a dealer or salesman to letters which win a job, from one point to another, clear through the field of letter writing, learning as we go how to arouse interest, impart confidence, and win cooperation, up to persuading people to buy something they had not considered buying, or to pay bills they had shown a disposition to postpone or maybe to dodge paying altogether.

By taking one point at a time just as it comes up in the natural order of things, beginning with the simplest and most obvious, *each point* in its turn will be equally *simple and obvious.*

Now then, starting at the beginning, what is the first thing to do in writing any business letter?

Obviously, it is to be sure we know, before we start to write, what purpose we want to accomplish. That's elemental, but that is just why we start with it. *It's the one thing we can all agree on,* and from that one point *the whole structure of how to write letters* will be built.

In other words, when you write a letter to anybody for any purpose, the job, reduced to primary elements, is to put something that you

  —*Know*   —*See*   —*Believe*   —*Feel, or*   —*Want*

into words and phrases that when signed, mailed, and delivered to the one you write to, will be

  —*Read*   —*Understood*   —*Believed*
  —*Agreed with, or*   —*Acted upon*

Your letter may be about only a barrel of sugar that you want a jobber to ship you; it may be about the way you want the sugar shipped; it may be about the belief you have that a certain prospective customer will find your prices lower than others; it may be about the fact that your machine will

THE WORK YOUR LETTER MUST DO

save time or labor for a prospect; it may be about a feeling you have that a certain debtor either must pay his bill at once or be sued.

But whatever it is that you know, see, believe, feel, or want, you can't make *the one to whom you write understand* it unless you first get it clear in your own mind—not a bit more than you can make a jobber understand what goods to ship you if you don't make either a written or a mental list of them before you write your letter.

Isn't that true?

You say, perhaps, "Why, no sensible person would write a letter without knowing why he is writing it."

But you are wrong.

Many men do. Not intentionally, of course, and not always completely. But often a man writes with only the bare "high spots" of his letter in his mind, and, by not having settled in detail *all that he wants his reader to understand* or to believe, or to agree with, or to act upon, he omits some small but vital point that leaves his letter open to misconstruction.

For instance, suppose Smith wrote you and asked you to lend him $100 and, after having thought it over, you decided that you trusted Smith implicitly and were glad to be able to lend him the money. A *good letter* to Smith will not merely convey the news that a check is enclosed, but will convey *that decision of yours—that trust which you feel* for Smith and that *gladness you have* at being able to lend him the money. That is what may be called *the "load" your letter must carry.*

Every letter has a certain "load" to carry—whether it be a letter ordering goods, complying with a request, asking a favor, enclosing a catalog, answering an inquiry, soliciting an order, asking payment of a bill, settling a complaint, following up a prospect, inspiring a salesman or a dealer, or trying merely to create good will, or any other kind of letter. Indeed, every advertisement has its "load." So has every sales talk and every speech.

BUSINESS CORRESPONDENCE

SPENCER HEATING COMPANY
General Offices
SCRANTON, PA

A. L. Wallace,
Chicago
Dear Sir

    Enclosed you will find the heater booklet you asked for

    Heaters often LOOK alike Heater claims may SOUND alike to anyone not personally conversant with the various makes But once see a Spencer in operation — once talk with the man who OWNS or RUNS one, and you will ask yourself these questions

    Why should any reasonable man buy a boiler requiring the large expensive sizes of coal, when the Spencer will give steadier, more even heat with the fine cheap sizes of Pea and Buckwheat #1?

    Why buy a surface feed boiler which will supply a varying temperature, when the Spencer will maintain a steady even temperature all day, and all night if desired?

    Still more, in the mild weather of the Spring and Fall, you can run half the Spencer boiler and secure all the heat you need with minimum fuel cost.

    Why should I be expected to shovel coal every three or four hours, when I can get a Spencer which will require coaling but once a day in ordinary weather, and twice in severe?

    In short, you will not consider seriously any boiler but the Spencer once you thoroughly realize what "Spencer Service" is.

    Our Chicago office, in the Railway Exchange Building, will take pleasure in giving you further details Will you not avail yourself of their advice on this important question of heating?

    Yours for Efficient Heating,
                        SPENCER HEATING CO

Panel 1

A GOOD LETTER

Above you find the first of a series of powerful, effective business letters which form an integral part of this book on applied business correspondence In this first chapter we do not deal with the actual writing of letters, but we do supply a number of examples to illustrate the fact that sizing up a letter's "load" is the first work of any correspondent

THE WORK YOUR LETTER MUST DO

NATIONAL LEATHER COMPANY
Office of the President
GRANDVIEW, OHIO

H. B Willis,
Waukesha, Wis.

Dear Sir

Answering yours of the 15th:

Are enclosing herewith descriptive booklet which may prove of interest and assistance in supplying your wants We have illustrated and described some of our leading styles, but if you do not find the style or kind of Pad wanted, please bear in mind we make a great many others The booklet also contains other valuable information for owners of horses.

In reference to prices we would refer you to your nearest harness dealer. That class of trade as well as many retail hardware and also general stores handle Pads. If your dealer is not in position to furnish what is wanted, please give us his name and address and we will co-operate in seeing that your wants are cared for It will be much more satisfactory, and economical as well, for you to secure the Pads in the manner proposed rather than attempt shipping from here Transportation charges on small lots are very much higher proportionately than when shipped in larger quantities.

Are confident you will find our goods satisfactory in every respect Our aim has always been to maintain a high standard of quality and workmanship and our registered trade-mark, Rex, as branded on our Pads, is a guarantee of such The word Rex is stamped plainly on the side of the Pad and unless it is stamped thereon is not genuine Insist upon your dealer furnishing this kind of Pad and accept no other.

Yours truly,
NATIONAL LEATHER COMPANY

Panel 2

A BAD LETTER

Above is a letter which failed utterly to sell its product Do you see why? If not, this book on applied business correspondence will show you There's a big lesson for you in this letter and the one on the opposite page When you finish the text in this chapter, turn back and read them in the light of what you have just learned In later chapters we'll refer you to them.

BUSINESS CORRESPONDENCE

For that reason, just as a shipping clerk sizes up the load to be shipped before selecting the packing and wrapping materials, so a good letter writer or ad writer or salesman or speaker should first size up the "load" his letter or advertisement or speech is to carry. And he can't be too sure that he has the "load" clear in his own mind before he attempts to select words or enclosures with which to impart it to someone else.

Surely we are all agreed on that much. Some of you may think it too plain, too obvious. It is elemental, but it's the step at which good letter writing begins.

This first panel you will find is the beginning of a wonderfully helpful chart which is to be built up in the pages which follow. With this chart as a background, every step from checking the most subtle sales letters of great national advertisers to studying the most powerful collection letters of the shrewdest collection men will be as clear and easy as this first step.

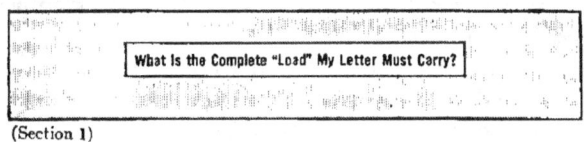

(Section 1)

Panel 3

After you have laid out in your mind, or on paper, what *thoughts or facts or decisions* you want your reader to get, as Panel 3 above suggests, then, like the shipping clerk sizing up the case or the kind of packing or quantity of padding to use on his load, it is time for you to size up:

—*How willing* the man you write to is going to be *to read* your letter.
—*How hard* it will be for him *to understand* your letter.
—*How readily* he will *believe* your letter.
—*How quickly* he will *agree* with your letter.
—*How ready* he will be *to act* on your letter.

That follows quite naturally.

THE WORK YOUR LETTER MUST DO

Of course, if there is nothing you want the reader to act upon, dismiss all bother about that step. If what you say has nothing about it that needs the reader's agreement, dismiss that part. If there is to be nothing about what you say that might be doubted, dismiss that part. The same is true as to his understanding it or reading it. But you should always decide on these points before you start to write or dictate.

As to how willing a man is to read your letter: in the case of a grocer sending an order to a jobber, or in the case of a letter to your friend Smith conveying the decision that you trust him and are glad to lend him the money he asked for, anyone can see how foolish it would be to waste much effort on attracting the reader's attention, or holding his interest. The "load" of such letters is a light one in this respect, as Smith is eager to have your reply, and any merchant is eager for orders. Therefore in the first jobs of letter writing to which we come, *the problem of getting letters read* is merely a matter of having them properly addressed, stamped and dropped in the mail box

But you can easily see that if Smith, instead of being a personal friend, were merely a casual inquirer for your catalog or if the grocer were writing to a list of residents in his city whose trade he wanted, then you couldn't be so sure that the letters would be read. Such letters should be started in a way that *will draw the readers into them.*

So now you can see that the second thing to do, before you can write a good letter, is to consider the *person to whom you are writing*, your relations with him, and just how much *self-interest* he will feel when he sees a letter from you; and so we can add a step to the chart which we are building, and Panel 3, with the addition, will look like the drawing on page 12.

Now where do we stand?

For all letters we see that first we must work out clearly what thoughts or facts or decisions our letter is to carry. Then we must size up the position the one to whom we are

BUSINESS CORRESPONDENCE

GEO. STUHLER'S SONS COMPANY
GROCERIES CROCKERY THREE-STORES SHOES AND CLOTHING
MONTICELLO, IOWA

Mr. Henry Williams
Monticello, Iowa

Dear Sir:

If you do as Arnold Bader did - he lives five miles northeast of Monticello on the Bowen road - you will have very little trouble with your clover and you can start a field of alfalfa that will grow.

For three years Mr. Bader had been trying to get a catch of alfalfa and clover. His clover came up better than his alfalfa,- but both were thin in spots. Either they didn't last through the winter - or the scorching sun of July and August burned them out.

Just about a year ago we received our first bottles of Farmogerm which is nothing but a trade name given to nitrogen-gathering bacteria which all clovers and alfalfa demand, if they are to succeed.

Mr. Bader used Farmogerm with his alfalfa and clover seed last season. The results were better than we dreamed of. He got three cuttings from his alfalfa. His clover was good and he received from 12 to 14 pounds more of cream a week from the same cattle this winter than he did last. Think of it - 14 pounds more of cream a week from the same cattle!

How Mr. Bader succeeded with these two hard-to-start crops is pretty well explained in the pamphlet enclosed. Be sure to read it. On the first pages you will find why Mr. Bader used Farmogerm - what Farmogerm is - how it is applied - what it will do - and all about it. If your time is worth anything, it will pay you to study this pamphlet.

Figure what a good catch of clover means to you. It means a hay crop of high feed value, that will build up muscle and beef and increase the yield of milk. Clover like alfalfa is a great soil improver - it renovates the soil - it gathers moisture from the deep subsoil below - it adds humus (the same thing you add when you apply manure) - it draws nitrogen from the air and deposits it in the soil. It will build up worn out land besides giving you a valuable hay crop. Read what the U.S. Department of Agriculture has to say about Farmogerm and soil transfer on pages 4 and 5 of the pamphlet.

Farmogerm is clover and alfalfa insurance. Figure up the cost of putting in a crop - the work - the time - the cost of clover and alfalfa seed. And then figure out how much you actually lose if you do get a catch and it winter-kills or burns up, or if it comes up thin and you have to plant it all over again.

When Mr. Bader bought his first bottle of Farmogerm, he was in exactly the same position you are. He didn't know whether it would do any good or not. But he knew that something was needed. He realized that it was his soil that was wrong more than the weather and that Farmogerm promised to correct the trouble. Today he is glad he tried it. He is going to use more this spring. And you will feel exactly the same way after you have given it a trial.

To introduce Farmogerm, we are enclosing a coupon check good for 50 cents worth of garden seeds with every bottle. You can mail us your order if you want to. It will receive just as careful attention as if you were here in person trading at the store. It's easy to fill out the order blank. Just put down the kind of garden seeds you want and the number of bottles of Farmogerm.

Yours very truly,

GEO. STUHLER'S SONS CO.

GRS/OT

Panel 4

THE WORK YOUR LETTER MUST DO

Dear Sir.

Such good results were obtained by our customers using Reedman's Nitrogen Fertilizer last year that we have arranged to increase our capacity for production this year   A large proportion of those who used it last year have voluntarily written us giving us an account of increased crops obtained through its use   We have arranged for the production of a larger amount this season and accordingly have decided to reduce the price on larger orders.

In the future our five-acre bottles will be furnished for $6 instead of $9 as heretofore   Fifty acres will be furnished at one time for $55, and one hundred acres at one time for $100. The price for single acres remains the same — and the garden size 50 cents.

It is important that you send us your order as promptly as possible that we may have the nitrogen prepared and shipped from the laboratory to you when you want it.

Spring planting is now coming on, so that you should have the nitrogen on hand, ready for use when the weather is just right. Reedman's Fertilizer is the best and cheapest way for you to increase this year's crops.

We enclose booklet and order blank which we hope you will use now without laying it aside

                          Yours truly,

                          REEDMAN FERTILIZER CO

                              By J. Q R
                              Harding, Ind.

Panel 5

A SUCCESSFUL LETTER AND A LETTER THAT FAILED

By way of contrast, compare this letter with the one on the opposite page used in selling a culture of nitrogen-producing bacteria for use with clover or alfalfa seed. The letter on page 10 sent to 1,500 farmers by a general store in Iowa made 20 sales by mail and brought 150 men in to ask for further information It satisfies all the requirements of a good sales letter   The above letter is from the producer of another brand of nitrogen bacteria   Though his profit from effective letters might have been a hundred times that of the Iowa merchant's, his opening is weak and hackneyed, and his argument unsupported by any evidence   The one selling point which he puts forward is price reduction.

BUSINESS CORRESPONDENCE

writing will take towards our letter; that is, whether he will be willing to read the letter without being teased or surprised or influenced into doing so.

Ordinary business letters, such as regular correspondence with customers, dealers, salesmen, and others, are practically sure to be read. If the reader did not have an interest

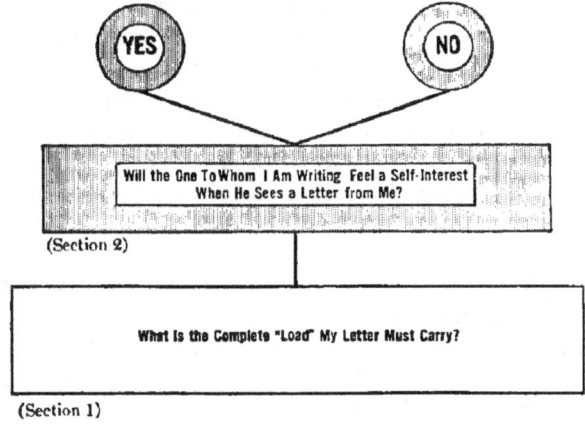

Panel 6

in them they wouldn't be written. There are, of course, many letters in which he won't take a natural interest, but we'll leave that point till later. But be sure that *what we have written will be understood*—why, that, to be sure, is still another matter. Let's make that a little plainer—suppose, in granting the loan to your friend Smith, you simply wrote:

```
Dear Smith:
    Yours received.  Enclosed find check for $100.
        Yours truly,
            Brown
```

Smith might not understand your decision at all. He might think that you begrudged him the money. Remember, your decision was that "you trust Smith implicitly and are glad to be able to lend him the money." That is the "load" of this particular letter, and if Smith does not understand that

THE WORK YOUR LETTER MUST DO

you trust him *implicitly* with the money and are *glad* to be able to lend it, then your letter has not carried its "load" properly.

And that's the trouble with so many letters. Their writers know what they want to say, and, in fact, think they've said it. But the English language is inexact, elusive, and often letters written with the best intentions in the world not only fail to carry their point but do harm, not only fail to smooth out a situation but make it worse.

How *many, many letters fail*—just because *they don't carry the "load."* There is the credit man's letter that fails to carry his sincere belief in the justice of his claim, or perhaps his belief in the debtor's honesty; there's the salesman's letter that fails utterly to carry the big point of superiority in his goods; there's the merchant's letter announcing the arrival of spring styles, written because the merchant really believes he has such an attractive stock that any man will profit by inspecting it, yet getting no further than to convey only a cold or silly "invitation." And in many cases the only fault with the letters has been that the writers failed to express their *ideas or feelings in words*.

That knack of expression is what makes some men's letters have life and warmth, like the heater letter on page 6, while those of other men are but cold typewriting, like the letter adjoining it. That knack in the letter of one business house *refusing* to exchange an unsatisfactory article makes *you feel good toward the house in spite of the refusal*, while the letter of another house, even though *consenting* to an exchange, creates in you a sense of the firm's grudging condescension or its suspicion of your honesty or maybe its feeling that you are a nuisance

That knack makes one letter or one advertisement describing a machine so impress you with the *reality* of the machine's qualities, that you *see* its parts and visualize it in action (as the automobile advertisement at the top of the next page makes you do); while the description of a similar machine in another man's letter or advertisement gives you only a blurred im-

BUSINESS CORRESPONDENCE

Why I Drive a Gladiator

HERE IS ONE MAN'S OPINION of the Gladiator car. He is not a racing driver—not an expert. He is a typical owner—typical of the thousands of hard-to-suit keen buying men who have bought Gladiator cars.

"I bought my Gladiator car eight months ago after a careful investigation of all other standard makes.

"The car sold itself to me without any help from a salesman. I got into it and drove. It was the easiest driving car I had ever handled.

"I rode in the back seat over a particular stretch of road, for example, which I knew made every other car rattle and shake. The Gladiator—here and everywhere else—wiped out the shocks with a long easy swing.

"I knew the company behind the car—knew of the experienced automobile men who had bought up all its stock—figured that here was a permanent, honorable business which would take care of Gladiator owners—if they needed it.

"So I bought the car.

"DURING THE PAST EIGHT MONTHS I have done about ten thousand miles in all weathers—over snow and ice—city and country—in traffic and on the open road. The Gladiator is what they said it was—the car of all cars made to satisfy the owner.

"I like to drive now that I don't have to struggle with controls. My wife likes to drive—now that she has a car she can handle in comfort—and with safety.

"To me it is a positive luxury to know that the Gladiator means road dominance. Not only speed, mind you. I don't want over fifty at most—and that seldom. I want sustained power—so even pace uphill and down—the same easy swing up hills as on the level.

"I want pickup and snap—for my pride and my safety too. There are times when I want to jump *out* of trouble—when I want my motor to snap that car out of a tight bit of traffic at a touch. That's why I drive a Gladiator car.

"It's good. It's as good now as when I bought it. It's a quick alert powerful comfortable. It's a car I'm glad to drive and glad to ride in. I like to show it off to my friends. It meets my needs, day in and day out, with a higher grade of motoring than I had thought possible."

THAT'S JUST ONE MAN'S OPINION. It is typical of thousands. That's characteristic Gladiator "owner talk."

Absolutely the only way the Gladiator can sell itself to you is by personal test in direct comparison with every other car made. The more you know about cars the quicker you will be to get the dominant Gladiator owner features—for your satisfaction.

If the car is what this man says it is you want one. Find out—today.

GLADIATOR MOTOR CAR COMPANY

Dominant Dollar-Value In This Beauty-Car

The new Emperor has shown itself supreme in beauty-value, in performance-value. From this supremacy comes dominance in dollar-value also.

You sense this fact with your first glimpse of the car. Closer study is wholly convincing. The Emperor does dominate in dollar-value. No room is left for doubt.

In January the Emperor became the year ahead beauty-car. Long before by performance it had won distinction as the world's best Four.

A Year Ahead In Beauty

Look about you. Mark the cars you see. In salesrooms and on the street. Try to put them on the same beauty plane with the Emperor. The more you see of others, the higher looms the Emperor.

Beauty is sound value today. Emperor beauty is year ahead beauty. We added 25 style features, many exclusive. Even next year and the next, allowing for new refinements, its style will be good.

That is why beauty in this case is value.

To get this extra beauty this greater value, we increased our production. We built factory additions. We installed new machinery. We invested almost another million in buildings and equipment. To build more cars and absorb the cost of greater beauty without lowering quality.

So you get more than the year ahead beauty-car. You get all the old-time Emperor goodness. You get the year's most brilliant performer.

Holds Its Lead In Performance

The Emperor has won not only over other fours. It has won over sixes, eights, twelves. The new Emperor holds the same supremacy.

Again and again it has demonstrated its superior pulling power in deep mud and stubborn sand on high hills and mountain climbs. Not alone in dealer demonstration but in owner service everywhere.

The Capital-to-Capital tour was a national demonstration. It demanded 20,000 miles of travel in four months. It proved Emperor performance and endurance as these qualities were never proved before.

Facts That Will Prove Themselves

Beauty-value, performance-value, dollar-value. Some cars give you one or another in some degree. The Emperor gives all, in heaping measure.

It is the year-ahead beauty car. It has proved its sheer mechanical ability to dominate in performance. It stands at the top in dollar-value. These facts are unquestioned.

Test it and compare it as you like. We are confident of the outcome.

Panel 7

Good letters and good advertisements are so nearly alike that often good points in one will suggest good points in the other. In this book we will not turn our entire attention to letters. Often we will illustrate the text with advertisements. These are the first. The text explains why they are reproduced

THE WORK YOUR LETTER MUST DO

pression, as does the automobile advertisement at the bottom of the same page.

That knack is what makes some collection letters force you to realize the importance or the necessity or the good grace of sending a remittance at once, while others don't cause you a second's thought.

In short, through all business correspondence—indeed, through all business intercourse, and through all social intercourse, too, whether by correspondence, advertising, salesmanship, or casual conversation—the knack of expressing ideas or feeling in words is of first importance.

What's the use of accommodating a man with a loan and then of making him feel you begrudged it? What's the use of exchanging goods for a dissatisfied customer if you make him feel grouchy towards you by doing it? What's the use of sending a prospect a description of your goods if you don't *make the description mean something to him?* "There is none," you will say and you are right.

In the next part the specific ways by which we can convey an idea so it goes right home to a man or convey a feeling so that it wraps itself, right around a man's heart, will be pointed out. But we must pave the way for it—we must lay the foundations so that no one can misunderstand, and no one can misuse the principle involved.

At any rate, you see now, if you didn't before, that in all letters there is some central feeling or some big idea that must be searched out before you start to write or to dictate. You see how necessary it is, even in such a simple matter as Smith's loan, to have definitely settled in your mind, not only the "load" your letter is to carry—that is, what facts or decisions—but what *specific feeling* or what *concrete idea* you want the reader to get from your letter.

And just remember this. back of every advertisement, back of every newspaper article, back of every short story or long novel, and back of every speech that is worth while, this same principle holds true. Before anyone starts to write or even plans to write, the big idea or feeling must be de-

BUSINESS CORRESPONDENCE

cided upon so that all one says will help to develop it. Panel 8, which is another step in the chart we are building, will help us keep this point in mind. You will find it below.

Now, you see that I had an object in starting with simple affairs such as Smith and his loan, for it is fundamental principles we are after, and it is always easier to

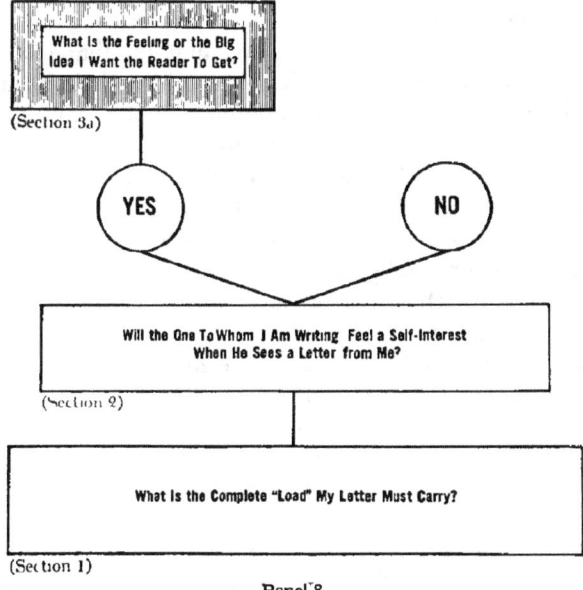

Panel 8

get at fundamental principles of letter writing from a simple letter than from a letter complicated by many individual conditions or circumstances. When we put this Smith letter together *right*, on the right principles, as we shall do later on, it won't be much trouble to substitute a "sample of goods" or an "explanation of an error" or an "offer to exchange" or an "invitation to come in and look over stock" or a "request to look over catalog" or any of a thousand other business letter "loads" in place of your imaginary "loan to Smith." Conditions, words, phrases, and dress will all

THE WORK YOUR LETTER MUST DO

change; but you will see the same fundamental principle used in all—*a principle you can then adapt* to your own letter needs.

Right here a word about this book on applied business correspondence. Be guided by my judgment and experience. You will find many things in this book that you already know. But it is absolutely essential that everything be told in its proper place in order to get all of the points rightly related to one another.

So do not skip anything, no matter how familiar it already is to you. Go through every detail as laid out, from first to last, or better by far waste no time on any of them.

I say this now because so many times I have had new men in my organization—men who were really good letter writers even before they joined me—ask to be excused from the more elementary part of my instructions. But every time the men are excused, trouble follows.

To continue with the charted plan for sizing up letters: When we reached Panel 8 on page 16 we had concluded that after deciding on the "load" and determining the reader's degree of willingness to read that letter, the big idea or central feeling the letter is to convey had to be decided upon. And instantly that brings up the point of whether or not the prospect wants even to consider the Big Idea. Because there are always some who don't.

Remember, we are learning the knack of writing letters for practical business purposes, and not merely to build up ideals. Therefore we must learn to meet and cope with the *difficulties that business letters have to face* in real life. And one of the greatest of these is the attitude of the reader.

He may be already prejudiced against the idea you want to convey—because of habit or inclination. This is often the condition of prospects of a retail store who live or work in another section of town; or prospects of a manufacturer who are accustomed to buying at home; or consumers who are used to cheaper goods.

The reader may be *indifferent to considering your idea*, as in the case of prospects who have already had one or more letters

BUSINESS CORRESPONDENCE

```
STUART H HEIST PRESIDENT                    CHAS H GUMMEY SECRETARY
CHARLES KROPP VICE PRESIDENT                LEE H HEIST TREAS & GENL MGR
```

Blaisdell
PAPER PENCIL CO
WAYNE JUNCTION
PHILADELPHIA

American Sash & Door Co.
16th & Bellefontaine St.
Kansas City, Mo.

OUR PROOF:-   If the altitude of a cone

               Is equal the length of a cylinder

               And the diameter of base of cone

               Is equal the diameter of cylinder

               Then, the cubical contents of cone
               is just one-third that of cylinder.
               Therefore, every time you use a knife or a
               machine to sharpen a lead pencil you lose
               just two-thirds of the lead.

               YOUR PROOF -   Q. E. D.

               Make a comparative test of the
               Blaisdell PENCILS - samples of which
               we have mailed - with wooden pencils
               of equal grades you will find that
               one Blaisdell will outlast two wooden
               pencils. Needle points are not re-
               quired for ordinary work.

                    Yours very truly,
                         Blaisdell Paper Pencil Company

Panel 9

THE OTHER MAN'S WAY

Here is an idea for you Don't miss it even if you do not happen to be in the particular line of business actively involved The value of this book on applied business correspondence lies in the fact that it makes you think The text will tell you how to write letters The illustrations, like the one above, will supply ideas, not to copy, but upon which to build

THE WORK YOUR LETTER MUST DO

```
                    CONGER AND COMPANY
                    MANUFACTURERS' AGENTS
                          HOSIERY

    E  H. Graham & Co.,
    Milwaukee, Wisconsin.
    Gentlemen
            You believe in buying the best and cheapest
    hosiery you can possibly buy, don't you?
            But how about the goods you have been buying,
    were they entirely satisfactory?
            When we started in business we were thoroughly
    convinced that the public cares as much for quality as
    for price, with that belief behind us we selected as
    our motto (QUALITY FIRST) and we think we are right,
    the public does want quality — you want quality in
    whatever you buy.
            We handle (2) grades of 200-N. half hose, made
    from selected combed yarns, (1) grade of 144-N. hose
    looped or sewed toes, in either grades sizes run from
    9 to 11½, also (1) grade of Misses' Ribbed Hose made
    from a frame spun yarn, sizes run from 5 to 9½, put
    up in bundles of 2/12 doz. or (1) doz. boxes, sizes
    in code or regular figure, price, terms, and samples
    will be sent on request.
            Remember that the very life of our business
    depends on giving absolute satisfaction as to price,
    quality, promptness, safe delivery, close attention to
    details and the fair treatment of every customer,
    so we guarantee you satisfaction.
            Please write us, whether you order now or not,
    you are sure to have some questions you'd like to ask,
    and we will be glad to answer them   Let us know
    exactly how we can serve you
            May we look for your letter in the return mail?
                          Very truly yours,
                                CONGER & COMPANY
    DHH/E                        D  H  H
```

Panel 10

BURNING STAMPS

The best thing about the other man's mistakes is that they often show up our own. That's why we print the letter above The writer of it might as well have burned the stamps which carried it Its fault? That's easy The "I" point of view throughout. Later chapters will show you how to substitute for the "I" attitude, the "you and I" attitude.

BUSINESS CORRESPONDENCE

from you without responding; or, as in the case of specialty manufacturers whose prospects think they are getting along well enough without your article; or, as in the case of debtors who have ignored your statements and letters.

You cannot go far in practical business letter writing or in straight selling or in talking to the public in any capacity, without meeting such indifference or opposition; and merely to bombard it with *repetitions* of your original selling idea or collection idea is *wasted energy*

You must consider your reader's position; and when you conclude, either from circumstances or from previous correspondence, that a condition of indifference or opposition

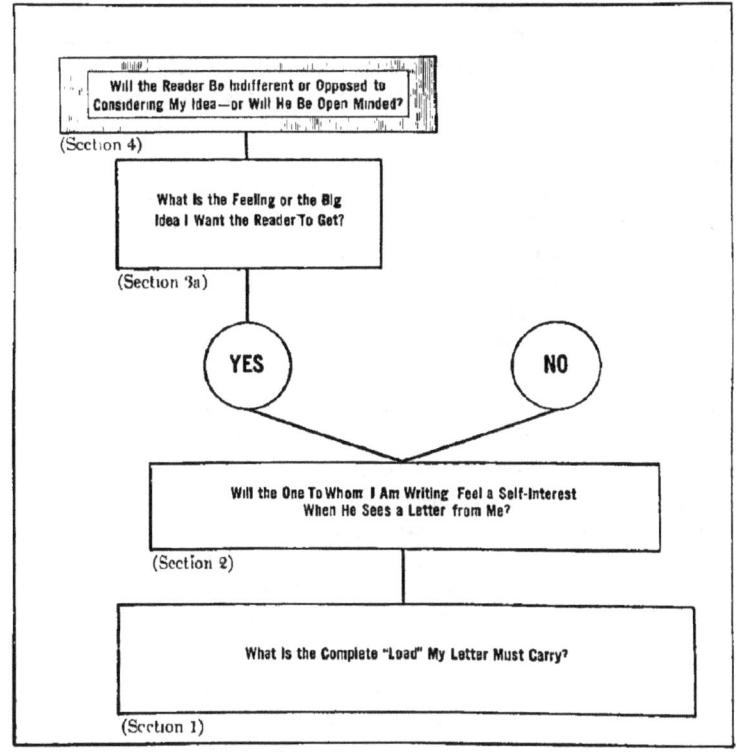

Panel 11

THE WORK YOUR LETTER MUST DO

exists, then your idea should be presented by more indirect or visionary or negative methods for the purpose of *overcoming indifference or opposition.*

Conveying an idea or expressing a feeling in a direct, graphic way will be gone into in detail in the next chapter, as I have said; and then in a further chapter I shall tell you how to put the idea over even to indifferent readers. But before you can grasp the principles to be brought out we must lay down the whole system of letter construction in skeleton form. And so in Panel 11 on the opposite page you'll see another step (Section 4) added to the chart we are building.

The next step, in starting to write, is to make sure that our letter will be understood by the reader. We must, in other words, consider *the nature of the idea or feeling* we want to convey and the amount of mental effort necessary for the person or persons to whom we are writing to grasp it.

Because right away in considering different people, we think of some who can't understand unless things are plain.

Before we start writing or dictating to people about our goods, we must consider how much or how little they know about such goods; before we start to write our motives or reasons for a certain act or desire, we must consider how familiar or acceptable such motives or reasons are.

For instance, in expressing trust and cordiality to Smith in connection with his loan it is easy to be quite clear. But when it comes to letters about merchandise or machinery or service—or anything of that nature—we all have a natural tendency to use trade expressions, descriptive phrases, technical terms, or similes, that mean much to ourselves but little to the person outside the business.

Then, too, it is easy to get so close up to your own business; for details of your proposition to get to be such an old story to you; for those little preliminary explanations that you went over for yourself before you started writing to become such a matter of course to you; in a word, it is easy to be so full of your subject yourself that you go on talking or writing to the other man as though he knew all about your business,

BUSINESS CORRESPONDENCE

or all that had passed through your mind, as well as you know it.

Not one of us but has this trouble, and to avoid it we must, in getting ready to write, size up our reader's knowledge of, or sympathy for, what we are going to say to him. This is an extremely important point, and yet it is so frequently overlooked that it has been made a separate step in the chart which we are building. Notice it in the panel below. Of course, in this sizing-up process which we are learning in

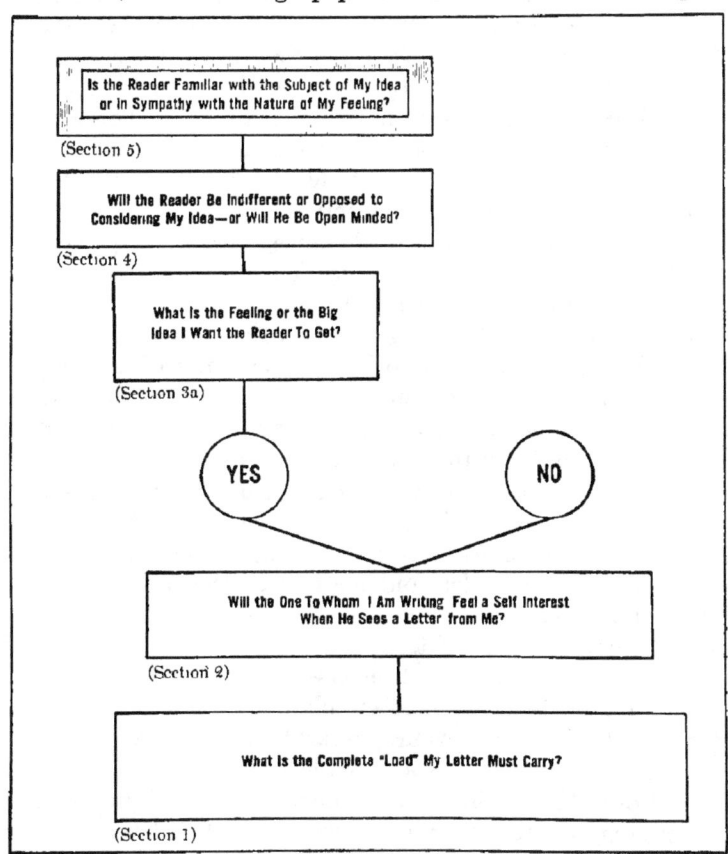

Panel 12

THE WORK YOUR LETTER MUST DO

this chapter we can hardly stop for everything. It is enough to know that this point hasn't been overlooked. In the fourth chapter it will be covered carefully.

We shall learn there how to make use of what we know about the reader; that is, *how to adapt our style or our tone or our phrases or our very words to his understanding* so that we can make our letter appeal to him the way the Stuhler letter shown on page 10 appealed to the farmers it was written to; or we can build up our idea to fit exactly our reader's turn of mind, as does the Blaisdell Pencil letter on page 18. We shall learn from simple, clear principles how so to *construct our sentences and phrases*; so to choose our words, so to *group our ideas*; and so to put together our statements from first to last, that what we write or dictate will mean to the other man, when he reads it, exactly what *we* meant when we wrote it—and can by no chance mean anything else.

Well, we have covered quite a distance, measured by pages of print, and still seem to be only getting ready.

But don't think we are wasting time.

I have found, in organizing the correspondence work of many different businesses, and in training many of the men who have been developed in SYSTEM'S own organization, that the most important part of making effective business writers is training them to analyze their work.

Of course, the preliminary steps I am outlining here are not always necessary for the construction of every letter.

For many letters a quick size-up is all you will need, but even for such letters the order and method of the system now being outlined will give you a more accurate route along which to guide your thoughts.

But for the more important letters—letters involving large issues, or letters to be used in circularizing—you cannot do better than to work out your preparatory steps exactly as they are here set forth. Experience has taught this.

In addition, the outline you are now getting will give you a better grasp on the specific instruction that follows. We shall soon be deep in the mysteries of graphically expressing ideas in words, meeting psychological problems, choosing words, and so on; and such mysteries could never be made simple and clear if we did not have all these steps straight behind us, every one of them based originally on the simplest of letter problems.

Now let us see how far along we are.

If, on the chart we are gradually building up, we were sizing up the work some actual letter had to do, we would know what idea or feeling we had to convey; what steps to take for overcoming indifference or opposition; and what style of language and phrasing to use. In the case of the grocer placing a complicated order for goods, or in the case of granting our old friend Smith his loan, we would be ready to write.

But instead of lending Smith the money, suppose you decided that you trusted him implicitly and would like to accommodate him, but that you couldn't really spare the money. Or, suppose our grocer friend, instead of ordering goods, were about to write a prospect that he could save money or get better goods or more prompt service at his store. Then we would find ourselves face to face with the problem of *not only making our reader understand, but making him believe.*

That is second in importance only to being understood—in advertising, and in selling, and even in ordinary conversation, as well as in correspondence. If only we can make people believe, then our power to sell, our power to collect money, our power to calm irritation, our power to influence by what we write or say, becomes tremendous. But if people don't believe, then our most vivid descriptions, our most alluring offers, our most specious excuses, become as mere "sounding brass or a tinkling cymbal."

You can readily see, in Smith's case, that even if you make your position in not lending him the money perfectly clear to Smith's understanding, unless your style of expressing yourself impresses your sincerity upon him, he may angrily think, "Oh, I know! He's just making excuses—he doesn't *want* to lend me the money."

THE WORK YOUR LETTER MUST DO

Similarly, a dissatisfied customer, after reading your letter of explanation, may say, "Rot! they simply have my money and now don't care whether the goods make good or not!" Or a prospective customer may, on reading a sales letter, think, "Oh, that's what they all say! He probably doesn't have any better goods than anyone else!"

Such conditions arise continually, and hence the safe thing to do before writing a letter is to continue the size-up of your letter problem and see whether or not your letter may have to meet such a reception. So that you can't forget this point, a sixth section has been added to the chart we are building. Notice it in Section 6 on the following page.

Where you see *the possibility of your reader's doubting your assertions* then, in addition to watchfulness over the clearness of your idea, you must exercise care in making your style express sincerity. In the fifth part we shall learn the knack of illustrating our points and clothing our assertions or our arguments, so that they win full confidence and breathe the very spirit and atmosphere of honesty, truthfulness, and sincerity.

This brings us to another important point that should be decided upon in advance.

Suppose that Smith, instead of being just a friend, were a customer whose trade we wanted to hold, and instead of a loan, wanted bigger credit than we felt he was entitled to or good for.

Or, suppose our grocer friend were writing to a customer who had been offended and who had stopped trading with him, and the grocer wanted to win back his trade. Or, suppose we were manufacturers of a machine or a piece of merchandise, and a prospect thought our price was too high, or that we took too long to deliver.

Business correspondence is full of such conditions which must be met—conditions that require letters which not only put over the big idea and get it believed, but get it agreed with. And in the sixth chapter we shall take up the writing of such letters, and *learn the principle of exercising persuasion.*

BUSINESS CORRESPONDENCE

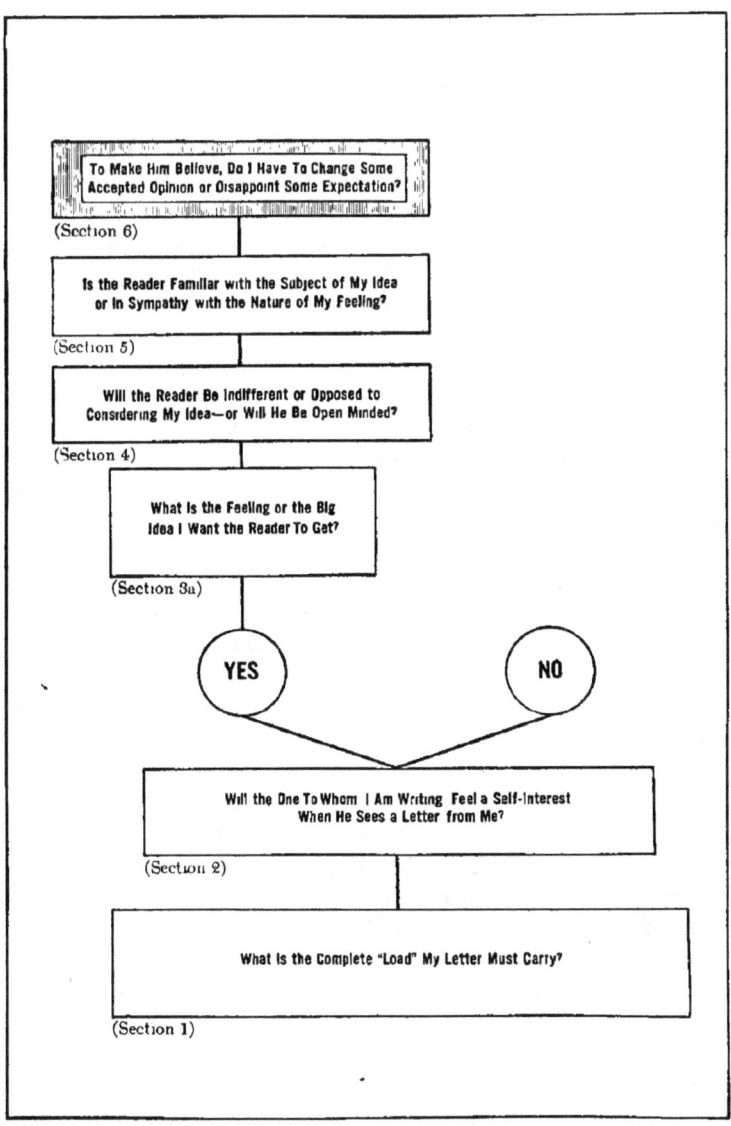

Panel 13

THE WORK YOUR LETTER MUST DO

We no sooner find ourselves masters of the art of exercising persuasion, than we meet the necessity for another faculty in order to get our ideas agreed with. That is *arousing conviction*.

For instance, suppose our old friend Smith is transformed into one of your salesmen—a good salesman, capable of big things, but fallen into a slump or into careless ways. There comes a time when your letters trying to make him see and agree with the advisability of waking up and going to work, must do something more than exercise persuasion—they must arouse conviction.

Or, going back to the fourth step in our chart (Section 4, on page 20) suppose you are writing a sales letter or a collection letter to one of those types you have had to classify as opposed to your idea. You might be a merchant tailor writing to a man, or to a list of men, in the habit of buying ready-made clothes. Or you might be the ready-made dealer going after the buyers of custom-made clothes. You can imagine endless cases under this head.

To get such readers to agree with our idea requires a peculiar twist to our arguments that *makes* them carry hard, cold conviction.*

As it stands now, the chart shows us just what elements our letter is going to require in order to be effective to the highest degree, up to the point of getting some action.

Hence we must now add two elements—persuasion and conviction—that will have to be used in many letters—sometimes one and sometimes the other. So to know when to use either we must size up our letter's load from the angles called for in Sections 7a and 7b in Panel 14, which you will find on the next page.

Before we attempt to shape finally, not only the close of the letter, but its whole general policy, we should determine whether *the "load" of the letter requires a specific action*. Too many writers leave the whole matter of getting action until

---

*How to put that twist into your letters is explained in a later chapter from the bottom up, until it is made as simple as the very first step we took at the beginning of this chapter

BUSINESS CORRESPONDENCE

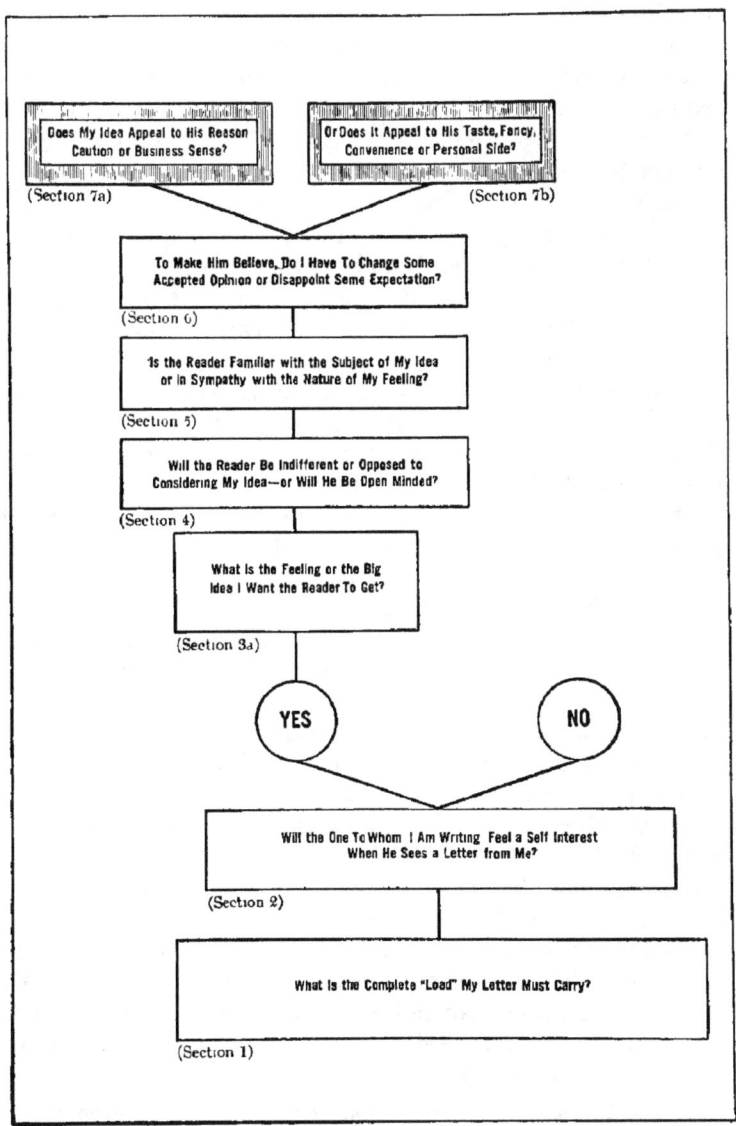

Panel 14

THE WORK YOUR LETTER MUST DO

the close, when it might be much more effective if the whole framework of the letter were adapted to lead up to it.

This is particularly true where the action desired is one that requires sustained willingness for it on the part of the reader. Take letters from manufacturers or wholesalers to their dealers to enlist cooperation, or to encourage the use of a window trim or the distribution of advertising matter; or, take letters to consumers seeking to make them ask their dealers for a particular brand of goods; or, take letters to salesmen to promote greater efforts—all of these cases, and many other similar ones that you can easily imagine, require the *knack of inspiring enthusiasm*.

And you cannot inspire enthusiasm by writing the body of your letter in a plain, matter-of-fact way, depending on a "ginger up" or "hurry up" paragraph at the end to carry over this part of the load. Your whole style must be adapted to it. Enthusiasm should be incorporated into your efforts at persuasion—into every paragraph and every sentence of a letter. Moreover, these points should be decided in advance.

Where the action is definite, one that can be decided and completed at once—as in returning an order card, writing a letter, or sending a remittance—it need not always be mixed through the whole letter—it need not always demand the inspiration of enthusiasm—often such things are entirely out of place. A subtle psychological "push" is the best "puller" of results in many types of letter.*

Action, then, is the capstone of the chart we are building. In Panel 15, on the next page, you see it so placed as a sort of perpetual reminder to us. Now there remains but one step and our chart will be complete.

No doubt you noticed long before this that we have been assuming right along that a letter is sure to be read. Of course, more often than not a writer will have to admit that his prospect will not feel a self-interest strong enough to cause him to be sure to read the letter.

---

*In Part VII we shall get a clear insight into such cases, and into suggestive ways of stimulating action.

BUSINESS CORRESPONDENCE

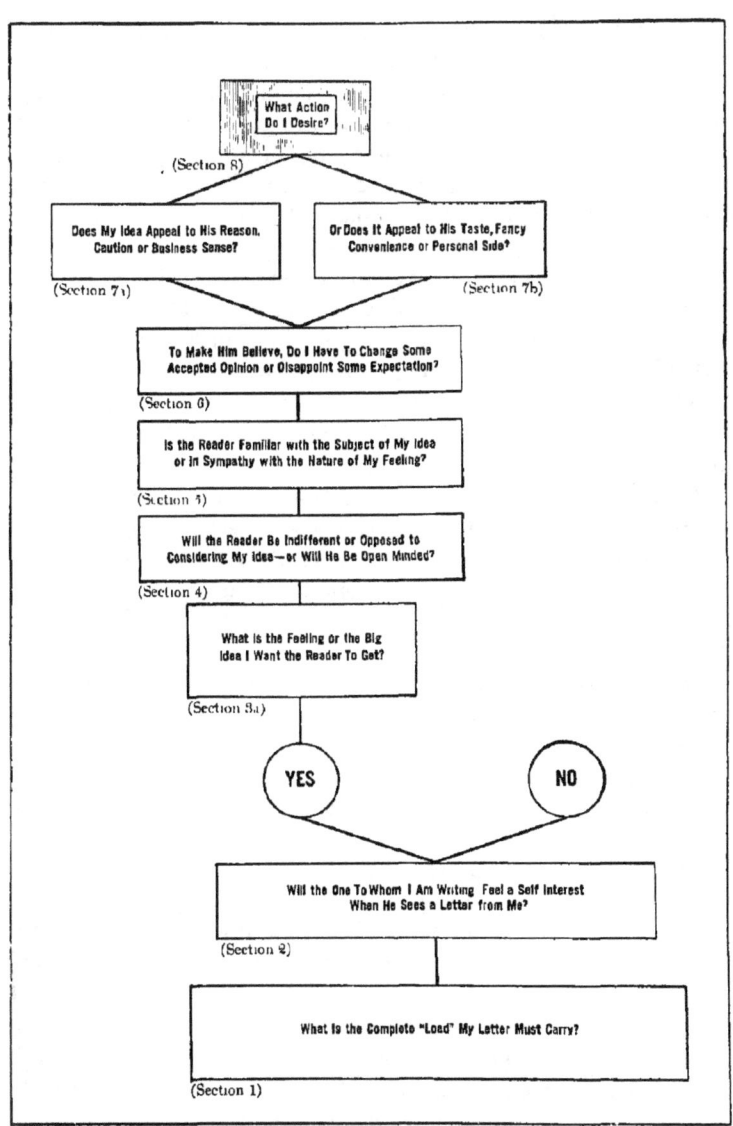

Panel 15

THE WORK YOUR LETTER MUST DO

Smith will eagerly read your letter answering his request for a loan. The man who owes you money will often read your letters, because, even though he doesn't intend to pay he may be interested in what you are going to do. But just suppose that Smith were only one of many customers of yours, and, instead of asking for a loan, had asked for a sample of a certain article you sell. Your decision is to send him the sample and call his attention to its good qualities. In that case you are not so sure he will read your letter—he may merely take out the sample, give your letter a casual glance, toss it aside, and look the sample over from his own viewpoint, totally disregarding what you wanted him to observe in it.*

Or, suppose he hadn't written you at all—that his name merely appeared on a trade list.

Then we must answer "no" to the second question in the chart (Panel 6, page 12) and *create some self-interest* for him in our letter In other words, we must face the job of *gripping attention*. By adding a memorandum to that effect to the chart, (Section 3b) we complete it. You'll find it illustrated on the next page

Don't pass too quickly from this chart. Let all that it graphically calls up sink in. See how it fits your needs, how it allows you to *size up*, in the most thorough, efficient way, that long experience has been able to devise, *practically any letter* that any business proposition which you encounter will require.

All of the factors or elements shown in the chart do not, of course, enter into every letter. But it is of prime importance that you find out—before you start to write or to dictate—which ones do enter into your letter and which ones do not.

And that is why the chart is such a big help. It practically decides for you the "load" your letter is to carry and the conditions it has to meet, before you even begin to think

---

*The knack of finding points of interest that will make your letter stick up over the commonplace of your reader's mail will be worked out in a later part of this book.

BUSINESS CORRESPONDENCE

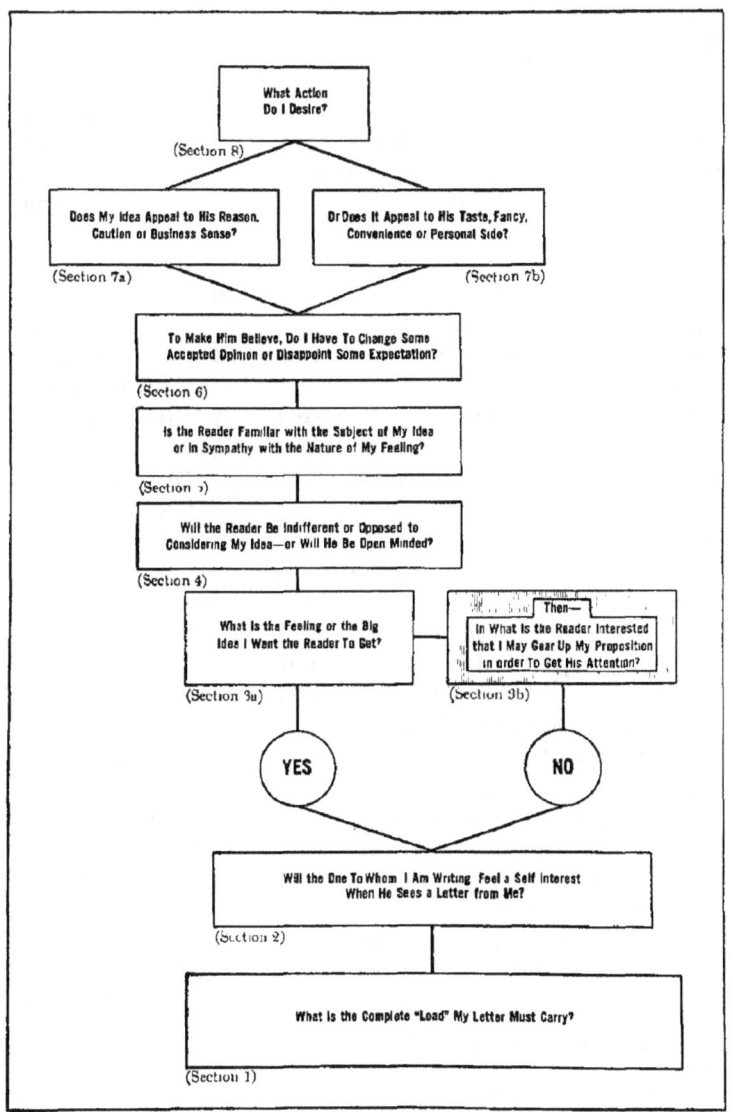

Panel 16

THE WORK YOUR LETTER MUST DO

of how you are going to write or how you are going to word your letter.

Look at the matter this way: it is unreasonable to expect an automobile to show equally good results on all manner of roads if it is kept on one gear. A good driver looks ahead, and when his car is on a long, steep hill, or a congested street, he throws in the low gear; but when it is on a level, straightaway stretch, he puts in the high.

So with letters.

An experienced letter writer neither fiddles away time on attention-getting schemes for a level stretch proposition he knows his reader is interested in; nor wastes space on detailed description for a clear-road proposition he knows his reader understands; nor uses effort in heavy argument or attempts to arouse enthusiasm for easy grade propositions that he knows his reader feels a pressing need for. In such cases a good letter writer throws in the high speed and gives his reader the gist of what he wants to know in terse, concise form. But when he sees ahead a steep hill of reader's indifference for his proposition, or a narrow roadway congested *with counter arguments or prejudices or skepticism*, then he doesn't attempt rashly to plunge through, but throws in the slow gear and winds in and out carefully with picked arguments and vivid descriptions, or pushes up the hill slowly with convincing, detailed reasons.

That's the first step to take when you plan to write a letter—look ahead and analyze what kind of "going" the letter will have to meet when it reaches the reader's hands. And that's what the chart on page 32 does. It shows you how best to take that "look ahead."

In concluding this first chapter let us consider some practical examples of actually using the whole chart. That will make the various points clear and perhaps indicate right off the bat to you how you can use the chart in your own business. Take a look at the letter on the next page—it is an actual letter from FACTORY's own file. In Panel 18, on page 35, see the way the planner of it sized up its work by using the chart

BUSINESS CORRESPONDENCE

THE MAGAZINE OF MANAGEMENT
A.W. SHAW COMPANY PUBLISHERS
New York   Chicago   London

H. W. Higman,
Chicago, Ill.

Dear Sir:

Men are cutting the ground from under manufacturing precedents.

The Tabor Mfg. Co. cut its shop force from 100 men to 70, and at the same time increased its OUTPUT 300% — by Scientific Management.

An eastern machine shop, in one department, increased output 25%, lowered labor cost 10% to 20% and increased wages 25% — by Scientific Management.

A competent authority charges that American railroads waste a million dollars a day in inefficient operating methods. The Canadian-Pacific is SAVING these wastes — by Scientific Management. A keen observer of conditions in Europe and America says —

> "Today the American business man faces a crisis. The increased cost of living demands a readjustment of salaries and wages. Increased efficiency appears to be the only way out."

What does it all mean to YOU? The page proofs of a new book that answers the questions are now on my desk. For this book, "How Scientific Management is Applied", not only explains PRINCIPLES of Scientific Management — not only shows specifically how Taylor, Gantt, Emerson and others have changed the whole aspect of costs, profits and wages for many manufacturers — not only shows how such plants as the Bullard Machine Tool Works, Sayles Bleacheries, Yale & Towne, and others ARE applying these principles — but shows how YOU may apply Scientific Management to YOUR plant.

Five hundred copies of this book are now ready. NONE will be sold. There is no price that can buy one.

But the book is FREE.

A subscription to FACTORY, the Magazine of Organization and Management, brings you "How Scientific Management is Applied" without cost, even transportation prepaid.

Sign and mail the enclosed blank TODAY.

Very truly yours,

Merritt Lum

Circulation Manager

F-D
Encl. 93.2

Panel 17

THE POWER BEHIND THE PEN

If you were building a house would you try to put up the roof first? But, when writing letters, don't many correspondents practically do what amounts to the same thing? They write or dictate a first draft, revise it once or twice, and then send it on its way   A letter should be as well planned and built as any structure   Before setting pen to paper every phase of any letter should be thought out and then it should be built solidly from the ground up   This ability to see a proposition from all sides—to consider, to weigh, and to select—that is the power behind the pen   That power was applied to the successful letter above   The plan behind it is to be found in Panel 18   Study it   See how the chart which we built up was used   Make this method your own

THE WORK YOUR LETTER MUST DO

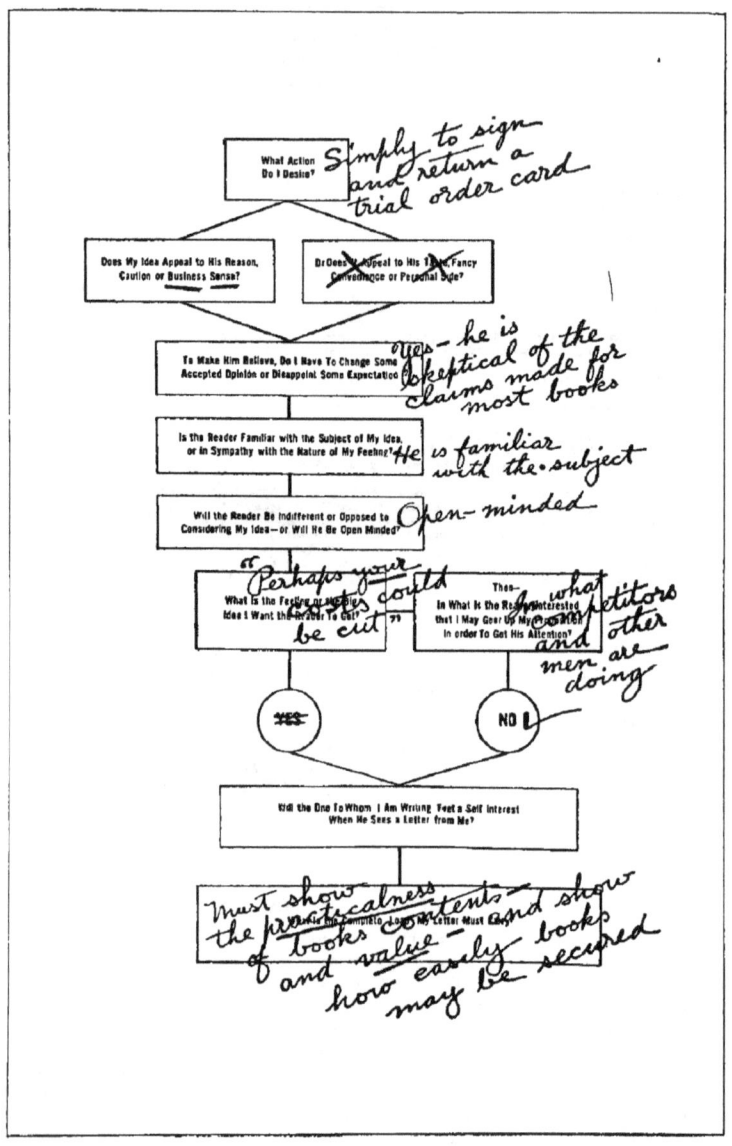

Panel 18

on page 32. How simply the method and chart work out! How effectively it brought all the ramifications of the letter's work to the mind of the writer of it so that he was able to start writing with an exact knowledge of just where he had to begin, all that he had to get into it, and just where he had to end.

Of course, complete consideration of such a letter must be reserved for later chapters of this book, but letter and chart do make us see right here and now how great a help is the chart on page 32, and how practical it is.

Do you not see how your use of such a chart, or at least your use of its principles, would save you time, and keep you from making an error—or an omission?

That's one side of the question. On the other side, take the simple case of writing to Smith that you can't spare him the money he wants to borrow.

Imagine Smith, a friend of yours, appealing to you in an emergency. Imagine your position. Smith has done you many favors ungrudgingly. You have looked forward to paying him in kind, but now that the call has come you can't respond.

There's a situation that would tax the ability of the best of us. How should such a letter be written? What must be said and what must not be said? How can we make him understand? How appease his disappointment and how appeal to his reason?

On the opposite page is a chart of such a letter. See how every condition has been provided for.*

Don't you see how quickly you could accustom yourself to going at every letter that way, so that after a time you would not need the chart to guide you; so that your analytical ability would develop into always going right to the bottom of the proposition?

That is the Big Idea of the chart—to make us analyze, and the Big Idea of this book, as you will find, is to show us how to analyze.

*A letter to Smith based on this chart will appear in the fifth chapter.

THE WORK YOUR LETTER MUST DO

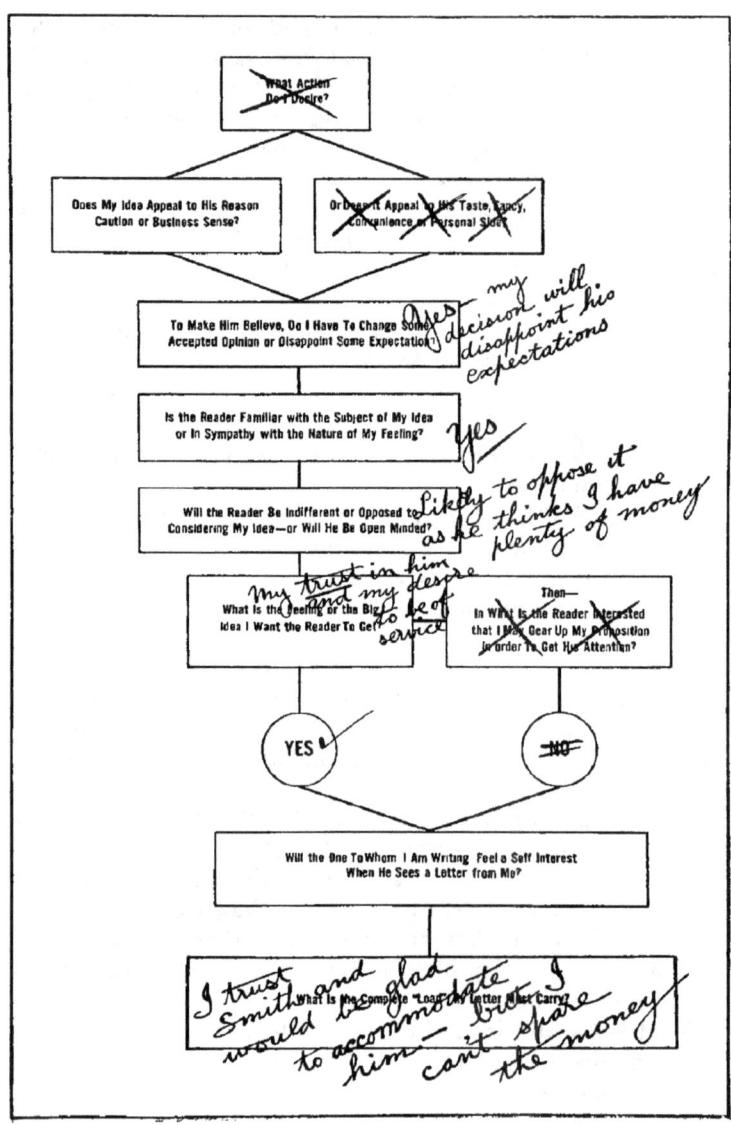

Panel 19

BUSINESS CORRESPONDENCE

In the next chapter we shall begin to make use of our knack of sizing up the letter's load by actually writing—and learning to put so graphically into words an intangible idea, or an almost indescribable feeling, that a person a thousand miles away can see what we want him to see as plain as day, or feel what we want him to feel as powerfully as we feel it ourselves.

SUMMARY

IN this chapter we have learned that before we start to write or dictate a letter we should size up the work our letter must do. We found that there are 10 elements that may enter into the work of any letter. Among them are the "load" of the letter, the reader's interest or lack of interest in it, his willingness to believe what it says, his tendency not to agree with a letter even when he believes, and so on up to securing action, the purpose of practically every letter

Frankly, in this chapter we have been dealing with fundamentals. But we studied fundamentals, not because some of them were unknown to us, but because we wanted to find a common ground from which any letter writer, no matter how great, no matter how small, his experience, could start. Now that we have found that starting place, we are ready to go on.

In the next chapter then, we will begin our study of actual letter writing and learn how to express feeling and ideas in words. How often have you felt, as your written page baffled you, that if you could only put your man in front of you and talk to him, how quickly he would feel the point you were trying to make or how quickly misunderstandings would thin out. Well, these are some of the topics we take up in the next chapter. When you are through with it you will not only know what successful men have done when confronted by situations similar to those in which you may have often found yourself, but you will know *how* to work out of such situations the next time you encounter them.

PROBLEM SECTION I

IN working out this book on applied business correspondence, every principle was based on the actual writing of men who are concededly masters of their craft, and on actual letters that have been used by practical business men and business firms.

In these problem sections, however, we shall practise the *application of the principles* learned from the chapters. We shall often *write entirely imaginary letters* to illustrate a point, or *rewrite* other people's letters from our own point of view.

In this way we can put principles into practise with a little more freedom than if we had to confine ourselves to actually used letters.

A complete part, then, will consist of, first, a *study of principles* found in the writings and letters of others, as covered in the chapters; and, second, practise in *the knack of applying those principles* to any and all kinds of letters. In this way we shall get a good working *combination of Theory and Practise.*

Neither should be neglected.

It is absolutely necessary, in order to understand *what makes a letter pay*, to study into the principles of writing; and in order to understand why letters pay it is necessary to study the same principles in the successful letters of others. But that is only half of the work. We don't want to be mere imitators. We don't want merely to adapt the successful letters that others have used. We want to be able *to create successful letters* of our own. So every time a principle or rule is developed in the chapter, we shall in the problem section haul it in, so to speak, examine it more intimately and try applying it to some everyday business affairs.

BUSINESS CORRESPONDENCE

In each problem section I will look ahead and find, from the examples of letters which appear here and there in this book, good illustrations of the application of each principle brought out in the chapters I shall then give you the facts necessary to work out a fair application of the principle, and propose that you work out such an application of your own. Then in the following problem section I shall point out the letter in which the principle was successfully used under the same conditions and discuss it.

In that way you can not only practise, but you can *correct your practise* of the principles developed.

In this first problem section, then, we want to accustom ourselves to, or "get the hang of," using the chart shown in the first chapter; that is, sizing up the work the letter must do.

Perhaps you will be puzzled over making a brief of your letter's "load"—you will be inclined, perhaps, to put *all the details* down as part of the letter's "load," when you should put down only the heads of the points to be covered But these you will find are enough to remind you, when you come to write, of the details necessary. If you get confused, see the size-up of "the complete load" in the charts on pages 35 and 37.

I know that some people, when they look at the chart, will think it is too complicated, or too "ginger bready," for a practical person to bother with But if you will just bear patiently with it for a time you will see its true simplicity and its real value.

Let me give you a practical example of its worth. A man in New York showed me just recently a letter he had received from a business associate in Oklahoma that showed how even very able men could profitably use such a chart The writer of the letter is a man of large affairs, long experience, and great ability. At the top of the next page is the letter with just a few things changed in order to disguise it.

Now it was not the vagueness about the property that worried the men who received this letter, as the writer of it

THE WORK YOUR LETTER MUST DO

Dear George.

　　Can you and your partner take $5,000 each, and lend me $5,000 on a $20,000 deal? It is a 1/32 royalty on a piece of property right near the Dunkley farm and already has five producing wells, yielding 670 barrels a day, and will likely develop not less than 20 wells by next year. The sixth well will be shot next week. Two dry holes so far. It looks good to me and I would like to get a half in it but happen not to have the ready money just now. If you don't feel like making me the loan, would you two take the three quarters for yourselves? Let me know at once as I have to give an answer by the 22nd.

　　　　　　　　　　　　　　　Hastily,

was a trusted friend on whose word alone they were accustomed to invest in oil royalties. But for the life of them they couldn't tell whether the writer wanted to borrow $5,000 from each of them, or only $5,000 from both.

It made a big difference to them at the time, and they had to wire for an explanation. The delay was just enough to make them too late to get the royalty.

The facts—as they were finally developed—were that the 1-32 royalty was offered for $20,000, the man on the ground wanted to take half but only had $5,000 available, so he wanted his New York friends to take half for $10,000, and lend him $5,000 between them so that he could swing his half.

Now let me show you what sizing up the work of that letter would have done for that man—or will do for any man.

On the chart on page 42, I have sized up the work that his letter had to do.

With such a size-up, could any sensible man have been as ambiguous as the oil man?

Wouldn't anyone, from that chart, have naturally dictated a letter about like the one at the top of page 43?

You see even the ablest of men can sometimes fail to write an important letter so it carries its "load," if they don't take the pains to work out that "load" carefully in advance. And don't you see how our method of charting the "load"

BUSINESS CORRESPONDENCE

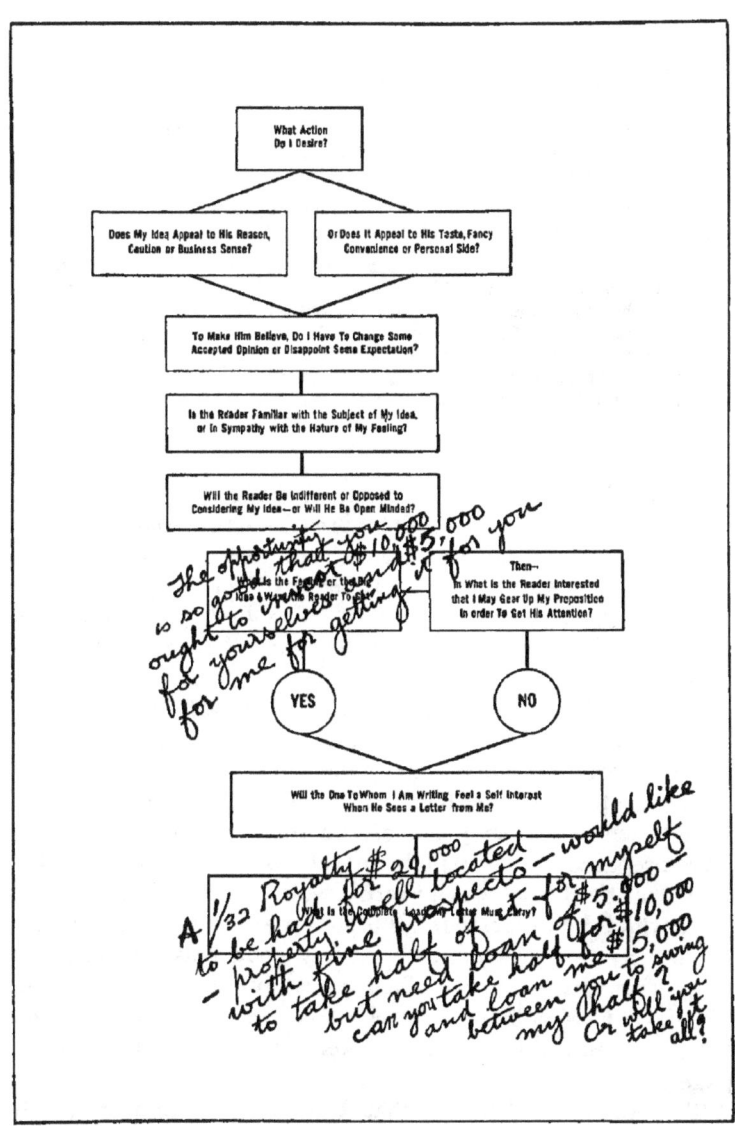

Panel 20

THE WORK YOUR LETTER MUST DO

Dear George:

    There is a 1/32 royalty offered for sale on a piece of property right near the Dunkley farm. It already has five wells producing 670 barrels a day, with prospects for at least 20 producing wells by next year. Only two dry holes found so far. A sixth well is to be shot next week.

    $20,000 swings the deal and it looks so good to me that I would like to get in on half interest.

    Now can you and your partner take a half for $10,000 and then lend me $5,000 to help me swing the second half? — I haven't the whole $10,000 available right now but can raise $5,000. The deal must be closed quickly. Write or wire at once as I must give an answer by the 22nd. If you don't want to lend me $5,000 do you want to take three-quarters for yourselves?

                       Hastily,

helps to do such work by reminding one of every point to look for and settle on? Compare the chart and my letter carefully. In this simple letter but two points had to be kept in mind, the first—a statement of the proposition; the second, its effect on the reader. The first point was suggested by the first question on the chart, "What is the complete "load" my letter must carry?" Then and there I wrote down that "load." Because "George" is a friend I ignored the question about self-interest and went on to the third step in the chart, and, across the panel which brought the point, wrote the feeling I wanted him to get. Easy, isn't it?

But before I turn you loose on some original problems I have prepared, let me explain another use of the chart. In the first chapter I spoke of granting Smith, a friend of ours, the loan which he requested. But suppose I haven't the money, or for any one of a number of very good reasons can't possibly grant the favor. Then a real problem is before me. To show how valuable the chart becomes in such a case I have charted a refusal. Let's look it over. You'll find it on page 37.

The complete "load" is that I trust Smith and ordinarily would consider it a privilege to lend him money on account of

BUSINESS CORRESPONDENCE

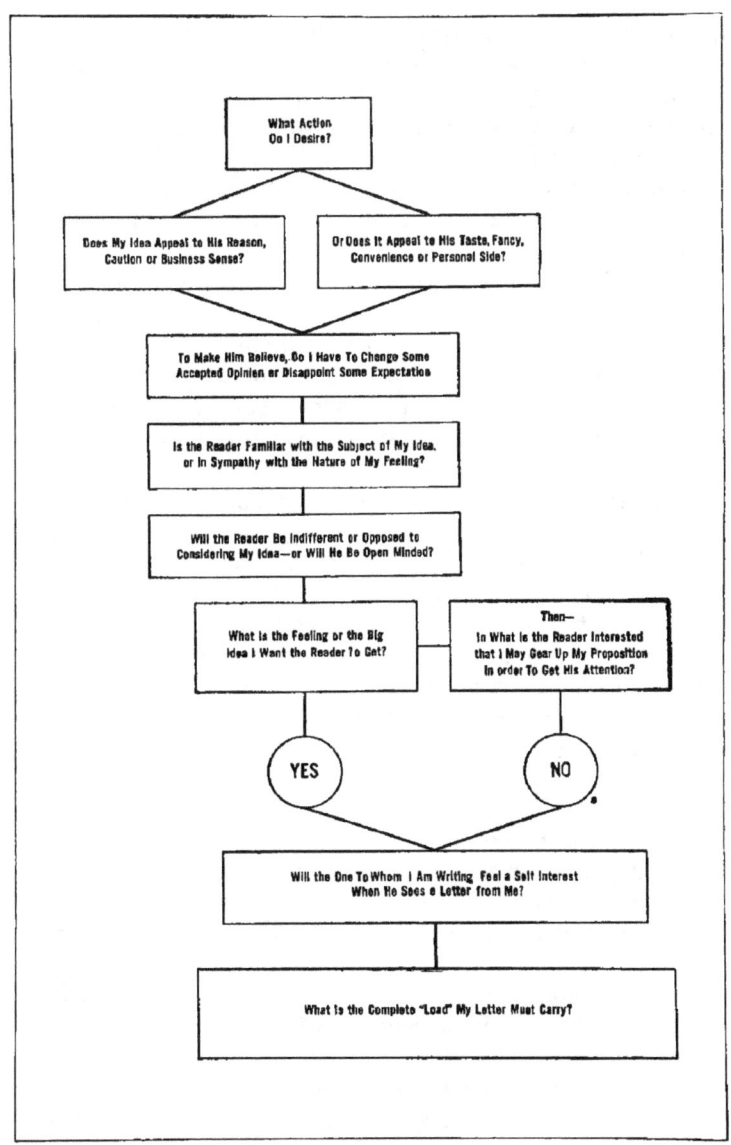

THE WORK YOUR LETTER MUST DO

many favors I have received. Self-interest can, of course, be ignored in this case, but trust, as the chart suggests, can't be too carefully implied. The other questions on the chart also present points which must be taken into consideration if Smith's friendship is to be retained. Read the chart carefully, and as you read, keep in mind all the little helps it brings out, so that a sincere, friendly letter to Smith almost writes itself.

One more chart and then I'll let you try this plan for yourself. On page 34 is a letter from FACTORY'S own files which was very successful in selling a business book. Compare the chart on page 35 and this letter See how the chart helped to bring out every selling point made. You can trace each step in this clever, powerful letter just as easily as you traced the steps in the Smith refusal.

Now then: As you have three charts before you running from the simple to the complex, you may now try your hand on analyzing the "load" of a letter by means of a chart. Take the simple case of lending Smith the $100 he asked for. Remember that your decision is that you trust Smith implicitly and are glad to be able to lend him the money and are enclosing the check. Sketch out a complete chart like that on page 44, or write up a number with carbon paper on the typewriter, and on it make a size-up of the letter's work, from which you could write or dictate a letter that would cover every point you want covered and give Smith every impression you want him to get.

You will find a correct size-up of such a letter on page 78. Compare it with your own in every detail, then, if you have made any mistakes, you can profit by them on the future practise work.

Now let me explain how to keep your practise problems in such a way that I can later refer you to them as new points come up.

Buy from any stationer 12 heavy manila folders which are chiefly used for filing letters. On the outside cover of the first folder write or print the words "Material File" On the second folder write boldly the figure "1" and below the number write plainly in smaller letters the title of the first chapter, "Sizing up the Work Your Letter Must Do." On the next folder write in the same way the figure "2" and the title of the second chapter, "Expressing Feeling or Ideas in Words." Continue by writing the numbers and titles of the remaining chapter on the other folders. You may abbreviate the titles if you care to.

When you have finished, slip the 11 folders inside the first and make them into a serviceable book by passing a rubber band around the lot.

Take the size-up chart just made, write on it "Size-up of Smith Letter," so you will recognize it easily again, and file it in the second folder—"Expressing Ideas"—as in the second problem section you will find the correct size-up of the problem. Do the same with all other practise problems, which you come to in this problem section. This will make it easy to refer to them in working out other problems.

But that is only one part of the use to be made of the file.

The titles of the 11 folders are also the 11 elements of work that enter into letters and doing business with letters. So, in the folders, you should file all the good letters or advertisements you run across, and all the information, hints, and suggestions you get for applying each of those elements.

Thus the little file will become the start of the most scientific kind of Data File or Material File, or Work File—whatever you want to call it—that you can have.

Of course, the little file that you have made will soon be outgrown, but you can expand it on the same principle, or improve on it for your own purposes, as you see fit. Any stationer can supply you with equipment for making your file just as big and as useful as you may need.

Now you are ready to do your first constructive work. On pages which follow, you will find four typical letter problems Size up the "load' the letters will have to carry. Don't try to write the letters. Details are reserved for future problem sections.

THE WORK YOUR LETTER MUST DO

Problem 1

Assume that you have a men's shoe store and at the opening of the spring season you wish to circularize a list of men in your city, telling them that your new spring stock has arrived and is complete in every line, and that you want them to come to your store for their spring shoes. We will assume that this list comprises names of men who have never traded with you, and who are unknown to you.

On a blank chart like that on page 44 (write up a few with carbon paper on a typewriter, or have this done for you) make a complete size-up of the work such a letter must do. Write at the bottom of it: "Size-up of Men's Shoe Store Letter." File it and in the next chapter I shall not only give you a correct size-up, but I shall also show a letter actually used for such a purpose by a big city store. Then we shall take up this very letter, and from what we shall have learned about expressing an idea in words, we shall rewrite it, as far as its big idea is concerned, as it should have been written in the first place—and we are going to see why.

Problem 2

Next assume that you are selling land—Louisiana corn land, we shall say. Suppose that you have been advertising in northern farm papers, and want to write an answer to the inquiries received, so as to get prospects interested in the opportunity for bigger, better crops offered by your new land, the greater prosperity in view, the ideal climate, and so forth.

Using a blank chart which you have prepared, make a size-up for such a letter, paying particular attention to what *idea* to convey. Be sure to write at the bottom of the sheet: "Size-up of Louisiana Corn Land Letter."

Always identify your size-ups in this way so that you can recognize them quickly when you want them. File the chart just completed in your Material File. In the next chapter I shall show you such a letter as it was successfully used, so that you can see how your size-up works out in actual cases. We shall also see how to develop and write the idea for it.

BUSINESS CORRESPONDENCE

Problem 3

Again, for example, assume yourself to be a tire manufacturer. Assume that a user of your tire, through careless treatment, has rim-cut his tire and then sent it back to you with a nasty letter. Suppose you want to show him his error, yet hold his good will by making a partial adjustment, such as giving him a new tire for part cash.

Size up the work such a letter must do on one of the charts you have prepared. Of course, in this letter, as in the others, there are many details you would have to know before you could really write the letter. But for practise in using the chart, we only expect you to cover the idea. The job now is to get accustomed to analyzing in a logical way. File the chart just completed in your Material File, writing as usual "Size-up of the Manufacturer's Letter," and in the next chapter you will not only see an actual letter used for such a purpose with which to check up, but you will also be shown how it was constructed.

Problem 4

This time let us say you are a fire insurance agent and on your books are several people who have failed to pay the premiums due on their policies. You have written them several times without result. You still believe they are intending to pay but are putting it off, so now you want to wake them up.

Size up on one of the prepared charts the work of such a letter. File your completed chart, for in the third part we shall have just such a letter to analyze and study, and don't forget to write at the bottom of the sheet: "Size-up of Fire Insurance Agent's Letter."

You are not going to find it the easiest task in the world to make either this size-up or the others on preceding pages. But the more you do it the easier it will become. I have purposely been rather vague in giving you the facts from which to make your charts, as I don't want you to bother too much yet over details. You will get them later.

THE WORK YOUR LETTER MUST DO

And now again, as we conclude this problem section, let me caution you against taking too lightly the matter of analyzing, or "sizing up" the work a letter has to do.

More poor letters are caused by not analyzing the work properly than by any other one cause. More *wrong* letters are caused by it—letters that are too long, or too short, or too impatient, or too good natured, or letters that offend, or give false impressions, or mishandle the subject, or letters that simply take up space without getting anywhere

That one point of forcing yourself to fix on one big idea or central feeling around which to shape your letter, will do more to improve the quality of your letters, especially dictated letters, than any other one point I know of—it helps you to "concentrate your fire," instead of drifting about in a sea of words.

And after you have acquired the habit—for it will come to be a habit in time—of sizing up letters carefully and fixing on a definite idea for each one, you will find it easy to apply the same principle to other letters or advertisements you write—and to your speech, as well. The best advertisements, as well as the best letters, are those based on one big idea, and the best complete campaigns of either advertising or selling are often those based on one big idea.

In the next part we take up the matter of ideas more specifically—how to choose the idea to convey, and then how to express it in words as clearly as an artist could paint it. So make yourself as familiar as possible with the use of the size-up chart, because you will need it.

PART II

EXPRESSING FEELING OR IDEAS IN WORDS

CHAPTER II

EXPRESSING FEELING OR IDEAS IN WORDS

IN the first chapter of this book on applied business correspondence, we turned all our attention to the importance of sizing up the "load" of a letter before starting to write or dictate. We found that there are 10 important points to keep in mind and that the chart which we worked out provided a sure guarantee that we would not overlook any of these points in future letters.

So we are now agreed, it is probably safe to say, that analyzing a letter according to the points shown in the chart on page 32—beginning at the bottom and working right up to the top—is the surest way there is of getting a complete understanding of every essential a letter must perform. When you have charted the essentials on the chart, you virtually have a blueprint of your letter as it ought to be written.

In handling that difficult FACTORY letter, illustrated on page 34, the value of the chart was apparent at once. On the other hand, its assistance in writing even the simplest letters can hardly be overemphasized. For instance, in writing Smith your decision to lend him the hundred dollars he asked for, you can see from Panel 40 on page 78 how *absolutely accurate* this method is. The chart, as you have discovered, shows at once the *simplicity* of the letter required, and it also shows at once just what feature in it *demands care*.

This prolonged discussion of such an elementary letter as the reply to Smith may seem uncalled for, but if you will recall how you began the study of arithmetic, you will remember how much time and how much blackboard space the teacher used to demonstrate that "one plus one makes two." Simple and tiresome, indeed, but how important you found it!

BUSINESS CORRESPONDENCE

ADDRESSOGRAPH COMPANY
"Prints from Type"
CHICAGO, ILLINOIS

Mr. C S Childs,
St. Joseph, Mo.

Dear Sir·

    Take a handful of address plates — 20 or 30 — slip them into the magazine — place the envelope, postcard, statement, or whatever you wish to address, at the printing position and "typewrite" names and addresses — at a speed of 30 per minute.

    This is the way the Hand Addressograph will address your list. With it you can do in a few minutes' work that which you now spend tedious hours doing by hand. It is so simple in operation that your list can be handled by any boy or girl without the possibility of mistakes or omissions

    This hand model costs very little — yet it is a COMPLETE Addressograph It prints from standard card index metal address plates embossed with permanent typewriter style type You can depend on it to stand the hardest usage — to print accurately and NEATLY

    Possibly you have certain questions which you would like to ask regarding the Addressograph We are anxious to take up these points in detail with you — will you write us about them?

    If you have decided upon a particular model simply note your selection on the enclosed card and send it in to us Or, if you will write us more in detail about your requirements, we will gladly recommend the exact equipment which will save you most

    The return envelope enclosed is yours to use.

                    Very truly yours,
                            ADDRESSOGRAPH COMPANY

Panel 22

EXPRESSING FEELING IN WORDS

This letter to Smith is the "one plus one makes two" of the whole art, or science, of good letter writing—of good writing of all kinds, and of good speaking and good talking, too. If you can write a good letter to Smith, you can write a good letter on almost any subject. For that reason you'll find the Smith letter referred to again and again.

Now one of the first questions we considered in sizing up the reply to Smith, and one of the first questions to be considered in writing any letter, is· "What is the Feeling or Big Idea I want the reader to get?" That point is so important, and yet so often overlooked, that I have made it the subject of this second chapter; for the ability to express yourself in a letter, or an advertisement, or an after-dinner speech, or in an informal conversation, in such a way that other people *see what you describe, or feel what you depict*, is often the backbone of personal strength and character and efficiency.

Before I show you how to cover this important point, however, I want you to read the four letters I have illustrated in Panels 22, 23, 24, and 25. First read the letter of an addressing machine manufacturer reproduced on page 54. As you read the first and second paragraphs can you not see, almost as if the machine were working in front of you, the points which the writer is trying to convey to you—the simplicity with which the machine is operated, the efficiency with which it works?

Then read the letter from a motor manufacturer on page 56. Do you get any very definite idea about the motor described? No, nothing but dry information. Just to get a real strangle hold on this point read the letters on pages 57 and 58. They are the "Answers to Inquiries" of two corset manufacturers. Compare them for yourself to see how from the letter on page 57 you *get the feeling of comfort, good health, and smart style;* while from the other you get nothing but statements.

Don't you know some men whose conversation is like the letters on pages 56 and 58—merely a recitation of statements —and other men whose talks to you make you *see or feel or virtually live* things they say—not merely hear them?

BUSINESS CORRESPONDENCE

INTERNATIONAL MOTORS CO.
FACTORY AND OFFICES
KINZIE, NEB

Mr R L Chadwick,
St Louis, Mo

Dear Sir

    As requested in your letter of the 12th inst , we take pleasure in sending you, under separate cover, a copy of our latest catalog, and here attach a price list of our different models

    As you will notice, the Oceanic is built in three sizes, of 2 HP, 3½ HP and 4 HP The 2 HP and 3½ HP motors are of the 1-cylinder, 2-cycle type, whereas the 4 HP motor, our 1916 addition, is of the 2-cylinder, 4-cycle type

    The 2 HP motor we usually recommend for ordinary rowboats up to 18-20 ft in length, whereas the 3½ HP size was especially designed for boats for heavy commercial uses Both motors develop a speed of about 7 miles an hour

    For those customers who desire more speed than either of the above motors can develop, we are just bringing out the 2-cylinder motor of 4 HP This motor, having been constructed especially for speed, is more particularly intended for competition with the 2 HP motor, rather than the 3½ HP one — that is, we expect it to be used on about the same size boat as you would ordinarily use the 2 HP size for

    All our motors are built for use in salt water — very economical in the use of gasoline, simple in construction, thoroughly tested before shipment, and fully guaranteed.

    Holding ourselves at your disposal for any additional information that you may desire, and asking that you kindly state in your order for which market the motor is intended, we remain,

                  Yours very truly,

                       INTERNATIONAL MOTORS CO.

EXPRESSING FEELING IN WORDS

EDWARDS & COMPANY
REGINA CORSETS
DETROIT, MICHIGAN

Mrs. H. A. Murray,
Madison, Wisconsin.

Dear Madam:

    Thank you for your inquiry just received in regard to Regina Corsets.

    You need not wear an uncomfortable corset to be fashionable. Style, comfort, and good health are all combined in the Regina Corset. No corset or corset waist could be safer for the growing girl, more reassuring for the mature woman, or more perfect as a foundation for fashionable gowning.

    In our new catalog you will find among the many attractive models the one which suits you best. Ask your dealer if he has that number in stock or will get it for you. If he cannot supply you, order direct from us.

    When you ask for a Regina Corset be sure you are shown the genuine, bearing the label Edwards & Co. There are a number of inferior imitations which are frequently sold as Regina Corsets because this is to the dealer's advantage. The genuine has better material and workmanship and will fit better and wear longer. Edwards & Co. are the originators and sole manufacturers of Regina Corsets.

    We pay postage on all orders in the U. S. Every garment is fully guaranteed.

    Trusting we may have the favor of your order, we remain,

                           Very truly yours,
                           EDWARDS & COMPANY

BUSINESS CORRESPONDENCE

What fundamental principle lies back of this difference? If we have a machine or a corset or a shoe or a service to sell, or if we have an experience to relate or an anecdote to tell or a yarn to spin, how can we speak of it or write of it so as to make the other man see the Big Idea or sense the Feeling we want to convey—rather than to make him merely read our words or listen to our voice?

Let us begin at the bottom and work up to our answer.

Suppose we were on a sightseeing trip and were writing to a friend at home our impressions of the things we saw. Suppose that on a fine, clear, autumn day we came to a prosperous looking farm with everything about it conveying the idea of the plenty and prosperity of the land, and the comfort and peace and good living it provided the owner; and suppose that we desired to give our friend at home that same idea or feeling about it.

Let us see how we could go about it Let us see how, without any great writing ability or any highly developed imaginative powers, we could make that distant friend see and feel

---

BEEHIVE DEPARTMENT STORE
DETROIT, MICHIGAN

Mrs. F O. Reed,
Champaign, Ill.

Dear Madam

Replying to your favor of recent date, we are pleased to send you, under separate cover, copy of our catalog showing the new styles for spring Should you make a selection we will be glad to furnish a corset to you through your local dealer, or, if there is any objection to this, we will send it to you direct on receipt of the retail price.

Thanking you for your letter and trusting you may find something to suit your needs, we remain,

Very truly yours,

BEEHIVE DEPARTMENT STORE

Panel 25

EXPRESSING FEELING IN WORDS

the atmosphere of plenty and comfort and peace and good living that we saw and felt as we looked at that prosperous farm scene.

Any of us can tell what it was that we felt—that is a natural part of feeling it. Therefore, in big type in the panel below, I have set down a statement of the *feeling or the idea* that we are to convey.

THE IDEA

Prosperity; plenty; comfortable, hearty living

Panel 26

That much, at least, is easy.

Now, if our friend were riding with us at the time, to make him see and feel the prosperity of the land and the comfortable living of the owner, we probably would have pointed out the *evidences* of prosperity and good living; that is, the sights that made us think of prosperity and good living. If you recall similar experiences, you see how naturally you would have said: "Just look at those apples—" if the abundance of apples had caught your eye first and had made you think of a big store of fruit in the cellar for the winter. Probably you would have added, "The trees are still full of them; and see all those in barrels and boxes; and those in piles, probably for cider." And then, as your eye wandered over the broad acres, you would naturally enough have exclaimed about the corn, and about the pumpkins between the rows of corn.

Any of us on such an occasion could run our eyes over a scene like that and point out *the big, interesting features* apples, corn, pumpkins, buckwheat, for example.

In the panel on the next page, I have set down those four features—which we may say are the things that would stir up in our minds the *idea or the feeling* of prosperity and comfortable living that we want to convey.

BUSINESS CORRESPONDENCE

Do you follow? In the first two panels I have simply listed the natural trend of thoughts that arise when one looks at an autumn farm scene. Could anyone look at such a scene and not be able, later, to set down at least four outstanding "features" of it? That is all I have done in the panel below.

But now we are getting ready to write; and we remember that *our object in writing is not merely to state that we saw* apples, corn, pumpkins, buckwheat, *but to make our friend see and feel*

THE "FEATURES"
Apples   Corn   Pumpkins   Buckwheat

Panel 27

the visions of prosperity and plenty and comfortable, hearty living that the apples, corn, pumpkins, and buckwheat made us see and feel.

That is why I put "The Idea" on page 59 in such big type—so that we cannot get away from it and so that when we write about "apples," we shall remember to put something in the description that will make those apples and the corn, pumpkins, and buckwheat look plentiful to our friend and make him think of storing up such riches and of enjoying them.

It is the third step in our letter. It shows the connection of each "feature" with the idea to be conveyed—the idea of plenty.

How perfectly natural now to add to each "feature" a few words indicating its plentifulness. Is there anyone who can't do that much? No great command of language, no drawing on imagination, is required to do that, and yet we have begun to make the reader sense the abundance and plenty of the farm which we have set out to describe. That, you will notice, is what I have done in the panel at the top of page 62.

EXPRESSING FEELING IN WORDS

But we must remember *the second part of the idea* we are to convey—the good living that these crops provide. We must *call up thoughts* of enjoying the apples, corn, pumpkins, and buckwheat.

Is it difficult in describing these four things to include the thought of eating them, and also of taking others to market to exchange for luxuries? Well, hardly! And see in Panel 29 how simply, with the start already made, we can bring in the atmosphere of eating and enjoying—by just the suggestion of "stores of apples" instead of mere "apples"; by the reference to "cider", by the mention of "golden ears" of corn and "cakes and puddings"; by the hint of "honey and slapjacks."

What have we accomplished?

Bit by bit we have built up from the bare list of "features" in a farm scene—apples, corn, pumpkins, buckwheat—*a simple, plain description that not a man among us could not write*—perhaps not using the exact words used, but using words as good. Yet it makes the plenty and prosperity of the land, and the comfort, peace, and good living of its owner, as plain as day.

And *now I shall tell you a secret*—on page 63 you will see this exact description—elaborated a bit, dressed up a bit, polished a bit—made into one of the acknowledged masterpieces of English literature It is Washington Irving's description of the Van Tassel farm, in his famous "Legend of Sleepy Hollow"

Probably none of us could evolve this little gem in the expression of an Idea and the conveyance of a Feeling quite as the great Irving did it. But every one of us can be at least as graphic as Panel 29 if we lay out our ideas as carefully, and list our "features" as naturally, and then link the description of each "feature" with the Idea as I have indicated in the preceding pages.

In other words, we do not need to be a genius like Irving to be a vivid letter writer or a brilliant talker, if we but *cultivate the knack of visualizing the Idea or Feeling;* and then

BUSINESS CORRESPONDENCE

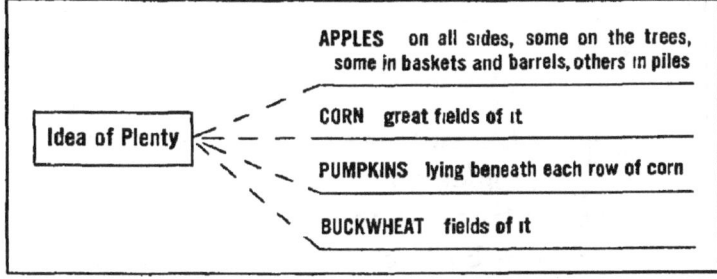

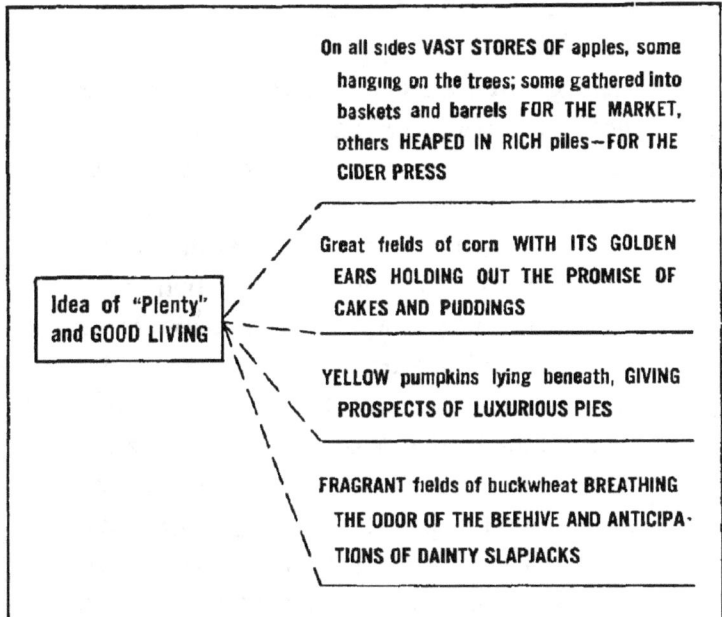

Panel 28 (upper) and Panel 29 (lower)

BUILDING THE LETTER

By beginning with four simple "features," such as apples, corn, pumpkins and buckwheat—as in Panel 27—and steadily filling in with new thoughts as they arise, a letter practically writes itself. Panel 28 (top) shows how the thoughts which call up the idea of plenty are attached to the original "features." In Panel 29, by filling in Panel 28, we approach the finished product, which is reproduced on the next page.

EXPRESSING FEELING IN WORDS

O**N ALL sides** he beheld **vast stores of apples;** some hanging in oppressive opulence **on the trees;** some gathered into baskets and barrels for the market; others heaped up in rich piles for the cider-press. Farther on he beheld **great fields of** Indian **corn, with its golden ears** peeping from their leafy coverts, and **holding out the promise of cakes and hasty-pudding; and** the **yellow pumpkins lying beneath** them, turning up their fair, round bellies to the sun, and **giving** ample **prospects of** the most **luxurious of pies;** and anon he passed **the fragrant buckwheat fields, breathing the odor of the beehive, and,** as he beheld them, soft **anticipations** stole over his mind **of dainty slapjacks,** well buttered, and garnished with honey or treacle, by the delicate little dimpled hand of Katrina Van Tassel.

—WASHINGTON IRVING

pick a few leading "features" of the scene or article, and simply describe them from the basis of the Idea or Feeling rather than haphazardly.

Now let me show you how the point I have made may be applied to *a plain, everyday business proposition.*

Suppose, instead of the imaginary Van Tassel farm of Irving's story, we have some farm land that we want to sell. Suppose, for example, it is Louisiana corn land and that we want to convey the idea to northern farmers of wonderful farming opportunities, such as big crops, ready markets, high prices, and fine climate, which await the farmer who moves to Louisiana.

First, let us visualize that idea as we did in tracing the Washington Irving description. Let us put it into the single, dominating thought which we want to pervade our letter—as in the panel below.

THE IDEA
Opportunity, wealth; good living

Panel 31

Now, just as we did before, let us determine on the "features" that make our land offer the wealth and good living we claim for it. We will suppose we know that the corn grown on the land can scarcely be exceeded in quality. The river and railroads and ocean ports offer easy access to the markets of the world, and for that reason prices will probably always be good. In addition, the fertility of the soil in the Mississippi Valley makes it one of the greatest agricultural districts in the world. The climate is also a deciding factor. These "features" I have listed in the panel on the next page.

The only difference so far between our "features" and those of the Irving description is that his were concrete objects, such as corn and apples, while ours are the abstract

EXPRESSING FEELING IN WORDS

qualities or properties of our land. This latter situation is true of most business propositions. The "features" are seldom visible, actual objects. For instance, the "features" of an automobile may be the ease with which one rides, the low gasoline consumption per mile, and so on The "features" of clothing, as another example, may be style, comfort, and durability

But you understand—and therefore we shall continue with the land letter. Let us apply the main idea given below

---

THE "FEATURES"

Quality of Corn   **Access to Market**
Prices   **Fertility of Soil**
                Climate

Panel 32

to each of the "features" we have listed. In other words, let us take "quality of corn" and so describe it that it arouses thoughts of "opportunity, wealth, and good living." Let us do the same with "access to markets," and so on through the list.

By combining Idea and "features" in the most ordinary way we get the result shown in Panel 33 on the next page. We are not writing literature, mind you, and yet step for step we are following the processes used by Washington Irving in building up that famous description of the Van Tassel farm.

Now by ordinary filling in of Panel 33, you could convey the idea of this land's wealth and good living so clearly that any farmer could *see it* and *feel it*

Have you any doubt about it? If you have, take a look at the panel on page 67 and see that it has been done! There you will find an actual and successful letter written to sell this very land. That letter attracted scores of northern farmers into lower Louisiana. Look it over carefully. There's noth-

BUSINESS CORRESPONDENCE

ing "Irvingesque" about it, to be sure. But the principle is there.

Skipping the first two paragraphs, not of interest to you until you study the ways of "Gripping Attention" and "Holding Interest," you see that we have been simply reconstructing the third and fourth paragraphs, just as we did in the case of Irving's classic description. And you see that, in this case—*the expression of an idea for practical business purposes*—the same process applies. In other words, what Irving's art did in "The Legend of Sleepy Hollow," what this land

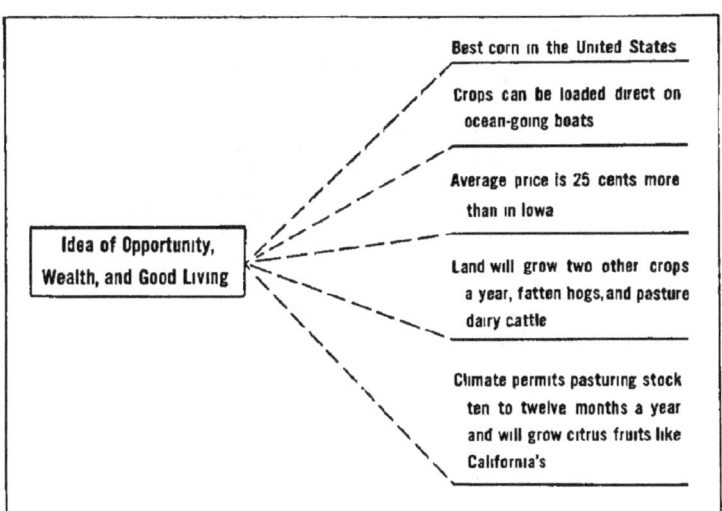

Panel 33

"HITTING ON ALL SIX"

Watch a mechanic correct the ignition system of an automobile At the end of the job he has six wires to the battery These must be attached to the cylinders of the engine Until each wire is properly connected with the right spark plug, the machine won't go Writing a letter is a mechanical job, in fact it is as mechanical as laying bricks or building a house, or fixing an automobile engine Each part of the letter must fit, each must join with others and work in harmony with them or the letter won't go The "features" are the live wires leading from you, a battery of ideas, to the printed word, your engine, which makes the message go When the "features" of a letter are known, thought out, found to be right, by testing, and connected to the Big Idea, the letter, like the auto engine, will hit on six cylinders.

EXPRESSING FEELING IN WORDS

DELTA LAND COMPANY
New Orleans, La.

Mr. R. L. Johnson
Riverside, Neb.

Dear Sir:

What has given the high selling value to Iowa farms? CORN. What has given the rapid advance in farm values to fill the central western states? CORN. What is the biggest factor in making the rich farm lands of Lower Louisiana advance? CORN. WHY? Because they are in "THE CORN BELT."

You hear your neighbors say, "I won't buy land out of 'The Corn Belt.'" That's why he will buy our Lower Louisiana land. It's in THE PROVED CORN BELT. This Lower Louisiana land will grow more bushels of corn per acre, at a smaller expense, than you can grow on a northern farm (and a dozen other crops that you can't grow there) and it will sell for more money a bushel

Do you know that the best corn in the U. S is grown in this Lower Louisiana country? That it will make No. 1 corn out of the field? That it can be loaded on an ocean-going ship for less than you can load your crop on the railroad? That the average price to the farmer is 25 cents more than the Iowa farmer gets? That the same field will grow two other crops the same year? That hogs will make the hog man pay for his land? That it is the best dairy country in America? That you can pasture your stock 10 to 12 months, two or three to the acre? These are facts that will make you sit up and take notice.

Remember this is a corn country with a climate finer than California's. It's a country with abundant rain and certain crops. It's a country with greater citrus fruit possibilities than either Florida or California. It's a country that pays three dividends a year instead of one.

It's land that you can talk to "HOME FOLKS" and friends. It's land that brings results. It's land that is better than an insurance policy, for it will take care of you and it will pay dividends to your children's grandchildren.

Have you read the booklet "RECLAIMED"?

Our offer on the back cover of the booklet is a fair one. It's purely a matter of business. You can't afford not to investigate this great soil, admittedly the richest on this continent, with this offer before you. Then, on top of that, is our special "Trip Receipt Plan."

Yours very truly,

DELTA LAND COMPANY

Panel 34

salesman's genius did for his corn-land proposition, we—any of us—can do. Not, maybe, so effectively as the land salesman has done it, nor so well as Irving has done it, but still, by careful preparatory work, we can do it well enough to *get results.* And that is what we all want In the problem section which follows this chapter you'll have the opportunity of practising the application of the principle so that you can adopt it at once in the letters you are writing.

Now you see the difference between letters that merely assert facts and *letters that make us see the idea or get the feeling.*

It is the same difference that marks the man whose conversation bores us from the man whose conversation interests or entertains us.

I don't mean to infer that good conversationalists consciously visualize each idea or feeling and then chart out its "features" as we have done Nor do I say that all good letter writers go through all the details of this process. To some men this visualizing process is intuitive. They do it unconsciously.

I do mean to say, however, that people who do not possess this intuition can create it by practising this process at every opportunity; that by going through the actual operations I have described—by writing them on paper, just as we have done it in this chapter—they not only will help to accomplish the vivid expression of the idea for any particular letter or talk, but also will, in time, train the mind to work that way unconsciously.

And for vitally important letters or speeches or even for informal talks in which you want to be sure to convey a definite impression, such a process is a measure of safety, no matter how good a writer or talker you may be, for if you have agreed to nothing else so far, surely you now agree with me that *expressing feeling or ideas in words is not a matter of fine writing.*

Just surely to drive this point home, I'm going to go over once more the principle we have been studying. This time I'm going to take it up from a negative point of view—I'll

EXPRESSING FEELING IN WORDS

show you how, by applying this idea, a bad letter may be made into a good one

Mind you, we are for the present going to ignore everything but *conveying the idea or feeling* Time enough to consider such matters as pulling power, attention-getting, and interest-holding, when we come to the study of those points—as we shall in due time. For the present we shall study just the idea or feeling that a letter should convey.

First of all, read the letter on the next page. It is a copy of a letter, disguised, of course, actually mailed by a city store to attract customers to a new shoe stock just placed on sale. Does the letter convey to you one definite idea or feeling?

Of course not, yet the language is fine The construction is good. Many of us couldn't write a letter that would sound so well. But *it does not convey a central feeling or idea.* The first impression is that the writer is trying to be smart. The second is a foggy knowledge that new shoes are on sale There's practically nothing that would pull any of us from our dealer into the letter writer's store.

Now let's try our constructive process on that letter and, although we know nothing about the shoe trade, write a letter that will attract customers and make them, at least, come in and look over our stock.

The first thing to do is to size up, as we learned to do in the first chapter, the "load" the letter must carry On page 71 you'll find the letter completely charted Notice how the first step allowed me to size up the "load" accurately, "To interest a man in new shoes and induce him to come here for them." That, certainly, is the "complete load" our shoe store letter must carry.

Now for the next step, the "Feeling or the Big Idea" we want our reader to get: "That our stock is so big and so complete that no matter what kind of a shoe he wants it must be here " That's what the writer of the original letter *tried* to make his reader feel, but a casual inspection of his work shows how he failed.

BUSINESS CORRESPONDENCE

KAYNOR'S
EVERYTHING IN SHOES
MINNEAPOLIS, MINN.

Mr. T. L. McRae
Minneapolis, Minn.

Dear Sir:

    We believe we <u>can</u> interest you —

    In shoes for spring, and to your advantage.

    This is not a toddling thought born of the wish —
— but a statement of a logical fact arising from the
knowledge of our position concerning men's boots and low
shoes for spring.

    Lines are now complete — lasts that are accepted
for the new season are here — in leathers that will
prove satisfactory — in effects that are new and pleasing — accompanied by a pricing that is consistent with
the quality, workmanship and finish of these fine
examples of good shoemaking.

    Here is a conscientious and skilled shoe service —
ready to fit you properly with shoes to suit your
inclination, whether it be for a last newly designed or
again the last which you are accustomed to wearing.

    May we have the pleasure of "showing" you?

    Especially ready at the noon hour.

                       Yours very truly,

                            KAYNOR'S

Panel 35

FINE WRITING?

Pretty phrases and flashy paragraphs are not what bring replies to the sales letter Your prospect may admire your literary touch, chuckle over your wit, and—chuck your letter into the waste-basket "Fine writing" is the besetting sin of the letter reproduced above It's clever It sparkles But where is the magnet that draws customers? Compare this letter with the one reproduced on page 74

    That letter has a hook in every line It's not clever, but it sells shoes

EXPRESSING FEELING IN WORDS

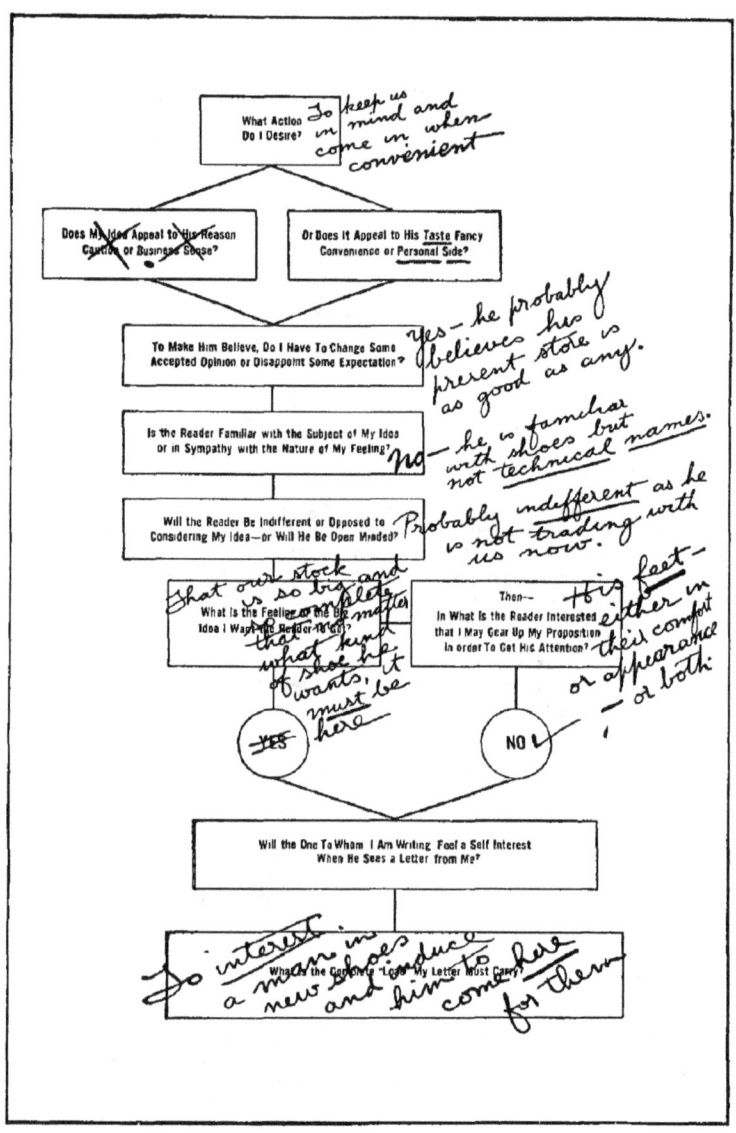

Panel 36

BUSINESS CORRESPONDENCE

As "feeling" in a letter is what we are concerned with at this time, we'll leave our chart right now and devote ourselves to developing this one section of it. In future chapters and future letters we'll take up the other points brought out by it.

Of course, there are a number of other good, strong ideas on which such a letter can be based—quality is one; service is another, but, as the reader's interest in new shoes is apparently what the writer of the letter had in mind, I stuck to it in drawing up my chart

It is important, always, to keep the "Feeling or the Big Idea" in mind this way as you lay out a letter. That is why, as you may have noticed, I print it and refer to it just as often as possible.

That is what you should do when you plan a letter—write out your visualization of the Big Idea and read it frequently while you are working out your letter and while you are actually writing it.

In the panel below is the idea the writer wants to convey. Now to select the "features" for it.

THE IDEA
Shoes for any foot, for any taste, for any purpose—if there is a particular kind of shoe ANYWHERE it must be here.

Panel 37

If you were really the shoe dealer writing this letter, your duty would be to go through your stock from front to back; if you were a machine salesman, your duty would be to inspect the machine, and, if possible, watch it in actual operation; if you were a book dealer, your duty would be to study the table of contents or even to read through the book again. Often from such steps you can conceive the idea or feeling you want to convey.

EXPRESSING FEELING IN WORDS

Remember this in writing a letter: No matter how many times you have done it before, *study your article or proposition again when you come to select the "features" of your letter.* Take my advice on this when you have letters to write and you will never regret it.

Therefore let us imagine ourselves going through a shoe stock. Here are the new spring styles—"A 50," we shall say, is a long vamp, narrow toe, and "A 51" has the effect of a narrow toe, but is wide and roomy—it is intended for a man who can't wear a narrow toe, but who wants to look in style —"A 52" is a buttoned shoe; "A 53" is laced, "A 54" is a fancy top; "A 55" is a plain shoe. The "B" models are Oxfords—tans, blacks, grays. (We are not trying to be accurate as to the merchandise, so those of you who are familiar with shoe styles please remember that it is only the principle you should look for).

Then come wide, comfortable shoes, running up into extra large sizes. And over here are extra narrow lasts; and beyond them come the "crank" shoes—shoes with arch supports; shoes with flat, low heels; and shoes without toe caps—all the "isms" of shoes. And after we have seen them all, probably we can't for the life of us think of a man who couldn't find somewhere among all those shapes and sizes just the shoe that would suit him. Isn't that about what the writer of the letter on page 70 had in mind when he wrote, "a logical fact arising from the knowledge of our position ———"?

And *there is the job of our letter*—to make the man to whom we write see all those shoes just as we saw them, so that he too will come to our conclusion.

Now, as you will remember, our next step is to list our features. To save time I've done the job for you. In the panel at the top of page 74, you'll see a list of our "features" just as we saw them.

Can't any one of us go through such a shoe stock of a retail store and see that much? And if we can *see it*, can't we *set it down on paper?*

BUSINESS CORRESPONDENCE

THE "FEATURES"		
Shoes—	Long narrow ones	Fancy tops
Long narrow toes	Health shoes	Plain tops
Wide toes that LOOK narrow	Arch-supporting shoes	Oxfords—tan, black gray
Buttoned	Flat heels	Roomy, comfortable shoes
Laced	Plain toes	Big—UNUSUALLY big shoes

    Here are the new, long narrow toes for those who want the very latest style· and for those who simply CAN'T wear those thin, narrow toes, here are comfortable broad toes, but so skilfully shaped that they have all the appearance of being narrow. Some are buttoned, some laced, so no matter which you prefer, you can have it. And here they are in rather extreme fancy tops, but if your taste is quieter, why, over here are the plain leather tops.

    And then oxfords -- oxfords in all shapes, tan oxfords, gray oxfords, and substantial blacks.

    But perhaps you don't run to STYLE so much as comfort -- for you, then, there are roomy, comfortable, sensible shapes, and in every size from unusually small to tremendously big, from broad, short to long, narrow.

    There are all styles of shoes with arch supports, and in anatomic shapes; and with square, low heels and for men with bunions, then in special shapes without toe caps.

Panels 38 (upper) and 39 (lower)

This letter is effective Its plain, simple language grapples the reader and ties him to you To understand its power read again the letter on page 70 See how this letter avoids "fine writing" and clings closely to this fundamental As you write keep clearly in mind the reader's point of view, constantly anticipate how each word, phrase, sentence, and paragraph will affect him.

EXPRESSING FEELING IN WORDS

Of course we can   And if we can set it down on paper, as in Panel 38, then any one of us can surely put those words together with simple adjectives and verbs so as to make readable sentences.

Let us try it

> Here are the new, long, narrow toes for those men who want the very latest style

Just *applying the idea* to the model described almost writes the sentence for us; for as soon as we start to write of narrow toe shoes, the idea of "shoes for any foot, any tastes," makes us think of bringing in the taste or the foot that narrow toe shoes will please   Then:

> and for those who want to be in style, but who simply CAN'T wear those thin, narrow toes, here are comfortable broad toes, but so skilfully shaped that they have all the appearance of being narrow!   .

In Panel 39, on page 74, you see the rest of the letter; that is, the part of it which develops the idea or feeling which we intend to convey. We'll not bother with the entire letter just now.

Before we leave this interesting topic, however, I'd like to have you turn back to the original letter on page 70 and compare it carefully with the letter on page 74. I'm sure you'll agree that the letter on page 74 is easily the better, although its language is cruder, it is far less studied; and it might have been written by a man who pays only slight attention to good English or to the principles of sentence structure.

And that brings up another point about conveying ideas or feelings which at first you might think we should take up right here—it is the *kind of language to use* and the *order in which to bring up "features."*   You might think that these are two separate points   But, strange to say, they are really one, as we shall see.   They both rest on one, simple, fundamental principle of letter writing, namely, *economizing the reader's mental effort.*

BUSINESS CORRESPONDENCE

It has been proved (we shall later see some interesting examples of it) that a reader or listener has, at each moment, but a limited amount of mental power available. Compare reading with looking at a picture. The eye sees and the eye apprehends the picture in a moment, but in writing we can only produce our effect by a series of small impressions, dripping our meaning—so to speak— into the reader's mind. A man's brain at the best is a narrow-mouthed bottle into which he can receive but one word at a time. If you want your reader to think of "apples," for instance, you must use no words that will take his mind off "apples"; and you must write no words that will force him to use mental power in associating their meaning with apples. If you do use such words, you are weakening your own case, because you are causing him to use up part of "the mental power available at the moment" for shifting your word around in his mind. He has that much less mental power with which to *catch the drift of your idea*

Do you see? Recollect how Washington Irving applied that principle. Just notice the simple, homely language he used in his description; yet no one could use bigger words than Irving could, if he desired.

Think how far the shoe dealer took your mind away from his shoes when he diverted your attention with, "This is not a toddling thought born of the wish," and again with, "a logical fact arising from our knowledge"!

We shall learn in later chapters why *simple language*, instead of being a handicap, is always *a strong point* in either writing or talking

And we shall also learn that the same fundamental principle requires that we *choose the order* in which we bring up our "features" so that the *reader will use the least possible mental effort in following the Idea*

I can't give you a better example of what I mean than that found in the addressing machine company's letter illustrated on page 54.

The writer of that letter *could* have said:

EXPRESSING FEELING IN WORDS

> "You can typewrite names and addresses at a speed of 30 a minute — simply take a handful of address plates," and so on.

But do you see what the reader would have done? He would have put his mind on "typewriting the addresses"; then he would have had to *jar that thought out of his mind* to adjust himself to thinking of using an addressing machine, before he could have grasped the idea.

But when the writer began:

> "Take a handful of address plates . . "

the reader easily calls up the image of doing it, then, with

> "slip them into the magazine"

he easily imagines the operation. Reading:

> "place the envelop, postcard, statement, or whatever you wish to address, at the printing position . "

he follows you with no mental effort·

> "and typewrite names and addresses at the rate of 30 per minute . "

gives him the whole idea with just the feeling you want to convey—"Well, how easy!"

This is so interesting and so *wonderfully helpful* that you may be impatient with me for not going on and covering it fully now. But experience has shown me that I must not. It comes under the head of "How to Make Your Meaning Clear," in the fourth part; and you can profit by it more after you have read the third chapter which deals with "Overcoming Indifference or Opposition" Making sure that we can apply the fundamentals of expressing ideas or feelings will keep us busy for the time Afterward there will be plenty of opportunity to learn how to perfect your style of expression.

We have now learned what to do to make the reader—or listener—grasp the idea we wish to convey. But, as we know, our knowledge applies mostly to actual objects—things we can describe.

It is time now to study the application of what we have learned to the more ordinary things that we have to write or

BUSINESS CORRESPONDENCE

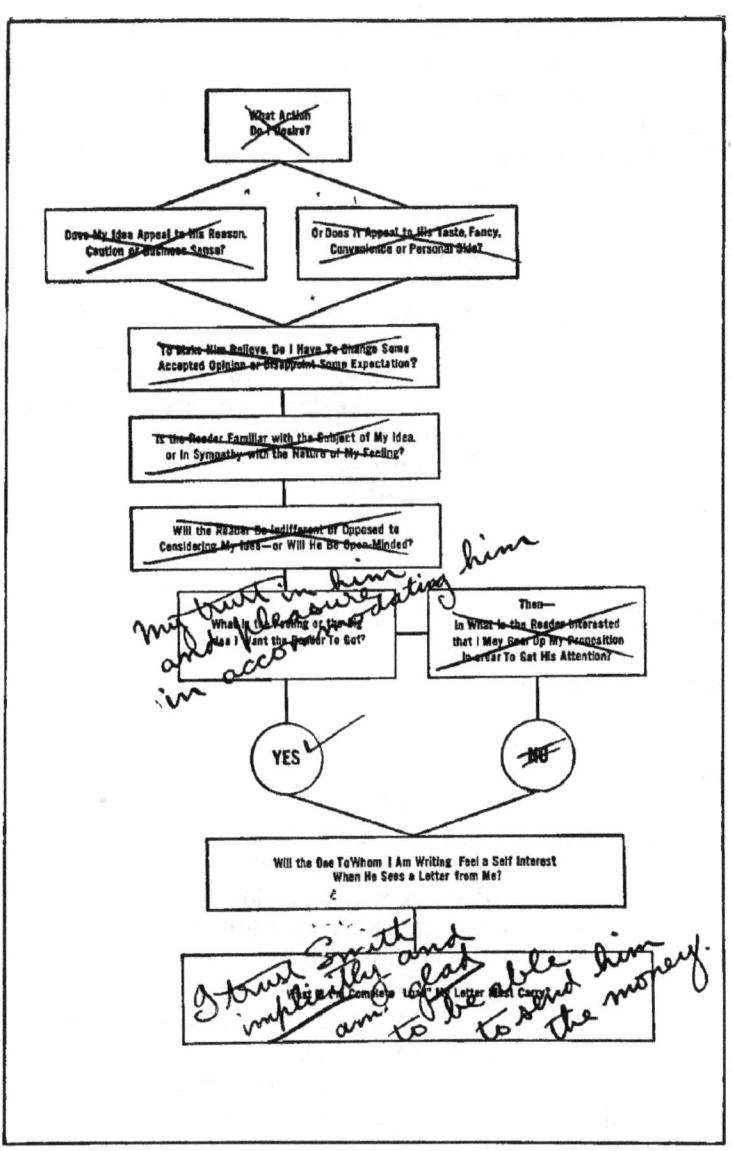

Panel 40

EXPRESSING FEELING IN WORDS

dictate about in the course of a day's work—collection letters, letters to smooth out complaints, in fact any kind of letter.

So back we go to the Mr. Smith, to whom we are going to lend $100. By the way I keep bringing that letter up and then laying it down again, while considering some other letter, you might think we really never were going to write it. But I have a reason. And as I have said, I have gone through all this so many times that I must insist on your letting me help you in my own way.

On the opposite page you will see my size-up of a letter to Smith granting the loan he asked. Study it. It is apparent at once that the feeling of "trust" and "pleasure" which the chart calls for can't be described as we can describe a farm or a machine or a stock of shoes. We can't, in other words, pick physical "features." But we can pick what *corresponds exactly to physical "features"*; that is, the *mental "features"* of the feeling we want to convey.

But before we write that letter let me make the principle behind our point very plain. An example will show you what I mean. The letter on the next page is one sent by a tire manufacturer to a man who had returned a used tire with the request that the manufacturer replace it with a new one.

Just suppose that you had fired the tire back at the manufacturer, feeling annoyed and disgruntled, and that you had received in return the polished, cordial, frank letter quoted! Wouldn't it have taken the edge off your annoyance? Wouldn't it have made you feel, "Well, those people are pretty square—I guess maybe I didn't take care of that tire the way I should—I'll study that bulletin"?

Now, let's see how it gets you to feel that way.

Reversing the process we used on Washington Irving's fine description, and on the land letter, and on the addressing machine letter will do the trick.

In the panel on page 81 you will see how this letter looks when "all the finishing touches" are crossed out. That leaves just the "features."

EXPRESSING FEELING IN WORDS

KENWOOD TIRE COMPANY
Boston, Massachusetts

Mr. E. M. Robinson,
Boston, Mass.

Dear Sir:

    Thank you for returning to us the 34" x 4" Pebbled Tread case, because it's easy to see you didn't receive the full service this tire was capable of giving and we want to see that you do get full service from every Pebbled Tread you use.

    In trying to find just what had caused the trouble, we noticed a good many little cuts in the tread, much like those described in the enclosed bulletin. You'll be interested in the explanation of what trouble these little cuts sometimes cause and of the best way to prevent their causing trouble in any of your other tires.

    Frankly, if you'll follow out the suggestions made in this bulletin, you will never have a tire give out before its time, as your old one did. Since we are interested, first of all, in seeing that you do get full service from your next tires, we'll gladly share your loss on this old one by sending you a new one of the same size for $17

                      Yours very truly,

                            KENWOOD TIRE COMPANY

EXPRESSING FEELING IN WORDS

How does the first "feature"—"Thank you for returning"—make you feel? Doesn't it make you at once feel that you are going to get a fair, courteous answer?

And from, "Easy to see you didn't receive full service," don't you unconsciously get the feeling that exact justice is going to be given you, no matter what it costs?

"We want to see that you do," gives the impression that the firm is looking after your interests, and from the phrase

---

THE "FEATURES"
Thanks for returning
Easy to see didn't receive full service
We want to see that you do
In trying to find out trouble we noticed
Way to prevent the trouble
Send new tire for $17

Panel 42

"in trying to find out the trouble," you almost see the painstaking effort that is being made to help you.

All these "features" build up just *the kind of feeling that makes you receptive* when the writer comes to telling you how you could have avoided the trouble, for he virtually convicts you of having injured the tire by your own carelessness, only he does it in such a diplomatic way that you feel not his censure but his desire to help you. And when he offers you an adjustment requiring you to pay $17 for a new tire, your whole feeling is one of satisfaction.

Summed up, then, the *feeling which the letter conveys visualized* as we have visualized the feeling for other letters, is shown in the panel on the following page.

If you study the "features" in the light of "The Feeling" to be conveyed, you will see that the writer first gives you an indication of his attitude toward your complaint in order to start the feeling he wants, then he simply reviews the steps he took from the time the damaged tire was received up to the decision he made on the adjustment, flavoring each "feature" with the feeling he wants to convey.

In short, as Washington Irving, in order to make you *see* the prosperity of the farm he was describing, *took objects* that caught his own eye and made them the "features" in

---

THE "FEELING"

That the manufacturer is fair, anxious to give justice, watchful in his customer's interest, and though the fault is not his, willing to be generous.

Panel 43

his description, the writer of the tire letter, in order to make you *feel* his fairness, his interest in you, and his generosity, *took mental steps* that led to his final decision and made them the "features" of his letter. But perhaps that is not plain enough so let us take a successful collection letter and see if a "demonstration" on it won't make the point clearer.

On the following page you will find a letter which is the fifth in a series written to delinquent accounts by a big Boston house. The "Idea or Feeling" to be conveyed evidently is that, although the debtor is just and fair, the claim also is just and fair and that it will be pushed to the limit. As in other cases I have given you, I have set down on page 84, (Panel 45) the Idea or Feeling so that we can visualize it better.

Now if you were the collection man, your first step would probably have been to look up the amount and the date of the bill; second, you would have looked up the letters sent and replies received; third, you would have satisfied yourself that everything was right about the claim, fourth, you would have decided what course to pursue

And that's just what the writer of the collection letter did. He first gave you an indication of his attitude, to *start the feeling* he wanted, then he simply *reviewed the steps*.

EXPRESSING FEELING IN WORDS

> ### WILSON TOOL COMPANY
> Omaha, Nebraska
>
> Mr. H. T. Morrison,
> Kearney, Nebraska.
>
> Dear Sir:
>
> We have decided to write you once more before handing your account to our Collection Department, where it cannot receive the same leniency that has heretofore been extended.
>
> According to our records, your account has been allowed to run behind. You have been notified of this and our several communications have failed to arouse you to a sense of responsibility. Please do not forget that you have signed a contract and that although the amount is small, it is as binding as though ten times the sum were involved. If you have lost interest in the contract it is through no known fault of ours.
>
> Our Collection Department shall not see the condition of your account if we can come to a satisfactory understanding now, without another week's delay. The matter rests with you.
>
>   Yours truly,
>   WILSON TOOL COMPANY

Panel 44

MAKING A START

Breaking into the game cannot be accidental, there must be a conscious plan, a new method, a radical bid for trade that will break through the public crust of indifference. The letter illustrated on this page, and those in Panels 41 and 46, will give you a start in the right direction in that fascinating game, letter writing Selected from thousands of letters, tried and tested in many ways, these letters have been chosen because they scintillate with ideas which override preconceived notions and worn out methods. The text explains the principles on which they were based. The problem sections allow you to test the worth of those principles

BUSINESS CORRESPONDENCE

Take another look at that collection letter on page 83 and you'll see that I'm right.

Do you not see where it gets its strength? Fundamentally it was constructed on exactly the same lines as the tire manufacturer's letter; yet it is a totally different type.

Now in concluding this chapter let us try this new principle on a letter to Smith granting the loan he asked. Our first

THE FEELING

We are fair, but our claim is a just one and if you don't pay, we will force you to

Panel 45

mental step is to decide that we will be glad to lend Smith the money if we can spare it.

Our second is to look up our bank balance to see if we can spare the money.

We find that we can spare it, and so our next step is to write a check and then a letter like this:

```
Dear Smith
    I'm glad to see you know how I would feel about
helping you out financially any time I can  My
balance in the bank happens to be pretty good, and
therefore you'll find a check for $100 enclosed.
Send it back at your own convenience
                        Sincerely yours,
```

By following the same principle used in the tire letter and in the collection letter, a letter like that just above almost writes itself. Yet does it not breathe the very feeling we want Smith to get?

To clinch the point let us take still another letter On the next page you will find one used with great success by a sales manager who had to make his men feel the necessity for cutting down their traveling expenses. Analyze the letter into the feeling conveyed and the "features" used

EXPRESSING FEELING IN WORDS

GREGG, WILSON AND FOX
Oshkosh, Wisconsin

F. T. Hopkinson,
La Crosse, Wisconsin.

Dear Frank

    Yesterday, the entire time of a conference was taken up with a serious discussion of rising costs, increased prices of material, and reduced profits And you may be sure that our sales organization came in for its share of attention

    Our selling cost was considered excessive. In fact, a good deal of criticism was aimed at me, and I am expected materially to reduce the cost of marketing our product

    Now, we will not consider for a moment the reduction of salaries or commissions I know that your earnings are not excessive for the service you are giving us; but I am going to ask you to reduce your traveling expenses if that is possible

    I am absolutely convinced that not a single member of our sales force would consciously spend a cent of the firm's money unnecessarily But I believe that expenses may be lowered if all expenditures are made after fully considering their necessity

    Understand, the company does not want you to sacrifice your comfort for economy We know that our salesmen are gentlemen, and we want them to travel like gentlemen If, however, you can curtail expense a little here and there it will help materially to reduce the excess on our bill for traveling

    I've been given to understand that selling costs must come down This is unpleasant news to me, and I know that you will do everything you can to prevent a repetition of the command.

    Every good wish for your continued success.

                Yours sincerely,

BUSINESS CORRESPONDENCE

to convey it and see how closely the construction of that letter follows the construction of other letters we have studied.

Now if we were to stop and chat for a while about what we have gone over in this chapter, you would probably ask, "Are all good letters as simple as these we have been looking at, are all good sales letters as direct, are all good answers to complaints as straightforward, are all good collection letters as frank, are all good letters to salesmen as conservative?"

No, they are not.

I know of many, many letters—every one of them *proved good* by results—which could not be reconstructed by the simple process with which we reconstructed Washington Irving's description, or by which we could reconstruct the works of Victor Hugo and other authors. Why is this?

Because the element of indifference or opposition to the idea on the part of the reader is a factor. Most of Charles Dickens' books, for instance, were written to attack some social system in the life of his times, and the general public could naturally be assumed to be either indifferent to the wrong or opposed to changing it. Therefore, his writing in such cases could not be rebuilt as we rebuilt Irving's narrative. And in a number of letters used in connection with the next chapter we shall see that the same sort of difficulties were met. You'll find four of them selected at random on pages 87, 100, 102 and 104. Look them over and see if you can detect the principle on which they were based. Each was written to a man or to *a list of men judged to be indifferent to accepting the writer's idea.*

When such an attitude exists in the reader's mind, experienced letter writers have learned, as great novelists have learned, as stump speakers and campaigners have learned, as many salesmen have learned, that a simple, direct expression of the idea will not get under the skin, so to speak. The "idea" must be approached from an indirect angle *How to work out this indirect approach* as a simple and easy expression of a direct idea will be covered in the next chapter We shall learn among other things how, from a simple, direct

EXPRESSING FEELING IN WORDS

sales idea on wrapping paper, to build an anecdotal or visionary approach for it, and just when it is right to do so. We shall learn when a subject like "fresh eggs" must, for best effect, be approached by the avenue of eggs that are not fresh, as in the letter below. We shall learn when a salesman's reproof or a "ginger-up" idea should be concealed under a cloak of bantering praise.

And, now, how far do you think you have progressed?

Can't you already begin to see where a big improvement can be made in many of your letters? Can't you now see why so many letters that you have seen and thrown into the

---

BROADACRES
STEVENSVILLE, OHIO
R. F. D. No. 2

Mr. F. C King,
Columbus, Ohio.
Dear Mr. King

  "An EGG VERSUS A PRETTY GOOD EGG."

 The eggs you buy as strictly fresh, coming by the usual channels of distribution, pass through the following hands from producer to consumer

  1 Collected by local dealers or the country store
  2. Shipped to commission houses at the big markets
  3 Sold to wholesalers and jobbers.
  4. Sold to retailers
  5. Held in retailer's store until delivered to customers.

 The time consumed is from two to three weeks for the first quality of fresh eggs.

    THIS IS A PRETTY GOOD EGG

 My eggs I collect twice a week from the farmers in my neighborhood — bring them to my farm, sort and pack them into cartons of one dozen each, and deliver them by auto the next day at your door, almost before the hen ceases to advertise her latest achievement.

     THIS IS AN EGG.
   TRY THEM AND SEE THE DIFFERENCE
      Yours truly,
         R T. STEVENS

Panel 47

BUSINESS CORRESPONDENCE

waste-basket failed to interest you? Can't you see the importance of putting at least one Big Idea or Feeling into every letter you write?

Go back over some of the letters you have written in past times and see if they really conveyed the idea.

Just try, for yourself, diagramming the idea of the very next letter you have to write, according to the simple little plan you have now learned and see if you can't make it much more vivid by the plan. Try the effect of picking out the "features" of your Big Idea and see if from them you can't make your idea much more clear. Take some event of your day that you want to describe to your wife in the evening, and on your way home just mentally resolve it into its "features" and see if you can't tell it to your wife much more expressively. Or take some humorous story that you have heard badly told and see if you can't bring out the humor of it much more pointedly.

There was never a story told, a speech made, an advertisement prepared, or a letter written or dictated, that could not be more pointedly or more eloquently or more expressively done if this simple little plan were applied to it.

And in the next part we shall learn still more about it.

SUMMARY

WE have found in this chapter that expressing feeling and ideas in words is almost entirely a matter of determining in advance the exact thought we want our reader to get and then selecting the "features" which will arouse that Big Idea in his mind. We have found that the chart we made up in the first part guides us to the Big Idea and that the Big Idea, in turn, suggests the "features" that aroused the idea in us. By writing down these "features" and connecting them by lesser thoughts, the interest paragraphs of a letter which awaken the Big Idea in the mind of the reader, practically write themselves

But there is another side to the proposition. We barely hinted at it in the latter part of this chapter. We have been

EXPRESSING FEELING IN WORDS

assuming that the reader was willing to listen, although we all know that there will be times when he will not be willing to hear what we have to say In the next part, therefore, we will take it for granted that our reader is opposed to our idea and so we will learn how to overcome his indifference or opposition.

Just as we turned to a master in this chapter to discover a fundamental of good writing, so in the next chapter we will turn to another master to find another principle. In this chapter Washington Irving was our guide In the next, a flash at Lincoln's Gettysburg speech and a glimpse at one of Robert G. Ingersoll's greatest orations will point the way. It may seem odd that the work of men long dead can show us how to write better business letters today, but odd as it may seem, it is a fact. The methods that Ingersoll and other great orators used to sway their audiences still stand They are being used, sometimes unconsciously, by the best letter writers. In the next part we'll discover what those methods are, try them, and prove them by pointing them out in tried and tested letters.

A word more Are you doing the work outlined for you in the problem sections of this book? Don't by any means overlook this very important work. Some of the tasks set for you are admittedly a little difficult On the other hand, they are intensely practical. Every one of them was selected because of the training in writing letters it will give you. And every problem, when solved, will make you better able to write letters that win.

PROBLEM SECTION II

IN the first problem section I charted for you the 10 important questions which should be answered in advance before writing any letter. Summed up, the answers to the questions constitute the "load" a letter must carry. We found that Panel 21, which grew out of the first chapter, *checks one up on each important part of the job of letter writing* and permits nothing that properly belongs to a letter's "load" to be left unsaid. The problems in the previous section proved the great practicability of the chart.

This book on applied business correspondence was charted before being written, exactly as I urged you to chart your letters. For instance, if you'll look at Panel 40 on page 78 you'll understand that in the first part we sized up the "load" this book must carry. The second section of the chart asks whether you as a reader feel a "self-interest" in this book. You do or you wouldn't be reading it.

I feel safe, therefore, in dropping this second question for the time being and going on to Section 3a of Panel 16, page 32, which asks, "What is the Feeling or the Big Idea I Want the Reader to Get?" On that question I'm going to rest and in this problem section show you exactly how to handle this important and extremely delicate matter.

Before I show you how to express ideas or feeling in words, let me explain my method once more. Bear this in mind: I'm not going to spend a moment at any time giving you rules of punctuation, laws of grammar or of rhetoric. You can find all that which you may need in books devoted to those special subjects. In this book *I'll deal solely with the principles of letter writing*.

EXPRESSING FEELING IN WORDS

From my years of experience in writing letters and teaching others to write them I've found that almost anyone can write a good letter if he is told what must be said in that letter. And that's what I'm going to do in this book. I'm going to devote most of my attention to showing you what to say, for when you know *how to analyze and how to find positively and definitely what to say*, saying it is comparatively easy. But don't misunderstand, there'll be times, of course, when much depends on the choice of words or choice of expression and I'll devote an entire chapter to that subject. What I want to make clear now is that we are not going to linger over the details of writing any one letter except as they show us how to write all letters. As a rule, throughout this book we shall drop details so as to be able to devote more time to principles. With the principles underlying good letter writing thoroughly understood, no matter what business or what line of work you are in, you'll be able *to write letters that are right*

Now we are ready to take up the actual work of this problem section. First, let's check up on the problems of the previous section.

Turn to your Material File which I told you to prepare and you'll find your size-up of a letter to Smith granting the loan which he requested. Compare it with the size-up which I have made on page 78.

Of course, you hit at once upon the "complete load" and wrote it across the bottom panel of your chart, for I practically gave you the answer when I submitted the problem. I'm also sure you didn't pause at the second question which brought up the matter of Smith's self-interest. The only possible question which might have stumped you is the third one, but if you read the foregoing chapter carefully you found the answer between the lines and decided that your trust and your pleasure in accommodating him was the feeling you wanted Smith to get.

Simple enough it seems, now that we've covered the point, and yet there is food for thought in that chart. How easy,

BUSINESS CORRESPONDENCE

in cases of this kind, to write a letter that humiliates or offends by apparent condescension on your part or by unwitting bruskness, all due to the fact that you didn't keep the Big Idea in mind.

Now look over the letter to Smith which developed from the chart. I showed it in the preceding chapter, but for your convenience I reproduce it again below:

Dear Smith:

I'm glad to see you know how I would feel about helping you out financially any time I could. My balance in the bank happens to be pretty good, and therefore you'll find a check for $100 enclosed. Send it back at your own convenience.

Sincerely yours,

There's a cordial handclasp in every line, there's your satisfaction, your gladness in being able to do a favor, and through it all runs a cheery "good luck to you, old man" that is bound to make Smith forget all about his embarrassment at asking a loan from you and that is sure to make him think of you as a prince of good fellows.

But you may, at once, come to the scratch with: "Oh, well, it's easy enough to make a loan, how about refusing it? There's the rub." Answering you, let me say that we are not through with Smith by any means. He'll bob up every once in a while. In the fifth part, however, I'll dismiss the matter by writing a letter that will make Smith understand our position and our real regret at not granting his request.

You are impatient to go on, I know, and so I'll pass on to the next problem. From your Material File take your "Size-up of Men's Shoe Store Letter" and compare it with my chart of the problem. You'll find it on page 71. Refer to it as you read.

This time the answer to the first question requires no discussion. The "complete load" of the letter is to interest the prospect in new shoes. But which answer—"yes" or "no"—

EXPRESSING FEELING IN WORDS

did you choose for the second question on the chart: "Will the one to whom I am writing feel a self-interest?"

I feel that there can be no debate on this point, for on a list of non-customers, personally unknown to a merchant, it is safe to figure that prospects will not feel much self-interest in his letter, and that as soon as they see that it is "only advertising," many of them will stop reading. In fact, for almost all circular letters to blanket lists of names, a writer should practically always answer "no" to this question. Notice that I answered "no," but *immediately made a "self-interest" for my reader.* What man isn't interested in his own feet? Comfort or appearance will get the interest of any man when shoes are the topic of discussion.

When I came to consider the Feeling or Big Idea, almost instantly, on account of the start I had made, the size and completeness of stock came to mind. The answers to other questions of the chart suggest themselves. Indifference, obviously, is the answer to the fourth question, just as the warning in the fifth question kept me, as it would have kept you, from being too technical.

As you continue to trace my work of sizing up this letter's "load" you'll see at once how the sixth question on the chart reminded me that I must disturb my reader's satisfaction with his present store in order to switch him over to mine. An appeal to his personal side, through his taste, leading to the action desired is suggested by the questions in the seventh and eighth panels at the top of the chart.

So you see, the chart, simple as it is, led me up to every problem which had to be solved in this letter. It is all so plain that further comment on my part is hardly necessary. You'll find the letter I wrote from it on the next page. Look it over. You'll find every feature I've mentioned incorporated in it.

Summed up, the chart of the shoe letter shows us: first, that the letter must have an opening that appeals to every man's interest in his feet; second, that it must convey the idea of how big the stock is; third, that the letter must not

BUSINESS CORRESPONDENCE

depend on the idea being enough, but that the writer must lead the man into it; fourth, that all shoe terms and descriptions must be translated into common, everyday language; fifth, that there must be an atmosphere of sincerity in the

> Here are the new, long, narrow toes for those who want the very latest style, and for those who simply CAN'T wear those thin, narrow toes, here are comfortable broad toes, but so skilfully shaped that they have all the appearance of being narrow! Some are buttoned, some laced, so no matter which you prefer, you can have it. And here they are in rather extreme fancy tops, but if your taste is quieter, why, over here are the plain leather tops.
>
> And then oxfords — oxfords in all shapes, tan oxfords, gray oxfords, and substantial blacks
>
> But perhaps you don't run to STYLE so much as comfort — for you, then, there are roomy, comfortable, sensible shapes, and in every size from unusually small to tremendously big, from broad, short to long, narrow.
>
> There are all styles of shoes with arch supports, and in atomic shapes, and with square, low heels, and for men with bunions, then, in special shapes without toe-caps.

letter; sixth, that as the reader's taste and personal preferences are being appealed to, the letter must exercise gentle persuasion and not use logic or argument; seventh, that as the action desired will call for sustained willingness, the reader must be inspired with enthusiasm, or he will lose his interest and lay the letter aside.

Now again read the shoe dealer's letter above and see if every point I mentioned (and all of them are on the chart) has been covered. You may notice that the letter lacks an opener I have purposely omitted it, but in a later problem section I shall bring up this letter again and, with you, work out an opener for it.

In the second chapter I devoted considerable space to an explanation of how to develop the Big Idea by dividing it into its "features" and then connecting idea and "features" to make a letter, or paragraphs in a letter. In this problem section I'll supply some ideas for you to develop, but before

EXPRESSING FEELING IN WORDS

I do that, I'll run over a good letter with you so that you'll be sure to do the work correctly.

On page 54 you'll find a copy of an addressing machine letter. Read that letter carefully, and follow the points in it as I bring them to your attention.

The Big Idea in the mind of the writer, you can plainly see, was "simplicity of operation, speed, and efficiency."

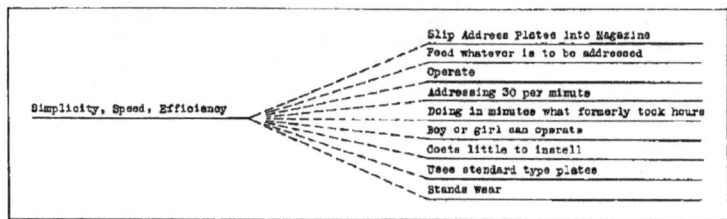

Panel 48

It is easy to pick the "features" that represent the machine's speed and simplicity, as the writer seems either to have watched or to have imagined a machine in operation and selected the exact steps taken to get speed, such as slipping the plates into the magazine, feeding, and operating. The "features" for the idea of speed are, first, the actual number of letters addressed a minute; and, second, the results of such speed on everyday work—"does in a few minutes what before took tedious hours."

The idea of efficiency is shown by, first, the cost of an operator—the fact that a young girl or boy can work the machine; second, the low cost of installation; third, the standard type plate used; and fourth, the machine's long life and durability.

I have outlined these "features" for you on the diagram above. Compare it with the addressing machine letter referred to in the previous paragraphs and notice with what extreme ease words shape themselves around "features" when the "features" of a letter are clearly before you. Make out a copy of that diagram and file it in your Material File, for it will provide a good example to follow if you are ever puzzled about building the Big Idea.

BUSINESS CORRESPONDENCE

You may think this is easy, but it's not. Follow me a moment longer before you try your hand at picking the features of the Big Idea. To reverse the process—for I want you to practise this plan from all angles—you will find on page 97 a letter that expresses its idea very clearly. Opposite that portion of the letter devoted to the Idea, I have drawn a bracket—you will find the "features" of the letter listed below the letter. From those "features" I want you to work out the Big Idea. (On a piece of scratch paper draw up a diagram like the one in Panel 48, and then write the "features" on the lines, following my plan for the Addressograph letter). File this diagram in your Material File.

Now, with the example fresh in your mind, see if you can, from the SYSTEM letter reproduced on page 98, pick out the "features" on which the writer built the expression of his Big Idea. That idea, to give you a lift on this first problem, was

```
You can learn from this book how to handle finances
and financial affairs with surer success.
```

The opening paragraph, of course, is merely an "attention getter." Diagram the idea into its "features," just as I diagrammed the addressing machine letter, and file your effort in your Material File In the next chapter I shall give you a correct diagram.

Because of the study and digging that I know you did to work the foregoing problem, you are prepared to take the letter of an insurance agent, reproduced on page 99, and make a complete diagram of its Big Idea with all the "features." In the next section I shall give you the correct diagram. Make a complete diagram of your letter and file it in your Material File.

You have now had experience in diagramming the "features" of the Big Idea and you have tried your hand at working out the Big Idea from its "features." The next thing to do is to write a letter, so we'll have a little practise along that line. To begin with, read the letter at the top of page 101 which I received from a retailer.

EXPRESSING FEELING IN WORDS

Dear Sir:

We are pleased to acknowledge receipt of your valued letter of April 20th, and agreeable to your request, are mailing you under other cover our HAYES Four-Wheel Planter book. It contains an honest and careful description and is of interest to every corn grower who would measure results in dollars and cents.

The HAYES Four-Wheel has been before the buying public twenty-nine years with constantly increasing sales. No article can be marketed profitably for so long a time unless it has the merit promised in advertisements and literature.

Few changes have been made in construction and only then when years of experience and actual field work have proved those changes to be improvements. We will not lower the high standard of quality of the HAYES Four-Wheel to add "talking points" and lessen the efficiency and dependability of the planter.

Thousands already know and every year corn growers are learning the wonderful advantages in HAYES Four-Wheel construction. How this planter plants every kernel exactly the same depth, drops all kinds and sizes of seeds accurately, never misses a hill, checks straight, and covers where all ordinary open wheels fail.

Why the HAYES Four-Wheel makes every acre a profit maker, saves time and trouble in planting, and produces a better quality and larger quantity of corn.

The HAYES Four-Wheel has fulfilled all these claims. Corn growers who buy this planter get what they expect. We guarantee it to fulfill every claim in your own fields or will refund the price paid together with freight.

We have no dealer in your town and are therefore pleased to enclose herewith NET PRICE LIST, freight prepaid to your R.R. Station. We have but one price, either direct or through the dealer, and everyone who buys the HAYES Four-Wheel knows he has bought at the minimum price.

Send us a sample of your seed and tell us the number you wish in a hill, and the distance apart if you drill, and we will select the sizes of seed plates best adapted to your needs.

Awaiting your favorable reply by early mail, we are

Very truly yours,

Panel 49

1—29 years of increasing sales
2—Few changes found necessary in all that time
3—Thousands in use
4—Plants every kernel same depth
5—Drops all kinds and sizes accurately
6—Checks straight
7—Covers where others fail
8—Saves time and trouble
9—Increases yield

BUSINESS CORRESPONDENCE

A. W. SHAW COMPANY
PUBLISHERS
CASS, HURON AND ERIE STREETS
CHICAGO

NEW YORK
BOSTON
PHILADELPHIA
CLEVELAND
A W SHAW CO., LTD.
LONDON

Oscar Jacobson,
Belleville, Ill.

Dear Sir:

Will you EXAMINE a copy of the unusual book, "How to Finance a Business," if I send it at my own expense?

In a perfectly frank, forward way 73 of America's foremost business men reveal their inside financing methods; tell you how to raise capital for new firms or secure additional funds to expand going concerns; their proved rules for avoiding financial troubles; successful yet simple ways of building credit; how to control the finances of a business in emergencies; specific suggestions for best applying for money at the bank; new unique ways of finding leaks and making savings; stock and bond issues; in all, 202 methods that have raised capital or extended credit, year in and year out, for 73 of America's most successful business men.

As you go through this book and find how 73 successful business men are meeting knotty financial problems you will find yourself intensely interested. But when you see how these shrewd men are meeting some of the very problems you now face -- and how easy it will be to adopt these same methods, adding their experience to your own, you will find yourself not merely interested, but SURPRISED.

Simply indicate on the numbered card enclosed the exact address to which I am to send your copy of this book.

No expense; no risk; simply mail the card.

But you should act today.

                Very truly yours,

                    A. W. SHAW COMPANY

Panel 50

EXPRESSING FEELING IN WORDS

R. W. WALDO
Chicago, Ill.

Mr. Herbert Watson,
Chicago, Ill.

Dear Sir:

    What's your summer-time hobby?

        -- Golf?
        -- Tennis?
        -- Fishing?
        -- Motoring?
        -- Baseball?
        -- Yachting?
        -- or plain, ordinary hikes over the country with camera or maybe with only a stick?

    Whatever it is, it increases the chance of accident Why not, then, increase your PROTECTION against LOSS from accident?

    Take out some additional accident insurance today. Drop me a line, or call me on the 'phone, and I'll have you fully covered by tomorrow morning.

    One out of every eight policyholders meets with an accident during the summer, on which indemnity is paid. Think of it -- one in eight!

    Call me up now and get yourself fully covered.

                          Yours sincerely,

                            R. W. WALDO

Panel 51

BUSINESS CORRESPONDENCE

MOORE PUBLISHING COMPANY
CIRCULATION DEPARTMENT
BOSTON, MASSACHUSETTS

Mrs. A. M. Brown,
Windsor, Ill.
Dear Madam.

    We regret we have not heard from you with a remittance in response to our bill for our magazine, Home Economics, sent you in March, but we presume that for some reason it was not convenient for you to remit the amount at that time. We can no longer carry this as an open account, and are again enclosing you a bill for the amount now due. We have, however, arranged a very easy plan of payment, whereby you can, without inconvenience, pay the entire amount in <u>instalments</u>.

    Your bill now amounts to $6, and we will consent to accept $2 every other month (only $1 monthly) until the whole amount is paid. We have made three notes, due 60 days apart, and enclose them herewith for your signature. Please sign and return them with the bill, using the enclosed envelop. We will receipt and return the bill and will forward the notes, as they come due, for collection. Or, if you prefer, you may send us three checks for $2 each, dated ahead and payable 60 days apart, and we will deposit them on the dates they mature We do not know whether you need or care to be thus accommodated. YOU may find it convenient now to send a check or a money order at once. We trust, however, you will appreciate this easy method that we offer for paying your account, and that you will send remittance either by note or by cash at once.

                  Very truly yours,
                MOORE PUBLISHING COMPANY

Panel 53

EXPRESSING FEELING IN WORDS

```
. . .. . .... . . . .... . . .. . ..... . . .
Dear Sir
           They've arrived —
           The new spring and summer shirtings.
           From these we are ready to make shirts to your
measure, to offer the assurance that your shirts will be
new and different in pattern and will fit.
           We are enclosing a few samples taken at random
from the many shirtings, from which selections may be
made in this Custom Shirt Section of ours.
           We shall consider it an especial privilege to
serve you in this matter this season, as we feel sure
we can meet your wishes in shirts made to measure at
prices consistent with what we deliver.
                                    Very truly yours,
--- ---------------- ----........ --- .. — — .- — . ....... — —— ---.- ...... ---------
```

Do you see how lacking it is in the expression of any real idea? Of course you do. Let's write a good letter for that proposition, that is, enough of a letter to convey a genuine idea to a reader. I wrote one. I shall show it in the next problem section and I would like yours to agree with mine, at least as far as the Big Idea is concerned.

The first work to do, of course, is to make a general size-up of the letter's "load." Get out one of the blank charts which you have already prepared and size up this letter's "load."

From my own size-up, which was based on a previous experience with just such a proposition, I suggest this:

> Our custom-made summer shirts will do as much for
> your appearance and comfort as a finely tailored suit
> of clothes does.

If you will first review the steps I took in building up other letters, you will agree that the next task is to decide on the "features." The first "feature" that makes one think of the appearance and comfort of a custom-made shirt is, perhaps, the way a cutter shapes his pattern to every curve, dimension, peculiarity, and position of his customer's shoulders, chest, neck, and arms.

The second "feature" is the cutter's personal skill in cutting and making the shirts to conform to the individual's pattern.

BUSINESS CORRESPONDENCE

ANGIER PAPER COMPANY
GRAND RAPIDS, WIS.

Henry Johnson,
Keokuk, Iowa

Dear Sir

It was a local between Philadelphia and Trenton

I sat in a smoker, which was half a baggage car At Frankford, an automobile tire was thrown on — a yard or two of its plain Kraft wrapper flapping in the breeze With my pocket camera I took a picture of it — see enclosed

And I said to the baggage man· "Does this happen often?" "Nearly every day," he replied, "we carry tires with wrappers loose, torn — and rubber exposed."

So I wondered "Does it pay a manufacturer to spend millions in building reputation, and then — to save a cent or two per tire — send his product broadcast over the land — imperfectly protected against light, dirt and exposure?"

Plain Kraft paper — even of a 50-pound basis — won't stand the strain of shipping But 30-pound Kraft — reinforced with yarn and waterproofed — will do the trick to perfection

Test the strength of the sample enclosed. Wrap it tightly around your wrist. Note the firm, strong, neat job it makes.

And six ounces will wrap a tire — right.

Tell us, please, the size rolls you use — diameter, width and core We'll then send you enough — without expense or obligation — enough for a thorough trial

Give Angier's Tirewrap the opportunity to prove its worth to you — as it has already done to Goodrich, Michelin, McGraw and others. The postcard is for your convenience.

Sincerely yours,
ANGIER PAPER COMPANY

Panel 54

EXPRESSING FEELING IN WORDS

The third is, perhaps, his genius for putting little improvements in a shirt, such as cutting the cuff of a striped shirt so the colored stripe instead of the white, comes at the edge —thus keeping the cuff's edge from showing soil so quickly —or cutting the front plait so the stripe or pattern exactly matches the body of the goods.

The fourth "feature" is the beauty and variety of materials one has to choose from. Below is a diagram of the idea and its "features":

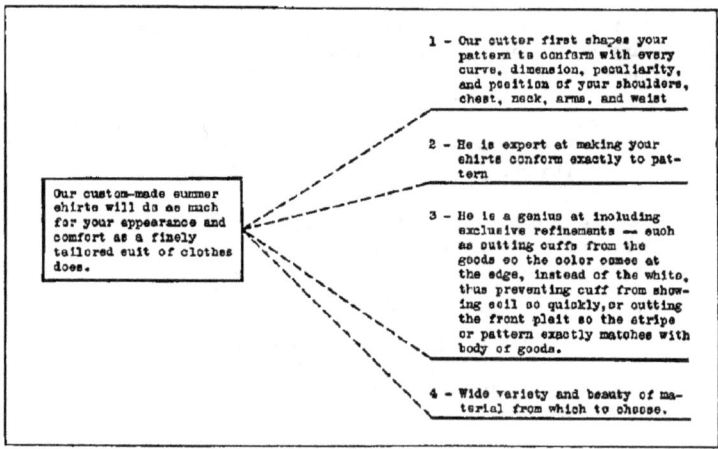

Panel 52

It will be interesting to see what you make of it. Write out only the expression of the idea by connecting up "features" and idea, just as you have been taught in this problem section and in the next problem section we shall compare notes. At this time never mind about the opening of the letter or its close. In concluding this part I'll call attention to two problems which follow. Work out these problems according to directions which I have given you and then in the next problem section you'll find the answers I have prepared.

Problem 1

Here are the conditions that faced a certain business man. Study them carefully, chart out a size-up of the work the let-

BUSINESS CORRESPONDENCE

GORDON & WILSON
The "Bestever" Line
ST. PAUL, MINNESOTA

Mr. A. T. Lanning,
Bangor, Michigan

Dear Lanning.

 Your report from Kansas City in one hand and a hammer in the other — that's a true picture of me right this moment

 "Everybody here buying close" — when I read that I raised an eyebrow. "Crop prospects bad" — when I read that I raised a fist. But when I came to your — "Think I was lucky to get even this much business" — I raised something worse than either eyebrow or fist.

 Nope, Lanning — You can't get any sympathy out of me on stuff like that. I got reports just like yours from every one of the other men, and I have just finished wiping off tears of sympathy for each one of them — except you and Burt.

 But any man who could drop into B. P.'s office after we had made that terrible bull of drawing a sight draft on them, and then drop out with old Pearson s re-order in his pocket — any man who can do the hundred other things you have done, and Burt has done, can't offer me talk about poor crop prospects and get away with any sympathy from me

 My sympathy glands freeze up when I get reports like this last one from YOU. You'd let poor crop prospects and generally tight buying stop you from getting big orders about as much as a good, well-brought-up mosquito would let a fly-screen stop him.

 You've been listening to some alibi-artist and got the microbe, that's the trouble WITH YOU. Forget it, and remember that Bestever Rompers and Blouses are as good a hard-time line as they are a prosperity line. And that Lanning is an all-kinds-of-times salesman. Spare me the "poor-crop-talk" — I'm deaf on YOUR side.

 Yours for a better alibi next time,

          L. R. T.

Panel 55

EXPRESSING FEELING IN WORDS

ter must do, diagram the idea into its "features"; then from that diagram, express the idea just as simply, yet as graphically as you can.

File your chart, diagram, and letter in your Material File. In the next chapter the actual letter will be found. You may compare it with your own and correct your mistakes, if you made any.

A cream separator manufacturer received an inquiry from his magazine advertising. He sent the prospect a catalog and a short letter, but did not get an order. He now wants to send a longer letter that will impress the prospect with the special qualities of the machine and that will differentiate it from cheaper machines which he suspects the prospect has also been investigating. The points about his separator are:

Made in a factory equipped with machinery adjusted unusually accurately;
Splendid material and workmanship used;
An unlimited guarantee as printed in catalog;
Separator gives more butter fat and cream,
Cheap separators get out of order and need repairs;
The guarantee ensures high quality and value;
No better separators made.

Problem 2

Now I want you to learn how to apply the same principles to a collection letter. Below I tell the conditions under which a certain collection letter was written. The letter appears in the next problem section. Do the same as you did for the sales letter—make a size-up chart, diagram the Big Idea into its features, then build up your letter upon them. File your memoranda in your Material File You will need them for reference later on.

There are a number of debtors on your books that have been sent a statement, followed by a second statement and a short letter. You, as a collection man, are going to send a third statement and a letter impressing the debtors with the fact that their failure to remit promptly is a hardship. While the accounts are not large in amount, the large number of them makes carrying them quite a burden. There is always a possibility, of course, in cases of this kind, of error in the bills, so that you, as the collection man, want to make the debtors see that if errors have been made, you should be told about it at once. If the account has only been overlooked you want to impress upon them that it deserves immediate attention.

With these test cases to practise on, I believe you will be able to work out others for yourself. Practise is what counts

You will not find it easy at first to pick out a concrete idea for every letter, unless you have been in the habit of doing that sort of thing. Nor will you probably find it easy to pick out the features that suggest the Big Idea. But practise will soon develop a knack that will amount almost to second nature with you. And every letter you write will show the results.

PART III

OVERCOMING INDIFFERENCE OR OPPOSITION

CHAPTER III

OVERCOMING INDIFFERENCE OR OPPOSITION

IF people always bought what they wanted, if people always did everything they would like to do, and if people always believed the simple truth when it was told them, writing sales letters would be only a matter of making see the desirability of your goods; writing collection letters would be only a matter of calling their attention to your account; answering complaints or writing any other kind of letter would be only a matter of stating facts.

And with what we learned in the first part about charting the "load" of a letter, and in the second part about conveying a Big Idea or Feeling, according to Washington Irving's methods, any of us could *handle about any kind of letter* we might have to write.

But the trouble is that people don't always believe what their reason bids them believe, or do even what they know they ought to do, or buy even what they are convinced it would be good for them to buy!

Don't you agree with that?

For instance, don't you know men who want an automobile and have money to pay for one, but who are not willing to spend the money for it? Don't you often see a man who wants new clothes, but for one reason or another makes his old ones do? Even when he has the money? And don't you often see people whose reason tells them they ought not to wear such tight shoes, or ought not to smoke so much, or ought to go to bed earlier, but who just sit tight and refuse to follow their own convictions?

Of course you do. Perhaps you have some of these amiable weaknesses yourself.

BUSINESS CORRESPONDENCE

Such conditions, at any rate, exist on all sides of us; and in letters, advertising, selling, even in friendly arguments and after-dinner table talk, we have to take them into consideration, if our letters, our advertising, our sales work, or our conversation is to be effective.

The *simple truth isn't always enough. Sometimes it must be staged.* Creating desire isn't always enough Sometimes the want for a thing must be made to seem a necessity.

So now having learned the fundamental principle of conveying a Big Idea or a Feeling, we must learn to adapt it, when necessary, to overcoming indifference or opposition on the part of people to whom we want to convey it. That is the fourth point I brought up in building up the chart on page 32, and that is the work of this chapter.

But do not forget, as you read this book, that simple descriptions like Irving's or concise, pithy letters like those we saw built up in the first chapter, by the same methods as Irving's descriptions were built, are the best way of presenting an idea—if they have an open, fair field ahead It is only when indications of the attitude, or character, or circumstances of our readers show us *the need for something more*, that we should get away from plain, straightforward methods.

To make this point clear, I shall discuss with you two great American orations. The first of them, Lincoln's address at the dedication of the Gettysburg National Cemetery, you will find with its "features" on the opposite page. The second, the close of Robert G. Ingersoll's great speech nominating James G. Blaine for the presidency of the United States, is on page 112.

Here are two of the world's masterpieces in eloquence; but how different they are! Note Lincoln's noble simplicity; on the other hand, note Ingersoll's rather florid style.

Just imagine Lincoln on the Gettysburg battlefield indulging in the flowery similes of Ingersoll's speech! But on the other hand, think how ineffective Ingersoll's speech would have been in that political convention if clothed in the solemn simplicity of Lincoln's words.

OVERCOMING INDIFFERENCE OR OPPOSITION

FOURSCORE and seven years ago our fathers brought forth on this continent a new nation, conceived in liberty and dedicated to the proposition that all men are created equal

Now we are engaged in a great civil war, testing whether that nation, or any nation so conceived and so dedicated, can long endure We are met on a great battle-field of that war We have come to dedicate a portion of that field as a final resting-place for those who here gave their lives that that nation might live It is altogether fitting and proper that we should do this

But, in a larger sense, we cannot dedicate, we cannot consecrate, we cannot hallow this ground The brave men, living and dead, who struggled here have consecrated it far above our poor power to add or detract The world will little note nor long remember what we say here, but it can never forget what they did here It is for us, the living, rather, to be dedicated here to the unfinished work which they who fought here have thus far so nobly advanced It is rather for us to be here dedicated to the great task remaining before us —— that from these honored dead we take increased devotion to that cause for which they gave the last full measure of devotion, that we here highly resolve that these dead shall not have died in vain, that this nation, under God, shall have a new birth of freedom, and that government of the people, by the people, for the people, shall not perish from the earth

—ABRAHAM LINCOLN

Loyalty to the national principles of liberty and equality, and to the men who died to save them
- The principles for which our nation was created
- The war that jeopardizes them
- The battlefield that typifies that war
- The soldiers who died on it
- What their sacrifice has done for us
- What we can do in return
- We must not let their deaths be in vain
- We must not let this government perish

Panel 56

BUSINESS CORRESPONDENCE

THIS is a grand year, a year filled with the recollections of the Revolution, filled with proud and tender memories of the past, with the sacred legends of liberty, a year in which the sons of freedom will drink from the fountains of enthusiasm, a year in which the people call for a man who has preserved in Congress what our soldiers won upon the field, a year in which we call for the man who has torn from the throat of treason the tongue of slander * * *

Like an armed warrior, like a plumed knight, James G Blaine marched down the halls of the American Congress and threw his shining lance full and fair against the brazen foreheads of the defamers of his country and the maligners of his honor For the Republicans to desert this gallant leader now is as though an army should desert their general upon the field of battle

Gentlemen of the convention, in the name of the great republic, the only republic that ever existed upon this earth, in the name of all her defenders and of all her supporters, in the name of all her soldiers living, in the name of all her soldiers dead upon the field of battle, Illinois—Illinois nominates for the next President of this country that prince of parliamentarians, that leader of leaders James G Blaine

—ROBERT G INGERSOLL

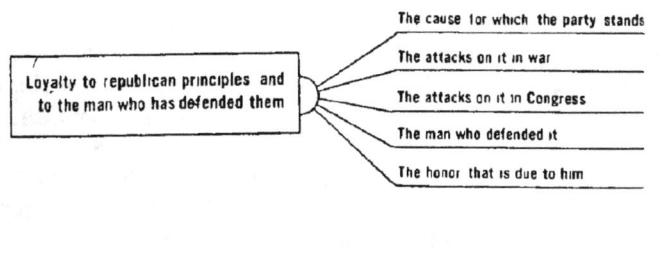

Panel 57

OVERCOMING INDIFFERENCE OR OPPOSITION

The probable attitude of the audience was taken into consideration by both men. Lincoln knew he would address a patriotic throng—a throng of saddened, solemn men and women looking up to him for light. To convey his idea he had but to make clear its "features." On the contrary, Ingersoll knew he would stand in the midst of a turbulent turmoil of political delegates, most of them committed against his idea and opposed to what he wanted. To convey his idea to them he had to arouse them, inspire them, stir them, and then when they were disposed to listen, make clear the "features" of his idea.

Now look over the diagram showing the Big Idea of each speech and its "features."

You see how similar they are. But when you compare them with the actual orations you see they were worked out differently. In Lincoln's you can easily trace the simple growth of the "features" into the finished masterpiece, just as you could in the Irving description, but in Ingersoll's you can scarcely trace the growth at all.

In this chapter, therefore, I'll show you what makes the difference between the two speeches, and then, just as I dug a great principle of letter writing out of Irving's masterpiece, I'll find you a great principle of letter writing from these masterpieces of oratory.

Now perhaps you are thinking, like the mother of the unwashed boy who answered the teacher's complaint as to his odor by saying that she sent her boy to school to be "learnt, not smelt," that we are here to learn about letters, not public speaking. And, in a way you are right, but bear in mind that *a writer has to do exactly what a public speaker has to do;* that, is to convey by words and style a definite idea or feeling in such a way that those addressed, whether by ear or by eyesight, will do, or think, or believe what the speaker or the writer wants them to. And the fundamental laws in each case are the same. There's plenty of proof of it.

For instance, as you have seen the wide difference in the working out of the expression of an idea as shown by those

BUSINESS CORRESPONDENCE

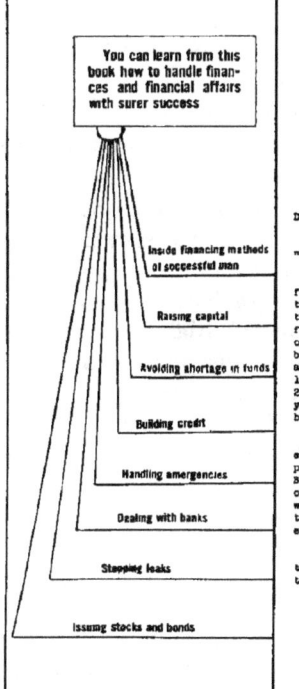

A.W. SHAW COMPANY
PUBLISHERS
CASS, HURON AND ERIE STREETS
CHICAGO

Dear Sir:

    Will you EXAMINE a copy of the unusual book, "How to Finance a Business" if I send it at my own expense?

    In a perfectly frank, forward way, 73 of America's foremost business men reveal their inside financing methods, tell you how they raise capital for new firms or secure additional funds to expand going concerns – their proved rules for avoiding financial troubles – successful yet simple ways of building credit, how to control the finances of a business in emergencies, specific suggestions for best applying for money at the bank – new unique ways of finding leaks and making savings, stock and bond issues; in all 202 methods that have raised capital or extended credit, year in and year out, for 73 of America's most successful business men.

    As you go through this book and find how 73 successful business men are meeting knotty financial problems – you will find yourself intensely interested. But when you see how these shrewd men are meeting some of the very problems you now face -- and how easy it will be to adopt these methods, adding their experience to your own, you will find yourself not merely interested, but SURPRISED.

    Simply indicate on the numbered card enclosed the exact address to which I am to send your copy of this new book.

    No expense; no risk, simply mail this card.

    But you should act today.

    Very truly yours,

    Merritt Lum

    Circulation Manager

Panel 58

OVERCOMING INDIFFERENCE OR OPPOSITION

two speeches, observe now the same difference in two business letters illustrated on pages 114 and 116.

Both are from SYSTEM's own sales letter files; and both were very successful letters. Read them over and look for the same difference in them you found between Ingersoll and Lincoln.

You can easily trace the growth of the "Will you examine" letter from its Big Idea and "features." On the other hand it's almost impossible to trace the growth of the "When you step into you office" letter. We noted the same difference in the development of Lincoln's and Ingersoll's speeches; and now we shall see why and how it developed and how to overcome it.

To make the matter clear, we'll first picture to ourselves the conditions that faced Ingersoll as he sat sketching his speech the night before the republican convention. He knew that the trend of feeling was against his candidate. He had sized up the one big idea back of Blaine's candidacy as Blaine's fights in Congress on the reconstruction question. But he could see the apathy felt by the delegates toward that idea. To impress it on them, to make them feel the advantages of Blaine's leadership, he—

Let me answer the question by asking you one. What do you do with a boy who hears your command and then shows an inclination to disregard it? You make him imagine the disadvantage of not obeying; do you not? That's *merely human nature.*

When little Willie says he will not wash his hands before going out, the wise mother says, "Then you shall not go out." When a patient tells his doctor, "Oh, I simply won't give up smoking," the wise doctor makes him see the consequences. When employees persistently violate an employer's rules, the wise employer pictures the discharge that will result from not obeying.

In other words, all through human nature we find that when people *decline or ignore the advantages* of something, the remedy is to make them realize the disadvantages of being

BUSINESS CORRESPONDENCE

A. W. SHAW COMPANY
PUBLISHERS
CASS, HURON AND ERIE STREETS
CHICAGO

You can learn from this book how to develop your personal efficiency

- The inner secrets of achievement
- Methods that fail
- Why they fail
- The simple laws of personal achievement
- Planning each day's work
- Arranging business deals
- Managing big enterprises
- The power to control and dominate

Dear Sir:

When you step into your office on Monday morning no doubt you have dreams of wonderful achievement — your step is firm your brain is clear and you have carefully thought out just WHAT you will do and HOW you will accomplish big things in your business. Perhaps the very plans you have in mind will influence your whole business career and you have visions of the dollars that will be yours rolling into your bank account

But do these dreams come true?

Are you always able to put through what you had planned to do — does your day's work have the snap and power you imagined it would have? Are you ever forced to admit that your dreams of big accomplishment are often shattered because of unexpected obstacles — new matters of pressing importance — perhaps little overlooked details that steal away your time and sap your energy?

How easy it is to think back and see how greater success was in your easy grasp if you had been able to better organize your work

It PAYS to know how to get the most from your own business ability — and and there is no surer, easier, less expensive road to personal efficiency than to get a copy of our FREE book "How to be Personally Efficient in Business" This remarkable book lays before your very eyes the inner secrets of business achievement — shows personal methods that MUST fail and then explains WHY they MUST fail — then rebuilds them before your own eyes into methods that WILL win and explains why they MUST win

And it explains the simple LAWS governing personal achievement which you can easily master

You can use this book to build up a successful plan for each day's work It will guide you in arranging business deals and managing big enterprises You will be able to develop business ability and strengthen your capacity for management At all times you will have added power to control the wills and dominate the actions of business men around you

The most progressive business men are the friends of SYSTEM And I should like our FRIENDS to be among the first to use this

So I am willing to do this Simply sign the enclosed card We will send you our book, "How to be Personally Efficient in Business," absolutely FREE — all delivery charges prepaid, and extend your subscription to SYSTEM one full year from its present date of expiration, at the price of SYSTEM alone $2. But only if this offer is accepted immediately — the price of SYSTEM will advance $1 per year on June 30th Save $1 by acting today

Surely no man who knows SYSTEM will neglect to continue his subscription So sending this card today means that you renew your subscription a short time sooner than you naturally would and you have the advantage of the low rate before the price of SYSTEM is raised

Send no money. Take no risk. Merely sign and mail the card — TODAY

Yours very truly,

Merritt Lum

Circulation Manager

Panel 59

OVERCOMING INDIFFERENCE OR OPPOSITION

without it. And that's what Ingersoll did. He made the delegates *see the disadvantages* of not nominating Blaine.

Students of advertising and selling call this "using the negative argument." Generally they condemn it.

I should like to condemn it, too. It is always nicer to make little Willie wash his hands by showing him how much better he will look. But if Willie positively ignores advantages, what is there left to do?

It is always nicer to sell your labor-saving device to a man by making him see how profitable it will be for him. But if he doesn't answer your letters—thus showing that he is indifferent or opposed to considering the advantages—what are you going to do to bring him around?

Can you ignore the primitive law of human nature that says: "then make him realize the disadvantages of being without it and, from that, *work him into considering the advantages* of having it"?

Well, hardly.

You suspect that there is a parallel between what a mother does to discipline an unruly child, what a letter writer does when it becomes evident that his *readers are opposed or indifferent* to his idea, and what Robert G Ingersoll, the past master in handling crowds, did when he realized that the delegates were cold to his idea, Blaine's candidacy. Let's dig it up.

First, be sure that you understand what Ingersoll did. Then we'll see how his method of approach exactly fits similar situations in letter writing. Merely a casual reading of the paragraphs on page 112 shows that instead of with realities, Ingersoll *approached his audience with a visionary image.*

As you read you see, first, a tender, patriotic vision of the trials our country has passed through; next you see a vision of a brave man fighting in Congress against foes of his country (we are not interested in the right or wrong of Ingersoll's beliefs); then you see a vision of republican principles being saved by Blaine, fighting alone, like a knight,

BUSINESS CORRESPONDENCE

and then—just as you get that vision, Ingersoll hurls at you. "For the Republicans to desert this gallant leader now is as though an army should desert their general upon the field of battle!"

Get well in mind how he played upon the imagination of the delegates in order to work them up to the point of picturing, *not*, mind you, the advantages of Blaine as a candidate, but the *disadvantages to themselves* of not nominating him. Just see how he worked them up to seeing themselves as soldiers on a battlefield deserting their general and then how he came down to a simple conveying of his positive idea. Magnificent, isn't it! And yet it's simple enough.

Now stop a moment and read that SYSTEM letter on page 116. The writer of it used the same principles that Ingersoll did Let's follow his work just as we followed Ingersoll.

The letter writer had his Big Idea and its "features," but he also faced the fact that the list of names he wanted to circularize had had three different letters built on that same idea. Some of his prospects had ordered each time, but now those that remained on the list, it was plain to be seen, were not willing to consider the Big Idea. In short, he faced the same conditions that Ingersoll faced on the night before his speech. And what did he do?

Why, like Ingersoll, and like the mother of the unruly boy, he *went back to primitive human nature* and decided that he had to play upon those readers' imaginations, and made them *picture the disadvantages* of being without the book.

Look over the points made (they are listed for you in the diagram at the left of the letter). Don't you get a vision of yourself setting out to accomplish big things? Then a vision of the success that is to come? Then a vision of your impotency, your failure to put the Big Idea over because of some trifling obstacle or little detail? Of course you do. And then you are jarred into reality by, "It pays to know how to get the most from your own business ability —and there is no surer, easier, less expensive road to personal

OVERCOMING INDIFFERENCE OR OPPOSITION

FRANCIS T SIMMONS & COMPANY
IMPORTING GLOVE MERCHANTS
CHICAGO, ILLINOIS

The Jamestown Dry Goods Co.,
Jamestown, Texas.

Gentlemen

    Ever had a good customer suddenly quit buying goods in your store? If so, what did you do? You waited until you saw him again and then said, frankly "We haven't seen you in the store lately, Mr Jones What is the matter?"

    You went at him STRAIGHT FROM THE SHOULDER in an attempt to find the real reason why he quit you Then Mr. Jones probably told you EQUALLY FRANKLY his reasons If his complaint was a just one and you had made a mistake — we're none of us perfect — you did your level best to make amends.

    This is just the attitude in which I am writing YOU this morning. I can't see you face to face, but I can TALK with you We haven't had an order from you since last fall, and I would certainly appreciate it if you told me "right out in meeting" WHY NOT If any department of this business has failed you, I want to know it.

    The fact that this business isn't PERFECT is surely not due to any lack of effort on our part, or because we aren't trying to make it so Every season finds us grown out of last year's clothes — literally so this year, when we had to move into larger quarters. Every season finds us selling better gloves and working harder WITH our customers to make THEIR sales larger, cleaner, and better.

    Just put yourself in my place for a minute or so Turn this sheet over NOW, and answer this letter as you would like to have it answered if you had written it Don't mince words Give it to me "hot off the bat " Enclosed is a stamped envelope to make an answer convenient.

    I am looking forward to hearing from you with the keenest interest.

                Very sincerely,
                FRANCIS T. SIMMONS & COMPANY

    P. S I am enclosing two yellow order blanks If, as I sincerely hope, nothing whatever is wrong, and you have merely overlooked filling in your stock, these blanks will be an easy way for you to tell us your needs Any gloves that we send you must please you, your sales people, and your customers, or we do not expect you to keep them

Panel 60

BUSINESS CORRESPONDENCE

FRANCIS T. SIMMONS & COMPANY
IMPORTING GLOVE MERCHANTS
CHICAGO, ILLINOIS

Murray Dry Goods Co ,
Thorp, Mich
Gentlemen.

    Have you ever been in this predicament? Busier than a frog on a fishhook, trying to do three things at once, bills to check, mail orders to fill, goods to check in, a window display to superintend, and — had one of your best customers rush up to you, shake a damaged pair of gloves in your face and come at you something like this.-

    "This is a PRETTY how-d'ye do! I've worn these gloves just ONCE NOW look at them Broken out in six places! I want a new pair " Were you ever backed up into this sort of a corner?

    Most probably you have been more than once. No wonder, with the obsolete, plain sizes When she bought the gloves she DEMANDED a pair two or four sizes too small for her The gloves were marked in plain sizes, and your clerk HAD to give them to her.

    They COULDN'T wear. They HAD to break, and YOU were "forced to make good " You knew it wasn't the gloves' fault, but who can argue with an angry customer?

    All would have been avoided if you had had the advantage of blind sizes The clerk could have LEARNED in our "CORRESPONDENCE COURSE" how to measure the hand, and how to give the woman the size she wore, not the size she WISHED she could YOU would have been saved the loss of the glove, an unpleasant argument, and worst of all — a dissatisfied customer.

    The French sizes are an EXCLUSIVE FEATURE of Simmons gloves We are wondering why you have waited as long as you have, without at least LOOKING Inquiry Card number three is attached and waiting to bring you samples AT OUR EXPENSE

                    Very truly yours,
                    FRANCIS T SIMMONS & COMPANY

Panel 61

RIVETING THE IDEA

Imagination! Study that word carefully There are as many ways of arousing imagination as there are colors in the rainbow A few primary rules might be evolved, but all of them would be subject to an infinite number of shadings For instance, all of the super-successful letters in Panels 60, 61 and 62 are based on one fundamental—the visionary approach There's imagination for you And—whisper—note the way of riveting the idea to the reader *His* experience is appealed to The answer to the puzzle *rests* in *his* judgment That's human nature Nothing is so important to a man as himself There is no subject on which he would rather talk—or listen

OVERCOMING INDIFFERENCE OR OPPOSITION

efficiency than to get a copy of our free book, 'How to Be Personally Efficient in Business'!"

And finally after you had been made willing to consider the Big Idea—the writer conveyed it to you in a very simple, clear way.

"Isn't this mere theory?" you ask.

It may seem to be, but it is not. But even if it were, flying was once merely theory to the Wright brothers. The steamboat was once merely theory to Fulton.

Every good idea is merely theory at first.

The wise man accepts an untried theory as only theory but says, "I will try it out." So don't scoff. Before I'm through I'll prove that it is a mighty good theory—a money-making theory.

Suppose you were a dealer and a good customer stopped trading with you. Could you use this "theory" in writing to him? You could and in this way the fact that the customer stops trading with you is proof that his attitude is against you—for one reason or another. Then if this "theory" is right, to write him a good letter you should arouse his imagination to a consideration of the disadvantages of his position toward you.

There you have this *"theory" pinned down to a good, practical, everyday business problem.*

On page 119 is an actual letter used in exactly such a case—in fact, on a whole list of inactive accounts. Read it. It starts creating a vision of an imaginary case in the reader's mind, exactly as Ingersoll started. It carries the vision on and up as Ingersoll did, and then, as Ingersoll at the right moment flashed his. "to desert this gallant leader now," so the letter flashes: "this is just the attitude in which I am writing you!"

That letter was mailed to 425 customers who had stopped buying. It brought back 32 direct orders amounting to $1,092, brought in 15 payments of small past-due accounts totaling $789, brought 103 answers from customers saying that they would order more gloves as soon as stock ran down;

BUSINESS CORRESPONDENCE

ADDRESSOGRAPH COMPANY
"Prints from Type"
CHICAGO, ILL.

Williamson Mfg. Co.,
445 Chestnut St.,
Philadelphia, Pa.

Gentlemen:

    Several times during the past year I have received circulars from a big Eastern advertiser. Each time my name and address on the envelop has been blurred and smudgy -- almost illegible.

    Every time I receive a poorly addressed circular from this prominent concern, I wonder how many hundreds of addresses they send out that CAN'T BE READ -- and as a result, how many are NEVER DELIVERED.

    What a loss inaccurate addresses must cause! Think of the wasted postage, the delays in mail delivery, and above all, the LOST SALES OPPORTUNITIES which are the result of faulty addressing.

    What a great percentage of this loss -- in your OWN advertising department -- could be prevented with the Addressograph!

    Why not determine NOW to eliminate the waste of hand addressing -- to secure the utmost in ACCURACY, ECONOMY and EFFICIENCY in handling your important lists.

    Today -- at no cost to you -- is your opportunity to learn how the Addressograph will help you. Mail us the enclosed card for more SPECIFIC information.

                         Yours very truly,
                         ADDRESSOGRAPH COMPANY

Panel 62

OVERCOMING INDIFFERENCE OR OPPOSITION

ROOT PIANO COMPANY
SYRACUSE, NEW YORK

Mrs. H F Fox,
Dayton, Ohio

Dear Madam

    We recently referred you to the dealer who sells our pianos in your vicinity. Will you kindly tell us whether you have bought one of him, or, if you have bought another make, what one you chose?

    We are having great success all over the country in competition with the few makers of high-grade work we have one of the best and one of the largest piano factories, we are a leading house, and we furnish the best thing at the lowest price consistent with quality. Therefore, we always like to know why, when we fail to sell a customer

    We enclose stamped envelope for reply, for which we thank you in advance.

                    Respectfully,

                          ROOT PIANO COMPANY

Panel 63

32 saying poor business was their only reason for not ordering; and 9 with specific complaints.

So you see that the principle, which is as clear in this letter as in SYSTEM's "When you step into your office" letter on page 116, or in Ingersoll's speech is more than "mere theory."

But let us test it again to prove my case. On page 120 is another letter from the same glove house. There was an entirely different purpose in this letter, but a probing of the reader's attitude showed the same conditions to be met. The list had already received several sales letters; this letter was to go to those who had not responded—in other words, to those whose attitude clearly was indifferent to considering the idea.

The letter on page 122 is still further proof of the right use of the "visionary approach." The value of the letter is proved

BUSINESS CORRESPONDENCE

NITEDAY ELECTRICAL FIXTURE CO.
CHICAGO, ILLINOIS

Mr. L T Darling,
Kansas City, Mo

Dear Sir.

    We presume that by this time you have either decided upon or formed your conclusions about your electrical fixtures

    Let us emphasize, we cannot do so too strongly, the fact that Niteday Electric Fixtures (selected everywhere for the better installations) are no more expensive than other makes. If some other makes, selling at a lower price and purported to be as good as Niteday really were as good, they could not be sold cheaper. Even for the exclusive patterns, no advance in price is asked

    Niteday fixtures can be furnished promptly This is a great consideration in many cases If you are told that they cannot be supplied promptly, kindly communicate with us and we will take a special interest in your case

    Remember we stand back of dealer, electrician, and you for any Niteday fixture you purchase

                    Yours very truly,

                    NITEDAY ELECTRICAL FIXTURE CO

Panel 64

YOUR READER

Most men like to read letters. To many people the arrival of a letter is an event But they can't, they simply can't read the average sales letter They rip off the envelop with interest, even with enthusiasm, and then, nine times out of ten, what do they get? A stereotyped opening A pointless proposition lacking real information, and a spineless close. The first annoys- the second irritates and the third simply adds to the speed of the fillip to the waste-basket Does that seem a little strong? Read the letters in Panels 63 and 64 and admit that the criticism fits On the other hand see how the letter in Panel 65 leads its reader to action

OVERCOMING INDIFFERENCE OR OPPOSITION

by the fact that although the list which received it had had five other letters and had been called on several times by salesmen, it brought 3½% returns!

Do you see how the letter follows that law of human nature by calling up visions of smudgy or unreadable addresses when the machine is not used, in order to make the prospect, who had been indifferent to direct appeals, wake up to a consideration of advantages?

Again you see the same fundamental principle used. Now let me prove it from a negative point of view.

In Panels 63 and 64, pages 123 and 124, are "second follow-up" letters for magazine inquiries. ("Second follow-up" means that the inquirer has received two letters already and has not accepted the idea) Only a glance at these letters shows how utterly they fail to arouse the reader, who has apparently dismissed the idea, into reconsidering it.

On the other hand, it is apparent at once that the "second follow-up" of a health appliance manufacturer shown on page 126 would affect a reader and make him reconsider.

What makes this letter so effective? What is lacking in the other two?

The first two lack imagination. The appliance letter scintillates with it. The first two ignore the negative argument. The other is a splendid example of it.

See how the imagination of the reader is worked up to picturing the disadvantages of being without the appliance. First she learns about one patient and his "$3,000 worth of treatment," then about another and another up to "what Mrs. Grant Johnson's son would say." And then see how the "load" is shifted over to the reader with the paragraph beginning "Even though your trouble may be slight compared with others." Why, the letter is enough to make a well person buy.

Of course, these *hard, practical, business-getting letters* don't ring like Ingersoll's famous speech, a speech that is quoted as a model throughout the English-speaking world. But

BUSINESS CORRESPONDENCE

B. H. STETSON MANUFACTURING CO.
DETROIT, MICHIGAN

Miss Elva Shanahan,
Chicago, Ill

Dear Miss Shanahan:

Do you hesitate to order our Appliance on account of the expense? Is that the real reason? The price should never stand between you and relief Do you think $25 seemed much to G. W Johnson after paying out $3,000 on other apparatus and treatment without relief? Read his letter inclosed.

Do you suppose Patrick J Gallagher of Woburn, Mass , would go back to his old time pain and helplessness for $25? Do you think E. T Brown of Peru, Ind , regrets the money he spent with us? — Get out that big sheet of letters I sent you and read what they say — What do you think Mrs Grant Johnson's son would say if his mother should demand that he go back to his terrible affliction so she could save the $25? Isn't it a mistake to put off what seems to hold such certain promise of relief?

Even though your trouble may be slight compared with others who have used our Appliance with great success it is of the utmost importance that it be attended to at once Spinal trouble, when neglected, soon becomes the cause of much suffering, of paralysis, liver, kidney, or bladder trouble, and headache and pains in the back develop These are usually due to pressure on the delicate spinal cord or on the small nerves which branch out from it to every vital organ

Medicine will do you no permanent good for it — will not remove the cause. Our Appliance permanently overcomes the trouble through the continual support and extension of the spine it gives. Just think what it would mean to you to be well again. Think how much easier and happier you could go about your daily duty if you were free from the pain and torture you suffer.

You will never be satisfied, and perhaps never be well, until you have used our Appliance

      Yours sincerely,
     B H. STETSON MANUFACTURING CO.

Panel 65

OVERCOMING INDIFFERENCE OR OPPOSITION

these men do adapt the *same big principle to their everyday affairs*.

Now you must admit that the points I have made are more than an untried theory.

Well, then, *how can we use this tested principle?* When prospects have failed to act on direct selling letters, or debtors have failed to respond to statements and plain reminder letters, or when prospective customers to be circularized live so far away from a store that we know they won't at first care to consider trading, or when a complaining customer has shown such heated annoyance that we know he won't want to listen to argument—in such cases and in others which are similar, how can we plan an appeal to their imagination?

The answer is at hand, but before going farther with this interesting matter of adapting our language or our style to the reader's attitude, let us take time to tie up loose ends and get everything shipshape for applying the principle to our daily needs.

If you will just stop to consider the points covered so far, you will recollect that we have divided prospects into two types—those who, so far as we know, are willing to consider our idea and those who are not willing to consider it. Panel 66, below, shows graphically our conclusions

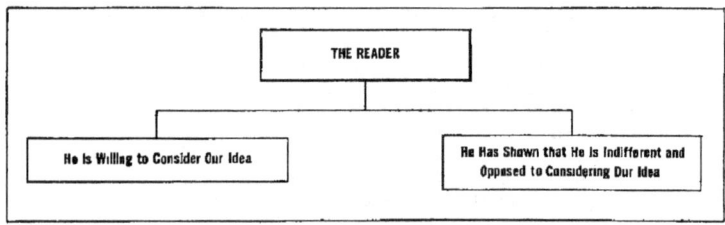

Panel 66

In other words, when from this chart we decide that a prospect or a list of prospects fall under the head of "willing to consider," then we can plan the expression of our idea along the simple, direct lines of Washington Irving's descrip-

BUSINESS CORRESPONDENCE

tion—or Lincoln's Gettysburg address—or any of the letters shown in the forepart of Chapter I. We can pick out the "features" of the Big Idea or Feeling and build them up as simply as possible, following the method of the SYSTEM letter which you found on page 114.

But when we find that our man, or our list of prospects, falls under the head of "not willing to consider," then, before we try to convey the Big Idea, we must get prospects willing to consider it. And that, as we have seen in the case of Ingersoll's speech, in SYSTEM's letter on page 116, the glove wholesaler's letters on pages 119 and 120, requires arousing their imaginations so that they will picture the *disadvantages of not considering* the idea.

Panel 67, below, graphically outlines the problem. Look it over and observe how it tells you that when a prospect is opposed or indifferent to the idea, his imagination must be aroused to a vision of disadvantages, and that this vision must be followed immediately with a vision of the advantages to be gained by accepting the idea. This chart is a kind of psychological map, and we can locate ourselves on it—that is, mark our position towards our readers—by checking it.

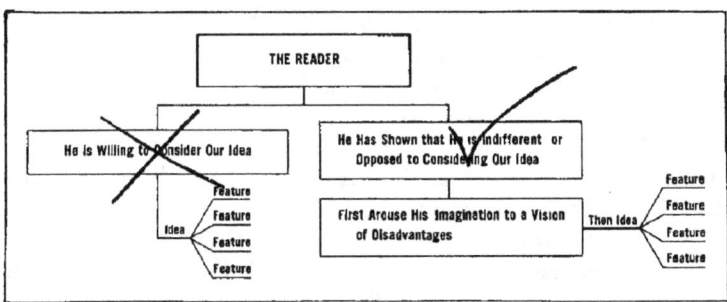

Panel 67

The check mark on the illustration shows, for example, the position in which a writer of SYSTEM's letters found himself when preparing to write the letter shown on page 116, it shows Ingersoll's position in preparing his great Cincinnati speech; it shows the position in which a writer of the Addresso-

OVERCOMING INDIFFERENCE OR OPPOSITION

graph Company's letters found himself when preparing the letter shown on page 122; it shows the position in which the writers of the other letters and the advertisement found themselves. And finding themselves in that position, all but two of them took the same course.

The writer of the piano letter and the writer of the electrical fixture letter, on pages 123 and 124, did not. Because they did not, their letters were weak. If you will now compare those two letters with the others, you will appreciate that fact. So, from the examples I have quoted and observations we have made, it is plain that overcoming indifference or opposition is largely a matter of *presenting the negative idea*.

We learned in the second chapter how easily a positive Idea or Feeling can be conveyed. We saw that it simply requires visualizing the Big Idea, picking out its "features," and describing each "feature" from the standpoint of the Big Idea or Feeling. To awaken the imagination to a negative idea should not be more difficult. And it isn't.

As a foundation on which to build, read the letter on the next page. It is a fourth collection letter used by a fire insurance agent. Since it is the fourth letter sent to policyholders who have not paid up a past-due premium, you'll agree that the writer could safely assume that his debtor was indifferent to the idea of prompt payment of the bill. That indicated the necessity for arousing the debtor's imagination to a vision of disadvantages. You can see for yourself how vividly it was done.

Now let us analyze the construction of that negative idea.

First consider the positive idea that the insurance man wanted to convey: "You ought to pay promptly the money you owe me." The debtor, having failed to heed it, the creditor impressed it on him by conveying the negative idea: "If I owed *you*, and should not pay promptly, how would you feel?"

Just as others we have mentioned, the insurance man, in order *to put his idea across*, created first a vision of such a

BUSINESS CORRESPONDENCE

R T WILLIAMS CO.
Pittsburgh, Pa

Mr. Roger Norton,
Cleveland,
Ohio.

Dear Sir:

    FIRE! FIRE! FIRE!

  Suppose the property on which we have insurance for you should burn tonight. I know you would want your money for the damage at once. The rule of this office is to pay losses very promptly, BUT suppose I asked you to wait for your money as long as you have made me wait for the money which you owe for this premium. Think it over.

  You owe us $9.

      Very truly yours,

       R. T. WILLIAMS CO.

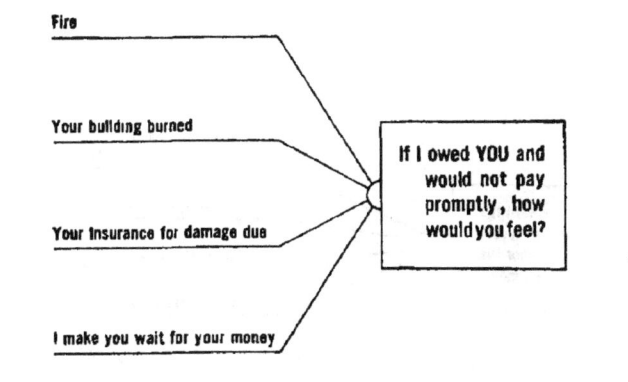

Fire

Your building burned

Your insurance for damage due

I make you wait for your money

If I owed YOU and would not pay promptly, how would you feel?

Panel 68

OVERCOMING INDIFFERENCE OR OPPOSITION

BENNETT COLLECTION CO.
Duluth, Minnesota

N. O Lucas,
Neenah,
Wis.

Dear Sir:

    The Boyce Mfg. Co. informs me that you have refused four requests for payment of your account. I think they must be mistaken. You have evidently forgotten the account was unpaid.

    I have been selling the public for twelve years and have found them treating me exactly as they themselves expect to be treated. Of course, there have been some dishonest people—people whose accounts you hand over to some wise collection lawyers to threaten and summon to court and who eventually pay in court costs four or five times the sum originally owing—but such cases have been rare. Certainly, neither you nor I understand what kind of a fool a man must be to pay $10 court costs and another $10 to the collection lawyer in addition to the original amount owing, because it has been shown that four letters went unacknowledged. Leave it to the lawyers to get it through.

    However, you are not that kind and I trust that this personal letter will call your attention to the oversight and bring your check, or half the amount due, anyway. I know that you have overlooked the last four letters and that is why I am making sure you will receive this one—from me.

    Let me hear from you by the 12th.

        Very truly yours,

          BENNETT COLLECTION CO.

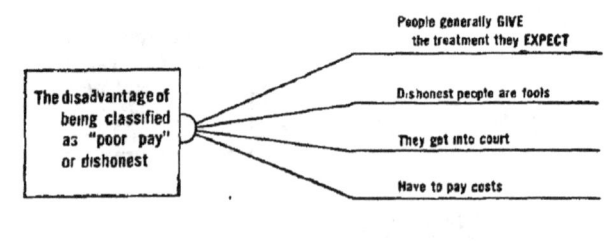

The disadvantage of being classified as "poor pay" or dishonest
- People generally GIVE the treatment they EXPECT
- Dishonest people are fools
- They get into court
- Have to pay costs

Panel 69

debt: "Suppose your building burned, the policy was due, and I held off paying you your insurance?" Then followed the positive echo.

Below the letter is a diagram of this visionary or negative idea and its "features." Notice that it is similar to the diagrams made for plotting positive ideas.

Before we continue with this, take another letter and with me trace out the negative idea and its "features." The collection letter on page 131 will serve. In this case the debtor ignored the bill; the second and third letters, which merely conveyed the idea of his indebtedness; and the fourth letter, which aroused the vision of his disadvantages.

He had to be shown that his attitude was rather stubborn. So the letter writer aroused in the debtor's imagination the idea of his loss in being put down as "poor pay." The diagram below the letter shows the connection between the Big Idea and its "features."

Of course, in looking over this Boyce letter, as well as looking over others at this time, remember *not* to consider the methods the writers have for opening their letters. That point will be brought up in a later chapter, so for the present we pass it by. We are now to study only the conveying of the idea.

We find now, from that speech of Ingersoll and the successful letters I have quoted, that when an antagonistic or indifferent audience is to be approached, a certain line of attack should be followed. I outlined it in the panel below which diagrams the thought of the letters we have studied

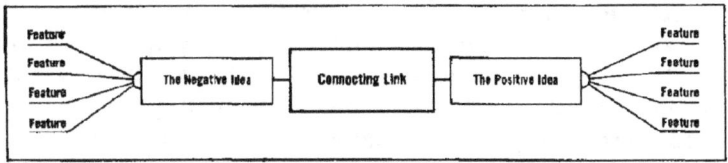

Panel 70

Now you see that in each case the author presented first a negative idea and followed it swiftly with a positive idea. We

OVERCOMING INDIFFERENCE OR OPPOSITION

also learn that the two ideas are closely connected or balanced on a phrase which I call the "connecting link."

Test the diagram on some of the letters on preceding pages. The glove dealer's letter on page 119 illustrates my point exactly, and so I plotted it for you in the panel below.

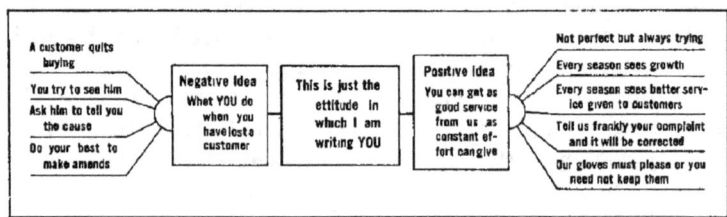

Panel 71

Just a moment's scrutiny of the diagram will show you, on the left, the negative idea of the letter, in the center, the connecting link; and on the right, the positive idea of the letter.

With this point in mind, turn back to Ingersoll's speech on page 112. See how he built up his visionary idea of what might have happened without Blaine's leadership; how he closed with the positive idea of "in the name of the republic," and so forth.

Observe *the sharp, awakening link* between the two—"to desert this gallant leader now is as though an army should desert their general on the field of battle."

Just to drive this point home, recall that SYSTEM letter on page 116. Trace the construction of the two ideas —positive and negative—and then again note the use of the same sort of connecting link "it *pays* to know how to get the most from your own business ability—and there is no surer, easier, less expensive road" and so on.

In short, you can go through all of these successful letters, built for many different kinds of business, for many different purposes, but all with a greater or less crust of readers' indifference to break through, and find that all are constructed on the same fundamental principle

BUSINESS CORRESPONDENCE

THE GEIGER JONES COMPANY
Canton, Ohio

S. A. Dennis,
Chicago,
Ill.

Dear Sir:

    Recently we sent you our book "Investing Under Expert Direction" and detailed information regarding the preferred stock at that time being offered by us. That security was typical of the conservative character of the 7% Cumulative Preferred Stocks which we have been selling for more than 11 years.

    We are not doing a general brokerage business but confine ourselves to the securities of a few well selected institutions which manufacture staple lines, and which have demonstrated their ability to pay regular incomes to their stockholders.

    A number of the requirements which we exact from these institutions for the protection of our clients are unique in the investment world. For example, - we always insist upon an actual investment of at least $200 for each $100 share of preferred stock issued. Second, we insist that the company create a surplus sufficient to pay the dividends upon the preferred stock for at least two years in advance, - as a reserve for the payment of dividends during years of panic and depression. Third, we always insist that our companies shall not have an indebtedness to exceed 20% of their total assets at the end of any fiscal year. This is an insurance against any disturbance of their financial condition during panics or depressions.

    Furthermore, we insist that our institutions manufacture only staple lines of common demand, insuring not only present prosperity but a future field. They must use modern methods of accounting to keep in constant touch with the developments of their different departments. This enables them to correct immediately any mistakes or weaknesses that may develop, in place of allowing them to grow during the entire year and afterwards to become a source of permanent weakness.

    We have demonstrated that a careful following of these methods insures permanent incomes to investors in this class of securities. Moreover, it has enabled us easily to re-market securities for our clients who find it necessary to realize and, best of all, although we have placed many millions of dollars worth of securities on the market, no client of ours has ever lost a dollar of principal or income on funds invested in our preferred stock.

    We will be pleased to have you make a personal investigation as to our methods of doing business and our reputation for fair dealing.

                            Very truly yours,

                                THE GEIGER-JONES COMPANY.

Panel 72

OVERCOMING INDIFFERENCE OR OPPOSITION

Now, how does it happen that *all* of these successful letters follow the same principle of construction so closely? This principle has never been charted out before. It has been known to a few writers and has been used by them, but it has not been generally known.

The answer is that writers and public speakers who are constantly meeting various problems such as testing different letters, and watching the effect of words on an audience, sooner or later arrive at certain definite facts regarding *ways to convey an idea*. In time they learn that one particular style pays here, another there Ten men in ten different businesses, each with an equal amount of experience will, almost invariably, either consciously or unconsciously, arrive at the same fundamental principles Superficially, their styles may seem to be radically different, but substantially, their methods of writing or speaking will be the same

And it is by watching the development of not ten but hundreds of such experiences and tracing them back to the great authorities of literature, oratory, and business, that the definite principles of this course have been worked out.

There are exceptions to them, of course But often these exceptions are more fancied than real. For instance, there has been many a successful letter written to people whose attitude had been shown to be opposed or indifferent to the Big Idea, without the use of an absolutely visionary or negative idea to carry it home. But in all such cases that have come under my observation, a visionary-negative idea has been unconsciously created by the very way in which the positive idea was explained.

On page 134 is a typical letter of this kind. It is a follow-up letter of a financial concern to *prospects who have failed to reply*. This letter does not in itself deliberately call up a negative idea; but read it carefully and see if the very way in which it states, "what we exact for the protection of our clients" doesn't set you unconsciously to thinking about what might happen to your money if you made an investment *not* protected by such exactions.

BUSINESS CORRESPONDENCE

HOME LAUNDRY COMPANY
Springfield, Illinois

Mrs. Howard McKay
Springfield
Illinois

Dear Madam:

    Figure it out for yourself'

    If the washerwoman comes once a week -- your home is hers for 52 days a year --

    -- almost TWO MONTHS of every year wasted -- spoiled.

    The next time you find yourself surrounded by the usual wash-day mess -- and the tranquillity of your household upset by the independence of the typical 1915 washerwoman --

    RESOLVE TO HAVE A CHANGE.

    If you haven't yet found the GENUINE solution for this annoying problem, there's a pleasant surprise in store.

    Don't give it up'

    Simply join the constantly increasing number of particular housewives who are taking advantage of our painstaking family service.

    Trust your priceless linens -- and your other washing -- to lifelong experts in fine laundering work --

    -- to an organization which has a service ideal to live up to -- and a reputation to maintain.

    If you want to find out how reasonably you can eliminate those weekly blue days --

    -- those days of steamy rooms and racked nerves --

    Draw a chair up to the telephone and call Main 444 this minute -- NOW.

    Let's talk it over while you have it on your mind.

                      Very truly yours,

                        HOME LAUNDRY COMPANY

Panel 73

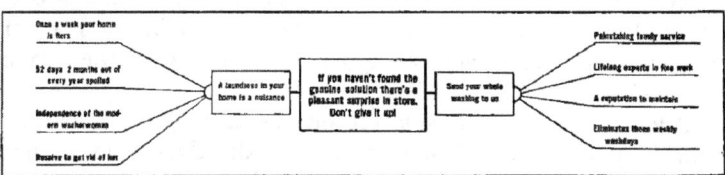

Panel 74

OVERCOMING INDIFFERENCE OR OPPOSITION

A good many writers adopt that method because of the prejudice against using the negative form. Yet if the *negative thought aroused is what gets the effect*, what is the use of beating around the bush? Certain it is that the man of only average writing ability runs the risk of missing the effect desired when he attempts a roundabout style. And until you become expert at getting word effects it will be best to use only the simple constructions illustrated by Panel 70 on page 132.

That is the method of construction found good enough by such successful campaigners as Ingersoll, Roosevelt, Bryan, and Billy Sunday. You will find that in their speeches before audiences inclined to be hostile or indifferent, or in offering *ideas opposed to generally accepted notions*, they all built their arguments on one plan, and that is the plan which has been charted for you. You will also find that Charles Dickens followed the same plan in his books which attack some solidly intrenched social or political system.

And in the practical, business-getting, or debt-collecting letters of the best letter writers you will find the same plan used.

The laundryman's letter on page 136 will clinch the point. That letter was sent as a follow-up to his straight selling letters. See in Panel 74, also on page 136, how its construction, too, follows the same simple plan which has been outlined.

What do you think of the "theory" now?

Doesn't it explain the pulling power of many letters whose results you knew but couldn't understand?

The letters on pages 138, 139, 140 and 142 will dismiss all remaining doubts. They were picked from the hundreds of good letters on which this book on applied business correspondence is based. Can't you now get a better idea of why and how they were so constructed and why they were successful?

Take the egg dealer's letter on the next page. See the simplicity of it, the bringing out of disadvantages in not buying his eggs; the connecting link, "this is a pretty

BUSINESS CORRESPONDENCE

good egg"; the plain, positive picture of the advantages of his proposition

That letter was built to introduce his proposition to people who were totally unfamiliar with it and hence assumed to be averse to changing their method or their dealer. From a social list of 800 names, usually a difficult list to get results from, it produced 48 orders and 20 permanent standing-order customers.

Study the other three letters (Panels 76, 77 and 78) in the light of our new viewpoint. In the sales manager's letter, see

---

BROADACRES
STEVENSVILLE, OHIO
R F D No 1

Mr. F. C King,
Columbus, Ohio

Dear Mr King

"AN EGG VERSUS A PRETTY GOOD EGG "

The eggs you buy as strictly fresh, coming by the usual channels of distribution, pass through the following hands from producer to consumer

1. Collected by local dealers or the country store.
2 Shipped to commission houses at the big markets.
3. Sold to wholesalers and jobbers.
4 Sold to retailers
5 Hold in retailer's store until delivered to customers.

The time consumed is from two to three weeks for the first quality of fresh eggs.

THIS IS A PRETTY GOOD EGG.

My eggs I collect twice a week from the farmers in my neighborhood — bring them to my farm, sort and pack them into cartons of one dozen each, and deliver them by auto the next day at your door, almost before the hen ceases to advertise her latest achievement

THIS IS AN EGG

TRY THEM AND SEE THE DIFFERENCE

Yours truly,

R. T. STEVENS

Panel 75

OVERCOMING INDIFFERENCE OR OPPOSITION

GORDON & WILSON
The "Better" Line
ST PAUL, MINN.

Mr. A. T. Lanning,
Ragnor, Michigan.

Dear Lanning·

Your report from Kansas City in one hand and a hammer in the other — that's a true picture of me right this moment.

"Everybody here buying close" — when I read that I raised an eyebrow. "Crop prospects bad" — when I read that I raised a fist. But when I came to your — "Think I was lucky to get even this much business" — I raised something worse than either eyebrow or fist

Nope, Lanning — you can't get any sympathy out of me on stuff like that; I got reports just like yours from every one of the other men, and I have just finished wiping off tears of sympathy for each one of them — except you and Burt.

But any man who could drop into B P.'s office after we had made that terrible bull of drawing a sight draft on them, and then drop out with old Pearson's re-order in his pocket — any man who can do the hundred other things you have done, and Burt has done, can't offer me talk about poor crop prospects and get away with any sympathy from me.

My sympathy glands freeze up when I get reports like this last one from YOU You'd let poor crop prospects and generally tight buying stop you from getting big orders about as much as a good, well-brought-up mosquito would let a fly-screen stop him.

You've been listening to some alibi-artist and got the microbe, that's the trouble WITH YOU Forget it, and remember that Bestever Rompers and Blouses are as good a hard-times line as they are a prosperity line And that Lanning is an all-kinds-of-times salesman Spare me the "poor-crop-talk" — I'm deaf on YOUR side.

Yours for a better alibi next time

L. R. T.

Panel 76

BUSINESS CORRESPONDENCE

ANGIER PAPER COMPANY
ORAND RAPIDS, WIS.

Henry Johnson,
Keokuk, Iowa

Dear Sir.

It was a local between Philadelphia and Trenton.

I sat in a smoker, which was half baggage car. At Frankford, an automobile tire was thrown on — a yard or two of its plain Kraft wrapper flapping in the breeze With my pocket camera I took a picture of it — see inclosed

And I said to the baggage man "Does this happen often?" "Nearly every day," he replied. "We carry tires with wrappers loose, torn — and rubber exposed."

So I wondered "Does it pay a manufacturer to spend millions in building reputation, and then — to save a cent or two per tire — send his product broadcast over the land — imperfectly protected against light, dirt and exposure?"

Plain Kraft paper — even of a 50-pound basis — won't stand the strain of shipping But 30-pound Kraft — reinforced with yarn and water-proofed — will do the trick to perfection.

Test the strength of the sample enclosed Wrap it tightly around your wrist Note the firm, strong, neat job it makes

And six ounces will wrap a tire — right.

Tell us, please, the size rolls you use — diameter, width and core We'll then send you enough — without expense or obligation — enough for a thorough trial.

Give Angier's Tirewrap the opportunity to prove its worth to you — as it has already done to Goodrich, Michelin, McGraw and others The post card is for your convenience

Sincerely yours,

ANGIER PAPER COMPANY

OVERCOMING INDIFFERENCE OR OPPOSITION

how the writer took the character and attitude of his man, Lanning, into consideration—knowing, evidently from previous experience, that this particular salesman would *not take kindly to direct reproof, or criticism, or ordinary "ginger talk."* See how, with the bantering negative idea, linked up by "my sympathy glands freeze up when—," and so forth, he led the salesman gracefully up to the positive idea.

And in the wrapping paper sales letter (page 140), can't you follow the construction on the same lines? Of course you can. It's so simple that perhaps you wonder that you didn't get the point before.

And then let us run over the collection letter I showed you in the second chapter and which I have reproduced again on page 142. You will recall that you worked out its Big Idea in the second chapter

Unless you have made a very deep study of collection letters, you were probably baffled when you came to trying to chart out the Big Idea and its "features." That is due to the fact that the *attitude of the reader* plays a very big part in its construction, and the use of the imaginary or negative idea is handled in an extraordinarily subtle way.

The letter was used on a list of purchasers of a very high-grade article which had been sold by circularizing a high-grade list of names. Before credit was extended, the purchasers were carefully investigated. Therefore, the debtors were known to be persons of means. But, having failed to pay up after several statements and letters, their attitude plainly was coldly indifferent to the importance of so small a bill.

Therefore, while the Big Idea of the letter was to make them realize that the bill, though small, deserved immediate attention, it was led up to by the visionary idea of their being classed, if the bill was not met, *as too poor to pay $6 at one time.*

Panel 79 on page 143, illustrates the construction of the letter. You can see that it is simple when the full attitude of the reader is considered, although, as we looked at it first, it seemed indirect.

BUSINESS CORRESPONDENCE

MOORE PUBLISHING COMPANY
CIRCULATION DEPARTMENT
BOSTON, MASS.

Mrs. A. M. Brown,
Windsor, Ill.

Dear Madam

  We regret we have not heard from you with a remittance in response to our bill for our magazine Home Economics, sent you in March, but we presume that for some reason it was not convenient for you to remit the amount at that time. We can no longer carry this as an open account, and are again enclosing you a bill for the amount now due. We have, however, arranged a very easy plan of payment, whereby you can, without inconvenience, pay the entire amount on the <u>instalment</u> plan.

  Your bill now amounts to $6 00, and we will consent to accept $2.00 every other month (only $1 00 monthly) until the whole amount is paid We have made three notes, due sixty days apart, and enclose them herewith for your signature. Please sign and return them with the bill, using the enclosed envelope We will receipt and return the bill and will forward the notes, as they come due, for collection. Or, if you prefer, you may send us three checks for $2.00 each, dated ahead and payable sixty days apart, and we will deposit them on the dates they mature. We do not know whether you need or care to be thus accommodated <u>You</u> may find it convenient now to send a check or a money-order at once. We trust, however, you will appreciate this easy method that we offer for paying your account, and that you will send remittance either by note or by cash at once

      Very truly yours,

        MOORE PUBLISHING COMPANY

OVERCOMING INDIFFERENCE OR OPPOSITION

And this chart brings up another point important to consider and that is the *brevity with which the positive idea may be conveyed* after the negative idea has paved the way for it. You will observe brevity in the collection letter, in the positive part of Ingersoll's speech, and in many of the letters quoted.

The *proper creation of the negative* idea in a reader's mind often makes him so ready and open to reconsideration of the

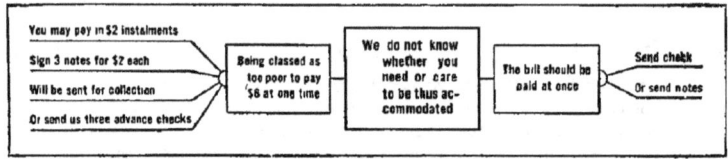

Panel 79

positive idea that only a sentence or two is necessary to convince him.

A good example of this is the clothing merchant's letter shown in Panel 80 on the next page. This letter was the sixth in a follow-up series of seven letters used only on a picked list of business men. The previous five letters had covered the proposition from all angles In this sixth letter, therefore, the businesslike vision of a strictly business situation was created, and after that the connecting link, "I am a clothing expert." Thus, *a few terse sentences conveyed the whole positive idea.*

Now, here is an interesting point which some of you may have guessed as you followed my explanation of a method of overcoming opposition. What we have learned in this chapter is really *the basis of all follow-up campaigns*—sales follow-ups as well as collection follow-ups. I'll prove it by going over a typical letter series with you.

In the first letter of a sales series you assume, or should assume, that the person to whom you are writing is open-minded; that is, neither for nor against the Idea So the first letter should be a simple conveying of the Big Idea or Feeling—like the letter shown on page 145.

BUSINESS CORRESPONDENCE

In preparing the second letter, the natural hesitation that people feel about saying yes or no to a proposition should be recognized, so a second letter should be only a more detailed, or more forceful repetition of the positive idea. The letter shown on page 146 illustrates the point.

For the third letter, conditions vary according to the proposition offered. If a proposition is a simple one, for a specific purpose or for a self-evident use—like a health appliance, a corset, a brand of underwear, or other clothing—something the purchase or use of which involves not more than one or two conditions—*after a prospect has had two letters* and has not responded, it may be assumed that he is indifferent or opposed. And in such case the third letter should approach him on the visionary or negative side. The method is illustrated by the health appliance letter on page 126.

McCANN, *The Tailor*
Peoria, Illinois

Mr. E. C. Edwards,
Decatur, Illinois.

Dear Sir:

    If a business expert said, "I can reduce your running expense one third" --

    You'd say, "Show me."

    I am a clothing expert.

    I've been telling you that I can reduce your clothes expense one third.

    Doesn't cost anything to be shown.
    What do you say?

               Very truly yours,

                    McCANN, THE TAILOR

Panel 80

OVERCOMING INDIFFERENCE OR OPPOSITION

CHALMERS MOTOR COMPANY
Detroit, Michigan

Mr. Harry K Goodall,
Elmhurst, Illinois.

Dear Sir:

    We thank you for the interest you have shown in Chalmers cars, and in accordance with your request are sending you one of our "Six-30" catalogs under separate cover You will find that it contains complete description and specifications of this car

    Of course, the best way and the only way to decide upon the car you wish to buy is to get into the car yourself — put it over the "bumps" so to speak Try it out for "get-away," hill-climbing ability, speed and power. That is what we want you to do. We have all the confidence in the world in our 3,400 R P.M. Chalmers — we know what it will do and we know that it will perform to your utmost satisfaction.

    Many of our "Six-30" sales have been made through the medium of our catalogs only — to customers who know the prestige of the Chalmers organization and who have faith in the ability of the Chalmers shops to build "quality" cars We mention this fact merely to illustrate the confidence the motor-buying public has in the Chalmers Company.

    The prestige we speak of has been gained through the Chalmers' long-standing policy to build "Quality" cars — cars that will stand up through hard service The "Six-30" is the lowest priced Chalmers ever put on the market — but no sacrifice has been made in quality The reduction in price is brought about through the wonderfully increased production facilities of the Chalmers plant.

    Our dealer, whose name appears on the enclosed card of introduction, will furnish you any further information relative to the Chalmers product upon request.

                        Very truly yours,

                              CHALMERS MOTOR COMPANY

Panel 81

BUSINESS CORRESPONDENCE

SPENCER HEATER COMPANY
General Offices
SCRANTON, PA.

Mr. L. I. Thomas,
Oak Park, Ill.

Dear Sir·

    Of all the experience that I have had as a manufacturer, this is the most perplexing —

    To have our engineers design a boiler that does positively reduce heating costs 1/3 to 1/2 by using the cheap sizes of coal — that usually has to be fired once a day, and one that will maintain heat for 10 to 12 hours at a stretch in zero weather without attention —

    And then to find that some jump at the conclusion that our statements are exaggerated.

    So I am writing this personally, for I know the Spencer Heater and what it will do, and I know that you and everyone else is anxious to reduce heating cost to a minimum.

    The fault must be with the literature — so I am sending you none, but would suggest that you write to some of the Spencer's owners whose letters we have previously sent you If you should like some testimony of someone nearer home, I will be glad to send you the names of some additional users

    We suggested this to an inquirer in Duluth recently and he wrote to every name given in the testimonial book When he finally placed his order he sent us the replies he had received with the comment that the original letters were lacking in enthusiasm when compared with his

    If you are not convinced that the Spencer will save you both time and money, it is not the fault of the heater but rather of the way we have presented the subject to you.

    If you will drop a line to me personally, asking me to explain any points that are not clear, I will indeed appreciate it Thanking you in anticipation, I am

                  Very truly yours,
                  SPENCER HEATER COMPANY

OVERCOMING INDIFFERENCE OR OPPOSITION

But some propositions are such serious matters—buying them involves so many consequences, as in the case of an expensive piece of machinery or a device that will require changes in operating methods or a *method* of buying necessities (as in changing from custom-made to ready-made clothes and vice versa; or shifting trade from a store where the prospect has an account)—that indifference may not safely be attributed to the prospect, even if he has had two letters without responding. He is often still open-minded on the matter, and simply is doubtful of the wisdom of the move. So, on such propositions, the best third letter is a direct positive-idea letter, only it should approach the idea from a different angle, so as to *give the prospect a new light* on it. The letter shown on page 148 illustrates this method.

As a matter of fact, this type of letter is considered by experienced follow-up men as the natural type of third letter. The type of third letter shown on page 126 (the health appliance letter) is really a fourth letter. In fact, whenever such letters are used, the third letter of the series is omitted and the time between letters is doubled. For instance, if between the first and second letters 10 days are allowed to elapse, and if the same period is allowed to pass between the second and third letters, between the third and fourth, it is usual to allow a double period, or 20 days. Therefore, you will usually find that *in a series for a direct, uninvolved proposition* where the third letter has the visionary or negative approach, a like period of 20 days is allowed between the second and the third letter.

But this whole matter of frequency of the letters is one that should be built up by study of the actual results in each case. Usually a letter series may be started on a 10-day basis; and then, as results show the necessity or wisdom for it, this basis may be extended or contracted. More will be said about this in a later chapter when mailing lists are considered.

But perhaps you will understand the whole proposition better by a study of the chart at the top of page 149.

BUSINESS CORRESPONDENCE

NUWAY SEPARATOR COMPANY
San Francisco, California

Mr. Guy C Williams,
Ragnor, Wash.

Dear Sir

    It would please us to learn if the copy of our special separator catalog, mailed recently, contained information of interest to you We trust you received it, and observed the money-making, time- and labor-saving features you will find only in the NUWAY.

    Could you visit our factory and see the accurately adjusted machinery, the splendid material and workmanship put into the separator, you would readily understand why we absolutely guarantee the NUWAY to be "the best." Please refer to page 6 of our catalog, and read our unlimited guarantee.

    The increased amount of butter fat or cream you will receive daily, and the perfect satisfaction you will enjoy in the long life and use of a NUWAY Separator, doubles the value of every dollar invested

    Please don't make the mistake of buying a "cheap" separator It will only be a continual source of annoyance and expense, repairs will soon be required, and much time and cream be lost in the separating

    Just as "STERLING" stamped upon silverware assures the customer of its pure, high quality and value, so NUWAY stamped upon a separator frame guarantees to the purchaser the finest separator ever built

    There are absolutely no better separators made than the NUWAY The man who knows separator values gets his money's worth when he buys the New Style NUWAY, and it will look good to you and all the family

    May we have the opportunity to quote you an attractive price on the separator you require for your dairy? How many cows have you and what size separator have you selected?

                    Very truly yours,

                         NUWAY SEPARATOR COMPANY

OVERCOMING INDIFFERENCE OR OPPOSITION

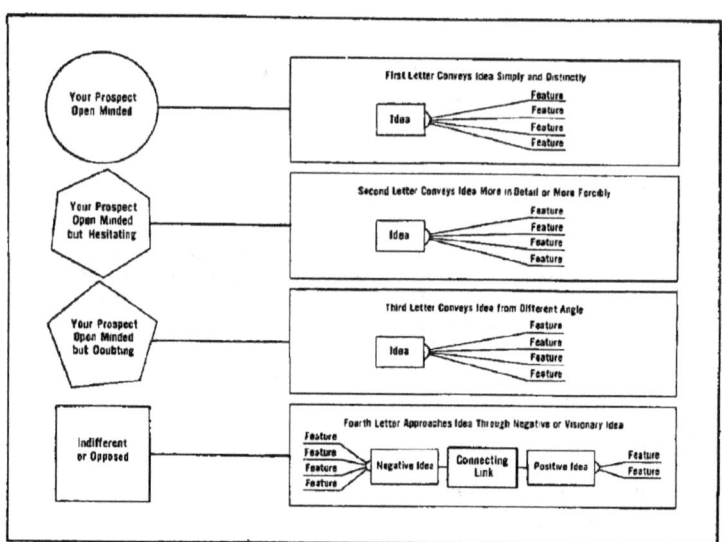

Panel 84

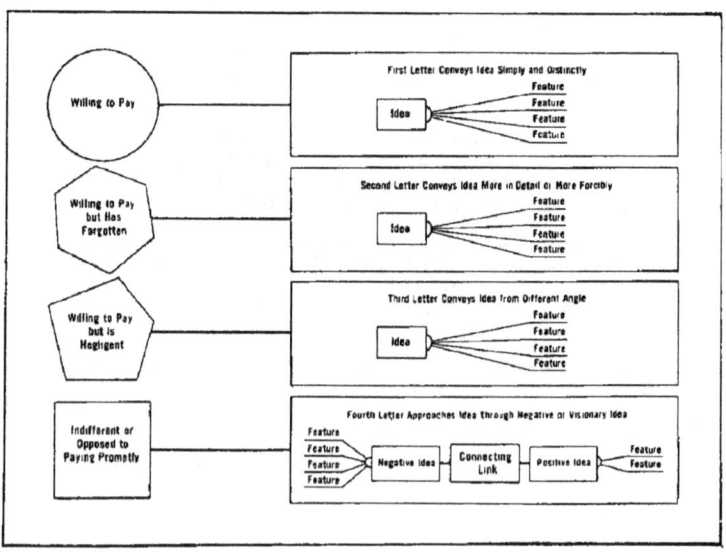

Panel 85

BUSINESS CORRESPONDENCE

It indicates the attitude of the prospect and the way the attitude may be overcome by four letters which begin with a simple presentation of the idea and end by presenting the idea through a visionary approach. In that chart you see that the prospect's state of mind can be assumed to change from open-mindedness, to hesitation, to doubt, and finally to indifference. The change from circle to square shows the reader's attitude and shows how the type of the letters should change.

To prove the point, trace this theory in the four reconstructed selling letters illustrated on pages 151, 152, 153 and 154 The angle of approach for each letter is the one proved by the advertiser to have paid best. Note how closely it follows the principle of our chart (Letters beyond the fourth in the series do not interest us yet. They involve the points which come up in later chapters)

A few pages back it was stated that the principles presented in this chapter apply to a series of collection letters as well as they do to single letters. In concluding this chapter I want to make this point clear and so I'll ask you to follow me in an *analysis of the first four letters of a collection series.* Before I begin, however, let me say this about all letter campaigns·

Too many follow-up series are built upon the hit-or-miss policy. As he is writing one letter a writer often thinks of a different or a better way to put his idea into words, and so he uses the new way in the next letter, regardless of the fact that what may be needed is *a complete change of approach.*

True as this is in sales letter series, it is even more true in collection follow-ups. A man starts out, in preparing a series of collection letters, to be as courteous and considerate as possible. This is right, but often he gets so interested in the process of seeing how courteous he can be that he almost *invents excuses for the debtor's failure to pay.*

Because that error is made so often, keep this point clear in your mind when writing collection letters. As he owes you an honest debt, it is for the debtor to make the apologies—not

OVERCOMING INDIFFERENCE OR OPPOSITION

KNIGHT KNITTING COMPANY
PORTLAND, OREGON

Mrs. H. M. Hopkins,
Grandview, California.

Dear Madam:

    It is a pleasure indeed to comply with your request for the new Knight-Knit Hosiery Booklet, and your copy is already addressed in the mail.

    Be sure to look on page 9 at the new striped models — these are the most stylish stockings of the year — a bit daring, but so pretty and charming and so MODISH THIS YEAR that every woman should have at least one pair In most lines they will cost you $1 to $1.50 — but page 9 in the booklet shows Knight-Knits at ONLY 75 CENTS PER PAIR! Think of it! 75 cents!

    Then on pages 5, 6 and 7 are beautiful mercerized silk stockings for everyday wear at 35 cents and 50 cents On page 8 are some fancy styles at 50 cents, and 65 cents. Then see the rich, sheeny, lustrous silk hose on page 10 at only $1 — and on up to $3

    But before you look at these pages read page 3 carefully — then you will learn why Knight-Knit Hosiery never grows old and faded looking — why Knight-Knits will never crock on your feet, or run in the wash And on page 4 you can see why Knight-Knits never develop those annoying "ladders" down the legs. In Knight-Knits you can have the beauty and style and comfort of FINE hosiery with all the wear and economy of coarser goods.

    As no dealer in your city is yet handling Knight-Knit Hosiery, we will gladly fill your orders direct at prices quoted. Simply use the enclosed order blank and your every wish will be carefully followed.

                    Very truly yours,

                            KNIGHT KNITTING COMPANY

Panel 86

BUSINESS CORRESPONDENCE

KNIGHT KNITTING COMPANY
PORTLAND, OREGON

Mrs. H. M Hopkins,
Grandview, California.

Dear Madam.

    No more of those horrid "ladders" starting at the knee, or where your garter fastens, and running down the leg of your stockings! No more stitches starting just below the ankle where the extra-ply heel is joined! No more toes poking through on the first day's wear and no more heels wearing out before you even BEGIN to get the value of your hosiery money!

    That's the good news that Knight-Knit Hosiery brings you. Where did you put the Knight-Knit Booklet you received? Get it out again now and see WHY Knight-Knits won't develop ladders — it's on page 4 See WHY Knight-Knits don't unravel at the ankle — it's on page 5 See WHY Knight-Knits are strong in the toes and tough at the heel — it's right there on page 5, too.

    Perhaps you didn't stop to realize the IMPORTANCE of those points before. But don't you see how much they will mean in saving you not only from buying hosiery so often, but in bother of mending, and annoyance over appearance? Knight-Knit Hose keep trim and shapely and NICE looking longer than any other stockings you ever wore

    And then if you'll just notice the PRICES of each kind you'll see they save you 15 to 25 cents a pair on ordinary kinds, 25 to 50 cents on the fancy kinds, and 50 cents to $1 on all-silk hose.

    Why NOT have stockings as good as these? Why NOT save the money that Knight-Knits save? Why not? Surely you like NICE hosiery — surely you dislike to see your stockings breaking out with "ladders" or unraveling at the ankle? Surely you hate to take your shoes off at night and see a hole facing you!

    Then you just try some of those plain Knight-Knits on pages 5, 6 and 7, for everyday wear, a few pairs of those pretty, dashing kinds on page 9, for special occasions, and a pair or two of the beautiful all-silk stockings on page 10 for real dressy times

    Make out a small order today and see for yourself how much better hosiery you can have, and STILL SAVE MONEY on them

    Money back — quickly and agreeably — if you feel the slightest dissatisfaction.

    Use the order blank enclosed.

              Very truly yours,
                  KNIGHT KNITTING COMPANY

Panel 87

OVERCOMING INDIFFERENCE OR OPPOSITION

KNIGHT KNITTING COMPANY
PORTLAND, OREGON

Mrs. H. M Hopkins,
Grardview, California.

Dear Madam

    Did the Knight-Knit Hosiery Booklet reach you? Have you had time yet to read it carefully?

    For surely if you have, one thing has impressed you — that you can have the QUALITY and the STYLE that every well-dressed woman wants in her stockings for less cost in Knight-Knit Hosiery than you ever saw before

    Just think of pure-silk stockings — as lustrous as a fine old piece of burnished ebony, as sheer almost as a piece of lace, as THOROUGHBRED as a seal coat, and yet as durable in the feet, and at the garter joint, and at the knee, as cotton hose — and so reasonable in price that anyone can afford a pair or two.

    Just think of the new, seasonable, striped patterns all shades and combinations, in dainty mercerized yarn, at only 75 cents a pair

    But Knight-Knits are not only stylish — in models 53, 54, 55 and 57, you may get your everyday stockings at wonderfully low prices — 35 cents and 50 cents for qualities usually sold at 50 cents and 75 cents

    And every Knight-Knit has the Knight top that prevents the garter fastening from starting a ladder down the leg; and the Knight reinforcing stitch where the extra-ply heel is joined so your stocking won't start raveling there, and Knight toes and heels so your large toe won't poke its way through, or your shoe wear out the heel.

    Knight-Knit Hosiery wears!

    Why not PROVE it for yourself? Make your selections row and fill out the enclosed order blank Remit only the regular retail price — we pay the express where there is no Knight-Knit dealer to supply you And if when you get the stockings they don't please you, send them back and we will refund every cent of your money. Or if when you have worn one pair, it doesn't wear just as we said it would, send them all back and we will STILL REFUND ALL YOUR MONEY

    No fairer offer could be made than this. Accept it today Make out your list on the enclosed blank and mail it now.

                   Very truly yours,

                          KNIGHT KNITTING COMPANY

Panel 88

BUSINESS CORRESPONDENCE

KNIGHT KNITTING COMPANY
Portland, Oregon

Mrs. H. M. Hopkins
Grandview
California

Dear Madam

    Four weeks ago -- just 30 days, to be exact about it -- we sent you our new booklet on Knight-Knit Hosiery And YOU -- you have evidently looked it over, then forgotten

    You MUST have been astonished to see such stockings as those on page 9 selling for only 75 cents -- but evidently you said "Oh, what's 25 cents or 50 cents or a dollar saved on stockings to ME -- I won't bother " You MUST have been delighted with the beautiful, lustrous, all-silk hose on page 10, and for a moment thought that with such stockings at $1 a pair or $1 50, or $2 or $3 you certainly would have, for once, all the fine silk stockings you wanted -- but evidently you thought "Oh, what do I want of fine silk stockings -- I'll wear cotton " You must have been glad to learn from page 4 that at last you could have stockings that would not develop "ladders" down the leg, or ravel at the ankle, or wear out at the toe and heel, before you got their worth in wear -- but evidently you then thought, "Oh, I don't mind -- all stockings wear out SOMETIME, so what's the difference if mine wear out before they should"'

    It seems as if you MUST have thought these things for otherwise wouldn't you at least have tried a pair or two of Knight-Knit Hosiery to see if all these wonderful points about them were really true?

    Of course, we know you didn't think those things -- though at first it would seem so   No careful woman would WILFULLY neglect the chance to get stockings that WEAR LONGER no economical woman would CARELESSLY ignore the opportunity to save 15 to 25 cents a pair on cheap stockings, and a dollar or more a pair on silk ones   No woman who loves to be well gowned would INTENTIONALLY pass by the chance of having such beautiful, such stylish, such "chic" stockings at the cost of commonplace ones

    It was simply that everybody hesitates at first about believing a manufacturer's claims. We don't blame you You don't know us So we will do this -- simply pick out the kind of stockings you would like best, in the booklet Put the size number on enclosed order card, sign it and enclose in the addressed envelop with the price of JUST ONE PAIR We will send you a pair of the stockings desired, Wear them, send them to the wash, wear them again, and wash them again -- then if you aren't as well pleased with them as when they were new, send them back and back to you comes your money

    That's the way to prove Knight-Knit claims That's the way to settle your doubts. That's the way to discover how to have prettier, better stockings than you ever had before, and save money on every pair!

    Will you do it? Certainly you will -- who could resist as fair and square an offer as that? Make your selection now -- fill out the card, mail it and get it done! And then you will see our claims come true   Thank you.

                                      Very truly yours,

                                      KNIGHT KNITTING COMPANY

Panel 89

OVERCOMING INDIFFERENCE OR OPPOSITION

you. A spirit of helpfulness and fairness should permeate your letters, but it should never grow so great in your mind that your letters appear afraid to demand the money.

With those points in mind, let us run through the general *policy of a collection follow-up*.

The first letter in a collection series faces the same condition as the first of a sales follow-up—one should assume that the debtor is open-minded; that is, willing to pay. Therefore, the first letter should be just a simple reminder of the debt. A statement in most businesses is enough as in the first letter, below, of the Archer series.

Statement

Mr. _Albert Moore_

In account with

A. H. ARCHER & COMPANY
New York City, New York

Oct. 1	Acc't. previously rendered	$ 119	39	

You must have overlooked the above. Won't you oblige us by sending check to cover?

A. H. Archer & Company.

Panel 90

BUSINESS CORRESPONDENCE

The second letter should assume forgetfulness, just as the second sales letter should assume hesitation, and it should be constructed on the same simple plan, as illustrated by the letters in Panels 91 and 92. Some houses make use again of the statement form. Also, in the second letter, it is often a good policy, by incorporating a solicitation for more business, to demonstrate in a practical way *a belief that the debtor has only overlooked the account.*

Now the conditions facing the third letter vary just as they do in sales letters. On a small account, or an account with a customer with whom you don't expect to do business again, you may skip the natural type of third letter, which, as shown for sales letters, conveys the same idea as the second letter with merely an approach from a slightly different angle. See the example shown in Panel 93.

ADAMS & BALEY
CHICAGO, ILLINOIS

Mr. Parker Johnson,
Glencoe, Illinois.

Dear Sir:

    The check you intended to send us covering the payment due on your book accounts has not yet arrived -- no doubt forgotten.

    Not a serious oversight, of course, but for the sake of uniformity in the handling of thousands of accounts promptness in remitting is greatly appreciated.

    Just pin check or money order to this letter and use the enclosed envelop for return.

    We thank you.

               Very truly yours,

                    ADAMS & BALEY

Panel 91

OVERCOMING INDIFFERENCE OR OPPOSITION

You will note that in all these letters, which have been picked carefully from the most successful "pullers" of concerns doing a large credit business in varying lines, none are discourteous, yet none of them *whine or fawn upon the debtor*. But they convey the idea of the writer's belief in the justness of his claim.

The fourth letter must assume indifference on the debtor's part. Therefore, it should approach the Big Idea through a visionary channel, just as a sales letter should. In Panel 94 you will find a letter to illustrate the point. The first para-

---

ADAMS & BALEY
CHICAGO, ILLINOIS

Mr. Parker Johnson,
Glencoe, Illinois.

Dear Sir:

    Perhaps you have not realized that several items on the statement enclosed have gone considerably past 30 days. They total $183.-29, as we have shown.

    Oversights like this creep in on all of us but now that your attention has been called to the matter you will no doubt let us have your check for this amount at once.

    And we trust you will keep us in mind with further orders, too. How are you fixed for canned soups? If the frosts do the damage that is predicted, as is not unlikely, canned soups will be at a premium. In sending your check you would do well to put in a reservation for as many cases of soups as you can use in the next few months.

                   Very truly yours,

                          ADAMS & BALEY

Panel 92

BUSINESS CORRESPONDENCE

graph, of course, is merely "an opener." The idea comes in the second paragraph, where you are made to put yourself in the creditor's place. The letter in Panel 95 is reproduced by permission from a book, "Collecting the Coin," by Louis Victor Eytinge, who has written many successful collection letters and who has helped many firms collect thousands of dollars in bad accounts In it, too, the presenting of the idea is very plain.

In the chart (Panel 85) at the bottom of page 149 I show the exact process of construction for the first four letters of a collection follow-up, just as I did for the sales follow-up. And

---

CARSON, MASON and OTIS
Los Angeles, California

Mr. W. A. Welsh,
Tacoma, Washington.

Dear Sir:

Permit us to again remind you that you are letting your account run behind. Please note the terms on your original bill. These terms were not decided on by us in any haphazard way -- they were carefully worked out as the basis on which we could AFFORD to do a credit business with our low margin of profit.

Now we are GLAD to have you take full advantage of your good credit with us, but when you let the account drag overtime like this it embarrasses us.

It will be so easy to forget again today about sending your check. Why don't you do it now, while it is still fresh in your mind?

Thank you.

Very truly yours,

CARSON, MASON AND OTIS

Panel 93

OVERCOMING INDIFFERENCE OR OPPOSITION

in Panels 90, 96, 97 and 98 is a series of four letters, built by combining the best points in the first four letters of three different collection series, each of which has been unusually successful.

Compare the policy back of each one with the general policy of the chart, see how they suggest a better way to make a collection series pay

---

R. T. CLEVELAND
Cincinnati, Ohio

Mr. A. G. Ackerman,
Woodstock, Ohio.

My dear Mr. Ackerman:

    I had surely expected your check would be in my office long before this time, as it is considerably over a month since your account became due.

    Unless you have conducted a similar business, you can hardly conceive of the mass of detail involved in handling the many thousands of these $3.50 accounts.

    The difference between profit and loss on such a business depends on the promptness of collections more than on any other one thing.

    I know you will not consciously be instrumental in working a hardship on any concern with which you do business and am quite sure that when you see your failure to remit is doing just this, you will send me a check by return mail.

    I should appreciate it if you will get it in the mail today.

                      Yours cordially,
                            R. T. CLEVELAND

Panel 94

BUSINESS CORRESPONDENCE

WILLIAMS BROTHERS COMPANY
Charleston, South Carolina

Mr. C. B. Singler,
Charleston, S. C.

Dear Mr. Singler:

If you forgot --

As I forgot --

And Tom, Dick and Harry all forgot as we forgot --

Say, wouldn't the business world be in a deuce of a fix?

Why, the whole commercial fabric of credits and discounts would go to pieces! Just fancy how great would be your difficulty in collecting what was rightly yours, if everyone were to say, "I forgot."

Now, I forgot to send you my usual stiff letter, when you forgot us last month -- when you forgot to send us check for $320 -- and because it was partly my fault, I'm writing this little note to prevent your forgetting this time! I don't want to draw on you simply because the money rightfully belongs to us. But -- am I not justified in expecting your check to follow this memory marker?

      Sincerely yours,

        WILLIAMS BROTHERS COMPANY

Panel 95

OVERCOMING INDIFFERENCE OR OPPOSITION

Don't you really feel that you could construct a better letter right now than you could before? Even though you knew, as some of you doubtless did, everything we have so far covered; doesn't having it all in clear, graphic form make using it a more simple matter?

Try out the plan of figuring out one Big Idea or Feeling for the next letter you write, before you start to write it, and see if it does not make that letter more graphic, more interesting, more human. Try the plan of diagramming the next Idea or Feeling you want to convey, with its "features," just as we have done, and see if the letter you build on it doesn't snap and sparkle with life more than the same kind

---

A. H. ARCHER & COMPANY
New York City

Mr. Albert Moore,
Kansas City, Missouri.

Dear Sir:

    You forgot --

    That check which you were to send us 10 days ago.

    We dislike to remind you -- but we dislike still more to have the involved and unnecessary bookkeeping expense attached to carrying one month's accounts over into the next. We will GREATLY appreciate your mailing us your check today.

    You needn't bother even to write a letter -- we understand how such oversights occur. Just enclose this statement and check in the addressed envelop.

                  Yours very truly,
                    A. H. ARCHER & COMPANY

Panel 96

BUSINESS CORRESPONDENCE

of a letter ever did before for you. Try out on the next "hard nut" correspondent to whom you have to write, the plan you have just learned of approaching him from a visionary or negative angle, and see if you don't get a stronger, more appealing letter than you could otherwise have written.

Prove it to yourself right now. Turn to the third problem section and get some practical experience in putting into practise the suggestions I have made.

A. H. ARCHER & COMPANY
New York City

Mr. Albert Moore,
Kansas City, Mo.

Dear Sir:

    Enclosed you will find the THIRD STATEMENT sent you on the overdue part of your account.

    The amount is not large, but the aggregate of a large number of such accounts makes a serious burden for any business to carry.

    If there is any error on this account, or any matter you are waiting to take up with our salesman, please let me know about it -- for an unadjusted claim should not stand open so long on our books. We mention this as it seems as if you would never let the matter run so long unless there were some sort of misunderstanding.

    But if you merely overlooked it, then, now that it has been brought to your attention, we feel sure you will let us have check at once. To avoid forgetting it again, why not send the check NOW?

                   Yours very truly,
                       A. H. ARCHER & COMPANY

Panel 97

OVERCOMING INDIFFERENCE OR OPPOSITION

A. H. ARCHER & COMPANY
New York City

Mr. Albert Moore,
Kansas City, Missouri.

Dear Sir:

How would you like my job?

Each salesman tells me, "Don't pester my customers about their bills -- they'll all pay." The sales manager says "We don't call on any man who isn't good -- why worry?" And the president always says, "Service -- that's our first duty -- think only of Service every time you call on a customer; think only of Service every time you write a customer."

But if our working capital is twisted up in overdue accounts, and our customer ledger spotted with items current, and items due, and items past due -- who's going to pay the freight?

There is $120.61 OVERDUE on your account. There is nothing wrong about it or you would have answered my last letter. Of course you are going to settle up -- soon. Of course I needn't "worry" about it. Of course I want to help render you "Service." But, to be perfectly blunt about it, I wish you would SEND ME YOUR CHECK TODAY. It would be better business for us, better business for you.

I know just how easy it is to let such payments slide along -- and yours has certainly slid quite a bit -- 60 days. Won't you attend to it today -- now, while you have it in mind? THANK YOU.

                    Yours very truly,
                    A. H. ARCHER & COMPANY

Panel 98

BUSINESS CORRESPONDENCE

SUMMARY

WE have now studied three of the secrets that have made a letter pull big results. In the first chapter we learned the 10 factors that determine how a letter should be written—whether we should bother about the way we begin it or "stage" it; how we should pick out some Big Idea; and whether we should present the Big Idea in a simple, direct way or work up to it through a visionary or negative picture. From the second chapter we learned how ideas or feeling can be expressed in words—how we can make our readers *see* the big point about our goods or *feel* the big point of our reason or explanation or argument We learned how to translate into words, by means of a simple little diagram, any intangible idea or human feeling we have to write

And now, in this third chapter, we have learned to present our ideas from a negative or visionary point of view so that they will be understood and accepted even when a reader is opposed or indifferent We have learned why experienced correspondents don't always come at their ideas straight from the shoulder, but make a reader or listener see the disadvantage of his position before presenting the Big Idea. And finally we learned how to chart and write a sales and a collection follow-up series.

Now one of the biggest annoyances in the correspondent's daily work is his inability at times to call up the exact word or phrase he wants. In the next chapter we will tackle and solve that problem

I will show you how you may prepare a Word File which will unfailingly present the wanted word This is a little brain partner found effective by many advertising writers and correspondents. The problem section will include instructions on how to use it After you have learned how to use it you will wonder why you hadn't thought of the system long ago.

The next problem section is the most interesting one so far. Be sure to read it carefully. Study the letter which has been incorporated in the text. Really, it's remarkable.

PROBLEM SECTION III

WE are now getting to a point where we can see some real results, don't you think? The knack of creating an imaginary ideal in the reader's mind, which I introduced to you in the third chapter, is one of the differences that distinguishes the really able letter writer (or advertisement writer, or speaker) from the prosy, set-in-a-rut man.

I speak from experience when I say you can't do very much with letters—whether they are for selling, collecting, answering complaints, turning down requests, or seeking favors—nor much with advertising, nor much with personal contact, if you can't make use of the imaginary, or the negative idea.

You have probably attended a banquet, or a lodge meeting, or gathering of some kind where everyday business men made speeches, and after the meeting heard someone say, "So-and-So made a fine talk, didn't he?" "Yes," the other man answers. "There was a lot of common sense in what Such-and-Such said, too, but some way he doesn't grip you like So-and-So."

My observation has been that those men who put a "lot of common sense" in what they said, but who couldn't make the people "get it," simply couldn't use the visionary or negative to *"put their common sense over."*

You'll find the same fault in letters. Many a man who has had the exact goods his prospects needed, or otherwise had facts or reason on his side, couldn't overcome prejudice and *make readers see things his way* because he failed to present his proposition right.

All through this book, therefore, I shall bear down hard on the right way to present an idea. It's of the greatest impor-

BUSINESS CORRESPONDENCE

tance. That's why I ask you in this problem section to follow me through several phases of it.

But before we practise with this absorbing principle, let us review the points made in the second problem section. We'll chat awhile over the problems, some of them "stickers," I suppose, which you encountered in that section

First, there is that SYSTEM letter selling the book, "How to Finance a Business." You visualized the Big Idea of it, diagrammed its "features," and then filed the diagram in your Material File Turn to your file. Get out your memoranda and let's talk it over.

With the start I gave you, I'm sure you had no trouble in working out the "features" of the letter. If you'll take a look at my diagram (Panel 99 below) you'll notice that all I did was to cut out the connecting words in the second paragraph and my task was complete.

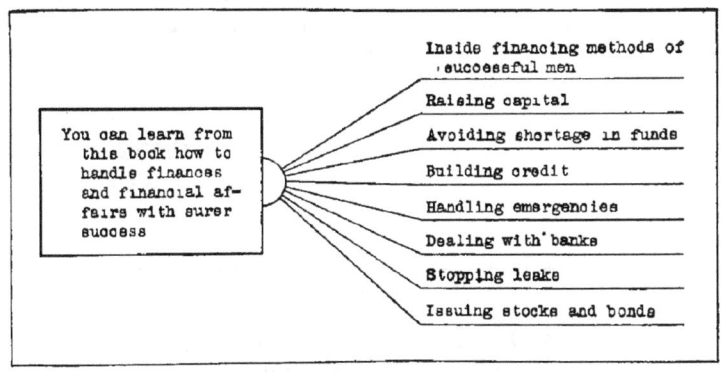

Panel 99

Now why did I ask you to do a task so easy? Why simply to prove to you again that any good written work, whether a short story, advertisement, oration, letter, or any other form, can be built up by writing down the "features" and connecting them up by a few explanatory clauses so as to make sense The first draft may not be flawless, but a little polishing up will fix that.

OVERCOMING INDIFFERENCE OR OPPOSITION

If you made any mistakes, read the forepart of the second chapter again. Trace the building up of the Big Idea in the Irving quotation and in the Delta Land Company letter Then compare your diagram of the SYSTEM letter with mine and see for yourself why I am right. If you do this you will be better able to criticize the results on the second problem.

This second problem, you will remember, was to work out the Big Idea in the letter answering an inquiry about Hayes Four-wheel Planters. The "features" for this letter were given you. Bring out the diagram from your Material File, where you put it and we'll look it over. Compare it with mine, below.

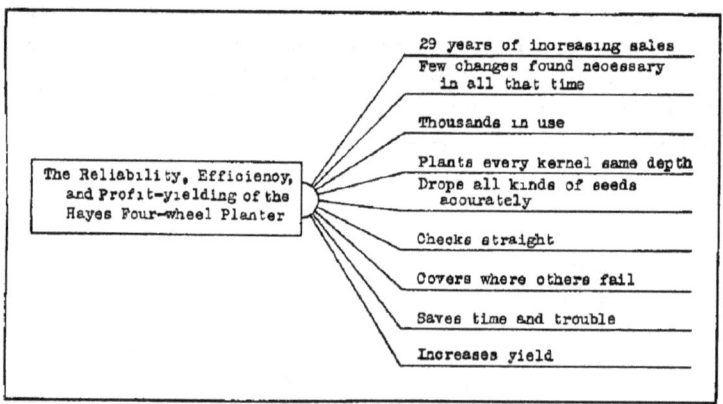

Panel 100

I am sure you had no difficulty with that job. In giving it to you to do, I had more than the mechanics of it in mind. I wanted you to see how readily "features," if selected right, tie back to the Big Idea. If you understand that, then the actual words you used to write the Big Idea are inconsequential.

The work you did on the SYSTEM letter and the Hayes letter must have lightened your load of sizing up the insurance man's letter on page 99. On the next page, in Panel 101, I give you the Big Idea and "features" as I took them from the letter. Nothing to it, was there? You should have this principle "down pat" by this time. Here is my diagram to compare with yours.

As you simply reversed the Irving process on this letter, I know you had it right. Of course, your wording of the Big Idea may have been, probably was, different from mine, but I believe most of you did it right. Analyze every good letter

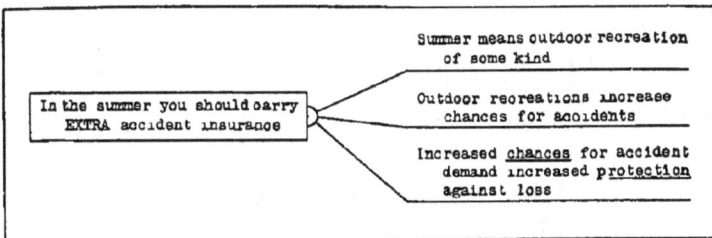

Panel 101

that comes your way until you fall into the habit of sifting ideas into their "features." It is all a matter of practise and habit.

And now we come to our first genuinely constructive work.

It is the letter—or the idea-portion of it—you were to write for a retail custom-shirt store, for which a diagram of Idea and "features" was furnished in the previous problem section

Bring out your letter, chart, and diagram from your Material File and compare it with my way of handling it as shown below. Now the first "feature" was this:

"Our cutter first shapes your pattern to conform to every curve, dimension, peculiarity and position of your shoulders, chest, arms, and waist"

When I started to *write that "feature" into letter form*, I looked down at the Idea section of my chart (Section 3a) and saw that the thought of appearance and comfort played a pretty big part in it. So I decided that, as nearly as I could, I would play up the "feature" of the cutter and his pattern in a way to make the reader think of standing up while an expert labored patiently to get every detail perfect—to make

OVERCOMING INDIFFERENCE OR OPPOSITION

the reader see himself being measured, to the fraction of an inch, and asked for his preferences, and so on—to make him think of having the services of an expert valet. So I wrote:

> "When our cutter measures you up for shirts — "

to create that thought of "being measured up", then:

> " — getting every curve, dimension, peculiarity, and position of your body down on paper — "

the "down on paper" to sound like accuracy, then

> "figuring just how much you need across the shoulders to give you full swing — "

the "just how much you need" to keep the reader in the picture:

> "and yet look trim and well tailored."

—"trim and well tailored" to make him see himself with proper pride. Then, I went on—but you can see how it all goes from the paragraphs of a letter I wrote from my chart and diagram.

Dear Sir

When our cutter measures you for shirts — getting every curve, dimension, peculiarity, and position of your body down on paper, figuring just how much you need across the shoulders to give you free swing, and yet look trim and well tailored, just how much across the chest to make your collar sit snug, just how much to give you around the waist to make your shirt look right SITTING OR STANDING:

And when he has cut your shirts to conform to every one of those details, and then made them up with such little refinements as watching to bring the color part of the pattern at the edge of your cuffs so they won't show soil so quickly, making the pattern on the plait match just right with the body, and so on

And when you get your choice from a variety of patterns that would almost bankrupt a ready-made shirt stock, and from materials of every description —

Why, then you get shirts that look as different on you as a custom-made suit of clothes, and make you FEEL DRESSED * * *

BUSINESS CORRESPONDENCE

Now the thing for you to do is to study over the comparison of my writing with your own. It would be hard to tell whether a letter finished up from either writing would bring results—that is always a matter of testing—which we will take up in a later chapter. But either outline will please you better than the letter we started from—the one in the second problem section. And we can see whether or not they express the Idea—and that's the point.

But this is a point that I want you to be sure to check up In putting your "features" into words, did you keep the Big Idea in mind all the time, so that thought of appearance and comfort was always there—and so that the reader himself was always in it?

That's the big point—you mustn't write just facts, you must write them as parts of the Big Idea. And the Big Idea is that "our shirts will do much for *your* appearance and comfort"—not for the appearance and comfort of some imaginary man.

And what I want you to be sure of now is that you got that "you" spirit into each "feature," and that thought of "appearance and comfort" into the "you."

Your words, your phrases, or your style needn't be anything at all like those of my letter to be equally expressive; yours could be more brief or more extended, your letter could be differently arranged—and still be exactly as good or better. But if yours hasn't that *man-to-man spirit in it that makes the reader see himself* in the idea, and see his appearance and comfort in it, then yours needs improving.

The next problem is the cream separator follow-up letter. In the preceding problem section you were given a synopsis of the conditions the writer of the letter had to meet and a rough idea of the selling points to be made. You charted the "load" of the letter, diagrammed its Big Idea and "features" and then wrote out the idea as completely as you could. Of course, writing a letter without knowing your merchandise first hand is always rather difficult, but it will do for practising ideas and that is our present task.

OVERCOMING INDIFFERENCE OR OPPOSITION

Take your cream separator letter from your Material File and check it "feature" by "feature" with the original letter to be found on page 148. If you have my idea, and I know you have it by this time, you'll find this checking up process so ridiculously easy that you may be a bit impatient at my requiring it

But just because the task I set seems easy is no reason for thinking it unimportant. If you find it easy, you have learned a *big principle in letter writing which will be useful to you* time and time again It is useful to you right now Prove it for yourself.

Problem 2 dealt with a collection letter. I asked you to go through the usual routine of charting the letter's "load," diagramming its "features" and building a letter.

Take letter and memoranda from your file and compare them with the letter on page 162.

Those of you who have nothing to do with credits and collections may balk at studying collection letters; nevertheless I urge you to work on this problem. Remember that we are studying the fundamental principles of business correspondence and, therefore, we must not overlook a single phase of it.

The problems that underlie a good collection letter are the same as those in a good sales letter, or in a good complaint letter, or in any other kind of good letter The collection man may profit by seeing *how sales letter ideas apply to collection letters* and the salesman can get valuable hints by studying the way collection letters may be turned into good sales letters.

All through this book on applied business correspondence I shall use letters of any kind that happen to illustrate best the point under discussion, and I want you to practise on all of the letters alike. The retailer can gain as much by writing a wholesaler's letter, or a banker's letter, or a manufacturer's letter as he could by practising solely on letters relating exclusively to retail problems. The same is true of a plumber, of a banker, or a garage man, or a man in any other kind of business.

BUSINESS CORRESPONDENCE

Now we are ready to *apply in a practical way the principle of the visionary or negative idea* which we discussed in the third chapter

First of all, I want to impress upon you the importance of the "connecting link." It, you remember, joins the negative, or visionary, idea with the positive idea

Although it may seem unimportant, the connecting link, when cleverly written, will often save the whole letter from the waste-basket. Much of the antagonism against the use of the negative has, I believe, come about because men who tried to use it failed to *gear it to the positive idea by an effective connecting link* I have seen many letters in which the writer created a good visionary idea fail, go up like a puff of smoke, simply because the writer did not tie up effectively the negative with the positive idea.

So I say, study hard on the connecting link idea which I explained rather carefully in the third chapter and upon which I'm going to dwell in this problem section. When you are sure that you understand the text, go back over the letters I quoted in the foregoing chapter and devote your entire attention solely to the connecting link. See how these links in every case have the effect of taking you by the shoulder, turning you right about and making you see the positive idea.

Here is another point for you. Have you noted that I often write "negative, or visionary" instead of just negative? My reason is that the term "negative" by itself does not express clearly enough, for all cases, the effect on the reader.

You will see by the clothier's letter beginning at the bottom of page 174 that, although the first idea is hardly what you could call "negative," still it has this effect: It makes you put yourself, not in the attitude of the dealer's customer, but of the dealer himself. In other words, you see the other side of the affair.

In the fourth letter of the Knight-Knit Hosiery series, on page 154, you will see another example of what I mean Notice that *you, as the reader, are made to criticize your own actions* as though they were those of another person.

OVERCOMING INDIFFERENCE OR OPPOSITION

That's the point. "Negative idea" as I use it means putting the reader of a letter on the other side of the argument. Whether you do it by picturing outright the direct disadvantages of not accepting your proposition, or by getting the reader to think of your idea from your point of view doesn't matter.

The collection letter on page 163, ("How would you like my job?") is another good example. And in the fourth chapter you will learn a great deal more about building up entirely visionary ideas.

Now in starting to practise on the connecting link principle and expressing the "negative-visionary" idea, pause for a moment to consider a problem on which you previously worked.

Problem 4, on page 48, dealt with a fire insurance agent's letter, one which had to collect past due premiums. You made a chart of it, marking the chart, "Size-up of Fire Insurance Agent's Letter," and filed it in your Material File. Take chart and problem from the file and refresh your memory by reading them over.

The conditions told you clearly enough that Section 4 of the chart, which asks whether the reader would be indifferent or opposed, would have to be answered affirmatively. The reader is indifferent. Well then, disregard all other notes you made on the chart and study the letter on page 130.

That letter was written to fit the conditions set forth in the problem. The negative idea, the awakening link, and the positive idea are so plain in this short letter that I shall not waste time in detailed consideration of them. But I won't let you off so easily.

Look over this letter thoroughly. Study the negative idea and the awakening link and jot them down on a piece of scratch paper. Lay your notes aside and then when you have completed all other work of this problem section, compare results with my diagram shown on page 130.

That will be a good test for you and if you find that your diagram checks up with mine, rest assured that you have gone a long way in your task of learning how to write better

BUSINESS CORRESPONDENCE

letters. File all your memoranda about this letter in your Material File.

Now try your hand at writing the connecting link between the negative and the positive idea. Here is a rough outline of the conditions a retail clothier faced.

Toward the end of the season the salesman from whom he bought a certain line of ready-made clothes wrote him that he could secure for him a small selection from the manufacturer's season's clean-up stock that usually went to two or three metropolitan stores. The prices were very low, and the quality high. The dealer accepted. Then he prepared (in addition to his newspaper advertising) to circularize his list of charge customers and also a list of non-customers. His regular customers having already bought their winter clothes, and the others being non-customers, you can see why a bit of the "visionary" was necessary.

I am reproducing below that part of his letter creating the visionary idea of the letter, and on the next page I am showing the positive idea.

Study carefully and put into practise what you have observed about "connecting links," by writing a strong, effective link between those two ideas

THE VISIONARY IDEA

Every year when the rush period of a busy selling season is over the big clothing manufacturers draw a deep long breath and begin to straighten up stock and warehouses. And nearly always they find suits set to one side during the rush, for some reason or another -- reserved, maybe, on some salesman's request for a particularly good customer and then canceled, -- or marked "hold" and the reason forgotten -- or often pushed out of sight by accident.

These suits are generally the very best of the stock. But they have to be disposed of quickly without regard to cost, to make room for the coming season's stock, for then space is more valuable than clothing.

OVERCOMING INDIFFERENCE OR OPPOSITION

THE POSITIVE IDEA

    There are some wonderful, dark, cloudy grays -- soft as down, light in weight almost as a feather, but warm as fleece. Linings of sheeny, rustly, silk serge. They sold for $40. I got them through my friend the salesman for $19 50 and have marked them $22 50 -- fair enough, isn't it? There are a few -- not many -- rich blue cheviots, a blue that you won't get next year -- deep and lustrous and warm. Same price. Then quite a number of domestic weaves in browns, grays and blacks, beautifully made up and finished, and tailored with the taste of custom goods These sold all season for $25 and $30 -- what do you think I have marked them now? -- $18!

    Come in and look them over. It's just like having a brand new fall stock to pick from -- at end-of-the-season prices, only no end of a season ever before had values like these.

    Come tomorrow -- Tuesday -- for they'll go quick

                       Very truly yours,

    Now you have had an opportunity to test out your newly acquired knack of building up a negative or visionary idea, and an opportunity to see how closely you can come to picking out the right kind of a "connecting link."

    To test your ability a little farther I submit another problem. Just below find the diagram of a letter sent out by the maker of a highly successful self-heating flatiron, called the Ajax Here you have the negative idea, the positive idea, and the connecting link between the two.

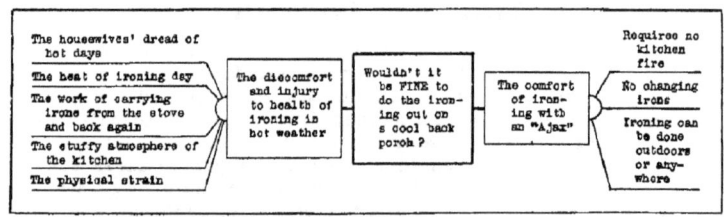

Panel 102

    From this diagram, the "features" of which are complete enough to give you all the selling points necessary to convey the Idea—write the complete letter just as good and strong as you can. In the next chapter you will be shown the letter from which the above diagram was made to compare with yours.

Problem 1

Next you should see what you can do in making a complete diagram of both visionary and positive ideas, with the connecting link and writing a letter based on them.

Take this as an outline of the "load":

A man received some goods of a certain house, but did not pay for them. After having received five duns, he has not even replied. A sixth letter is now to be written. The creditor wants to arouse in the buyer's mind a vision of the consequences his lack of attention to the bill will involve. It seems that as these goods were ordered by mail (if it can be shown that the debtor did not intend to pay for them when he ordered them) he is liable under U. S General Statutes Section 1581, for defrauding by mail. The creditor doesn't want to say that out and out in his letter, as he wants to give the man one more chance.

There you have a nice chance to practise your understanding of the use of the visionary or negative idea. Diagram it, write a letter based on your diagram, and then file all this material in your Material File. In the next chapter I'll show you how the problem was worked out by an expert on collections.

The foregoing problem and the two following I submit as typical of those which arise from day to day in the daily routine of the business correspondent. The practise you get in solving them will be sufficient to set in your mind the principles outlined in this part. On the other hand, you understand that these problems are only the beginning of the work that an ambitious person can do on this problem section.

Problem 2

Now here is another problem that will give you some good hard thinking along the lines of conveying the negative idea.

OVERCOMING INDIFFERENCE OR OPPOSITION

You are the manufacturer of a washing compound: Your product—call it anything you please—takes the dirt out of clothes without requiring them to be rubbed on a washboard. A housewife or a washerwoman may put three teaspoonfuls of it into a boilerful of dirty clothes, boil them 20 minutes, and have them "ready to rinse and blue and hang on the line " And, of course, your product won't hurt the clothes.

We will say that you have circularized all the women in a town, several times, but though in other towns the campaign has been successful, in this particular city results have been poor. So you decide to write a special letter for this town.

Make a complete size-up of this problem on one of the charts you have in reserve. Diagram whatever idea you decide on. If you say it calls for a negative idea, diagram that. Then write. Of course, not knowing any more about the product than I have told you, you can't expect to do as well as if it were your own business, but you will get some fine practise and it will be interesting

File your effort in your Material File, because in the next problem section I' l show you how this problem was handled by one such manufacturer, with phenomenal success.

Problem 3

One thing more.

Turn again to the custom shirt maker's letter on page 169. Suppose this letter were going to men who wore only ready-made shirts. How would you handle it?

Make a new size-up on one of your charts and then try to do all that the new chart demands. File this material and in the next problem section I shall give you my version of it.

PART IV

HOW TO MAKE YOUR MEANING CLEAR

CHAPTER IV

HOW TO MAKE YOUR MEANING CLEAR

IN this fourth chapter we are going to take up one of the most interesting elements of letter writing. Without leading you into the mysteries of grammar or rhetoric I am going to show you how to make every letter you write mean exactly what you say; nothing more, nothing less.

That's not only interesting, but important How many letters have you tossed into the waste-basket because you couldn't, in the rush of business, take time to translate a jumble of words into ideas? And as you recall some of the letters you have written—*letters which should have made good, but didn't*—perhaps you'll agree that a lack of clearness is what failed to put them across At any rate, coherence, that's what a school teacher would call it, is the first essential in any letter. Lacking it, letters that carry their "load" splendidly, that present perfectly their Big Idea, whether positive or visionary-negative, fail to make their reader act—go into the waste-basket.

Although books have been written on the subject and although there are scores of rules for attaining clearness, books and rules when boiled down amount practically to this: Clearness requires the use of the right word in the right place in the sentence. Substitute "right phrase" for right word and you have a definition of clearness in a paragraph. Substitute sentence for phrase and you have a definition of clearness in a whole composition.

Now why is the use of the right word and right phrase so very important? Simply this. When you speak or write to a man he can only comprehend one word or idea at a time As you talk, he builds a picture with the words you deal

BUSINESS CORRESPONDENCE

WONDER ENGINE COMPANY
St. Louis, Mo.

Mr Will T. Spencer
St Joseph, Mich

Dear Sir
* * * *

    The kind of fuel is an important item WONDER Kerosene engines operate on kerosene, distillate, solar oil, toppings and all fuels of like grade The principle of using low grade fuel by heating the air from the waste exhaust without any waste of fuel gives the WONDER engine an advantage over all other makes; Read carefully pages 10 and 11 of the catalog on this point Remember that WONDER Kerosene engines can be instantly changed back to use gasoline, distillate or motor spirits, so that to invest in a WONDER Kerosene engine enables you to use cheap fuels now and change to gasoline or other fuels in the future if conditions change. Do not overlook the big advantage of buying an engine suitable for all fuels

    But the price of the fuel, important as it is, is not the only thing to consider. The amount of fuel you use is still more important Therefore, be sure that the engine you order is guaranteed not to use in excess of one-tenth of a gallon per horsepower per hour If gasoline costs 15¢ your fuel cost per horsepower hour should not be over 1½¢ If you buy a Kerosene engine and use 8c fuel your cost of operating per horsepower hour should be far less than 1¢ Just think of it!

    Remember that only four-cycle engines with automatic fuel cutout can save fuel. Two-cycle engines take fuel in full charges every revolution, thus using double the amount The open air pipe damper engines (called throttling governors by some people) feed fuel continuously, only they increase or decrease the charge, and as a result are constantly feeding improper mixtures into the engine, which fouls, carbonizes the engine, and wastes from 30 to 50% of the fuel WONDER engines feed the fuel only when it is needed in full charges, which makes a perfect mixture, does not foul, keeps the engine clean, and cuts the fuel consumption to the lowest point Any engine that uses more fuel than we guarantee on WONDER engines cannot be classed as an economical power

                Very truly yours,

                    WONDER ENGINE COMPANY

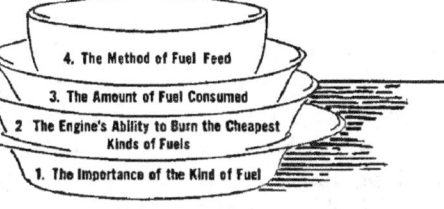

4. The Method of Fuel Feed
3. The Amount of Fuel Consumed
2. The Engine's Ability to Burn the Cheapest Kinds of Fuels
1. The Importance of the Kind of Fuel

Panel 103

MAKING YOUR MEANING CLEAR

him. Each word should fit snugly on top of another, otherwise the whole structure will totter. When a boy, you built towers with blocks. You quickly learned that each block had to be laid just right; the big ones at the bottom, the smallest ones on top. So with words and ideas in your daily work of letter writing.

Let me give you another example of what I mean, because I want you to get this idea firmly fixed in your mind. Never forget it.

Did you ever help carry the dinner dishes from the table to the kitchen? If you did, you will remember what a big stack of them you could carry if you piled them properly, the largest plates at the bottom, to hold on by, then the next sized plates, then smaller ones, then saucers, and so on. All you had to do to carry the pile was to get a grip on the bottom ones and hold on The others rested securely, one on another, without any effort of yours

But if you stacked them up at random, in any order they happened to come to hand, plates on top of saucers, large dishes on small ones, why then you probably spilled them or at least you had a hard time carrying them.

Well, in a homely way, that is just what psychologists say happens in a reader's mind *when a writer does not arrange his thoughts properly*—the tower tumbles and the idea to be conveyed is lost

For example, on the opposite page, you will find the idea-expressing paragraphs of a successful gas engine sales letter. Although this letter, to convey its Big Idea of economy and efficiency, gives you three different points to hold and carry in your mind at one time, it does so in such a way that you have no difficulty at all. After getting your mind to take hold of the broad, general point of the importance of the kind of fuel, the next point (the engine's ability to burn the cheapest fuels) rests on it just as a small plate rests on a larger one And that point furnishes a support for the next point—the amount of fuel consumed. And that makes a firm support for the next point—the method of feed. In short, you were

BUSINESS CORRESPONDENCE

JACKSON FERTILIZER CO
Racine, Wis.

Mr Paul B Beck
Whitewater Wis

Dear Sir

* * * *

    It is no uncommon thing for the use of 200 pounds of 'Big Four' fertilizer on corn to net an increase in yield of 20 to 25 bushels an acre   So you can see the great profits that can be made from its use   Land that produces a ton of hay an acre if properly fertilized will produce 1 1/2 to 2 tons

    The more approved way of applying fertilizers is to use a wheat drill and drill the fertilizer in prior to planting the corn   However many thousands of tons of fertilizers are applied in the drill row with the fertilizer attachment on the corn planter   It is much better when the fertilizer is drilled in the rows as they can be checked and cross-cultivated and the cross-cultivation tends to distribute the fertilizer between the rows

    We recommend our 'Big Four' Brand for use on corn at the rate of 150 to 200 pounds an acre and our 'Ajax' Brand for oats timothy and so forth at the rate of 200 pounds an acre   Either of these brands we can quote you at $1 60 per hundred delivered   In less than carload lots our terms are cash with the order

* * * *

Very truly yours

JACKSON FERTILIZER COMPANY

---

5. The Costs of Using
4. The Superiority of the Approved Way
3. Another Way of Using
2. The Approved Way of Using It
1. The Results of Using the Fertilizer

Panel 104

MAKING YOUR MEANING CLEAR

given a Big Idea, a foundation on which to build, then a smaller one to pile on top of that, and the least important idea to surmount the pile.

If you have not done so, turn to the letter and read it. Isn't it sensible? One can't help but get the writer's idea.

But let's look at the other side of the proposition before making a decision. Read the letter in Panel 104 on the opposite page. The panel contains the idea-expressing paragraphs of a letter used by a fertilizer manufacturer—used with poor reults, too. The reason for its failure is plain. It's only too evident that the writer *covered his points by dictating them just as they popped into his head* and without the least regard as to the kind of structure they would build up in the mind of the reader.

Didn't you find yourself halting, as you read, to "get the drift" of the letter? And when you were through, did you have half so satisfactory a grasp on the Big Idea as that which you got from the engine man's letter? Of course you didn't. And if you stop to think about it, the reason why the letter fails to get across is plain. The writer of that fertilizer letter piled plates on saucers. The letter is another case of piling big blocks on little ones—big ideas on little ones.

The point I make will be very clear if you will look over the diagrams at the bottom of Panels 103 and 104. In the lower part of Panel 103, I stacked the "features" of the engine letter in a pile just as plates should be stacked to show you the *mental burden the reader has to carry* and also to show you why the letter is so easy to read. A letter easy to read is, of course, easy to understand

Then at the bottom of Panel 104, I stacked the "features" in the fertilizer letter. It is plain how much juggling the reader of that letter had to do, in addition to reading, to carry the thoughts of the letter and to understand the Big Idea the writer of it intended to convey.

In plain terms, the writers of letters like the second one expect the reader not only to read the letter, but also to do part of the writer's own work; that is, think the letter. And

BUSINESS CORRESPONDENCE

that, many people decline to do. So, many a letter goes unheeded, many a story is laid down unfinished, many an audience yawns and wishes the speaker would finish, and many a man's conversation earns him the reputation of being a bore: simply because *the reader has to do too much* mental juggling and balancing to get the idea which the writer intended to convey.

Let that great philosopher, Herbert Spencer, make this plainer to us In his essay, "The Philosophy of Style," he put his finger squarely on the trouble. After citing many general maxims on how to write and speak clearly, he summed up all of them in the paragraph which I quote below:

"On seeking for some clue to the law underlying these current maxims we may see shadowed forth, in many of them, the importance of economizing the reader's or hearer's attention. To so present ideas that they may be apprehended with the least possible mental effort, is the desideratum towards which most of the rules point. When we condemn writing that is wordy or confused, or intricate—when we praise this style as easy, and blame that as fatiguing, we consciously or unconsciously assume this desideratum as our standard of judgment. Regarding language as an apparatus of symbols for the conveyance of thought, we may say that, as in a mechanical apparatus, the more simple and better arranged its parts, the greater will be the effect produced. In either case, whatever force is absorbed by the machine is deducted from the result. A reader or listener has at each moment but a limited amount of mental power available. To recognize and interpret the symbols presented to him requires part of this power, to arrange and combine the images suggested requires a further part, and only that part which remains, can be used 'or realizing the thought conveyed Hence, the more time and attention it takes to receive and understand each sentence, the less time and attention can be given to the contained idea, and the less vividly will the idea be conveyed"

Now, just as an experiment, for the last sentence substitute this: "The more time and attention it takes to juggle and balance each individual dish, the less time and attention can be given to maintain your hold, and the less securely can that stack of dishes be carried" There you have the same problem reduced to commonplace English

Spencer might be horrified to see his thought so twisted, yet in my homely, everyday illustration you have a simple *key to the cultivation of a clear, vivid, clean-cut style* of expression—

MAKING YOUR MEANING CLEAR

a homely key by which we ordinary people, without the genius of great writers, can, nevertheless, adapt the style of some of the greatest of writers to our everyday affairs.

Now then, just as we did in the three preceding chapters, let us get down to brass tacks, begin at the beginning, and take up the job of improving our style. First, let us see how we may make the description of any piece of merchandise, or any business service, or any other business want or demand that we may have to express, so accurate and so clear and so realistic that it will live in the reader's mind.

Suppose that instead of just a plain, everyday business man you were really a great writer, and suppose you had conceived the idea of some unusual situation—some situation that your readers never have experienced or heard of. You want to make them, even though it is entirely strange and unfamiliar to them, see it and feel it as though it were familiar. In business you often have to describe a machine or a package or an idea or a situation of some kind that the reader is totally unfamiliar with. Hence we are not going so far afield as it might seem.

Assume that you have conceived the idea of a great cannon breaking from its lashings on board a battleship at sea and creating terror and panic. You want to picture the damage it can do—rolling and pitching about the deck with the rolling and pitching of the ship; battering, smashing, and ramming; and to picture its danger to life—turning unexpectedly on its course with the tossing of the sea, running in circles or rushing from end to end; you want to make it seem like some dreadful wild beast; and you want to picture its might and power—with its enormous weight and frightful speed, and its unmanageableness; because, while it seems to have the power to move and to act like a creature alive, yet it is without the brain or reasoning power of a live creature.

In skeleton form, in Panel 105 on the next page, are your "features."

Of course you cannot begin your description with the "feature" you would naturally think of first—the damage the cannon can do. Your reader, unfamiliar with such situations, cannot yet comprehend the damage it holds. Remember, in the second chapter, page 77, how confusing and unconvincing the addressing machine company's letter became when we started it with, "You can typewrite names

---

THE "FEATURES"

The damage it can do
Its danger to life
Its likeness to a wild beast
Its power
Man's utter inability to manage it

Panel 105

and addresses at a speed of 30 per minute—" instead of first working the reader up to appreciating that speed?

Well, you have the same task now—you must start with the "feature" that will most easily work your reader up to the point of appreciating the danger of damage in the situation

So, just like the writer of the Addressograph letter, you must *begin with something the reader can understand for himself*—something he "can take hold of," like the bottom plate in the stack of dishes.

Recall how in Washington Irving's description, quoted in the second chapter, the author began with, "On all sides he beheld vast stores of apples." That was something the reader could grasp at once without effort.

Therefore, in the description of the terrors of a ship's cannon broken from its lashings at sea, as your reader is unfamiliar with shipboard conditions, begin with some "feature" that is familiar, with some "feature" that he can appreciate or grasp or picture easily. You must, figuratively, start with him on land and take him to sea with you.

Now, then, wouldn't the gun's likeness to some wild beast be such a "feature" to start with?

MAKING YOUR MEANING CLEAR

Any of us can vividly picture a wild beast at once. And if we get to thinking of the loose cannon as a wild beast let loose, we then can easily appreciate the danger of it.

So the best point to put first and foremost in the reader's mind is the likeness to a wild beast. The second point should be the one that will rest most solidly on the thought of a wild beast and that, of course, is power to kill and maim.

With a firm hold on the idea of a wild beast any reader can easily carry on top of it the idea of the beast's danger to life. Then, with the thoughts of dangers aroused, it is easy to attach those thoughts to a gun broken loose.

From a gun's danger to life your reader can easily go on to appreciate its ability to do the ship damage. That should come third. Consideration of the damage it can do will prepare your reader to take in and appreciate its unmanageableness. Although to start with, your reader knew nothing about the effect of a cannon broken loose at sea, he now has a clear grasp on the terrors you want him to feel.

See *how simp'y you can choose the order in which your "features" will be grasped* and held most easily by the reader, when you keep in mind that picture of a stack of dishes to carry?

Of course, in fancying you as a great writer about to describe the terrors of a ship's cannon broken loose at sea, I merely wanted to prepare you for an analysis of the style used by Victor Hugo in that wonderful description of his of just such a situation. On the next page I have taken that description of Hugo's, which you will find complete in his novel "Ninety-Three," and separated it into its "features" about as I did for the Irving, Lincoln, and Ingersoll quotations in previous chapters. I stacked its "features" to let you see how every one rests solidly on the preceding one—beginning with the gun's likeness to a wild beast, and going on to its dangerousness, its power to damage, its might, and its unmanageableness.

Begin reading at the bottom of the illustration. After you have passed the foundation "feature"—the biggest dish, read up, one step at a time.

BUSINESS CORRESPONDENCE

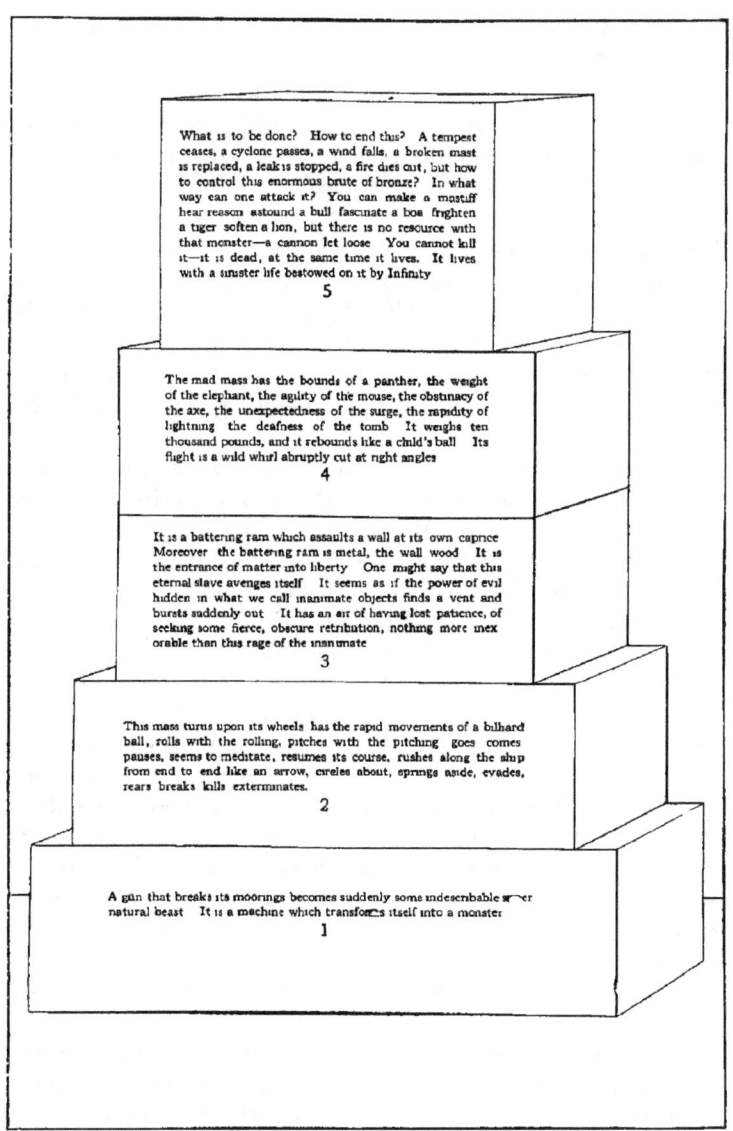

What is to be done? How to end this? A tempest ceases, a cyclone passes, a wind falls, a broken mast is replaced, a leak is stopped, a fire dies out, but how to control this enormous brute of bronze? In what way can one attack it? You can make a mastiff hear reason, astound a bull, fascinate a boa, frighten a tiger, soften a lion, but there is no resource with that monster—a cannon let loose. You cannot kill it—it is dead, at the same time it lives. It lives with a sinister life bestowed on it by Infinity.

5

The mad mass has the bounds of a panther, the weight of the elephant, the agility of the mouse, the obstinacy of the axe, the unexpectedness of the surge, the rapidity of lightning, the deafness of the tomb. It weighs ten thousand pounds, and it rebounds like a child's ball. Its flight is a wild whirl abruptly cut at right angles.

4

It is a battering ram which assaults a wall at its own caprice. Moreover the battering ram is metal, the wall wood. It is the entrance of matter into liberty. One might say that this eternal slave avenges itself. It seems as if the power of evil hidden in what we call inanimate objects finds a vent and bursts suddenly out. It has an air of having lost patience, of seeking some fierce, obscure retribution, nothing more inexorable than this rage of the inanimate.

3

This mass turns upon its wheels, has the rapid movements of a billiard ball, rolls with the rolling, pitches with the pitching, goes comes pauses, seems to meditate, resumes its course, rushes along the ship from end to end like an arrow, circles about, springs aside, evades, rears, breaks, kills, exterminates.

2

A gun that breaks its moorings becomes suddenly some indescribable super natural beast. It is a machine which transforms itself into a monster.

1

Panel 106

MAKING YOUR MEANING CLEAR

See how easy it is for you to grasp the situation although it is a totally unfamiliar one.

Probably no more vivid description has ever been penned. But the arrangement of "features," which makes it so vivid and so easy to understand, can be utilized in an ordinary business letter, as we shall now see.

In Panel 107 on the next page is the sales letter of a self-heating iron concern—or, more correctly, the idea-expressing paragraphs of it, as that is all we are interested in now.

Read the first paragraph. It conveys the negative idea of the strain and discomfort of old-fashioned ironing in the summer. Did it begin with the hard work of ironing in the summer, as you might have naturally expected it to? No. And why?

As the letter was mailed out in April, a woman would have had as hard a time appreciating that point as Hugo's readers would have had appreciating the danger of the loose cannon at sea. And as Hugo first called up the likeness to a wild beast as something the reader could grasp quickly, so the writer began with the *"feature" that women could grasp quickly* even in April· "How women do dread hot days!"

From hot days in general to ironing days in particular is easy. Now notice the progression from "ironing day" to "roaring hot fire"; from that to carrying the hot irons from the stove; from that to the likeness of the kitchen to a bake oven; from that to "hot, stuffy odor"; and from that, to "No wonder women hate ironing in the summer. No wonder women's health breaks down under such a strain." By the end of the paragraph *the reader has built up such a vivid picture* of ironing day hardships that she is hungry for a mental image of ironing without such discomforts.

In short, the reader has a stack of separate thoughts—an idea—that she carries without mental effort.

Although the description is one of a common, everyday situation, and although it was written by a plain, everyday business man, the method of putting the idea across is the same as Victor Hugo's.

BUSINESS CORRESPONDENCE

AJAX BRASS COMPANY
PITTSBURGH, PA.

Mrs. C L. Delvin,
Chicago Lawn, Ill.

Dear Friend

    How women do dread hot summer days! Particularly the weekly ironing days — when the stove must be kindled and a roaring hot fire made just to keep the old-fashioned irons hot. And then the long hours — trotting from hot stove to ironing board and back again — a trip almost every two minutes The sun sizzling down and the stove turning the kitchen into a sure enough bake-oven and the hot, stuffy odor of the ironing — enough to make one sick. No wonder women HATE ironing in summer. No wonder women's health breaks down under such a strain

    Wouldn't it be just FINE to do the ironing out on a cool back porch — or out under a shady tree, on hot days? Wouldn't it be a delightful relief to any woman to forget all about kindling a fire and then standing over a hot stove for hours at a time every ironing day in summer?

    If you had an AJAX SELF-HEATING FLATIRON you wouldn't have to kindle a fire — the ironing wouldn't have to be done in a blazing hot kitchen — there would be no need for continually running to and fro from ironing board to hot stove changing irons.

    With an AJAX SELF-HEATING FLATIRON the ironing could be done where one pleased — in the cool basement — out on the breeze-swept porch — out under the shade of the trees.

                Yours very truly,

                    AJAX BRASS COMPANY

Panel 107

AS TO ORIGINALITY

Originality that will make a letter pull is not a secret art locked in the mental store rooms of a few successful correspondents It merely requires study and applying a few definite principles In this chapter, two of those principles are fully explained One is that "features" of the Big Idea should be stacked in an orderly column The idea easiest to understand goes at the bottom of the column and the most difficult idea at the top, with others in the order of their importance, between The other principle is that time, study, thought should be given to words They supply color They awaken sympathy They lead to acceptance of your proposition The letter above and the one on page 193 are admirable examples of the application of both principles Note how easily the writers progressed from idea to idea and see how the words fit the idea, and help the reader to understand

MAKING YOUR MEANING CLEAR

N W. HALSEY & CO.
LA SALLE AND ADAMS STREETS
Chicago, Illinois

Mr. S. A. Dennis,
Chicago, Illinois.
Dear Sir:

Of all forms of public service, none constitutes a more vital part of the needs of a community than its water supply. Given then a water company, serving a populous and well-established community, operating under a favorable franchise, and with a conservative debt, its bonds are among the most stable and desirable forms of investment.

We are now offering an issue of first mortgage water bonds, the obligation of a company which has been in successful operation for 34 years, and now serving a population of about 70,000. These bonds, the State Water Company, First Mortgage 6's, mature in 1930, are available in denominations of $1,000, $500, and $100; and are offered strictly subject to prior sale and change in price at 100 and interest, to yield 6%.

The company furnishes the water supply, both for public and private purposes, to the entire city of Riverview and two smaller adjoining communities Riverview is a live, modern community, capital and largest city in the state The franchises of the company we extend beyond the maturity of these bonds and the value of the company's properties, on all of which these bonds are a first lien, have been conservatively appraised by independent experts at an amount largely in excess of the company's funded indebtedness Yet earnings are now 1 3/4 times the interest requirements.

Our own recommendation of these bonds, which is the outgrowth of exacting investigations into the affairs of the company prior to our purchase of the issue, is well substantiated by that of a number of the most conservative banks which have purchased the bonds freely, either for their own account or for redistribution among their clients, thus demonstrating their own confidence in the bonds and adding their recommendation to ours.

Here then is a bond, a first mortgage on all the properties of a company furnishing the most necessary form of public service to a substantial and progressive community, and having behind it a demonstrated earning capacity for a period of 34 years. These bonds are available at a price to return the investor a very liberal yield. We urge the necessity of a prompt acceptance by wire at our expense if you desire a reservation for either immediate or delayed delivery of some of the few remaining bonds.

Yours very truly,
N W. HALSEY & CO.

Panel 108

BUSINESS CORRESPONDENCE

Again I have proved that the principles underlying great literature and good letter writing are fundamentally the same If you understand principles, you can apply them to an ordinary business letter just as easily as you can apply fundamentals of arithmetic to any mathematical problem. Two times two is always four at any place, at any time, in any problem. The need of piling small ideas on big ones in any written work, always exists.

If you have the slightest doubts of this newest principle, take time to look for it in good letters which have been provided in this book Any letter shown you in previous chapters will prove my point. Letters such as the SYSTEM letters and the health appliance letter in the second chapter are especially good and will bear me out. Look them over, not now but later, with the new principle in mind.

Right now, however, we'll prove the principle by some new letters I selected from my collection. For instance, on page 193 is a letter used by a large bank. How often do

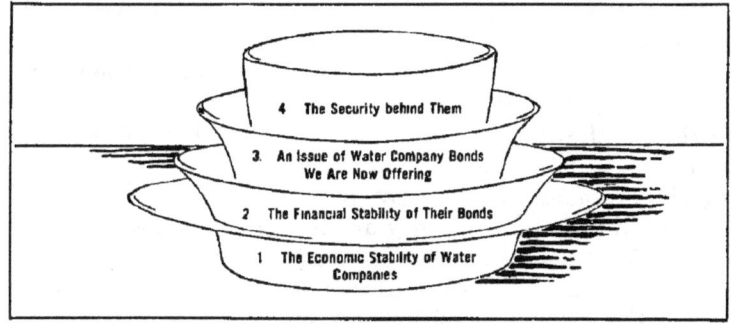

Panel 109

you see a letter on financial affairs that you can thoroughly understand without great mental effort—unless you happen to be an expert on investment matters? But you can *understand the whole idea of the letter* on page 193 without a bit of trouble. In the diagram above is the reason why you can grasp the letter's idea so easily. (Omit consideration of the last two paragraphs, as they are not part of the

MAKING YOUR MEANING CLEAR

idea, but involve arousing conviction and stimulating action, which will be taken up later).

If Hugo had been writing this letter, though his language would have been more vivid, undoubtedly his style of arrangement would have been practically the same.

The first thing he would have done—unconsciously perhaps, for to a man who is writing constantly, style of expression becomes almost automatic—the first thing Hugo would have done would have been to *select the best foundation "feature"* —a "feature" that could be grasped most easily and naturally by the reader. The economic stability of water companies is the easiest "feature" for men seeking investments to grasp, isn't it? Certainly it is, just as dread of hot days was the easiest "feature" for the women who would receive the self-heating iron manufacturer's letter to grasp; and just as the cannon's likeness to a wild beast was the easiest for Hugo's readers to grasp.

With the opening "feature" settled on, Victor Hugo would have next selected the "feature" most easily supported by the first one. Wouldn't you readily have picked for the second "feature" "the financial stability of water companies' bonds," if you were watching the piling up of your points so though they were dishes you wanted to stack up in solid form? And you, too, having this newest principle thoroughly in mind, would have picked the other "features" of your Big Idea just as they are shown in the diagram.

Now let's *give this principle another practical test.* Let's take that retail clothier's letter which you looked over in part in the preceding problem section.

Having secured some great end-of-the-season bargains in suits which you are going to offer at low prices, you want to *work your prospects up to an appreciation* of the unusual values you have secured. Begin your letter with this "feature," one that all business men can easily grasp:

"Every year when the rush period of a busy season is over, the big clothing manufacturers draw a deep, long breath and begin to straighten up stocks and warehouses."

BUSINESS CORRESPONDENCE

W. T. ROGERS CO.
MEN'S FURNISHINGS
Atlanta, Ga.

A. W Carlson,
Atlanta, Georgia
Dear Sir:

Every year when the rush period of a busy selling season is over the big clothing manufacturers draw a deep, long breath and begin to straighten up stock and warehouses And nearly always they find suits set to one side during the rush, for one reason or another — reserved, maybe, on some salesman's request for a particularly good customer and then canceled, or marked "hold" and the reason forgotten; or often just pushed out of sight by accident.

These suits are generally the very best of the stock But they have to be disposed of quickly without regard for cost, to make room for the coming season's stock, for space is more valuable than clothing Usually the big city dealers snap them up like lightning. But this year West, Winsor and Mack s salesman for this territory picked out for me the very cream of these suits.

There are some wonderful dark, cloudy grays — soft as down, light in weight almost as a feather, but warm as fleece. Linings of sheeny, rustly, silk serge They sold for $40, I got them through my friend the salesman for $19 50, and have marked them $22.50 — fair enough, isn't it? There are a few — not many — rich blue cheviots, a blue that you won't get next year — deep and lustrous and warm Same price Then quite a number of domestic weaves in browns, grays, and blacks, beautifully made up and finished, and tailored with the taste of custom goods These sold all season for $25 and $30 — what do you think I have marked them now? — $18!

Come in and look them over. It's just like having a brand new fall stock to pick from — at end of the season's prices, only no end of a season ever before had values like these.

Come tomorrow — Tuesday — for they'll go quick
Very truly yours,
W. T. ROGERS CO

MAKING YOUR MEANING CLEAR

With that "feature" as a foundation, the next, naturally enough, is what happens when the manufacturers begin to straighten up, like this:

"And nearly always they find suits set to one side during the rush, for one reason or another—reserved, maybe, on some salesman's request, for a particularly good customer and then canceled, or marked 'hold' and the reason forgotten, or often just pushed out of sight by accident."

Keeping in mind the analogy of "stacking up dishes" for your reader to carry, see how easily the second "feature" rests on the first. And on the opposite page is a letter containing these "features " Notice how *each point rests on the preceding one* as solidly as one plate rests on another.

Just see what a clear grasp you get of the Big Idea of it—and how tempting it seems! Then consider the letter on page 198. That is a letter used by a clothier in another city for almost the same purpose; but after reading it you don't even begin to have the grasp on the idea that you had after reading the other letter.

The reason for that is the disordered way in which the "features" are presented. What do we ordinary men know about "Kleinberg's wholesale surplus"? We don't appreciate that first "feature" any more than Victor Hugo's readers would have appreciated the dangers of a cannon loose at sea if he hadn't worked them up to it.

But we can imagine the straightening-up process that might be necessary to a manufacturer at the end of a busy season. That is the way the first merchant approached us.

In the second letter we must struggle to comprehend that "wholesale surplus." And then on top of it we are abruptly handed the thought of "prices so low" and "values so extraordinary." Of course, as we all know more or less about sacrifices made on surplus stock, we can, when we stop to think about it, take on that thought of prices easily enough, but at once the letter hands us more about "surplus"! It is just like getting another dinner plate added to our pile of dishes right on top of a small saucer!

BUSINESS CORRESPONDENCE

THE EMPORIUM
New Brunswick
New Jersey

G T. Peterson,
New Brunswick, New Jersey

Dear Sir.

    I want every one of my personal acquaintances and customers to know about the special sale of suits from Kleinberg's wholesale surplus The prices are so low, and the values so extraordinary that I feel sure you'll want some of the good things I can show you

    These are new goods — just made up surplus yardage of fine foreign and domestic weaves, beautiful stuff, fancy weaves and blues.

$15 now for $20 and $22 50 suits.
$20 now for $25 and $30 suits.
$25 now for $35 and $40 suits
And at $30 the very choicest, finest goods made.

    I can also show you at $13 50 some soft weave blues, with chalk-line stripes that are $20 values.

    Come in and see me, and I'll find the best thing we have for you.

                Yours very truly,

                              THE EMPORIUM

Panel 111

THE LOST IDEA

Looking for the proverbial needle in a haystack is easy when compared to finding the idea in some sales letters Compare the sales letter on page 196 and the one above There's a big lesson in them Both deal with the same subject, but see how the letter above loses you in a tangled web of words while the other leads you up, "feature" by "feature," to a complete understanding of the Big Idea. In reading the letters you write, must your reader grope in dark pockets of your mind for the lost idea? Must your reader *think* your letter as well as read it? Try in your next letter the new plan explained in this chapter of piling "feature" on "feature" Let the returns answer the question for you

BUSINESS CORRESPONDENCE

And then back again comes the letter to prices.

But there is still another reason why this letter does not impress you with its Big Idea as clearly as it should, and it is now time to consider it. You will remember that Herbert Spencer said:

> "A reader or listener has at each moment but a limited amount of mental power available. To recognize and interpret the symbols presented to him, requires part of this power; to arrange and combine the images suggested requires a further part, and only that part which remains can be used for realizing the thought conveyed Hence, the more time and attention it takes to receive and understand each sentence, the less time and attention can be given to the contained idea; and the less vividly will that idea be conceived."

Up to this time we have just been observing what an important effect the order of "features" makes in the reader's work of "arranging and combining the images suggested." Now in the clothier's letter reproduced on page 198, we see the importance also of not leaving too big a mental jump between one point and another.

The first thought that letter gives you is of the manufacturer's "wholesale surplus" The second is that the "prices are so low and the values so extraordinary."

As I said in our first review of the letter, if you once grasp the significance of "wholesaler's surplus" you can appreciate that a surplus stock might cause low prices But when you first read the letter, didn't you have to make a mental explanation to yourself of that relation of "wholesaler's surplus" to low prices, before it was well established in your mind? I'm sure you did. I know I did.

And the relation of other features to each other required mental calculation, too.

This seems like a trifle, I know, and yet the *whole matter of mental impressions is made up of separate trifles*, and, as Spencer says, "the more time and attention it takes to receive and understand each sentence, the less time and attention can be given to the contained idea." It is hard enough at best to get enough of a reader's attention to sell goods or to collect money or to create satisfaction by letter without making it harder than we need to, even by a trifle.

BUSINESS CORRESPONDENCE

HAHN & KENDALL
Peoria, Ill

Mr Albert Johnson,
Peoria, Ill

Dear Sir:

On your way to the Corn Exposition at the Fair Grounds you will pass two green cottages on Exposition Avenue between Main and Commerce The numbers are 110 and 114 Exposition.

This property, fronting 95 feet, considerably more than 100 feet deep, and partially looking down Commerce Street, can be bought for $15,500, or less than $165 a front foot

Inside property on Main or Commerce at this point, not so deep, cannot be bought for $200 a front foot. As practically all the traffic going out Main and Commerce turns into Exposition in front of this property, we consider it an exceptionally good purchase, even at the same prices prevailing on Main and Commerce. At $40 less a front foot it is just that much a bargain

213 front feet of new brick buildings are being constructed on Main Street at Exposition, and every foot of space has already been leased to substantial business concerns The Continental Gin Company, just one block away, has already commenced work on the $300,000 addition to its plant. A new 7-story warehouse on Commerce and the T & N. O. Railway was recently announced Don't you agree with us that this is a splendid piece of property to buy?

$3,500 cash, balance easy. The two houses help to carry the investment

Sincerely yours,
HAHN & KENDALL

Panel 112

WHICH?

In Panels 112, 113 and 114 there are two good letters and one poor one Without reading further see if you can pick the good one The letter in Panel 112 took hold of its readers at once because of its frank appeal to the reader's personal interest That collection letter in Panel 113 stirs by its mysterious warning of the federal courts Well, then, that leaves the letter in Panel 114. Did you pick it correctly? See how it buzzes from idea to idea like a fly at a picnic

MAKING YOUR MEANING CLEAR

But in the other clothier's letter—the one on page 196—you will find *no mental effort left to the reader.* You don't have to argue with yourself for even an instant to associate the end of a rush season with putting stock in order, nor to associate putting a stock in order with uncovering overlooked surplus stock, nor to associate the discovery of surplus suits set aside for "particularly good customers" with their being of high quality; nor to associate their high quality with the necessity for moving them quickly before they go out of style with the new season. And so on.

BENNETT COLLECTION CO.
Duluth, Minnesota

Mr. Ellis Oswald,
St. Paul, Minn.
Dear Sir

We have not, as yet, heard from you in response to our letter regarding your account for $9 20, now 60 days overdue

If there is any doubt in your mind as to the position in which you have placed yourself by your apparent failure to act in good faith, we suggest that you consult your attorney and ask him to read to you Section 1581 General Statutes of the United States and Section 5840 Revised Statutes of the United States This may cost you several dollars, but it will be money well spent

There may be some good reason why you have not paid. If there is, you certainly owe it to yourself to explain why you have not   Your continued silence will simply result in adding $15 or $20 to the claim in costs and penalties and having an execution and garnishment issue against you, to say nothing of having it known that the law must be invoked to compel you to pay your just debts

We have now warned you that this matter cannot be further ignored, and we disclaim all responsibility for any trouble which may ensue as a result of your continued disregard of your obligation and of our letters.

Yours truly,
BENNETT COLLECTION CO.

BUSINESS CORRESPONDENCE

On page 200 is a real estate agent's letter, further proof of the deductions we have made. Observe the opening "feature"—"*On your way to the Corn Exposition . . . you will pass two green cottages*"—something you can take hold of right away. And you don't have to pause the fraction of a second to associate the size of the property with what it can be bought for. Nor do you have to make an effort to turn your mind to what the neighboring property sells for and from that to a comparison of real worth and so on.

More proof from another source: take the sixth letter in a collection series, shown on page 201. "*We have not as yet heard from you*"—that is *something the debtor can take hold of quickly.* Contemplation of the position in which he

---

DEMPSEY & CLARK
Milwaukee, Wis

Mrs. J. O Thien,
Mequon, Wis
Dear Madam

    We have had some correspondence with you regarding Dempsey's Exercisers for children, as described in the enclosed folders This equipment has met with great success wherever it has been used. It embodies all of the essential features of the complete gymnasium, making possible the most beneficial forms of exercise and amusement

    We are again pleased to quote you the following low prices

Outdoor Exerciser, Complete Outfit No. 599W.......$14 00
Combination Exerciser.   ..   No. 623W   ...   8.50

    These prices are net f o b cars Remit 25% of the amount of order in advance and shipment will be made C.O.D for balance

    Our offer of a 10 days' trial at our risk, money to be refunded if you are dissatisfied, still holds good.

    Send in your order at once so as to be sure to get advantage of the above low prices.

                  Yours truly,

                        DEMPSEY & CLARK

Panel 114

MAKING YOUR MEANING CLEAR

has placed himself by the creditor's not having heard from him fits on the first thought naturally. The thought of legal difficulties and expenses associates itself with the contemplation of his position. And then the realization either of having no legal excuse, or, if he has, the advisability of stating it, has a place all made for it. And so does each other point pyramid on the original "foundation."

Reverse by looking over a poor letter. Read slowly the letter on page 202 and note the wide gaps between points—gaps that you must fill in by your own mental effort to make the letter effective What do you know about this equipment's success? You must take it for granted, out of a clear sky, or search your memory for facts about it. Then, when the letter hands you the thought of all the features the equipment embodies, you must refer somewhere else for the facts to fill in.

What is needed in this letter and what is needed in the clothier's letter on page 198 is not only a change in the order of points, but also the insertion of *more points of information* in between them—more "features." Those letters are like a moving picture film in which you would first see, say, Charlie Chaplin at the top of the stairs, then see him lying at the bottom without the details of his fall fitted in between the first and last scenes. Such pictures wouldn't get a laugh. Such letters can't get action.

Going back again to our analogy of the stack of dishes to be carried, you can see that these two letters make the idea as difficult to carry clearly in mind as it would be difficult to carry a tall stack of small butter plates balanced on a large dinner plate.

Panel 115

A mere glance at the panel above will call to your mind that such a stack of dishes

BUSINESS CORRESPONDENCE

is harder to handle than even a much larger stack would be; provided, that in the larger stack, between the very small dishes and the very large one, there were some medium-sized dishes to build on, as in the panel below.

In other words, either letter could be much longer and yet easier to understand, for the added length *would save the reader the mental effort of jumping mental gaps* unassisted. Notice how he must jump from "surplus stock" to "low prices" in one letter, and from "the equipment's success" to "what it embodies" in the other.

Now you see and now understand what an advantage length was in the clothier's letter reproduced on page 196.

Panel 116

Too often, in trying to be brief, letter writers violate the principle of supplying sufficient mental steps to allow a reader to build up the idea. By being brief they force their readers to supply the "features" omitted in the letter. That's *too much mental work for a reader*. It's almost if not quite as bad as mixing big ideas with little ones.

Of course, a long letter is not always best nor is a short letter always worst. Which to choose is a matter of judgment. Choosing, too, may be based on the answer Lincoln gave a friend who asked him how long a man's legs should be.

"Long enough to reach the ground," Lincoln answered.

And that's the way with letters, they should be long enough to do their work.

The man who argues that a short letter is always best generally says, "It's too much work to read a long letter." When he says that, he admits Spencer's argument that economy of the reader's time and attention is essential. And then he reverses himself by proposing to make his reader supply the missing part of the letter!

MAKING YOUR MEANING CLEAR

That's like cutting the length of a telegram so much that the man who gets it can't understand it. In trying to save a few cents the whole cost of the telegram is lost. *In trying to be brief, the Big Idea is lost.*

When you have made a correct size-up of your letter's "load," according to the method outlined in the first part, and know definitely the "complete load" the letter should carry, you should, when writing, *be sure that the letter does actually carry the "load"* selected for it. That is the only guide to the length of a letter.

There will be times when your chart will point out "features" which the reader will understand without much help on your part. Such "features" may then be just touched upon when you write, and your letter may be short.

More often, your chart or size-up will show you that there are "features" which cannot be easily understood by the reader. In such a case, write enough to be sure that the reader will understand you without effort even if you do lengthen your letter.

It is safer to depend on a man reading your letter than to depend on him using his memory to get your idea.

If you anticipate that a man won't *read* your letter if you make it too long, how can you expect him to take the trouble to *think* it if you make it too short?

Well, enough of that. Let's make this a resting point and review the points covered so far.

Starting from the broad principle, so clearly expressed by Herbert Spencer, that the secret of a clear, easy-to-understand style lies in saving the reader's or listener's time and attention, we began with learning how to arrange our "features"—so that the reader could carry all of them in his mind without confusion, or without effort to remember them.

We must not, of course, carry this principle to the extreme of thinking that a reader positively cannot grasp the idea unless the points are arranged just so—or that a letter is irretrievably ruined simply by error in arrangement. For we have already seen that with a correct selection of "fea-

BUSINESS CORRESPONDENCE

THE ANTOINETTE COMPANY
Chicago, Ill

Miss Elva Shanahan,
Chicago, Ill

Dear Miss Shanahan

    A woman's crowning glory is her hair, but she can never look her best unless it is attractively arranged. Thin, untidy locks make even the prettiest face unattractive, but no matter how plain the face, if it is framed in a soft, well dressed coiffure, it becomes instantly charming.

    We sent you our book "Hair and Beauty" some time ago and we hope that you have gone through it carefully and that you have found something in its pages that exactly suits your needs. There are very few women who do not find some sort of extra hair piece necessary, and we know that you too could dress your hair so much more becomingly if you had just the right additional hair piece Perhaps you cannot quite decide on the particular number that you need   If you will write us, shall be glad to make suggestions

    The transformation is becoming more and more popular The enclosed leaflet will explain just what a transformation will do for you or for any woman who is conscious of thinning hair about the face, or who is too much occupied to be able to curl and properly arrange her hair every day

    We shall be very glad to send you a sample of any of our goods because we want you to be the sole judge of the quality, style, and price All we ask is that a business or a bank reference accompany your first order.

    We should like to have your patronage and we hope that we shall hear from you very soon

                    Very truly yours,

                           THE ANTOINETTE COMPANY

Panel 117

MAKING YOUR MEANING CLEAR

tures," plainly and simply described from the point of view of the Big Idea, we can convey an idea or feeling quite graphically even without paying much attention to order.

But now we are seeking *to perfect ourselves in expression*, so that we not only make it possible for the reader to get our idea, but also make it easy and certain.

Observe the letter on the opposite page. It starts with a feature easy for a woman to take hold of—the crowning glory of her head. The next thought—that her crowning glory is poor glory indeed if it be poorly arranged, or thin and untidy—is solidly placed. But does not the third thought—about the booklet—jar you a bit? Were you quite ready for it? I hardly think so. Let us take the fourth "feature"—"there are very few women . . . . " and place it third—as in the panel on the next page.

Now read it. Doesn't it carry you along better?

It is such *finishing, workmanlike touches* that we are now seeking. And sometimes they become more than mere finishing touches, too—often they are all-important in a very particular letter. They may be just enough to *weight the scale in your favor* with a doubtful prospect, or any angry customer, or a recalcitrant debtor.

Well, we have taken Spencer's fundamental principle and by putting it into the homely analogy of giving a person a stack of dishes to carry, we have worked out a formula that gives us a good rule to go by. It cannot help but prevent serious errors in arrangement.

Of course, you may not use it on any but important letters. You may sometimes find you can score your point better by going quite contrary to our plan—in isolated cases. But when in doubt, test your letter by it. Some other arrangement may do, but one that will stand the test of the "stack of dishes" analogy is sure to be good.

We have also learned to apply the same rule in order to avoid omissions of essential features. That is important.

One of the most vexatious problems that the average man meets is that one of, *is my letter—or advertisement—too long?*

BUSINESS CORRESPONDENCE

THE ANTOINETTE COMPANY
Chicago, Ill

Miss Elva Shanahan,
Chicago, Ill

Dear Miss Shanahan:

  A woman's crowning glory is her hair, but she can never look her best unless it is attractively arranged Thin, untidy locks make even the prettiest face unattractive, but no matter how plain the face, if it is framed in a soft, well dressed coiffure, it becomes instantly charming.

  There are very few women who do not find some sort of extra hair necessary, and we know that you too could dress your hair so much more becomingly if you had just the right additional hair piece We sent you our book "Hair and Beauty" some time ago, and we hope that you have gone through it carefully and that you have found something in its pages that exactly suits your needs. Perhaps you cannot quite decide on the particular number that you need. If you will write us we shall be glad to make suggestions

  The transformation is becoming more and more popular. The enclosed leaflet will explain just what a transformation will do for you or for any woman who is conscious of thinning hair about the face, or who is too much occupied to be able to curl and properly arrange her hair every day.

  We shall be very glad to send you a sample of any of our goods because we want you to be the sole judge of the quality, style, and price All we ask is that a business or a bank reference accompany your first order.

  We should like to have your patronage and we hope that we shall hear from you very soon

      Yours very truly,

        THE ANTOINETTE COMPANY

MAKING YOUR MEANING CLEAR

Or, is it too short to tell what I want it to tell? And now you have a way to settle it.

The next time this question comes up, divide the Big Idea into its "features" and then see how those "features" fit on one another. If you don't like to sketch them out in blocks as I did—to sort of represent "dishes"—simply write them out on separate "dishes", that is, write them out on numbered slips of paper in the order in which they come in your letter. Then put them together and study to see if the first "feature" is one that your reader can readily grasp. Next determine whether your reader, having the first "feature" in mind, can easily grasp the next. Then see if, with two in mind, he can understand a third, and so on.

This method will expose any "gaps"; for if any "feature" does not balance easily on the preceding ones, then you know there is a point in between them that ought to be added.

On the other hand, if you detect a "feature" anywhere that does not advance the idea—one that does not take the reader a step farther toward grasping your whole idea—then you know it is unnecessary and probably can be cut out. (We will note an exception to this later when we come to studying the use of "repetition" to inspire enthusiasm or conviction or persuasion.) If you don't find such a "feature," you can rest easy in *the knowledge that what you have written is not too long*, which is a great relief on many occasions.

Now observe the advertisement on the next page to prove the point. It could just as well be a letter, and, as a letter, it would probably have paid as tremendously as it did as an advertisement—in fact, everything in this chapter applies to an advertisement, or an editorial, or a speech, or a sales talk, as directly as it does to a letter.

Now, that advertisement is long. But when it is separated into its individual "features" every single one of them takes you *a step nearer to the Big Idea*. Sometimes there is an apparent repetition of what the article does—but if you study it closely you will see that each time a "feature" is repeated it has a vital work to do right at that place.

BUSINESS CORRESPONDENCE

Madam—If YOU Had To Write This Ad, What Would You Say?

Suppose you had told a good friend of yours something, and your good friend turned up her nose and said "It isn't so!" What would you say?

Suppose you were the maker of SKITCH and had told me that SKITCH would save all rubbing of clothes on wash day, would clean my clothes beautifully, and wouldn't hurt them a bit—and I had said "Oh, it's a fake—can't anything do that!" What would you do about it?

That is my predicament

What I said about SKITCH is true SKITCH really *will* save all the rubbing of clothes SKITCH really *does* make your clothes as nice and clean as snow without a bit of rubbing SKITCH really *won't* hurt your clothes—SKITCH wouldn't, couldn't, positively *can't* urt the finest fabric ever woven

And yet you women of Aurora simply say "It isn't so!" Can you beat it?

What should I do about it?

There you go week after week laboring over a washboard—rubbing, rubbing, rubbing, bending, bending, bending And if you would simply use three teaspoons of SKITCH to a boilerful of clothes, then go about your other work or sit and read the newspaper if you like, in twenty minutes your clothes would be ready to rinse and blue and hang on the line as lovely and white as the best washing you ever saw

But you won't believe me!

You could get a 10-cent package of SKITCH from almost any grocer in Aurora and prove what I say, but you just won't do it! What on earth can I say to you?

Why, woman, woman! A 10-cent package of SKITCH will turn the drudgery of wash day clean out of your life, and more than that, it will save you three or four times its cost in the soap it saves! Listen, lady—it takes from one to three bars of soap just to rub out a wash, doesn't it? Well, all that soap you save every week when you use SKITCH, because with SKITCH you don't rub the clothes And a 10-cent package of SKITCH does from four to seven washings! My stars, madam, why don't you try it and see?

Instead of saying "it isn't so"—instead of believing some gossipy person who has told you those things are fakes"—just you be independent and get a 10-cent package of SKITCH from your grocer today and settle this argument for yourself

Other women in other cities have proved SKITCH and know to their joy on every wash day that SKITCH does just what I say In my home town, where everybody knows me, nearly every woman who has a washing to do uses SKITCH! Why, I could fill this paper up with letters that thankful women have written me in praise of SKITCH and in thankfulness for the work and soap it has saved them!

Get a 10 cent package of SKITCH today from your grocer and see Follow the directions absolutely They're simple and easy Don't try to improve on them If you follow the directions on every 10-cent package of SKITCH you won't have to rub your clothes on a washboard, and that is fact, pure fact

Now you go and try it You'd want me to do as much for you if *you* made SKITCH Go and do it and see for yourself—get a 10-cent package of SKITCH from any grocer, or send to me for free sample

Panel 110

MAKING YOUR MEANING CLEAR

On the other hand take a look at the printer's letter on the next page. It is very short, but analyze it carefully and you'll see that nothing could be added to make it plainer. Do you see?

You can't say arbitrarily that a letter or an advertisement should be short, or that it should be long. There is but one test. It must carry its "load"—and the "load" must determine how long or short the letter can be.

Now we have passed two conditions which must be kept in mind in order to make our meaning clear as we write or talk. Now for the third and last. It is, I believe, the most interesting of all—that is, *choice of words*. Get a glimpse of this fascinating topic by reading the advertisement you found on the opposite page.

After you get past that part which develops the "negative idea"—to the point where the "connecting link" between negative and positive comes in with, "What should I do about it?"—note the homely, "wash day" sort of words used. "washboard," "rubbing," "bending," "lovely and white," "nicer," "drudgery," and so on.

Note, too, the style of phrases which are used: "there you go"; "hang on the line"; "doing up your breakfast dishes"; "what on earth"; "clean out of your life"; "rub out a wash"; and so on.

All of those words and phrases sound like washing. Why, they almost smell like wash day!

Now turn back to the letter on page 193 and study the kind of words in that letter, from a bank to investors, and note these phrases· "vital needs," "favorable franchise," "conservative debt," "stable," "obligation," "maturity," "first lien," "demonstrated," "substantial and progressive community," "yield." They, in turn, sound like bonds and investments and safety.

But suppose the bank had used "everyday wants" in place of "vital needs," "sure thing" for "favorable franchise," "husky, live wire town," for "substantial, progressive community."

BUSINESS CORRESPONDENCE

KIER LETTER COMPANY
DIRECT ADVERTISING, PRINTING
Chicago, Illinois

Mr. Carroll D. Murphy,
Chicago, Ill.

Dear Sir

Did you ever ask your form letter printer to guarantee results?

Would he?

We will.

You write the copy — send us the order for processing and if you don't secure a larger percentage from our letters than you ever received from form letters, we will make no charge for the work

Our processing is not only better to look at but it pays our customers in dollars and cents to use our letters

Write your copy and the contest is on.

Yours truly,
KIER LETTER COMPANY

Panel 120
LONG OR SHORT?

The letters on pages 206 and 208 help to answer the question which bobs up at every conference, "Is the letter too long?" The letter on page 206, disguised of course, failed and narrowly escaped the waste-basket because it was too long Wiser heads saved it Rewritten, it pulled results Why? Because as it was written it made a rocky road for the reader to travel Revised, as on page 208, the reader buzzed along without fatigue and followed the writer's thought to favorable action That letter in Panel 120, above, represents the other side of the proposition Here the Big Idea trimmed to the bone drives home its point in one quick hammer stroke

MAKING YOUR MEANING CLEAR

Or suppose, on the other hand, that the Skitch advertisement had used "laundering" for "washing," "more nicely" for "nicer," "rubbing the foreign matter from the clothing" for "rubbing out a wash."

Probably the manufacturer of the washing compound is as dignified and educated a citizen as the banker, but *it isn't what you are that should determine your language.* It is what you are talking about and to whom you are talking.

In the panel on the next page is a curious and a very forcible illustration of the point I am making. Read the letter of a hosiery manufacturer to his retail trade. It is a splendid example of clear expression—logical order of points and language that literally sounds like merchandising. But that is not the point just yet. Read the letter of a haberdasher and tailor to his customers, on page 215.

Now here is what I'm driving at. The dealer who sent out that letter is quite possibly one of the dealers who received the letter reproduced on page 214, as he is both haberdasher and tailor. The clean style of that manufacturer's letter was just suited to the retailer, a practical, clear-thinking business man. The style of words—"increased sales," "decreased expense," "quick turn"—were *words he could grasp quickly and understand easily* because they are the language of his craft. If the manufacturer's letter to him had been dressed in words like those he used in his own letter he probably would have thrown it in the waste-basket, or he might have lost all confidence in the house. That manufacturer's letter is a letter about merchandising, written to a merchant, and it talks *merchandising talk* and *uses merchants' words*.

But the merchant's own letter is a letter about cheap flashy tailoring, written to a list of young, flashy, "sporty" men who try to be "swell" on a cheap plane—and it talks flashy-dress talk and uses a young "sport's" words.

Certainly you now see how the person to whom you are writing and what you are writing about should determine your choice of words and phrases, instead of your own preferences or a set style.

BUSINESS CORRESPONDENCE

HOLEPROOF HOSIERY CO.
Milwaukee, Wis.

Mr. Arthur Williams,
Reedsville, Mo

Dear Mr Williams:

    Because I believe you may not want to take the time to figure out just what increase you can make in your hosiery department by selling Holeproof Hosiery, I am attaching some figures showing the actual results obtained by a Holeproof dealer who kept close track of his sales of the jobbers' brands that he handled and his sales of Holeproof the year after

    The figures show clearly the increased sales, decreased advertising expense, small investment, quick turn of stock, large average sales, and decreased incidental expenses that result from the sale of Holeproof I believe they will show you also, if you study them carefully, <u>that</u> you <u>ought</u> <u>to</u> sell Holeproof.

    Now won't you think the matter over and in the meantime send me the enclosed card, which will bring you the fall and winter samples of this beautiful line of hosiery? The Christmas business this year is going to be a bigger thing with Holeproof dealers than ever before and that means a tremendous business, for the business these men have done in the past on Holeproof at that season has been enormous. There was never a more successful box on any proposition than the Holeproof box It's a dandy. Let us send you a sample along with the hosiery samples

    I'd like to see that card from you   Will you send it?

                      Yours very truly,

                          HOLEPROOF HOSIERY CO

MAKING YOUR MEANING CLEAR

JAMES T WILBUR
Windsor Park, Ill.

Mr James Jackson,
Windsor Park, Ill.
Dear Friend

    I'm no slinger of the big words   I'm just a tailor. Some folk criticize my plain, homely language, but I've got a plain, straight proposition — and here she comes at you

    $22.50 — $22 50, man, don't muff it — for a made-to-measure, cut-to-fit, finished-to-please-you suit of clothes that you can't equal uptown this side of $40.
There you are.

    If you're one of those chaps that can't believe a clothing ad unless it's dressed up in frills of fine words, and hung with beads of high-brow language, you won't like that But if you're just that far-sighted kind of fellow who can look naked facts in the eye without blushing, why look this way, for I'm going to raise the curtain.

  Look —

    If that suit that I cut to your measure, tailor to your taste for style, and finish to fit your every curve and bump, for $22.50 — if that suit doesn't fit you, doesn't suit you, doesn't simply tickle you stiff — if it isn't as racy and cocky and smart in its cut and as game and saucy in style as any suit you see this season;

    If when you put that suit on and look at yourself in it, feel yourself in it, walk in it, talk in it and shake yourself in it;

    If then, Mr. Man, you can't smile as you count me out $22 50 for it — then you just count your $22 50 right back in your own pocket and don't take the suit!

    Now there's my proposition stripped clean as the Gold Dust Twins

    Will you take me up on it? Come on Let me show you.

    I'm waiting,

                Yours truly,
                           JAMES T WILBUR

Panel 122

BUSINESS CORRESPONDENCE

On pages 217 and 218, is further proof. There you find letters of two different correspondence schools. The names have been disguised for obvious reasons and considerable "selling talk" has been omitted from each, as it is style of language, only, that interests us in them.

Both are directed to about the same type of men, and both are on the same subject. Now, it is always difficult to imagine yourself as being someone else, but just try to put yourself in the place of a young shipping clerk or mechanic or clerk in a store, and then see which of these two *letters would get right under your skin* most quickly.

If you were a young, untrained youngster on low wages, couldn't you grasp the idea more quickly from talk about "jobs," "the boss," "taking chances," "get ready for it," "where you work," and so on, than you could from that talk about "the eternal question," "bettering condition," "the life that confronts you," "solving"? Of course you could.

Now what I have said is not new. It has been known to writing men for years. My purpose is merely to emphasize the facts and to be sure you are making use of them. But to drive the point home, let us turn again to Spencer's Essay on Style and read what he says Speaking of the superiority of short, Saxon English, he says in part:

"The economy of the recipient's mental energy, into which are thus resolvable the several causes of the strength of Saxon English, may equally be traced in the superiority of specific overgeneric words That concrete terms produce more vivid impressions than abstract ones, and should, when possible, be used instead, is a current maxim of composition. As Dr Campbell says, 'The more general the terms are, the picture is the fainter; the more special they are, the brighter'

"We should avoid such a sentence as 'In proportion as the manners, customs, and amusements of a nation are cruel and barbarous, the regulations of their penal code will be severe' And in place of it we should write 'In proportion as men delight in battles, bull fights, and combats of gladiators, will they punish by hanging, burning, and the rack.'

"This superiority of specific expressions is clearly due to a saving of the effort required to translate words into thoughts As we do not think in generals but in particulars—as, whenever any class of things is referred to, we represent it to ourselves by calling to mind individual members of it, it follows that when an abstract word is used, the hearer or reader has to choose from his stock of images, one or more, by which he may figure to himself the genius mentioned In doing this, some delay must

MAKING YOUR MEANING CLEAR

GENERAL CORRESPONDENCE SCHOOL
New York City

Mr Oscar Koch,
Houston, Texas.

Dear Friend.

    Suppose a good job were open where you work. Could you fill it? Could you jump right in and make good, or would the boss have to pass you up because you lacked training?

    The man who is offered the big job is the man who has trained himself to hold it before it is offered to him

    Don't take chances on being promoted, don't gamble on making good when your opportunity comes If you want a big job that carries responsibility and pays good money, get ready for it.

    Pick out the job you want in the work you like best Then start right now to get, through the General Correspondence School, the training that will prepare you to hold it.

    Thousands of men have advanced through our training to the very jobs they wanted most What these men have done you can do. All we ask is the chance to help you. No matter where you live, the General Correspondence School will come to you and train you in your spare time in your own home.

               Very truly yours,
        GENERAL CORRESPONDENCE SCHOOL

Panel 123

BUSINESS CORRESPONDENCE

arise—some force be expended; and if by employing a specific term, an appropriate image can be at once suggested, an economy is achieved, and a more vivid impression produced "

Now how shall we apply this philosophy to our own work? First get clearly in mind that there are special *words for every idea we have to write about* or talk about. There are words that will fit best into your particular business and others that will fit best into mine, words that will suit your particular customers best and other words that will suit mine best

Again I'll let another man speak for me. In an article in SYSTEM, The Magazine of Business, W C. Holman wrote

"Words are almost living things There are weak words and strong words, pallid words and red-blooded words, words that are dull and words that smart and burn like vitriol There are words as splendid as precious

---

ACME CORRESPONDENCE SCHOOLS
Chicago, Ill

H B Charles,
Kansas City, Mo.

Dear Sir

What is the eternal question which stands up and looks you and every sincere man square in the eye every morning?

How can I better my condition? That is the real life question which confronts you, now, and will haunt you every day till you solve it

Read carefully the enclosed circular and be convinced that the "New Profession" — Traffic Management — answers this important life question which you and every man must solve if he ever expects to have more each Monday morning, after pay day, than he had the week before

The Acme Correspondence School is so sure that it can assist men who can meet the requirements of membership that it gives a Guarantee Money Refund Bond, assuring you of return of every penny for membership, if not entirely satisfied after taking advantage of the Practical Plan to help you

ACME CORRESPONDENCE SCHOOLS

Panel 124

MAKING YOUR MEANING CLEAR

gems, words as smoldering beautiful as the eyes of a sullen harem favorite. There are words as scorching as fire, words almost incandescent with heat and light—words that seem to have dropped hissing upon the page that holds them. There are words as dreadful as murderers, words that boil and swirl with meaning as dark as the black broth of a witch's caldron.

"And so in business there are all varieties of words for an advertisement writer's choosing. There are words as shallow as a pie pan and as meaningless as an idiot's chatter—words packed as tight with meaning as a machine-pressed cotton bale—words as evasive as eels—words as plain as old dog Tray—words as sweet and simple as a May morning.

"No matter what product you wish to describe, there are image-making words that will make the product fairly live in the imagination. There are words for use in describing food that will make the mouth water. There are words as dainty and filmy as the lace on a woman's dress. There are words for every product—every idea."

Mr. Holman not only spoke the truth, but also the very words he chose are good proofs of what he said. Just go back over them and see how your own feelings change as different words strike you—"words that soothe" make you really feel better, do they not? And "words that smart and burn like vitriol" are by their very sound painful.

Read the letter on page 220 and you'll find the idea applied and see how quickly the very words "cracks," "scales," and "ugly splotches" make it easy for you to call up the vision the writer wants to get in your mind. The forcibleness of the negative idea in that letter suggests the criticism that more specific terms could also have been found to convey the positive idea, in place of such words as "long lasting," and "good looking."

Finally, on page 221 see how specific is the letter to its subject of farming and to its farmer readers.

Now I have proved to you that *good writing depends largely on a choice of words.* Spencer argues for it in general. Holman and the letters I have quoted prove it in particular. Before I show you an easy way of choosing words and making your letters carry a punch that they may not have carried before, let me give you another test. This time, instead of turning from literature to letters, we turn from letters to literature. We'll look over the first three verses of one of the greatest poems ever written by an American:

BUSINESS CORRESPONDENCE

B. ARTHUR & COMPANY
Cincinnati, Ohio

Mr W T Adams,
Dayton, Ohio
Dear Sir

    Important as the color scheme is, it is not the most important consideration in painting a house. Durability of the paint is of first importance, for, no matter how attractively a house is decorated, its charm vanishes if the paint on it cracks, scales, and falls off in ugly splotches.

    How to make sure of long-lasting, non-cracking, non-scaling paint which retains its good looks is easy when one knows the facts about paint and painting. It is to our advantage as manufacturers of Sunshine white lead, the basis of a long-lasting, good-looking paint, to put you in possession of these facts Our experience has been that, once an owner or a prospective builder knows the truth, we are so much surer of another satisfied user of our product.

    The truth about paint and painting is told in simple, understandable language in a booklet that we publish, entitled "Painting — The Old Way and the New " This book makes clear what is and what is not paint. It also compares costs and illustrates inside and outside color treatments.

    A copy of the booklet is being reserved for you We will mail it immediately upon receipt of the enclosed card indicating that you are interested in avoiding the common and costly paint pitfalls
                  Yours truly,
                    B ARTHUR & COMPANY

Panel 125

SHORT WORDS—LONG RESULTS

"Words are things," Lord Byron said, "and a small drop of ink falling like dew upon a thought produces that which makes thousands, perhaps millions, think " In the letter on this page and the one on page 221, note the clever selection of words which make the reader draw mental pictures favorable to the Big Idea the letters present That first paragraph in Panel 125, for example, forces a picture of an unkept house to mind and creates unmistakably the suspense that leads the reader into the letter And in Panel 126, see how farmer talks to farmer in a message which clamors for a reply. Shakespeare knew the lesson these letters bring us. He said, "A word is short and quick but works a long result, therefore, look well to words "

MAKING YOUR MEANING CLEAR

CUTAWAY HARROW COMPANY
Higgananum, Conn.

Mr. D. S. Brown,
Three Oaks, Mich.

Dear Sir.

    Your interests and ours are identical — ever think of that?

    It is to our interest that you should make bigger crops with better tillage and thus make more money. The most successful farmers are the biggest buyers of CUTAWAY (CLARK) tillage implements — not because they are cheap, but because they are the best

    There is a CUTAWAY (CLARK) implement for every kind of tillage and a size to fit every possible requirement. Whether you are interested in a light one-horse harrow for garden work, or an implement for disking stubble, or a tool for orchard cultivation, or a disk harrow which will do the highest grade of work with a tractor, there is a CUTAWAY (CLARK) implement made for that particular purpose.

    The important feature of CUTAWAY (CLARK) disk harrows and plows were pointed out to you in our previous letter and in the catalog Remember the importance of the CUTAWAY forged-edge disks of cutlery steel which stay sharp Remember the dustproof oil-soaked hardwood bearings, the split lock bolts, the rigid main frame of the Double Action Harrow and other patented features which are essential for the best and most economical tillage and yet can be found only in the CUTAWAY (CLARK) line.

    Now won't you let us help you?

    If you have not already sent us the return postcard giving complete information as to your requirements, do so at once. It puts you under no obligation and it may mean dollars to you Thousands of satisfied users through a period of 35 years prove the value of our tools. We want to satisfy you also and cannot afford to do otherwise.

    Do not forget that CUTAWAY (CLARK) disk harrows and plows will, in nearly every case, save horses and at times a man, while at the same time doing superior work. Do not delay, therefore, in deciding on the tool which will fit your needs, and send your order.

    Very truly yours,

    THE CUTAWAY HARROW COMPANY

Panel 125

BUSINESS CORRESPONDENCE

Edgar Allan Poe's incomparable fancy, "The Bells." Even if you have read it before, and I'm sure most of you have, you'll enjoy it again in the light of what we have been studying. Look for words as you read.

See the poem in part on the next page. Read the first verse. Poe studied for days to find words like "silver, merriment, tinkle, crystaline. tintinnabulation" and "jingling sleigh bells."

Read the second verse of the poem to find words like "mellow, golden, happiness, harmony, balmy, molten-golden, gloats, swinging, ringing, chiming," that sound like wedding bells.

And, going on, find words that in themselves make one shiver and tremble with panic of fire, for in the description of fire bells we read words like, "clang and clash and roar, turbulency," and others. Every line carries flaming words.

Splendid! Magnificent! More than that in this case, absolute proof that the Big Idea will be more easily and quickly grasped by others if we *use words that instead of hindering, really help the reader* or listener to absorb the impressions we want him to have.

Go back to the Hugo description of the cannon broken loose at sea and read it again for words. When Hugo wrote this brilliant description he could take the time to search and search for the exact kind of French words to help express each kind of idea. When his translator was turning those descriptions into English, he, too, had the time to study the exact shades of Hugo's words and to search for corresponding ones like "rapid," when the movements of a billiard ball were to be called to a reader's mind, "rushes," to call up the thought of an arrow's movement, "assaults," for the action of a battering ram; the "bounds" of a panther, the "agility" of a mouse. But a man with a score of letters to write couldn't do that.

When Poe wrote that most wonderful—that almost incomparable of poems, "The Bells," he could study for days, if need be, to find the words he needed. Probably it would be

The Bells

Hear the sledges with the bells
Silver bells!
What a world of merriment their melody foretells!
How they tinkle tinkle tinkle
In the icy air of night!
While the stars, that oversprinkle
All the heavens seem to twinkle
With a crystalline delight
Keeping time time time
In a sort of Runic rhyme
To the tintinnabulation that so musically wells
From the bells bells bells bells
Bells, bells bells—
From the jingling and the tinkling of the bells

Hear the mellow wedding bells
Golden bells!
What a world of happiness their harmony foretells!
Through the balmy air of night
How they ring out their delight!
From the molten golden notes
And all in tune,
What a liquid ditty floats
To the turtle-dove that listens while she gloats
On the moon!
Oh from out the sounding cells
What a gush of euphony voluminously wells!
How it swells!
How it dwells
On the Future! how it tells
Of the rapture that impels
To the swinging and the ringing
Of the bells bells bells,
Of the bells bells bells bells
Bells bells bells—
To the rhyming and the chiming of the bells!

Hear the loud alarum bells
Brazen bells!
What a tale of terror now, their turbulency tells!
In the startled ear of night
How they scream out their affright!
Too much horrified to speak
They can only shriek, shriek
Out of tune
In a clamorous appealing to the mercy of the fire
In a mad expostulation with the deaf and frantic fire,
Leaping higher higher, higher
With a desperate desire
And a resolute endeavor
Now—now to sit or never
By the side of the pale-faced moon
Oh the bells bells bells!
What a tale their terror tells
Of Despair!
How they clang and clash and roar!
What a horror they outpour
On the bosom of the palpitating air!
Yet the ear it fully knows
By the twanging
And the clanging
How the danger ebbs and flows
Yet the ear distinctly tells
In the jangling
And the wrangling
How the danger sinks and swells —
By the sinking or the swelling in the anger of the bells,
Of the bells,
Of the bells bells bells bells
Bells bells bells—
In the clamor and the clangor of the bells!

—EDGAR ALLAN POE

BUSINESS CORRESPONDENCE

more correct to say that Poe's genius for words rather than for study and search, developed this almost sublime discrimination in their use, although it seems probable that it was a combination of genius and study. But a man cannot write poems while the stenographer is waiting.

So how can we, who are not gifted with the genius of a Poe or a Hugo, and not permitted the unlimited time to study dictionaries and synonyms every time we have a letter to write, or an advertisement to prepare, or a talk to make—how can we *ordinary business peop'e make a choice in our words* sufficient at least to help us land an order or to satisfy a complaint, or to collect a bill, or to secure a concession, or to win backing for our opinions? Why in this simple way.

In the organization of modern business, most of us, like actors in a play, are cast in certain characters We have a certain number of matters to talk about, or write about, and a certain kind of people to whom we must talk or write

The man over there sells machinery· his letters are about mechanical things· they are sent to men in a certain kind of business, men who know as much about machinery as he does.

The man over here sells a particular class of merchandise to one particular class of dealers Another man sells one line of goods—like groceries—to one class of consumers—say the working class of his neighborhood. And still another is a credit man. handles a certain type of credits with a certain class of buyers. And so it goes Each one of us has a definite position in a definite field.

Now *each field has its own language.* Farmers "crop their fields," "pasture their stock," "harrow" and "fallow" and "turn under." Their cattle "freshen," their seeds "catch." The merchant "turns his stock," "buys futures." "closes out," "takes his discounts," "gets better datings." The manufacturer "installs," "charges off," "figures overhead," "cleans up" The financial man handles "paper," distinguishes between "liquid" and "fixed"

Those are but a few illustrations of the way *language of the craft* creeps into every business or occupation.

MAKING YOUR MEANING CLEAR

Now no man would be considered a master of his business if he had not mastered its trade terms. So why not go farther? Why not master, for your particular article in your trade, the terms that will best express its particular qualities to the particular kind of people you sell?

If you are selling shock absorbers for automobiles, why not take the trouble to gather and file all the words that sound like shock—shake, shiver, bump, thud, jar, jolt, crack, bang, and so on. Then all the words that sound like the opposite of shock—smother, pillow, soft, ease, resilient, undulation, billowy, smooth. In short, whatever your business, *there are words for your business*—for your article—for your article's points of superiority—for your kind of customers. There are doubtless dozens, possibly hundreds of words that you could pick and choose from, so that you could always use genuinely expressive words without tying yourself down too much—if you only had them handy.

A thesaurus, a book of synonyms, or even a dictionary, of course have the words in them, but they leave you with the work of selecting from those that express the feeling you want, those that will be best understood by your readers.

So the best thing to do is *build up a little dictionary* of your own, similar to the one illustrated on the next page. Any stationer can supply you with the materials for it.

All you need is a pasteboard card index file, half a package of white cards and half a dozen each blue and salmon guides. Use the blue guides for listing Big Ideas for your product, the salmon guides for a list of "features" of each idea, and the white cards for words and terms which you find useful in everyday correspondence.

First analyze the type of letters that you have to write most and then *settle on the principal ideas that you have to express* in them. With what you have already learned from the first three chapters you ought to be able to make a fair start.

For instance, when a man comes to work for the A. W. Shaw Company, he soon learns, if he is put in the circulation department, that he most frequently uses ideas on efficiency,

BUSINESS CORRESPONDENCE

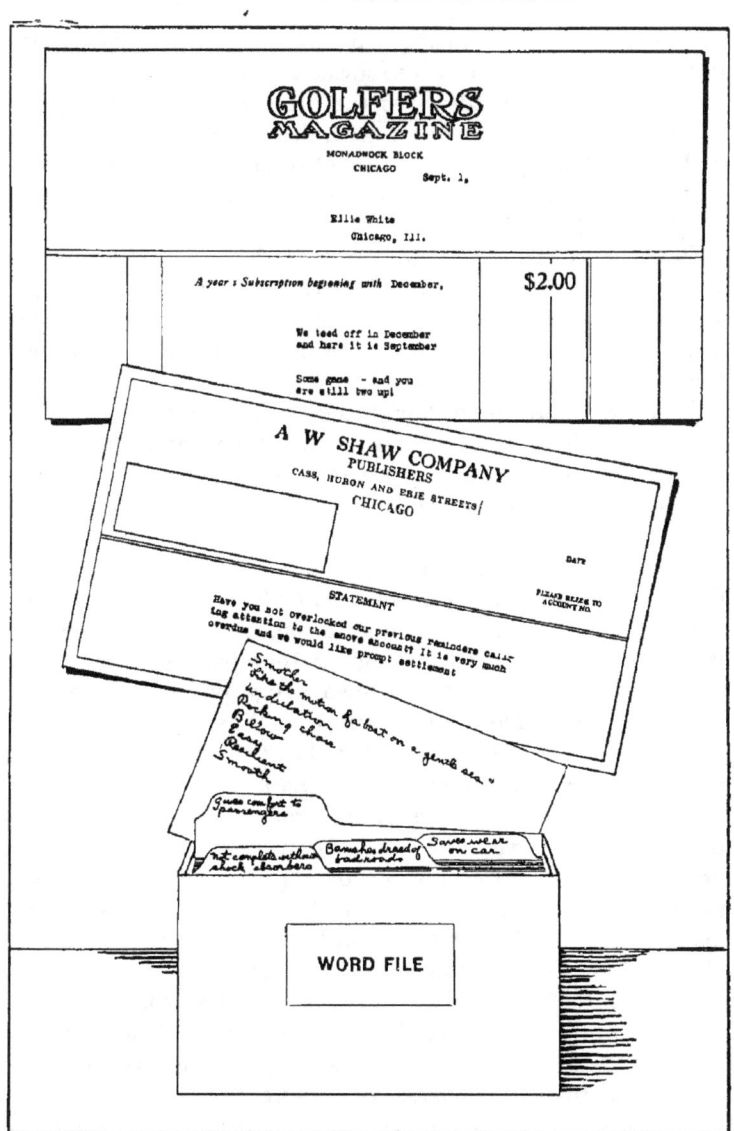

Panel 128

MAKING YOUR MEANING CLEAR

cost cutting, sales producing, value of system, and progressiveness in business. And those ideas are the first ones he puts on his blue guide cards. On the other hand, if you were in charge of the correspondence with dealers in a hosiery manufacturing plant, you would probably start your blue guides with such ideas as profit to the dealer and value of your magazine advertising.

In other words, to use this file, sort the ideas that you find you most frequently have to convey, and make out a blue guide card for each one—like the illustration on the opposite page. If you find that you make use of negative ideas, get them down on guides also.

You may have to start with only one or two But before long you will think of others. Now take each one of the ideas, and work out, in a general and rough way, the features that describe each one; and for each "feature" use a salmon-colored guide.

Then for each "feature" allot a few of the white cards. On those white cards set down *every really good word you know*, that by its sound, or its association, or its appearance in type, calls up the kind of thought that will help the reader to hold the idea. And set down every phrase or simile or metaphor that has a like effect. (When you learn the knack of this file you'll find often that one word like "rocking chair" for shock absorbers will *suggest an entire letter*).

As you write words on your cards, remember that it is better not to classify the words or phrases, but to put them down one after another just as you happen to run across them, for then when you go searching for an adjective you will, maybe, see a verb that comes in handy, or pick out a whole phrase that just hits the spot—or suggests another one.

The white card in the illustration shows the method of entering words. You may have to start with only a few words for each "feature." But if you keep your eyes open you will soon build up an extensive Word File.

You can *find everywhere words and phrases that just suit the* "features" of the ideas you use most. You'll find them in

BUSINESS CORRESPONDENCE

other people's letters or advertising, in newspapers, in books, in magazines, in poetry. You'll get them from public speakers, from salesmen, and from the Bible. The Bible is the greatest piece of literature in the world. Remember it has convinced more people, persuaded more people, won the confidence of more people, and got more people to act than all the sales letters, collection letters, advertisements, booklets, catalogs, editorials, campaign speeches, and salesmen the world has ever produced. And so its words, its phrases, and its construction can give many an inspiration for your Word File. In making up your file be sure to remember your readers. Don't fill the cards with words or phrases that only mean much to you—study, before you accept them for your file, *how much they will mean to your reader.*

Suppose the haberdasher and tailor to whom the hosiery manufacturer wrote in business language as in the letter on page 214 had written their prospects in that language! Such letters would have surely failed. Compare the wording of the two "collection reminders" on the statements at the top of page 226. The language of the golf magazine would be ridiculous if used by the publisher of business books, but isn't it appropriate for golfers when writing to them about a golfer's magazine?

Learn your people's habits of speech! In addition to your other efforts, make it a point to read all the letters you can that your customers or prospects write. Observe how they talk about your product—the phrases they use, the words that seem to come most naturally to them.

Then try to write to them according to their mental needs as they have voiced them and not according to the way you want other people to write to you.

SUMMARY

TWO big points in writing good letters have been brought to light in this chapter. Both of them, when applied, allow the dullest prospect to get a firm grasp on the idea and a clear understanding of your letter. The first point is that

MAKING YOUR MEANING CLEAR

"features" of the idea should be arranged in logical order, the "feature" easiest to understand first and others stacked on it in the sequence which will make them readily understood. The second point is that choice of words is one of the greatest factors in good letter writing. Edgar Allan Poe and Victor Hugo on one hand, and letters and advertisements on the other, were quoted to prove that the use of the right word is one of the greatest helps in effective writing. Then we found that each trade and craft has its own vocabulary. Finally, we learned how to develop a vocabulary that will enable us to use words in our letters that will mean to a reader exactly what we meant when we wrote them, just as surely as red means danger or a finger on the lips means "be silent."

As we completed this chapter, we found that we were rapidly getting away from prosy, matter-of-fact methods and were getting closer and closer to methods which make the reader act as we want him to. Analyzing the "load" of a letter was the first step we took in this direction, finding the Big Idea and selecting its "features' was another and the method of approach was the third. The fourth step we learned in this chapter, and so we are ready for the fifth: making letters sincere.

In the fifth chapter, out of 5,000 or more letters collected from various sources all over America, I have selected the best of those which carry conviction by their sincerity. They are reproduced with explanations that show what elements of character make people sincere and confidence-inspiring. And then by means of examples, I have shown you how to put those elements in written words so that your letters will have the same quality. You'll find no extracts from great writers in the next chapter, but you will find a score of sample letters in which the fundamentals of sincerity are so plain that any one of you can immediately apply them to letters of your own. In this fifth chapter, also, I dwell on the correct use of the so-called "you" element in letters. In explaining it, new light is thrown on this oft-discussed subject, and we find why the "you" element fails in its purpose when it is used carelessly.

PROBLEM SECTION IV

ALMOST every practical-minded business man with whom I have discussed the points brought out in the fourth chapter, has at first doubted the application of them to everyday business. And so I have no doubt that you, too, are thinking that we are getting overmuch into "fine writing"; that poetry and French novelists are a bit out of place in the study of letters to sell goods, collect money, adjust complaints and so on But I can convince you that I'm right just as I have convinced others. Here goes.

I had an experience once with a restaurant man that is so typical of results which can be gained by following the instructions in the fourth chapter and which had results so astounding, that I will tell it to you to prove my principle. The simple selling letter I wrote brought *122 customers out of a list of 385 names* into the restaurant the very next day. In final results it almost doubled the restaurant man's business. This experience I believe is so applicable to an automobile tire, a bank, a farm implement, a retail store, a food, a service, or a letter proposition of any kind, that I am going to take you through it in detail, pretending that you are the restaurant man.

Now, here is where you stand: You have a restaurant in a middle west city. It feeds about 250 people a day, but it has a capacity of 400 to 500 a day. You have compiled a list of about 400 professional men in the downtown district, lawyers, doctors, dentists, architects and the like. You had coupons printed, each good for 10 cents on a luncheon check, and mailed them to your list of men, but they didn't come in with the coupons You are up against it.

MAKING YOUR MEANING CLEAR

Here is where I come in, "I" meaning anyone who will *try applying to a practical business what we are learning from this book*

First I size up the "load" the letter must carry, on the chart we learned to use in the first part. I find from my chart that I must make those men want what the coupon will give them. But such men don't value a dime highly enough to make them do much to earn one. Your past results proved that to you. So I must make them want, not the dime, but what the dime stands for at your restaurant.

What does a dime stand for at your restaurant? A cup of tea you tell me, a sandwich, a piece of pie, and so on Which one of these 10-cent articles are you particularly proud of—which one do you think would be the biggest, best dime's worth? Well, you tell me, you have the best pie maker in town.

Now don't let the fact that we are talking about a restaurant bore you. I could put a "savings bank," or "6-cylinder car" in place of restaurant, and *dig into its sales possibilities* in exactly the same way.

We are in search of a Big Idea, and this method of search can be applied to any letter proposition. "So you have the best pie maker in town, have you? Now, we're coming to an idea. What makes you think he is the best?" It isn't a "he," you tell me, but a woman—Anna, by name— and if I'd ever eaten one of her pies—say, a lemon pie— I'd know why she's the best.

So I say—for every letter you want a big, concrete, central idea that will stick in the reader's mind, and here you have one: "the coupon is good, not for 10 cents, which is but a trifle, but for a piece of Anna's lemon pie—the best lemon pie any man ever tasted "

Do you follow me? That's the exact way, with only the superfluous conversation left out, in which the Big Idea of a wonderfully successful letter was worked out. And it's *the way to work out the Big Idea* for any letter or any other written work so far as that goes.

BUSINESS CORRESPONDENCE

For instance, how do you suppose the Big Idea back of the Prince Albert Tobacco advertising was worked out? I happen to know. I had a chance to work it out myself—and failed. The tobacco was submitted to a number of advertising men—I was among them—with a request to work out an idea for advertising it. I was young and conceited and never thought of getting a big concrete idea for an advertisement or a letter. I smoked some of the tobacco, read up clippings of other tobacco advertising and then wrote copy. It was returned with thanks—it was just "copy."

But another man started after it, as I later learned to start after the restaurant man. "Why do you think men should buy this tobacco?" he asked the manufacturer.

"Because it's mild," the manufacturer replied, "it's pure, it doesn't bite the tongue."

"Why doesn't it bite the tongue?" broke in the advertising man.

"Well, we have a special process—" and the Big Idea of "Prince Albert, the National Joy Smoke," saw the light.

In practically that way the big "30% oversize" idea of Goodyear tire advertising of a few years ago was born. Similarly the big, "try this treatment on your face" idea in Woodbury's soap advertising came into being. The "Valve-in-head" idea in Buick car advertising of a year or two ago was developed in the same manner. So was the "brown bottle" idea in Schlitz beer advertising of a few years ago.

But we must remember that we are writing a pie letter, so let's get back to the subject of what Anna can do. We dug up the Big Idea for your restaurant letter—"a coupon good for a piece of *Anna's* lemon pie." Anna's pie is individual—it's yours, just like the "patented process" which is Prince Albert Tobacco's own individual property. So you say, "Go ahead and write a good letter on it."

But I hesitate. Will those 400 professional men take an interest in Anna's pie or any lemon pie? No. They won't be thinking about things to eat when they get the letter. I must *create a visionary idea* for them—the vision of how good

MAKING YOUR MEANING CLEAR

Anna's lemon pie is and how poor other pies are by comparison with hers. You say, "That's good, now let's see you write a letter—good and hot." But what are the "features" of the Big Idea which is, "How good that lemon pie is"?

I have a pie baked and eat it and see. It tastes "fine." What makes it taste "fine"? I analyze carefully, and conclude that the "features" of its taste are.

The tart lemon flavor
The sweetness and fluffiness of the meringue
The delicious coming together of the sweet and sour
The flaky crust
The delightful sensation to the palate.

"All right," you say, "now go ahead and write your letter."

But wait. I've got to find *which of these features will be easiest for the reader to grasp and appreciate.*

"Oh, come now," you say, "don't get too much fine-spun theory into this—get busy."

"You think it's fine-spun theory, do you? Well, suppose *you* were one of those doctors, lawyers, or architects and you got a letter that started by telling about a pie's tart lemon flavor. Would you appreciate what that means? Suppose the letter started by telling you of the sweet meringue. Would it make your appetite wake up? Now be honest and admit that to an ordinary man lately come from breakfast and not thinking of eating or enjoying food, the thought of tart lemons by itself is not pleasant, and the thought of sweet meringue by itself is a bit sickish."

What must I do?

Why, I'll begin by getting a man's thoughts tuned up to eating. When he's thinking of eating, he can appreciate pie. When he is thinking of pie, he can appreciate the details of the pie—meringue, lemon flavor, the blending of sweet and sour, the crust, just as Victor Hugo—

"We're not writing one of Hugo's novels," you say, "but I suppose it's reasonable to take the points up in the right order. Now, go ahead and write."

BUSINESS CORRESPONDENCE

Again I pause. I have a big job ahead in making those men value a piece of Anna's lemon pie so highly that they'll prize the little 10-cent coupon that entitles them to it. So I must *choose words that help along* the good-to-eat thought.

"Cut out the fancy words and write plain English," you say.

"But words have such a big effect," I reply, "take Poe's poem—"

"I don't want any poetry in my business—my customers don't want poetry—they want food. You're giving me a lot of bosh."

The conversation I have detailed is almost exactly what occurred in the incident I mentioned, but I won't stretch out the details any farther. I patiently made the restaurant man understand that I didn't intend to write like the great masters of writing, but that I was only trying to learn from them. I got him to read Lamb's Essay on Roast Pig so as to see for himself how things could be made really to sound good to eat by the right sort of words. Finally he understood and then we went to work to express our ideas

```
"What a pleasure to top off a good luncheon with a
piece of Anna's lemon pie!"
```

Our first "feature," we decided, was to be the sensation to the palate of Anna's lemon pie, but as we were to lead into it by giving the reader an easy thought to grasp in the shape of eating "atmosphere," we began.

It was not hard to settle on that—in fact the restaurant man himself suggested it.

Then to describe our "feature" of "sensation to the palate" we wrote: "A mouthful of that pie is just a mouthful of delightful tastes."

But do you see how rather unpalatable that sounds? "Mouthful" sounds greedy, not fine and delicate. We thought of "bite," but bite made it appear that the pie was hard and tough. So we didn't use either, but decided on "When the lips and tongue close on a piece of that pie—"

MAKING YOUR MEANING CLEAR

What does that suggest to you? It suggested to me the thought of all the good tastes being squashed out in a gush of delightful sensations. "Squashing" didn't sound appetizing, however, but it led me to think of "a fountain of delightful tastes," and we wrote:

"When the lips and tongue close on a piece of that pie it's like a little gushing fountain in your mouth, deluging your palate with delightful tastes."

Sounds pretty good to eat, doesn't it?

Then we took up the second "feature"—the meringue. *Thought by thought, almost word by word, we built up* the expression of the visionary idea of how good that lemon pie was, until we were sure it would make a man's mouth water and make him think our little 10-cent coupon was worth something much more than merely 10 cents. Then we took up the positive idea—the coupon good for a piece of Anna's lemon pie.

How did we convey it? What are its "features"? We decided they were:

What the coupon is worth
How to use it
Why it is given.

At once we were confronted with: which of these "features" will be easiest for the reader to grasp? If we tell him just what it is worth, he may be contemptuous—10 cents is so small. He may be offended and ask, "why send me these dime coupons?"

Obviously that *"Why" "feature" was the best* one to start his grasp of the idea, because it followed so naturally on the visionary idea. That would lead to the worth of the coupon, and that lead to how to realize on it.

So we began: "I'd like to have you just taste a piece of that pie—so much so that if you'll use the enclosed coupon, it won't cost you a cent. Just come in for lunch today and present the coupon as payment for the dessert."

But now, does that language fittingly carry out the Big Idea? No. The idea, you remember, is not that a 10-cent

BUSINESS CORRESPONDENCE

coupon is much ordinarily, but when it means a piece of Anna's lemon pie, it's a great deal. So that the words would give that impression of good-natured challenge—we changed them to this:

> "How I'd like to see you tasting your first piece of that pie! By George, I'll pay for it, if you'll come in today — have your luncheon and top off with a piece of Anna's lemon pie, then simply hand in the enclosed coupon with your check in payment for the dessert."

Do you see how the freedom of "How I'd like," "By George," and "simply hand in," make the whole thing sound less like a "free 10-cent coupon," and more like a gentleman's good-natured challenge?

Well, that was the way we built up the expression of our ideas. So you see you must not look at what we can learn from the great masters of description and the artists in words as purely "literary." The best literature is that which does not impress us at the time as literature, but impresses us only with *the idea*. And that is *what we want for a good business letter*.

What was done in that letter for the idea of eating that lemon pie, and the idea of using the coupon, can be done in exactly the same way for the idea of eating anything, of using a machine, wearing a garment, trading at a certain store, owning an insurance policy, driving a car, doing business at a certain bank, pardoning an error, paying an overdue bill. There is *always a Big Idea* to work up if you will dig into the proposition and find it. There is *always an order of "features"* that will be clearest to understand if you will compare them, watch them and test them. There is *always the right kind of simple words* to help the idea if you will take pains with them.

Pure genius has written many successful letters. But *taking pains* has written many, many more. In fact, although I used to misunderstand what was meant, I am beginning to believe that the old saying, "Genius is the capacity for taking infinite pains," may be the truth after all.

But our restaurant letter was not finished when we had the **idea** expressed. It was too impersonal. It lacked sincerity.

MAKING YOUR MEANING CLEAR

We will learn in the next chapter why a matter-of-fact description of something never convinces us as much as a description that has personality in it. Below you'll find the first draft of the letter, as we have now seen it composed.

> Dear Sir:
> What a pleasure to top off a good luncheon with a piece of Anna's lemon pie!
> When the lips and tongue close on a piece of that pie it's like a little gushing fountain, deluging the palate with delightful tastes.
> First the frosting of cool, snowy, vaporous sweetness. Then quick the refreshing, lemony tartness. Then sweetness and tartness get crushed in together and Pouf! they join and blend in an entirely new taste that gradually melts away somewhere down your throat and only a soft happy memory remains — until the next mouthful.
> Then the crust — when you put it into your mouth it seems as though it had only been making believe to be crust after all. For where is it? It crumbles and flakes away and gives itself up to the rest of the pie like a sacrifice, to help make one grand, complete taste of paradise for you
> How I'd like to see you tasting your first piece of that pie! By George! I'll pay for it if you'll come in today—have your luncheon and top off with a piece of Anna's lemon pie — then simply hand in the enclosed coupon with your lunch check, as payment for the dessert.

In the next problem section we will take up the above letter again and see how personality and sincerity were injected into it. Then in the sixth problem section we will go farther and see how persuasion—the clincher that made 122 out of the 385 men who received the letter, actually come to that restaurant for lunch the next day and use the coupon—was incorporated in it. Then you will have seen the *complete, inside construction of a letter that almost doubled the business* of the restaurant—increasing the permanent net profits by more than $75 a week, simply by the proper use of the Big Idea and the application of the principles of clearness, sincerity, and persuasion.

Now let me help you apply my idea to your own business. In place of the list of prospects for that restaurant, I want you to substitute your list of prospects. In place of the

BUSINESS CORRESPONDENCE

restaurant, put your business. In place of the lemon pie, put the biggest, strongest selling idea of your proposition. Then work out the expression of that idea on the same methodical basis. Compare it with the idea in the best letter you can write by the old "inspiration" way of working and see which is best. The difference, I promise, will be so marked that anyone can see it Then just for further practise, try this:

Problem 1

If you were a mail order manufacturer of baby carriages and were going to write a letter to mothers of new-born babies, and had these "features" for your Big Idea:

We sell direct, thereby saving you middlemen's profits.

Being manufacturers, we offer you a wider variety of styles and finish to choose from than a dealer can offer.

We have been making baby carriages for 20 years and have learned how to cover all the little points of comfort and convenience that mothers like.

The pride we take in devoting ourselves exclusively to the making of good baby carriages.

The selection of the carriage your baby is to ride in is next in importance only to baby's food and clothes.

In what order would you put these "features"? Write such a letter complete and see how close you come to choosing the same kind of words for appealing to a mother's love and pride in her child, as were used in a successful letter that will be reproduced in the fifth chapter. File your letter in your Material File, for you will use it again.

Problem 2

Here is another nut for you to crack Suppose that you had been appointed chairman of the mission this government sent to Russia after the revolution in that country, and were going to prepare the address to the Russians that Mr. Elihu Root made. Suppose the "features" of your address were to be those of Mr. Root's masterly speech, namely:

MAKING YOUR MEANING CLEAR

America's desire to help the Russian people
The object of the mission
Our joy in Russia's new freedom
Our love of liberty in all lands
Our faith in democracy.

What order would you have selected for those points? Think it over carefully, put them down, and file them, for in the next chapter I will reproduce part of the address and show the order in which Mr. Root approached them.

This may seem like an odd problem to put before you, but you will see as you go along that *you can app'y what you are learning* to all forms of public expression of ideas. With the length of time we have taken for constructing the restaurant idea and the amount of study you should put in it, you have enough to do and I'll not offer more problems in this section.

But now let me see how you came out on the previous problem section work. Your first job was to construct a letter for the "Ajax" self-heating iron, from the diagram I gave you in the preceding problem section, and which you filed in your Material File. Take it from your file and then turn to page 192 where you will find the original "Ajax" letter. Refer to letter and diagram (Panel 102) as you read. The close of the letter has been omitted as it makes a special premium proposition which has no connection with this problem section. You can learn considerable from a careful comparison of your own letter with this one, as it is a *good examp'e of a well bui't, successful puller of resu'ts*. With the diagram to refer to, you can see the points the writer made are clear, so that detailed comment is not necessary. I don't mean to say that study of the letter and diagram is not necessary for you, because it is.

Another problem of the last problem section was to construct a strong "connecting link" between the visionary and positive ideas of a retail clothier's letter. Take your memorandum from your Material File. Notice that the connecting link should be something like this:

BUSINESS CORRESPONDENCE

> Usually the big city dealers snap them up like lightning. But this year West, Winsor & Mack's salesman for this territory picked out for me the very cream of these suits

It seemed to me at first that I could have put a stronger link in between the two sections, but probably if I had written the letter I wouldn't have thought so. It often happens that when a letter is all completed, by going back and separating it into its parts, we can *often rewrite one part of it much better* than we had it originally. I have rebuilt and restrengthened many letters in just that way.

If you are particularly interested in this problem you'll find the complete letter on page 196. If you are not especially interested, let's continue by looking over the collection letter you were to construct for the conditions outlined in the preceding problem section. How does your letter compare with the real one as shown on page 201?

This letter was used by a big collection agency, and for this particular type—threatening, yet giving the debtor one more opening to save his face—is a strong one. Did you construct one equally strong? Check yourself up very carefully, for it can teach you a great deal as to *just how far you can go with a threat* and still be within the law.

Next, from your Material File take your chart, diagrams, and the letter you built up for the washing compound proposition outlined in the preceding problem section.

First take up your chart: If you analyzed the conditions carefully—remember it was assumed that you had circularized your prospects with a *complete campaign that had brought the business* in other places, but had failed with it in this case—you should have sketched the "load" your letter had to carry about like this:

To make them realize that it is foolish not to try Skitch, at least, and to see that it really does save all the rubbing and hard work of wash day, really does make the clothes clean, and really won't hurt them—when women in other cities have used it so successfully.

MAKING YOUR MEANING CLEAR

Your answer to the question "Will they feel a self-interest in receiving a letter from me?" should be "No." We are not yet to touch the method of meeting this condition, however. Simply be sure that you have answered the question my way.

The Big Idea, in view of the letter's load, should be something like this:

It is *foolish* not to find out if Skitch will do all these things —save the rubbing, save the hard work, not hurt the clothes.

But, of course, since the prospects have had a complete campaign already on the subject, you should have seen that they are indifferent or opposed to considering the proposition, and therefore should have *arranged for approaching them through a Negative or Visionary Idea*. You may have hit on a Visionary Idea different from the one I used, one equally good or even better. If so, you can congratulate yourself. Compare yours with this one and see if you got this thought in it:

Suppose I had done to you what you are doing to me— heard your claims and then just said "They aren't so," without making an effort to find out.

The balance of your chart we won't stop to consider now, for it comes up in later chapters. But compare now your actual letter with the original material which you will find on page 210.

Of course, the illustration on page 210 is an advertisement; but, as explained in the fourth chapter, it might just as well have been a letter as far as its principle is concerned.

If what you wrote doesn't now seem to be as attractive and gripping as this advertisement that completely met the conditions outlined and, with four subsequent advertisements, *turned that city into a profitable market* for the advertiser, then try applying the method outlined in the fourth chapter on the problem I gave you and see how much you can improve your copy.

The last bit of work you were given in the previous problem section was to take the letter for the custom shirt maker

BUSINESS CORRESPONDENCE

and add to it whatever paragraphs would be necessary to make it an article for use on a list of men who wore only ready-made shirts

I expected you to see at once that in such a case the readers could be assumed to be indifferent or opposed to the idea of paying the extra cost of custom-made shirts—and hence a Visionary or Negative Approach would be needed in order to make them see things your way.

I went at it this way. If those men don't believe in custom-made shirts now, then we ought to make them see themselves dressed in poorly fitting shirts—if they are stout, then make them imagine the ridiculous appearance of the commonest misfit large men meet; if they are slim then make them see the funny appearance of a man in a shirt too big for him. Here is the way the problem worked out for me:

```
        You take a man who is big-muscled or corpulent, and
nine times out of ten when he sits down his stomach will
stretch a ready-made shirt until it gaps in front, show-
ing his undershirt, or worse.  Ready-made shirts are not
made with room enough for him   Then, with a slim man,
chances are there's too much goods, and when he sits,
his shirt billows out in front like one of those pannier
effects on a woman's skirt. You've seen how funny men
with such shirts look, haven't you?
        And how sloppy a man looks when his shirt is too
broad across the shoulders for him — but how skimped and
pinched he looks and feels when it isn't broad enough.
Sometimes a man's collar makes two homely furrows
running V-shaped across his chest
        And yet SOME MEN STILL THINK custom-made shirts
don't pay!
```

Then, for the Connecting Link, I wrote this:

```
        If you have a figure like a fashion plate which any
shirt will fit, maybe custom shirts don't pay. Or if you
don't get good custom-made shirts, maybe they don't
pay. But —
```

Then in the seventh problem section we shall add a strong "closer" for it.

PART V

HOW TO MAKE YOUR LETTER SINCERE

CHAPTER V

HOW TO MAKE YOUR LETTER SINCERE

A CRITIC once said to me, "Why leave the matter of sincerity till the fifth chapter in your book? The necessity for it should be taught from the very start." He misunderstood.

It is *not* the moral attribute of being sincere in what you say, that we are to deal with in this chapter. That is part of honest men's characters. It is the faculty of *impressing your sincerity upon your readers* that we now seek. And that's important, for some people who are as honest and sincere as the day is long, and whose honesty and sincerity cannot be mistaken for an instant when they talk to you man to man, seem utterly unable to convey the same impression when they put their thoughts on paper, or address an audience. A certain formality creeps into their words—a stiffness amounting sometimes almost to coldness.

So, having learned in previous chapters how to select the "load" of a letter; how to choose the Big Idea and how to present it, our aim now is to learn the knack of saying what we have to say in such a way that a reader, or individual listener, whichever he may be, will get the same impression of frankness and truthfulness that he would if he were looking straight into our eyes.

Now, when a man talking to us face to face wins our complete confidence in his assertions, we generally say afterward, "His frankness won us over." And when we see a man win confidence and make friends on all sides, we usually say, "He has a frank, open, friendly personality."

Did you ever stop to analyze the source of that impression of frankness, friendliness, and openness? Most of us have.

BUSINESS CORRESPONDENCE

Those of us who have not, need not make a very deep search to find it. I simply mention it to show that just as we can find exactly what makes us feel that this or that man is frank and honest, so we can get that effect in our letters, and make our readers think and feel that our letters are frank and honest.

First let us agree on *the source of the impression of friend'iness and sincerity* that some people give us. Unquestionably it comes from their manner of acting and speaking. But when we study a bit deeper we find something else. We find that the man to whom we quickly extend our friendship and in whom we quickly place complete confidence, is almost invariably a man with whom we have *points of mutual agreement* or sympathy.

For instance, if you like dogs probably you don't distrust every man who does not like them, but you do warm up to a stranger more quickly when you find he, too, is a dog lover. Looking at the matter from another point of view: laboring men, politicians find, are more quickly interested in a cause by a speaker who is identified with labor, like Samuel Gompers, than by a speaker who comes from the capitalist class. Bankers give audience more readily to a man who shows he knows banking. We even find shrewd sales managers sometimes utilizing Irish salesmen for Irish trade, Jews for the Jewish districts; Italians, Polish, Scandinavian, or other nationalities, for the trade in communities settled by people of their respective tongues.

Now, it is not because Jews consider all Jews more truthful, or farmers consider all farmers more honest, or dog lovers believe truth goes only with a love for dogs, or laboring men trust other laboring men more implicitly, that the avenue of approach spoken of is generally followed. It is not that any class trusts its own class more than others. It is because, in the course of their relations, a point of mutual sympathy or understanding is more likely to develop.

When two people begin to find sympathies or interests in common, they begin to like each other, and if they like each other they usually trust each other.

HOW TO CONVEY SINCERITY

You see, *two minds or personalities coming in contact* with each other are just like two cog wheels in a machine. The cogs are their sympathies. If those sympathies, or cogs, match each other, then the meeting is enjoyable and interesting, and creates confidence. If you like dogs and horses and flowers and outdoor life, while the man you meet has no taste for them at all, but likes dancing, cards, society, and midnight frolics—you can see that when you come in contact with each other: neither of you will move the other to any interest or liking. (What appear to be contradictions to this rule are not in fact contradictions. When two people of opposite tastes are close friends, the opposite tastes are dominant, but down in the hearts of each person will be found a secret interest in the other's tastes.)

But if you have even one taste in common, though the rest be contrary, that one mutual interest is often enough to carry you over the gap of the non-mutual ones. Salesmen use this principle of psychology right along—knowingly and unknowingly. They seek to *find "a point of contact" with the prospect* that will create sufficient mutual interest to keep the wheels of personal relationship going. They sometimes agree, against their own inclinations, with an opinion of a customer in order to gain strength on another point.

In all probability, therefore, mutual tastes, or sympathies, or interests, are the secret of what we call "personal charm," or "likeability" or "popularity." The person who possesses that enviable quality is quite likely to be a person who has naturally, or who has cultivated, a broad liberality and almost universal sympathy with things—so that no matter what the foibles and notions, or likes or dislikes of others are, he sees some good in them, or some sense, or some quality of one kind or another that makes mutual sympathy. Therefore, he is liked and trusted.

But now, can this secret of personal charm, personal friend making, personal confidence winning, be applied to practical business letters? That's what we want. Can we so use it in everyday dictation or writing, that the prospect will believe

BUSINESS CORRESPONDENCE

> Pontiac, Ill.
>
> Clark & Dearborn
> Chicago, Ill
> Gentlemen.
>
> By same post I am returning the white gloves, as I do not care for this quality. The gloves I wanted were the line you stock at $1.25, and which you advertised as your special line at 89 cents.
>
> The hose I ordered were also another special line. You advertise in the papers that country clients may avail themselves of these reduced prices, but on this, my first occasion for ordering, you cannot supply either
>
> If you can't send the goods ordered, kindly return my money.
>
> Yours truly
> (Mrs.) M E White

Panel 129

THE CUSTOMER SAID—THE STORE REPLIED

Customers worth having are worth satisfying No legitimate business transaction is complete until the customer is satisfied Above, see a complaint letter written to a Chicago store Exasperation permeates every line The complaint is a just one, but the situation unavoidable from the store point of view But read the answer on the next page Notwithstanding the impossibility of an absolute adjustment the customer's way, that letter, by its consciousness of the customer's attitude and its genuine endeavor to be fair, not only made plain the store point of view, but satisfied its reader Behind that letter is this thought "A satisfied old customer represents more business than a book of new prospects" Picture the customer. Mentally seat him beside your desk Then talk to him. The writer of the store's letter takes just that attitude He acts as if the customer came personally to the office There is no chance for a quarrel. He is fair and open-minded and he shows the complainant that he really sees things as she does. Most people recognize a fair proposition when they see it. It is not hard to show that you have given all that you have agreed to give if you go about the job in a courteous, tactful way

HOW TO CONVEY SINCERITY

CLARK & DEARBORN
CHICAGO, ILL.

Mrs. M. E. White,
Pontiac, Illinois.

Dear Madam:

    We have your letter with reference to goods ordered from our Sunday advertisement. It MUST be exasperating to you and it certainly is exasperating to us — for you could not want the goods more than we want your trade and good will.

    But, you see, when standard lines like these are advertised at such prices, hundreds of women want to take advantage of them, just as you did, and while you are writing your order, hundreds of others are doing the same. So the stock goes quickly. The only thing we can suggest is to hurry your order into the mail just as early after the advertisement appears as you possibly can.

    We are sorry, but we cannot get a single additional pair of gloves of the style advertised, at any price. We have secured a few more of the hose of the style advertised, but the price on the white will be 32 cents, black 37 cents. Even at that slight advance they are still remarkable values.

    If you wish we will gladly send them on approval. This is against our usual custom, but we want to go out of our way to remove the bad impression you have received.

    Let us know your wishes and in the meantime we will hold your remittance to your credit.

                           Yours very truly,
                              CLARK & DEARBORN

all we say about our merchandise? That the debtor will believe that what we ask him to do is right? That the dissatisfied customer will believe that our answer to his complaint is fair? Will this principle "work" in a business letter, so that we can make what we write seem to look the reader straight and unafraid in the eye, so that when it is read by a perfect stranger, days after it was written, and miles away from the writer, it will still carry *the impress of a strong, sincere, winning personality?* Let us see.

In Panel 129 on page 248 find a letter received by a city store from an out-of-town customer. You can see exasperation—even suspicion—sticking out of every line of it. The letter had to be answered although the store simply couldn't supply the gloves advertised and the only hose of the style advertised that could be supplied were at an advanced price. So you see what a difficult job the store's correspondent had in order to tell the plain truth and yet hold the customer's confidence—for the plain truth looked very much like the very untruthfulness which the customer suspected.

But it was done. The customer not only wrote a cordial letter in reply, but accompanied it by an order for more goods. Let us consider the letter that did it. You will find it on page 249. The concrete impression the letter gives is frankness. It impresses us as the talk of a friendly, frank man.

Now let us see where that impression of friendliness and frankness—of human personality—comes from. Where do you first begin to feel it? Isn't it right in the first paragraph, where the letter says, "It *must* be exasperating to you—"?

The *effect of that sympathetic admission* in the letter is exactly that of the salesman who looks you straight in the eye and says "I won't deny for an instant" some opinion of yours. It's like the frankness of a man who in telling you about a dangerous experience remarks, "I admit I was scared stiff—if there'd been any place to run I'd have run—but— "

The confession to a feeling that you think you probably would have felt in such circumstances, provokes a sort of

HOW TO CONVEY SINCERITY

mental chuckle and the impression, "Here's my kind of fellow —he's telling the straight truth."

And then you tend to believe implicitly in the courageous action he afterwards describes. If he had left out that little touch of human feeling that established sympathy or mutual understanding between you, you might have disbelieved his story.

Now study again the effect of the letter on page 249. See how showing sympathy with the customer's feeling established *a basis of mutual understanding.* "It *must* be exasperating to you" is a cog that fitted in with a similar cog in the customer's mind and then, "And it certainly is exasperating to us"—why, one feels, this isn't a cold-blooded bit of typewriting—this is a real person talking to us!

And notice the other high lights of the letter: "But, you see—"—"hundreds of women want to take advantage of them just as you did"—"And while you are writing your order, hundreds of others are doing the same—." The writer's sincere, frank friendliness disarms suspicion, makes the reader see things his way. In fact, the whole effect of the letter—as we can judge for ourselves, and as its result with the customer showed—is of a real personality, looking one straight in the eye, and telling the simple truth.

So much for the complaint letter. Now to look for the same principles in a sales letter. The letter on page 252, selected from a score of similar letters, will serve. This letter is successfully used by a baby carriage manufacturer who sells his product direct by mail. He secures the birth records of his territory and within a few months after a baby's birth he starts a follow-up series to the mother, beginning with the letter on page 252 As he has to *draw his trade away from its natural outlet,* the retail store, he has a good, hard job to perform in winning complete confidence in his claims

I might stop to comment on the choice of words used for the appeal to the mother of a young babe—as the sentiment of mother love is faithfully mirrored in them. And we might stop profitably to observe the logical arrangement of "fea-

BUSINESS CORRESPONDENCE

BETTER CARRIAGE MFG. CO.
PHILADELPHIA, PA

Mrs D. E. Crilly,
Chicago, Illinois.

Dear Madam.

After baby's food and baby's clothes, the most important thing you have to decide upon is the little cart that baby is going to ride in — is going to be seen in — is going to be admired in

Never a child came into the world but was worthy as good a cart as could be afforded We take pride in the handsome, comfortable, stylish little carts we make We would rather make a good cart for a little round babe than the best automobile that runs, and no one, we honestly believe, makes a better one

For twenty years we have been making them — experimenting with them — learning to make better ones all the time. All the little points that make for baby's comfort and health — all the little points that go to make a proud, stylish, little turnout for the most inspiring sight in all the world — a mother and her child — have been observed and considered by us.

Devoting ourselves entirely to the making of children's things, we appreciate full well the importance of price to you.

And we long ago determined that our policy should be to offer every mother the chance to have for her child a cart that is fully worthy of the occasion, at a fair and reasonable price.

We early determined to save her the unnecessary profit that the middlemen usually make — the wholesaler and the retailer — to sell our carts direct to the customer. Another advantage in this method is the wide range in selection of color and grade of upholstering. You don't have to offend your good taste, as you probably would if you had to buy what a local market affords.

The catalog sent you illustrates and describes our many handsome styles We know that you will read it carefully — because such an important matter as the selection of baby's cart requires care, doesn't it? Then, when you have picked out just the one you desire, our order blank gives very clear directions so that there will be no mistake about getting just what you selected.

And we ship promptly and all charges prepaid

Yours sincerely,

BETTER CARRIAGE MFG. CO

Panel 131

HOW TO CONVEY SINCERITY

tures." But just now we are most interested in tracing the reasons for the letter's impression of frankness.

In it we see again *a letter that seems to look us straight in the eye* like an honest man; and seems to be good friends with us like some cordial, sincere, human being. In short, the letter has personality. Why? Why because, by a sympathetic understanding of mother's pride and love for her baby, it starts up the cog wheels of personal friendship and trust. Feel for yourself the *human touch of the opening paragraphs.* Turn to the letter and read them again.

That first paragraph, for example, not only gives the mother "features" she can grasp easily, but it gives them to her in a way that makes her fall right in with them.

If, instead of part of a letter, these "features" were a part of a personal interview, can't you just imagine the writer leaning down to pat the baby's cheek and saying, "What a fine child"? And that personal touch is exactly what he has to put into the cold typewriting of his letter. Notice that first the letter talks of baby carriages, not merely as something the manufacturer has to sell, but also as something the mother has to choose—two cogs working in unison. Then the fine workmanship on the carriages is not only a matter of the manufacturer's pride, but it also concerns "baby's comfort and health" and it helps "to make a stylish turnout for a mother and her child " The *prices are not only bargains, they are also opportunities* for "every mother to have for her child a cart worthy of the occasion at a fair and reasonable price." The selling method is not merely buying direct from the factory, it is "to save the middleman's profit and give a wider choice."

All through the letter, mutual understanding and sympathy are created between writer and reader. And that's the principle, we agreed, which underlies personal friendship and trust. Compare the letter with the one on page 249, and see how similar they are. And observe the printer's letter on page 254. Still different is this one—a strictly business letter to strictly business men.

BUSINESS CORRESPONDENCE

THE RECORD PRESS
CHICAGO, ILL.

Winslow Brothers Company,
Chicago, Illinois.

Gentlemen

    I'm tempted to write you a long letter telling you just why you ought to use letterheads that give people a good impression of your business, how these first impressions grow into confidence and confidence into cash

    But what's the use?

    You know, beforehand, about what I would say You already know that your letterhead has as much significance to the person reading your letter as the appearance of your store front has to the passer-by

    The point is this   I've studied office stationery so long and printed so much of it, that I know how to give it all the prestige and power that is possible to put into a small piece of printing

    I want your order because I know I can give you as satisfactory work as you ever paid for.

    What shall it be, how many and how soon?

                    Sincerely,

                          THE RECORD PRESS

Panel 132

THE SINGLE AIM AND THAT WORD "YOU

Suggest that you can help the reader in your letter and you have his attention   Tell how and you have his interest. Prove it, and you are likely to have his signature   The letter above is especially good because it not only meets the test of the foregoing statements, but also makes its strong and convincing appeal in a few words. It has one end in view—to crystallize wants—turn desire to decision —to get results, the order, now   "You" is the second most important word and the second oldest   As an attention-compeller it is without a peer, but it is a word with which one may not take liberties. The writer of sales letters must remember that he is generally addressing a stranger, and that while a friendly, natural, man-to-man attitude is desirable, nothing that verges upon familiarity will be tolerated   "You" is familiar   It will, without doubt, get the reader's attention   Therefore, be sure that it gets the right sort of attention   Study how it was handled on the next page

HOW TO CONVEY SINCERITY

WILLIS-JOHNSTONE COMPANY
SPRINGFIELD, MISSOURI

Mrs. F E. Ross,
Whitewater, Missouri.

Dear Madam

There is only one way to find the best store in which to do your buying.

Call on every dealer in town, compare qualities and prices carefully, then buy where your dollar goes the farthest

Don't let any firm feel that it has a MONOPOLY on your trade. Don't let any firm consider you a sure customer.

Make the men you deal with win your trade each time, over and over again. Don't buy even a second time from any firm before you have made the other fellow figure at ROCK BOTTOM for your order.

The firm that considers you as SURE may not think it necessary to give you the lowest price, which another firm would quote to get your trade

Each firm you visit will claim—each must claim—that they can save you money. Your business is to look for the house that says·--"WE TAKE THE LEAST PROFIT " That is the only firm you will find that really will and does SELL CHEAPER

The WILLIS-JOHNSTONE COMPANY believes in selling to EVERYBODY and making small profits rather than in making big profits and selling only to a few.

That is why we are writing to you personally. We are trying hard to get your business We want you to know it is to your benefit to see us before buying house furnishings of any kind We promise that it will pay you well for walking a few steps out of the main business district to look over our stock and prices

      Yours truly,
      WILLIS-JOHNSTONE COMPANY

P S.--If you need matting this summer, either by the yard or in made-up rugs, we have patterns and pieces we are sure will please you.

BUSINESS CORRESPONDENCE

What *made that letter win confidence when other letters had failed?* Why the same sort of mutual understanding—mutual sympathy Notice the opening lines. "I'm tempted to write you about so and so, but what's the use—you know it all—." With one sweep the writer establishes a feeling of "now, this fellow is sensible, let's see what he has to say about it."

The letter on page 255 offers further proof. Here is a successful letter of a house-furnishing goods dealer who had to make his readers believe that it was to their interests to go out of their way to buy from him. Why should this letter have pulled so much better than most retailers' letters—where does its frankness and sincerity come from? Where, but from the same sort of *effect of mutual understanding and sympathy*. This time the prospect's confusion between the conflicting claims of rival stores is made the issue. The secret of personal magnetism can be applied to letters—that the *reasons why each of those four successful letters won their readers' confidence* and friendship are just like the reasons for the friendship and trust we feel for a strong personality.

You see, sincerity is a personal quality. A stone wall cannot express sincerity. Nor can a typewritten sheet of paper. You can't make a letter, or an advertisement, or a speech, ring with sincerity, therefore, unless you can make it sound like a real person. It has to have personality. That quality we call personality requires two people—one to shine it and one to reflect it.

Robinson Crusoe, when he was alone on his desert island, practically was just a human machine. But when his man Friday appeared, and Crusoe took an interest in him, thus awakening a return of interest on Friday's part, then, and only then, did Crusoe begin to express his personality. And a letter that talks entirely about the writer or entirely about the writer's interests, of what he can do and what he can't do, what his merchandise is or what it isn't, is like Robinson Crusoe puttering about on his desert island with no one to observe, or admire, or obey, or care a snap of the fingers about him.

HOW TO CONVEY SINCERITY

There can be little personality of the writer felt in a letter which treats solely of the writer's interests, because there is *no reader's personal interest created* upon which to shine it But when the baby carriage manufacturer took his Big Idea of the better satisfaction a mother could secure by buying a cab direct of him, and made each "feature" of it a matter of mutual interest between himself and the mother, then the letter took on the air of *a friendly talk between two people* with mutual sympathies. The writer's personality was felt—and the result was confidence in his claims, and orders for his goods.

On page 249 you can see how the store's complaint adjuster, recognizing the customer's exasperation, made it a mutual affair between them by gearing it to the store's own exasperation. Then he made the big rush of orders for the bargains advertised a mutual affair between the customer and the store by gearing to the store's dilemma the customer's own desire for the bargains. And on page 254 you can see how the printer, recognizing the average business man's objections to being preached to about the value of good printing, created a mutual interest by his "you know it, already." You can easily chart the effect of the other two letters in the same way, showing that *the same psychological law that creates liking and trust between two persons, creates liking and trust in a letter.*

Now we have pared away the husks and are down to the meat of our proposition. We have agreed upon the qualities which make some people likable and confidence inspiring. We have seen that the same qualities may be put in a letter with the same effect. We are ready, therefore, to find out how we can *apply these laws now, at once,* to everyday affairs and how to take the "features" of a letter's Big Idea and make them not only our interests, but also the reader's interests. Frankly it's a big job. It is bigger and deeper than what has been called "Putting the 'you' element into letters," for that expression, "the you element" only half covers the task.

BUSINESS CORRESPONDENCE

FAIRY FLOUR MILLS
CHICAGO, ILL.

Mrs. H. A Swartz
Whiting
Indiana

Dear Madam

     If only I could make a mere letter tell you how much of your cake-making troubles Fairy Flour would save!

     Just think — Fairy Flour takes all the mystery, all the difficulty, all the bad luck out of cake making. It doesn't pay to fuss over a cake in the old-fashioned way, even if you are a fine cake maker For Fairy Flour, without the work, makes as delicious a cake as you could make with all your fussing.

     But if you aren't a successful cake maker now, why Fairy Flour is a godsend! Anyone can make cakes that are light as a feather and simply delicious, with Fairy Flour.

     You just add water, mix gently, then bake. That's absolutely all. It seems impossible, doesn't it? But one package will show you I am telling the truth. You add no milk — the milk is all in it, in powdered form You use no eggs — the eggs are in it, in powdered form You do no work — for the work has all been done, by expert cake makers!

     It sounds like a Fairy tale — but it's only the genuine truth of Fairy Flour, and I am going to prove it to you Go to any of the grocers on the list at bottom of this letter and get one 25-cent package of Fairy Flour. Use it just as I have said and if it doesn't make you as splendid a cake as you ever saw, the grocer will refund your 25 cents — on your mere say-so

     Will you do it? Why, it's worth while if only to marvel at this new wonder! Go to any one of these grocers — today

                        Very truly yours,

                             FAIRY FLOUR MILLS

Panel 134

HOW TO CONVEY SINCERITY

A letter that is all "you" and "your" is just as one-sided and hence just as impersonal, and just as insincere to the reader, as one that is all "I" and "my."

Let me repeat that personality, or sincerity, or confidence—call it what you like, requires two people. You can't have confidence without having someone hard by to have confidence in, nor can you inspire confidence without having someone at hand.

We have all seen letters that bristled with the word "you" that said "you this" and "you that"—and advertisements that pointed fingers at us and said "you need this" or "you want that." But there wasn't much personality in them after all. They were just as cold and impersonal as a letter that says nothing but "I this" and "I that."

For instance, here is an extract from a letter I once had to revise, seeking to sell an automobile accessory:

> "You don't like to have the springs of your car squeak, do you? You like to have it roll silently along as still as a bird flies. But you don't like to have to spend a half a day down under your car oiling springs, do you? You'd like some easy way to keep your springs well oiled without the muss and bother of present methods, wouldn't you? Here is what you have been waiting for."

The word "you" is in the letter often enough to suit the most exacting, but are you, yourself, in it? Certainly not. You don't get the least impression of the manufacturer's sincerity, his friendliness, his frankness. About all the element of personality you get is that of a rather conceited young person gratuitously telling someone whom he calls "you" a great deal about that person's own business. And yet this manufacturer wondered why automobile owners didn't believe in his product and buy it on receipt of that letter!

Compare the paragraph I have quoted with the letter on the opposite page. It sells a different product, but it has the same sort of labor and trouble-saving idea to convey and the same sort of *skepticism to meet*. In that letter the housewife doesn't hear herself called "you" quite so often, but she does feel her interests and her problems so closely linked up with the merchandise, and her doubts so much more sympathetically appreciated, that she feels much more of the real "you" interest in it. And isn't the sincerity, and frankness, and friendliness of the manufacturer, more humanly expressed? *That letter isn't a "you" letter, it's a "you and I" letter.*

Now then, suppose you owned an unoccupied building in a certain district and I were a real estate agent who wanted to secure the handling of your property. Suppose I wrote to tell you that I knew how to rent property better than your present agent did. Suppose I filled my letter with statements about myself, the same sort of statements probably made by your present agent. Would you believe me? I hardly think you would. That would be *the kind of talk you were accustomed to.*

Looking at the proposition another way, suppose I told you all about your own problem—things you already knew—such as, "Your building is vacant," "You want a tenant," and so on. Would you believe I was a better agent than the one

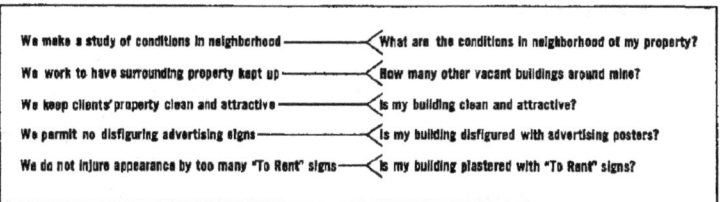

Panel 135

you already had? Hardly! That would be the plain "you" attitude which is so often misused and which we have condemned.

But suppose that I was a more careful student of letter writing. Suppose that after I had diagrammed my Big Idea —my knowledge and experience in handling property—I had charted out your probable attitude. And suppose my chart showed me that as you already had an agent—who had

HOW TO CONVEY SINCERITY

probably given you the same idea about himself as I want to give you about myself—your tendency would be to think, "all real estate agents are alike."

Just assume that I had gone that far. Then let us assume I had said to myself, "Well, in that case, I will win my prospect's confidence by not talking entirely about my own idea, or entirely about his own needs, but will link the two together." Under such conditions I'd set down the "features" of my Big Idea as in the panel on the opposite page. Then, as far as I could, I would find a connecting link for my "features" and your interests as an owner, as shown.

If I did all that before I wrote my letter to you and thus made it easy to put each "feature" up to you in a way that *touched your personal interests as much as they did mine*, then you would begin to take some stock in the idea of my knowledge and experience.

Now I never wrote a letter like that, but on the next page is one exactly like it that was used by a Texas real estate firm. It won the confidence of owners. It brought many appreciative replies indicating that it had created good will. More than that, it secured a number of good accounts.

I don't know whether the man who wrote it worked out his plan in the way I have outlined. Probably he didn't, as many men have a natural intuition when it comes to *appealing to human nature*. But I know you could build up as good an appeal, even without that intuition, if you follow the plan we are now learning. Are you beginning to see how it works?

Suppose, just to take another concrete example that happens to be at hand, we were seeking to increase the business of a bank. Suppose we were going to circularize all our safety deposit vault customers in the interests of other departments.

You might say that surely a bank does not have to worry about people believing its letters. But when a bank wants to convince a man that it really wants to be friends with him, that it really seeks his business, that it really wants to be

BUSINESS CORRESPONDENCE

KENDALL & COMPANY
DALLAS, TEXAS

Mr. W. B Brown,
Dallas, Texas

Dear Sir

  Our firm has just completed a survey of the central business district of Dallas on Elm, Main, Commerce, Akard, Ervay and Harwood Streets, with a view of suggesting to interested owners individual action which would improve the appearance of vacant properties and increase the chances of their rental   We have made this survey and are making these suggestions in the interest of the general situation rather than with the idea of any immediate individual gain
to our own firm

  For your information we will state that owing to conditions which prevail, there are today within the district mentioned ONE HUNDRED AND FOUR FIRST FLOOR VACANCIES   The need, therefore, of active, intelligent effort on the part of property owners is perfectly apparent

  This letter is not written as a request to you for any change of agency   If you are receiving satisfactory service from your present agent we believe you will find your interests greatly subserved by permitting his sign and HIS SIGN ONLY on the building   If our firm is that favored agent, we will do our best to render you efficient service.

  In order that we may intelligently prosecute this work to a conclusion, we want to ask if you will not be good enough to drop us a line in the enclosed stamped envelope, advising us your views and what action you are taking in the premises

      Yours respectfully,

         KENDALL & COMPANY

HOW TO CONVEY SINCERITY

more than an institution of marble and granite and steel to him, then indeed a bank does need to get personality and sincerity into its letters.

On the next page is a very successful example of a letter that arouses those emotions. What gives it that *human touch, dignified, as it should be, yet intensely personal?*

Separate the Big Idea into its "features" and you find that for each one an interest or sympathy of the reader has been found, just as in the real estate letter. So instead of the usual bank phrases, "we solicit," "this bank does" and so forth, the writer has put himself in the customer's place In the first paragraph he hits exactly on what the customer does really think of the institution; and all through the letter the customer's side is always joined to the bank's side. Interests are made mutual.

To some of you, perhaps, putting yourself in the reader's place and cultivating a sympathy with his position or an understanding of it may seem like some difficult psychological undertaking. But, as a matter of fact, it is easy. It means only *a perfect understanding of your own proposition* If you properly size up the work your letter has to do, according to instructions in the first chapter, you must, in doing it, consider whether or not the reader is likely to be skeptical of your claims—and you can't decide that without considering his reasons. And when you know and appreciate his reasons for being skeptical, it will become as easy and natural for you, in conveying the "features" of your Big Idea, to cover them both from the reader's and your own point of view, as it is to talk on any mutually interesting subject with a friend.

The banker who wrote the letter on the next page knew the true nature of his business so thoroughly that when he came to conveying the idea of the bank's personal services, he knew that the customer would be skeptical because the Big Idea of the bank would be a cold steel and marble institution. So the banker *linked up that thought of the customer with his own thought* of "flesh and blood and brain behind it all." He knew the customer must have a feeling of security in the safety deposit

BUSINESS CORRESPONDENCE

GLENCOE NATIONAL BANK
GLENCOE, ILLINOIS

H. E. Flint,
Glencoe, Illinois.

Dear Sir

As a patron of our Safety Deposit Vaults, we wonder sometimes if your only thought of us is for the stalwart steel cage that holds your valuables safe, the massive iron doors that swing shut behind you, the locks, the bolts, the mechanical system, that protect you.

There is flesh and blood and brains behind it all. There is knowledge of business needs and experience in business undertakings that might serve you in other ways with the same efficiency, and the same solid security, that our Safety Deposit Vault serves you

Our Bond Department not only has for sale at all times a carefully selected line of securities, but can offer you sound and helpful advice and counsel in the investment of your funds; it both sells and buys stocks and bonds on commission

Our Mortgage Department has money to loan at all times upon improved real estate, and can often make the quick negotiations of a loan a great convenience to you.

Our Trust Department offers the most reliable stable service as Executor, Administrator, Guardian, Trustee, etc In the Peoples National Bank and the Peoples Savings Bank, both of which institutions are owned by this company, we can offer you the accommodations of every proper banking facility.

We thank you for the patronage already extended us, and sincerely hope that we may sometime have the pleasure of serving you in any further capacity that our facilities can offer you.

                    Yours truly,
                    GLENCOE NATIONAL BANK

Panel 137

HOW TO CONVEY SINCERITY

vault, so he linked it up with the thought of there being the same security and efficiency in other departments. The real estate department, as his letter describes it, does not merely perform certain functions, but it "can often relieve you of worry" by performing them. The bond department does not "sell and buy" merely—"it can offer you sound and helpful advice" in buying and selling.

The banker made his letter a personal, human, friendly communication simply by getting a clear understanding first of the "features" of the idea he wanted to convey, and then of the reader's attitude toward them or interest in them. You can write in the same way with scarcely an effort if you make an equally clear size-up.

Here, then, we have at our service *one of the most prized assets of a good letter writer* or eloquent public speaker—the art of putting personality into written words or words addressed to a body of people where personal contact is impossible.

And when you stop and think about it, it is quite logical that it should be so. For what makes the strength of personal contact, but a mutual understanding and sympathy? We like and place our confidence in only those people who can understand us and whom we can understand—with whom we feel in sympathy and who show themselves in sympathy with us. And so our letters, to carry the magnetism of personality, and the impression of frank sincerity that goes with it, must create the same atmosphere of mutual sympathy or understanding.

To some people the knack of creating this atmosphere is as natural as breathing. They have a talent for writing. But for those who haven't that talent, the size-up chart which you were taught to use in the first chapter supplies the deficiency. Once you get from the chart a thorough understanding of why your readers are likely to be skeptical of your Big Idea, or doubtful of any of its "features" you can then bring out those "features" not in direct opposition to the reader's attitude, but as a mutual give and take—just as in the successful letters reproduced in this book. Your letters

BUSINESS CORRESPONDENCE

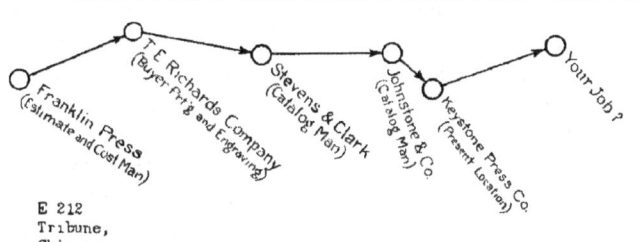

E 212
Tribune,
Chicago

    It looks to me as though, through every experience I have had since I left school, I have been aiming right for the position you advertise.

    When I was estimator and cost man for the Franklin Press, figuring the SELLING PRICES on printing jobs like you have to buy every day, the T. E. Richards Company picked me as a good man to do their buying of printing and engraving. My knowledge of shop processes and costs enabled me not only to buy intelligently, but to save considerable money through better layout of the jobs -- you have probably seen how much more some of your jobs cost when the layout man doesn't know how to save printers' time.

    That success as a layout man secured me, two years later, the position of catalog man with Stevens & Clark. You know probably that while their catalog is not as big as yours, they have to get rock-bottom prices for top notch paper, engraving and printing.

    I made a good enough record in three years to get me in at Johnstone & Company at a much higher salary. But it was too high for them -- maybe you have done that yourself -- paid a man a salary to get him that you were sorry about afterwards. It made relations unpleasant and I left in two months' time.

    I took my present position as a place to tide me over until I could find a location in which I could use all my past experience.

    Yours is just that place. I want a chance at it and won't haggle about salary to start -- I can prove my worth if I once get started.

    Will you give me ten minutes' personal interview to back up what I have said in this letter?

                        Yours truly,
                            J. H. Cross

Panel 138

HOW TO CONVEY SINCERITY

then become, not mere cold statements of fact on the one hand, or fawning subserviency to the reader on the other, but *virile, interesting, man-to-man talks* based on the same fundamentals that, as we saw on page 249, control our personal relations.

The mails every day are full of proofs of the point I make. As a good example, read, on the opposite page, a letter of application which *out of 54 replies to an advertisement got first attention* and won its writer the job. The little map at the top is merely an attention getter; the way to originate such stunts will be shown in a later chapter, but the body of the letter—the part that won confidence and impressed the personality of the applicant on the employer—is constructed exactly according to the same principles we have just learned.

Study that letter, and you will see how (if you had to write it) you could put the same "you and I" sympathy into every "feature" of the idea, once you had seen from your size-up that the employer would have many applications all stating similar experiences, and doubtful as to which applicant really was the best man. Or observe the piano letter on the next page and see how the same principle applies to another selling letter. Here a size-up would show that because the piano was neither so high priced nor so widely known as others there would be a natural tendency on the part of high-grade prospects to doubt its claims to quality.

See how that *understanding of reasons for the prospect's doubts* is used to give personality and sincerity to the whole letter— how it gives warmth, not alone to the beginning of the letter, but to each separate point. "You can *pay* more—," "you can secure a piano bearing a more widely advertised name"—such phrases make the letter seem almost like the frank, honest talk of a friend to another. And how much more truthful they make the subsequent paragraph seem. Then again, "But that, perhaps, will exaggerate our claims—," "it is a piano modestly advertised, moderately priced—," *how forcible those assertions make the next one*—"but nobly built!"

BUSINESS CORRESPONDENCE

VERDI PIANO COMPANY
NEW YORK CITY

Mrs. A B. Foster,
Syracuse, New York.

Dear Madam

    The piano that is going to grace your home for a good many years to come--that is going to be the evidence to your friends and visitors of your taste and musical discrimination--that is going to be the pride of your family and have a far-reaching effect on the cultivation of the family's musical ear--the purchase of that piano, we know, must be considered from more ways than the price you pay
    But it must also be considered from more ways than the <u>mere</u> <u>name</u> on the front of it
    You can <u>pay</u> more for a piano than you would pay for a Verdi. You can, by paying a higher price, secure a piano bearing a <u>more widely advertised</u> name But will the fact that you selected for your piano the one with the most advertising back of the name and the biggest figures on the price, necessarily mean that you selected the <u>piano in best taste</u>?
    Not always. The Verdi is essentially the piano of the music lover. Its presence in the home bespeaks the family's genuine taste for <u>music</u> Its full, rich tone, its singing qualities, its truth, go right to the heart of the music lover. Its touch, its response, its splendid ability to rise to the highest demands of the artist, give it an immediate charm to the player.
    But, of course, to the uninitiated the Verdi has not the glamor of reputation
    It is like the difference in tastes for restaurants Here in New York there are many gilded, garish cafes where <u>everyone</u> goes--the out-of-town visitor and the diners who follow the crowd. While the <u>connoisseurs</u>--those who know--turn aside to some side street, to a small dimly lit cafe--they go not for <u>name</u>
but for <u>quality</u>
    But that gives an exaggerated idea of our claims--the Verdi is not the <u>best</u> piano. It is only <u>one</u> <u>of</u> <u>the</u> <u>good pianos</u> It is a piano modestly advertised, moderately priced, but <u>nobly built</u>--a piano for the discriminating but not at all for the showy
    It may be just the piano for your taste--if not now, then later when your musical taste has become more difficult to please If so, you will be disappointed indeed if you permit yourself to be led away from it now
    Why not let us place one in your home for trial? We again extend our liberal offer Consider it—can you afford to judge rashly? Our local dealer is ready--let him send a Verdi to you now.
                        Very truly yours,
                          VERDI PIANO COMPANY

Panel 139

HOW TO CONVEY SINCERITY

On the next page is a letter, the last of a series used by a manufacturer of automobile tops for Ford cars, that glows with the writer's sincerity—because of exactly the same expressed understanding and sympathy with the reader's position. This letter, with just one slight change—instead of enclosing a sheet of paper for reply, merely suggesting that the prospect write his reply on the back of the letter—according to latest reports had been *mailed to 1,973 names and had pulled 723 replies*—36%—and made 181 sales, or about 10% of the total list. That letter also has personality

Before I go any farther let me answer one objection I have heard made, an objection you may make yourself. It is this. Some men believe that they are above the need of what they call "artificial ways of winning confidence." A banker put his objection in this way· "These are tricks—they may be necessary for some people, but they would not be becoming in the letters of a bank. We tell the truth and we expect people to believe it."

That sounds like a valid objection, but as a matter of fact it is not. As I told you once before, the simple truth is not always enough. Sometimes it must be staged. Your reader's believing you is a matter of the conditions the letter must face when it is read.

If you have made an accurate size-up of the letter's work and in that size-up have seen no reason for your reader's doubting, or disliking to believe your claims, or if you don't care whether he doubts or not, then, of course, you need not take the trouble to convey the impression of your sincerity, aside from actually being sincere.

But if your *size-up does show a reason for your reader's being doubtful*, or a chance that he won't want to believe, or if you don't want him to get the impression that you are cold and indifferent to his interests, then if your letter is to do its work properly, you must exercise care in putting the impression of sincerity into it. And that means putting your personality into it—no matter how dignified or how weighty or how just your proposition may seem.

BUSINESS CORRESPONDENCE

FOUTS & HUNTER
TERRE HAUTE, IND.

Mr Henry Eberlein,
Warsaw, Indiana.

Dear Sir

Today your correspondence was laid on my desk. I have before me your original inquiry, and copies of my several letters to you I see that we have sent you our catalog and some of our literature. For some reason, that we don't understand, you have not responded

I want to help you to be fully informed if you plan to buy some sort of a new vehicle before long But it is not my wish to burden you with my letters and our literature, if you are not interested. Will you do me the kindness to write me why you have not sent us your order, or asked for more information?

Does it seem to you that our prices are not attractive? Or is it the terms? Or the description of quality?

Doesn't the Cozy Cab appeal to you as the ideal all-weather buggy?

Are you going to buy some kind of a buggy a little later, but are not quite ready to place the order now? If so, when will you be ready for it?

I am enclosing a sheet of paper and a stamped envelope to make it easy for you to answer these questions, if you will do me this courtesy Please do it before you lay aside this letter. I will be governed by your reply.

       Sincerely yours,
        Sales Manager
        FOUTS & HUNTER

Panel 140

GUNS OF ARGUMENT

Irresistible appeal, "you and I" talk, pleasant personality, qualities which can be acquired when they do not come naturally, are what made the letters in Panels 138, 139 and 140 lure the reader to favorable action In them the guns of attractive argument and effective salesmanship are aimed directly at the reader Behind each letter is the thought "If I show a knowledge and interest in his affairs he will take an interest in mine." So the reader does not get out of the way, but stands and takes the shot It may be selfish, but the nearest subject to me is *me* The ace-high theme with you is *you* Played upon skilfully that theme not only collects today's profits but tomorrow's good will

HOW TO CONVEY SINCERITY

For instance, one can hardly conceive of a more dignified mission than Mr. Elihu Root's journey to Russia at the opening of America's entry into the war, or a more dignified bearer of it than Mr. Root. Yet in his address to the Russian people upon his arrival, knowing the Russians' reasons for doubting his sincerity, and knowing that some of them would not want to believe him at all, he did not deem it unbecoming to his dignity to do exactly what we have seen done in these business letters.

We can analyze his address into a Big Idea and "features," just as clearly as a good letter can be analyzed. Notice my analysis at the top of the next page. Also notice that for each "feature" of the Big Idea the Russians' *attitude or reason for doubting it was sized up, and a point of mutual sympathy established* just as in the letters we have analyzed. If you will read the first paragraph of that part of his oration reproduced on the next page you can see how he handled the first "feature" of his Big Idea:

Now, let us look beneath the surface of the presenting of that "feature." You remember that the Russians had been made doubtful of Mr. Root's sincerity by the charges that the government in America was a capitalistic government.

How did he meet it? Certainly not by stubbornly standing on his dignity and ignoring possible doubts. But, by a sympathetic understanding of the reasons for those doubts—Russia's passion for democracy—he got the Russians' own *greatest interest right with him* by describing the President as chosen at an election in which more than 18,000,000 votes were freely cast and fairly counted, by universal, equal, direct, and secret suffrage. In effect he says, "you doubt the democracy of our government—what do you think of this for democracy?"

Isn't the underlying principle exactly that of the real estate letter on page 262, which meets the owner's doubts of one real estate agent's being better than another, by: "our firm has made a survey of the vacant property in the district where your property lies, and finds so and so"?

BUSINESS CORRESPONDENCE

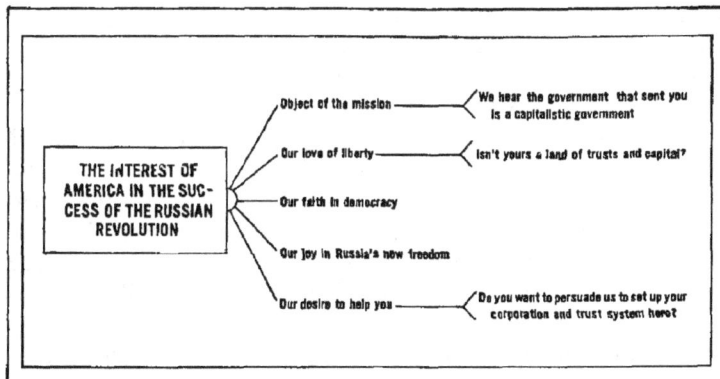

Mr Root's Speech

"The mission for which I have the honor to speak is charged by the Government and people of the United States of America with a message to the Government and people of Russia The mission comes from a democratic republic Its members are commissioned and instructed by a President who holds his high office as Chief Executive of more than 100,000,000 free people by virtue of popular election, in which more than 18,000,000 votes were freely cast, and fairly counted pursuant to law, by universal, equal, direct and secret suffrage

"For 140 years our people have been struggling with the hard problems of self-government With many shortcomings, many mistakes, many imperfections, we still have maintained order and respect for law, individual freedom and national independence Under the security of our own laws we have grown in strength and prosperity But we value our freedom more than wealth We love liberty and we cherish, above all our possessions, the ideals for which our fathers fought and suffered and sacrificed, that America might be free

"We believe in the competence of the power of democracy and in our heart of hearts abides faith in the coming of a better world in which the humble and oppressed of all lands may be lifted up by freedom to a heritage of justice and equal opportunity

"The news of Russia's new-found freedom brought to America universal satisfaction and joy From all the land sympathy and hope went out to the new sister in the circle of democracies And the mission is sent to express that feeling

Danger Threatens Both Nations

"The American democracy sends to the democracy of Russia a greeting of sympathy, friendship, brotherhood, godspeed Distant America knows little of the special conditions of Russian life which must give form to the Government and laws which you are about to create As we have developed our institutions to serve the needs of our national character and life, so, we assume that you will develop your institutions to serve the needs of Russian character and life "

Panel 141

HOW TO CONVEY SINCERITY

Which in effect says, "You think all real estate agents are alike—what do you think of this for efficiency?"

Then consider the next "feature" of Mr. Root's idea—"our love of liberty."

Stories had been told in Russia that America is a land of trust magnates and millionaires, not a land of working people. Do you see how he created a mutual understanding, by practically admitting the great wealth of America, but indicating that it was through democratic laws that our wealth grew? So he continues "feature" by "feature" until he comes to the last "feature," "our desire to help you." See how he anticipated possible hostile criticism of this "feature" and overcame it in the last paragraph I have quoted on the opposite page.

Stop and consider that he was here answering the complaint of certain Russian leaders against the corporations and trust system in American institutions, exactly as the letter on page 249 answered the complaint of a customer against the store's methods. He *used the identical principle in the store letter* when it said sympathetically, "hundreds of women want to take advantage of our bargains, just as you did, and while you are writing your order hundreds of others are doing the same." In short, we see that what was called by all the diplomatic world "*a masterpiece in winning the confidence of a nation,*" is a clear, simple example of the same principle we have now learned for making our business letters win confidence.

By this time I feel sure that every one of you is convinced of the practical value of the principle I have explained and by the same token is anxious to see how it will work out in a letter Well, I've been saving the hardest answer to that Smith request for a loan—remember it in the first chapter?—for just this purpose. I'll show you how to refuse him. Your reason is that you cannot spare the money he asked you to lend him.

Turn again to the chart on page 37, which I drew for that letter in the first chapter. The Big Idea, you will see from that chart, is to make Smith feel your trust in him and

BUSINESS CORRESPONDENCE

your desire to be of service. We learned in the second chapter that the way to select the "features" which convey a Feeling or a Big Idea, is to *review the mental steps* that lead up to them. So we will just imagine that the "features" in the panel below are the basis of your trust in Smith and your desire to serve him:

THE "FEATURES"

Long friendship
Warm appreciation
Respect for his character
Many favors received from him

Panel 142

But we see also from the chart why Smith may not believe in our financial inability to help him—why he may say "It's only an excuse." (Our chart shows that our decision will disappoint him bitterly) So we must *not coldly state the facts*, but must get a mutual understanding of them.

Knowing from our size-up how Smith feels, it would be pretty safe to expect that our first "feature" of "long friendship" will provoke the thought in Smith's mind of "Well, two such old friends ought to help each other out—I'd have done it for you." Wouldn't that be about what we could say he would think? Then our "feature" of "Warm Appreciation" will likely be met with the thought in Smith's mind of "That's how I felt toward you—that's why I came to you for help." And "Respect for his character" will probably provoke a similar thought. "Many favors received" will likely make him think "Why not return them?"

You see that when you have a size-up made, as we have in Smith's case, it is a simple matter to judge of your man's reception of the "features" of your idea. And with the "features" selected and an answer to them anticipated, you

HOW TO CONVEY SINCERITY

can then build up a "You and I" letter—*a "give and take"* argument—a letter of mutual sympathy and understanding, as we have seen done in other letters or by Elihu Root.

I'll write the Smith letter to prove how easily it is done. We have decided on Smith's probable attitude toward our first "feature." To overcome his objections, we'll start the letter by explaining the first "feature" in this way:

```
Dear Smith
        The bitter thing for me in having to write
you this letter is the knowledge that at any time
in the course of our long friendship I would only
have had to ask you and you would have loaned me any
money I needed.  I have always had just that
feeling —
```

See how easy it is to create mutual understanding and sympathy, when you have what you want to say, and what your man thinks about it, right together in your mind!

We have now *struck a responsive chord* in Smith's heart—he says to himself, "That's right."

His thought of "I'd have done it for you" is now *working with the development of our idea, instead of against it.*

Then we come to the second and third "features," and we understand his thought about them, too. So we add.

```
        — that's the appreciation I have felt for your
friendship and the respect I have felt for your
character — and it's what I am glad to think,
from your having written to me now for this money,
that you have felt toward me
```

Again see how deftly the reader's attitude can be worked into your "feature" simply by understanding it. We didn't wait for Smith to say, "That's how I felt—that's why I came to you." We encouraged him to think it and answered him before he could give voice to his idea.

Finally, as we know the next "feature"—"the many favors received from him"—will make Smith think "Why not return them?"—it is simple to write:

```
        You have done me so many favors that I'd gladly
lend you the very clothes off my back, if I could.
But the fact is, that as things are with me, I
could spare the clothes off my back just about as
handily as I could spare $100 just now.
```

BUSINESS CORRESPONDENCE

SHERWOOD, EDWARDS COMPANY
NEW YORK CITY

H. R. Fraser,
Joliet, Illinois.

Dear Sir.

    I have tried to convince myself in every way possible that it would be right for me to pass for shipment your recent order given to our Mr. Morinski, but I simply can't do it until you have been able to reduce your present open account.

    I know you will be disappointed, but I do not want you to feel at all hurt It is not a question of confidence in you — our past relations show that. But it is simply not discreet in the present trade conditions to carry an open account of more than $3,000 for a store doing your volume. I have been strongly tempted to do it because of my great respect for you personally, but my better judgment tells me it would do neither of us any good

    As none of your April invoices will be due for some weeks, I suggest that you send us a 30-day note for their total, $1,127 32, which will permit us to fill the present order at once.

    You may feel that we are being too stiff over this matter — but if you will think it over I believe you will see that what is a safe credit for us to give is a safe credit for you to take and anything over that is a bad indebtedness for you to assume in the present state of the market.

    Trusting to hear favorably from you as to the notes for April invoices, I remain,

                              Yours faithfully,
                                 Credit Department

HOW TO CONVEY SINCERITY

We have now conveyed our idea of our trust and our desire to help, and have done it in a way that makes it sound sincere. Read the various "features" through consecutively now and see if we haven't paved the way for Smith's believing our reasons for not sparing the money, whatever they might be.

The personality of the letter is, of course, that of one intimate friend to another, but you can probably put the *same sentiment in any other letter*, if you have sized up conditions carefully and have your idea clearly in mind.

Others have done it and what others have done you can do. Here's proof. On the opposite page is a letter dictated by a credit manager to cover conditions a great deal like those in the imaginary case of Smith. In this letter, however, *the writer's personality had to be that of a broad, firm business man.* It brought back the settlement desired, with a letter from the customer beginning, "In reply to your very frank letter, I enclose—."

Why did that letter impress the merchant with its frankness? Why, for the reason that your letter to Smith would impress him with your frankness. If you have the slightest doubts, diagram the "features" of the Big Idea of that letter, then make a table of them and their effects on the reader, and you will see the same principle of mutual understanding.

See how the personal tone—the ring of sincerity—in the garage man's letter on the next page can be traced out by the same kind of table. You'll find one below his letter. I could show you others, but I'm sure you now agree that you'll find the same principle in all of them

And *getting that principle down on paper is not "a trick"* as the banker said. It is simply applying to letters the law which we saw governs the pleasantness of relationship and degrees of trust between friends. There is only one slight difference. In personal relationship the mutual sympathy is developed unconsciously from the natural trend of conversation, and in a letter we can't hear the reader's opinions from his lips

BUSINESS CORRESPONDENCE

WAYNE SUPPLY COMPANY
BENTON HARBOR, MICH.

Charles Hickey
Stevensville
Michigan

Dear Sir

     Try to get in to see me in the next day or two   I have a new tire that I want to show you

     It is one the Goodyear people have put on the market and is an ideal tire for big luxurious cars

     IT IS THE GOODYEAR FORTIFIED TIRE WITH HEAVY DOUBLE THICK ALL-WEATHER TREAD

     The extra large blocks wear for thousands of miles, and when they finally do wear down, there is still the thickness of a plain tread beneath   They will give you the kind of mileage you are entitled to

     On your car these tires will show up in fine style They are in perfect harmony with the car's finish   The big, sharp edged, deep cut blocks accentuate the clean cut lines of your chassis   They fairly "breathe" distinction and dignity

     You can get them from me without delay   I have Goodyear Tires in all sizes   Come in and see them, that's all I ask

                    Sincerely,

                    WAYNE SUPPLY COMPANY

    P S — Note these tires on large cars   There's a reason

A new tire	I don't need tires now
Goodyear Fortified -- heavy, all weather tread	How does that interest me?
The extra large blocks wear for thousands of miles, and then there is still the plain tread	Will they pay me?
Their appearance	Would they improve my car?

Panel 144

HOW TO CONVEY SINCERITY

or see them in his actions, so we must estimate them in advance, and *deliberately plan on the development of mutual sympathy*.

Although this sounds formidable, we have seen how simple it can be made by means of the size-up chart on which our letter's work is planned. In almost every letter you write you can use that method to help make your letter more personal, more human, more confidence-winning.

The personality may be that of a dignified institution—like that expressed in the bank's letter in the panel below. Or it

---

OLD HARBOR STATE BANK
OLD HARBOR, MAINE

R. T. Sawyer,
Old Harbor, Maine.

Dear Sir:

Perhaps it is because we know more about you than you know about us, that we have written you so many times without a response.

A bank must choose its customers with almost as much care as a business man must choose his bank. We have taken the pains to satisfy ourselves thoroughly as to the desirability of YOUR account to US, so possibly we have the advantage of you.

But Old Harbor has many business houses that can tell you of the character of service this bank renders — the real help and the practical service it extends to its customers. Why not talk with some of your friends who do business here? Ask them about us. Put us to as severe a test as we have put YOU. We are anxious to abide by the results

Sincerely yours,

OLD HARBOR STATE BANK

Panel 145

BUSINESS CORRESPONDENCE

HARTFORD INSURANCE CO.
HARTFORD, CONNECTICUT

Ronald Thompson,
Milwaukee, Wisconsin.

Dear Sir:

Did you ever — as a kid — sneak up alongside an old mill pond and heave what Penrod Schofield might call a "good ol' rock" far out into the middle of its placid surface — just for the fun of seeing all the mud turtles on all their sunny logs drop off into the water with one loud individual PLUNK!

If the humble mud turtle formed no part of the backyard fauna of your youth, we reckon there was something mighty similar to engage your budding talents Just as you find now, in your grown-up days that the pursuit of your business aims often involve the same emotions that lent interest to your activities in the eyes of your early neighbors.

For example, we want to point out to you a few of the prospects that are basking along the banks of the Hartford mill pond — prospects that are waiting only for you to heave in the good ol' rock before they slide off into the pond and leave your pockets bulging with commissions.

It's vacation time, and there's just as much certainty of your winning HARTFORD ACCIDENT COMMISSIONS among the men about to leave home, as there was of the turtles rolling off their logs when you punctured their placidity with a cobblestone.

It's easy to learn who is going away. The man who sells fishing tackle and golf balls, the man who sells trunks and bags, the man who puts touring cars in a touring condition, the tourist agent and a score of others, can help put you wise as you go quietly mouching about They are leaving home — the place that stands for safety and security in their minds — they are panting for accident policies

So put a bunch of Hartford application blanks in your pocket Bildad, and go straight to every man you know who can tell you who is going on a vacation Then see every prospect who is about to leave town — in short, drop in your rock, and if some of them don't slide off their logs with a noise like a Hartford commission — why then I'm a mud turtle myself.

Yours truly,
HARTFORD INSURANCE CO

Panel 146

HOW TO CONVEY SINCERITY

may be that of a hearty "good fellow" sort of man—like that on page 280. The spirit of each of them can be analyzed by exactly the same method, and a spirit similar to that in any of them can be created by the same process of tabulating the "features" and the reader's attitude toward each.

The process itself automatically develops the style of personality to be expressed.

The knack of doing this can easily be cultivated. It will be a matter of pure labor at first. But as you keep doing it—persisting in it for each letter until you have it complete—doing it over and over again until you have it right—all at once you will be surprised to find that you do it almost without conscious effort. And then from having to use pencil and paper every time you write, you will suddenly find that as you dictate rapidly to a stenographer or to a dictating machine, your thoughts will shape themselves automatically along the personal line.

Then your letters will leap the level of commonplace and take on a tone of personality, individuality, and above all, sincerity.

SUMMARY

WE have learned in this chapter that the sincerity of letters is not a moral attribute at all. A man may be ever so sincere and not be believed, and another be entirely false and still attract followers by the score. In short, sincerity in a letter is not so much a matter of the writer's thoughts and feelings as it is of the reader's. Aside from being sincere which, of course, is taken for granted, sincerity depends upon a writer's ability to call up corresponding thoughts in his reader.

Analyzing to find the method of impressing the reader with the genuineness of our beliefs, we found that the source of the impression of friendliness and sincerity that some people give us lies in their ability to understand, to appreciate, to sympathize with other people's problems. We turned this thought to good account and, in letters which we wrote or studied, established or found "cogs" of mutual contact. These "cogs" in a letter arouse in readers' minds the emotions a writer feels as he writes or dictates his letter.

In discussing these "cogs" we established another important truth, namely, that a letter which is all "you" or all 'I" cannot create the necessary personal touch between reader and writer. The "you and I" spirit is needed. The best way to get it is to look over the "features" of the Big Idea in a letter and link each one up to the probable thought that it will arouse in a reader's mind. In other words, if we understand how to impress our sincerity on a reader, the "you" element in a letter will generally take care of itself.

In the next part we shall have another bit of human nature to study. We are to consider the question of exercising persuasion, and that, we shall find, will lead us into a study of human motives What these motives are, what forms they take, how they may be appealed to by the letter writer, are all taken up in great detail.

PROBLEM SECTION V

WELL, in the last problem section you, as a restaurant owner, and I, as your letter expert, built up paragraphs of a letter which we figured would make our prospects' mouths water. Recall that we worked over the sales possibilities of Anna's lemon pie, that pie which we said seemed "a little gushing fountain in your mouth just deluging your palate with delightful tastes." In roughing out that letter we learned that the methods which we decided to adopt were the same as those used successfully in well-known advertising campaigns. And we learned how to apply the principles of the pie letter to any other letter we are called upon to write. In this problem section I'll show you how to inject personality and sincerity into the pie letter and in the letters you have to write as part of your daily routine.

Before I take up that fascinating topic, however, I'll run over the two problems I set for you in the last problem section. The first dealt with the conditions which faced a baby carriage manufacturer. Reach for your Material File and take the baby carriage letter you wrote for me. Lay the letter itself face down until I tell you to refer to it, and, turning back to page 238, refresh your mind on the problem so that you will have its points well in mind as you read.

The "features" on which the letter should be built (the bottom plate on which other plates should be stacked) is, I believe, the one at the bottom of the list—the importance of selecting the right kind of a carriage. My reason is that the importance of everything pertaining to her young baby is a thought uppermost in every mother's mind and so it is easy to bring the carriage into her mind through this channel.

BUSINESS CORRESPONDENCE

When you have the mother thinking of the importance of baby's carriage, the "feature" of your own pride in the "making of good baby carriages" stacks on it. That "feature" leads easily to the third, "twenty years' experience." From that, you progress naturally through the "feature" of selling direct to the final "feature," "wide variety of styles offered."

Now then, how close did you come to this order of stacking "features"? Turn over the letter you wrote and see. If you hit my explanation fairly closely, turn to page 252 and read the letter you find there. Compare it with your own for words and general style of expression. But if you did not get the order of "features" I have indicated, I suggest that you rewrite your letter according to these new directions before passing from this problem. After you are finished with it, return your letter to your file.

The second problem was a novel one. You were to select the order of "features" for Mr. Elihu Root's address to the Russians. You'll find the part of his address I promised you on page 272. Turn to it and make your comparisons as before.

And now, if you will go back to the first draft of the restaurant letter on page 237, we'll try applying to it what we have just learned about personality and sincerity.

The first "feature," the one that opens the letter, is the delightful sensation of Anna's lemon pie on the palate. In the preceding chapter you will recall, we are warned that the first precaution in writing a letter is to anticipate the reader's possible attitude to and his reception of your "features." Hence, as you run over in your mind the possible attitude of the reader of this letter don't you think he would be likely to say to himself, "What's that got to do with me? What do I care about Anna and her lemon pie?" It strikes me that way.

Now the letter, as it is written, opens with a statement which any reader is almost sure to doubt or contradict. Imagine a busy man opening his morning mail and being greeted with the defiant statement, "What a pleasure to top off a good luncheon with a piece of Anna's lemon pie." He's

HOW TO CONVEY SINCERITY

not interested in lemon pie and certainly not seeking advice on the subject

In the last chapter, however, we were taught that a good letter should have a give and take element in it. If it challenges, it should complete the job and answer the question it arouses. Revision of that first line is necessary, but in revising we'll keep the thought of the original statement and supply the answer. In short we'll tell the reader what Anna's lemon pie has to do with him. Like this:

> If you'd drop in here for lunch some noon I'll bet you'd say you <u>never</u> <u>ate</u> <u>anything</u> <u>better</u> in your life than your first piece of Anna's lemon pie!

By the change, you see, a mutual interest has been awakened. Instead of a cold, impersonal exclamation about that lemon pie, as before, we now have a challenge, a two-party opening to the letter, one in which both the reader and the writer are concerned.

Quickly, before the interest that any one feels on receiving a challenge can turn to resentment, we'll show our sincerity in making the statement. The second paragraph offers the opportunity and so we'll open it like this.

> My, what lemon pies that woman can bake!

and before he can challenge that statement we'll make him feel a warm, human relation to Anna's pie by making him think of no one eating it but himself. The second paragraph of the original letter supplies the idea, therefore we'll add it unchanged to the opening sentence. The revised paragraph will then read like this:

> Why, man, when you close your lips and tongue on a piece of that pie it's like a little gushing fountain in your mouth just deluging your palate with delightful tastes.

Compare that with the original letter as far as we've gone and see how much personality we are getting into our idea.

Next we come to the "feature" of meringue. That, we decided, was second in importance. What is the reader going to think about meringue? Isn't it likely to be something like,

BUSINESS CORRESPONDENCE

"Yes, same old sugary concoction"? So we'll just let him think it, and revise the third paragraph to answer him like this:

> First the frosting — not that sugary sort of meringue you're thinking of, but <u>frosting</u> — of cool, snowy, vaporous sweetness "

Now we've got him coming our way. Let's hold him by continuing the process with the other "features" of our letter. The third "feature," "the tart lemon flavor," if left unchanged, is almost sure to remind him at first of sour lemons, and turn him from the letter. So we'll change our first draft to answer the objection like this:

> Then quick the refreshing lemony — not sourness, mind you, that's too strong a word — but rather a wild, pleasing tartness

Do you see how easily our letter is becoming like a conversation—in which each has his own say? The next "feature" in our original draft was the blending and melting of the combined tastes. It's pretty good as it stands and so without change we'll add it to the letter:

> Then sweetness and tartness are crushed in together, and Pouf! they join and blend in an entirely new taste that gradually melts away, somewhere down your throat and only a soft, happy memory remains — until your next mouthful.

A reader is pretty likely to wonder, "How can this pie be so different? Is it true?" We'll anticipate such a thought by adding an answer like this:

> Yes, Anna certainly has a knack about lemon pies that's all her own

Of course, all this is interpreting the reader's attitude according to my own judgment and, therefore, I am suggesting the allusions that fit my own views of the case. You understand, I am sure, that my method of solving the problem is *not* the only method of getting the results we are after. There are, actually, dozens of ways of leading the reader on. If you should interpret the reader's attitude to Anna's pie, in

HOW TO CONVEY SINCERITY

a different way, and if your attitude typifies a natural, human feeling and you really answer it, you will get an equally good effect.

For instance, in regard to the "feature" of combined tartness and sweetness you might have thought the reader's attitude would be "Oh, I don't believe it—it's bunk!" In such a case it would be entirely proper to answer in some such way as this: "Wait until you taste your first piece and you will see!"

This new sentence accomplishes the same purpose as mine, only in a different way. Substitute it for "Yes, Anna certainly has a knack about lemon pies that's all her own." You will find it sounds just as personal and sincere as the sentence I wrote.

In brief, the big point I am driving at is that to make your letter sincere you must get the viewpoint of the reader. When you do that it is easy to shape the points of interest to his viewpoint.

Bear what I have said in mind as we work over the last "feature" in the letter. As we consider the "feature" of the flaky crust, we can guess that the average man thinks of pie crust as being of one of two kinds—the crisp, flaky kind and the tough, heavy kind. As we rewrite our original draft of the "feature" it is easy to show this sympathetic knowledge of such a belief. This is one way:

> Then the crust — I must call it crust, I suppose, as if it were like other pie crust — it's crisp, of course, like good pie crust should be, it's flaky — but Anna's crust, when you put it into your mouth seems to have only been making believe to be crust after all. For where is it? It crumbles and flakes away and gives itself up to the rest of the pie like a sacrifice — to help make one grand, complete taste of paradise for you

That's all I'll do with this letter at present. I feel that I don't need to explain the few changes made in the expression of the positive idea. Read the revised draft of the letter at the top of the next page and you can easily see what a marked effect our simple work in this section has had.

BUSINESS CORRESPONDENCE

Dear Sir

    If you'd drop in here for lunch some noon, I'll bet you'd say you never ate anything better in your life than your first piece of Anna's lemon pie

    My, what lemon pies that woman can bake! Why, man, when you close your lips and tongue on a piece of that pie it's like a little gushing fountain in your mouth just deluging your palate with delightful tastes

    First the frosting — not that sugary sort of meringue you're thinking of, but frosting — of cool, snowy, vaporous sweetness. Then quick the refreshing lemony — not sourness, mind you that's too strong a word — but rather a wild, pleasing tartness. Then sweetness and tartness are crushed in together and Pouf! they join and blend in an entirely new taste that gradually melts away somewhere down your throat and only a soft, happy memory remains — until your next mouthful.

    Yes, Anna certainly has a knack about lemon pies that's all her own.

    Then the crust — I must call it crust, I suppose, as if it were like other pie crust — it's crisp of course, as good pie crust should be, it's flaky — but Anna's crust, when you put it into your mouth seems to have only been making believe to be crust after all.

    For where is it? It crumbles and flakes away and gives itself up to the rest of the pie like a sacrifice — to help make one grand, complete taste of paradise for you.

    Yes, sir — I would like to see you tasting your first piece of that pie! By George! I'll pay for it myself if you'll come in today — have your luncheon and top off with a piece of Anna's lemon pie — then simply hand in the enclosed coupon with your lunch check as payment for the dessert

PROBLEM 1

As you have learned how easy it is to put personality and sincerity into that pie letter, try the plan for yourself. Suppose you made apple cider and wanted to sell it to a lot of city people. Suppose your Big Idea was "There couldn't be a finer drink than our apple cider"—and that its "features" were about as follows:

The taste of good old apple cider

Our cider is even better than the old-fashioned kind

HOW TO CONVEY SINCERITY

We wash the apples and sort out the rotten ones

Bottled by a process that will keep it without getting hard for two years

Non-alcoholic—can be enjoyed by ladies and children

Fine for weak stomachs.

Tabulate your reader's attitude towards each of those features, then write them in a way to establish a personal sympathy with his thoughts. In the next chapter you will find such a letter, and a very successful one, too, with which to compare the results of your own efforts.

Problem 2

For the second problem, suppose you had a collection letter to write to a customer who had had two notes fall due and both were still at his bank unpaid, while he had written you no explanation. Suppose the idea you wish to convey is "the injury he is doing himself by such neglect" and the "features" are:

Two notes remain unpaid without explanation

We must either take legal steps or have a reason for not doing so

Leaving us without explanation prevents us from helping you.

You want the debtor to believe in your idea—how would you establish the personal feeling between him and you, that would make him believe you? In the next chapter you will find a letter that has done it many times.

File your work on these two problems in your Material File and we will discuss them in the next problem section.

PART VI

HOW TO MAKE YOUR LETTER PERSUASIVE

CHAPTER VI

HOW TO MAKE YOUR LETTER PERSUASIVE

AS we have learned in previous chapters how to convey ideas in our letters, how to inspire interest in the ideas conveyed, how to make the expression of those ideas clear and easy to understand, and how to put the ring of personal sincerity into them, it is time to learn to put into them the knack of exercising persuasion.

What is persuasion? To understand my definition, consider the automobile. It can be made to go in one of two ways. It can be propelled by an outside force or it can be moved by starting the engine and gearing it to the wheels. Utilizing the motive power of the car is, of course, the more pleasant and more efficient method. Now, the average man is somewhat like an automobile. he can be moved to action by outside force or he can be *moved to action by starting a motive power within him*. The latter method is exercising persuasion.

Certainly this method is by far the more satisfactory and efficient method of influencing people When you know how to use it, you have at your command one of the most powerful assets, either for business or for social success, that exists in the world of human affairs But nowhere is its use so full of possibilities as in the printed or written words of business. business letters or business advertisements.

In buying an automobile, first you have a look at the engine. You study it to learn how it makes the car move. In *learning to influence people*, you can hardly do less; therefore, let us study a bit the motives which prompt human actions Behind every voluntary action lies a motive You won't find such a law taught in academic books on psychology, but you will find it taught by every practical experience of

BUSINESS CORRESPONDENCE

NEW IDEA HOSIERY
HOBOKEN, N J

Mr. Herbert Watson,
New York City

Dear Sir:
    I am indebted to Mr J M Edmunds for your name.

He has formed the New Idea Sock habit, and being of a rather generous nature, wishes to pass on a good thing to you

    Under separate cover I am sending you a catalog describing the various styles we manufacture

    A dollar bill attached to this letter, with the outline of your foot, or the size of the hosiery you wear, will bring you two sample pairs, any weight, which will tell their own story.

    May I be favored with your reply?

              Very truly yours,

                    NEW IDEA HOSIERY

Panel 147

A SIEVE FOR THE MAILING LIST

In the letter above comparatively few propositions can be sold   It's enough to stimulate the prospect's interest and get him to reply   Letters like the one illustrated above and the one on page 295 are first letters   They are sent broadcast to find the people who are interested, or who can be interested in the proposition they put forth. A reply shows that the sender of it is worth, at least, the expense of a follow up series   But compare the two letters and you will see clearly why the one in the panel above failed   To get a reply, a motive for replying must be presented   In this first letter where is it? In the second one, however, any man engaged in stock raising has, handed him, a real motive which appears in the phase of bettering his stock   There's more about motives in the text   At this time bear in mind that inquiry letters are really the sieve for your mailing list   To find whether your sieve is right, read your inquiry letter from the standpoint of the man who is to receive it   Ask yourself if you would answer it. Test it for a reason, an inducement

MAKING YOUR LETTER PERSUASIVE

FIELD STOCK FOOD COMPANY
MINNEAPOLIS, MINNESOTA

H. D. Horton,
Antigo, Wis.

Dear Sir:

    At the request of a neighbor of yours we are sending you a book. You will notice on page 2 there is a valuable coupon that will entitle you to a free prescription and letter of advice from our Dr. Smith on any matter relating to your sick or injured animals. All that is necessary is that you enclose a 3-cent stamp for reply.

    From pages 3 to 8, inclusive, there is a discussion of how our present modern feeding methods do violence to nature, why heavily fed animals need a tonic. Dr. Smith has supplied, in his Tonic, ingredients that promote digestion, by acting on the liver, the kidneys, the bowels, ingredients that expel worms.

    Then on the bottom of page 8, how it is sold on a guarantee.

    From pages 9 to 21, inclusive, we tell how to feed Dr Smith's Stock Tonic. On pages 22 to 29, inclusive, Dr Smith discusses some of the most common ailments of stock and their treatment.

    On page 30 we give you the formula for Dr Smith's Stock Tonic and what authorities have to say about these ingredients.

    Finally, on the last page is our written guarantee.

    We believe that you will find this book of considerable value.

    We shall be pleased to receive your order for any quantity of Dr. Smith's Stock Tonic or any of our other preparations, remembering that every article bearing the name of Dr. Smith is sold subject to our written guarantee.

                  Yours very truly,
                    FIELD STOCK FOOD CO.

Panel 148

BUSINESS CORRESPONDENCE

business. Of course, there are times when you say, "I had no motive in doing so and so," but that is purely a form of speech. I am sure that you usually mean that you had no *conscious* motive. But a motive you had and have every time you so much as raise your hand, though it may be only instinctive, or subconscious. *A motive your prospect must have* or he won't send you an order for your goods, clip and mail a coupon for your catalog, ask his dealer for your brand, specify your line in his contracts, or come to your store to trade.

A *motive* your debtor must have or he won't send a remittance for your bill. A *motive* your customer must have or he won't disclose the confidential credit information you want. A *motive* your dealers must have or they won't push your goods A *motive* there must be in each person from whom you want an action of any kind, before that person will be willing to do what you want him to do.

And the whole secret of persuasion, as distinguished from brute force, is to *arouse the motive* that will prompt the action you desire, and set it to working for you in the reader's or listener's mind. This is the mission of your letter, if your letter is to persuade someone to do something he has not intended to do, just as to start his engine is the automobile driver's work, if he is to make his car move.

Now some of you may be confused by *the difference between motives and ideas.* To understand, bear in mind that "motive," as I use the word, is a reason for acting which you create in the reader's mind. On the other hand, an "idea" is a statement of fact which may or may not arouse a motive in a reader's mind. For example: in Panel 147 on page 294, is a letter (its identity disguised), used by a certain manufacturer. Its purpose is to get the reader to watch for and to study the manufacturer's catalog, the catalog being the real sales literature in this case. To try out a notion I had about it, I had the names of 40 men put on the manufacturer's list and had the letter sent to them. Later on I found that although they had received the letter, only one of them had been persuaded by it to save the catalog from the waste-

MAKING YOUR LETTER PERSUASIVE

basket and to study it. Yet each man was a good type of potential customer for that particular article.

In just a minute I'll tell you why that letter failed. You'll get my point better, however, if you'll turn your attention to page 295. There is a letter with almost the same purpose, but a similar test on a list of live stock owners showed that the *letter secured attention for the catalog* from *28 out of 32 names.* (The number of orders was not investigated, as that was the catalog's work.)

Now I should say, off hand, that the letter on page 294 is a better piece of English composition than the letter on page 295. But good composition does not always make a good letter.

Let's see what was lacking in the hosiery manufacturer's letter. We can all see quickly that there is no Big Idea conveyed by it. We learn merely that a friend of mine has formed a habit and has had data on the habit sent to me—that's as much of an idea as this letter conveys. As a matter of fact, the friend who supplied my name to the manufacturer had not only formed the habit of wearing this manufacturer's socks, but also his feet had been helped by them. The letter, however, does not convey that idea.

Since you already know how to get a Big Idea into a letter, the fact that the letter lacks one deserves no more than passing comment. What interests us now is the fact that the letter does not arouse a real motive for bothering about the catalog. We find a lot of ideas and that is all. I might have been told that my friend had formed the opium habit, but that would arouse no motive for studying facts about opium. But if, in addition to being told that he had formed the opium habit, I were made to believe that the habit was killing him, and that I might save him by studying the facts about opium, then a motive would be aroused, *a motive that prompts so many human acts—'ove of a friend or family.*

Do you think the Love Motive does not enter into the realm of cold, practical business? Observe the successful letter of an insurance agent shown on the next page and see that it does. That letter not only conveys a Big Idea about

BUSINESS CORRESPONDENCE

JAMES B. THORSEN
Insurance Counselor

Mr. D. A. Stanley,
Chicago, Ill.

Dear Mr. Stanley:

    I have a seasonable suggestion for you. It is this — a Life Insurance Policy to provide
A CHRISTMAS ANNUITY
for your wife, daughter, or someone you wish to safeguard; a Christmas gift that will come after you, every year for many years; a reminder of your wise discrimination and loving foresight.

    Such a policy to provide an Annuity of, say $1,000 a year, payable to your beneficiary every Christmas, will cost from $250 to $500 a year; larger or smaller amounts in proportion.

    If it appeals to you at all, let me show you how simple it all is; how big the satisfaction; how small the cost.

                  Yours very sincerely,
                            JAMES B THORSEN

Panel 149

A HUMAN NOTE

How human are you? Do you analyze yourself when you have a letter to write? Have you learned to look into your own heart, choose from among the emotions you find there and put them down on paper so that your letter sounds the human note? The human appeal may be made in many different ways but in a no simpler way than by touching one of the six prime motives described in this chapter and listed on page 306   The letter above and the one on the opposite page are two successful letters which drew on account of their humanness   In each is to be found a powerful appeal to motive   In Panel 149 the drive was made on the Love Motive. In Panel 150 you can easily detect the strong play on the Gain Motive   To write human letters is not easy   For some of us long practise is required   But this truth will always hold   Make the prospect see in your letter the direct relation to himself or his business   Put a motive in every letter that seeks to persuade

MAKING YOUR LETTER PERSUASIVE

CLEVELAND & CO.
Philadelphia, Pa.

T. A. Lardner,
Philadelphia, Pa.

Dear Sir:

When the Dominion of Canada unconditionally guarantees both interest and principal; you can be reasonably sure that the obligation will be met.

Any note or bond that is secured by such a guarantee may be considered safe.

The CANADIAN NORTHERN RAILWAY is about to issue a one-year note that will be amply secured by collateral carrying the Dominion of Canada's unconditional guarantee.

We do not know, at this writing, just what these notes will yield, but we expect them to be on a better than 6% basis.

If these notes do yield over 6% interest, you will be making an excellent investment by placing your order for some of them.

We shall send you full particulars as soon as they are out and in the meantime shall be glad to enter your order, subject to the above description and interest rate You can purchase these either outright or on our investment savings plan, whichever is most convenient to you.

Very truly yours,

CLEVELAND & CO.

Panel 150

life insurance, but it also persuades prospects to investigate, by arousing the world-old motive of love

Again, suppose I were given the idea that our friend had formed a habit of buying certain supplies at a certain store, and then I were made to think that he was saving money by it or was getting better goods and that I could do the same. That would be arousing a real motive for investigating—the Gain Motive See, on page 299, how a financial house arouses this powerful motive by *a letter which gets one to wait for and to study a follow-up announcement.*

Do you begin to see the difference between mere ideas or interest or desire, and a real motive? Do you begin to see why the hosiery manufacturer's introduction—the interest of a friend—although a very good introduction, was *not* the motive to persuade readers to trouble about his catalog?

Referring again to the letter on page 295, we see that the writer of it apparently did not value the fact that the prospects' names were supplied by a friend except as an introduction. But he did put a value on the arousing of a genuine, human motive—in this case the preservation and protection of the reader's live stock. Constantly in that letter you see brought up the thought of protecting and benefiting your stock—the *motive for studying the catalog.* In the first paragraph you see this motive aroused by the suggestion that the catalog may afford an opportunity to help one of your sick or injured animals; in the second paragraph you see it aroused again by the thought that the catalog may show you how to save a sick animal.

"Self-preservation," an old proverb says, "is the first law of Nature"—and self-preservation includes the preservation and protection of one's property, one's interests, and one's opportunities. So this manufacturer persuades prospects to read his catalog by *arousing the Self-Preservation Motive.*

You see, not even the newest and most intricate development of business—advertising and letter writing—can get away from the world-old verities of human life. In the three practical business letters that we have just observed, we see

MAKING YOUR LETTER PERSUASIVE

LYON & HEALY
Chicago, Ill.

Dear Sir:

In making the customary examination of our books July 1, your account showed a balance of $34.61, part of which, at least, is past due and entitled to adjustment.

An early remittance would be greatly appreciated, and while it is always our aim to be as agreeable and lenient as possible with our customers, we are obliged to observe certain rules regarding settlements. A laxity in this respect would make it very difficult for us to give our patrons the Lyon & Healy service we are so justly proud of, and which, in fact, can only be maintained by keeping the transactions between our customers, our creditors, and ourselves on a proper financial basis

If in your mind there is any reason why the account above mentioned should not be liquidated, we wish that you would write us promptly, giving full details so that we can govern ourselves accordingly. On the other hand, if the amount specified is correct, your cooperation in the form of a remittance to reach us within the next few days will be gratefully accepted.

With thanks for past favors, and awaiting your further commands, we remain,

Yours very truly,

LYON & HEALY

Panel 151

BUSINESS CORRESPONDENCE

the primitive motive of self-preservation being employed in one; love being employed in another, and gain in another.

And on page 301 we may read an appeal to still another motive. Read the letter, the fifth of a collection series used by a Chicago house which conducts a huge credit business with a surprisingly small percentage of losses That letter has persuaded many honest but slow pay customers to act with dispatch in settling their overdue bills because it arouses the primitive, human, Duty Motive. In

---

ROGERS PEET COMPANY
New York City

Mr. Kendall Banning,
New York City.

Dear Sir:

    We want to be neighborly, so have opened a charge account for your convenience at our 34th Street store

    The enclosed card of introduction to Mr. Magill, manager of the 34th Street Store, will not only identify you, but will assure you of the friendliest welcome.

    We should add, however, that all four of our stores are at your service and that your account is available at any one of them.

                    Respectfully,

                    ROGERS PEET COMPANY

Panel 152

SAY TO YOURSELF

Say to yourself before you write or dictate, "I am going into this man's office He does not know me and does not know that I am coming This is my one big chance to make good I must try hard to concentrate my talk I must make him understand. I must give reasons Above all, I must supply a motive for acting" In the letters illustrated in Panels 151, 152 and 153 the writers visualized their prospects in that way These are form letters and yet they smack of individuality Note the stress on motives In Panel 151 the appeal is to the Duty Motive, in Panel 152 to the Pride Motive and in Panel 153 to the Pleasure Motive

MAKING YOUR LETTER PERSUASIVE

Panel 152 is the short, terse letter of a New York store that stirred many a man to bring his trade to that store because it arouses the old, old Pride Motive—pride in the tribute paid to the reader's standing and to his credit. Also, on page 304, we see the very successful letter of a western business-farmer which, mailed to a list of 2,000 prospects, persuaded 250 of them to order, because of its appeal to the Pleasure Motive.

In short we find that *to make readers act we must supply a Motive*. We can convey to a man the *idea* that our machine will save him money, that our tailoring will improve his appearance; that our tobacco will taste good; that our bill is past due, that we will make good a defect in his purchase, if he will send it back and give us a chance. But if he is to act our way, he must either have, or we must arouse in him, a *motive for acting*, or he won't buy even what he believes in or desires, or he won't even send a check which he knows is due.

Now here is a point which you may have picked up as you read the preceding pages. The motives which make people act are as definite and limited as the number of fingers on your hand. You may lose some, but you will never have more. They may take various forms, but fundamentally their nature is unchanging.

Look at the matter this way. we can create new ideas. We can create new wants. We can create new methods of buying We can create new plans for collecting. But the motives that persuade people to act on our ideas, fill the wants we create, order by the method we originate, or pay on the plan we devise, are limited and as old as humanity.

If you haven't given this thought your attention before, prove it for yourself some day by this simple but interesting test. Analyze any letter that has really persuaded people to perform some act they had not already planned to perform, analyze any political speech that has persuaded people to change their votes, analyze any sales talk that has persuaded prospects to order what they hadn't expected to order; analyze any sermon or book or tract or play that has worked a reform—and you will find it has accomplished its end by

BUSINESS CORRESPONDENCE

ORCHARD FARM HOME
SOUTH HAVEN, MICH.

Mr. H. K. Wilson,
Racine, Wis.
Dear Sir

    DO YOU REMEMBER

    Your boyhood days, and how, armed with a long straw, you lay on your stomach and sucked your fill of good old apple cider as it trickled from the press?
Good, wasn't it?

    "Shucks, no such cider nowadays," you say

    You're wrong!

    Granddad never did press such cider as Frank Pyle's Apple Juice. He didn't wash the apples--I do. He didn't sort out the rotten ones. I do

    Do I hear you say "Maybe you do, but no chance for my getting a glass of it before it's hard as a rock"

    Wrong again!

    When those clean, sound, rosy-cheeked apples go "squash" and the juice comes a rushing, I get busy and bottle it before there is a chance to start fermenting. I have figured out a way to make it keep just so (without using chemicals in the process) till year after next, if you can hold off of it that long

    Friend wife can draw it on the W. C T U or the club ladies on her "at home" afternoons and make them say nice things

    The kiddies will naturally mob the cook for it, with ginger bread and doughnuts. It will give them the apples' rosy cheeks

    Your stomach is not as good as it was in the old days--you have to favor it these times Forgot that old saw, "An apple a day keeps the doctor away," didn't you? Well, Frank Pyle's Apple Juice is the "cream of the apples," so just make a glass a day your rule and throw away the pills and ills

    Better have a shipment on the way Write how much on the enclosed order blank, slip it into the addressed envelope with check, cash or stamps for the proper amount. Mail it right now

              Yours truly,
              ORCHARD FARM HOME

Panel 153

MAKING YOUR LETTER PERSUASIVE

arousing some form of one of the *six prime motives of human action* which I have listed for you in Panel 154 on the next page.

More often than not in business these motives are given either simpler or more complex classifications, or different names In psychology they are called "instincts." But, looked at in a broad way, the classification we have shown will *cover sufficient'y for practica' use, the motive for every human action*. You will find that much of the secret of persuasion lies in sufficiently arousing the one that will prompt the action you desire.

For example, on page 307 is the follow-up letter of a local sales agent, on the inquiries turned over to him by his home office. It employs the Satisfaction of Curiosity Motive (a form of the Self-Indulgence Motive) with considerable success. And on page 308 is a similar letter used by the same insurance agent who wrote the letter shown on page 298.

In both cases the Curiosity Motive was aroused—curiosity in one case to know the rather mysterious "matter in which you are interested," and in the other to know which really are the six best insurance companies. In both cases curiosity was a strong enough motive to induce the simple action of granting an interview, which is all that was desired, because both salesmen banked heavily on their ability to close after the interview was secured. On the other hand, it would have to be an unusually strong booklet, or catalog, that could successfully produce sales if examined purely out of idle curiosity, wouldn't it? Or you can hardly conceive of a man's paying an overdue debt out of curiosity. You see that *circumstances can affect the se'ection of the motive* to be aroused.

Now that we have agreed that persuasion depends on arousing the proper motive to act, and now that we know what motives are and how they have been applied, let us go a step farther and find *how to apply our new learning.* This we can understand clearly after we have an insight into the methods of arousing motives in the minds of readers or an audience. We encounter this thought of motive many times every day.

BUSINESS CORRESPONDENCE

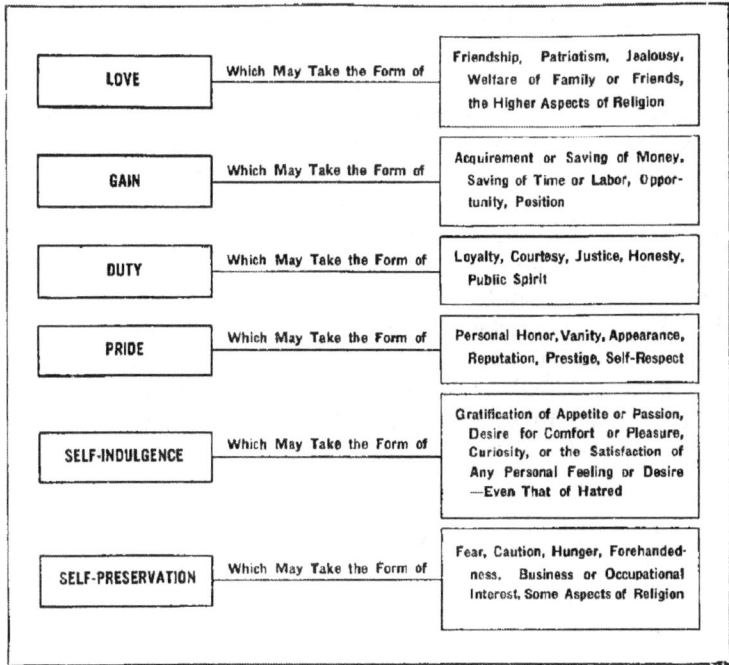

Panel 154

THE TEST OF A LETTER

The first step to take in persuading a reader is to study what you want him to do and then to determine which one of the six prime motives listed above will most readily impel him to do it. Before you write apply these tests to your proposition:

Will it protect his life, his health, his property, or his interest? If so the Self-Preservation Motive must be stirred.

Will it help his wife, or children, or country, or someone or something else that he loves or is grateful to? If so, the Love Motive must be aroused.

Will it make money or save money, or any of the equivalents of money for him? If so, the Gain Motive must be aroused.

Will it fulfil his sense of loyalty or courtesy or justice or honesty or obligation? If so, the Duty Motive must be aroused.

Will it satisfy his self-respect, add to his reputation or prestige, or cater to his vanity? If so, the Pride Motive must be aroused.

Will it appease an appetite or passion, yield comfort, satisfy curiosity, or gratify any other personal whim or desire? If so, Self-Indulgence must be played upon.

If it fills the requirements of more than one of these six motives, which one of them will exert the power, or which is the most easily aroused?

306

MAKING YOUR LETTER PERSUASIVE

What, for instance, arouses the motive to act in one letter when another, which puts the proposition equally as clearly, gets no response? *What is there in one sa'esman's talk that persuades us to sign on the dotted line* although another salesman who knows the goods just as well, and perhaps explains them better, gets "No" for his answer? Why do thousands of people listen through years to sermons, day after day read editorials; and time upon time hear lectures on the value of leading a moral life, without altering one jot or tittle of their habits, and then, suddenly, after hearing one sermon by Billy Sunday, feel themselves moved by fear, or love, or duty, or some other motive to pledge themselves to reform?

I have been an interested observer of the methods of persuasion used by the famous "Billy"—not from any enthu-

---

D. A. FIELD
Chicago, Ill.

```
Mr  C. R. Paxton,
Chicago, Illinois

Dear Mr  Paxton

    I should like to have a personal talk with
you regarding a matter in which I understand
you are greatly interested.  Will you kindly
call me on the telephone upon receipt of this,
so we can make an early engagement to our
mutual convenience?

    You can reach me at my office, 'phone
Central 6501, until 8 this evening, and any
other day from 11 a.m. to 5.30 p. m.  If you
should desire to call me up in the evening you
can usually reach me at my home, Hyde Park
9560.
                    Yours very truly,
                        D. A. FIELD
```

Panel 155

BUSINESS CORRESPONDENCE

JAMES B. THORSEN
INSURANCE COUNSELOR

Mr. E C. Hine,
Beaver Dam, Pa.

Dear Mr. Hine·

          THORSEN'S SIX

   There are almost 200 regular Life Insurance companies.

   Many of these are perfectly safe.

   Some of them are both safe and good, but there are
          SIX BEST.

   Six in a class by themselves   I know them and I know why they are best

   I am not the paid agent for any _one_ _company_, therefore I am free to tell the _truth_

   If you want the best there is in Life Insurance, you've got to take one of
          THORSEN'S SIX.

             Yours very truly,
                 JAMES B. THORSEN

Panel 156

HOW TO USE THE SELF-INDULGENCE MOTIVE

Strong letters, attractive offers, in fact a whole campaign may fail because too much emphasis is placed upon the presenting of the proposition Some propositions can't be put effectively in a letter There's too much to tell or to explain, to get an intelligent yes" or "no" from the prospect But a letter can do much in picking live prospects who, at least, will give ear to a salesman That is what the letters illustrated in Panels 155 and 156 do When searching for the motive that will put your message across, remember that not the least of these is Self-Indulgence in the form of mystery We all love to probe the unknown The letter in Panel 155 strikes this motive with compelling force. The letter mailed by special delivery touches curiosity to the quick It gets the reply and the salesman for a correspondence school has the opportunity he had been waiting for As for the letter in Panel 156, you'd like to get some expert advice on this subject, wouldn't you?

MAKING YOUR LETTER PERSUASIVE

siasm for his logic, but purely to learn how he gets results. For think what we may of the final effect of his work, one fact we all must admit—he persuades more people to do what he wants them to do, than any other living preacher. He not only has the knack of conveying his ideas forcibly, and the knack of making powerful use of the Visionary Idea to get interest, but also he plays skilfully with the great human motives. If you study his sermons you will find that each one is based on one of the *Six Prime Motives* we have just been considering.

In some of his sermons he strikes the Self-Preservation Motive, in some the Love Motive, in others a high form of the Gain Motive, in many the Duty Motive. Even Pride is made the motive of some, while a few of his sermons utilize the motive of Self-Indulgence, although in a rather spiritual sense.

As the Reverend Mr. Sunday is about as successful in getting the action he wants as anyone we know of, let us dismiss all thought of approval or disapproval of his creed and look analytically at one of his successful sermons to see how it works. His sermon "Eternity" is one most successful in getting action. Hence, on the next page, I have reproduced a series of extracts from it. These extracts occur at intervals in the sermon, in the order I have shown them, the last one at the close.

If you should read that sermon with those extracts crossed out of it, you would find it an ordinary evangelistic sermon. I doubt that it would make a dozen converts. But when the extracts are inserted in the sermon you can at once see why so many people are persuaded to immediate action— you can then *actually feel the powerful pull of the aroused motive—Self-Preservation* in the form of the fear of damnation.

What are these extracts? What part of the sermon do they represent? Analyze them closely and you see that they are *not* reasons. Nor are they any "features" of any particular idea in the sermon. They are simply what psychologists call *suggestions*. They suggest to the reader, or tell the

BUSINESS CORRESPONDENCE

"WHAT shall be the end of them that obey not the gospel of God?" Will you say, "God, I didn't have time enough?" "Behold! Now is the accepted time." Will you say, "God, I had no light?" But "light is come into the world, and men love darkness rather than light."

WHAT shall be the end of them that obey not the gospel of God?"

WHEN Voltaire, the famous infidel, lay dying, he summoned the physician and said, "Doctor, I will give you all I have to save my life six months."

The doctor said, "You can't live six hours." Then said Voltaire, "I'll go to hell and you'll go with me."

WHEN King Charles IX, who gave the order for the massacre of St. Bartholomew's day, when blood ran like water and 130,000 fell dead, when King Charles lay dying, he cried out, "O God, how will it end? Blood, blood, rivers of blood. I am lost!" And with a shriek he leaped into hell.

FRANCES E. WILLARD cried, "How beautiful to die and be with God."

THERE is a way that seemeth right unto man, but the end thereof are the ways of death.

"WHAT shall the end be?" Listen! Listen!

YOU can't stand before God in the Judgment and say, "Jesus, were you down there in the tabernacle? In my home? In my lodge? Did you want to save me?" Behold! Behold! A greater than the governor is here. Jesus Christ, the Son of God, and he waits to be gracious.

WHAT shall the end be of them that obey not the gospel of God?"

A MAN said, "I cannot be a Christian. I cannot obey God." That is not true.

YOU can be a Christian if you want to, and it is your cussedness that you are unwilling to give up that keeps you away from God.

DON'T tell God you can't. Just say you don't want to be a Christian; that's the way to be a man.

TELL GOD you are not man enough to be a Christian. Don't try to saddle it off on the Lord. You don't want to do it, that's all; that's the trouble with you.

EVER since God saved my soul and sent me out to preach, I have prayed him to enable me to pronounce two words, and put into those words all they will mean to you; if they ever become a reality, God pity you. One word is "Lost," and the other is "Eternity."

WHAT is your life? A hand's breadth—yes, a hair's breadth—yes, one single heart-beat, and you are gone, and yet you sit with the judgment of God hovering over you. "What shall the end be of them that obey not the gospel of God?"

WHAT shall the end be of them that obey not the gospel?" And the gospel of God is, "Repent or you will go to hell."

SOME people deny that their suffering in the other world will be eternal fire. Do you think your scoffs can extinguish the flames of Hell?

THERE may be a Hell. I'm ready; where do you get off at?

WHAT shall the end be of them that obey not the gospel of God?" What will some do? Some will be stoical, some will whimper, some will turn for human sympathy.

Panel 157

MAKING YOUR LETTER PERSUASIVE

listener, the fear of what may happen after death. They don't tell him to be afraid. They don't picture any particular thing to be afraid of. They are simply "fuel" for the motive for reforming—the motive of Self-Preservation, or fear of damnation. (I prefer the term "fuel" to "suggestion" because it is more graphic). Call it what you will, Mr. Sunday feeds this fuel to the flames of the Fear Motive, until that motive is the dominant power in the yielding listener's mind. Then he acts.

But we are not learning to be evangelists. Therefore let us see how all this applies to practical business Read Panel 158 on the next page From that letter, used successfully by a farm implement manufacturer, I have taken exactly the same sort of purely suggestive material that I extracted from the Billy Sunday sermon. The letter as it now stands clearly expresses the idea. But do you feel any persuasion to act on it? Certainly not.

Therefore, read the letter as it was actually used—you'll find it on page 313. See what a spur to action the suggestions give the letter. Why do they prod the reader? Why, because they carry exactly the same thought as the extracts from Sunday's sermon—they are *fuel for the Fear Motive*. In this case the prospect is made to think that he may lose the opportunity to buy

These suggestions, or this fuel, mixed with the "features" of the idea of the letter, as air is mixed with the gasoline in an automobile motor, *generate the driving power—the motive to act* just as carburetion of air and gasoline provide the power to drive an automobile. Review any of the letters already shown in Panels 148 to 156, and you will see this same mixing of suggestions and ideas, the net result of which, on the reader, is not only a grasp on the idea, or an interest in it or a belief in it, but an actively aroused motive.

So much for selecting the motive to be aroused; now for the second point in exercising persuasion, finding the fuel which when mixed with the "features" of an idea will *arouse the motive* for acting. To begin with, suppose we take that

BUSINESS CORRESPONDENCE

GIGANTIC MANUFACTURING CO.
SAN FRANCISCO, CAL.

B. R. Millard,
Orange Grove, Cal.
Dear Mr Millard·

  There is no doubt what a Gigantic will do. You will be satisfied to reflect that the increased land value alone pays for your time and the cost of the machine. The crops are pure velvet — clear profit, and every year sees these profits increasing Your new land in the next four years will return bigger yields than your best old land.

  Don't tell me it s too expensive when acres of your land are lying idle — actually depreciating in value right at this time — when in the next two years the price of all farm products will break every known record, owing to the great European war.

  Why, it's enough to arouse every drop of aggressive blood in a business farmer's veins when he thinks of the immeasurable demands, the immense opportunity to feed and clothe the world, and acres and acres of his stump land, the richest on his farm, actually losing more money now if not cleared than for ten years heretofore

  Every day some energetic man picks up a pocketbook that the crowd has walked over for hours

    OPPORTUNITY KNOCKS ONLY ONCE
     AT EACH MAN'S DOOR

  It is knocking now at your door.

  If you don't want to spare the full price now, then send a deposit and order for one at the low price for fall or winter delivery Pay the balance when you have it shipped later

      Yours truly,
      GIGANTIC MANUFACTURING CO

Panel 158

YOUR PAPER SALESMEN

In the above and opposite letters you have opportunity for practising the analysis of a letter The letter above makes a brave effort to present a brisk selling talk In many respects it's a good letter, but still it misses the mark Scrutiny of that letter will point out its gravest fault—lack of motive See how the letter opposite sounds the Fear Motive By the first line the reader is teased to action through fear of losing an opportunity to buy at a low price The letter as it stands is a "go-getter" of good business

MAKING YOUR LETTER PERSUASIVE

GIGANTIC MANUFACTURING CO.
SAN FRANCISCO, CAL.

B. R. Millard,
Orange Grove, Cal.
Dear Mr Millard

<u>LAST CHANCE</u>

Now's your last chance to get a Gigantic Stump Puller at the low price There is no doubt what a Gigantic will do You will be satisfied to reflect that the increased land value alone pays for your time and the cost of the machine The crops are pure velvet — clear profit, and every year sees these profits increasing. Your new land in the next four years will return bigger yields than your best old land

Don't tell me it's too expensive when acres of your land are lying idle, actually depreciating in value right at this time, when in the next two years the price of all farm products will break every known record, owing to the great European war.

Don't you know that all of Europe will have to come to the American Farmer for food and clothing? In spite of that fact we Americans are neglecting the greatest opportunity of centuries by wasting our stumpy land, letting it grow up in weeds, brush, sprouts and second growth.

Why, it's enough to arouse every drop of aggressive blood in a business farmer's veins when he thinks of the immeasurable demands, the immense opportunity to feed and clothe the world, and acres and acres of this stump land, the richest on his farm, actually losing more money now if not cleared than for 10 years heretofore

Every day some energetic man picks up a pocketbook that the crowd has walked over for hours.

OPPORTUNITY KNOCKS ONLY ONCE
AT EVERY MAN'S DOOR

It is knocking now at your door The low prices for the Gigantic Puller, the only machine with power enough to do all your work is about to be withdrawn. Higher prices are inevitable after June 30.

If you don't want to spare the full prices now, then send a deposit and order for one at the low price for fall or winter delivery

The enclosed sheet with order blank will show the amount of deposit if you want us to hold one of the offers at the low price Pay the balance when you have it shipped later, but whatever you do, don't miss this chance. Don't fail to send before June 30 next.

Yours truly,
GIGANTIC MANUFACTURING CO

Panel 159

same form of the Self-Preservation motive that we have already seen so skilfully handled by Billy Sunday and by the writer of the letter on the preceding page—and see how we can arouse it for ourselves. Let us write *a last lettter to a debtor* before bringing suit for a delinquent account

The Big Idea, we will say, is: "You have exhausted our patience—suffer the consequences." Suppose we had developed the "features" of that idea as shown in the panel below.

THE "FEATURES"

We have used every honorable means to induce you to protect yourself
We have appealed to your honor.
We have tried to arouse your self-respect
Apparently you are careless of both.
We will now refer the account complete to the courts

Panel 160

But when an account has gone to such a point, we know that the mere idea of being sued is not going to get action. We must arouse a motive, and we have decided it is going to be the *fear of what may happen.*

What fuel do we require? We have seen the fuel used by Sunday—we have seen the effect he attains by not defining the danger exactly, but leaving it to be built up by imagination. If Sunday had stated specifically what he thought would happen to "them that obey not the gospel," it would not have seemed half so bad to the average man. Mystery always adds to fear. So, suppose we *develop that same suggestion of mystery* in what will happen to this debtor if he doesn't pay his bill. First, say, give him this to think of:

> The time for the final action on your account has come.

MAKING YOUR LETTER PERSUASIVE

That is better fuel for his sense of fear than to say "We are now going to bring suit." Then

> We are through. We shall not ask you again for payment.

That has the same gruesome tinge of the unknown. "What are they going to do, then?" is the probable question.

To increase the mystery is our task and so instead of coming out flat-footed with the statement "will now refer the account to the courts," we shall say, instead·

> We shall now refer the matter to the proper authorities

The word "authorities" is so indefinite that to many a dishonest man it suggests the thought of police or deputy sheriffs, rather than civil courts, of which he may not be afraid.

This *thought can be encouraged and more "fuel" added* to the Fear Motive, by an inference, like Sunday's, of "what you will wish you had done," such as:

> and you can explain to them, which, in view of certain circumstances, we think you will suddenly find yourself very anxious to do

Concluding, we'll take another leaf from Sunday's methods and close with an ominous repetition of the mystery.

> We are sorry that you have made this necessary. You have evidently miscalculated. But no other course is open to us. The time for final action is here.

Scatter these bits of fuel for the motive among the main "features" of the idea, and you have—not a theoretical letter, but the master-copy of an actual letter used successfully by a large collection agency on its extreme cases In the panel on the next page you'll find it.

You see now, don't you, why I went so far afield as to analyze an evangelist's sermon? You see now that the same motive that brings people into Sunday's fold, brings orders to one business house, and collections to another. And the same method of arousing that motive is useful to both. Nor does that method apply only to that one motive.

BUSINESS CORRESPONDENCE

> **Motive**
> Self-Preservation—Fear of What May Happen If Account Is Not Paid

The time for final action on your account has come.

We have used every honorable means to induce you to protect yourself We have appealed to your honor. we have tried to arouse your self-respect Apparently you are careless of both

We are through. We shall not ask you again for payment We shall now refer the matter to the proper authorities, and you can explain to them, which, in view of certain circumstances, we think you will suddenly find yourself very anxious to do.

We are sorry that you have made this necessary You have evidently miscalculated But no other course is open to us The time for final action is here

Panel 161

MAKING YOUR LETTER PERSUASIVE

Try it on *another everyday example*—persuading through the Self-Indulgence Motive—the satisfaction of an appetite or taste. Assume that we are retail grocers, and that we have a new brand of coffee, which we want to use as a leader.

Our Big Idea is the fact that we have secured the exclusive sale of this superior coffee, and that as the supply is limited by the roasters, we offer it only to a select list. And let us say that we are going to arouse interest in the Big Idea by a Visionary Idea of the taste, fragrance, and appearance of such coffee. Not to bother with too many details, we'll just say that our rough-out of the letter runs like this:

> Last summer, when my wife came back from visiting her folks down East, she brought a couple of pounds of coffee they were using down there.
>
> I'll own up that it made the best grade of coffee I had in my store taste like a cheap imitation. I made up my mind right away to stock it.
>
> It had a fragrance that would bring us hurrying to breakfast in the morning — you know how the odor of real good coffee starts your appetite. Its color was almost as red when you poured it as old port wine, and just as clear — turning to a beautiful brown when you added cream. And such flavor!
>
> Only by sending the empty package to a trade paper did I learn where to get it, but it was worth the trouble. I now have the exclusive sale for this city — Ozama Coffee it's called — and it's just as good as the sample my wife brought home. It's 40 cents a pound, but you never tasted coffee like it at any price.
>
> I am not going to advertise it generally. I am just going to offer it personally to my regular trade and to a few selected families whose trade I should like to get.
>
> I want YOU to try just one pound.

Now I think you'll admit that the idea is pretty clearly conveyed in that much of the letter, and that the atmosphere of personality and sincerity runs all through it.

But we want our prospects not only to believe this is good coffee, but to be so persuaded they ought to get some at once that they won't forget it or grow disinterested or let their allegiance to any other store stand in the way. We

BUSINESS CORRESPONDENCE

want to arouse the motive of Self-Indulgence—the appetite for good coffee—to such an extent that it *swamps all objections* to coming to our store, and so that people won't delay in satisfying their self-indulgence.

You remember how Billy Sunday selected as fuel for the Fear Motive the sort of points that left the reader to conjure up his own notions of what he had to fear? Well, let us see if we can't adapt that same method in selecting fuel for the Pleasure Motive, and let the reader conjure his own notions of what the coffee will do for him. Just as others built up the fears for the unknown, so we shall build *anticipations of pleasure over the unknown.* We'll begin by throwing the charm of the unknown over our coffee:

> No one in this part of the country had ever heard of this coffee There was no roaster's name on the package.
> I wouldn't stop hunting for it — wrote my wife's people, got the grocer's name and wrote him but could get no satisfaction.

A real lover of good coffee is going to feel an appetite for tasting such a hard-to-get coffee, don't you think?

Then, suppose we add more of such fuel by bringing out whatever points will make him think of the coffee as very exclusive:

> The coffee is a special blend of a little old firm of importers in New York
> They are old fashioned and have followed the methods for sixty years.
> Every dealer has to say in advance how much he will need during the year. He can get just that much during the year and when that's gone he gets no more till the next year.

Isn't that good fuel for the motive that will bring the customer looking for such coffee? Then:

> From the way my regular customers are taking to it, I doubt if I made my year's order as big as I should.
> Take my word and try one pound now

And then, as we learned from Sunday's way of closing with a repetition:

MAKING YOUR LETTER PERSUASIVE

> No one else in this part of the country has this coffee, and only a few can have the privilege of enjoying it.

Now mix those chunks of fuel for the motive among the visionary and positive ideas of the letter and what do we have? Panel 162, on the next page, shows the complete letter —a letter that the grocer who used it says was the best paying piece of advertising he ever put out.

I believe you are now better able to appreciate why I made the scientific c'assification of motives to be found on page 306, for you cannot help having seen, I think, how much help, in selecting fuel for the motive, it is to *know the type of motive you must arouse* For example, in the grocer's letter we have just been studying, the decision that the Self-Indulgence Motive was to be aroused showed that the fuel should be a kind to appeal to the more selfish, pampered side of the reader. Hence, the emphasis on facts that made the reader think of having something that others couldn't have and of having something hard to get. If we had left the motives unclassified and so perhaps thought of the motive for that letter as being only the coffee appetite, it would scarcely have suggested so accurately the proper shade or tone of the "motive fuel"

And in the collection letter on page 316, our tabulation of motives suggested Self-Preservation, and that led up to the tone of "something is about to happen."

On page 321, also, you can see how knowledge of the general type of the motive *gives value to the "motive fuel"* in the constant suggestion of "orders," "more orders," "advertising built our business," etc. This is an old letter—one used when SYSTEM was just becoming known—but an extremely successful one It is interesting to note that even then the SYSTEM type was followed: a positive idea—"our advertising experts will help you in your advertising"; a visionary idea—"what our advertising experts have done for our business," and through it all the fuel for the Gain Motive in the form of the possibility of ideas or suggestions.

BUSINESS CORRESPONDENCE

MOTIVE
Self-Indulgence—The Appetite for Good Coffee

Last summer when my wife came back from visiting her folks down East, she brought a couple of pounds of the coffee they were using down there.

I'll own up that it made the best grade of coffee I had in my store taste like a cheap imitation. I made up my mind right away to stock it. But no one in this part of the country had ever heard of it and there was no roaster's name on the package.

It had a fragrance that would bring us hurrying to breakfast in the morning — you know how the odor of real good coffee starts your appetite. Its color was almost as red when you poured it as old port wine, and just as clear — turning to a beautiful brown when you added cream. And such a flavor!

I couldn't stop hunting for it -- wrote my wife's people, got the grocer's name and wrote him, but could get no satisfaction. Finally, by sending the empty package to a trade paper, I learned where to get it. The coffee is the special blend of a little old firm of importers down on Coentie's Slip in New York. They are old fashioned and have followed the same methods for sixty years. Every dealer has to say in advance how much he will need during the year. He gets just that much and when that's gone he gets no more till the next year.

But it's worth the trouble. I now have the exclusive sale for this city — Ozama Coffee, it's called — and it's just as good as the sample my wife brought home. The importer fixes the price at 40 cents a pound and won't let it be changed. I could get 50 cents if they'd let me, for you never tasted coffee like it!

Now, from the way my regular customers are taking to it, I doubt if I made my year's order as big as I should. So I am not going to advertise it generally this year. I am just going to offer it personally to my regular trade and to a few selected families whose trade I would like to get.

I want you to try just one pound — I believe that when you have tasted it you'll so appreciate the chance to get such coffee that you'll maybe later try me out on other things, too.

But take my word and try out one pound now. No one else in this part of the country has this coffee, and only a few can have the privilege of enjoying it.

Panel 162

MAKING YOUR LETTER PERSUASIVE

Motive
Gain—More Business

If you will sign, stamp and mail the enclosed postal card, a way will be opened up to you to get MORE orders

I believe that in our Advertisers' Service Bureau are three of the brightest advertising writers and business-getters in the country   At least, they are the best that I have been able to find

You have seen our advertising everywhere — letters, circulars, booklets, magazine and newspaper space. This advertising has built up our business. And these men, who conceived and wrote and laid it out, I believe can increase YOURS

Will you let them try?

There is absolutely no cost to you for their suggestions. For I am so confident that they will suggest some new copy or selling scheme to you that it will pay — and pay well — to advertise in SYSTEM, that I am warranted in making this quite unusual offer

Why not accept it?

Panel 163

BUSINESS CORRESPONDENCE

The contrast between the small amount of motive fuel in this last letter, and the much greater amount in the grocer's letter on page 320, may puzzle you. If you turn back through the various letters shown in this chapter you may be still more puzzled. In Panel 161 you see but little fuel, in Panel 159, considerably more, in Panel 156, very little, in Panel 155, even less; in Panel 153, again quite considerable. And so the variation goes. I don't know whether the men who wrote these letters were merely acting on instinct or intuition, or on knowledge gained by tests, or on scientific certainty. But when the amount of fuel for a motive is under consideration there is a pretty safe rule that can be followed.

In every normal person the Six Prime Motives exist. The successful pleader doesn't create a motive for making people act—he merely arouses it and makes it so active that it is dominant for the time over the other motives Now as to how much fuel or effort it will take to arouse that motive to the dominant pitch depends on the relative activity of the other motives.

Let me put that in another way: If the Gain Motive is active in your mind and prompts you to stick closely to your business, the man who wants to persuade you to leave the office and play a game of golf will not find you very susceptible to the Pleasure Motive. He can only persuade you by heaping on the fuel of the Pleasure Motive until it becomes more active than your Gain Motive, or, as we usually say, "overcomes your objections." But if the same friend should approach you on a day when your business ambitions were low, he would not need to use nearly as much persuasion. This principle, unchanged, applies to letters. For instance, collection men find that it requires but a little motive-fuel to rouse the motive of fear of lawsuits in the mind of a man enjoying a good position, but with an irresponsible, naturally dishonest man the counter motive of Gain is so active that it smothers the other motives.

The motive that governs our action at any one time is the motive that is so active that it dominates and crowds out

MAKING YOUR LETTER PERSUASIVE

the claims of all other motives. So we see that *the quantity of motive fuel a persuasive letter requires* depends on the susceptibility of the reader to the motive—on how much counter motive must be overcome. If the motive you are seeking to arouse will have but little competition, as was the case with the SYSTEM letter on page 321 in which the prospects were known to be already advertising for more business, then but little fuel is needed.

On the other hand, the insurance man who used the clever letter reproduced on the next page knew that his list of prospects had already shown the Self-Preservation Motive in the form of Thrift to be active, by going so far as to have had him figure the cost of a policy. So he depended on but a small amount of fuel to rouse that motive to dominance. But for the grocer's letter on page 320, it was evidently known that counter motives—such as the prospects' loyalty to their present grocers, low prices at another store, and so on—would have to be overcome. Therefore, much "fuel" was fed to the Pleasure Motive.

Mail order houses, for the same reason, have found it necessary to feed the motive for buying from them—usually a form of Gain Motive—to the utmost extent in order to overcome the activities of counter motives. This is *why mail order letters are often so full of repetitions.* There is, however, a purpose for those repetitions. Experience has proved that the Gain Motive for buying by mail is smothered by counter motives—fear of sending money in advance, or of not liking the goods, loyalty to home trade, and so forth—unless it is fed up to overwhelming dominance.

This same rule must be followed in collection letters. The man who is naturally dishonest is so much under the domination of the Gain Motive that strong "fuel" is needed in order to make dominant the fear of being beaten in courts. Hence we see the need of such letters as that shown on page 316, for extreme cases.

Where the debtor is known to be responsible, however, or where the presumption is that way, counter motives will be

BUSINESS CORRESPONDENCE

VANDERBILT AVENUE BUILDING
NEW YORK CITY

Mr Kendall Banning—
  Dear Sir.
      The circled day is an important date for you—keep it in mind—

DECEMBER						
SUN	MON	TUE	WED	THU	FRI	SAT
						1
2	3	4	5	6	7	8
9	10	11	12	13	14	15
16	17	18	19	(20)	21	22
23/30	24/31	25	26	27	28	29

Any Northwestern policy issued <u>after</u> that date will cost you a good deal more money—age changing.
      Yours very truly,
        Brevoort B. Barr

Panel 164

MAKING YOUR LETTER PERSUASIVE

much less active, and we find such letters as that on page 326, or that on page 327, proving effective. And in some *cases where the class of customers is high,* even as small an amount of fuel for the motive as that shown on page 328 has proved successful.

In short, the number of statements or letters that the debtor has received without acting on the account, other things being equal, determines the collection man's judgment as to the best motive to be aroused, and how difficult it will be to arouse it. As we learned in the third part, the first four letters of a collection series are usually confined to conveying the idea of the debt's claim to attention. The presumption is that the debtor intends to pay, that he has a sufficient motive, and that he has only overlooked the matter.

But *after a debtor has received four letters,* the collection manager has a right to assume that the Honesty Motive is overruled in the debtor's mind by the Gain Motive, and hence the fifth letter should attempt the active work of arousing a counter motive—usually the Pride Motive in the form of reputation and self-respect, as you can see on pages 326, 327 and 328. This failing, the sixth letter resorts to the Fear Motive—as we saw on page 316.

In a sales follow-up the same principle applies. When a prospect inquires about the goods, the presumption is that the motive for buying is active. Hence, the first four letters, as we learned in the third part are confined usually to conveying the Big Idea of the goods But *after the fourth letter,* this motive is assumed either to have never been strong enough really to prompt buying, or to have become passive. So the subsequent letters must exercise persuasion.

For example, I sent an inquiry to a watch manufacturer in response to a magazine advertisement. The first letter enclosed the booklet and gave me very briefly the idea of the watch's quality. The second letter enlarged on the same idea. The third letter conveyed the same Big Idea to me, but this time approached it from the angle of price. The fourth letter opened up on me with a visionary idea of what

BUSINESS CORRESPONDENCE

MOTIVE
Self-Preservation—Fear of Lawsuit

This is the FIFTH letter we have sent you requesting remittance on your account

There are four payments now due amounting to $15

As you have entirely ignored our letters there is but one step open to us — to refer the account to our attorneys

This, therefore is to inform you that unless we receive settlement within the next ten days, we shall with reluctance be compelled to take the usual legal measures

Frankly, have you left us any other course to pursue?

Panel 165

TO GET THE MONEY

In the collection letter, show your man that you mean business, impress upon him that you intend to give him a square deal and that you expect the same Show him that it is to his advantage to settle the obligation. Remember the "you" and "I" element, but emphasize the "you" by pointing out to the debtor that it is to his interest to settle the account and keep his record clean A proper play on the "you" element is always aided by a proper selection of motive and fuel for it Read the letters shown in Panels 165, 166 and 167 **with motive in mind** All of these letters brought **in the money.**

MAKING YOUR LETTER PERSUASIVE

MOTIVE
Self-Preservation—Fear of Lawsuit

There must be some reason for your permitting two of your notes to remain unpaid after maturity and at the same time ignoring our requests for payment or explanation

If we knew the reason, we should know what to do — either take steps to enforce our contract rights or get together with you in an effort to protect both of us

There may be some very good explanation, but you can't expect leniency when you won't even write us We are anxious to help you Please don't prevent us from doing so

Payment or satisfactory explanation simply must be made immediately

Panel 166

BUSINESS CORRESPONDENCE

MOTIVE
Pride—Dislike of Losing Reputation

No reply has been made to the statements previously sent you. Do not, through further neglect, force the use of severe and aggressive measures to collect this account.

Panel 167

I would lose if I paid more for a watch, or if I bought one with less quality. In the fifth letter, it was assumed that any motive I might have had for buying was dormant, and you will see from the letter on the next page how the Gain Motive was appealed to, in order to persuade me to action.

This follow-up principle, of course, does not apply invariably. There are some *propositions that by their nature attract curiosity or information inquiries*—no real buying motive existing at the time the inquiry is made. Many farm implements attract the inquiries of farmers who only want to compare the implement with one they own; automobiles and new automobile accessories attract many such inquiries; bicycles, motorcycles, motorboats, boys' goods, fashion catalogs, and sporting goods all draw this kind of inquiries. Wise sales correspondents recognize this condition, but also recognize that many such prospects can nevertheless be turned into good customers, and hence build their follow-up letters on the Persuasion Motive right from the beginning.

In such cases the construction of the first four letters is not different from the general plan shown in the third chapter, except that the fuel for a buying motive is incorporated in each one—or at least from the second letter on. On page 330 we can see an example of this in the second letter of a cream separator manufacturer.

MAKING YOUR LETTER PERSUASIVE

Motive

Gain --The Big Value Offered

Three cents a week

That's not a great amount to pay for correct time and the satisfaction of owning a high grade, modern up-to-date watch, is it?

Yet that's about the way your investment figures out.

Suppose you buy a 19-Jewel South Bend Watch adjusted to four positions in 20-year gold-filled case for $28 75

Under average conditions the movement will last you a lifetime, while the case is good for 20 years

But let's be conservative and figure but 20 years of usefulness for both That means more than 1 000 weeks and less than 3 cents per week   Can you think of any other article that will serve you as well for as little?

If it cost double the money it would still be a good investment, wouldn't it?

So why not decide now to send us your order today? We sent you a folder describing this special watch value some little time ago   We are enclosing you another folder herewith that gives some additional facts

We know there is no better watch value in the world than these 19-jewel watches offer   We were oversold on them at several different times last year   We don't know how much longer we will be able to fill orders on these watches   So make sure by ordering now   Just pencil your order on the blank below and mail today

Panel 168

BUSINESS CORRESPONDENCE

> **Motive**
>
> Gain—The Increased Yield of Butter Fat

Why not stop this waste?

With any cream separator, excepting our SUCTION FEED, unless you operate them at exactly the certain set speed, you lose, through the poor skimming resulting, an enormous amount of butter fat. And 4,000 authentic tests have proven that over 95% of all separator users turn their separator under speed.

Think of what this means — over $1,500,000 wasted in lost butter fat (which could be saved by our SUCTION FEED) by dairymen every year

The enclosed circular will explain this new separator marvel of ours to you in interesting detail. For the benefit you will derive — read it through carefully

Now, surely, you do not want this waste to occur in your dairy. You don't want to throw money away. Take the precautionary step therefore Use the enclosed self-addressed envelop — write us and ask us to show you just how much it will save for YOU We can give you some mighty interesting information

Panel 169

SELL YOURSELF

No matter what kind of a letter you have to write, keep this fact in mind never use an argument that does not seem irresistible to you Know your goods from the source of the raw material to the delivery of the finished product. In selling them look at the proposition through the eyes of the prospect Sell yourself the order and you will find the talking points that win.

MAKING YOUR LETTER PERSUASIVE

Then there is the follow-up series which is mailed to lists of prospects, not originated by an inquiry. In such letters, of course, no buying motive can be assumed to be active, hence every letter must have the elements of persuasion in it. Panel 170 shows the first of a very successful follow-up series soliciting new accounts for a clothing manufacturer. Observe how the Self-Preservation Motive in the form of business caution is fed in this letter.

And here, again, the question of *selecting the best motive for a letter* is brought up. A merchant stocks a certain line usually through the Gain Motive, and yet this letter seeks to move him to action through a different motive. But examine the letter closely and you will see that while selling is the ultimate aim of the letter, the immediate action desired is investigation, and the very nature of investigating implies caution, open-mindedness, or foresight. Therefore, in this case, the Business Caution Motive is probably more easily aroused than the Gain Motive would be. The whole question of what motive to arouse should always be settled on the basis of what available one can be most easily aroused in the case at hand. That is why I left the discussion of selecting motives until after you had seen the ways of arousing them.

As we now know that a reader's susceptibility to any motive at any given time depends on the activity at that moment of all the counter motives, we can easily see what effect his previous attitude toward us, or our knowledge of his interests, his habits, his location, must have in determining our choice of motive. *The debtor who has ignored* many statements and letters we know to be unsusceptible to the plain Duty Motive. The man who has bought extravagantly from us in the past we know will not be so easily susceptible to the Gain Motive as to the Pride or the Self-Indulgence Motive. The merchant who is already stocked on one brand of goods, and who is making money from it and feeling perfectly satisfied, will not be so susceptible to the Gain Motive when we seek to interest him in a rival line as he perhaps would be to the Business Caution Motive. On the other

BUSINESS CORRESPONDENCE

> ## Motive
> Self-Preservation—Being Sure You Have the Best Line

You have so many manufacturers trying to sell clothing to you that you may have decided to "let well enough alone." That's a very good policy in business, provided you're sure it is "well enough."

The fact is, we've made our name and line so much of an asset in popular favor that we don't hesitate to say that whenever a merchant identifies himself with us, his business begins to increase. And we're pretty sure, no matter how "well enough" you're doing, you'll not object to doing better.

It's one of those things in business which is important enough to find out about because it represents very definitely and very certainly more volume for you, and that ought to sound good.

We'll be glad to tell you more about it by correspondence, or by having our representative arrange to see you when the men start on the fall selling trip.

It pays to be informed. Shall we give you the facts, or will you talk with our salesman when he comes your way? Let us know how you feel about it.

Panel 170

hand, if our line were one that represented the possibility of entirely new business to the merchant, then probably the Gain Motive would be our easiest channel.

As a matter of fact, *the experience of most advertising men and salesmen* has been that the Self-Preservation Motive is the most difficult to arouse, if the action desired is serious or costly.

Strange as it may seem, the average person apparently buys less frequently because of future protection to health, future safety of his business, care for old age, and so forth—any of the purely precautionary motives included under the head of Self-Preservation—than for any other motive.

For instance, I did considerable work once for a manufacturer of a catarrh remedy, and I learned that advertising and letters based on any form of the Self-Preservation Motive —such as the dangers of catarrh bringing on tuberculosis, causing deafness, and so forth—got but little response. But copy that told how obnoxious the catarrh sufferer was to his friends; pointed out that people often changed seats in a street car to get away from him; showed that people disliked to eat at the same table with him, *brought orders rolling in.* In other words, protection against future suffering— Self-Preservation—was *not nearly so effective a motive as Pride.*

Salesmen of efficiency appliances find the same condition— business men would rather spend money for a machine because it will produce profit, than because it will safeguard them.

I have also found that either the Pride or Duty Motive will *arouse the average man or woman to pay a bill more quickly* than will the fear of consequences. This does not contradict what has already been said as to the manifestly dishonest person, because the dishonest person is not average.

Experienced salesmen, advertisers and letter writers will usually choose the best motives, where there is room for a choice, in this order: Love, Gain, Duty, Pride, Self-Indulgence, Self-Preservation. That is, if more than one motive is available for the proposition, they will choose the one nearest the top of that list, other things being equal. For instance, if a proposition might appeal both to a man's love for his wife and to his desire to gain, the Love Motive would be played upon first. I don't know why it should be so, and maybe it isn't always so. But experience tends that way and it makes a good basis to start planning from—letting circumstances or judgment alter the rule as seems wise. But always *remember to distinguish between the idea that the reader is to be sold on, and the motive that persuades him to sign the order.* The idea that makes a business man want to possess an office appliance may be the safeguarding of his records, while the motive that makes him forget all counter motives and buy might be his pride in having top-notch equipment.

It all goes back to what has been said before, that we don't buy everything we want. We buy only that part of those things we want, that Self-Preservation, Love, Gain, Duty, Pride, or Self-Indulgence sweeps us on to buying over the resistance of all counter motives.

Therefore, in writing letters to persuade, first see that the right idea is conveyed, and then inject the "fuel" for the motive in order to get action.

SUMMARY

IN this chapter we have seen: First, that all human actions are prompted by one of six Prime Motives which have been listed for you on page 306. This you can prove by analyzing your reasons for any act you ever perform. In some phase or other, one of the Motives will always apply;

Second, that to persuade a reader to act in the way we want him to do, we must arouse one of those six motives, choosing the one that will surely prompt such an action, the one that will have the least interference from counter motives, and therefore the one that will be most easily aroused;

Third, that a motive for action is aroused in the reader by mixing with the expression of the idea, the kind of thoughts or suggestions that will make the motive active in the reader's mind—in other words, the task of the letter

MAKING YOUR LETTER PERSUASIVE

writer is to feed fuel for the motive into the general trend of the letter;

Fourth, that the amount of fuel must be regulated by the writer's judgment as to how active the motive is in the reader's mind and how much counter motive must be burned out.

All this may sound complicated when considered in bulk, but if you will start practising at the very beginning—first selecting a motive, then the fuel, and then going on one step at a time, you will find it soon becomes very easy. Invariably a student will write a better letter by following this system of exercising persuasion. First attempts, of course, will be, generally are, far from perfect, but each subsequent trial of the method will show an improvement.

In the next chapter we shall continue our study of motives, but from another point of view—the close of the letter. We shall see that the close depends largely on giving the reader at the right moment an impulse to act. This question we shall trace to its beginning and after showing why an impulse is necessary, show how it may be prepared. Without anticipating too much, it may be said that this rests on giving the reader's motive some easy task to do. This new work is interesting, easy to understand, and the chart for closing a letter which is explained in detail, will enable you to put the new principle into practise right away.

PROBLEM SECTION VI

BEHIND every voluntary action there is a motive. Let us all agree to that. Of course, there are times when people's motives are hard to understand, and at first thought motives may seem to be lacking. But search deep enough and you will invariably find that the underlying cause of any action is due to one of the six motives we read about in the last chapter

These in their order, you will recall, are *Love, Gain, Duty, Pride, Self-Indulgence, and Self-Preservation* Some of you may be inclined to argue over the order in which motives should be placed, holding, for example, to the proverb that "self-preservation is the first law of nature." I'll not debate with you on that. I'll leave that to the professors. I am a business man and I hold that from a plain, ordinary, business standpoint the motives which prompt human action may be listed as I put them

Now, of course, the talk of motives in this problem section has but one purpose. *The right motive is at the bottom of successful persuasion.* And we'll practise in this problem section on how to persuade customers to buy goods, or service, pay bills, accept an answer to a complaint, and so on. We'll begin with the knack of picking the motive by working over a letter with which we are familiar and then pass on to original problems in this fascinating subject.

As interesting a letter as any is that pie letter that we began in the fourth problem section. In the past two sections we put personality and sincerity in it; now we'll make it persuasive. With the start we've made, the job is easy. It merely hangs on the selection of a motive. The letter as it

MAKING YOUR LETTER PERSUASIVE

stands is on page 288, where you can refer to it as we proceed in our work of completing it

In the first place, the action we want from the reader of that letter is the presentation of that little 10-cent coupon. What motive will persuade him to do that? To decide, we'll look over the list of motives to find that four of the six instantly can be dismissed from our calculations. Probable motives then become *Gain and Self-Indulgence* (I believe that my choice of motives is plain without a discussion. Certainly, Love as a motive need not be considered in this case. Equally valid objections are apparent for the other motives.)

Now consider the possibilities of the first remaining motive, Gain. How shall we apply it? Gain of the dime's worth? That would be worth considering were it not for the fact that our list consists of doctors, lawyers, architects, dentists, and other professional men, who can't be influenced by the prospect of gaining that 10 cents. Therefore, we'll reject Gain as a motive and turn to Self-Indulgence, which seems to fit the bill.

But merely selecting the motive is not all of our task. Motives have many phases, hence it is necessary to *select the proper phase of this Self-Indulgence* before going farther. Self-Indulgence may take the form of gratification of appetite or passion; desire for comfort or pleasure, satisfying of curiosity or any other personal feeling or desire, including hatred. Of course, this list is not a complete tabulation of the forms Self-Indulgence may take. There are many others, but the list will do for us, for the key to our problem is to be found in it.

It pays to be cautious, however, for we can easily go astray. For instance, gratification of appetite seems to be the exact point of attack. But it isn't. Why? Because when it comes noon, men of this type may forget all about the appetite we created. Noonday lunch with most of them is a sort of social hour—they go where friends go so that they can visit and chat and joke while they eat.

Therefore, we must arouse the Self-Indulgence Motive in some other way. Why wouldn't that desire for a good time at lunch—the humoring or indulgence of sociability—be *the motive that would have the least resistance* at noon? That appeal looks good to me. How about you?

Suppose we work our readers up to considering the use of the 10-cent coupon as a sort of sporting proposition—one good fellow's dare to another of, "I'd give a dime to see you tasting your first piece of Anna's lemon pie."

If we can get that form of the Self-Indulgence Motive working—indulging the sociable and sporting inclination—at noon our prospects may say to their usual luncheon companions, "This fellow says he'd give a dime to see me eating a piece of Anna's lemon pie—here's the coupon. Let's go up and see what 'Anna' is like, and make him come across with the dime "

Don't you think, with that class of men, such a motive might work better than a more serious one?

See how *a study of motives opened a broader vision* of our job for us? It brought out not only the difference between ideas and motives, but also the difference between motives and reasons Reason is cold, dispassionate. Motive is as warm and human as humanity itself. We want reasons before doing things—but we won't do them after we have the reasons, unless we have a motive.

Now none of those professional men will come to our restaurant with his 10-cent coupon unless he has a reason. And reason we have given him in the Big Idea that the coupon is good for a piece of Anna's pie and in the visionary idea that Anna's pie is so good.

Since his reason has made him willing, we must now arouse a motive for acting. Let us see what "fuel" will arouse that motive. The very words in which we thought of the motive would be good "fuel," wouldn't they? No doubt about it. Therefore, we'll redraft the letter and begin it in this way:

```
    I'd give a dime to see you eat your first piece of
Anna's lemon pie.
```

MAKING YOUR LETTER PERSUASIVE

The next two paragraphs of the letter hit the mark just as they were written. We'll drop them in the new letter without change. But we'll not forget our motive and the "fuel" it requires. Therefore at the end of the third paragraph we'll add this:

    You'd say it, too — I'll bet a dime you would!

That keeps the motive blazing and we can slip in another paragraph previously written, the one about the crust.

Then we hit the coupon idea and to make it stick we'll add more "fuel" by opening the final paragraph with this sentence:

    Yes, sir, I'd gladly give a dime just to see you taste your first piece of that pie —

And we'll revise still more to add this "fuel" to the motive:

    I'll put it right in this letter — or a coupon as its equivalent

Here is still another urge to the reader. We'll get it in that last paragraph, too.

    By George! I will give a dime.

Now, I'll incorporate all of the "fuel" for the motive into the letter to show how much persuasiveness it adds to it. Below I print the letter in full, as far as we have gone. Study it over. Next time we will learn how to construct the proper close for the letter—a close that will fire the motive into action.

    Dear Sir:
        I'd give a dime to see you eat your first piece of Anna's lemon pie.
        My, what lemon pie that woman can bake! Why, man, when you close your lips and tongue on a piece of that pie it's like a little gushing fountain in your mouth just deluging your palate with delightful tastes?
        First the frosting — not the sugary sort of meringue you're thinking of, but frosting — of cool, snowy, vaporous sweetness Then quickly the refreshing lemony — not sourness, mind you, that's too strong a word — but rather a wild, pleasing tartness Then sweetness and tartness crushed in together, and Pouf! they join and blend in an

BUSINESS CORRESPONDENCE

> entirely new taste that gradually melts away somewhere down your throat and only a soft, happy memory remains — until your next mouthful.
>
> Yes, Anna certainly has a knack about lemon pies that's all her own. You'd say it, too — I'll bet a dime you would!
>
> Then the crust, I must call it crust, I suppose, as if it were like other pie crust — it's crisp, of course, as good pie crust should be, it's flaky — but Anna's crust, when you put it into your mouth seems to have only been making believe to be crust after all. For where is it? It crumbles and flakes away and gives itself up to the rest of the pie like a sacrifice — to help make one grand, complete taste of paradise for you.
>
> Yes, sir — I'd gladly give a dime just to see you taste your first piece of that pie! By George! I will give a dime! I'll put it right in this letter — or a coupon as its equivalent — and if you'll come in today, have your luncheon and top off with a piece of Anna's lemon pie — you can simply hand in the coupon with your lunch check as payment for the pie.

Now I think you have my idea in practise as well as in theory, which was explained in the last chapter. You see the job in persuading is *to select* the right motive from the list; *to analyze*, as I did just now for the pie letter; and *to choose* the right angle or phrase or feature, whatever it may be called, of the motive and *to app'y* it to the purpose of the letter. It's not as easy as it looks. There's plenty of opportunity for originality on the job, as you'll find before you finish this problem section.

Later on I'll give you a chance to test this principle for yourself, but first I suggest that we clean up the other problems begun in the last problem section. In the first place you were supplied with the "features" of the idea used in a letter to sell apple cider. Your problem was to tabulate the reader's attitude toward each "feature" and word the "features" in a way that would establish a sympathy with the reader's thoughts.

On page 304 you will find the actual letter on which this problem was based. Of course, it would be absurd to expect that any two people would arrive at the same sort of phrases

MAKING YOUR LETTER PERSUASIVE

or even at exactly the same tone in a letter, but in the successful letter on page 304 you have *a general standard by which to measure.*

By studying the letter and by comparing it with the problem I set for you in the last problem section, you will see that its intimate, personal atmosphere can be traced from the table of the "features" and the reader's attitude toward them in the panel below:

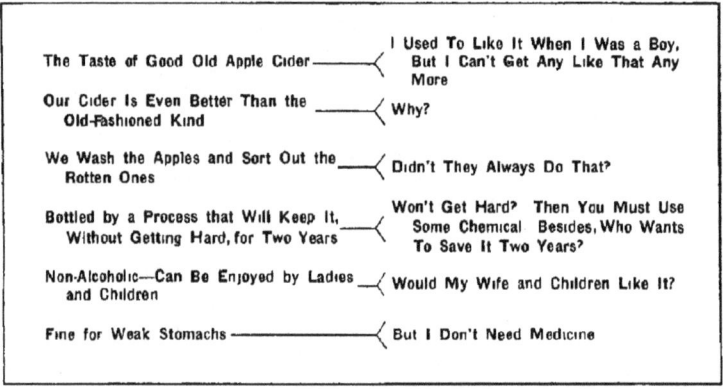

Panel 171

How nearly did your table come to that one? It should have been something like it, at least. If it wasn't, try again. Test this new principle on your letters until you are sure that you have it.

Your next problem was to tabulate the reader's attitude toward the "features" of a collection letter that was outlined for you. You will find the original of the letter on page 301. A comparison of your work with the finished result will, I believe, answer any questions that may have come up. If you need more practise, you will find many other letters in the foregoing chapter which you may analyze into a tabulation of reader's attitude.

This mention of extra work reminds me of a point that I have spoken, of before, but which I'll state again. The prob-

BUSINESS CORRESPONDENCE

lems in this book are purposely limited. They are only suggestions, so to speak. Even if you are sure that you understand everything perfectly, it will be well at times to apply on some of the letters in the book the principles which the problems brought to light. That's the way to get most out of the work you are doing.

Now, I think you are ready to tackle the real work of this problem section. You have found that this question of motives is not mere theory, but that it is *a practical phase of everyday affairs*. The matter of selecting the proper motive to play upon leaves room for errors of judgment, no doubt, but so does every important step in business. Keener judgment can be cultivated along this line by painstaking study of your proposition, of the people with whom you deal, and of the motives used for various purposes in other successful letters.

Problem 1

You will find, in the panel below, the main portion of a very successful letter used by a purchasing agent. He really

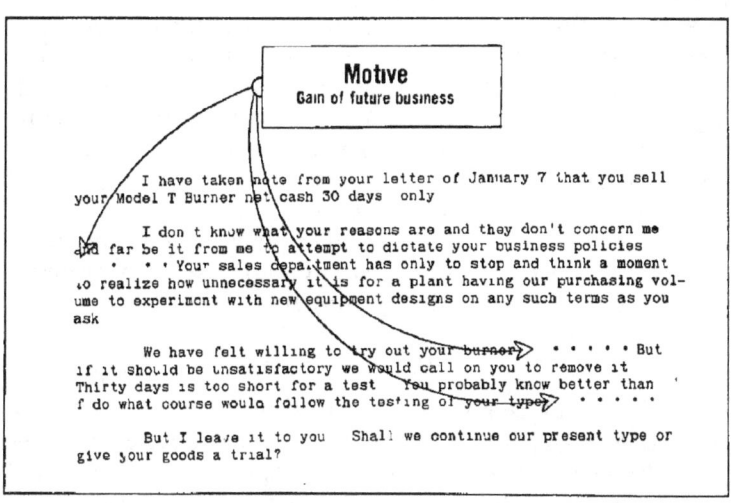

Panel 172

MAKING YOUR LETTER PERSUASIVE

wanted to buy a trial order from this firm, but wanted better terms. In his letter he tried to persuade the seller to alter his terms. I have indicated the motive of the writer at the top of the letter, and by the lines I show the points in the letter where the motive's "fuel" was supplied. Try your skill now at inserting at those points the kind of "fuel" that will arouse the motive.

File this letter in your Material File. In the next chapter you will be given the original letter to correct your work by.

Problem 2

As we are practising in this book on a variety of styles of letters, let us now try one written to get agents. In the letter on the next page I am going to let you select the proper motive as well as supply the "fuel" for it. Remember to consider carefully what kind of action is sought for, and what the results of that action are going to be for the reader, and to choose your motive accordingly. Remember, also, to choose the motive that is likely to have least resistance with the particular type of reader reached.

You will find in this letter, and usually in all letters, that inserting the "fuel" for the motive after the body of the letter is decided on, calls for minor changes in the original wording. You probably noticed this as you watched the building up of the restaurant letter. *In actual business*, when you have all the principles of a good letter in hand, you will *simply lay out all the various steps of a letter* in a preliminary outline and then incorporate them in your letter as you write or dictate. Just now, of course, we must use each principle by itself to get accustomed to using it.

Problem 3

On page 346 is another letter which I have treated in the same way as the previous example. Here you see that although the Big Idea is the applicant's ability and experience, the motive aroused for giving him his chance is a

LUSINESS CORRESPONDENCE

> **Motive -- ??**

We were very much pleased to receive your inquiry and shall do our best to give you the information you wish Under separate cover we are sending you our latest catalog and we enclose some literature we feel will be of interest to you

As you will see by our catalog, we manufacture a complete line of hosiery and underwear We sell our goods through our representatives not through storekeepers We have been selling our goods this way for the past twenty-one years and have built up an enormous business in all parts of the United States. . . . . .

Our goods are not peculiar in any way They are what everybody wants Just high grade hosiery and underwear of fine quality and remarkably low price. so you see you do not need any experience to sell them They are easy to sell and those who buy them almost always become steady customers

 . . . . Selling our goods is not hard If you only show them to people, they will see at once how much better they are than anything the local dealer can sell at anywhere near the price, for our goods bought from regular dealers with all the middleman's profits attached, would cost 50% more than you would sell them for

As to our terms, we give you a commission of 25% . . . . . . We prepay all the shipping charges so that you actually make one-fourth on all you sell Doesn't this seem like a fair proposition?

You may be sure we will help you to the utmost if you take up the work We will supply you with literature selling arguments, samples of the goods, in fact give you the full benefit of our experience and advice and every advantage that has made possible the success of our representatives

We only ask you to deposit a small amount for a sample outfit as an evidence of good faith This money is returned to you when you have sold a certain amount of goods, so the samples really cost you nothing We take all the trouble and risk so that you can begin the work at once, for we know that if you will make a start you will make a success of the work

Panel 173

MAKING YOUR LETTER PERSUASIVE

form of the Duty Motive—business fairness. *Try your hand at developing this motive.*

PROBLEM 4

Now for the next problem I want you to do still more of the work. Here is a brief of a letter I'd like to have you write:

Certain customers of an ice company have let their bills run too long—the new monthly bills are almost due. The Big Idea of the collection letter is that the bill will have to be paid at once. Its features are.

Your last month's bill is unpaid
Customers must not get behind
In order that the remittance will not be confused with current bill, the enclosed special blank should be used.

Out of these "features" you ought now to be able to visualize very clearly the idea that the bill will have to be paid at once.

The motive selected by the writer of the letter, after many experiments, was a form of the Self-Preservation motive—saving oneself from embarrassment. I will give you this much of a hint as to the "fuel"—it encouraged the customer to think she had only overlooked the payment. The enclosed remittance blank put the words into her mouth, "I had forgotten." With that much information, try writing the complete letter

PROBLEM 5

For the next problem I am not even going to give you the Big Idea. I shall simply tell you the purpose of the letter and let you map out its "load," its Big Idea, the motive for action, and write it complete. Here it is.

A manufacturer of a dairy supply circularizes his dealers for lists of their customers to whom he proposes to mail a series of letters selling his product—call it D D. It is quite an effort to get the dealers to make up and send him such

BUSINESS CORRESPONDENCE

Motive

Duty (Business Fairness)

To cause one of your employees to lose his job is not my intention But if any of your employees has MY job — then it isn't his
* * * * *

If you have a copy writer working on mail order accounts who can't write a piece of copy as good as the sample enclosed, marked Exhibit 1 and which brought back inquiries at a cost of 53 cents for which sales were closed at a cost of $6 10, when the lowest cost per sale had previously been around $10—then he has MY job and his job is somewhere else * * * * *

Exhibit 2 pulled 144 inquiries from the Cosmopolitan, 28 from the Motion Picture Magazine, 33 from Argosy Average cost about $1 40 Exhibit 3 is the only piece of copy that paid out on this proposition last year — it is the only one I wrote, but two other copy men had had a try at it before it came to me

If you have a copy writer who is producing mail order copy that doesn't pay like that, HE HAS MY JOB * * * * *

I have other samples I could show you -- in five years' experience I have handled about every sort of mail order proposition there is going * * * * *

My name and address is

    H A Hornsby
    555½ Cochin Avenue
    Brooklyn

My age is 27   Graduate of Williams

Please put yourself in the place of an advertiser and consider me as a solicitor for your agency -- and then write me whether or not you will give me a show to prove that we are both losers if my real job is with you and I'm not filling it

Panel 174

MAKING YOUR LETTER PERSUASIVE

lists, although the advertising he proposes to do is really to the dealers' advantage. Often the dealers fail to follow directions—they send too long a list. Sometimes they merely tear pages from the rural telephone directory. Such help is impracticable, for the follow-up series consists of four mailings costing $2\frac{1}{2}$ cents apiece.

To revise, the dealer must pick names from a list of his best customers. The manufacturer also has to know the kind of dairying each man engages in.

A special blank is enclosed for the purpose. This blank is also enclosed with the original request for a list, but it has been ignored. Therefore, a special effort must be made to make the dealer see why he should use it.

Plan the whole letter and then in the next chapter we shall see how nearly you have come to a form that represents the product of long experience on this particular job.

PART VII

HOW TO MAKE YOUR LETTER GET ACTION

CHAPTER VII

HOW TO MAKE YOUR LETTER GET ACTION

RESTING on the edge of a precipice, a rock is a potential avalanche. But there it rests. There it rests for possibly hundreds of years until one day a tiny impulse—a wind, a vibration, a slight shifting of the earth beneath—starts it moving, and the rock starts an avalanche.

So with an audience of people. In it are all the potentials of a great ovation. But those potentials remain only potentials—as the motive to cheer the orator or applaud the play grows and swells—until interested friends start a ripple of hand clapping. That is the impulse needed. The applause bursts forth.

The *need of an impulse at a critical moment* has been recognized and used for all kinds of purposes for many, many years. It occurs in many, many forms. Probably at some time in your life you have stood before the entrance of a circus side-show and heard a "barker" describe all the wonderful things to be seen inside the tent. Analyze such a talk and you will find that it consists of *a series of vivid visionary ideas, paving the way for the positive idea* that the show must be worth seeing. Strung cleverly through the talk you'll always find the fuel of some potent motive for paying the admission price, and always at the close of the "spiel," you will recall, as the barker begins the old formula, "step up now, ladies and gentlemen ———," there comes a general push forward.

The man back of you pushes forward. His advance starts another and another moving forward, and you, too, find yourself moving forward. At exactly the right moment, just as the "barker" has aroused a motive for going forward, that general motion of the crowd starts you and the aroused motive, now working, carries you on.

As a matter of fact, the impulse that starts the crowd at such times is supplied by carefully placed "shills," as they are called in circus slang. The "shills," employees of the circus, are scattered among the crowd and at the given cue they begin pushing and crowding forward, thus setting the whole crowd in motion towards the ticket seller. Each person in the crowd thinks that all the others are going into the tent, so, he concludes, that as he is started he will keep on. Thus do people who hadn't intended to visit the side show at all, once started, soon find themselves paying over their money for admission.

The explanation, however, is simple enough. To understand it, recall a point I made in the last problem section. We agreed that human motives could be compared in some respects to the engine in an automobile. Well, if a motive is a mind engine, then the impulse is the self-starter. In other words, *when you have picked the right motive* and worked on it in the body of your letter you may say that the fuel is ready, the spark ready, and all that is needed is the impulse to start the engine going.

Applying this thought to the circus crowd, we find that we have, although in the crudest form, the scientific "close" for any persuasive argument, whether in the form of letter, advertisement, sales talk, or speech. The salesman who ends his clinching point with, "Now how many will you need?" or, "which style do you prefer?" thus starting you into action by getting you to decide how many or what kind, follows this method. The salesman who deftly inserts a fountain pen in your hand, pointed straight at the dotted line, thus starting you at the first step of writing, has also adopted this principle to his use. The promoter who lays out his long subscription blank at the closing moment and sets you reading off the names of those who have already subscribed—thus accustoming you to the thought of adding your own signature to the list—also *applies the old, old principle* behind the theater's claque, or the circus "shill." They are starting the engine after the gas has been regulated and the spark set.

Hence, a letter that seeks to persuade the reader to act should follow that same course. With what we have learned from the sixth chapter, we know how to arouse the motive for action. Therefore, if we now supply, in the form of a "close" or "clincher," *an impulse that starts that motive working*, we come as close as humanly possible to making sure that our letter will bring results.

Looked at from this new point of view, the matter of writing "a strong close" for a business letter becomes a simple matter. The new point of view, in fact, allows us to set a definite standard by which to measure the exact effectiveness of any proposed close. That standard is this:

The more nearly a close comes to actually starting the motive for action, the better it is.

With that rule in mind, let us examine the close of the letter illustrated on the next page. The motive aroused in that letter is gain—the gain of quality in a particular style or separator and the gain of profit from its use. The action sought is the selection of the writer's separator in preference to others.

Now just consider the last paragraph of that letter, the close, by itself: "Your reply will have prompt attention. What size shall we price you?"

If the Gain Motive has been aroused, as we shall assume it has been, by the fuel scattered through the letter (the Gain Motive keeps saying "better choose this separator, choose this separator, choose it") can't you see how the subtle suggestion of, "your reply will have prompt attention" starts that motive power at work thinking of "your reply"?

In other words, that phrase turns over the reader's mind-engine once, to use the automobile analogy. And the motive power of the mind has something easy on which to begin to work.

Now consider the last sentence of the letter, "What size shall we price you?" By that the engine gets a good, brisk

BUSINESS CORRESPONDENCE

NUWAY SEPARATOR COMPANY
SAN FRANCISCO, CALIFORNIA

Mr. Guy C Williams,
Ragnor, Wash

Dear Sir:

 You were interested to write recently regarding a Nuway Separator and your inquiry was given prompt attention--but we do not recall receiving your reply. Did you receive our catalog?

 If you could understand, as we do, just the kind of material and workmanship we put into the latest Nuway, and the profit and satisfaction you will enjoy in its use, we know you would decide upon the latest Nuway, and nothing else.

 Where can you find such a broad, unlimited guarantee--that we are ready to fulfil at any time--as we offer to the purchaser of a Nuway? Does it not show our unlimited confidence and desire to give a square deal to all purchasers of Nuway Cream Separators? Kindly refer to page 6 in the catalog mailed you.

 Improved Nuway Separators have large capacity, are easier to operate and easier to wash clean, consequently, they save you time and labor, and their life of usefulness is prolonged.

 There is no way that larger net returns can be secured from your herd than by separating the cream and using the warm, sweet, skim milk for feeding purposes, raising your best calves, and developing them for future milkers, or fattening well bred hogs for market

 Nuway Separators actually make and save money, Mr Williams, and viewed only from a standpoint of dollars and cents, there is nothing that will pay so well as the latest Nuway Separator.

 Your reply will have prompt attention. What size shall we price you?

      Very truly yours,
       NUWAY SEPARATOR COMPANY.

LETTERS THAT GET ACTION

spin. The Gain Motive—selecting the best size—is now actually at work. Easily *the prospective buyer finds himself actually engaged in choosing,* one of the processes of buying. It is then quite natural for him to complete the transaction.

If we apply to that close our standard, "*The nearer a close comes to actually starting the motive for action, the better it is,*" we can say that the close which we have just considered is most effective. Unfortunately, it happens that this particular letter is one of the few quoted in this book on applied business correspondence on which it was impossible to secure a statement of the actual results. But I would be willing to go on record as believing that if the letter did not produce results, it certainly was not because of a weak close.

We shall not, however, stop to debate the question, for the letter on page 356 can be analyzed in the same way. I know its record. I know that it really did pay. It happens to be a collection letter instead of a sales letter, but this newest principle, like all others that we are learning, applies to all letters.

The letter on the next page has been used—with slight variation to fit the specific conditions in each case—for |more than a year by a large wholesaler, and in nearly all cases it brought a satisfactory settlement.

Study the close, the last paragraph of the letter, carefully, and you will see that it has exactly the same effect as the close of the sales letter on page 354. In the collection letter close, the customer's motive—protecting his credit—is started on the task of settling the account. The customer is set to deciding whether it would be better to send a check or let the creditor draw, and if to draw, how it would be best to have the drafts come. The cases in which this letter did not bring back at least a letter declaring the debtor's intentions or desires were extremely few—and even that result is valuable to a credit man. But in most cases it brought a prompt settlement.

Just to prove the *effectiveness of the letters built on these new principles* and illustrated on pages 354 and 356, let me quote

BUSINESS CORRESPONDENCE

KREIDELL COMPANY
CHICAGO

Johnson Dry Goods Co.,
Thorp, Mich.

Dear Sirs

    There are two invoices on your account which are overdue, as you will note from the enclosed statement.

    Feb 5 .... $131 26
    Feb 22 .... 234 10
             Total $365 36

    We realize that your purchases must be heavy at this season of the year and are glad to note a continuance of orders coming our way, but we must, both of us, see that we do not lose sight of the terms on which your trade can be profitably handled

    Will you, therefore, look over the enclosed statement and see if you cannot send us a check for the overdue balance, or write us on what date we may draw on you.

    If you prefer not to send a check at once, shall we draw on you for both overdue invoices together at a convenient date — say April 10 — or for one invoice on that date and the other 10 days later?

                Yours very truly,
                KREIDELL COMPANY

Panel 176

THE POWER OF SUGGESTION

Classroom psychology, with the implicit confidence it teaches in the power of suggestion, must be diluted when applied to hard business Experience shows that while mere suggestion, as is claimed, may control experimental subjects in the laboratory, it will not, in business, make many people draw dollars out of their pockets and spend them In the laboratory the constantly reiterated suggestion to a student-subject, "You should let your beard grow," may soon fructify in a set of whiskers on the student's face as it is said to have done

LETTERS THAT GET ACTION

the close of other letters which have come under my observation. For example, I have before me a collection letter of a Boston wholesaler in which the writer went after the debtor in unmistakable terms. But here is the way he closed:

"Thanking you in advance for your prompt attention to this matter, we are ——"

Do you think that spineless ending out of the ordinary? Well, then, read this close of another collection letter, otherwise strong:

"We do a large volume of business at the very lowest possible margin of profit and we simply have to make close collections in order to buy goods of standard manufacturers and at the same time keep our large stock up to the standard at all times. We remain, ——."

In both letters it is easy to see that an impulse to start the reader's motive is lacking. On the other hand, the thought in that second close, if put in the body of the letter, might, I dare say, have been converted into excellent fuel for the motive.

Now the close of the two collection letters is not out of the ordinary. The same fault occurs in sales letters and others which appear in the mails every day. As a final example, read this close of a sales letter:

"Trusting you will see fit to accept our offer and assuring you of our prompt attention, we beg to remain ——."

There you have another close which dashes water on a flaming motive.

Summed up, the trouble with each of the three poor closes I have just quoted is that the reader, instead of a stimulus to action, gets a real "let-down." How many letters fall into that class! I have in my file hundreds of them, and I suppose that if I had access to all the correspondence written in a single day, I would find thousands of letters that, in the final paragraph, retard the reader's motive for action. Many such letters, no doubt, convey a vivid idea, express it clearly, and have plenty of fuel for feeding a strong motive to act.

BUSINESS CORRESPONDENCE

McKAY & HOWARD
DETROIT, MICH.

The R. B. Jameson Co.
Chillicothe, Missouri.

Gentlemen:

I note from your letter of January 7 that you only sell your Model T Burner net cash 30 days

I don't know what your reasons are, nor do they concern me, and far be it from me to attempt to dictate your business policies. But you have only to look us up in Dun's or Bradstreet's to get an idea of what our purchasing volume must be; and your sales department has only to think a moment to realize how unnecessary it is for a plant having that purchasing volume to experiment with new equipment designs on any terms such as you ask.

We have felt willing to try out your burner and, if satisfactory, to make it standard equipment, but if unsatisfactory, to call on you to remove it Thirty days is too short for a test You probably know better than I do which course would follow the testing of your type. I should think it would pay you, if you have confidence that your burner will stand up for us, to make an effort, and even a sacrifice, to get it established with us.

But I leave it to you. Shall we continue to use our present type, or give your goods a trial?

                Sincerely yours,

                   McKAY & HOWARD

Panel 177

LETTERS THAT GET ACTION

But at the wind-up they leave the motive resting on a dead center.

Mind you, I am not maintaining that a letter which does not supply an impulse for action is bound to fail. I have seen many letters closing weakly that, nevertheless, brought results. But I have also seen results secured by letters that made not a single tangible effort to arouse an action motive. That kind of letter never pulls against competition, or against indifference, or against unwillingness to spend money or pay a debt. It fails when the reader is unwilling, as we might say, to get out and crank his own engine.

That thought of cranking the engine is a good one to keep in mind when you anticipate that your reader's mind-engine will be hard to start. In such cases, of course, you must be careful to close with as strong an impulse to action as possible. For other letters you may be more careless—if you are ever willing to be careless. Personally, I believe that every single letter that is written or dictated should be made as nearly right in every respect as there is time and ability to make it. Better to take too much pains than too little. Let me give you an example to prove my case.

One of the best letter writers I have ever known is—what do you suppose?

A purchasing agent!

He has nothing to sell, nothing to collect, no complaints to adjust, no salesmen to coach. He dictates every letter—but he dictates carefully and almost every letter he dictates is a masterpiece for its purpose. On the opposite page is a letter from his file. That letter was sent to a firm from which he wanted to get certain terms, those terms being contrary to the seller's policy. Read the letter carefully and observe how one big, concrete idea is conveyed, just as in a sales or collection letter. That idea, of course, is that the buyer can and will buy elsewhere unless his requirements are met—yet nowhere does the letter specifically so state. In other words, he gives a very definite idea that he will not buy unless his

BUSINESS CORRESPONDENCE

A W SHAW COMPANY
PUBLISHERS
CASS, HURON AND ERIE STREETS
CHICAGO

NEW YORK
BOSTON
PHILADELPHIA
CLEVELAND
A W SHAW CO.,LTD
LONDON

Mr W T Mallers
Sheboygan
Wisconsin

Dear Sir

    We are just putting to press the most important set of books for manufacturers that I know of — "The Library of Factory Management "

    After three years' work by a trained staff, the editorial work is almost complete and we are able to give FACTORY subscribers this chance to secure the books in advance of other manufacturers

    "The Library of Factory Management" consists of six profusely illustrated half-leather volumes (technical book size) detailing the most advanced practice in Production at every point from planning factory buildings to balancing estimated costs with the financial accounts The first two volumes now being delivered, and the other four volumes still in manuscript or proof form show that the set will take a place at the top among books on factory management for profit

    But I need not go into detail The editorial staff has done that in the attached postscript Better yet, you can see for yourself free of charge We do not ask you to buy these books We do ask you to see them — to inspect them as you would a new machine, and satisfy yourself that they will add dollars to your bank account month after month We have not invested in them blindly and we shall be well content with your decision after you leaf through the first two volumes

    So we make you this wide-open offer — we assume the full burden of proof — we do everything we know how, to show our absolute confidence that these books will make money for you Just put your pen to the enclosed card and mail it The first two volumes of "The Library of Factory Management" will come to you AT ONCE for five days without charge You can browse through them at will — and even that cursory examination will give you ideas which are worth money in your plant ESPECIALLY JUST NOW

    Never mind your check book — take no money risk Sign and mail the card As a straight business proposition, won't you do this now?

                            Very truly yours,

                             Thomas S. Rockwell

                                    Manager Book Sales

Panel 178

LETTERS THAT GET ACTION

terms are met, but he leaves the way open to return and buy later on the seller's terms. Still the anxious seller would not ordinarily get that thought.

See also how the buyer arouses a motive for accepting his terms by saying:

"You have only to look us up in Dun's or Bradstreet's to get an idea of what our purchasing volume must be."

Combustible fuel for the Gain Motive—gain of future business—don't you think? Then the writer adds:

"We have felt willing, if satisfactory, to make it standard equipment."

More good fuel to feed the desire for gain. And the writer keeps the motive blazing with this thought:

"——it would pay you, if you have confidence that your burner will stand up for us, to make an effort, even a sacrifice, to get it established with us."

No pleading or bulldozing in that, but just fat, rich fuel for the flames of the desire to sell. And now observe the *impulse that starts that motive actually working:*

"Shall we continue our present type or give your goods a trial?"

That close, before one realizes it, starts the motive of gain for business answering, "give our goods a trial." Not to accept the writer's terms requires the reader deliberately to stop the wheels of his mind-engine and to reverse himself—a hard thing to do. (It might be well to mention that the letter did persuade the seller to ship the goods on the terms wanted by the purchasing agent).

The purchasing agent's letter brings up a second point which must be considered in shaping the close of a letter, that is, to *make it hard for a reader to decline the action* desired. You have seen an example in the purchasing agent's letter. You may see it repeated in the close of one of FACTORY's letters, on the opposite page. In that letter the manufacturer's Gain Motive is started on the simple action of, "Just put your pen to the enclosed card—," "never mind your check book—," "as a straight business proposition—," and

BUSINESS CORRESPONDENCE

HARPER TOOL COMPANY
ST. LOUIS, MISSOURI

Mr. T. L. Vance,
Grant Park, Illinois.

Dear Sir:

    Since you persist in ignoring our letters requesting peaceful settlement of your account, we can only conclude that you prefer the troubles of a brush with our attorneys to paying this debt a day before you have to.

    Yours is the choice.

    One way, you have the use of our money for a few weeks longer at the expense of trouble, very likely notoriety, and certainly legal costs. The other way, you pay your debt now, and have the satisfaction of knowing it is out of the way.

    Which will you do? Not hearing within 10 days, we shall conclude that you prefer the first course we have mentioned and our attorneys will be instructed to proceed against you.

                    Yours truly,

                    HARPER TOOL COMPANY

Panel 179

PRACTICAL PSYCHOLOGY

You know that to start an automobile engine after your fuel is regulated and your spark set, you first apply an outside starter. In simple, untechnical terms, you give the engine an artificial push to give the real motive power a chance to get in its work. From that first light task it soon gains full headway—and your car is ready to move. That is physics. And likewise you know that if, instead of trying to start an automobile you were trying to sell one to a prospect, you would not wisely say at the close of your first talk, "Write a check for $2,000 at once and get your car." You would probably say "Let me give you a demonstration." In other words, you start his buying motive off on something easy. That is psychology. In both cases you have followed one principle—helped the motive power to get started on some light, easy task, then directed its momentum into the larger, the final action. That is the idea behind every good close to a business letter.

LETTERS THAT GET ACTION

HARPER TOOL COMPANY
ST. LOUIS, MO.

T. L. Vance,
Grant Park, Illinois.

Dear Sir:

Since you persist in ignoring our letters requesting peaceful settlement of your account we can only conclude that you prefer the troubles of a brush with our attorneys, to paying this debt a day before you have to.

Yours is the choice.

We have placed all data in our attorney's hands with instructions to proceed against you in 10 days. You can now either ignore this letter, later answering in person either to the attorney or the court, and in the end paying both bill and costs — or you can simply send us the amount of your bill by return mail. Merely fold your check or money order into this letter and the whole matter is settled.

But be sure you do it BY RETURN MAIL or it will be too late.

Yours truly,

HARPER TOOL COMPANY

Panel 180

BUSINESS CORRESPONDENCE

so on. For him to decline to go through with the action requires him to reverse action and say, practically, "I don't care if it is a straight business proposition, I don't care if all I have to do is sign the card—I won't do it." And that is generally hard for many men to say or do.

To hark back for a moment to the crowd in front of the circus show, such a close at the end of a letter which has really aroused a motive for action, is just like the unseen pushing of the "shills," which starts one moving forward to the ticket seller. Such a close puts one in the position of the man outside the tent. *It makes it easier to continue to act* than to come to a stop, turn around, and go back.

To make this point still plainer, look over the letter illustrated on page 362. It was written and tested by a New York publishing house. The writer made an effort to supply in his close an impulse to start action, but his close was like a self-starter that doesn't quite start. Study carefully this paragraph:

"One way you have the use of our money for a few weeks longer at the expense of trouble, very likely notoriety, and certainly legal costs. The other way you pay your debt now, but you have the satisfaction of knowing it is out of the way."

You can see that the paragraph gives a slight impulse to the debtor's Self-Preservation Motive by encouraging the decision to take the less troublesome course. Note, however, the final statement, which reads:

"Which will you do? Not hearing within 10 days we shall conclude that you prefer the first course we have mentioned and our attorneys will be instructed to proceed against you"

That close leaves the motive hung on a dead center. A test of that letter showed only fair results. The letter was then changed to the form shown on page 363. *Results increased nearly 60%.*

Now in the light of what we have already learned, it is easy to see how this latter close not only supplies the impulse to act, but makes it actually easier (mentally) for the debtor

LETTERS THAT GET ACTION

to continue on that action and really mail the remittance, than to stop and resume his former attitude.

In the close of the letter as first written, the phrase "not hearing from you in 10 days we shall ———" makes it easy for the debtor to say "All right, start something." But in the close of the revised letter, his *Self-Protection Motive is started on the ease and simplicity of winding up the affair*—"simply sending the remittance—," and, "merely folding check or money order —," and at the end he is led to consider a necessity for taking those simple steps quickly. In other words, keeping on and finishing the job is made easy.

Now we are aware of two big points that go to make the close of a persuasive letter stimulate action. We have found that *a letter to get action should first supply the little impulse*—the push—the psychological self-starter—that sets the wheels of the motive in actual movement, even though that movement is directed only to deciding some minor or preliminary point of the real action. We have also learned that the close of the letter should make following the preliminary action easier for the reader than stopping and going back.

Before going on and showing you how to apply these principles to your letters, let me give you one more example of what I'm driving at. On the following page you will find in a letter applying for a job, an excellent example of the application of both principles I outlined in the preceding pages.

Note that although the Big Idea conveyed is the writer's value as a copy man, the motive he seeks to arouse in order to persuade the employer to give him a chance is the Duty Motive in the form of business justice. See how *his close* beginning in this way *stimulates action:*

"Please put yourself in the place of an advertiser and consider me as a solicitor for your agency ———."

With that sentence he sets the employer's motive of business justice at work on the simple little job of thinking how *he* would like to be treated. And what advertising agent cannot quickly say to himself how he would act toward a

BUSINESS CORRESPONDENCE

555 COCHIN AVENUE

Mr. James R Early,
Montreal, Quebec.

PERSONAL

Dear Sir·

    To cause one of your employees to lose his job is not my intention But if any one of your employees has MY job--then it isn't his--every man has a place somewhere, and I want my own.

    If you have a copy writer working on mail order accounts who can't write a piece of copy as good as the sample enclosed, marked Exhibit 1, and which brought back inquiries at a cost of 53 cents, from which sales were closed at a cost of $6.10, when the lowest cost per sale had previously been about $10--then he has MY job, and his job is somewhere else

    Isn't that about right? Isn't that the basis on which YOU go after accounts?

    Exhibit 2 pulled 144 inquiries from the Cosmopolitan, 28 from Motion Picture Magazine and 33 from Argosy The average cost is about $1.40. Exhibit 3 is the only piece of copy that paid out on this proposition last year--it is the only one I wrote, but two other copy men had had a try at it before it came to me

    If you have a copy writer who is producing mail order copy that doesn't pay like that, HE HAS MY JOB Wouldn't you feel that way if another agency had an account for which you could get better results?

    I have other samples I could show you--in five years' experience I have handled about every sort of mail order proposition there is. All I ask is a chance to show you Isn't that all you ask of a prospective client?

    My name and address is
               H A Hornsby
               555 Cochin Avenue
               Brooklyn

    My age is 27. I am a graduate of Williams

    Please put yourself in the place of an advertiser and consider me as a solicitor for your agency--and then write me whether or not you will give me a chance to prove to you that we are both losers if my real job is with you and I'm not filling it

               Yours respectfully,

                             H. A. HORNSBY

Panel 181

LETTERS THAT GET ACTION

solicitor if *he* were the advertiser? Then the applicant continued:

"— and then write me whether or not you will give me a chance ——."

The employer, remember, has been set to thinking how fairly, if he were an advertiser, he would treat an agency's solicitation of his business. So it is much easier for him to continue with that declaration and give this applicant "a chance," than to reverse himself and refuse the applicant an opportunity to demonstrate. The letter worked out that way and the copy writer secured the job.

Now, then, when you *boil down what we have learned so far* about the close of a letter, you'll find that every good close of a persuasive letter ties very closely to the particular motive the letter has sought to arouse. In short, a close properly constructed not only supplies the impulse to act, but also it supplies some little job for the motive to act upon. That's a rather difficult point to grasp, I know, but if you will review with me that sales letter on page 354, my point, I think, will be clear at once.

The motive of the letter is gain of quality in the style of separator to be bought, and gain of profit from its use. Now, by having that motive clearly in mind, the writer's simple task in closing was to pick some job on which that motive could get busy. He did it by pointing out the model on which the most gain would be likely, if a purchase was made. Is that clear?

Let me repeat that thought The writer whetted the farmer's appetite for making the money offered by this type of separator. That was the motive. *The impulse, the whip to action, the job for the motive* is the way he set the farmer to deliberating over the size that would give the most gain. That was a job which the motive would pick up easily.

You'll find the same idea in the letter on page 356. As this letter aroused the debtor's Self-Protection Motive (protecting his credit) the writer had to find a job which would set that motive speeding to action. He chose the

BUSINESS CORRESPONDENCE

FREDERICK H BARTLETT & CO.
CHICAGO, ILL.

Mr C H Jasper
Oak Park
Illinois

Dear Mr Jasper

    Suppose that for a long time you had considered buying a certain something — an automobile let's say All of a sudden you make up your mind you want it You go with the money in your pocket to buy But you find that one machine — the car you'd built all your dreams around — gone! And you couldn't buy one like it anywhere without paying a great deal more than the regular price

    How disappointed you'd be! How much more eager than ever you'd be to get such a car — eager probably to the point of being willing to pay the extra amount asked

    Of course, you can hardly expect to MAKE money out of an automobile — that's where a good investment beats it But you can't have even the faintest desire to own either automobile or investment until you have thoroughly posted yourself on its every feature And once you've done this, it hardly pays to delay acting — buying

    In two previous letters we told you just a little of a tremendously promising investment opportunity — Bartlett's big new, realty development — the "Fortune Spot " We prefer to think these letters somehow never reached your hands, for the response to each was so surprising that it seemed as though almost everyone who got them answered

    These letters briefly dealt with a superb money-making chance open only to comparatively few The few were to be picked from among Advance Inquirers to whom we offered "ground floor" privileges and a special "inside deal "

    As we said before hundreds inquired They wanted the facts They got them And influenced by nothing else but the facts, hundreds invested

    There are however several choice investment chances still open That these would be snapped up in a few days is a moral certainty — if we published broadcast the complete story of the opportunity itself!

    But to increase YOUR profit and to bring this BIGGER profit to you QUICKER —

        — we are withholding any and all definite public announcements to make this last one in private

    We will furnish full information —

        — we will give you the entire advance "Fortune Spot" story —
        — we will tell you simply and plainly the whys and wherefores of its money-making certainties its golden possibilities —
        — we will make you a Preferred Customer of the big Bartlett organization and clearly explain how richly you can profit thereby —

        — and we will do all this without the least bit of obligation to you —

    if you send in the enclosed card and say that you want merely to consider the proposition with an open mind

Panel 122

LETTERS THAT GET ACTION

thought of estimating which method of protecting credit would be most convenient. He was successful.

You probably have used that identical principle a thousand times quite by instinct. For instance, you may have tried to persuade a friend to go with you to a ball game. You tried your best to get your friend's Self-Indulgence Motive (the sport of seeing the game) aroused. You seemed doomed to fail until you craftily asked, "Who do you think is going to win, Bill—the Giants, or the Cubs?" And Bill's sporting motive got started into action on the job of picking his choice of teams. And he yielded to your invitation.

A *good salesman also makes use of the same principle.* Have you ever had a book salesman work you up, unconsciously, to weighing the relative merits of the red leather binding and the green buckram—not that you had any intention of buying either, you thought, but just as a matter of preference? And then before you could stop he had you signed up for the set you had picked as your preference?

He simply started you deciding your preference in bindings as a suitable kind of job for the motive he had aroused. And that is what you have to do in constructing a good close for a letter. Let us see how it works.

On the opposite page is the body of a successful real estate operator's letter. How could we go about constructing a close for it that would stimulate action?

We have learned that *the first thing to do is to consider the action-motive aroused by the letter,* and then seek for some easy preliminary task upon which that motive can be set at work. Well, we can see that the action motive in this letter is a form of Self-Preservation—fear of losing a chance to make money. What is suitable as a starting task for that motive?

What is more suitable, or more natural, than to set the motive at guarding against overlooking any possibility to make money?

Let's see, then, how near we have come in that deduction to the kind of close this letter really had. On the next page you will find all but the final paragraph of the close actually used.

BUSINESS CORRESPONDENCE

Do you see how that close does exactly what we decided that it should? See how it sets the reader's fear of losing an opportunity at work—deciding not to take a chance on being prejudiced.

> Now do you, or don't you?
> If you want to forget once and forever the whole business
> Or if you want to pass up till it's too late an an opportunity that must take first rank among any you have ever had —
> Sign the "No" side of the postal
> But if you like to have before you the complete facts for calm, unprejudiced study —
> And if you are in position to allow a favorable later decision make money for you —
> SIGN THE "YES" SIDE OF THE POSTAL!

But now *the second step in constructing a strong close*, we learned, is to make it easier for the reader to continue the action already started, into the complete action desired, than to halt and go back.

In studying the difference between the closing paragraphs of the collection letter shown on pages 362 and 363, we saw this effect very clearly obtained by the final sentence on page 363. It directed the reader's mind into considering some particular phase of the action just as though he were in the midst of it In that letter, after the debtor's Self-Preservation Motive (protection to his credit) had been started at work on planning the ease of settling the affair, it was deftly set to considering the necessity brought out by the final sentence:

"But be sure you do it by return mail, or it will be too late."

In the letter of application that we studied on page 366 we saw this same effect obtained, after the employer's motive had been set at work considering himself as one of his own customers and the applicant as a salesman. That close set him to thinking about what he should write the applicant, as though it was quite settled that he should write.

Now let us apply that simple principle to the real estate letter close printed on page 368 and see how it works.

LETTERS THAT GET ACTION

The *close so far has reached the point of the alternative*—"Sign the 'yes' side of the postal."

What should be done to make the prospect consider some phase of that action as though he had already decided on doing it? If our principle is right, it should be some thought of how, or when, or why, or some other point about signing "the 'yes' side" of the card. Below I show the ending of that letter. Our principle is the one that was followed.

    Sign it now and see that it's dropped in a mail box
    before the last collection tonight.

Now do you see how simple it is to work out that much discussed and much argued problem of "a strong close?" Of course, as we become more and more used to applying this principle we shall not always stop at the mere settling of the essentials for our closing paragraphs. In order to get away from an appearance of sameness in our letters, or, in letters of extra importance, to get our "starting impulse" working with as little appearance of eagerness on our part as possible, we shall rapidly *learn to shift the essentials of a good close into many different forms.*

For example, on the next page you will find a close for a very effective follow-up letter which was used by a western manufacturer.

Now, at first glance, that close does not seem to fall in with the principle we have just discussed. But let us go beneath the surface of it. In previous letters a special discount had been offered the reader. In the opening paragraph of this letter the prospect is told that the rising costs of raw materials will necessitate withdrawing the special discount, but he will be given 15 days in which to take advantage of it. *The action desired is a trial order* for the manufacturer's goods. The motive for immediate action is Self-Preservation (fear of losing an advantage).

Figure A

We shall say that Figure A, above, graphically represents the final action desired. Figure B, on page 373, is the motive.

BUSINESS CORRESPONDENCE

I don't want to hurry you, but I have issued instructions that this pattern must be held for fifteen days until I have time to hear from each person in the territory where this special offer was made. Your acceptance will not obligate you -- if, when delivered, your judgment tells you that you can afford to do without it, send it back at our expense.

I trust that I have explained fully my reason for writing you at this time -- I do not want you to feel that we are unreasonable in cutting off any advantage which was extended to you before these new conditions came up.

I would rather have you wire the order at our expense than to cause you to lose this opportunity on account of my oversight. So you need not hesitate a moment to use the telegraph blank enclosed.

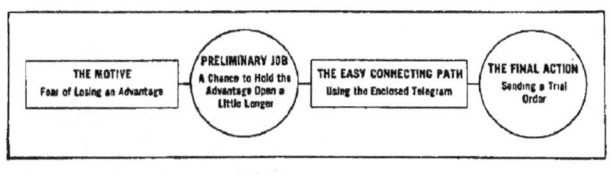

Panel 183

LETTERS THAT GET ACTION

Now analyze the close which I show on the opposite page, but for the time being omit consideration of the last sentence. The writer really does set the reader's motive at work on a preliminary job. In this example the thought is that a trial order will hold the opportunity open a little while longer. The writer did not say that in so many words—he did not want to appear too eager—but the effect of such a statement is there.

> THE MOTIVE
> Fear of Losing an Advantage
>
> Figure B

Hence, in Figure C, below, I have placed the preliminary job of this letter; namely, a chance to hold the opportunity open a little while longer.

Logically, the next point to consider is a method of linking motive and preliminary job to the action desired. In this case the last sentence "So you need not hesitate a moment to use the telegraph blank enclosed" does the work as indicated by Figure D.

> PRELIMINARY JOB
> A Chance to Hold the Advantage Open a Little Longer
>
> Figure C

Now all that remains to be done is to put these figures together in the order I've mentioned and we have a complete diagram, not only of this particular close which we thought at first was different from the others, but of every good close shown in other letters in this chapter as well as a good close for any kind of a persuasive letter you may have to write. You'll find it at the bottom of the opposite page.

> THE EASY CONNECTING PATH
> Using the Enclosed Telegram
>
> Figure D

When you have an important close to write, simply lay out on paper, or in your mind—paper is always preferable—the final action you desire from the reader, whether it be to send you an order, pay a bill, go to a dealer, instruct subordinates, call you on the telephone, write a letter, give you a job, or merely to do a personal favor. Next, write down just as we did above, the big motive for the reader's performing the action. Then think out some minor action you could set that motive busy on—just as we have seen done—and write it as before And finally, plan some little suggestion or encouragement

BUSINESS CORRESPONDENCE

KNIGHT KNITTING CO.
PORTLAND, ORE.

Miss C L. Murray
Geneva
Wisconsin

Dear Madam

    We were very much pleased to receive your inquiry and will do our best to give you the information you wish   Under separate cover we are sending you our latest catalog and we enclose some literature which we feel will be of interest to you

    As you will see by our catalog, we manufacture a complete line of hosiery and underwear   We sell our goods through our representatives, not through storekeepers   We have been selling our goods this way for the past 21 years and have built up an enormous business in all parts of the United States

    Several thousand representatives, both men and women are making money for themselves and for us by selling our goods   They have built up a steady trade for themselves and they find that every year their profits become greater and their work becomes easier

    Our goods are not peculiar in any way   They are what everybody wants   Just high grade hosiery and underwear of fine quality and remarkably low price   So you see you do not need any experience to sell them   They are easy to sell and those who buy them most always become steady customers

    Just a willingness on your part to do your share in making the goods known in your town will go a long way toward giving you permanent and profitable business with a steadily increasing income and financial independence   Selling our goods is not hard   If you only show them to people, they will see at once how much better they are than anything the local dealer can sell at anywhere near the price, for our goods, bought from regular dealers with all the middle men's profits attached, would cost 50% more than you would sell them for

    As to our terms, we give you a commission of 25%   For instance, when you sell $100 worth of our goods, you make $25 for yourself   We prepay all the shipping charges so that you actually make one fourth on all you sell   Doesn't this seem like a fair proposition?

    You may be sure we will help you to the utmost if you take up the work   We will supply you with literature, selling arguments and samples of the goods, in fact we will give you the full benefit of our experience and advice and every advantage that has made possible the success of our representatives

    The same success awaits you if you are willing to make a start

    We only ask you to deposit a small amount for a sample outfit as evidence of good faith   This money is returned to you when you have sold a certain amount of goods, so that the samples really cost you nothing   We take all the trouble and risk so you can begin the work at once, for we know that if you will make a start, you will make a success of the work

                                            Sincerely yours

                                            KNIGHT KNITTING CO

Panel 184

LETTERS THAT GET ACTION

that will furnish *an easy mental path* for the continuance of the preliminary action.

When you have that diagram made for your letter's close you can then put it into any phrasing or wording that may seem expedient—but if you stick to the form of the diagram, you cannot help but get an effective close—one that stimulates action.

Of course, you can point out to me, and I can point out to you, hundreds of letters that seem to have been effective without such an airtight close. I can also point out to you hundreds of big paying letters that close in just the way we have now diagrammed. For instance:

On the opposite page is a letter from an underwear and hosiery house that was unusually successful in getting women agents to sell its goods. The close of the letter has been omitted. Suppose we diagram in the panel below what a good close for it should be like·

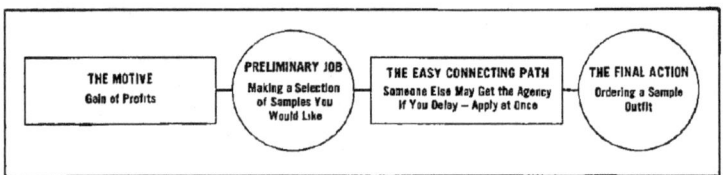

Panel 185

That's the kind of close our diagram would indicate, isn't it? Now, let's see what the man who wrote the letter did. Here is the close he actually used:

```
       We suggest that you make a selection of the
  sample outfit you think best fitted for your re-
  quirements, fill in the enclosed application-for-
  agency blank, and send them right in to us
       We protect our representatives in their terri-
  tory and if you delay writing us, someone else in
  your town may get the agency. So let us hear from
  you by return mail
```

You see with what absolute certainty one can construct the effective close with the aid of a diagram. But there is another point brought up now by this letter and by others,

BUSINESS CORRESPONDENCE

DANIELS & DICKSON
UTICA, NEW YORK

Mr. F. S Ross,
Beaver Dam, Pennsylvania.

Dear Sir

    We gratefully acknowledge your mailing list of D D prospects for circularizing purposes

    Now we want to make this list bring you in as many paying customers as possible, so we are returning it first to you for you to pick out the best names on it, then you send this SELECT list to us separately We have found that it pays the dealer better to have his BEST prospects worked hard than to have a big list worked only a little, so, of course, you will want us to know which are the names it would pay best to work hard for you.

    Four times, we have found, is the right number of times to send mail to good prospects, and as each piece of mail costs us 2½ cents, we will spend for you 10 cents on each prospect. This runs into big money very fast For instance, 1,000 names worked once will cost $25-- worked four times, it will cost a total of $100 We expect you will soon be doing enough business on D D to warrant spending that much, but at the very start we think selected names are better to start on, for then we can hammer them hard and make them into real customers.

    We feel sure, therefore, that you would rather pick out those you know to be the most progressive farmers and the best prospects, than to just have us take any names. Use the enclosed mailing list blank form, for it will save errors. Also, as far as possible, in order that we can send the most effective advertising matter to each name, check them thus, in the column indicated

    "A" -- for "sells cream to creameries"
    "B" -- for "sells whole milk to cheese factories"
    "C" -- for "sells whole milk to bottlers"
    "D" -- for "sells whole milk and cream to

consumers"

                Very truly yours,

                        DANIELS AND DICKSON.

Panel 186

LETTERS THAT GET ACTION

too. You probably have noticed often in what we call on the diagram "the easy connecting path," a reference to something enclosed. In the close last noted it was to the "enclosed application-for-agency blank." In the close previously studied it was to an "enclosed telegraph blank."

On the opposite page is a letter used by a large manufacturer of a dairy supply, to fulfil a very delicate mission. He solicits his dealers to send him lists of prospects for circularizing, and solicits them very persistently. But often a dealer, when he finally does send a list, sends in so many names that it would be out of the question to circularize them all. After working so hard to get any names at all from the dealer, to persuade him to revise the list requires delicate handling. After much experimenting, this manufacturer has found that the above-mentioned letter secures the dealer's cooperation in almost every case—in fact, during the previous year, although nearly a hundred of these letters had to be used, only one dealer refused to make out the new list.

You can readily see how absolutely the close of this successful letter follows our diagram of an effective close, but also note how effectively "the enclosed mailing list blank" cooperates in making an easy path for the action to follow.

In fact, in many cases, *a form of reply blank that helps to make action simple and easy may be of a'most as much importance as the wording of the close.* It is really part and parcel of your "easy connecting path." In the dairy supply manufacturer's letter to dealers, for instance, his close has started the dealer's Gain Motive—getting free advertising from the circularizing—at work on the consideration of what names are best, and has blazed an easy path for continuing this action by the suggestion about checking the class of dairying done. So the mailing list form, on which all this checking can be done easily and quickly, is just another encouragement to actually set about revising the list.

The telegraph blank—all worded in accordance with the offer and ready merely to be signed and handed to a messenger boy or telegraph operator—which is enclosed with the letter

BUSINESS CORRESPONDENCE

PHOENIX ICE COMPANY
NEW YORK CITY

Mrs. Thomas Caswell
New York City

Dear Madam:

Pardon us for calling attention to the fact that you have forgotten last month's ice bill, but this month's bill is soon to be made up and accounts must not be in arrears

We know how easy it is to overlook these small matters. But now that you have it in mind won't you attend to it at once? Just fold your remittance in the enclosed blank, using the self-addressed envelop, so it will not be confused with the current month's bill. Thank you.

Yours respectfully,

PHOENIX ICE COMPANY

Phoenix Ice Co.

My July bill **$1.67** was overlooked. Credit enclosed—☐ check ☐ m. o. ☐ currency—at once to order to bring my account up to date.

Signed _____

Put Stamp Here

PHOENIX ICE CO.
817 Greenleaf Street
New York

THE OLIVER TYPEWRITER COMPANY

☐ Ship me a new Oliver Nine for five days free inspection. If I keep it, I will pay $49 at the rate of $3 per month. The title to remain in you until fully paid for.
My shipping point is _____
This does not place me under any obligation to buy. If I choose to return the Oliver, I will ship it back at your expense at the end of five days.
☐ Do not send a machine until I order it. Mail me your book—"The High Cost of Typewriters —The Reason and the Remedy," your de luxe catalogs and further information.

Name _____
Street Address _____
City _____

Full Length Ribbons—3 for $1, Postpaid

THE R. A. RICHARDS CO

GENTLEMEN:—You may send us postpaid for enclosed $1, three RICHARDS' Best Typewriter Ribbons. If we do not find same satisfactory in every respect, and equal to any typewriter ribbon we have ever used, we shall return same to you, at your expense.

Record or Copying _____ Name _____
Make Machine _____ Address _____
Color _____ City _____
Width of Ribbon _____ State _____

Panel 187

LETTERS THAT GET ACTION

whose close was studied on pages 371 and 373—is just a continuation of the letter's close.

In Panel 187, on the opposite page, the remittance blank and self-addressed envelop play an important part for the collection letters of a large ice company, in smoothing out the way for prompt action. This form is an evolution of long experience. It secures payment of delinquent bills without embarrassment. It helps *materially on small collections*.

This same sort of help in the way of a simple, easy-to-understand and easy-to-fill-out order form or inquiry form would make action easier for many selling propositions. Many good selling letters, instead of being helped, *are handicapped by the order form or inquiry blank* enclosed—simply because the care and study given to the preparation of the letter was omitted when it came to the enclosure. I have seen order blanks and inquiry blanks so complex that I would not dare attempt to fill them out without long, careful study, even if I were quite worked up to buying. And requiring long, careful study by the reader will often stop the work of the aroused motive.

This is particularly true in cases where specifications are part of the order. Almost any nature and quantity of specifications can be reduced to the comparative simplicity that makes it seem easy for the prospect to fill out and sign the order, if you go at them with the determination to make them simple. See how much more helpful to the action-motive of the letter is the order form for typewriter ribbons shown on the opposite page—than the usual commands to state "what machine you use," and so on. The same sort of simplicity and clearness could be imparted to a list of specifications several inches long.

Even the legal requirements which enter into the order forms of some propositions—as in the case of goods sold on instalments or on conditional sale—can be reduced to a less forbidding appearance if a conscientious effort is made. The order form of the typewriter company on the opposite page is a perfectly safe legal contract for all but a few states, yet

BUSINESS CORRESPONDENCE

NO!

Don't inform me further on your unusual investment opportunity Even if there is a chance for me to make money through it I can t possibly see my way clear to invest at this time So let s forget it!

Name

Address

YES!

Send me, at once complete advance information on the Fortune Spot so I may consider it at my leisure This is a simple request for the facts understand please, that *it is not to obligate me in any way* If my judgment tells me your proposition is worth further consideration *later*, I'll let you know

Name

Address

INSURANCE CO OF NORTH AMERICA, Philadelphia
Enclosed is $7.50 for which send me book of 100 coupons which insures 100 packages valued up to $10 each

Name

Address

The Arnold Co. Milwaukee Wis.
I attach flyleaf of my telephone directory Its thickness is ___ inches Please tell me how I can profitably advertise with Arnold Removable Phone Book Covers

Name

Address

Business

THE COLORADO TIRE & LEATHER CO
MANUFACTURERS OF
Durable Treads
DENVER, COLORADO

Special Introductory Cash Certificate

This entitles

    Mr. H. C. Steinway,   Chicago, Ill

to the Special Introductory Discount of 30% from the regular price of the new 1917 Full Cover Model Durable Treads

This Cash Certificate when attached to the Information Blank will be accepted by us as 30% of the regular price whether or not cash is sent with this certificate

        THE COLORADO TIRE & LEATHER CO

Panel 188

LETTERS THAT GET ACTION

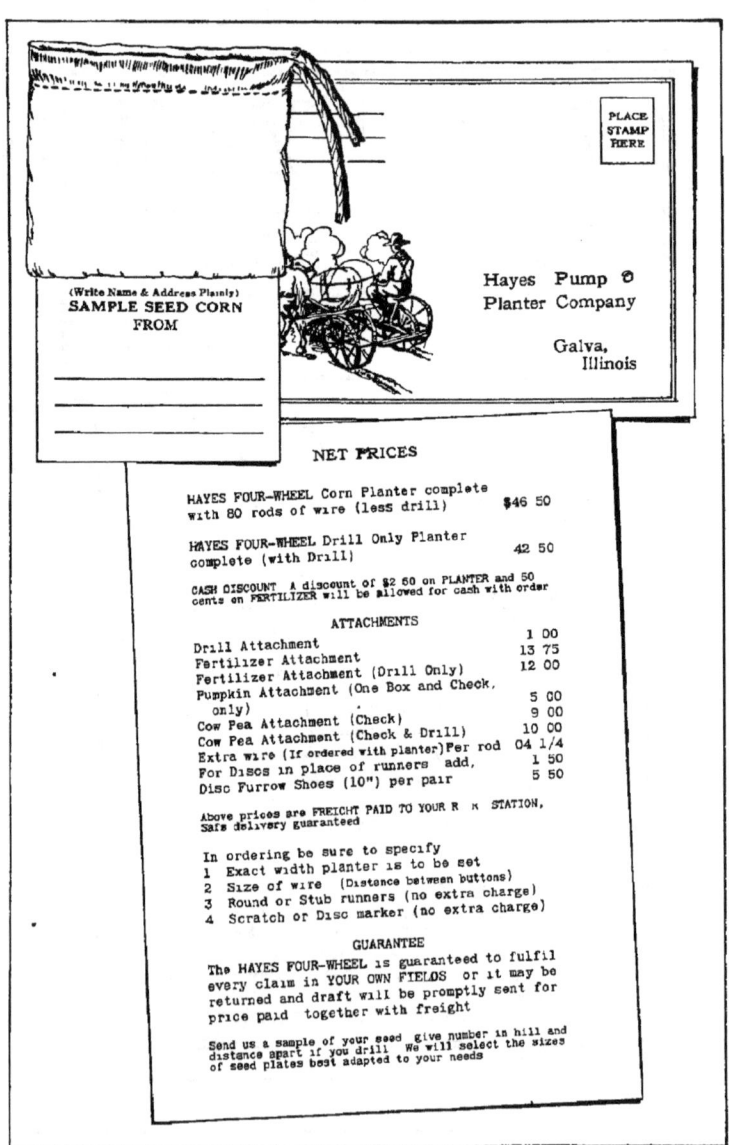

Panel 189

BUSINESS CORRESPONDENCE

so simple that after the letter or advertisement has encouraged you to act, you find no cold water thrown on you when you come to sign. And what a world of detail is covered in the space of two lines in the concise little corner-coupon of an insurance company which you will find in the center of page 380.

In short, the secret of building an effective order card, or coupon for an advertisement, or remittance form for collection letters, is to start where your letter or advertisement ends, **and then work your card or coupon as a natural easy answer to it.**

The order card, which was used with a SYSTEM letter, shown below, and the Arnold Company form, on page 380, are both good examples of how easily such a form can thus be constructed.

Any number of conditions, options, and restrictions that you may have to use, if put into free, easy language appearing to come from the signer, will not seem so formidable to a man or woman—and particularly to a woman—as fewer

---

FREE EXAMINATION COUPON

A W SHAW COMPANY,
Wabash Ave and Madison St, Chicago

Send on for examination, at your expense, the six handy volumes of "The Knack of Selling" I'll dig into their plans and methods and see whether they'll help me to increase my sales If this set does not reveal new ways by which I can sell more goods, increase my ability, instill in me a greater confidence and give me more power, I'll return them, again at your expense But if the books explain new and more effective schemes and methods in selling that I can apply to my own work, I'll remit $3, payment in full I am to be the judge—my word is final

Name _____ Firm _____

Street & No _____ Position _____

City & State _____ Business _____

(Canadian orders, $3 20, duty prepaid, U S Colonies and Foreign, $3 20 cash)

☐ Check here if you want full particulars about the use of "The Knack of Selling" in training salesmen

Panel 190

LETTERS THAT GET ACTION

and even simpler conditions will, if stated in formal terms and in the third person.

At the top of page 380 is the return card enclosed with the real estate firm's letter shown on page 368. Turn back and read the close of that letter, and see that it was worked out on the principle we have learned.

Also on page 380 you will find an enclosure sent in addition to an order card. A special discount has been offered and this extra enclosure helps to keep the Gain Motive working by adding to the impression of value.

Of course, we do not need to consider here any such enclosures as descriptive circulars, "stuffers," and so forth. Such enclosures are taken up in the ninth chapter. All we are now interested in is the little order or inquiry or remittance forms that make the action desired easy for the reader —that *supplement* the effect of the close.

Such helps also have an additional and initiative value all their own. For while the busy man with a big mail may ruthlessly throw away all enclosures that he has decided not to act on, the ordinary man or woman who receives much less mail has a natural dislike to throwing away "a perfectly good envelop" or neat order card The result is the envelop or order card often lies about the desk or reading table, to bob up every now and then and cause the whole question of using it or not using it to be reopened in the prospect's mind. Hence, the more appearance of importance and value you can put into such enclosures without going too high in cost, the better they will pay.

That Hayes' Pump Company group on page 381 is a fine illustration of how such enclosures work. On the printed slip is an easy-to-grasp resume of exact prices for the many different kinds of equipment that is supplied with the planter, and a clear statement of just what information to supply with an order.

As this information includes the kind of seed to be planted, a little cloth sack is enclosed in which to send an actual sample of the seed the farmer uses!

BUSINESS CORRESPONDENCE

This is a letter we have written for you to mail back <u>to us</u>! Funny thing to do, but read it. See if you don't feel perfectly willing to send it—
a stamped and self-addressed envelope is inclosed herewith

Chicago, Ill

Gentlemen

Like probably everyone else in the world I want to make money   I haven't much to invest nor am I particularly anxious to invest anything at this time

Any investment proposition I even consider must not only be sound but also safe — so safe that I'm protected against loss besides having a better-than-usual chance of profiting handsomely

I've heard that you have a big new realty development under way — the biggest and most promising that Chicago has ever seen   I'm told it's city property, only 24 minutes from the loop, with really wonderful transportation facilities   I've learned about the tract being so peculiarly situated that quick and certain value increase is inevitable

I'm told that the rest of the story is a business secret given only to advance inquirers and that those who do inquire are put on your Preferred List, entitled without cost or obligation to special privileges and an unusual "Ground Floor" deal

Make me one of the "Insiders"!

Send me ALL the FACTS please, at once   You will understand, however that in making this request, I am not to be in the least obligated   But if the facts — the confidential story, the location of the Development, its possibilities, the prices, terms etc — lead me to believe your proposition is worth further investigation I'll notify you in due time

Yours very truly,

James M Lee

891 Brompton Ave

Panel 191

LETTERS THAT GET ACTION

Just imagine for yourself the effect this neat little cloth bag is going to have on a prospect. It is too nice to throw away. It is too small to use for anything else. It acts as a constant appeal to make use of it in the only way it can be used; in sending a sample of seed back to the manufacturer with the order.

A coin carrier attached to order blanks for articles costing but a small sum, or enclosed in collection letters for small bills; ready-written telegraph blanks with letters asking hurried action; mailing envelops for photographs where the prospect is asked to let the writer plan the painting or decorating of his building or other property; all such conveniences have the same effect as this little bag

Of course such enclosures probably won't secure an order by themselves. But they help.

A real estate operator went to an extreme point along this line in the letter shown on the opposite page. This was one of a vigorous follow-up series, and really was a "kicker" for the previous letter, rather than a letter in itself. You see it furnishes the prospect a complete, signed letter to mail, worded in a way the prospect can have no objection to using, while the wording is also a very clear expression of the big idea behind the whole proposition. That is the secret of all good enclosures for helping to stimulate action. Make them dovetail with the idea of the letter, and word them as a natural reply to the letter's closing argument.

SUMMARY

WE are now at the top of the hill so far as this book on applied business correspondence is concerned. From now on, the load we have to carry will be less heavy, but not the less interesting. Faithfully following the chart which was described in the first chapter, we have taken up, step by step, the fundamentals of letter writing. We have gone over seven such steps ranging from the "load" of the letter described in the first chapter, through clearness, sincerity, and persuasion down to drawing a strong close which was the "load" of this chapter.

Closing the letter, we found, goes way beyond the psychology of the classroom. And so we added to that the stern realities of business. Classroom teaching with the implicit confidence it places in suggestion may control experimental subjects in the laboratory, but in business it will not make people draw dollars from their pockets and spend them. In business we find that a thousand bare suggestions to act often are instantly wiped out by one suggestion of a motive to act.

Therefore, in this chapter we discarded mere suggestion and for it substituted two simple rules for the close of a letter. These are: 1. To supply an impulse that will set the reader's motive in action, 2. To direct this activity to the result we plan to attain.

The impulse to act, we found, depends upon the selection of a proper motive, as explained in the preceding chapter. To direct the activity, we must supply some easy means of action so that the reader will find it easier to act on the suggestion than to refuse to do so.

It may seem strange now, but in the next chapter, we'll jump back to the beginning of the letter and take up the matter of gripping attention. Although some authorities will disagree, winning attention, as a matter of fact, is the least important point to consider when planning a letter. But for the few cases in which attention must be gripped by some mechanical means it can be secured by following the author's plan of building a stopper for the prospect's attention-rays. How this may be done, the thought behind it, how the stopper hooks the reader to the Big Idea is told in the next chapter, and on completing it, we will have gone a long way in our task of making our prospects stop and read our letter.

PROBLEM SECTION VII

A WORD about motives, by way of review, before we settle down to work on this seventh problem section. You will remember that we decided in the sixth chapter that every human action can be laid to one of six underlying causes or motives. These in their order are: Love, Gain, Duty, Pride, Self-Indulgence, and Self-Preservation. A successful pleader, or more to the point, *a successful persuasive letter* in some way or other invariably plays upon one of these motives. Each one of them appears in life every day in scores of different phases. The real trick, after selecting the motive, is to pick the phase most likely to appeal to the reader.

Motive and motive phase picked, the rest of the job of starting the reader your way is comparatively easy. The fuel, that is, the suggestion which will make the selected motive dominant in the reader's mind, need only be applied at various stages of the letter.

In this problem section we take up the method of securing action by the reader. We shall find that this ties back closely to what we have already learned about motives. Action, we shall find, depends largely upon giving the reader *an impulse to act*. When this urge has been given, an easy means of acting should be supplied. This may be a simple order blank, an enclosed stamped envelop, or any other little task for the aroused motive to work on. However, I think we all understand this matter of motives and are ready for actual practise on the theories we have learned. Our first work consists of checking up the light tasks set in the last problem section.

BUSINESS CORRESPONDENCE

Of the five problems we worked over, the first was that of a purchasing agent's letter. You were to select for the Gain Motive the fuel which would make the seller alter his terms. Now get your work out of your Material File, and compare it with the original letter to be found on page 358.

I should be disappointed if your fill-in at the first break in the letter was not approximately the same as in the original, for the necessity of proving your worth as a customer is essential. It is quite likely, however, that you did not think of the reference to Dun's or Bradstreet's, or if you thought of it, did not like it. You see the necessity of it now, I am sure, for you see that the main point is to have thought of some way in which the seller's desire for gain from your future purchases could be started "licking its lips," as we might say. A suggestion as to the volume of those purchases is, it seems to me, the best sort of fuel, and that is the kind the original letter supplies.

The second stop for fuel holds out a prospect of big orders, naturally enough. At the third fuel station the thought of getting well established with the buyer's firm is certainly necessary.

Let us, then, turn to the second problem I gave you. This dealt with questions relating to a letter of application. In this problem I rather expect you to have come wider from the mark. The motive is unusual for such a type of letter, and requires skilful treatment or it might react on itself. It has been handled in a masterly manner in the letter shown on page 366.

"Every man has a place somewhere, and I want my own," has a *ring of independence and self-reliance* about it that avoids all suggestion of the objectionable sort of pleading for a chance, yet it does arouse the motive of business fairness, or duty, in an employer's mind.

The fuel, "isn't that about right? Isn't that about the basis on which you go after accounts," is free of all tendency to "sob" or beg, yet it has a subtle effect on the employer's motive of business fairness.

And so with the other points. This letter is worth careful analysis in comparison with your own attempt.

In the third problem you were to select both the proper motive and the fuel for it, in a letter to secure agents. The original letter on page 374 speaks for itself.

Next was the collection letter for the ice company. I let you compose the whole letter from a mere sketch of its features in order that you might test yourself on your ability to judge how much motive fuel was necessary. You will see from the original at the top of page 378 that a very little was sufficient to do the work. Why?

Because the customers of an ice company can be assumed to believe that bills must be paid sometime, and hence the motive of saving embarrassment over delayed payments should be one quickly aroused.

The fifth problem gives an example of using more fuel for the motive. The original with which to compare your attempt will be found on page 376.

The Big Idea of that letter, as you will see, is that "It will pay to have the names on your list selected carefully." Its features are:

Experience shows that a few good names thoroughly circularized pay better than many names insufficiently worked.

Four mailings is the most effective number.

Cost of four mailings makes it impractical to cover more than your best names at present.

Now with the idea conveyed by means of these features you will see that the motive for actually doing the work of revising the list, is gain of the free advertising the dealer gets from the circularizing. Compare the fuel you chose for your letter with this:

"So, of course, you will want us to know which are the names it would pay best to work for you."

"We will spend 10 cents on every name for you."

"We will hammer them hard and make them real customers for you."

BUSINESS CORRESPONDENCE

Study the close of this letter in the light of what you have read in the last chapter. Forego study of the opening of the letter This topic will be considered in the next problem section.

Now it is time to turn to our restaurant letter and see how the proper close to stimulate action was constructed. That letter, as we left it in the last problem section, is to be found on pages 339 and 340. Before we do any more writing, refresh your memory by studying over the diagram of a perfect close in the panel below. Then, in this restaurant letter step by step we will follow the rules for closing which I outlined in the preceding chapter.

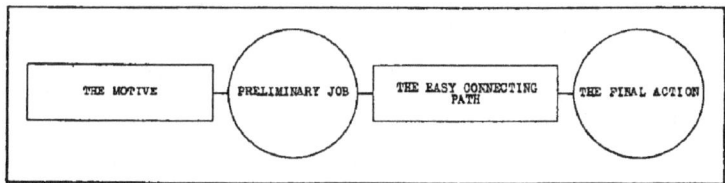

Panel 192

In drawing the close to the restaurant letter, the first thing to do is to set down the final action desired and the motive. The final action in this case we know to be the presentation of the 10-cent coupon. The motive, on account of previous work done on the letter, we know to be Self-Indulgence in the form of the gratification of the prospect's sociable, sport-loving instinct.

The second step, as we learned in the foregoing chapter, is to plan some easy little task to set the motive at work.

Let's see. The reader's sport-loving instinct is aroused, so why not give it this easy little job: "Well, I've got to eat somewhere—why not have the fun of calling this fellow's bluff?" Like this:

    You've got to have lunch somewhere — come on along
    and have it here today and call me on my bet.

Wouldn't that arouse the reader's motive for the bigger action? Thirdly, we must provide his motive with an easy path to

LETTERS THAT GET ACTION

the final action. We have seen in the last chapter how effective is some inference that the action which is desired has already been decided on, so how would this be?

> Come on — this noon — when we'll be sure to have Anna spare no pains — and bring a friend with you — same offer holds good for him. Come ahead!

Below you'll find the complete letter.

> Dear Sir:
> I'd give a dime to see you eat your first piece of Anna's lemon pie.
> My, what lemon pie that woman can bake! Why, man, when you close your lips and tongue on a piece of that pie it's like a little gushing fountain in your mouth just deluging your palate with delightful tastes!
> First the frosting — not the sugary sort of meringue you're thinking of, but frosting — of cool, snowy, vaporous sweetness. Then quickly the refreshing lemony — not sourness, mind you, that's too strong a word — but rather a wild, pleasing tartness. Then sweetness and tartness crushed in together, and pouf! they join and blend in an entirely new taste that gradually melts away somewhere down your throat and only a soft, happy memory remains — until your next mouthful.
> Yes, Anna certainly has a knack about lemon pies that's all her own. You'd say it, too — I'll bet a dime you would!
> Then the crust — I must call it crust, I suppose, as if it were like other pie crust — it's crisp, of course, as good pie crust should be, it's flaky — but Anna's crust, when you put it into your mouth, seems to have only been making believe to be crust after all For where is it? It crumbles and flakes away and gives itself up to the rest of the pie, like a sacrifice — to help make one grand, complete taste of paradise for you.
> Yes, sir — I'd gladly give a dime just to see you taste your first piece of that pie! By George! I will give a dime! I'll put it right in this letter — or a coupon as its equivalent — and if you'll come in today, have your luncheon and top off with a piece of Anna's lemon pie — you can simply hand in the coupon with your lunch check as payment for the pie.
> You've got to have lunch somewhere — come on along and have it here today and call me on my bet Come on — this noon — when we'll be sure to have Anna spare no pains Bring a friend with you — same offer holds good for him. Come ahead!
> Yours truly,

BUSINESS CORRESPONDENCE

No especial beginning was put on it—for a reason that you will learn later. It was mailed as it stands—405 letters in all, of which 20 were returned because of incorrect address or other cause, leaving a net list of 385. And 122 coupons were used. But one of the biggest results was the spirit created—nearly all these men had good-natured comments to make as they threw down the coupons, and that good-natured spirit was a part of the trade thereafter.

It required several days of intermittent fussing and arguing to produce the letter, but as in the end this fussing turned the tide of business from the mediocre to the prosperous, they were days profitably spent.

Problem 1

Now you may try putting into practise the way we have learned for charting out a strong close—one that stimulates action. To begin, I'll give you an easy task. Below is the main portion of a letter sent to mattress manufacturers by the manufacturers of a packing case. I want you to work out an effective close for it.

"The railroads think so much of the Sefton box for shipping mattresses, they are changing the classification to accommodate it.

Your competitors are enthusiastic about the results they obtain by its use.

The retailer is delighted with it.

If anything further is necessary to convince you, read our proposition in the next paragraph, look inside this letter, and then act on your best judgment.

Without cost or obligation, we will send you a Sefton mattress box."

In Panel 193, on the following page, you will find the diagram of the close. Motive, preliminary job, and final action have been filled in for you. All that remains is to suggest the easy connecting path. Write it down, and file it

LETTERS THAT GET ACTION

in your Material File. In the next problem section we will see how closely you came to the proper answer.

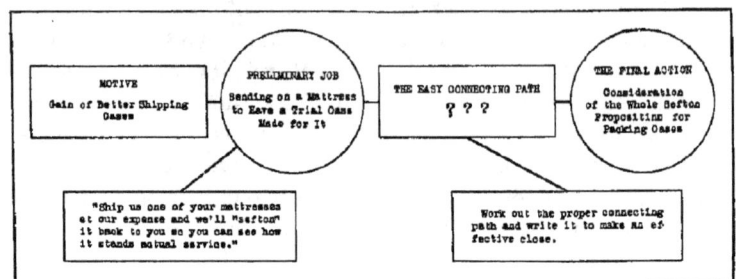

Panel 193

Problem 2

Now we'll go a bit further. I have reproduced, below, the body of one of System's own letters, and in the panel on the next page, I have charted out the complete close. I want you, from that chart, to write the close the chart suggests to you. File this also in your Material File and next time we will see how the Mail Sales Department of System did the work.

```
Dear Sir
       That vexing question answered
—that business problem solved
—directly, accurately, instantly — and you need not even
leave your desk
       Of all the mediums ever devised for keeping the busy
man in live-wire touch with every business fact or figure
necessary to his day's work, nothing has ever yet been
published that proved quite as reliable and handy as the
"Business Man's Encyclopedia"
       These books answer all those questions that pop up un-
expectedly every day, the little business puzzlers that
harass and hinder you most, how to key an ad, how to buy
for a quick turnover, how to say the right thing in a busi-
ness letter, how to collect a bad debt without causing un-
pleasantness, how to get a testimonial from the customer
who complained
       Ready for quick references are hundreds of just such
subjects, all indexed and awaiting but a turn of the page and
a glance of the eye — to get just what you want  You are
given a complete business dictionary, all kinds of weights
```

393

BUSINESS CORRESPONDENCE

and measures; important facts and pointers on business law, correspondence, proof reading, copyrights, patents, corporations, banks, drafts, checks, exchanges, insurance, leases, common carriers, interest, lightning calculation methods This mere letter could not even hint at one-tenth part.

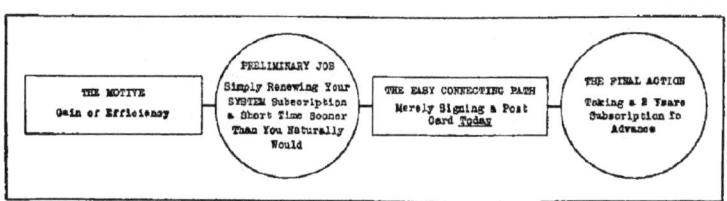

Panel 194

Problem 3

For your third practise problem I reproduce below the body of a book publisher's sales letter. I want you now to try doing all the work of starting action for it. Chart out the complete close and write it. Then file your work in your Material File. In the next problem section we will see how nearly you came to the one actually used.

Dear Sir

You own six volumes of Kipling's works which we gave you.

When Mr Kipling learned that so many Americans were receiving these six volumes he consented to an arrangement by which you can add in uniform style, all of his other books, 19 volumes, so that you will be the owner of a magnificent 25-volume set of Kipling's COMPLETE works — all that have been published.

The royalty payments on the other volumes have heretofore been so large as to preclude a low price. One set of 25 volumes has been sold at $50 The Seven Seas Edition, a limited edition, is being subscribed for at $138

If you will promptly take advantage of Mr. Kipling's special arrangement for your benefit, we will ship to you 19 new volumes, thus making a 25-volume Kipling set in absolutely uniform type, paper and binding, for only $1 a volume, payable $1 a month

Furthermore, you will have a guarantee from us that you can add any future books that Mr. Kipling publishes, uniform with your set, for $1 per volume.

LETTERS THAT GET ACTION

This is a great opportunity   It means actually that for $19, payable at $1 per month, (or $17.10 if you prefer to pay in cash,) you can own all the Kipling volumes published, for which others have paid $50, practically the same except for paper and binding, that others are now paying $138 for

THIS IS THE FIRST TIME THAT A COLLECTED SET OF KIPLING HAS EVER BEEN OFFERED AT THIS LOW FIGURE.

When Mr Kipling's cable came we made one edition out of paper purchased at the old price. (The price has more than doubled now)   Some sets of that edition remain, and you can have one if you are prompt   POSITIVELY NONE CAN BE FURNISHED AT THIS PRICE WHEN THESE REMAINING SETS ARE GONE.

Problem 4

For the fourth and last problem I am reproducing the body of another letter—a farmer's. I want you this time not only to chart and write a complete close, but also to lay out and write the proper kind of Return Order Card. In the next chapter you will be shown the one actually used with great success, with which to check up your progress.

My dear Mr Allen

I have eggs to sell for Easter, which will be new-laid just before the holidays.

Since you have not yet tried Sycamore Farm eggs, brought from the farm to your door in an hour, will you consider this special Easter offer?

I am not going up on my prices for eggs during the Easter holidays. On the contrary, if you order four dozen (or more) of my eggs, using the enclosed order blank, I will deliver them at your door the Friday or Saturday before Easter for 30c a dozen

These eggs I will guarantee to be not more than from one to three days old on delivery at your door. In addition to their absolute freshness, all my eggs are large and brown and of the best possible flavor, as they are produced by hens fed a balanced grain ration approved by the Department of Agriculture. The nests are kept entirely fresh and clean, and free from all alien matter or disinfecting agents. This is an important point in egg production, as eggs very quickly absorb flavor and bacteria from an unsanitary condition of the nest and hen houses. Eggs should be as carefully guarded from contamination as any other food product

BUSINESS CORRESPONDENCE

```
Do you know where your eggs come from, and how they have
been cared for?
   Easter is a time when eggs are plentiful and the prices
low   But it is also a time when you should insist on get-
ting only the best and freshest   If you do not keep hens
yourself and have your own eggs, why not take this oppor-
tunity to get Sycamore Farm eggs?  One trial will convince
you of the difference between store eggs and these eggs
straight from the farm
```

When you complete your work on the order card and have charted and written a close which pleases you, file your work in the Material File. In the next problem section you'll be handed a letter which brought orders rolling in although the list to which it was sent was extremely difficult to pry orders from.

Completing work on this problem section is another milestone in your self-imposed job of writing better letters. In the next chapter we'll take up the matter of gripping attention and then I'll supply some different problems.

PART VIII

HOW TO MAKE LETTERS GRIP ATTENTION

CHAPTER VIII

HOW TO MAKE LETTERS GRIP ATTENTION

NOW that we are ready at last to take up the question of making letters grip the reader's attention, it may be well to state why in this book the study of a letter's beginning has been put off so long. It is because most letters do not require a studied method of attracting the reader.

For all letters written to answer inquiries, for all letters written to regular customers on ordinary subjects, for all letters written to present claims, to pay bills, to explain, to adjust, to acknowledge, and to record—even for many important letters written to sell goods or to collect money—the letter itself is enough. In fact, for 90% and perhaps more of the individual letters written or dictated in business, a properly addressed envelop and a postage stamp will insure the attention of the person addressed.

The big job for most of us lies in expressing the idea and getting it understood, or believed, or acted upon.

Therefore, until we had learned to make a letter explain our idea and to make that idea appeal to an indifferent reader, or to make that idea clear to readers to whom it was new, we could well afford to defer a study of attention-winning schemes. Until we learned how to make our letters seem truthful and frank when the confidence of the reader had to be won, or to make our suggestion seem a good thing to do in case action was necessary, or to get action started in case prompt action was wanted, study of attention-winning stunts would have distracted us from more important matters.

In short, until we had learned how to make a letter carry its "load," a study of how to attract attention to it would have been about as fruitless as teaching a student

BUSINESS CORRESPONDENCE

of oratory how to attract a big crowd before he had learned how to address one

But now that we have covered all the foregoing points it is time to take up the remaining 10% of letters. Under this list come all *which we may reasonably expect will be ignored* unless the reader's attention is deliberately attracted to them.

Of these letters probably the most important are circular letters—in other words, form letters mailed to unknown people, either for direct orders or for general advertising effect. Naturally, it is not safe to assume, as a general proposition, that such letters will meet with an attentive reception, although from many people all letters, circular or otherwise, do get close attention.

Also classed among the remaining 10% are the last letters in a long follow-up series to inquiries, when the inquirers may be assumed to have become tired of considering the proposition.

In this category also belong the final letters of a collection series. The debtor may be assumed to have become callous to the duty of paying his bill

And finally comes a type of letter that may be written to people who can be depended upon to give a careful reading to the letter as a whole, but for which a *special kind or degree or attention* is wanted.

In this chapter we are going to meet all those varieties of letters and see how a proper send-off can be planned for them, so that they will be lifted off the humdrum plane of circular letters and so that they may be made *to grip the receiver's attention.*

You notice that I say *grip* the receiver's attention, *not* attract it. Think well of that distinction, because it is going to have an important part to play in the kind of opening we learn to plan for a letter *We don't want our letters merely to attract attention.* A poorly written, or poorly spelled letter, or mussy, soiled stationery, or a bizarre, rainbow-colored letterhead might *attract* attention. An applicant

LETTERS THAT GRIP ATTENTION

for a job might attract an employer's attention by appearing in a clown's suit.

But *gripping* attention requires holding it and controlling it. That is what we want our letters to do. Hence the method by which we attract must be harmonious with the idea our letter conveys—else the attention attracted will not be gripped but later will be repelled. I shall give you a few examples of what I mean.

On the next page is a letter which falls into the second class of letters I mentioned; that is, one of the last letters of a follow-up series. Notice the thumbprint near the top of the letter. Now I warrant that you are tempted to say that getting attention by means of a thumbprint is a freakish way of attracting, instead of gripping, attention. And so it would be, I believe, in most cases. But study the letter. See how the thumbprint on the letter sheet blends with the thumbprint feature of the idea.

Instead of being annoyed by having your attention attracted by the thumbprint because the idea of the letter is totally unconnected with the means of attracting your attention, you find *a logical development of the attention-getter into the idea.*

On pages 404 and 405 is another letter that at once draws the attention. In this case the attention is drawn by the unusualness of those colored panels and arrows. A frivolous method, you may say at first. The letter seems to attract attention by its oddity—like a man wearing "loud" clothes. But consider further. Each panel, on closer inspection, shows something worth noticing to anyone who has been interested in this proposition. And the arrows, instead of deceiving us, point to something additionally interesting. The attention that was drawn by the panels and arrows is not disappointed. Investigation, at least, seems to be very much worth while.

The reader looking over his mail gets a series of impressions just as you might if—let us say—you were driving along a country road. While driving, probably every once in

BUSINESS CORRESPONDENCE

NATIONAL LEAD COMPANY
CHICAGO

Mr William Prindeville
Chicago Ill

Dear Sir

SMUDGY FINGER PRINTS, SIMILAR TO THIS ONE soon appear on interior walls Every year owners of buildings pay out thousands of dollars to have these and other unsightly marks covered over by paper or paint, because paper and many paints will not stand washing

White-leaded walls, tinted or white, are washable Lukewarm water and mild soap will clean, freshen and sanitate them, without injuring even the most delicate finish

Frequent painting is considered unnecessary Right there is one dollar-saving reason why you should have your architect specify Dutch Boy white lead throughout (walls as well as woodwork) for the apartment house that is being built for you at 1210 Franklin Avenue

Another reason, equally as important, is that Dutch Boy white-leaded walls do not chip off or crack The paint dries hard but is still sufficiently elastic not to break Moreover, paint made of Dutch Boy white lead excels in beauty of finish, whether flat or gloss It costs no more per gallon It spreads farther and covers better It lasts longer

Yours very truly,

NATIONAL LEAD COMPANY

P S — We maintain a staff of paint specialists whose entire time is devoted to owners who have paint problems or who desire color suggestions It will be a pleasure to assist you in any way without obligation on your part If necessary, we will send a representative to consult with you.

Panel 195

LETTERS THAT GRIP ATTENTION

a while your attention would be suddenly attracted by a fleeting glimpse of what promised to be an interesting scene. You'd stop at once for a better view. If the glimpse, on closer inspection, led on to a vista that interested you, you'd be glad you stopped and you'd observe every detail of the scene. But if your attention had been attracted by only an odd glimpse of an otherwise dull scene, you'd probably be disappointed, give the scene but one look, and then move on and forget it.

So with letters. The two on pages 402 and 404-405 which we have just looked at attracted attention by a glimpse—nothing more—but the glimpse led on, not to a different idea than we expected, but to one that developed quite consistently from the glimpse.

Here, then, we plainly see two elements to be considered in planning to make a letter grip attention.

1. The receiver's attention
2. The idea to which his attention must be led.

Therefore, the opening, or the arrangement, or the heading, or the illustration, or whatever it is with which we attract attention, must be designed to lead without disappointment to the idea we want our reader's attention to grip. Only in that way can we *both attract and grip the attention.*

Now what is attention? That's a familiar word. We all have our own definition of it, but probably few definitions would agree. Therefore, before going further, let us analyze and agree on what we mean by "attention," so that we shall know what we are about when we set out to attract it.

I spoke a while back of riding in the country and having the attention suddenly attracted by a glimpse of scenery. Why should such a glimpse stop one? How does it? What part of the mentality of a man constitutes the attention that was stopped? Perhaps this personal experience will best answer the question for us.

Once I traveled down the Mississippi River. There happened to be but few passengers on the boat and the captain

BUSINESS CORRESPONDENCE

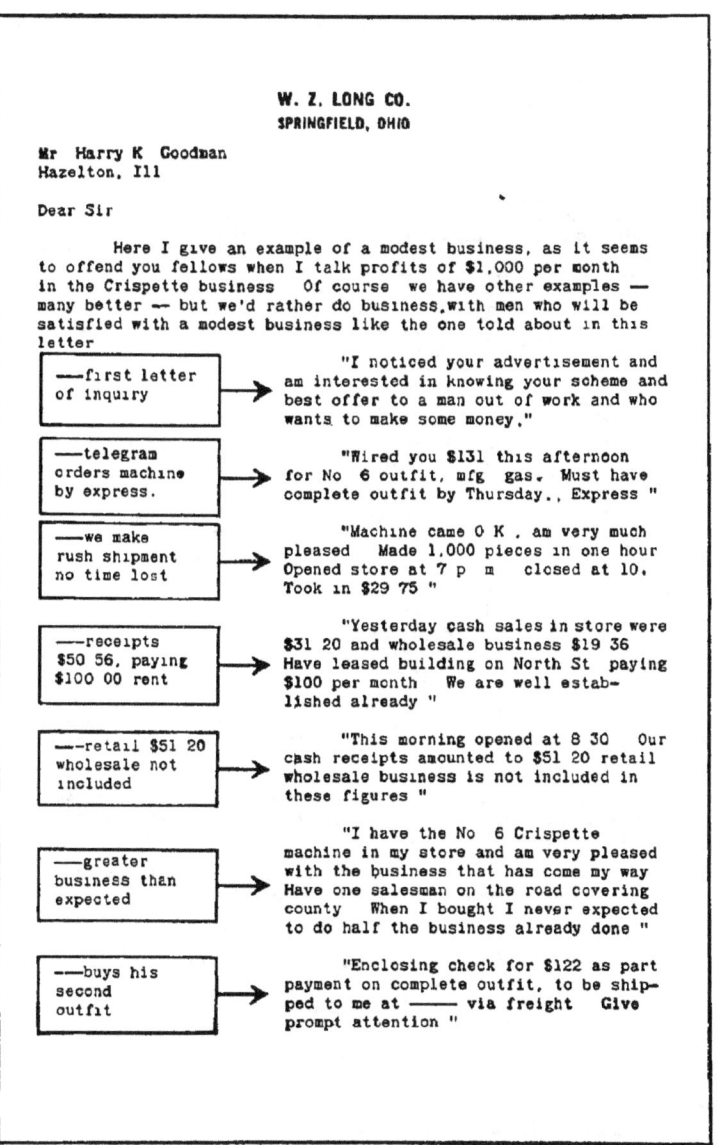

Panel 196A

LETTERS THAT GRIP ATTENTION

Mr Harry K Goodman - 2

——cash sales retail only $39 16	"Convinced there are barrels of money in the Crispette business My cash sales alone in the store today were $39.16."
——telegram, asks cash price on 3rd machine	"Did you make shipment Crispette machine to ————————? Quote best price on another for cash by wire Going to pay cash for 3rd machine Doing biggest business ever known "
——telegram, orders 3rd complete outfit	"Have wired cash Ship today to ———————— All mail to Pittsfield Confirm by wire as soon as possible "
——"going some" looking for job a month ago	"I am doing business which I believe no other Crispette man ever did I am backed up with $10 000 cash Refer to Dun's or Bradstreet's "
——sales never under $50 daily	"I will have a photo made of my store and my employees then you can judge the business I am doing. My sales never drop under $50 a day in the store "

These letters and telegrams are all from one man How's that for a small town, in the middle of winter? There's no good reason why you shouldn't do as well There are hundreds of locations all over the country

Read this man's first letter "Out of work" — "Want to make some money " He got the machine and followed instructions The letters and telegrams tell the story.

There's an order blank with this letter Send it with your remittance today We will ship promptly.

Yours very truly,

W Z LONG COMPANY

by———————————

Panel 196B

BUSINESS CORRESPONDENCE

let us amuse ourselves with the searchlight in the evenings. As we swung its rays over the shore, every once in a while at the very edge of the light would appear some object that looked *alive*. Immediately we would turn the full glare of the light on that object. Sometimes we would find something alive and interesting; other times we would discover that our attention had been attracted by only a light-colored bush or other inanimate object, and then we would swing our rays forward again. Always we hunted for *something alive* to be picked up. That's what I mean by attention.

The constant sweeping of the searchlight's rays as we went down the river typifies to me the attention of the normal human mind. With its rays it is continually sweeping the sky line of life for indications of something worth turning its concentrated light upon.

For instance, a man sits at a window apparently looking at nothing. Ten men pass and he hardly sees them. The eleventh comes along and something about that eleventh man makes the man at the window think of a soldier. He is interested in soldiers and he stops his attention—his searchlight—and turns its full light on that man. Or, picture a man at his desk looking over his morning mail. The first six circular letters receive a glance that sweeps over their contents, and then they are dropped into the waste-basket. His glance sweeps on to the seventh—but the seventh is that letter on page 402. It has a smudgy fingerprint on it that stops his attention as it is about to swing on over it to other things

"What's that?" he wonders. Then he turns back to the letter and reads:

"Smudgy fingerprints, similar to this one, soon appear on interior walls— " So they do, he agrees

"Every year owners—" and in the full glare of his attention now turned on the letter the Big Idea is lighted up.

Have I made myself clear? I'm sure I have. To fix my point unforgetably, however, I'll illustrate it for you. At the top of the next page I have pictured a searchlight and

LETTERS THAT GRIP ATTENTION

its rays (the attention of a business man who is opening his mail). Below, in Panel 198, I have indicated for you the Big Idea of a letter you've sent him. Your reader's attention as he takes up your letter is sweeping on. It will sweep right on over your idea and beyond it, unless there is something about your idea that sticks up into one of those rays and *causes his attention to stop.*

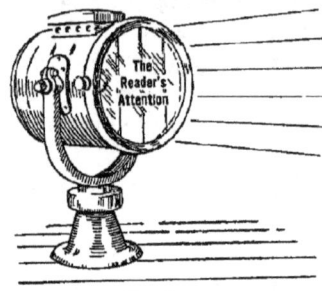

Panel 197

Now as we know, 90%, or thereabouts, of all the letters we have to write are for the purpose of conveying ideas that in themselves come within range of the receiver's attention-ray. So we don't need to worry about them. But the other 10% are just like the little obscure houses on the shore that the steamer's searchlight never stopped for; or the 10 men who passed our man at the window without ever making him take notice. No doubt each of the houses or each of the 10 men had something interesting about them, but whatever it was it *didn't stick up into range of the observer's attention-rays*

Now the 10 men who passed unnoticed very likely didn't care for the observer's notice But that isn't true about that 10% of our letters. They need and want the receiver's notice. We want him to stop and turn the full glare of his attention on them

Therefore, in writing letters which are planned to attract the reader's attention we must devise something that will stick up from the ideas in those letters into the range of one of the reader's attention-rays and attract and stop his attention as it swings along.

The Big Idea of Your Letter

Panel 198

407

BUSINESS CORRESPONDENCE

That something I call the *Stopper* of a letter or an advertisement. I have pictured my idea in the panel below. You'll notice that I have merely made a small addition to the illustration seen on the preceding page

Remember, however, as you plan attention-stoppers for your letters that the *same devices will not stop the attention-rays of all people*. One woman's attention may be stopped at the slightest hint of dress styles. The attention-rays of another woman will sweep over the hints of styles and clothes without lighting up a single corner of them, but anything that smacks of cooking, housekeeping, or home making, will stop her attention at once. Some men will pick up immediately, with their attention-rays, anything bearing on business or money making, while others miss everything but indications of pleasure or sport.

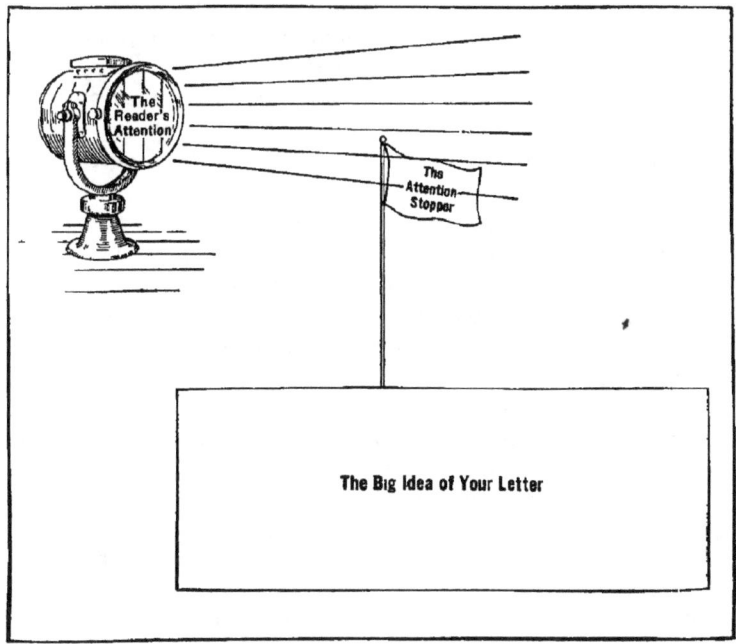

Panel 199

LETTERS THAT GRIP ATTENTION

The usual explanation for this difference in people is that it is due to a difference in powers of observation.

But it is no such thing. Science has shown that a normal human mind is always busy. Our attention searchlight is always working, though sometimes we scarcely know it. What it lights up most quickly for us depends upon the character and intensity of our various attention-rays. All of us have, through tendency or by concentration, sharpened and strengthened certain of our natural attention-rays, and by disuse have dimmed the intensity of others.

For example, the woman who overlooks all the indications of housekeeping interests may be as earnest a housekeeper as another who never misses a recipe in the paper, or a housekeeping scheme in the magazines. But through constant anxiety, and eagerness about styles and clothes, she has intensified her attention-rays in those directions at the expense of others. That condition, as I have said, is typical of all of us. And it is also true that there are times when all of us are susceptible to certain kinds of interests and almost oblivious of others. That is because we have temporarily concentrated upon one kind of attention-ray and let others get dim.

Hence, in planning a Stopper for a letter or an advertisement—or an after-dinner speech—yes, or for our ideas in a general conversation—we must first consider the people we are trying to reach, what their most vivid attention-rays are, or at least *which rays will be most intense* at the time we reach them.

If we are writing to the owner of a business it is easy to guess that his most active and intense attention-rays have been trained to look for sales, collections, bills, and any of the other details that make up his business. So, in form letters that have been most successful in circularizing owners of businesses, we find Stoppers adapted to catching that kind of attention-ray.

The letter on the next page is a splendid example of what I mean. The opening sentence, "The letters you mailed

BUSINESS CORRESPONDENCE

QUALITY PRINT SHOP
PROSPER, OHIO

John M. Jones & Co ,
Prosper City, Ohio.

Gentlemen·

    The letters you mailed from your office yesterday probably cost between $4 and $7 per hundred for postage, typewriting, letter paper and envelops The stationery used cost only about 10% of the total — 40 cents to 70 cents per hundred — yet it represents a very important element in business correspondence.

    A letter written on attractive stationery starts right — it immediately creates an Impression of Confidence in the Quality of your Product. It is not possible to measure this value with exactness, but we know that it exists, and as the cost of well-designed and well-printed stationery is only a fraction of a cent per letter, you cannot afford to use anything but the best

    That is the kind designed and printed by

        THE QUALITY PRINT SHOP

Panel 200

WRITER AND READER

When you are planning the method of stopping attention for your letter, remember that the ways of gripping the reader may be reduced to a few general methods Each method can be varied according to the ingenuity of the writer Among the successful ways of gripping the reader to the Big Idea of the letter are the following The mental shock the idea is to put a "stop—look—listen' sign at the top of the letter as on page 402 The catch line the opening of the letter on this page falls into this class The attention may be gripped by the startling way in which the proposition is stated The letter on page 412 is an example The reader is reminded of one of the greatest problems of his business Attention can be gripped often by a reference to news of the day or some other familiar allusion Freight rates is an interesting topic to any business man Notice the use of it in the letter opposite But remember all the attention-stoppers in the world won't make a man read your letter if you cling too closely to rambling sentences and loose paragraphs They have sent many an excellent letter to the graveyard

LETTERS THAT GRIP ATTENTION

SEFTON MANUFACTURING CO.
CHICAGO

U. B. English
Utica, N. Y

Dear Sir.

    The railroads think so much of the Sefton box for shipping mattresses that they are changing the classification to accommodate it.

    Your competitors are enthusiastic about the results they obtain by its use.

    The retailer is delighted with it.

    If anything further is necessary to convince you, read our proposition in the next paragraph, look inside this letter, and then act on your best judgment.

    Without cost or obligation we will send you a Sefton mattress box and you can see for yourself. Or, ship us one of your mattresses at our expense and we'll "Sefton" it back to you so you can see how it stands actual service.

    Give the necessary instructions now -- you are a busy man and might forget it if you put it off.

                 Yours very truly,

                      THE SEFTON MFG. CO.

BUSINESS CORRESPONDENCE

GEORGIA INVESTMENT CO.
ATLANTA, GA.

Mr D C Heath,
Atlanta, Ga.

Dear Sir:

You are a rare and resourceful man if you are as clever at investing money as you are at making it Most men have all they can do making enough so there will be some left to invest

Still you must invest your savings, and you probably have some bonds Why? Not because you are well posted about bonds in general, nor because you know all the facts about the bonds you own. You would be the last man to claim such knowledge You bought bonds because you had to invest in something, and bonds looked good

But in business can you imagine yourself shipping a $1,000 order to a new customer just because you have heard of him before? No You would look him up first And if you had known that there is a way to look up bonds before you buy, you probably would have looked them up the same way

Here are a few facts about our service along that line — security reports You can get the idea in a couple of minutes, and the enclosed postal card will bring the rest of the story

You may ask for particulars about our service, or for a special report on any bond, without any obligation on your part.

Yours truly,
GEORGIA INVESTMENT CO.

Panel 202

LETTERS THAT GRIP ATTENTION

from your office yesterday," can hardly escape catching the reader's attention.

And for another good example read the opening of that letter on page 411. How quickly the man engaged in manufacturing mattresses, and constantly interested in freight classifications and railroad rates is going to be stopped as his attention-rays catch on:

"The railroads think so much of the Sefton box for shipping mattresses that they are changing the classifications to accommodate it."

Of course, in many instances it is difficult to decide just what the prospect's most vivid attention-rays are. Hence we cannot always plan a Stopper so specific as the two examples I have given you. In such instances we have to build our Stopper just that much higher from the letter's idea. We have to get that much farther away from the subject matter. Observe, for instance, the letter on the opposite page.

The receivers of that letter may not be acutely interested in investments at the time of getting the letter. Other business problems may be so much more important that the attention-rays for investments are dim. Yet their *attention will be stopped* by it.

That first sentence, "You are a rare and resourceful business man" sticks up so high and so prominently that, dim and dull as the investment attention-rays may have been, they caught the interest in that opening and caused attention to be stopped.

So now, you see, the first step in planning a Stopper is to visualize the prospective reader, or in the case of a circular letter or advertisement, the general type of the whole list, in some such way as we showed on page 407. We must take all that we know about those readers—their characters, their pursuits, their purses, their interests in life—or all that we can find out or all that we can guess—and from that information *set down* what we think should be their *most intense attention-rays*.

BUSINESS CORRESPONDENCE

For example, we shall say that our list is made up of women. Now from what everybody knows about women, we can easily assume that most of them will have quite intense attention-rays for dress fashions, some for literary subjects, some for art, some for domestic hints, some for care of babies, some for cost of living, and so on. I am sure that I have mentioned enough for the purpose of illustrating my point.

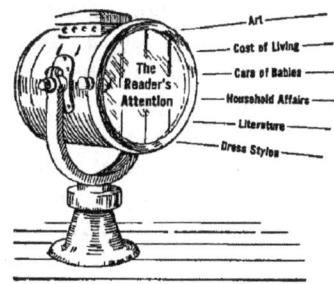

Panel 203

For the purpose of this chapter I've sketched these rays in the panel above. And that's a good thing to do whenever you have an attention-gripping letter to write.

First: Visualize your prospect. Second. Write down the things he or she is interested in. Of course, you needn't put them down as rays of a searchlight as I have done, but don't fail to jot them down on a scratch pad. Third: Study the Big Idea in your letter to see what feature of it or what fuel for the motive, or what mutual sympathy can be built up or enlarged upon to make a Stopper for one of the attention-rays you have selected.

The Big Idea

"This Pneumatic Dress Form Makes Dress Fitting Easy—Whether You Make Your Own Clothes or Hire a Seamstress."

Panel 204

For instance, assume that we have an attention-gripping letter to write to women. Assume the Big Idea of the letter to be that which I have set down in the panel at the left. Consider it carefully. To which of the attention-rays for women listed above can we build up most easily from that idea?

As the idea has to do with dressmaking, it is quite safe to choose the attention-ray of Dress Fashions as the easiest to reach.

414

LETTERS THAT GRIP ATTENTION

Our problem has now resolved itself down to this: *what feature or motive or sympathy in our letter can be most easily built up* to constitute a Stopper for the reader's interest in fashions? And right there is an interesting point, for right there is where so many inexperienced letter writers make a mistake. They don't build their Stoppers high enough or strong enough.

Get this point well in mind. A real Stopper in this case must do more than merely mention fashions, and in other instances the Stopper must do more than merely mention the attention-getter. You, for example, may be interested in making money, but that does not mean that you will stop to listen every time you hear the subject of money mentioned. But if something is said about money that applies to your own money-making plans, you are almost sure to give attention at once.

Therefore, a real Stopper for the attention-ray of Dress Fashions must have in it something interesting to the reader about fashions. For this particular letter we should choose, for instance, some new mandate of fashion that can be attained by the reader by accepting the proposition we made her.

You see, it is rather a simple affair, after all, this building a Stopper that will make our letters grip the prospective reader's attention. And on the next page you see how *an actual letter, built up on this system,* looks in type.

But suppose our letter had been one for which no Stopper for the Dress Fashion attention-ray could be erected. Suppose our letter had to be about a baby food. Wouldn't it have been equally simple to decide that Care of Babies was the attention-ray to strive for? Then we could have arrived easily at something like this Stopper, which was used in one of the successful Nestle's Food letters:

```
Dear Madam:
    How is your baby getting along?
    We are always interested in babies — and we are
especially in your baby because you sent for a
package of Nestle's Food
```

BUSINESS CORRESPONDENCE

THE FASHION SHOP
CHICAGO

Miss Elsie Carter,
Chicago, Ill.

Dear Miss Carter

  The tight-fitting waist is Fashion's latest decree, thus making it necessary to be fitted perfectly at the waist line A delicate task for the dressmaker, requiring many fittings, and a hard one for the home dressmaker. But "Susie," The Pneumatic Dress Form, will solve both difficulties.

  "Susie" will stand in your place at the dressmaker's — or she will stand in front of you at home to be fitted to perfection. For "Susie" can be adjusted to represent your own figure to the fraction of an inch, to the slightest curve of your form. Once adjusted, a waist fitted to "Susie" is a waist fitted to you, just as if you had stood for a score of fittings.

  Just think how PERFECT it makes home dressmaking! And think how much easier it is to let your seamstress fit your clothes to "Susie," your Pneumatic Figure, while you have your time to yourself, than to have to stand and stand for fittings.

  "Susie" is helping thousands of women to have better-fitting, more stylishly made clothes Let her help you. Read the descriptive offer enclosed Then simply fill in the order blank and mail to us with $5 If not perfectly satisfactory, return at our expense and your money will be refunded

  Send now so you can have one of the new tight-fitting waists fitted over "Susie" — that is the test which tells.

      Very truly yours,

          THE FASHION SHOP

LETTERS THAT GRIP ATTENTION

Or suppose our letter wasn't one that offered a chance to stop either of the attention-rays which were effective on these first two letters. Suppose it was to be written to win customers for a retail merchant. What could we do about a Stopper for such a letter?

Why we'd follow the regular course. We'd first determine the **Big Idea** of the letter. Suppose it to be low prices on provisions. Now just starting off with assertions about our prices would be just like mentioning fashions in the dress form letter on the opposite page—it wouldn't be enough to stop attention. But we know—or have guessed—that one of the attention-rays of our prospective readers is for Cost of Living That makes it easy to decide on a Stopper like this one used in a very successful retailer's letter:

```
Dear Madam
    If you have your last butcher's bill handy and
will compare the prices with the following "Specials"
I am quite sure you will see where you could have saved
some money by trading with me
```

Now I must admit that all the examples I have quoted so far have been of an easy type. You can't always locate, in every business, an attention-ray of your prospect that links up so directly with the idea in your letter. Nor is the first one that offers such a link-up always the best one to work for.

For instance, *in planning a circular letter to business men*, SYSTEM's correspondents can always write down in a visualization of the prospective reader's attention-rays, ones like Efficiency, Economy, More Sales, and so on. And there is usually a direct link-up between any one of these attention-rays and the idea their letters have to convey. But the very directness of that link-up results in so many Stoppers being used on it, by so many different firms, for so many ideas, that sometimes it ceases to be useful. You can imagine that if you were taking that Mississippi River trip and playing the searchlight along the shores, and had uncovered one certain kind of object, say a log cabin, several times, you would soon cease to stop the light for a closer examination of log cabins.

BUSINESS CORRESPONDENCE

A.W. SHAW COMPANY
PUBLISHERS
CASS, HURON AND ERIE STREETS
CHICAGO

NEW YORK
BOSTON
PHILADELPHIA
CLEVELAND
A W SHAW CO.,LTD.
LONDON

D S Brown
Dayton Ohio

Dear Sir

That vexing question <u>answered</u>
— that business problem <u>solved</u>
— directly accurately <u>instantly</u> — and you need not even leave your desk

Of all the mediums ever devised for keeping the busy man in live-wire touch with every business fact or figure necessary to his day's work nothing has ever yet been published that proved quite as reliable and <u>handy</u> as the "Business Man's Encyclopedia "

These books answer all those questions that pop up unexpectedly every day the little business puzzlers that harass and hinder you most how to key an ad how to buy for a quick turnover how to say the right thing in a business letter how to collect a bad debt without causing unpleasantness how to get a testimonial from the customer who complained

Ready for quick references are hundreds of just such subjects all indexed and waiting but a turn of the page and a glance of the eye — to get just what you want You are given a complete business dictionary all kinds of weights and measures important facts and pointers on business law correspondence proof reading copyrights patents corporations banks drafts checks exchanges insurance leases common carriers interest lightning calculation methods This mere letter could not even hint at one-tenth part

Our first offer is to SYSTEM'S subscribers I am particularly anxious that each of our friends have the first opportunity to secure a copy of this new set of books—first to examine the very methods that have already increased efficiency for men in practically every line of business So I am willing to do this Simply sign the enclosed card We will send you this new three-volume set of the "Business Man's Encyclopedia ' absolutely FREE — all delivery charges prepaid and extend your subscription to SYSTEM two full years from its present date of expiration at the price of SYSTEM alone $4

But only if the offer is accepted immediately — the price of SYSTEM will advance $1 per year on June 30 Save $2 by acting today

Surely no man who knows SYSTEM will neglect to continue his subscription

So sending this card today means that you renew your subscription a short time sooner than you naturally would And you have the advantage of the low rate before the price of SYSTEM is raised

Will you not sign that postcard TODAY?

Very truly yours,

Merritt Lum

Circulation Manager

Panel 206

LETTERS THAT GRIP ATTENTION

A. W. SHAW COMPANY
PUBLISHERS
CASS, HURON AND ERIE STREETS
CHICAGO

NEW YORK
BOSTON
PHILADELPHIA
CLEVELAND
A W SHAW CO. LTD.
LONDON

D S Brown
Dayton Ohio

Dear Sir

One year and ten days ago I sent you an IMPORTANT letter (see EXACT reproduction attached). Since that time exactly 32 726 keen business men have accepted my offer and received FREE the "Business Man's Encyclopedia " and for each of these men these books have helped to solve many a BAFFLING business problem that it would have taken hours perhaps days even to ACCUMULATE THE NECESSARY DATA from which to START finding the solution

And now at this time with future business conditions so crowded with possibilities shrewd business men are more than ever alive to the need for authoritative FACTS on which to base their judgments and their actions so I EXTEND this same offer — even MORE

— for in our bindery we have the New Eighth REVISED Edition Enlarged re-edited amplified — statistics corrected and VERIFIED — these books should be as much a part of your labor-saving equipment as your desk or your telephone (Note the paragraphs marked)

And to friends of SYSTEM is offered the opportunity to get these famous books FREE Simply fill in and return the convenient card We will enter your subscription for a FULL year and send you the two volumes at once

But send the handy card NOW and grasp all advantages to yourself and to your business that the facts in these books bring you Mail the card TODAY

Yours very truly Merritt Lum
Circulation Manager

new three-volume set of the Business Man s Encyclopedia, absolutely FREE — all delivery charges prepaid and extend your subscription to SYSTEM two full years from its present date of expiration at the price of SYSTEM alone $4

But only if the offer is accepted immediately — the price of SYSTEM will advance $1 per year on June 30 Save $2 by acting today

Surely no man who knows SYSTEM will neglect to continue his subscription

So sending this card today means that you renew your subscription a short time sooner than you naturally would And you have the advantage of the low rate before the price of SYSTEM is raised

Will you not sign that postcard TODAY°

Very truly yours Merritt Lum
Circulation Manager

Panel 207

BUSINESS CORRESPONDENCE

And so it is with the *Stoppers used commonly on certain obvious attention-rays*. Around about Christmas time the magazine advertising pages are filled with headlines arranged to stop the attention-ray of Christmas gift buyers. "Give him this" and "Buy this for mother," the advertisements say. The Christmas gift attention-ray soon becomes wearied of them.

Good advertising men who have made a study of their business realize the similarity between this tendency and the old fable of the boy who cried "Wolf!" too many times. So they look for *new or different attention-rays or new and different Stoppers*.

SYSTEM, for the same reason, has often found it expedient to get away from the more obvious Stoppers for the attention-rays of Efficiency, More Sales, and so forth, in such ways as this:

```
Dear Sir
        "Don't worry! I'll get around to it some day"
         — thought Mr. C. H. Curtis, a Wisconsin mer-
    chant, as he realized that growing competition made
    it necessary for him to reach out for new business.
```

You can easily see that a retail merchant's attention-rays for ideas about More Sales, Bigger Business, and so on, may have become jaded through the constant repetition of such introductions as "Do you want more business?" or "How are you to meet competition?" He has stopped the searchlight of his attention so many times for such direct appeals before that now his attention-rays fail to notice them. But you see what a *fresh and striking effect* the Stopper above quoted would have on the same attention-rays.

Other good examples of how SYSTEM has made its study of this principle of Stoppers pay, are shown on the two previous pages. First just note the letter on page 418. See how the *attention-rays of the average business executive* have been visualized, and then a Stopper built up from one feature of the Big Idea to attract just one of those rays.

The letter was tested and found successful and then mailed to a large list of business men. It paid. But the proposition

LETTERS THAT GRIP ATTENTION

was considered so important to all executives that a few months later it was decided to test the same letter again on the same list. But the Stopper of the letter did not this time stop the prospective reader's attention so quickly. The attention-rays were evidently dulled to it by having seen it before. So the test did not show good results.

What was to be done? The idea of the letter was known by previous results to be right, so simply a more striking, more forceful Stopper was needed. This new Stopper was printed on a flap and folded over the upper part of the letter, as shown on page 419.

The new Stopper caused attention to be again focused on the idea, and the letter yielded even better results than the original mailing.

So much for the theory of Stoppers.

Before going farther, let us review a bit and then I'll show you how to build up Stoppers for letters of your own.

As far as we have gone we have uncovered *four principles of attention-getting*, as follows:

A good idea in a letter will not pay (if the idea is not one that in itself stops the receiver's attention) unless an artificial Stopper is built for it.

A poor idea in a letter will not get results, no matter how forcibly the attention is stopped.

A forceful Stopper and a good idea combined will not get results if the attention that is won by the Stopper is not the kind of attention that will intelligently light up the idea.

A good idea to which attention is attracted by a Stopper that catches the right kind of attention-rays, will get the very best kind of results.

Those facts seem now to be perfectly clear. Let us see how they work out for us.

To take a concrete case, suppose that we are the manufacturers of a wrapping material for freight and express shipments. Suppose that we have to circularize a list of large nurseries. We shall assume that we have charted the work our letter must do; we have selected for the Big Idea the thought that·

"Our wrapping material has proved the best and most economical for other nurseries and will prove best for you."

We have picked out the features that convey that idea, arranged them, and found the ways to inject mutual sympathy and hence sincerity into them. We have selected the proper motive, inserted fuel for it in the letter, and we have started the motive to action. In other words, we shall assume that we have proceeded with our letter about as far as the copy in the panel below.

The enclosed letter, voluntarily written us by the Gardner Nursery, tells the story of their satisfaction with Quickwrap.

Now we don't ask you to use Quickwrap because they do, for our packing problems must be decided on their own merits   But of this we are confident.

Quickwrap will do for you exactly what it has done for many of the world's largest nurseries   Give you the most complete packing service it's possible to secure.

It will enable you to make a neater, stronger package, cut down shipping weight, save time, twine, moss, and straw, as well as eliminate all need of burlap, which costs from 25 to 50% more.

Quickwrap is Waterproof, Frostproof, Verminproof, and Dirtproof. So it prevents moisture from soaking through, protects your stock from every exposure, and gets to its destination in perfect condition.

You have already seen samples of several grades   Now we send you a new one, K1690 — the strongest that we make. Price, 100 yards by 36 inches, $4 32, 40 inches, $4.65, with 5% discount on 10 rolls or more

Decide on this or others for your spring packing, and order a small quantity for a trial   Remember, we'll take back all unused rolls, if you are dissatisfied in the least.

How many rolls, what grade, how wide?

Panel 208

LETTERS THAT GRIP ATTENTION

The letter as written is pretty good. The Big Idea ought normally to stop a nursery man's attention. But on further consideration we decide that as our list consists of new prospects who don't know our goods, we won't take a chance on the letter. Hence we plan a Stopper for it.

The first thing to do in planning the Stopper, we have learned, is to visualize, as nearly as we can, the attention-rays of our prospective readers, and, in the upper part of the next page, I have charted the probable attention-rays of our list. When you know the general type of your prospects, such a chart is not difficult to make.

So far, then, we have the body of our letter written It expresses a Big Idea It enlists mutual sympathy in its features It arouses a motive for action It has a close that starts motive going. We have the attention-rays of our prospective readers visualized. We must *now build up a Stopper* to catch one of those attention-rays.

To which one of them can we build most easily and logically from the idea in our letter?

Examining the illustration of attention-rays we note "Meeting Competition" and "News of Competitors." And studying the idea of our letter we note that one of its most important features is a testimonial letter written by a big nursery, probably a competitor of every prospect on our list. It is easy to see in it the *opportunity for our Stopper.*

Suppose we open our letter with the name of the big nursery that wrote the testimonial letter, and add some fact about the nursery that would lead consistently to its letter Wouldn't that stop the prospective reader's attention-ray of "News of Competitors?" It would. It did.

At the top of the next page, you'll see how such a Stopper was actually constructed to lead, with a slight change, into the body of the letter as we have already seen it written

The letter was furnished by Mr. Edward H. Schulze, director of "Making-Letters-Pay System" of New York. It was one of a successful series of follow-up letters which, on

BUSINESS CORRESPONDENCE

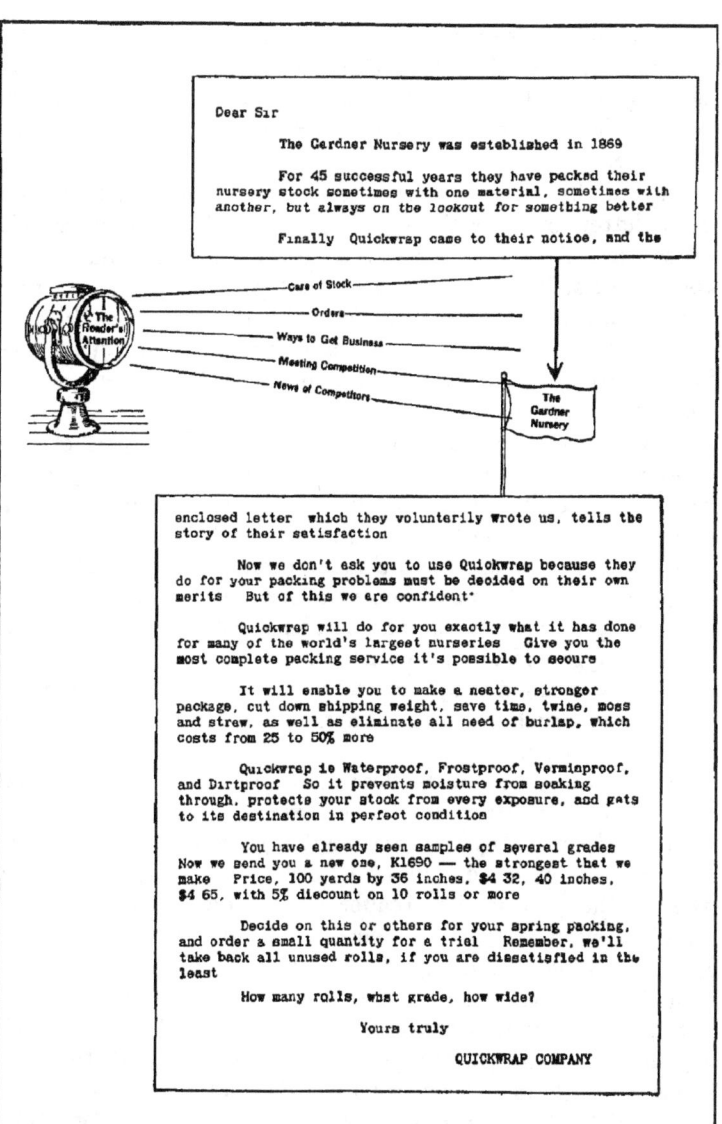

Dear Sir

    The Gardner Nursery was established in 1869

    For 45 successful years they have packed their nursery stock sometimes with one material, sometimes with another, but always on the lookout for something better

    Finally Quickwrap came to their notice, and the enclosed letter which they voluntarily wrote us, tells the story of their satisfaction

    Now we don't ask you to use Quickwrap because they do for your packing problems must be decided on their own merits But of this we are confident·

    Quickwrap will do for you exactly what it has done for many of the world's largest nurseries Give you the most complete packing service it's possible to secure

    It will enable you to make a neater, stronger package, cut down shipping weight, save time, twine, moss and straw, as well as eliminate all need of burlap, which costs from 25 to 50% more

    Quickwrap is Waterproof, Frostproof, Verminproof, and Dirtproof So it prevents moisture from soaking through, protects your stock from every exposure, and gets to its destination in perfect condition

    You have already seen samples of several grades Now we send you a new one, K1690 — the strongest that we make Price, 100 yards by 36 inches, $4 32, 40 inches, $4 65, with 5% discount on 10 rolls or more

    Decide on this or others for your spring packing, and order a small quantity for a trial Remember, we'll take back all unused rolls, if you are dissatisfied in the least

    How many rolls, what grade, how wide?

    Yours truly

    QUICKWRAP COMPANY

Panel 209

LETTERS THAT GRIP ATTENTION

a list of 1,000 nurseries, *produced 275 orders totaling $19,246.44.* So we must agree that this letter "carries its load." Certainly the Stopper is effective. We can see how simple its effectiveness is when we see its construction charted as on the opposite page.

An equally effective Stopper can be constructed for any other letter, or advertisement, or speech, if the same simple process is followed. On the next page is a letter that pulled good results, in spite of a close that probably could be materially improved. But the letter conveys its Big Idea so clearly, and arouses so strong a motive, and its opening—its Stopper—so rivets attention, that the absence of a strong close was overcome.

Analyze that Stopper and you will see how perfectly it conforms to a chart of its work. A chart of the prospective reader's attention-rays would manifestly show that all owners of fine property have a strong attention-ray for anything bearing on the condition of their property. Hence a Stopper that will draw that attention-ray to the matter of preserving the trees on the reader's estate almost immediately suggested itself to the writer.

You see, a good Stopper, or "opener," as some people call it, is not so much a matter of genius and cleverness as it is of careful attention.

When you have one to devise, simply remember that first the idea of the letter should be clearly expressed, the points of mutual sympathy or agreement injected, and the fuel for the motive inserted. Second, the most likely things to attract the prospective reader's attention—"his attention-rays" as we have named them—should be considered. This is not a difficult matter at all. You will know from your past dealings with the prospect, or if you are circularizing a list of names you will know from the character of the list, at least some of the things that can be assumed to be of interest to them—to constitute "attention-rays" for them. And, third, when you have clearly before you the body part of your letter and a chart of the prospective reader's atten-

BUSINESS CORRESPONDENCE

THE DAVEY TREE EXPERT CO.
KENT, OHIO

Mr W. A. Bond,
Sea Cliff, N. Y.

Dear Sir:

    A casual glance at the beautiful trees on your estate indicates that some of them are in a serious condition, concerning which you should have full information.

    Our representative will be in your vicinity again in the near future and will take pleasure in making a thorough inspection of your trees, if you so desire, and submitting a full report on the conditions as he finds them. There is no charge in this connection.

    The trees on your estate are of the utmost value. They cannot be replaced by trees of like size and beauty if they are allowed to be destroyed through physical weakness or decay or insect enemies or disease Our representative will be pleased to make such an inspection and report to you if you will send in your name on the enclosed postcard. This will not obligate you in any way

    Real Tree Surgery is Davey Tree Surgery There is no second best We have treated and saved the trees on the Capitol Grounds and White House Grounds at Washington, D C , and on the Parliament Grounds at Ottawa, Canada, and on thousands of private estates, country clubs, parks and cemeteries throughout the country.

    Awaiting your early reply, we are,

                Very truly yours,
        THE DAVEY TREE EXPERT COMPANY

Panel 210

LETTERS THAT GRIP ATTENTION

tion-rays, to find a point of contact between your idea and some one of those attention-rays is a matter of common sense.

Occasions do arise—quite frequently, in fact—in circularizing lists of prospects or in preparing advertising copy for newspapers or magazines, when you cannot be certain that the one most suitable attention-ray is common to all the prospective readers. In mailing large lists of business executives, for instance, SYSTEM knows from experience that not every man of them will be keenly interested in increasing his own efficiency. But if the proposition to be sold demands such an interest on the part of the buyer, then SYSTEM has no hesitation in building the Stopper for its letter to attract only that one attention-ray. Because those who would not have their attention stopped by an interest in increased efficiency most probably would not spend money to secure increased efficiency—no matter if their attention has been attracted by some other means.

In the panel on the next page, for example, see a Stopper built solely for the attention-ray of Care for Valuable Papers. But if some of the men on the list have no active attention-ray for this subject; that is, if they have a safe deposit vault, or perhaps have no valuable papers, the Stopper would not stop their attention, would it? Assuredly not, but neither would they then be prospects for renting a safe deposit vault.

On page 430 is another good example. Here we find a Stopper built up on the supposition that most of the merchants addressed have *active attention-rays for anything bearing on good buying* Perhaps with some merchants on the list such an attention-ray is not very intense—but if it isn't, then there is little likelihood of the manufacturer securing an order from them on the price basis.

In short, these latter examples all go back to the third condition for attention getting I stated on page 421; namely, "a forceful Stopper and a good idea combined will not get results if the attention that is won by the Stopper is not the kind of attention that will intelligently light up the idea."

BUSINESS CORRESPONDENCE

THE FARMERS' BANK
DANVILLE, ILL.

W. R. Adams,
Danville, Wis.

Dear Sir:

Unless you have a safe deposit box, you certainly must have papers and valuables at home or in your office, which if lost or damaged would cause you a lot of trouble to replace, even if they could be replaced at all.

Our safe deposit vaults afford absolute protection and are within a few steps of your office.

The expense of a box is very small compared to the service it gives you.

I wish you would drop in and look over our premises anyway.

Yours very truly,

THE FARMERS' BANK

Panel 211

JUDGE AND JURY

After you have attracted attention and secured the interest of the reader, you have made a good beginning, but only a beginning, you then have the hard task of holding that interest, explaining your proposition, pointing out the superiority of the goods or the service you are trying to sell and making an inducement that will bring in orders. Your case is in court. The jury has been drawn. The judge is attentive. The opposing counsel is alert. It is up to you to prove your case. And when you present your case, remember what you learned in the fourth chapter. Interest your man quickly by close-coupling his interests to yours. Then give him clear, concise statements in snapping words and crackling sentences that will make him keep his searchlight trained on your thoughts.

LETTERS THAT GRIP ATTENTION

Therefore, in planning a Stopper never risk attracting a kind of attention that will not result in business after it has been attracted. That is, *never attract attention merely for the sake of attracting universal attention.* Do not, as a rule, plan to meet an attention-ray of all the names on a list, or all the readers of a magazine, but plan to reach the right kind of attention-ray of possible buyers.

To illustrate this point still more clearly: if we were advertising a corn remedy in the newspapers it would be foolish to use space for a big heading and expensive illustration just to attract the general attention of all readers, when perhaps a smaller heading and simpler illustration would attract a specific buying attention from readers who had corns. And the same principle applies to letters.

Probably more flagrant mistakes are made in this respect in magazine and newspaper advertisements than in letters, but they are often to be observed in both. The most certain way to avoid them is through the use of the illustration on page 408. It requires you to consider not only the prospective reader's attention but also the idea for which you want his attention. And in constructing a Stopper according to the diagram, you will naturally build from idea to the Stopper, and the danger of a strained or forced or absurd attention-getter will be practically overcome.

So far we have only applied our principle of the Stopper to the opening paragraph of a letter—which, of course, corresponds with the heading of an advertisement.

But, just as advertising often requires an illustration or unique typographical arrangement or use of white space, so in letters *the work of the Stopper may sometimes be made to begin before the receiver of the letter begins to read* This is particularly true when the letter is to go to lists of names that have been circularized many times before, or to lists that you believe have been circularized frequently by others. There is always, in such cases, the danger that your prospects will spot your letter as "another of those circulars" and dismiss it without a glance.

BUSINESS CORRESPONDENCE

FRANCIS T. SIMMONS & COMPANY
CHICAGO, ILL.

Crockett Company,
Raleigh, S C.

Gentlemen

What does your women's glove department pay for a "dollar glove"? How does the glove you buy stand up? Is it making friends for you? Or is it a constant source of annoyance?

We have been offering to sell you gloves and give YOU our usual salesman's commission of 8%. You haven't "taken us up "

Here, then, is a definite proposition· We will prepay the parcel postage on a sample order of two dozen of our Touraine "dollar" women's dress gloves-- in black and tan--lay them on your shelves FREE

Your cost will be per dozen.

Our regular price	$9 50
Less 8% salesman's commission	76
	8.74
Less 3% discount for cash	26
Net cost per dozen	8 48

Have your girls sell these gloves IN COMPETITION with the ones you now carry. If the Touraine glove doesn't please you, your salespeople, and your customers better than the ones you now handle, send them back COLLECT before you are asked to pay one cent on the bill.

Please TRY Simmons Gloves at our expense via the attached card

      Very truly,

      FRANCIS T. SIMMONS & COMPANY

P. S --Mail the enclosed "Correspondence Course" card also. The Course is free but valuable to you. We want your head glove saleswoman to profit by it.

LETTERS THAT GRIP ATTENTION

THE AMERICAN
REVIEW OF REVIEWS
30 IRVING PLACE NEW YORK

A Cable from
Rudyard Kipling

Mr Henry Allison
Pittsburgh, Pa

Dear Sir

    You own six volumes of Kipling's works which we gave you

    When Mr Kipling learned that so many Americans were receiving these six volumes he consented to an arrangement by which you can add in uniform style all of his other books, 19 volumes so that you will be the owner of a magnificent 25-volume set of Kipling's COMPLETE works — all that have been published

    The royalty payments on the other volumes have heretofore been so large as to preclude a low price One set of 25 volumes has been sold at $50 The Seven Seas Edition, a limited edition, is being subscribed for at $138

    If you will promptly take advantage of Mr Kipling's special arrangement for your benefit, we will ship to you 19 new volumes, thus making a 25-volume Kipling set in absolutely uniform type, paper and binding, for only $1 a volume, payable $1 a month

    Furthermore, you will have a guarantee from us that you can add any future books that Mr Kipling publishes, uniform with your set, for $1 per volume

    This is a great opportunity It means actually that for $19 payable at $1 per month (or $17 10 if you prefer to pay in cash), you can own all the Kipling volumes published, for which others have paid $50, practically the same except for paper and binding, for which others are now paying $138

    This is the first time that a collected set of Kipling has ever been offered at this low figure

        When Mr Kipling's cable came we made one edition out of paper purchased at the old price (The price has more than doubled now) Some sets of that edition remain, and you can have one if you are prompt Positively none can be furnished at this price when these remaining sets are gone

    Send no money Simply sign the enclosed application The 19 volumes will be sent express prepaid, and after you have received them and found out that everything is satisfactory, you can send us the first payment of $1

    But for the reasons stated above, please act at once

                        Yours truly
                        The Review of Reviews Co

    P S — If your six volumes are worn or you have given them away let us know and we will see that you get the entire 25-volume set at $1 a volume

Panel 213

BUSINESS CORRESPONDENCE

On the preceding page, however, is an example of how one firm has successfully handled such conditions. Here the main Stopper is displayed so as to stop the attention of all those interested in authors and books before they have a chance to think that the letter is just an ordinary circular letter.

The idea behind it may be stated in this way: After you have once decided that the list of prospects demands a Stopper outside of your opening paragraph, the principle of constructing it is identical with the principle we have already learned.

In the case of the letter above mentioned, for instance, the writer, after deciding that his list of prospects would probably dismiss any ordinary book proposition without a hearing, decided to get his attention gripper at work before the reader could know what the letter was about. He made a clever use of the illustration on page 408. It showed him that as his Big Idea was a special opportunity offered by Mr. Kipling himself, and that as the prospect's attention-rays were an admiration for Kipling, an effective Stopper could be made by working up some graphic representation of a message from Kipling.

The exact typographical or illustrative method of getting such an effect might have varied with each one of us according to our tendencies, but I don't believe there is a single one of us now who could not have achieved the same final effect, if he had his chart as a basis to work from.

And on the next page you will see another effect of the same kind—this time results were secured by pasting a photograph on the letter. If you should chart out the prospect's attention-rays in connection with the Big Idea of the letter you'd see how *easily such unique and effective Stoppers can be originated.*

Exactly the same principle can be applied to working out the headings or illustrative ideas for advertisements, for postcards, circulars, "envelop stuffers"—even for envelops. There is a danger that prospects may throw away a letter without even starting to read it unless the attention is stopped.

LETTERS THAT GRIP ATTENTION

The Automobile Directory
"It Hangs Everywhere"

Mr Fritz:

    Meet Mr. Esserman, purchasing agent of the Motor Car Equipment Company, New York.

    Excuse the interruption, Mr. Esserman, but I wanted this gentleman to actually see how a big purchasing agent has solved his catalog problem.

    Mr. Esserman told me that he started to keep his catalogs on the top of his desk. In a short time it was full. Then he tried filing them. They soon filled the files and He could never find anything when he wanted it.

    Now each consignment of literature takes the path that this morning's pile is destined to take — to the receptacle directly beneath it.

    Now notice the hook that Mr. Esserman has screwed into the side of his desk conveniently near his left hand. This efficient hook holds the solution of his buying problem — one complete crossindexed, condensed, <u>essence</u> of all the thousands of catalogs that are sent him — The Automobile Directory

    If he wants to buy spark plugs he reaches for the "Red Book." In two seconds he has a complete list of every single manufacturer of spark plugs, trade names, buying information.

    The same holds good not only with every accessory, but also with every complete automobile and every other article large or small that is bought or sold in the automobile industry

    There are 50,000 Essermans in the automobile trade. There are a thousand Essermans in the automobile factories. Their combined purchasing power runs into many billions of dollars.

                        Yours very truly,

                                  President

    P. S. — If you will sign and mail the enclosed postcard, I will tell you how you can turn the <u>buying</u> service that The Automobile Directory gives to these men into a tremendous <u>selling</u> power for you.

Panel 214

BUSINESS CORRESPONDENCE

SYCAMORE FARM
TRENT OHIO

EGGS NEW-LAID FOR EASTER

Mr Eric Allan
Boston Mass

My Dear Mr Allen

　　　　　I have eggs to sell for Easter which will be new-laid just before the holidays

　　　　Since you have not yet tried Sycamore Farm eggs brought from the farm to your door in an hour will you consider this special Easter offer?

　　　　I am not going up on my prices for eggs during the Easter holidays　On the contrary if you order four dozen (or more) of my eggs using the enclosed order blank I will deliver them at your door, the Friday or Saturday before Easter for 30 cents a dozen

　　　　These eggs I will guarantee to be not more than from one to three days old on delivery at your door　In addition to their absolute freshness all my eggs are large and brown and of the best possible flavor as they are produced by hens fed a balanced grain ration approved by the Department of Agriculture　The nests are kept entirely fresh and clean and free from all alien matter or disinfecting agents　This is an important point in egg production as eggs very quickly absorb a flavor and bacteria from an unsanitary condition of the nests and hen houses　Eggs should be as carefully guarded from contamination as any other food product　Do you know where your eggs come from and how they have been cared for?

　　　　Easter is a time when eggs are plentiful and the prices low But it is also a time when you should insist on getting only the best and freshest　If you do not keep hens yourself and have your own eggs why not take this opportunity to get Sycamore Farm Eggs?　One trial will convince you of the difference between store eggs and these eggs straight from the farm

　　　　Order at once and make sure of the best eggs for Easter　I can guarantee to fill only the early orders

　　　　An immediate reply on the enclosed postcard is all that is necessary to bring the eggs to your door the day before Easter

　　　　　　　　　Very truly yours

Panel 215

434

LETTERS THAT GRIP ATTENTION

There is, occasionally, a chance that they may never take it from the envelop.

On the opposite page are two examples of how the Stopper has been made to *begin its work on the outside of the envelop*. However, none of these special schemes are anything but a physical or typographical adaptation to the one fundamental principle of Stoppers that we have learned. In the book letter, on page 431, and the trade directory, on page 433, the Stopper is merely an application of our principle—the novel "stunts" by which the Stoppers in these two cases were illustrated is only a matter of the physical layout.

On the envelop at the top of the opposite page see how the Stopper is purely a result of matching the Big Idea of the letter—the great charm and originality of O. Henry's books—with a visualization of the prospect's attention-rays—one of them being for all interesting literature. This would easily suggest the value as a Stopper of some peculiarly original quotation from O. Henry. Then to caricature this quotation and put it on the outside of the envelop, where it would surely be seen, was a logical sequence that could occur to almost any of us.

In the second example, the same process of charting and thinking is shown.

It is *concentrated thinking* of the Big Idea in your letter in connection with the attention-rays of your prospect that *makes Stoppers effective*. Our system of visualizing the prospect's attention-rays as though they were the rays of a searchlight is merely an aid in pinning your thoughts down to essentials.

Try this plan in every letter that you fear may not grip the attention it deserves, and you can hardly fail to think up an effective, often a unique and original Stopper.

But do not fall into the error of thinking that something unique and original is necessary or always best. Often, if you have arranged the features of your idea in accordance with the principle laid down in the fourth chapter, the feature you have found to be one most easily to be grasped will prove

BUSINESS CORRESPONDENCE

also the best kind of a Stopper from the prospect's attention. Here, for example, is the way a successful letter from a business college opened:

```
Dear Miss Swineford:
    Yesterday we received four calls for young women
stenographers and bookkeepers
```

This opening was simply one feature in the Big Idea of the letter—that the school's course insured success. It had been selected as the easiest feature with which to begin unfolding the idea. A chart also showed it to be an effective Stopper for the prospect's attention-ray of Opportunities to Earn Money. The utmost striving for something unique would not have bettered the effect that was suggested by the chart.

This thought holds particularly true when the visionary or negative idea is used—if the visionary idea itself has been carefully chosen it will nearly always have *a leading feature that has possibilities as a Stopper.*

Then, too, when pains have been taken to enlist the reader's sympathy to or agreement with the features of the idea, as we learned to do in the fifth chapter, it often gives the opening feature the effect of a Stopper. I have in front of me one of the follow-up letters of a binder manufacturer that illustrates this point. The Big Idea in it is that:

"In the catalog you received recently are illustrated the best types of looseleaf binders, no matter for what purpose."

One of the first features, of course, had to be: "You recently received our book of binders "

Now, in analyzing the reader's probable mental reaction to each feature it would be easy to see that the prospect's most probable reaction to that first feature would be something like, "Well, what of it?" So *to establish a mutual feeling,* the wording of the feature was changed to:

"Do you remember sending in a request for our book of binders a short time ago? It was mailed the same day and we assume it reached you o. k."

LETTERS THAT GRIP ATTENTION

You see what an effective Stopper that simple feature becomes for the business executive's attention-ray for details of his business.

Here is another example: A manufacturer, whose prospects are women wage-earners mostly in small towns, took the same kind of Stopper for his third follow-up letter. He said:

```
Dear Madam
     It is really your turn to write, but as you have
not answered either of my former letters I am going to
write again.
```

Notice that the writer simply took a feature of his Big Idea, namely, "I have written you twice explaining my proposition"—and engaged the reader's sympathy by changing it to "It is really your turn to write." Then, knowing that one of the attention-rays of his particular class of prospects was for what we might call "doing the right thing by a friend," he has let the first feature of his idea serve as the Stopper for attention—and it served the purpose well, too.

This brings up a point that may prove helpful to you, that is, *limiting the possible attention-rays of prospects*. In charting the probable attention-rays of your prospects don't try, don't think it necessary, to consider every attention-ray possible to your prospects. You can use only those that have some possible bearing on your proposition. So, by first getting your Big Idea down on paper, its features arranged, and all other points covered, you can then confine yourself to charting out only those attention-rays that offer some chance of being useful to you.

As a rule, it is always better to *leave all thought of attracting attention until the rest of your letter is complete*. Then you may find, as in the example just noted, that your Stopper is ready. Or, if not that, you may find that you have the nucleus for one.

The letter on page 434 is a good illustration of what I mean. In this instance fuel for the motive for the first sentence of the letter was selected as "I shall have eggs which will be new

BUSINESS CORRESPONDENCE

laid just before the holidays to sell for Easter." Later on, when visualizing the prospects' attention-rays which would have a possible bearing on the proposition, naturally an attention-ray was disclosed for "things to do for Easter." See how simply this suggests the typewritten line at the top of the letter: "Eggs new-laid for Easter."

This *use of some bit of the motive-fuel as an attention-stopper* is often possible. In that restaurant letter which we studied in detail in recent problem sections, for example, a complete and effective Stopper was supplied, without addition or change, by this motive-fuel:

"I'd give you a dime to see you eat your first piece of Anna's lemon pie."

Many other successful selling letters have their attention-stoppers built in this same way—either from the motive-fuel itself, or based upon it.

Now you see the advantage of postponing all thought of how you may attract the prospect's attention, until you have all the other points in your letter carefully worked out.

Not until the letter is otherwise complete, need you visualize the attention-rays of your prospects that have any bearing on the idea or motive in your letter. Then, when you have to consider gripping attention, consider that the attention of your prospects is just like a big searchlight and that each ray represents some one particular kind of interest or curiosity. Then study which one of those rays is nearest in line, or most closely related to, the Big Idea or the motive in your letter.

When you have, by this process, found the attention-ray that will most surely light up the necessary interest or curiosity in your letter's Big Idea or motive—or, in other words, when you have found what kind of interest or curiosity your letter's Big Idea or motive will most quickly appeal to—your job is to see that *an appeal* to that interest or curiosity *is brought into prominence* at the very start of your letter.

If the opening feature of your Big Idea, or the opening motive-fuel constitutes such an appeal, then that is your best Stopper. But if it does not constitute such an appeal,

LETTERS THAT GRIP ATTENTION

you must add something to it—build an artificial Stopper, just as highway commissioners paint white the fences near a dark or risky pass in the road, or an outdoor advertiser puts lights on a sign at night. When you fear that the prospective reader's attention might not get as far as reading the opening sentence of your letter, put the Stopper at the top of the letterhead, as we have seen some writers do. If you should fear that the prospect's attention might not even get so far as to open the envelop, then put the Stopper on the envelop itself, as we have also seen done. That is the simple formula by which you can be as nearly sure as you can be sure of anything in doing business at a distance, that your idea will get full attention from the one to whom you write.

SUMMARY

WE have now covered the eight essential requirements in the knack of writing good letters.

We have seen the advantage of sizing up a letter's complete work—the "load" it must carry—before starting to write or dictate, and we have learned a system for making that size-up. When the work is simply to convey a plain idea to one who has a self-interest in the idea, we have the plan described in the second chapter of picking out the essential features that distinguish the idea. When the idea is one to which our size-up indicated the reader may be indifferent or opposed, we can apply the principle in the third chapter of arousing interest through a Visionary or Negative Idea.

In the fourth chapter we saw how to make our meaning clear to the reader when we anticipate that our idea will be quickly grasped by a person unfamiliar with it. We all know that if a man is described to us having a wooden leg and cross-eyes, we are pretty sure to recognize him no matter which feature is described first.

But if he is described to us by the shade of his eyes, contour of his face, set of his chin and his general bearing, then for us to get a recognizable idea of him we must have his features described in proper order.

BUSINESS CORRESPONDENCE

Then we came to the work of making our letters express sincerity—which is identical with making them express an honest and agreeable personality, by means of creating mutual sympathy between ourselves and the reader. When a letter must not only convey an idea and win confidence in it, but also must secure a definite action, we can apply the knack of exercising persuasion—by discovering the motive that would prompt such action and then feeding to that motive the fuel which will impel it. And in the preceding chapter we saw how to start a motive into action—by the right kind of close. Now we have seen how to stop attention and focus it on our Big Idea.

It would be nice if we could stop there. But, we are only now at the stage of a manufacturer who has perfected his product. As he must then design shipping packages for his product, so we must know how to design a proper dress for our letters. In the next chapter, therefore, we shall see the relation between the ideas in our letters and the stationery on which they are written, and the relation between the motive aroused by our letters and the circular matter that accompanies them. And then all those principles and formulas, that we have taken up one at a time, will be put together.

PROBLEM SECTION VIII

IF you have ever studied courses in business correspondence or read other books on the subject, you may think that I have been disagreeing with some of them. Well, you're right. I do disagree with some things that have been taught, but not always as a matter of theory. However, we must not forget that some splendid theories don't work out.

Because theories are dangerous in a work of this kind, I have eliminated them and confined my work in this book to testing and proving just three kinds of principles. These are:

1. Principles I have learned and proved through my own personal experience;

2. Principles learned and proved by SYSTEM through its correspondence with thousands of firms and individuals,

3. Proved principles that SYSTEM's editorial investigators have found in use by other firms.

Where this book differs most from other books on business correspondence is in the relative importance placed on various points and the order in which they are studied. Other writers, for instance, begin with the opening of a letter, but it has been my experience that expressing the idea is more important. A good beginning is always important, but we all know that even with a bad beginning we have a chance for success if we know how to carry the job through to completion. And it is equally true that a bad beginning in a letter does not necessarily ruin it if the idea is put across with force and vigor.

Some other writers lay stress on the "you" element in a letter, but practical experience has taught me to prefer a "you-and-I" atmosphere.

BUSINESS CORRESPONDENCE

Also, others attach much importance to good English and to avoiding hackneyed, stereotyped phrases. But I have learned by hard business experience that if the idea is conveyed by the necessary features, then stereotyped phrases and even poor English will be overlooked. It is said that Lincoln had a very unattractive speaking voice and that he made a poor appearance on the platform because of his ungainly limbs and crude gestures. But my! How he could convey his ideas, create sympathy, and arouse the motives for action.

Now the style of construction and grammar of a letter, or any other written work, is parallel to a speaker's modulation of voice, his gestures, and stage presence The better English you use the better for you—but *English is the finishing touch to a letter!* And as I told you at the start, it is not the purpose of this book to make you a finished writer, but to teach you how to *think* out letters that bring home the bacon.

If your command of English does not happen to be good, or if your knowledge of grammar and composition is weak, you ought to study English. However, I don't mean to urge you, a busy man, to devote your leisure hours to the classroom or to writing "compositions," as so many teachers of English require. You can learn English by reading good books. And when you read books for the sake of the English, notice the author's way of expressing himself. Note the length of sentences. Observe his word choice. Study the verbs he uses. Or, after you have read over your mail for the day, go over the letters again and pick out words or tricks of expression which please you (Here is where that word file you outlined in the fourth chapter will come in handy.) A third method of improving English is to get a college textbook on English. Keep it on the library table and read it once in a while. But even if you don't study English, if you prefer to cling to your own style of writing letters, even if it be crude, put in some good practise on the fourth, sixth, and seventh chapters. Creating sympathy and arousing motives for action are really the fundamentals of good letter writing.

LETTERS THAT GRIP ATTENTION

Let me caution you. If you take up the study of composition, or have taken it up, never get so engrossed with writing "crisp, snappy, business-building English" that you put it ahead of visualizing the Big Idea, expressing sincerity, exercising persuasion, stimulating action, and gripping attention. It is very easy to make such a mistake.

I know a sales manager—or rather an ex-sales manager—of a large business, who was originally a writer of masterly sales letters. But they were crude and full of hackneyed, conventional phrases such as "Your esteemed favor to hand," "In reply to yours of recent date I beg leave to say," and so on. After they got in action, his letters did convey the Big Idea so clearly and expressed so much sincerity and human sympathy, and worked on motives for action, so well, that they kept customers in line and kept the sales force on its toes.

Unfortunately for him, this sales manager became interested in using better English. Ordinarily that is commendable, but in his anxiety to write correctly he made his sales letters and bulletins examples of good English instead of stimulants to action. The results were noticeable in the attitude of the men toward him and in the tenor of customers' replies. Realizing that something was wrong, he determined to find out at one of the summer conventions of salesmen. At the first session he told his men he noticed that they weren't showing as much "pep" and as much sympathy with him as formerly. "Now," he asked, "what do you do when you get my weekly sales bulletin? What do you do, Cooper?" and he singled out one of his best men.

"Why," replied Cooper, who was too valuable a man to be afraid to tell just what he did, "the first thing I do is get out my dictionary and look up the big words."

That is a true story, and, as I said, the man is now an "ex"sales manager.

The moral I draw from that story is this: if you now write in a labored, conventional style, or don't use good grammar, learning to express your ideas by visualizing the features of them is enough to study at first. These new methods will

BUSINESS CORRESPONDENCE

automatically breed the habit of using less hackneyed phrases and unnecessary verbiage. Let this habit take its natural course. After you have it started, study the simple rules of composition, but don't try to apply all the rules at once Take your time. Grow into the habit of writing well.

A man learning to write better English is like a left-handed base-ball player learning to bat right-handed. If the ball player changes gradually he soon acquires the knack of batting right-handed, but if he tries to change suddenly and if he forces himself continually to think about the change, he runs the risk of batting at the balls right-handed, but only batting at them. So with English. Try always to write simple, grammatical English. But be sure not to let your endeavor to write good English interfere with the purpose of your letter The idea of the letter—not the English in which it is written—comes first.

Now let's turn to a review of our work in the previous problem section. I gave you the body of a certain letter—that of a packing case manufacturer—and then charted the elements of an effective close for it. I then quoted the way "the preliminary job" in this close had been worded and left you to work out "the easy connecting path" between that and the final action desired. The complete letter as it was used is shown on page 411. Turn to it and compare the original work with your own. The easy connecting path between the preliminary job and the final action, you remember, is to make it easier for the reader to keep on the path and to take the final action, than to refuse.

See how true to form is the close of the letter. Consider the last two paragraphs. Easily the reader is started to thinking that sending a mattress for specimen packing is easy. The experiment costs nothing and the rest of the paragraph is rather indefinite—something that can be done at any time later. But, the last paragraph beginning "give the necessary instructions now" starts to pin the reader's indefinite resolution down to a serious consideration of the proposition "You are a busy man and might forget it if you put it off," has just the effect

LETTERS THAT GRIP ATTENTION

we have learned to strive for—it subtly puts in the prospect's mind the thought that he has really determined to consider this packing idea seriously—and makes it easy for him to turn to his secretary and issue the order.

A little practise and you will find this idea of charting the close to be a wonderful help.

The answer to the second problem—the close of a SYSTEM letter which was charted in the preceding problem section—will be found on page 418. In giving you this problem I wanted you to test yourself in translating a chart of the close into suitable wording.

In the third problem you had a chance to try yourself on both charting and writing. You will find the complete letter reproduced on page 431 I want you to study very carefully the comparison of your own close with the one used.

If you did not get the proper elements from your chart, make a new chart with the successful close to guide you, and study into the "why" of each step. Disregard the postscript on the original letter, as this is a special offer with which we are not concerned in this work.

Give the same careful study to the comparison of your fourth problem with the close of the original letter shown on page 434 with the order card enclosure.

If you have found any shortcomings in your own work, check them up with the foregoing chapter, for every close in these letters is a good interpretation of the principle explained. Mere differences in wording are not shortcomings—the big point is to see that the fundamentals of the closing paragraphs you have planned agree with those shown in the actual letters.

There is no better practise work possible that I have ever seen. Submitting your practise work to a teacher for criticism, as is done in most correspondence school courses, seems a little more complete, but when applied to a subject like letter writing it does not fill the requirements of a practical business man. You would then get only the opinions of another man, and opinions, even from the most expert letter writer, can be nothing but opinions until put to the test of actual use.

BUSINESS CORRESPONDENCE

But by practising on the problems given in this book and then seeing how those identical problems have been successfully met in real business, you get not the help of an individual, but the help of practical experience.

As in the next chapter we must devote all the space possible to samples of effective letterheads, envelops, and enclosures for all kinds of business, I am going to take our practise examples in Gripping Attention from the preceding chapters. But please work out your own solution carefully and fully before you refer back to the actual letter—this is for your own benefit and it is important You'll find these letters illustrated in preceding chapters

Problem 1

For the first problem, I'll give you the body of a letter applying for employment. In the panel on the next page I have charted the probable attention-rays you could safely attribute to the reader of the letter or, in fact, to any manager of a business depending on advertising and customers' good will. Read the letter which you find below, and then pick out the attention-ray to which you could most easily appeal and try your hand at building up a forceful Stopper from the Big Idea which you find in the letter.

```
    If any of your employees has MY job -- then it isn't
his -- every man has a place somewhere, and I want my own.

    If you have a copy writer working on mail order ac-
counts who can't write a piece of copy as good as the
sample enclosed, marked Exhibit 1, and which brought back
inquiries at a cost of 53 cents, from which sales were
closed at a cost of $6 10, when the lowest cost per sale
had previously been around $10 -- then he has MY job, and
his job is somewhere else

    Isn't that about right?  Isn't that the basis on
which YOU go after accounts?

    Exhibit 2 pulled 144 inquiries from the Cosmopolitan,
28 from Motion Picture Magazine, 33 from Argosy.  Average
cost about $1.40.  Exhibit 3 is the only piece of copy
that paid out on this proposition last year -- it is the
only one I wrote, but two other copy men had had a try at
it before it came to me
```

LETTERS THAT GRIP ATTENTION

If you have a copy writer who is producing mail order copy that doesn't pay like that, HE HAS MY JOB Wouldn't you feel about that way if another agency had an account for which you could get better results?

I have other samples I could show you -- in five years' experience I have handled about every sort of mail order proposition there is going All I ask is a chance to show you. Isn't that about all you ask of a prospective client?

My name and address is

    H. A. Hornsby,
    555 Cochin Avenue,
    Brooklyn.
    My age is 27.
    Graduate of Williams.

Please put yourself in the place of an advertiser and consider me as a solicitor for your agency -- and then write me whether you will give me a show to prove that we are both losers if my real job is with you and I'm not filling it.

                Yours respectfully,

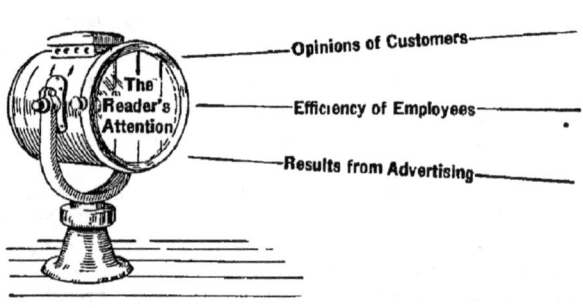

Panel 216

When you have performed the work just outlined, to the best of your ability, turn to the seventh chapter, where you will find the original letter on page 366. You may have thought that as the Big Idea of the applicant's letter was his ability to produce results from advertising, the attention-ray for that subject was the best to strive to attract. The writer of the original letter did not build his Stopper on that Idea and he was right. That is why I picked this letter as a problem for you.

447

BUSINESS CORRESPONDENCE

I want you to see for yourself the necessity for studying the attention-rays and their relative value for your proposition

Any manager of a mail order business, we grant, is probably more interested in the results of his advertising than in any other phase of his business. But if you study the situation as an applicant should do before writing his Stopper, you will appreciate that the attention-ray for results of advertising is undoubtedly being played for and "flagged" by more seekers of business from the mail order man—by advertising solicitors, printers, paper houses, and so on—than any other attention-ray. So to get a keener brand of attention and lift our application out of the rut from the very start, a Stopper built to catch the attention-ray of Efficiency of Employees would be indicated by close study of the chart This important point was brought out in the preceding chapter.

PROBLEM 2

Now below is the body of a sales letter for a baby carriage manufacturer. This letter was mailed to a list of new mothers secured from the birth records. With that knowledge of who the prospects are and what idea should be conveyed by the letter, you are to chart the attention-rays, select the best one to "flag," and then write the Stopper.

> Never a child came into the world but was worthy of as good a cart as could be afforded We take pride in the handsome, comfortable, stylish little carts we make. We would rather make a good cart for a little round babe than the best automobile that runs, and no one, we honestly believe, makes a better one
>
> For 20 years we have been making them — experimenting with them — learning to make better ones all the time All the little points that make for baby comfort and health — and all the little points that go to make a proud, stylish little turnout for the most inspiring sight in all the world — a mother and her child — have been observed and considered by us.
>
> Devoting ourselves entirely to the making of children's things, we understand full well the importance of price to you.

LETTERS THAT GRIP ATTENTION

> And we long ago determined that our policy should be to offer every mother the chance to have for her child a cart that is fully worthy of the occasion, at a fair and reasonable price.
>
> We early determined to save her the unnecessary profit that the middle men usually make — the wholesaler and the retailer — to sell our carts direct to the consumer. Another advantage in this method is the wide range in selection of color and grade of upholstering. You don't have to offend your good taste, as you probably would if you had to buy what a local market affords.
>
> The catalog sent you illustrates and describes our many handsome styles We know that you will read it carefully — because such an important matter as the selection of baby's cart requires care, doesn't it? Then when you have picked out just the one you desire, our order blank gives very clear directions so that there will be no mistake about getting just what you selected.
>
> And we ship promptly and all charges prepaid.
>
> Yours sincerely,
> BETTER CARRIAGE MFG. COMPANY

The original letter for your second problem will be found on page 252. If you are growing familiar with the principle of Stoppers, explained in detail in the foregoing chapter, your work on this problem should be pretty accurate.

Problem 3

For the third problem, I am giving you, below, the body of a letter used by the Addressograph Company. This letter is mailed to lists of firms that are known to be doing direct advertising and circularizing. You are to chart the attention-rays of such prospects and select the best ray to "flag" and perform the work. This is going to be a fine test of your mastery of the last chapter, so work it out carefully.

> Several times during the past year I have received circulars from a big eastern advertiser. Each time my name and address on the envelop has been blurred and smudgy -- almost illegible.
>
> Every time I receive a poorly addressed circular from this prominent concern, I wonder how many hundreds of

BUSINESS CORRESPONDENCE

>   addresses they send out that CAN'T BE READ -- and as a
>   result, how many are never delivered.
>   What a loss inaccurate addresses must cause! Think
>   of the wasted postage, the delays in mail delivery, and
>   above all, the LOST SALES OPPORTUNITIES which is the
>   result of faulty addressing
>   What a great percentage of this loss -- in your OWN
>   Advertising Department -- could be prevented with the
>   Addressograph!
>   Why not determine NOW to eliminate the waste of hand
>   addressing -- to secure the utmost in ACCURACY, ECONOMY,
>   and EFFICIENCY, in handling your important lists?
>   Today, at no cost to you, is your opportunity to
>   learn how the Addressograph will help you. Mail us the
>   enclosed card for more SPECIFIC information.
>   Yours very truly,

When you have that last problem worked out, turn to Panel 62 on page 122

You will notice in the letter which you will find there that no "artificial" Stopper at all was used. One of the attention-rays of such a list would surely be for Other People's Circulars If you didn't have such an attention-ray charted, it was because you had not studied the situation carefully enough. And when you had picked such an attention-ray, a study of the "features" of the idea should have shown you that that first "feature" of "Circulars received from an eastern advertiser" was Stopper enough—none could be stronger.

Next time, after we have analyzed the matter of letterheads, envelops, and enclosures, we are going to make a general review of all the points covered and learn how to put them all together.

PART IX

PLANNING LETTERHEADS, ENVELOPS AND ENCLOSURES

CHAPTER IX

PLANNING LETTERHEADS, ENVELOPS AND ENCLOSURES

WITH the details of thinking and writing letters disposed of, we shall turn in this chapter to the mechanical side of our problem and devote all our attention to stocks, layouts, colors, and other items that make up a well-balanced business letter. First I shall give you ideas on letterheads and envelops and then I shall turn to enclosures.

So that we may start from common ground and get the correct viewpoint on how a letterhead and an envelop should be planned, let us go back to the very rudiments of letter writing.

We write and mail letters for just one purpose—to transmit our ideas. If the necessity for transmitting an idea to someone by mail came to us suddenly, as it probably did years ago to some business man, our only concern—outside of expressing the idea, winning confidence for it, persuading action on it, and getting attention for it—would be to secure a piece of paper big enough to contain the letter's "load" and an envelop big enough to contain the piece of paper. But as this necessity for transmitting an idea to one person developed into the necessity for transmitting ideas to one person every day, then to two a day or six a day or a dozen a day, we would soon be put to the necessity of selecting and laying in a stock of paper and envelops that would make our work easier.

So far so good. We should then have arrived at that stage in the history of letter writing when firms and individuals began to standardize their letter sheets and envelops.

But at that stage, the effects—the results—of our letters would have assumed an increased importance. When a job has to be done several times every day, doing it effectively becomes much more important than when it has to be done only occasionally.

So, in addition to being as careful as possible to convey our ideas clearly, to win confidence, exercise persuasion, and grip attention, we would have to take more pains to see that the *paper and envelops* by which our letters' "loads" were transported were *safe, efficient vehicles*.

Isn't that about the way letterheads and envelops were developed? At any rate, that is the present basis on which to decide the effectiveness of a letterhead or an envelop. Ask yourself, "Is it a safe, efficient vehicle for transporting the 'loads' of my letters?"

In other words, as your letterhead or envelop is the means of transportation for your letters, it should be chosen just as transportation for merchandise is chosen. A manufacturer does not order his goods transported by express or by freight or by mail merely because he likes one method better than the other, or merely because one method is cheaper or speedier.

He considers first the goods—what method of transportation is *safe* for them, second the customer's convenience—what method would be *prompt*; third himself—what method would be *economical*. And his choice is the method that most nearly fits all three requirements.

So with letterheads. In selecting them you should first consider what sort of "loads" your letters carry. If in your business you have nothing to transmit by letter but plain, positive ideas—if you do not intend to solicit new business, if you have no complaints to mollify, no personal or business prestige to create, no action to persuade—then, as far as your letter's "load" is concerned, a letterhead bearing your name and address, like that at the top of the opposite page, will serve.

But be careful Before deciding definitely, you should consider the people to whom you write. If they know your business or know why you are writing and can quickly connect up a letter from you with their own interests, or if the kind of

LETTERHEADS, ENVELOPS, ENCLOSURES

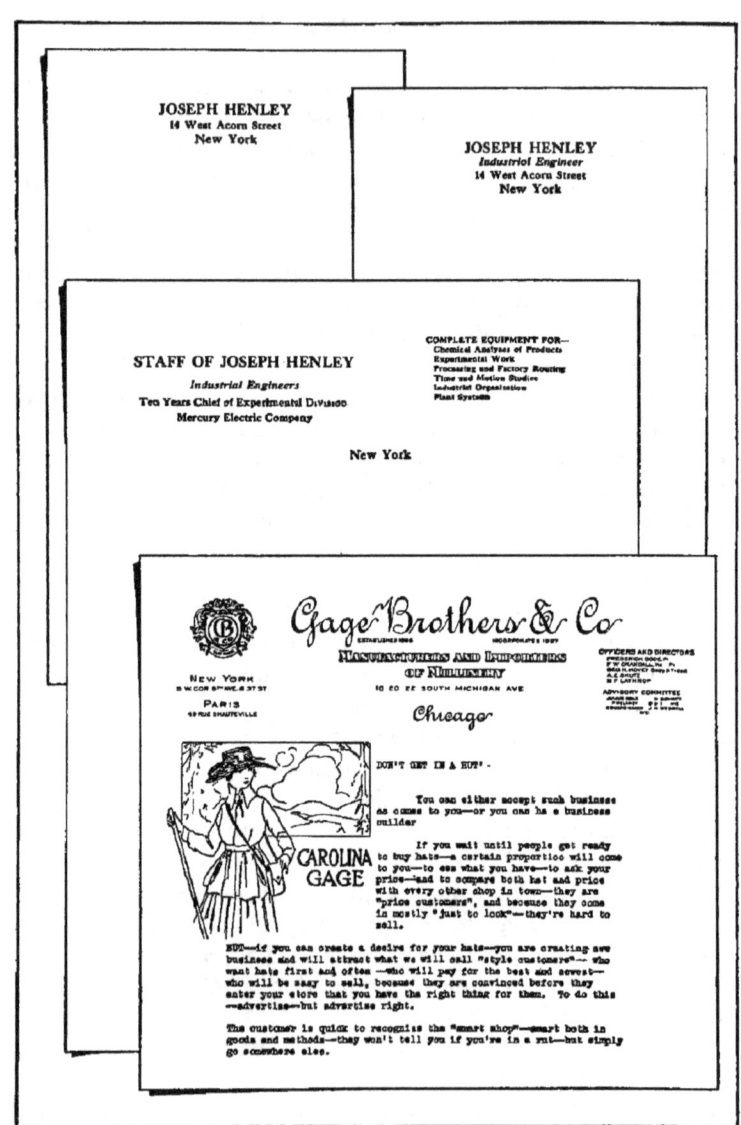

Panel 217

"loads" your letters carry do not require any such knowledge on the reader's part, then the plain name and address card is enough. But if your letters go to people who are strangers and who might not be able to grasp the full significance of your idea until they know your line of business, then you'll need letterheads like the one second from the top of the preceding page.

Finally, as you decide upon a letterhead for even such simple propositions as those we have been considering, that is, when no solicitation of business, no persuasion, no particular seeking for personal trust, is required, you should consider the letterhead question from a third angle. You must consider it from your own point of view. *How elaborately can you afford to go into the letter and envelop proposition*, and how elaborately do you want to go into it?

You might personally want to go into it on a very moderate, *economical* scale, using light, cheap paper and plain printing But if the nature of the ideas you have to convey to your reader is such that cheap paper and poor printing would hurt their reception, then you should compromise between the kind of stationery you would like to buy and the kind that would help most to put your ideas across.

Or, your own taste might lean to the use of the very best paper and *expensive* embossing, whereas the nature of your letters demanded an impression of careful efficiency, or your profit from the correspondence required most rigid economy. There again you would have to compromise.

Now, in a general way, we have the basic principle of efficient business stationery. We have seen how stationery evolves, in the case of a simple, personal business, into the plain, clean-cut letterheads at the top of the preceding page. Now, just imagine the business not so simple Imagine that you had to solicit business by letter.

To do that, the plain name, business and address card would hardly be a safe medium of transportation for the "load" some of your letters would have to carry. A part of that "load" would be the *establishing of confidence* in your

LETTERHEADS, ENVELOPS, ENCLOSURES

ability, resources and experience. And if all the people from whom you had to solicit business were not familiar with your ability, resources, and experience, a plain, uninforming letterhead might retard the creation of confidence. And also, if you really possessed extensive ability, had ample resources for performing your work, and had had long and valuable experience, could you not make your stationery demonstrate those qualifications for you?

In such a case our basic principle of letterheads would surely point to the third Henley letterhead illustrated on page 455.

Or, to go in the opposite direction, suppose that you were in some highly competitive line—wholesale millinery, let us say.

Considering first the character of "loads" to be carried by a millinery concern's letters, it is easy to see that included in the "load" of practically every important letter from the business would be the task of *building up or protecting the firm's reputation* for style leadership and style authoritativeness.

Then, considering the people to whom letters would be written, we can easily see that any ideas concerning style would be more difficult to absorb from a formal, commercial looking letterhead than from one reflecting daintiness and originality. And, third, considering the firm itself, if it really had claims to leadership in style, it should have an organization and facilities capable of supplying latest styles.

Do you see how logically and how surely you arrive at the general tone most desirable for such a letterhead? It should be artistic, probably hand-lettered; it should, if possible, show its offices in, or connections with the leading style centers, like Paris or New York. An illustration of some seasonable and exclusive model would be appropriate. With such an understanding it would have been easy to have given an artist the clear directions that would have produced results like that shown at the bottom of page 455.

How far you can go or wish to go in dictating the actual execution of your letterhead plan must depend, of course, on

BUSINESS CORRESPONDENCE

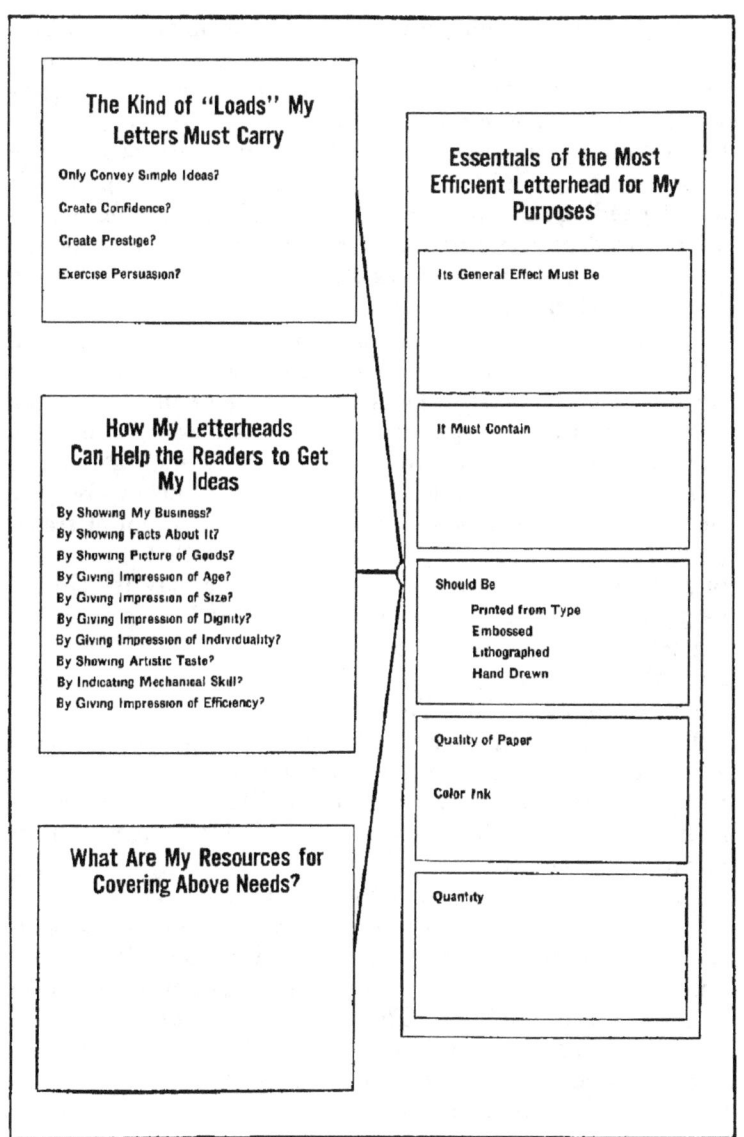

Panel 218

LETTERHEADS, ENVELOPS, ENCLOSURES

your own artistic ability, knowledge of printing colors, lithography, engraving, and so on. The average business man may well leave those points to his artist or printer. But he should *dictate and control the effects* to be obtained. The leaving of not only the style of lettering or drawing, or the choice of types and colors, to the artist or the printer, but also depending on him to produce the final effect, often secures a letterhead perfect perhaps from the artist's or the printer's point of view, but it almost as often results in a poor medium for transporting business ideas.

Therefore, it is not my purpose, in this chapter, to dwell on the technique or art of designing letterheads, but to show you *how to specify* the general nature of the design and to be sure that the general effect, when done, will be a help in conveying the ideas in your letters, and not a hindrance. In other words, I shall show you how to be sure that your stationery is a safe and efficient medium of transportation for your letters' "loads." That is all that the average business man should attempt to know. He may let himself be guided in the actual execution of the plan by the advice of a good artist, printer, lithographer, or engraver. When you have this problem up for consideration, however, look over your files and see what others have done

But no man will ever absolutely know the best general effect to secure from letterheads, nor will he know whether the artist's or printer's work has insured the best effect unless he has carefully studied and analyzed the requirements of his particular business.

The simplest and surest method of doing this is to graphically *chart the work that your letterheads ought to do*, on some such form as the diagram on the opposite page. (Make out a number of blank forms of this diagram; you will need them in the problem section). The items enumerated are not intended to constitute a complete list of the points to be considered, as special items exist for each line of business. But those shown indicate the character of the items that should be considered.

BUSINESS CORRESPONDENCE

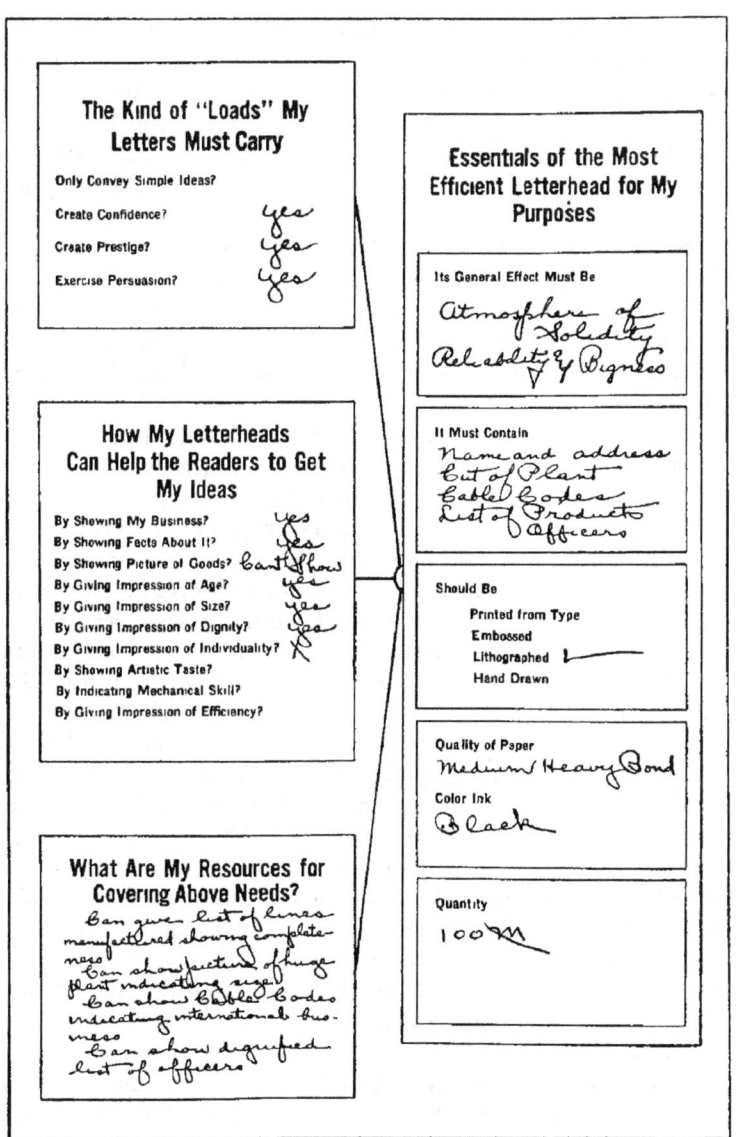

Panel 219

LETTERHEADS, ENVELOPS, ENCLOSURES

When you have checked off or written in on a chart the various points that your letterhead should cover and when you have checked off against the various points the extent to which you can go in covering them, then you will be able to set down on the right-hand side of the chart the essentials that should be embodied in a letterhead most effective for your business.

Is that clear? Let us see how it works and then we shall be sure. Suppose we are pottery manufacturers, making a complete line of pottery and distributing our goods through plumbers and plumbing supply houses. We want an efficient letterhead for our business. Let us check off our imaginary requirements on the chart.

First we ask ourselves, "Must our letters convey only simple business ideas?" Our answer obviously is "No." We shall assume that we have much *sales correspondence* with dealers and that as we are advertising in the magazines, undoubtedly we shall have *correspondence with consumers.* Hence, it is quite likely that our letters will frequently have to create confidence and prestige and exercise persuasion. Therefore, we shall check the kinds of "loads" our letters must carry, as shown in the upper left-hand square of the chart on the opposite page.

Second, for the reader's convenience, how can our letterheads help in transporting our letters' "loads?" By showing our business? Surely. By giving facts about it? If possible. By showing pictures of goods? This can't be done if our line is large, especially as pottery includes so many items. Would the impression of our business age help? Yes, if ours is an old firm. Size of the business? Yes, if it is a large one. Dignity? Somewhat. Individuality? Hardly. Artistic taste? No. Mechanical skill? Impossible to show in our line. So we check the second square of the chart as you will see on the opposite page.

Now how can we cover all the points we have listed? Why, in the bottom left-hand square of the chart are shown our letterhead resources.

BUSINESS CORRESPONDENCE

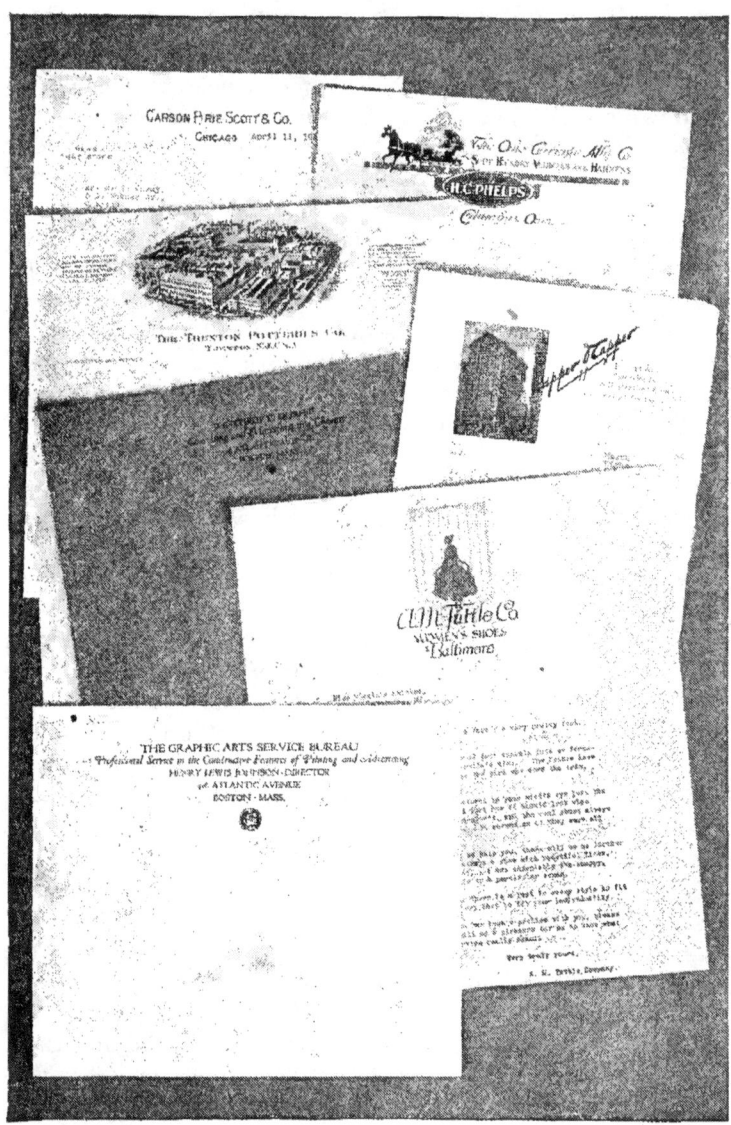

Panel 220

LETTERHEADS, ENVELOPS, ENCLOSURES

Now turn to the right-hand side of the chart for the third consideration—ourselves and our pocketbooks. Do you not see how easily *the essentials of an efficient letterhead* could be set down on it? There you have a plan of what our business requires of our letterheads as far as we can supply it. The choice between printing, embossing and lithographing brings up a question on which expert advice should perhaps be sought. Getting competitive bids from different letterhead houses generally opens a way of settling the question. The arguments and the prices of rival houses often give the information on which to base a decision. But with the plan of the essentials scientifically charted, we can let a contract for our stationery with certainty that we know what we want and that we will know it when we get it. Near the top of the opposite page you will see the letterhead we have built up.

I have often heard and read long arguments by artists and typographical experts about the advisability or folly of encumbering a letterhead with *lists of officers or a list of products*, but you now see the clear, businesslike answer to the problem. You can see that it is not a problem that concerns the artist or typographical expert at all. It is a problem to be decided by the owner of the business, or the buyer of his stationery, according to a chart of the requirements of the business. When a list of officers will add a needed touch of dignity to the letterhead, then a list of officers should be shown regardless of any outside person's arguments that "no one cares who your officers are." But if such a list is not needed for such a purpose, then it is a detriment.

The same holds true as to lists of products, lists of branch houses, cable codes, date the business was established, cuts of the products manufactured or sold, photographs of the founder of the business, and so on.

A man should determine whether such points are needed for the particular work his letters have to do, and for those which are needed, let an artist or typographical expert undertake the task of arranging and reproducing them with good taste. The designing of letterheads is an art in itself, hence

BUSINESS CORRESPONDENCE

a discussion of this subject would be out of place here. There are, however, many books published on the subject. Most of them are available in public libraries.

We have just seen how a chart would pave the way for the Pottery letterhead. At the top of page 462, at the right, is a different type. Here is a concern selling buggies by mail. Confidence and prestige must be created and persuasion exercised. The firm's business should be indicated to the prospect, and any facts about it that will indicate quality and style will be helpful in selling the reader Also, as in the sales letters, the president's *personality is made a factor*, and as all letters are signed by him, anything that will help along the atmosphere of his personal prestige will be helpful.

Now, then, let us again put ourselves in another man's place and this time imagine ourselves the owner of this business and see what our resources are for developing a good letterhead. First, we shall assume that our chart has shown that we want something to indicate quality and style. We can state our policy of making only split hickory vehicles, to indicate quality, and we can show a photograph of a stylish model and handsome turnout to indicate style. We can help along the atmosphere of the president's *personality by* indicating that the letter comes direct from the president's private office Our chart of essentials would then demand:

1. A general effect of Style and Quality.
2. Matter to show:
    (a) Name and address
    (b) The slogan "Split Hickory Vehicles"
    (c) Illustration of stylish turnout
    (d) "Office of the president "

We need go no further to see how such a chart would lead to the letterhead of the Ohio Carriage Mfg. Co.

To go to the other extreme, we see by the letterhead in the upper left-hand corner of page 462 how the same kind of chart would indicate a totally different type of letterhead for another firm. Carson Pirie Scott & Company is a department

LETTERHEADS, ENVELOPS, ENCLOSURES

store known to probably every man, woman and child in Chicago, and there is nothing the store could put into its letterhead to add to its prestige further than to use the finest steel-die embossing and heavy quality paper.

But now, let's imagine ourselves the owners of a smaller store—an exclusive men's specialty shop in the fashionable shopping district. A chart of letterhead essentials in such a case would demand an effort of style and exclusiveness, a need of impressing the address on the reader's mind, and a statement of the kind of merchandise sold. See from the rough reproduction of the Capper & Capper letter shown on page 462 how these demands have been met by artistic arrangement, an etching of the building in which the store is located, prominence given the address, and the trade-mark of the store printed in red.

Hence, this is *the science of efficient stationery:* to analyze carefully the character of work your letters must perform; the character of the impression you must create, the resources you possess for creating that impression; to specify the essentials your analysis has shown to be both needed and possible and from those specifications to build up your letterhead with the assistance of a good printer or artist.

If you work on such a plan, your letterhead will be as simple as your business permits. And *simplicity* should be the ideal to be striven for. Nothing that your analysis does not show is needed should ever be put on a letterhead. If your name and address alone will fill the requirements, anything further is not only unnecessary, but unwise. If only your name, address, and nature of your business fill the requirements, do not add anything else. But when further details are shown to be valuable don't hesitate to add them.

On the next page are two effective letterheads that contain much material—but as it is of value, why should it not be there? The letter at the top of the page shows details of all the products manufactured, but as much of the correspondence is with consumers who might not know of all these products, an analysis would show the need for such cuts.

BUSINESS CORRESPONDENCE

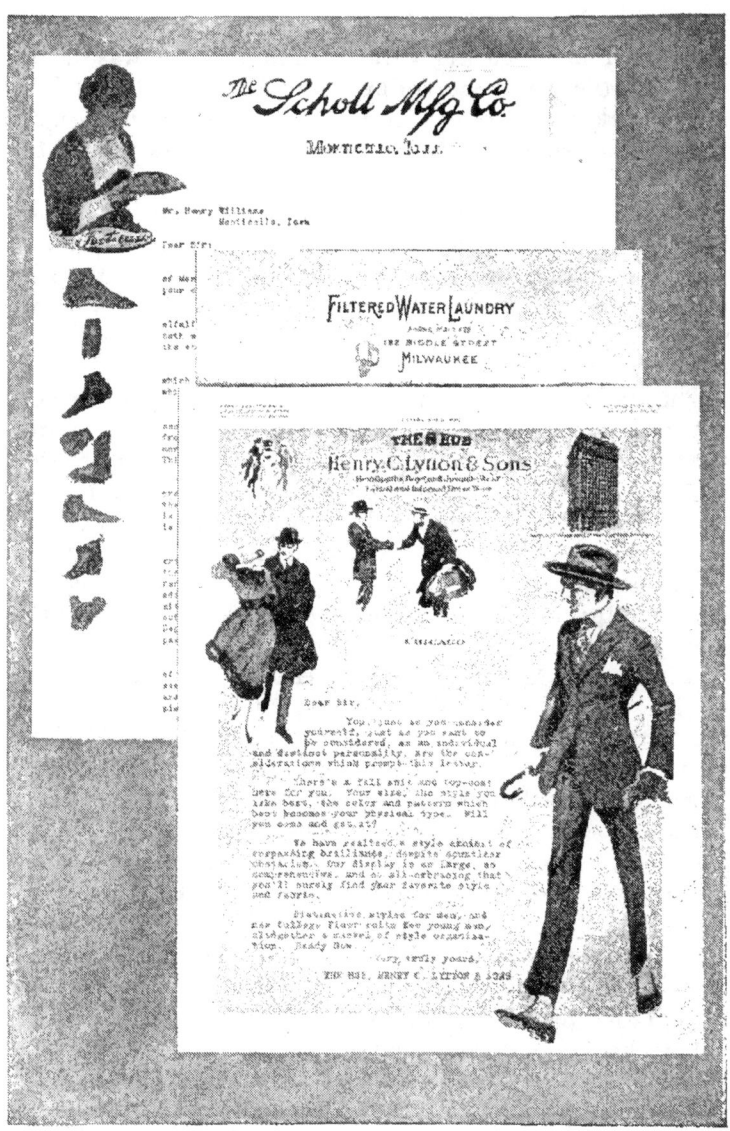

Panel 221

LETTERHEADS, ENVELOPS, ENCLOSURES

The letter at the bottom of the page is designed for a special form letter in which the attractiveness of styles was the big idea. So the many cuts, printed in colors, helped materially in the work of the letter. In the laundry letter simplicity is the keynote—and a chart of essentials would show that all the letter needed is the atmosphere of quality workmanship.

Put the letterheads you are now using in your business to the *test* of such an analytical chart of requirements and possible essentials and see whether you are lumbering them up with *unnecessary details;* or, on the other hand, see whether you are missing some of the help that you could get from a more complete letterhead.

The matter of envelops follows the same principle—nothing not vital should be on them. A plain return card to match the letterhead is enough unless your chart demonstrates that a *trade-mark, cut, slogan, or other matter* can be useful in helping your letters to accomplish their work. When your goods do have an individual point that can be easily illustrated, one that will help focus intelligent attention on the contents of the letter, as in the auto letter on the next page; or when your proposition has some distinctive feature that can be emphasized, as in McClure's letter, then it is good judgment to sacrifice simplicity on your envelop, just as you would on the letterhead. You remember we had needs of this kind illustrated in the preceding chapter in which we studied ways of gripping attention.

Putting attention-gripping devices on envelops or letterheads has proved to be so valuable that many large business houses do not hesitate to prepare both special letterheads and special envelops for the mailing of a circular letter when an analysis chart shows that the letter requires points not needed on the firm's regular stationery. The clothing letterhead on the opposite page was planned to fit such a case.

For the same reason, different departments of the same business may, when a careful chart of letterhead essentials is made, show such widely varying needs, that the business is not only warranted in having, but is almost compelled to

BUSINESS CORRESPONDENCE

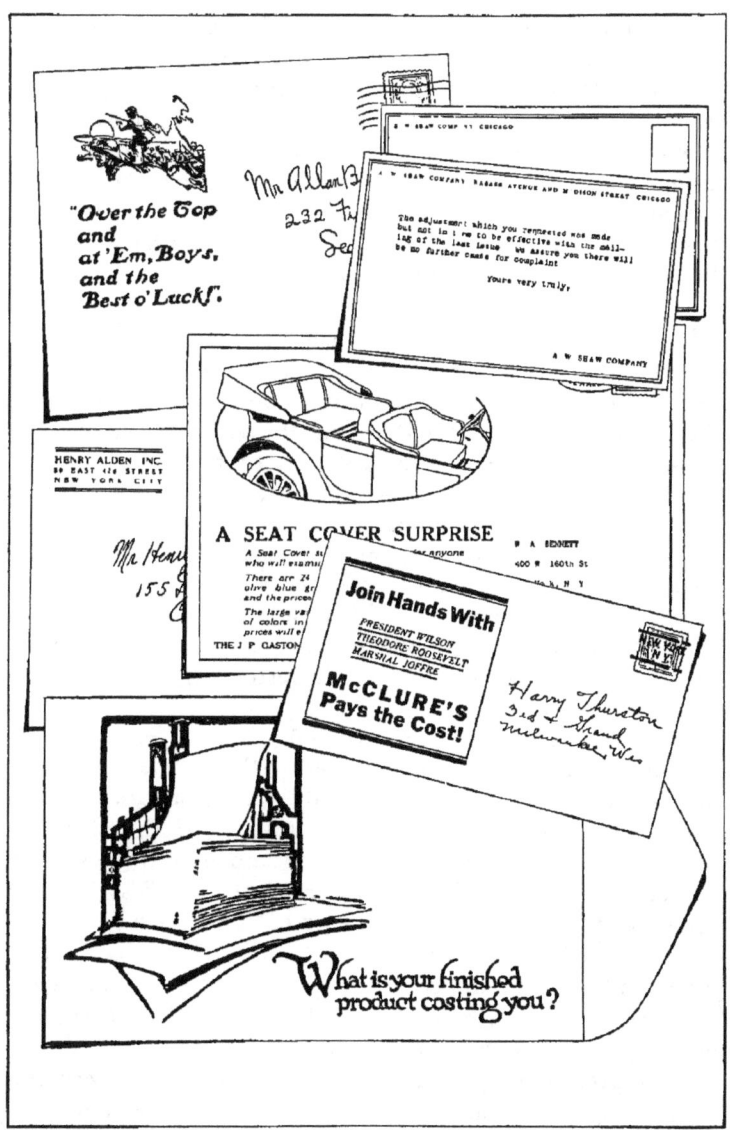

Panel 222

LETTERHEADS, ENVELOPS, ENCLOSURES

have, different types of stationery for them. The sales department, for instance, may need colored illustrations of the products, an advertising slogan, and so on, which would be out of place on the correspondence of the credit department. When the business is big enough to make such differences important, it is big enough to justify two or more types of stationery. A chart of the stationery's essential requirements, such as we have learned to make in planning a letterhead, is the surest way to bring such needs to light.

Varying the character of stationery has been found particularly important to advertisers using a long series of follow-up letters. The firm's stationery, if unvaried, might not only fail to give the full cooperation demanded by varying types of the different follow-up letters, but it also may easily become so quickly recognized by the prospect that he will toss it to one side as "another of those letters from so-and-so" before the letter itself gets a chance.

If the *follow-up-work* is big enough to warrant the expense, when the series has been planned according to the principles already outlined, each letter in it should be submitted to a chart of stationery requirements, and a form color scheme, size and shape laid out to fit each letter and give variation to the whole series

So far we have not given thought to *size and shape* of stationery. It can be correctly settled by exactly the same method of charting the requirements and resources. Merely add to the items in the first two squares of the chart on page 458, an estimate on the general amount of typewritten matter your average letters will require. If most of your letters will be short, medium length, it is useless to have letterheads of the standard size $8\frac{1}{2}$ x 11 inches. You waste paper and mar the appearance of your letter. "Note size" letterheads—$5\frac{1}{2}$ x $8\frac{1}{2}$ inches—will look better, save you money, and save much time in folding.

But if your average letters are long, then the full size letter sheet will be, not only more economical, but also more convenient than handling many two-page letters.

BUSINESS CORRESPONDENCE

Here again your chart, if carefully worked out, may indicate the advisability of employing both sizes of letterheads. For if you have many long letters to be written, and also many short ones, it is obviously inefficient to waste stationery in making one size do for both

SYSTEM has not only found, by analysis of its own requirements, that different types of letterheads for its different departments not only pay, but also save much money. And for certain types of short communications—like acknowledgments of change of address, and so on, where no carbon copy is necessary or advisable, an individual form postcard has been found a convenience and an economy.

The window envelop comes under the same category of efficiency stationery. For filled-in form letters, and also for regular correspondence where the volume is large, the window envelop saves typewriting the address on the envelop, and the carbon copy of the letter is always a carbon of the address to which the letter was mailed. Remember, however, that there is some prejudice against its use.

But before any size or style or quality or form of stationery can be said to be efficient, you must analyze the requirements, not only from your own viewpoint, but from the viewpoint of the character of your letters, and of the reader's convenience.

The chart on page 458—adapted, of course, to the peculiarities of your own business—is the surest way to avoid mistakes.

With the make-up of letterheads and envelops disposed of we next turn to a consideration of enclosures. But remember that in studying the enclosures that should go with a letter, we must eliminate order cards and reply cards. From experience I have learned to consider them as really part of a letter's close, and they were treated as such in the seventh chapter.

The enclosures that are up for our consideration now are those that have an entity of their own—that could be read intelligently even if entirely separated from the letters they

LETTERHEADS, ENVELOPS, ENCLOSURES

originally accompanied. These I divide into three types, according to the character of the work they are designed to do:

1. *Missionary enclosures*
2. *Reenforcement enclosures*
3. *Selling enclosures.*

Missionary enclosures are what some people call, and I think miscall, "envelop stuffers." They are those inexpensive little circulars illustrating or describing briefly some particular product or some one unique feature of a product to be inserted in the regular day's mail, or in the monthly statements, or in all answers to inquiries, or in mailings of form letters, without any particular reference to them in the letter, but just on a chance that someone in need of such a product may be attracted, or someone just wavering in doubt may be swung over by the particular feature illustrated. The missionary enclosure may have nothing to do with the idea conveyed in the letter with which it is enclosed It is merely—a missionary preaching its message wherever it happens to be.

The reenforcement enclosure, just as its name suggests, is an enclosure made to reenforce the work of the specific letter with which it is enclosed. Just as an army may need reenforcements to enable it to storm some particular trench, so a letter often needs a reenforcement enclosure to enable it to accomplish some particular phase of its work. One feature of the letter's idea may be a point of mechanical construction that a photographic illustration and detailed description would make much stronger; or it may be the style of a garment that a drawing would enhance; or it may be the testimonial of a customer that a facsimile letter would make more convincing In such cases only a printed circular can offer the necessary reenforcements to the word-features of the letter.

The selling enclosure is an enclosure designed to be able to make a sale by itself. It may be used primarily as a reenforcement enclosure, but if entirely separated from the letter or if mailed alone would have all the elements of a complete sales canvass, including the order-coupon. This is the kind of enclosure particularly in vogue with mail order houses, but

BUSINESS CORRESPONDENCE

Panel 223

LETTERHEADS, ENVELOPS, ENCLOSURES

its great strength can also be used by other business houses as well.

Now, with this rough idea of the three types of enclosures—which will be made clearer as we get into a study of how to construct each type—we must learn when each type should be used. It is poor business to go to the trouble and expense of enclosing a circular with a letter if the circular is not the right kind; it is poor business to go to the trouble and expense of enclosing a circular when none is really needed; and it is equally poor business to send a letter without an enclosure if a selling enclosure would bring in more orders, or a reenforcing enclosure help the letter do its work, or a missionary enclosure bring an occasional new inquiry.

Consider first *the missionary enclosure*. View it in the light of your *business as a whole when enclosures are planned*. Ask yourself if there are any products in your line that would benefit by being called to the attention of your regular customers, or that might interest those who inquire about other goods. On the opposite page, I illustrate how one publisher treats such a case. A little four-page leaflet telling about his books is enclosed in the answer to every inquiry for his advertised products. Printed simply in plain black on light paper, the cost is so small that he can afford to insert them in every letter even if only an occasional order or inquiry results.

Another question to consider is whether there is some particular feature of your business that your casual correspondents, or even regular customers, might overlook if it were not called especially to their attention. At the bottom of the opposite page I show how one retailer uses a missionary enclosure in his regular mail to call attention to the facilities of a charge account. The other illustrations on that page I'll pass without comment, for it is very plain that all of them carry out in varying detail the principle I've outlined.

Also, if you make or sell more than one line, it is best to decide whether customers for one line would be *possible customers for other lines*. If you think they would be, then include in your circular letters, or in your regular mail, or with

BUSINESS CORRESPONDENCE

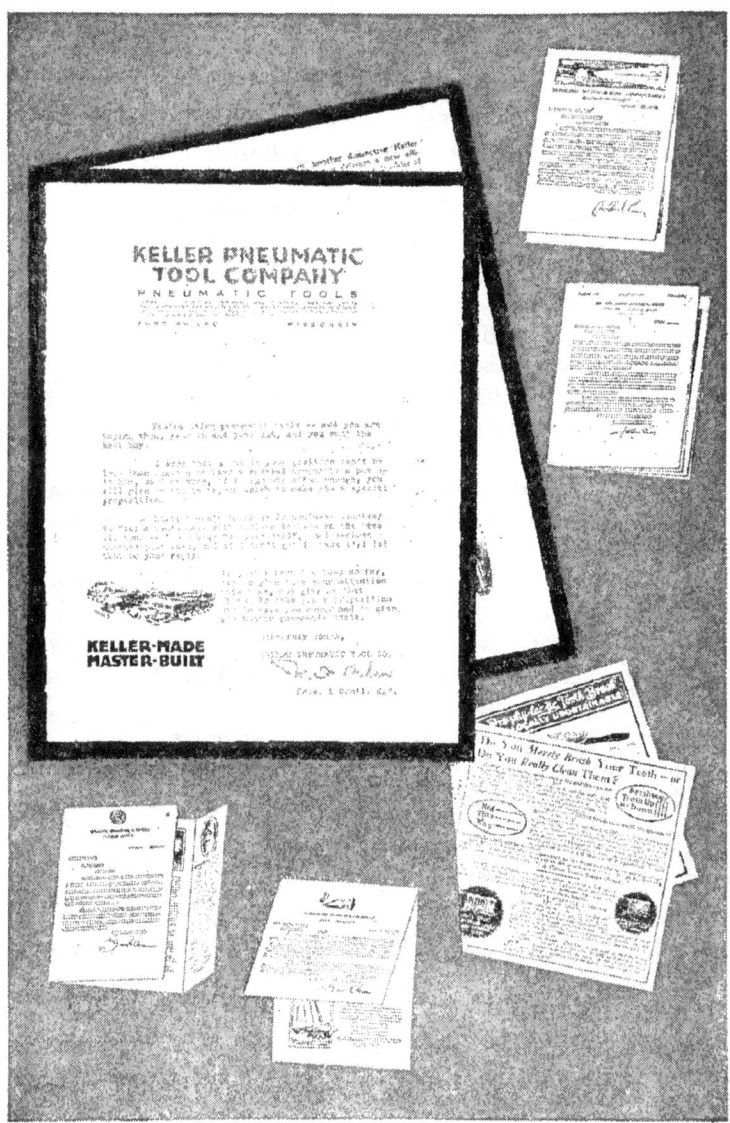

Panel 224

LETTERHEADS, ENVELOPS, ENCLOSURES

your monthly statements, a missionary enclosure for some one of your other lines, changing the enclosure in each letter sent the customer.

At times you should ask yourself if you have a seasonable specialty that would be benefited by a missionary enclosure in all mail sent out during its season.

In short, the success of the missionary enclosure depends on its being so inexpensive that the cost of using it is a trifle; so light in weight that it does not add to the postage cost of the letter; and so simple and brief that it does not "clutter up" the letter. Hence, if there is any opportunity at all to help the sale of your goods, or help the usefulness of a department, or promote the understanding of an individual feature, you should take advantage of it by using missionary enclosures in your letters.

Many successful houses have a series of four or six missionary enclosures prepared at the opening of each new season, one perhaps for each product, or one perhaps for each distinctive feature of the main product. These are used in rotation, one form for all mail going out the first month, another during the second month, and so on, so that every customer or correspondent of the house is likely to get one of each form of enclosure.

Next: study the reenforcement enclosure. After you have examined into the enclosure needs of the business as a whole to see if you can profitably use one or more missionary enclosures, you should consult the *needs of specific letters* and determine whether they can be benefited by reenforcement enclosures.

Ask yourself if there is a feature of the idea to be used in your answers to inquiries that needs more detail to make clear than you can put in a letter. In the panel on the opposite page, you will see how a tooth brush manufacturer encloses a circular with his answers to inquiries in order to reenforce his letter by explaining and illustrating the details of one feature of the selling idea more completely than could be done in the letter itself. On other occasions the letter itself

BUSINESS CORRESPONDENCE

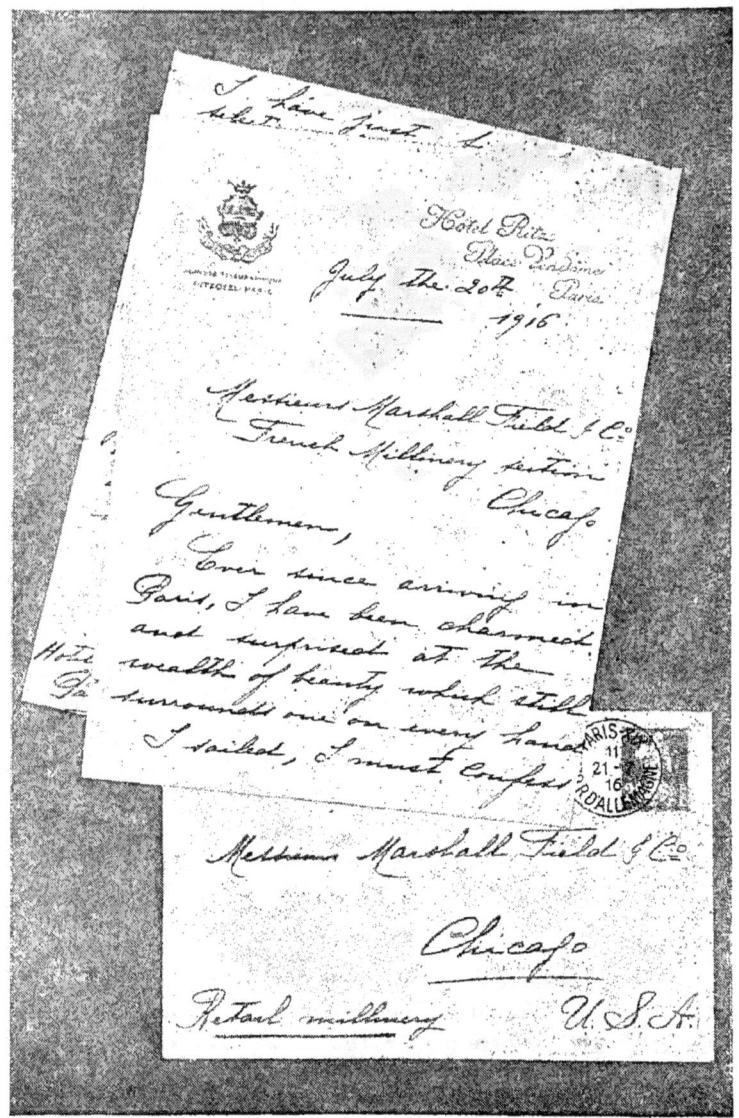

Panel 225

LETTERHEADS, ENVELOPS, ENCLOSURES

may be increased in volume to four or more pages and reenforcement data supplied as in the Keller Pneumatic Tool Company letter. Extension pages on letters are becoming more and more popular. For some lines they are especially useful, as by not filling in the addresss at the top of the letter they can be mailed as third class matter. Various ways of making up extension letters are illustrated on page 474.

Are there more detailed specifications than you can cover in a letter? Are there more specific price and discount lists than a letter can carry? Would photographic illustrations of the product, or detailed drawings of its parts, help in conveying the Big Idea? If so, make use of a reenforcement enclosure.

Would facsimile reproductions of the endorsements quoted or referred to in the letter reenforce those features in the letter? It has often been found profitable in the case of a testimonial from some influential firm or individual to go to great lengths in getting an impressive facsimile, as witness the illustration on the opposite page. This hand-written letter from an eminent French modiste was reproduced in its entire three pages, with letterhead and envelop, all in the original colors, and enclosed as a reenforcement to the selling idea of which the testimonial was a feature.

Then comes the question, are there so many individual features requiring reenforcement, or so many styles or models or prices, or so many *descriptive details necessary* in our proposition that a booklet to cover them all would be justified?

Going to the expense of a booklet, or even of a modest leaflet or circular, simply because it seems the conventional thing to enclose, has never appealed to me as very good business. Nor have I found it wise to go a single step further, in the elaborateness and expense of either circular or booklet, than efficient reenforcement of the letters makes necessary. If an analysis of what your proposition really requires shows an expensive booklet to be needed, then you should have one; if it shows an economical booklet or even just a four-page

BUSINESS CORRESPONDENCE

Panel 226

LETTERHEADS, ENVELOPS, ENCLOSURES

circular—say with a letter on the first page, as illustrated on page 474—to be enough, then that is all you should have, but if the analysis shows that no booklet or circular at all is necessary from a practical point of view, then it is folly to indulge in one simply because others have them. This brings us to our third point, consideration of a selling enclosure.

This may be a circular or booklet that covers your proposition so thoroughly, with all the elements of idea, sincerity, persuasion and action in it, that it can be looked to to produce orders by itself. Your conclusion as to whether your proposition needs or could effectively use such an enclosure, calls for a careful study of its sales possibilities.

If a proposition is one that can be covered in every detail in short enough space, its features built up one on the other in such a connected form that a prospect can and will read it through at one sitting, and get from it *a complete visualization of the whole proposition*—then an out-and-out selling enclosure will pay. In the panel on the opposite page is the selling enclosure of an automobile accessory proposition. It has all the elements of a complete sales talk or sales letter—it has a Stopper for attention, mutual "you-and-I" sympathy, fuel for the action motive, and an action-stimulating close. Above all, it not only conveys a big central idea, but conveys it in complete, consecutive detail, in reasonably short space.

But don't let the idea of a selling enclosure get the best of you. As I said, selling enclosures are very useful additions to a letter when they describe some simple or comparatively simple proposition. But too often selling enclosures are used to describe some article that really needs a booklet or perhaps a catalog to do it justice. Then selling enclosures are as useless as they are useful when used correctly.

For instance, consider the enclosures you have received with letters on such propositions as automobiles, addressing machines, and other articles involving many separate features and many of the features requiring voluminous details. Such propositions could not be conveyed to you in compact, complete, ready-to-be-acted-upon form. Therefore, a selling enclosure was impractical for them. The only practical enclosures for letters about such propositions are reenforcement enclosures which may be either circulars covering one or several of the most prominent features, or booklets covering all features.

Primarily, the selling enclosure is for use with a letter on the same proposition, and it has both a reenforcing and selling power. But if it can be condensed into small enough size—say into a 6 x 6 leaflet, or even smaller, which when folded once goes snugly into the folds of a letter—it can be used also as a missionary enclosure with all mail. Mail order houses thus do much effective missionary work for low-priced specialties. Book publishers and others make effective use of it. Wholesale houses use it profitably for combination assortments. And many manufacturers doing no mail order business or direct advertising, print such missionary selling enclosures in large quantities, and by imprinting a certain quantity with each of their dealers' names, induce the retailers to use them with bills and monthly statements, and even for counter hand-outs. In the form of little booklets, sometimes they bring in big returns. I illustrate several forms of this business-winning enclosure on page 478.

Now as to *selecting the enclosures that will fit* your particular letter. After your letter has been sized up and written, if you are planning a circular form letter; or after the general nature of your daily correspondence has been sized up, if you are planning the routine letter work of the business; or after you have planned your stationery to fit the requirements of the letter, you should, as the first step in planning the enclosure, analyze the possibilities of enclosures as outlined in the preceding pages..

Bear in mind, as you make your selection, that the type of enclosures to use is exactly parallel with the efforts of a salesman calling on trade—if he can possibly get an order he tries for it and it is only when he knows he can't get an immediate order that he is satisfied to try to pave the way for getting an order on another visit. And it is only when he knows he

LETTERHEADS, ENVELOPS, ENCLOSURES

can't do either that he is content to do mere "missionary" work for the distant future.

Therefore, in analyzing the needs of a circular letter or the general correspondence of a business we should first study to see if a selling enclosure can possibly be used to advantage Referring to the chart on the next page, we should give a careful, closely thought out answer to the question in the first large square If we can answer "Yes" to it, then we trace the dotted line to the "Yes" square and learn the kind of enclosure to prepare.

If we must answer "No," we trace the dotted line to the "No" square and then just as carefully answer the questions in the second square. If we can answer "Yes" to any one or more of them, trace the dotted line to the "Yes" square and there is the kind of enclosure our letter needs.

If we can answer "No" to the questions in the first two squares, then, by tracing the dotted line to the "No" square, we should again give a careful answer to each of the third set of questions. If we can answer "Yes" to one or more of them, the dotted line to the "Yes" square will lead us to the need of one or more missionary enclosures.

But if our answers are all "No," then the "No" square indicates the necessity and, therefore, the wisdom of putting no enclosures at all in our letters other than the order or inquiry cards needed.

Just a moment's consideration will prove to you the *dollar-saving business efficiency* of analyzing your enclosure needs in this way Often, too often, in planning the mailing of a circular letter, or laying out a system of follow-up letters, a man thinks to himself, "Now I must have a printed circular to enclose." And thereupon he proceeds to prepare one. Sometimes his printed circular covers only the same ground covered by the letter, repeating, perhaps, but not reenforcing where reenforcement is needed. Sometimes the enclosure is so vague as to be no more than a missionary enclosure, when a strong reenforcing, or even selling enclosure, would be valuable.

BUSINESS CORRESPONDENCE

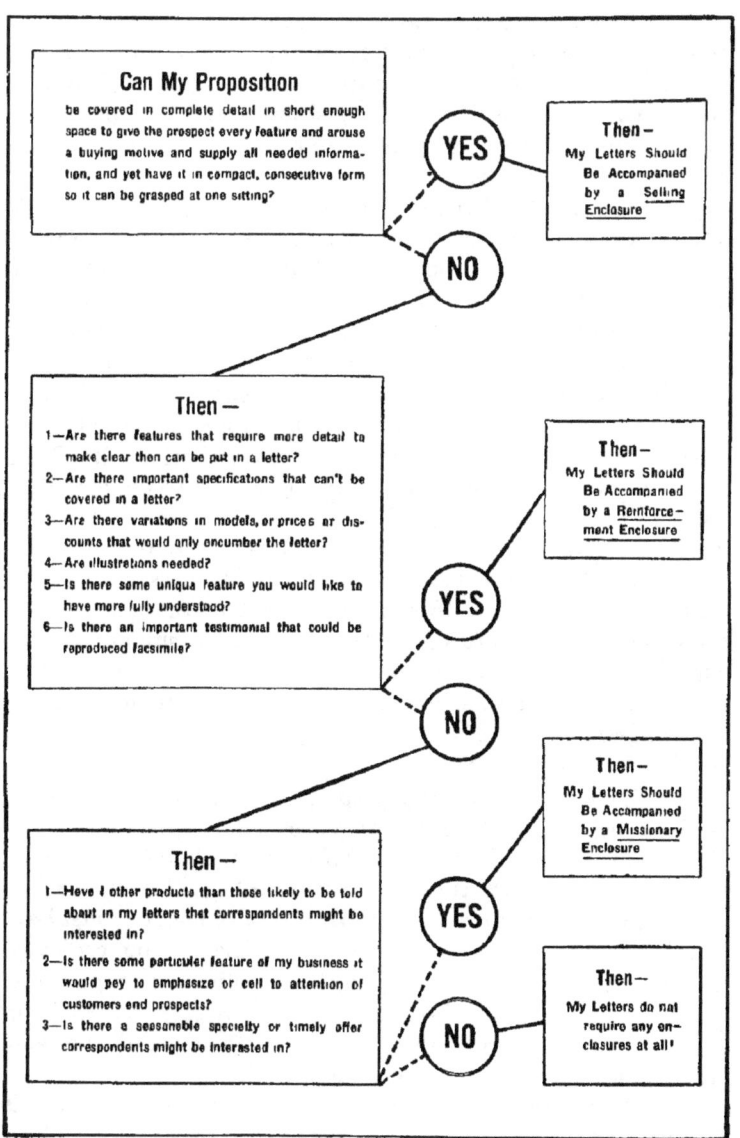

Panel 227

LETTERHEADS, ENVELOPS, ENCLOSURES

Such enclosures are a waste of money. The enclosure, no matter what it is, should perform a needed part of the work. But it will not, in all probability, perform that work if you don't chart out the entire proposition and learn definitely what particular work is needed, and construct the enclosure with that job in mind.

The *construction of any enclosure*—whether missionary leaflet, reenforcing folder or booklet, or selling circular—once its work is sized up and known, follows largely on the lines of a letter's construction. As in the case of a letter, you know the work to be done on the reader's mind, and, in the case of a letter, a Big Idea must be chosen for carrying the enclosure.

If it is to be but a missionary enclosure telling of some product you make or handle, or some department of your business, or a *unique feature of your methods*, then the Big Idea must be along the lines of "Here is a thing you will find useful," or "Here is a quality of so-and-so that will please you," or "Here is a piece of such-and-such that you can't beat," or "Here is a department of our business you should take advantage of." Because the object of the enclosure is missionary in its nature, the idea should be simple and its expression brief. Unless the proposition is so simple that missionary work and selling can be combined in small space, on a missionary enclosure, no attempt should be made at persuasion to immediate action.

For the reenforcement enclosure, the *features that need to be described in detail,* or the facts, specifications, price lists and so on that need extended explanation, should be treated exactly as you would treat the features of an idea in a letter. Being a reenforcing circular, its Big Idea, of course, must be a supplement to the idea in the letter—never too radically different, yet never too nearly the same to be mere repetition.

The selling circular should convey *the biggest idea in your proposition* regardless of the letter—in fact, it should be constructed altogether as an independent selling unit.

With both reenforcing and selling enclosures, a strong Stopper for attention and a powerful visionary or negative

BUSINESS CORRESPONDENCE

idea are essential to get interest. The prospect generally takes up printed matter in a listless or indifferent frame of mind, often before he has read the letter, so the printed matter should be ready to drive away that indifference right from the start.

In a word, then, you should proceed in planning and writing the matter for an enclosure exactly as you would in planning and writing a letter The big difference comes only in its physical make-up. In the printed enclosure your matter must be arranged with an eye to typographical effect, colors, and the shape and size of the pages. Illustrations also must be arranged.

After the nature of the enclosure is settled on and the proper copy written, then you must stop, and as in the case of the letterhead, come to a decision between what you would like for the job in the way of printing, cuts, colors, paper stock, and so on, and *what practical business will allow you to spend*

The best way to decide is to write on a piece of scratch paper a list of the features of your enclosure. For illustrations, decide on those which you prefer to have appear as plain black and white drawings, those you would like to show in color, those you would like to have illustrated from photographs Then select from samples of paper which any printer, paper dealer or paper manufacturer will gladly furnish you, or from printed matter of other houses, the kind of paper stock you think would be appropriate.

Estimate roughly the number of pages your matter will require, if for a booklet; or estimate, if for a folder or leaflet, the size sheet Then ask your printer to give you a rough idea of the cost for both cuts and printing

Reduce this figure to the *cost per piece*, see how it compares with the possible benefit—and then decide whether you can afford to spend that much to tell one person the points your copy brings out. Consider the gross cost again—is the volume of business you ought to get from many prospects big enough to warrant the expenditure on top of the cost of letters and postage and labor?

LETTERHEADS, ENVELOPS, ENCLOSURES

Of course, these estimates are only preliminary guesses. No printer could or would give you an absolute figure on such hazy data, and no business man can tell just how well his mailing is going to sell before he has tested it*—you can't be certain that you want all the copy and cuts you have arranged for.

But the estimates serve as a *preliminary basis* from which to work. Nine times out of ten, my experience has been, you will find the cost going altogether too high. So you must start trimming. First look to the things for which substitutes can be found. Ask your printer, any paper dealer, or any paper manufacturer, for samples of cheaper paper that might do as well. Find out if you can't substitute line cuts for half-tone engravings of some illustrations. See if between you and the printer you can't make up a dummy that would cut more economically from stock or that would require fewer impressions on the press, or that would save folding or assembling.

Then, if after all the *possible substitutions*, the cost is still too high, you must at last come to economizing in big things. Try omitting one color, or by Ben Day screens or tint blocks or process printing, to get the effect of the extra color without the cost—your printer or engraver, or a good artist, if you are to employ one on any illustrations, can help you if you are not expert on these things. And last take up the omission of illustrations that are least important, and copy that might be spared so that you could cut down the size of the job.

When you have made the approximate cost come within the approximate amount you want to spend, then the real work commences. You must make your "layout."

If you are dealing with an artist in regard to illustrations, or if your printing job is to be a very large one, the assistance of the artist or the printer should be called in on a circular or booklet layout—unless you are an expert yourself. But assuming that you have to do it all yourself, your next step should be to have a dummy made up on the stock you have selected, which any printer will be glad to do for you.

*Various methods of testing will be explained in the next chapter.

BUSINESS CORRESPONDENCE

FIGURE A

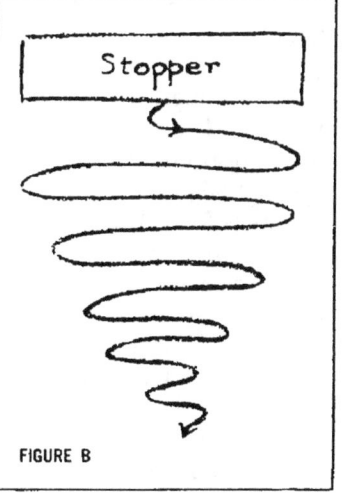

FIGURE B

FIGURE C

FIGURE D

Panel 228

LETTERHEADS, ENVELOPS, ENCLOSURES

Now the problem of *getting your copy arranged on the dummy* begins.

The most important point in making a layout, whether it is for a folder, booklet, or magazine advertisement, is to see that in the completed work you don't retard the reader's grasping your idea. The *best layout* for a piece of copy, of course, helps the reader to grasp the idea—that is what a layout is for. But many men rush into the matter of layout with their minds so bent on getting something unusually striking or unusually artistic, that they lose sight altogether of the reader's convenience, often getting so much layout effect on the eye that they kill the copy effect on the thought.

Now I can't show you how to make artistic layouts. I don't know how to make them myself. When I have a job that calls for something really artistic I hire an artist—and you had better do the same although you can pick up a lot of information on this subject by studying what other people are doing. But what anyone can learn, and what we all ought to know, is how to make a layout that helps our copy do its work as far as plain business sense can help.

It is not very difficult. Remember what we said was the *most important point about a layout*—doing nothing to retard the reader's grasp of the idea. Now what is the reader's mental process in grasping an idea?

We have already seen that when one of his attention-rays has lighted on something of interest, he brings his full attention to a stop and proceeds to look for the idea. He sees a bright light, for instance, and says, "What's the idea of it?" and proceeds to look for explanatory details. If your Stopper were a line of type, the reader would start from that point looking for the Idea. We all know that the eye, in looking at things, naturally moves from top to bottom. It has been trained that way. We read a letter by beginning at the upper left-hand corner and traveling down, as I have indicated in the Figure A on the opposite page.

Therefore, copy, in an advertisement or booklet, should be prepared according to the same plan. It should be laid out

BUSINESS CORRESPONDENCE

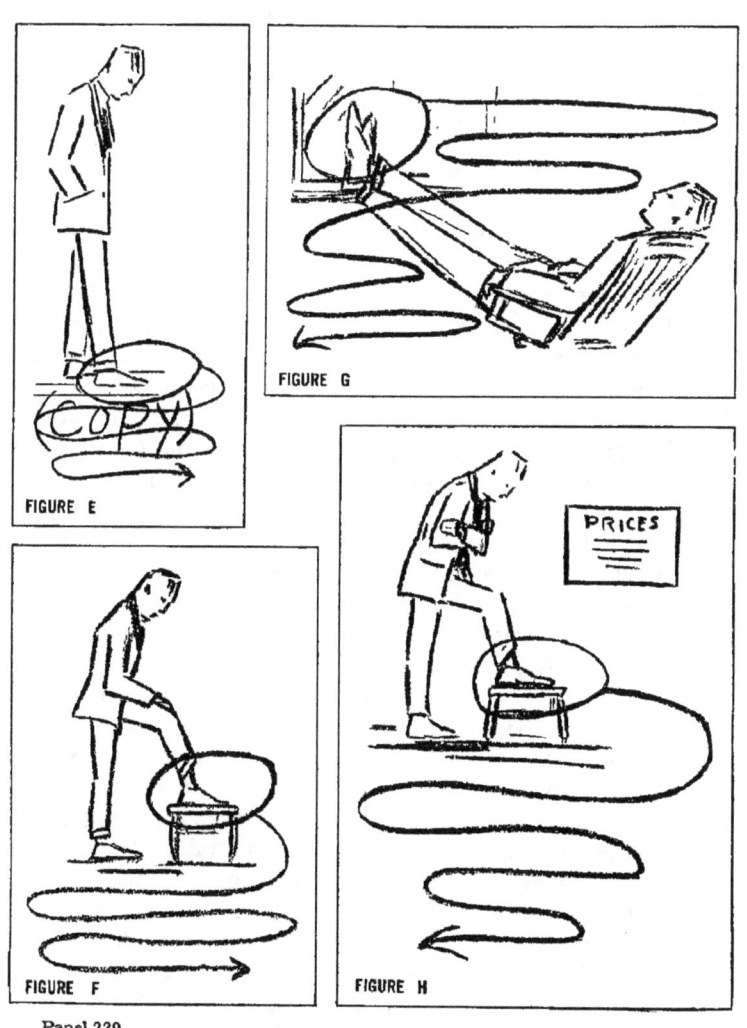

Panel 229

ENCLOSURES, LETTERHEADS, ENVELOPS

so that the features of it will unfold, from the Stopper down Figure B, then, represents roughly the general plan of a good layout.

Now suppose we were laying out a shoe circular and our Stopper were to be the picture of a man admiring the appearance of his new shoes. Let Figure C (page 486) represent it. The attention of the reader is going to travel quickly to the shoes, isn't it? The eyes of the man in the illustration point that way, and probably we would have the cut made so the shoes were the most prominent part of the picture.

Then if we carelessly put our copy alongside the cut we would force the reader to move his attention as shown in Figure D (page 486)—manifestly an unnatural course for him, and therefore one that would cause a feeling of discomfort. He might be quite unconscious of the cause, he might even be unconscious that his feeling was discomfort—just as in your sleep, when a wad of bed clothes bothers you, you don't feel exactly conscious of pain or discomfort, yet you know something is wrong and you toss or roll away from the cause of the trouble without knowing why.

Very often we get this impulse to "move away" from a circular or advertisement without knowing why—the real reason being that the layout has irritated our reading or observing instinct, by trying to drive it the wrong way.

Hence, if our attention-stopper has focused the reader's attention-rays on the shoes, we must arrange our layout to let his desire to "get the idea of them" move downward in its natural method, for instance as it would in Figure E on the opposite page. But such a layout might be impractical, as it uses up so much space in length. The shape of our circular or the size of our advertisement might not permit it. Then it is up to us to arrange the picture differently. Figure F shows one way of doing it by showing one of the man's feet on a bench or chair. Or we could save still more space by a layout, as in Figure G, representing the man sitting on a chair with his feet up in front of him on a window sill.

BUSINESS CORRESPONDENCE

But at any rate you see that when we know what we have to do we find it easy to shift and shape until we have done it.

So the sum and substance of the first principle of making a layout is to help the reader to grasp your idea by "routing" it in accordance with the direction in which his eye naturally moves. That is, when you have placed a Stopper on your folder or advertisement or booklet on which the reader's attention will be first focused, arrange the features of your Big Idea from that Stopper down—don't require the reader's eye to move upward before he can begin to see your idea unfolding.

Far be it from me to claim that a wrong arrangement will prevent your circular or advertisement from being read. Probably the average prospect would read it just as quickly when wrongly arranged as when rightly arranged. But there are always some who are in just that state of rising indifference in which the slightest difficulty—the slightest encouragement to quit—will send them away from your advertisement or prompt them to toss your circular to one side. And as we always want all the business possible, we want our layouts to offer no possible obstacle to the interest of any possible prospect.

So far we have been considering only the layout of relations between the Stopper and the Big Idea. We know why the features that convey the idea should never be placed above the Stopper, nor, unless otherwise impossible, should they come to the left of the point where the Stopper leaves the reader's attention focused. The reader's eye should be allowed to move toward the right, and downward, to the main idea. But this does not necessarily mean that the Stopper must be the topmost point of the circular or advertisement.

Just as we have seen a necessity for reenforcement details for the main features of a letter's idea, so there are reenforcement details often needed for the main features of a circular's or advertisement's idea. Such reenforcement details not only can be placed in the spaces left vacant by your layout of

LETTERHEADS, ENVELOPS, ENCLOSURES

Stopper and Big Idea, but also they are often more valuable there than elsewhere.

Just for example, suppose we were laying out a shoe circular on the lines shown in Figure F on page 488. We will say that the Big Idea is, "Black Joe shoes are made all comfort inside but all style outside." Now from the Stopper down we want to convey the Big Idea clearly. Well and good. But after that idea is conveyed to the reader we know he'll ask, "Wonder what they cost?"

Now it is always true that when you have just been imbued with an interesting idea you don't immediately move on, or start talking to someone else, or push the advertisement to one side. You contemplate the scene that gave you the idea, or talk further generalities about it with the man who imparted it, or take another general look at the advertisement that conveyed it. So if in our shoe circular we just put a little box or panel or paragraph up in the space above the Stopper, as shown in Figure H on page 488, and in it give that reenforcing detail of prices, we shall not have disturbed the grasp of our idea at all, yet we shall have made use of that vacant space—and when our prospect takes his second contemplative look he will find his question answered.

If the Big Idea has been bargain prices, and the reenforcing detail the point about comfort, or perhaps quality, then we would reverse the operation.

There you have the key to the layout of those details which don't help to convey the idea yet are essential in helping the prospect make up his mind. You have seen advertisements that had perhaps several reenforcing details placed in apparently isolated spots, quite unobtrusively, and maybe have wondered why.

You have seen circulars—say a book circular as indicated in the layout on the next page—where the Stopper and Big Idea of the book's helpfulness followed in good order, but the description of binding came in a little spot up on the left-hand side of the illustration, and the detailed contents came in a panel below. You can now understand the why of it.

BUSINESS CORRESPONDENCE

Theorists often say, "Don't make your layout look choppy." From the viewpoint of artistic balance they are right. And they are right from all viewpoints if they mean that a layout should not be a speckled conglomeration of boxes and panels and squares, or that the features of the Big Idea should not be "chopped up" needlessly into separated blocks of type.

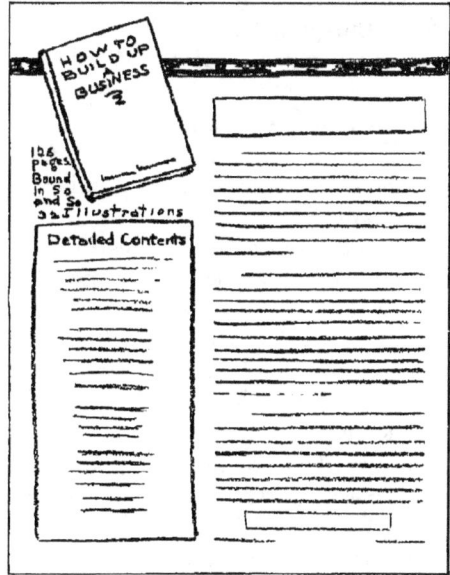

Panel 230

But if there are reenforcement details that do not play a part in conveying the main idea, a good layout will arrange them where they will not impede or obstruct the absorption of the main idea, even though artistic balance has to be sacrificed.

So far, then, we have learned that laying out a folder or booklet or advertisement requires:

1. Preparing the copy and cuts to convey the Big Idea, and also the reenforcement details.

2. Planning an Attention-Stopper.

3. Arranging the Stopper and the features of the main idea so the reader's eye moves naturally from one to the other.

4. Arranging any reenforcement details so they do not interfere with the main idea, but will be seen when the reader, having grasped the idea, takes his "second look."

If you will compare this method of laying out the presentation of a business message on the printed page with the way a good salesman arranges the presentation of his selling talk, you will see they are exactly parallel. The experienced salesman does not clutter up his canvass by dragging in all his ammunition as fast as he can. He first puts over the Big Idea of his proposition. Then, when he knows that if his presentation is taking effect the prospect will be in a contemplative mood, the salesman begins to bring out his reenforcing points.

Experienced public speakers follow the same plan. Those who know how to hold and influence the thoughts of an audience convey the main idea of the speech or sermon before getting down to the finer details.

Thus the audience has a visualization of the idea in mind into which to fit the details. But if a speaker or preacher goes laboriously into all the details of each feature before going to the next feature, the audience does not get a grasp of the complete idea until the very end—and generally not until it has become wearied, and has lost interest in the struggle to keep details connected.

My aim has been to show you how to lay out your copy so that the reader, directly his attention has been stopped, will receive the Big Idea of your proposition before he gets down to the supplementary or reenforcing details. If you put your Big Idea over to him, and it is a good idea, you need not fear his failing to look back for the supplementary details. And if he doesn't get the idea, or if the idea does not strike him as worth while, then it doesn't matter about the details—you have lost him anyway.

After you have progressed this far with the layout, you come to the matter of color Now by "color" I don't mean merely the colors of the spectrum—red, blue, yellow, and so on. I mean—to put it not quite accurately but in a way we can all understand—contrast.

We have just been considering the effect of a speech or lecture, so let us use it again You know how monotonous and ineffective a speech would be if delivered in one tone of voice. The speaker has to emphasize his more important points. Now his emphasis does not come altogether from a loud tone and vehement gestures. It comes from the contrast between those loud tones and vehement gestures and the even tones and quiet demeanor just preceding. If he bellowed and gesticulated from beginning to end, there would be no emphasis at all. And further, if he bellows and gesticulates too frequently the emphasis is lost.

Now a printed circular or advertisement must get its emphasis in the same way. If you use too much black face type or too many display lines you kill the effect of it all. If you want to emphasize one particular point by display type, see that it is preceded by either small, light face type, or white space. And after you have given such emphasis don't immediately start to emphasize another point—give the reader a rest.

If you are using colored inks for either illustrations or type, the same rule applies. Don't think that you must "get your money's worth" of color by using the color in every possible spot. Put it only where it helps the reader appreciate your point—in an illustration either to show an actual color of your goods or to throw another color out by contrast; in type matter, only as an orator would use an unusually emphatic gesture.

Good taste has something to do with it, but good business judgment has more. The best method for getting yourself started right on the arrangement of color, or contrast, is to first go through your copy carefully marking those features needing emphasis, and those parts for which you would like headlines Then roughly estimate on your dummy about where the headline and the emphasis is going to fall If they are going to bring masses of color too closely together you must either arrange a way of separating them, or if the order in which they are arranged cannot be changed without hurting the copy effect, then you must omit the color emphasis on some

By making typographical effect and copy effect give and take with each other, a final balance can be struck.

LETTERHEADS, ENVELOPS, ENCLOSURES

SUMMARY

WITH the simple fundamentals explained in this chapter we have gone as far in the matter of the preparation of letterheads and enclosures as the layman needs to go. The principles laid down do not cover the whole subject, but few practical business men want to go into the details of typography and art. What we all want is the fundamentals that will be a guide to learning and a standard by which we can measure our own and others' work.

And so in this chapter we have seen what constitutes an efficient letterhead for any business and how, by following a simple chart, it is possible to build up the essentials of a letterhead. We have seen that enclosures fall into three classes, missionary, reenforcement, and selling enclosures, and how scientifically to discover which of the three will make the most efficient kind of enclosure. Then we took up the problem of layouts and saw how to prepare copy for the printer and how to lay out copy so that the reader will quickly grasp the main idea.

In the next chapter we shall see how to make preliminary try-outs of our letters, of our circulars, of our booklets, before we have spent too much money on them; how to organize our work—whether it be the daily dictation of routine letters or the mailing of one circular, or the directing of a whole campaign, or conducting a follow-up system, how to determine the relative advantages of using sealed, first-class letters, filled-in or unfilled-in letters, individually typewritten letters, or imitation typewritten letters, and so on.

All that we may know about writing letters and planning enclosures may go for naught, however, if we don't know how to use our knowledge most efficiently. Therefore, the next chapter will consist of instructions about the practical, everyday conduct of business by means of the mails. We'll trace the growth of a correspondence department from the one-man office to the huge corporation office. Then we will be ready to take up testing, idea lists, material sources, and the other big ideas which are included in the final chapter.

PROBLEM SECTION IX

I AM not one of those who go so far as to say that a man's business stationery is one of the most important adjuncts of his letters. In fact, I know better from experience. While working as a correspondence organizer or in writing sales and collection letters, it has often been my lot to find a client stocked up with stationery as poorly adapted to the needs of his proposition as you could well conceive, and financially unable to junk it for new stationery. Yet his letters, by having the right stuff in them, overcame this unnecessary handicap and were made to pay

The same conditions may have come under your observation.

You have probably seen salesmen or collectors whose clothes were shabby or whose toilet was neglected, but who could get the business just the same. There was a ball player some years ago with the New York Giants who was deaf and dumb—a pitcher, at that—yet he made good

But such exceptions don't prove that a ball player doesn't need to hear, or that a salesman shouldn't be neat and clean, or that a business firm's stationery shouldn't be appropriate. I cited the instances merely to show that the claims of specialists as to the absolute *sine qua non* of their particular specialties, are sometimes exaggerated.

You probably will not fail in business if your stationery isn't perfect. But if your stationery is perfectly adapted to your requirements, you will find doing business by letter easier and more economical.

And if careful planning of stationery will help a business even ever so little, who would be so careless as to neglect this simple precaution?

LETTERHEADS, ENVELOPS, ENCLOSURES

The Kind of "Loads" My Letters Must Carry

Only Convey Simple Ideas?
Create Confidence? *Yes*
Create Prestige? *Yes*
Exercise Persuasion? *Yes*

How My Letterheads Can Help the Readers to Get My Ideas

By Showing My Business? *Yes*
By Showing Facts About It? *Yes, our lines*
By Showing Picture of Goods? *Can't—too many*
By Giving Impression of Age? *Yes*
By Giving Impression of Size? *Yes*
By Giving Impression of Dignity? *Yes*
By Giving Impression of Individuality?
By Showing Artistic Taste?
By Indicating Mechanical Skill?
By Giving Impression of Efficiency?

What Are My Resources for Covering Above Needs?

Date business was established. Founded in old colonial days. Complete line carried.

Essentials of the Most Efficient Letterhead for My Purposes

Its General Effect Must Be

It Must Contain

Should Be
    Printed from Type
    Embossed
    Lithographed
    Hand Drawn

Quality of Paper

Color Ink

Quantity

Panel 231

BUSINESS CORRESPONDENCE

Hence to understand thoroughly the principles covered in the last chapter is just as important in its own place as to understand the principles that have gone before. And in this problem section I'll give you an opportunity to practise them through the use of the charts which I described in the foregoing chapter.

First, let me see how thorough a grasp you have on the principles of drawing up the specifications for a letterhead after its requirements have been charted. Suppose you were planning the stationery for a hardware and household supply store. We shall say that this is an old New England store founded back in colonial days—1784. It carries hardware, cutlery, kitchen utensils, household goods, and garden supplies.

On the previous page I have checked off on a chart the requirements of the letterhead. To test your mastery of the subject, fill out the specifications side of the chart, on one of your blank forms, according to the method I followed in the last chapter for the Trenton Potteries Company and the Ohio Carriage Company. File it in your Material File, and in the next problem section we shall find a letterhead built up for just such a store and we shall see how near your specifications came to being right

Then let's try your skill still further Suppose this time you were going to order stationery for a bank. I shall just give you the general outline of conditions: the bank is a big, solid one with $2,000,000 capital and $1,500,000 surplus; it owns its own handsome modern building, and its directors are among the most substantial business men of the community in which the bank is located

In this case I offer no suggestions at all Work out the specifications for a letterhead from one of your blank charts, and then in the next problem section we shall see how accurate you have been, by a study of the actual letterhead of just such an institution.

For your third problem I am going to make you do practically all the work. I shall simply give you the name of

LETTERHEADS, ENVELOPS, ENCLOSURES

a well-known manufacturer, and let you figure out the probable conditions and requirements for yourself.

We will select a firm that we all have heard about, the Gillette Safety Razor Company—but whose letterhead I don't think many of you have seen, as its correspondence is mostly with the trade.

Work out the whole letterhead proposition for it, using one of your blank charts, and in the next problem section I shall reproduce the original and see how well you now know how to handle the problem.

The matter of choosing the kind of circular to enclose with a letter is one that is so clear and simple when worked out by the chart shown in the last chapter, that I am not going to ask you to spend your time on working out test problems on this feature.

As a practical man you will find plenty of tests for the chart right in your own business, and there is enough real work for you to do on this subject without asking you to take up imaginary problems that would do you no particular good.

What I think you should do, however, is to submit to the test of the chart the enclosures you have previously used, or seen used in your line of business. Many fundamental errors in the character of enclosures are constantly being made, and you will find it worth while to study and to see if you yourself have been making them.

But I am anxious to have you understand clearly the principles of arrangement on a circular or booklet. You should know enough about layout to be able to check up the work of any artist or printer you employ, and in the preceding chapter I have given you some sound principles to guide you.

Just to see how good a grasp you have on it, I want you to work out this test case. suppose that you were a retail haberdasher and were sending out a letter on your line of fall hats. Suppose that you also had the agency for a fine line of union suits that your regular hat trade might be interested in. Obviously, a little missionary enclosure on the union suits would be valuable, wouldn't it?

BUSINESS CORRESPONDENCE

Well, we'll say you have a nice cut showing the union suit folded in its individual box, the top cover off to display the goods. And we'll say that the manufacturer has furnished you with small swatches, or samples, of the fabric.

Your missionary circular is to be, say, 6 x $3\frac{1}{4}$. Now lay out the most effective arrangement of cut, sample, and about six lines of copy. Next time we'll take a look at a very effective circular of just such a kind and see how closely you came to getting the most efficient layout.

Then for a booklet cover or frontispiece. Suppose you were getting up one on hand-made quilts. All the copy that is to be on the page is this.

The irresistible charm of beauty and individuality in the hand work of exclusive designs. Your cut, we will say, will show a number of girls quilting by hand.

Make a layout to show where you would place copy and cut on a page $9\frac{1}{2}$ x $6\frac{1}{2}$. We'll see the original in the next problem section. And then you can check up your work.

PART X

ORGANIZING CORRESPONDENCE WORK AND TESTING LETTERS

CHAPTER X

ORGANIZING CORRESPONDENCE WORK
AND TESTING LETTERS

IN the previous chapter we saw how to plan scientifically the sort of business stationery that would prove the most efficient transportation medium for our letters, and the sort of circular or enclosure that would most efficiently back up our letters.

We had already seen how to stop the prospect's attention and focus it on the idea in our letter, how to make our letters exercise persuasion, how to express warm, personal sincerity, how to make our meaning clear, how to overcome indifference by means of a visionary or negative idea, how to convey an idea in words, and how to size up the work a letter has to do.

In other words, we know the fundamental principles of producing the copy for a letter and preparing the stationery and enclosure for it. The next step will be how *to use with the greatest efficiency the letters we write or dictate.*

Just as we began with the very simplest of letter problems in uncovering the principles of writing letters, working up through the most difficult ones in the order in which they appear in practical business, so in learning to properly organize our work we shall begin with the simplest conditions and work up.

If you were about to start yourself in a small, one-man business you would probably find that even before you rented an office or store there would be a letter or two to write. Probably you would take pen and ink and write them—and if they were important you would possibly make copies by hand. But as writing letters became a regular job with you the work of making hand copies would soon occupy too much

BUSINESS CORRESPONDENCE

of your time and you would then take your first step in organizing your correspondence—installing a copying machine.

And in a way the whole matter of organizing correspondence is mirrored in that first step—installing the old-fashioned letter press. The smallest going business you can think of recognizes—has to recognize—the value of a copying press when more than a letter or two a week is to be written Copying letters by hand takes the time of someone who could be better employed, and it also opens a way to make mistakes. Every step in organization, every installation of machinery, every employment of a stenographer or typist or mail boy, every short cut in arranging personal work, should be dictated by the same reasons—*to save the time of someone who could be better employed, or to save the risk of mistakes.*

No step in organizing a correspondence department should be taken that one, or both, of these reasons does not dictate, nor should any step that one, or both, of these reasons dictates be omitted

For instance, in the small one-man business just taken as an illustration, when the number of letters grows to a point that even the time for writing them in longhand begins to infringe on the time needed for other affairs, or when the appearance of handwritten letters begins to give an erroneous impression of the business, then more machinery should be installed—longhand letters should give way to typewritten letters. Simultaneously, the old hand-copying press will be superseded by the carbon copies that can be made with a typewriter, and the primitive letter book will give way to a correspondence file.

If you will keep that one general principle of time or labor saving in mind as we follow the development of correspondence organization to its point of highest systematization, you can easily tell just *which stage of organization is fitted to your own needs.*

There is no practical need for incurring the expense of time-saving or labor-saving devices or systems if the time or labor thus saved cannot be profitably used at something else

ORGANIZING WORK

In the panel at the top of the next page, there is represented all the organization necessary for the small one-man business which requires only an occasional letter—you see it is no organization at all. The manager does the entire job. But in the chart at the bottom of that page, you see how a greater demand on the manager's time has caused him to organize more closely. The dotted lines represent what would probably have been his first step—installing a typewriting machine to perform the hard work of transcribing and of making file copies. This would have been but a temporary organization, followed, as business increased, by hiring a stenographer to take over the typewriting, to make file copies, and to attend to the mailing. In the final scheme of organization the manager has left himself only the work of preparing the matter for his letters and dictating it to the stenographer.

This is all the organization that is ever given to the correspondence work of some business managers and department managers. The number of stenographers may be increased to a dozen or a hundred, but the plan is the same.

But is it enough? For a business with no settled routine—a business in which each letter is unlike any other letter in the questions it answers or the idea it conveys or the action it seeks—for such a business it is enough. But how many businesses or how many departments are like that?

Very few. In almost every business the matters which have to be handled by correspondence are limited to certain definite classes or types.

A sales manager today has to write Jones a letter of reprimand for quoting unpermissible terms to a certain customer. The idea he wants to convey to Jones, we will say, is that Jones has not studied the firm's sales manual carefully enough or he would have known that such terms were more than they could give. That's the Big Idea, we shall assume, just for an example. The sales manager gives careful thought to expressing that idea—selecting the salient features by which it can be visualized, and arranging them in such a way that the idea will be burned into Jones' mind. So far, so good.

BUSINESS CORRESPONDENCE

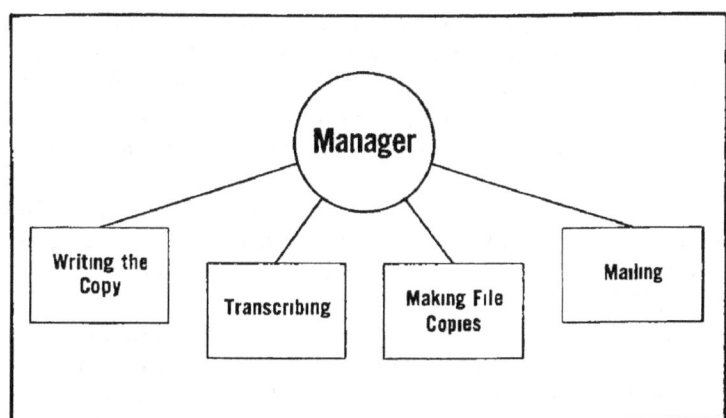

Panel 232

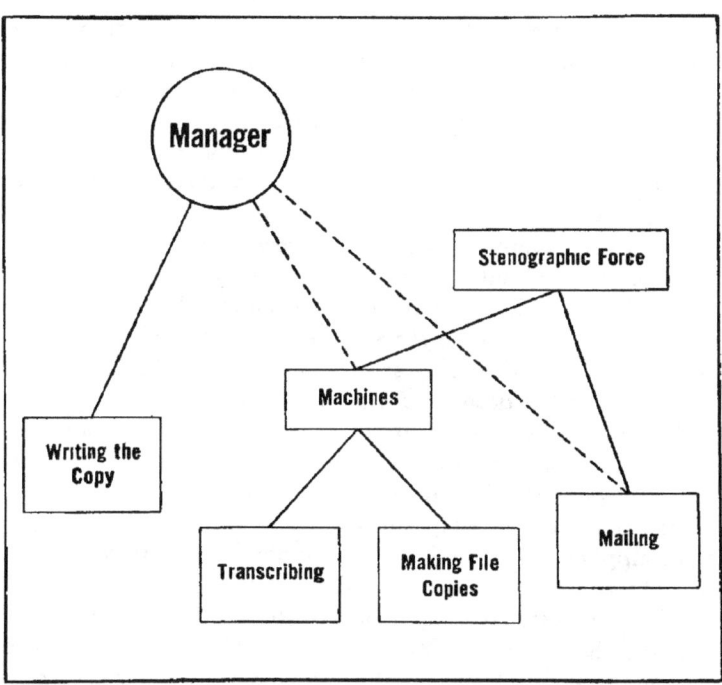

Panel 233

ORGANIZING WORK

But tomorrow, another salesman, Smith, sends in an order in which he, too, has made a concession which the house cannot accept. It is not the same error that Jones made, but its cause is the same—that is, carelessness in studying the sales manual—and the Big Idea the sales manager will want to convey is the same.

Now, if the sales manager goes to work and thinks out the expression of that idea all over again, isn't he duplicating his yesterday's work? Isn't he spending time on something that he could better leave to a system? Certainly.

That's a typical problem. With a staff of salesmen on the road, the questions which come up between them and the sales manager will, in a year, be largely of the same nature And with a list of a hundred or a thousand customers, the same sort of similarity will crop up in correspondence

I have cited the sales manager's case merely as an example. In any department of any business the *general correspondence* will similarly fall into *certain fixed types*. Exceptions—new and unprecedented conditions—are bound to come up, but the bulk of all dictated letters in any one business will be merely adaptations of a certain number of ideas, motives, and sympathies

Therefore, assuming that the correspondent's time is valuable enough to make a waste of it costly, the next step in organizing his work is to install a system by which the features of an idea, used frequently and carefully worked out, can be turned to instantly, thus saving the work of thinking them out again, or the danger of expressing them in a careless way.

So, on the next page, you see a chart showing the organization of correspondence work for a man who finds his letters or a certain portion of them, running mostly along fixed lines.

Such a system was explained in the fourth chapter and you were supplied with a skeleton card index for it. If you will go back to the outline of that index, which I called a "Word File," and refer to pages 225 and 227, you will recall how simply it works. You have only to analyze the nature of your everyday letters and dig out the Big Ideas they have

BUSINESS CORRESPONDENCE

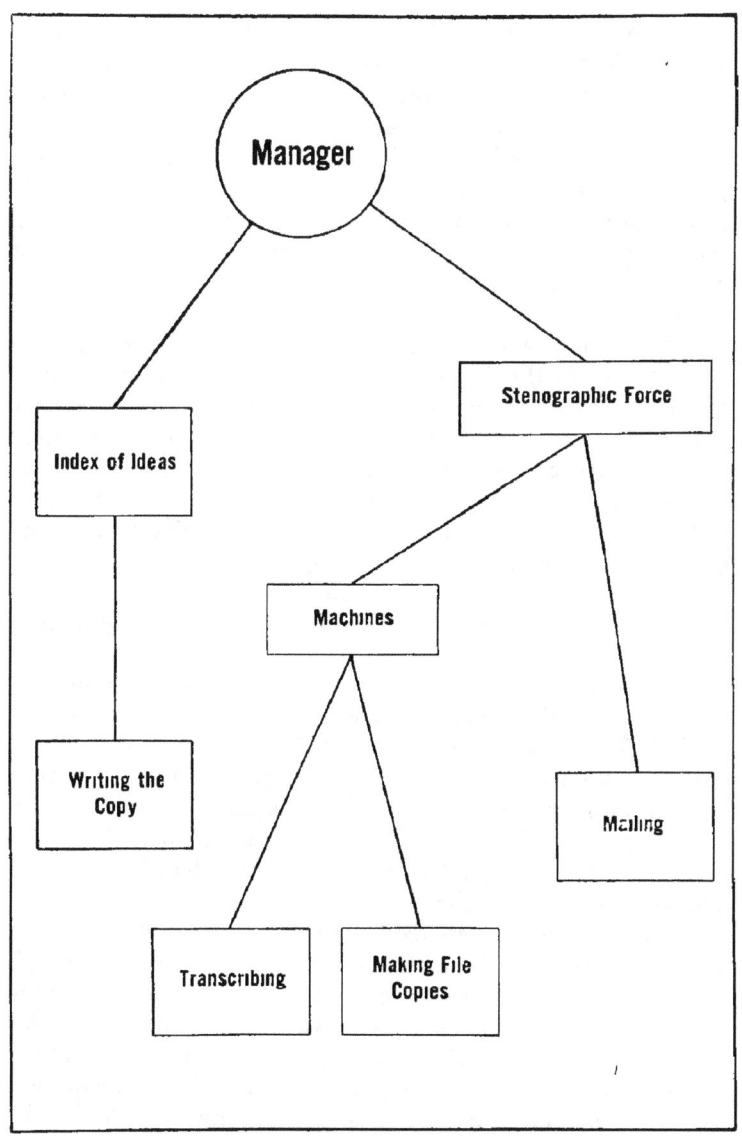

Panel 234

ORGANIZING WORK

to convey. Then for each Big Idea, work out in your leisure time the features that visualize it. For each feature, index, as they occur to you, words, phrases, illustrations, similes, and so on, that help to express it

With such a Word File at hand, after you decide on *the Big Idea to be conveyed in any routine letter*, you simply refer to your index and look up that particular idea. The file will show you just how to go about conveying it in the clearest way, without having to do your original thinking all over again.

This method, you see, relieves you from thinking out over and over again the features for each individual idea. Use of the Word File permits you to *throw the work on a system*. After you have selected for some important idea in frequent use, the features which visualize it and the words and phrases which express it, you can utilize your work on a thousand subsequent letters and make each one as forcible as if it had been given hours of individual study.

Such a system is particularly valuable for the head of a big business whose letters mostly involve ideas on the big policies of the business.

Where correspondence is mostly with a limited number of people—as a sales manager's correspondence with his men, or a small firm's correspondence with its few customers, such a flexible system just fills the bill. The repeated use of identical phrases would be unwise in such cases, but with the index of each Big Idea's features, the writer has *a guide to the feature to bring out to convey each idea*, and he can reshape his phrases and sentences to suit the case.

Where such conditions exist, the next logical step forward in the organization of correspondence work is a form paragraph system. A *form paragraph system* merely requires putting between your Word File and your work of preparing copy for your letters, a system that will relieve you of working out the wording and phrasing of features of ideas in frequent use. The chart on the next page graphically states my idea. The correspondent's work, with such a system, is reduced first,

BUSINESS CORRESPONDENCE

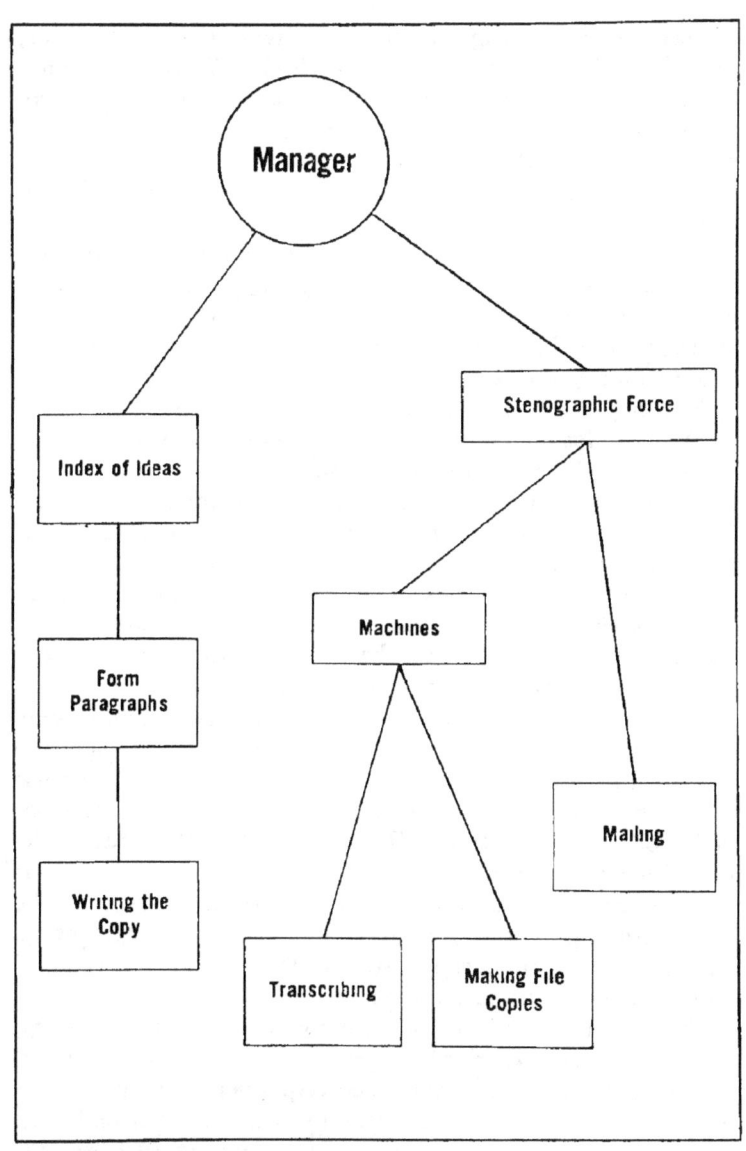

Panel 235

ORGANIZING WORK

to settling on the Big Idea to be conveyed by each letter; second, to looking up its features in his Word File; and, third, from the completely worded paragraphs in the form paragraph system, to reading to his stenographer the paragraph worked out previously. He dictates only what is necessary to link them up or to cover the individual points of the case at hand

This is the very simplest of form paragraph systems, one which can be used to advantage by any man with enough correspondence to employ a stenographer. It is not merely a saving in work but, what is equally as important, it *standardizes the quality of letters*

No one can dictate equally well at all times—especially when many letters are greatly alike. The mind tires of them, the best of phrases sound stale, the most vivid of words seem commonplace, and the dictator slides over points, or endeavors to use new phrases or new words. The result is that the standard of his letters at the end of his dictation falls far below the standard of those dictated when his mind was fresh. But with the expression of his ideas' features carefully worked out once for all, in the very best possible form, he can keep every letter up to the highest standard

As I said, I hardly know of any man with letters enough to dictate to keep one stenographer busy, who cannot make efficient use of that much system. And as he develops its use he can generally expand and extend it to take in much more of his ordinary dictation. He will soon find that, just as he is making use of only certain Big Ideas in his letters, he is seeking only a certain few actions with them. And thus the form paragraph system may be used with equal efficiency on standard closing paragraphs, standard openings, and standard motive-fuel paragraphs, and so on.

The most unhandy part of a general form paragraph system, according to my experience, is *getting the right form paragraphs quickly and easily.* I have seen correspondents compile a comprehensive collection of excellent form paragraphs and then make ineffective use of them because they lacked a graphic index The men overlooked the fact that the more complete the average form paragraph book or file becomes, the harder it is to find just the paragraph wanted without as much work in searching for it as it would be to write it.

The ordinary system I have found in use in offices I have investigated consists of allotting a number to each form paragraph Paragraphs are filed either in a looseleaf book or a vertical file in numerical order. The dictator's index shows these paragraphs divided into classes, such as "openers," "closers," "acknowledgments of orders," and so on. Under each of those class headings, the paragraph itself is indicated by its first line and a short description. Thus, under the class heading of "acknowledgments of orders" would be "shipment delayed," "are holding order for fresh stock "

But after a few days of actual work I have nearly always found that if the file of form paragraphs is at all complete, the correspondents have considerable trouble in picking out the best form paragraphs for a letter I have found that most of them have to refer pretty frequently to the actual paragraph to see how the wording fits

The trouble with the indexes is that they classify the form paragraphs according to what the paragraphs say, although the correspondent, as he looks for the right paragraph, thinks of it in terms of *what the reader is thinking* or what he wants the reader to think

For instance, if a customer had complained that the wrong goods had been shipped and if you wanted to write him a letter confessing the mistake, but giving him the idea that it was very unusual and would not occur again, in looking for a good opening paragraph you would probably think of it as one that would put the customer in sympathy with your idea. But in the ordinary index to a form paragraph file you can't look for it that way, for the index is made according to the facts or decisions stated in the form paragraphs which have been written. Your predicament, you see, is a good deal like trying to find a man's name on a list that has been classified by towns or states.

ORGANIZING WORK

Now I have invented what I think is *a better method of indexing form paragraphs.* Wherever my plan has been installed it has saved work and resulted in better dictation

Its principle is simple. I index the form paragraphs according to the purposes for which they are wanted instead of according to what they say.

We know that the first thing to do after a general size-up of the letter's work, is to fix on the Big Idea it is to convey

Therefore, when you are ready to start dictating and want to pick out *the best form opener* for that letter, you will naturally look for one that will make a good introduction for the Big Idea. Hence, you should index all your openers according to the idea they are to introduce.

To make my point clear, I am showing roughly in the chart on the next page an index, according to my system, to the form paragraphs of an investment house. The details are not carried out very far, partly because I cannot now recall them all and partly because they would only be confusing to you. But I have set down enough specific details to allow you to catch my idea. You can see how *the same general system would apply to any business* or any department of a business.

The index should be laid out on a single sheet, mounted on heavy cardboard about as you see the skeleton index as I have drawn up the illustration.

The dictator, when he has settled on the Big Idea to convey, puts his finger on that idea in his index. In the next column his form-openers, adapted especially to leading up to that particular idea, are classified according to the question or attitude or frame of mind that is indicated by the prospect's letter.

Each of these openers is written to lead sympathetically to a specific answer to the prospect's question or doubt, and from that answer to lead to the Big Idea. Hence, the correspondent has but to run his finger along the list until he finds *the opener that meets his prospect's question.*

With the opener settled and noted by its index number, the correspondent then moves his finger across to his list of

BUSINESS CORRESPONDENCE

Ideas	Openers	Features	Motives	Motive-Fuel	Closers
A- "My Money Will Be Safe — While It Will Still Be Earning Me Good Interest."	A-1000- Wants to Know if He Can Realize on His Bonds at Any Time A-2000- Wants to Know What Would Happen to His Money if Property Should Burn A-3000- Doesn't Understand "First Mortgage Bond"	A-100- Nature of Security A-200- Age of Company A-300- Number of Investors A-400- Amount of Money Invested A-500- Not a Single Loss A-600- Capital Back of Guarantee	A-10- Gain of 6% Interest Rate A-20- Gain in Having Money Constantly Working A-30- Safety A-40- Duty to Family A-50- Pride in Having Invested Capital	A-10.1- Difficulty of Finding Sound 6% Investment A-10.2- What 6% Means in Cash A-10 3- Difference between 6% and Savings Bank Interest	A-1- Giving 3 Good Offerings to Select from A-2- To Make Selection from Enclosed List A-3- Showing Loss by Delay in Accrued Interest

Panel 236

ORGANIZING WORK

features of the Big Idea, and, depending on how much or how little of the idea the prospect seems to understand, selects by their index number the paragraphs to follow.

As in most concerns every answer to a prospect's inquiry letter makes an effort to close an order, the correspondent can by this index move his finger across to the *list of possible Action-Motives* After he has selected the best one to arouse, immediately to the right he finds a list of form paragraphs of fuel for that motive. From this list he can order any persuasion paragraph inserted wherever it seems to fit to best advantage. Then, immediately following the form paragraphs of fuel for each motive is a *list of closers* especially written to start that motive in action.

So by merely deciding on his Big Idea, the correspondent can quickly and easily find all the other best form paragraphs that go with it

If any of these form paragraphs fit equally well with two or more general ideas, they should be listed separately in the index along with each idea, and a separate copy should be put in the file under each proper index number. In this way the correspondent has only to search through but one section of the index to find the paragraph he is looking for

The *paragraphs may be numbered by the decimal system;* that is, thousands for openers, hundreds for features, tens for motives, decimals for various fuel paragraphs of each motive, and units for closers—as in that way there is the least possible chance for making mistakes in index numbers Both correspondent and typists soon learn such a system, and the danger of mistaking "one thousand" for "one hundred," or "ten" for "one" and vice versa, is much less than would be the danger of misunderstanding numbers that run in direct sequence

In some systems it will be found advisable to have on hand different wordings of the same paragraphs, just to secure variety, and such variations can be graphically indexed by merely adding a decimal to the index number, just as was done in the index on the opposite page, with the fuel paragraphs of various motives. Thus, if you want to word each feature of an idea in several different ways *to fit different types of intelligence* in your prospects, or different business interests, this system gives you practically unlimited flexibility.

A good system of form paragraphs, however, cannot be built up in any haphazard way. My own method in studying a business whose correspondence work is to be freshly organized or reorganized is to begin with an analysis of letters in each department to find the Big Ideas that are, or should be, most used. This means going over enough of the past correspondence to give a fair average. In some departments where correspondence is heavy, just the accumulation of a few days' correspondence will be fairly representative of a day's average work. In others, where the volume is light, the correspondence for a period of 30 or 60 days must be analyzed to get an average.

Next I have the files of letters brought out for the period which I have decided will make a good average showing. I include both the letters received and answers to them. Then I size up each of these letters to discover the Big Idea in them. If, as is quite likely, the writer was not particular to put a Big Idea into every letter when those letters were written, I try to find what Big Idea should have been conveyed in each reply.

This analysis, if you follow my plan, should be done carefully and painstakingly. Of course, it will take time. One complaint manager I know occupied his evenings for a whole week just on this analysis of ideas. But as it ultimately enabled him to *build up a system of best answers to every letter* that came to him in the next two years, and his work so increased the profits of the house that he was promoted to a big-salaried position, the time paid for itself many times over.

In your business, which I assume is an average business, no one department's routine letters will be found to be utilizing, or call for the utilizing, of more than six or eight Big Ideas. Often a department will utilize not more than two or three.

When you have analyzed your letters or the firm letters and found the Big Ideas standard in all your correspondence,

ORGANIZING WORK

and have studied the Big Ideas from all angles until you are fairly certain you are right, then set these Big Ideas down on your index.

As your next step, *pick out the salient features of each Big Idea and visualize them in words.* The best of all the letters your files have disclosed should be gone over carefully, to find what features consciously or unconsciously used in the past seem to make the idea clearest. If you have any circular letters or advertisements based on a similar idea that have paid, they too will help you to locate the best features. Sometimes to write out an expression of the idea by using several different combinations of features, and then to study them or submit them to friends, will put the final touch of accuracy on your choice.

That is another period of hard work for you, but when it is done you will find that even if you go no further you will have improved the effectiveness of your letters by 50% or more.

When you have selected for each standard Big Idea the best standard features with which to visualize it, these should be listed by titles according to their nature, as you saw done with the features in the index on page 514. You cannot add them to your permanent index sheet as yet, as you must first work out the form-openers. But no attempt at writing openers should be made until the features have been written, as the openers should be planned to lead naturally into the features of the idea.

Hence your next step is to *write out the best and most graphic wording for each feature of each Big Idea* When this is done you can go back to the matter of openers.

Here again you must make a thorough size-up of the letters received—this time to get at *the writer's mental attitude*, principal interest, reason for doubt, or the question that is bothering him. For in all letters in which you do not have to make a deliberate plan for stopping attention, as I showed you in the eighth chapter—and answers to inquiries, complaints, and customers' questions certainly are of that kind—*the best opener* is one that awakens a bond of sympathy between the prospect's

BUSINESS CORRESPONDENCE

mental attitude and the Big Idea you are about to convey to him.

So you must analyze your customers' or prospects' letters closely and find the general types of mental attitude they represent. There will not be many. Seldom have I ever seen in any one man's correspondence more than 10 general types and usually less. In a collection department they run along the lines of "did not understand terms," "wants extension of time," and so on; in a complaint department they run along the lines of "shipped the wrong size," "goods not received," "order incomplete," and so on.

One hundred different customers may state their mental attitude in 100 different ways, yet all have the same type of attitude. It is for you to dig through their different ways of stating or asking things and to find the fundamental type represented—just as you saw the types of mental attitude represented for the openers in the index on page 514

When you have a list of the types of mental attitude your customers' letters represent, then, knowing what ideas you have to convey, to write an opener that will show sympathetic attention to the customer's attitude or question or complaint at the same time it enlists his sympathetic attention for your idea, is merely a matter of applying the principles of the fifth chapter But to *keep the paragraphs from having a jagged or fragmentary effect* when made a part of a letter, I have found it best to write them into two or three complete letters, so as to get into them the rounded-out style that one is likely to lose if he writes them as single paragraphs. After they are molded to your satisfaction the individual paragraphs can be extracted.

The same process applies as to finding the standard Action-Motives and the same methods should be used in writing the paragraphs of motive-fuel. In writing these it is particularly advisable to write complete letters embodying them, and then copy them rather than try to write them by themselves.

To select the best types of "preliminary actions" on which to build action-getting closers, and thus to write the closers themselves, the same processes are to be used

ORGANIZING WORK

And then you have a set of form paragraphs that represent the best thought and best work that is in you.

The next step is completing your index of them. You have already seen the system I recommend. The best form for the index is a question which I have not fully settled to my satisfaction. A large sheet in diagram form, as shown on page 514, is the most convenient to consult and trace your thoughts upon, but it usually has to be so wide that correspondents find it too unwieldy.

In its place they use a small card index on exactly the same lines as the Word File to be found in the fourth chapter. I think probably the plan that will work best in most cases is to lay out your index while it is in process of construction, on such a diagram as that on page 514, and then when done to transfer it to a card index.

The method of indexing by numbers may be modified to suit yourself The plan of indicating ideas by letters of the alphabet, openers by thousands, features by hundreds, motives by tens, closers by units, and then all subdivisions of a class by decimals as in the case of motive-fuel paragraphs, is one that experience shows causes the least confusion and fewest mistakes, and is also the easiest to memorize.

When each paragraph has been given its number or letter, a typewritten copy should be made for each stenographer or typist. The usual policy is to paste each paragraph on a 5 x 8 card and then file each classification in order behind tabbed guide-cards.

Just how complete a dependence should be placed on a form paragraph system of the type we have just discussed, is a question that you must answer for yourself and for your particular business.

In some large mail order and jobbing houses, where each correspondent has a huge volume of mail to be answered and typed each day, and where a day's delay in getting a reply off to a customer may mean lost business, the system is used to the exclusion of all personal dictation on a large percentage of letters.

BUSINESS CORRESPONDENCE

PARA-GRAPHS		
1	1	25th
2	133	
3	130	$1 50
4	170	
5	52	
6		
7		
8		
9		
10		

FORM LETTER

ENCLOSURES Bot #19 Cur #34

SP DEL Y | REG | ORDINARY

Waterman Catering Company
1694 Kennedy Street
Columbus, Ohio

Columbus
February 25, 1918

... Superior Street,
Buffalo, N Y

Gentlemen

Increasing business makes it necessary for us to purchase additional cooking equipment As soon as possible will you ship to us two No 26 Gas Ranges, as listed in your catalogue No. 18? Enclosed herewith is our check for $94.50 which according to the catalogue

... Kennedy Street
Columbus Ohio

Gentlemen

We acknowledge herewith the receipt of your order of the 25th Our warehouse stock of No 26 Gas Ranges is exhausted just at present. In order not to keep you waiting a minute longer than necessary, we have sent word to the factory to ship your goods direct. They should reach you in a very few days, almost as soon as if they were coming from our own warehouse

In checking over the amount of your remittance we find you have sent us more than enough money to cover the cost of the goods. We are, therefore, returning the balance ($1 50) herewith

That you will be pleased with the quality of these goods, we are thoroughly confident. If there is anything at all in connection with the shipment that puzzles or displeases you, let us know at once and we shall see that the matter is promptly straightened out to your complete satisfaction

We thank you for this order, and ask that we may be allowed to serve you again in the near future

Yours truly

Panel 267

ORGANIZING WORK

Paragraphs are prepared in such detail that *the correspondent may build a complete letter* from them simply by noting on an instruction slip their various numbers or names in order, and inserting specific details, like amounts of money, merchandise, line numbers, dates, and so forth

At the top of the opposite page is a reproduction of how the system is applied by a large wholesale house; (this illustration is copied from "The Automatic Letter Writer," a book published by the A. W. Shaw Company, to explain the workings of the form paragraph systems).

The instruction slip is clipped to the letter to be answered. On the line opposite the number of each form paragraph to be copied is a notation of any specific data necessary. (The master copies of the paragraphs are written to show the place for such details)

Below the letter of inquiry is the complete letter written from this instruction slip. You see how nearly it approaches a personally dictated letter, although a letter like this takes hardly a tenth of the time it would require to dictate it. Also letters of this kind can be written by a low-priced typist instead of an expert stenographer; therefore the money saving alone is considerable.

But this method, remember, is one in use in a big business, a business where the points covered by letters are set in very definite grooves, and where *promptness in answering letters* counts for almost as much as the quality of the answer I am sorry to say that I have seen the same method used in smaller businesses, or in businesses where more personality was needed for the letters, with results that did not seem good to me.

For a correspondent whose volume of work is not so large as to make the matter of getting through each day's correspondence a great difficulty, and for a correspondent whose business demands avoiding all earmarks of mechanical handling, I am personally always in favor of using the form paragraph more as a master guide to good dictation than as a finished part of a letter.

BUSINESS CORRESPONDENCE

- **1000 – Quality of Goods**
  - 1100 – Not What Was Ordered
    - 1101 – Correct According to Order
      - 1101 1 – Return
      - 1101 2 – Can't Return
    - 1102 – Our Mistake
  - 1200 – Damaged
    - 1201 – Offer Cash Concession
    - 1202 – Return for Exchange
    - 1203 – Return for Refund
    - 1204 – Recover from Railroad
    - 1205 – Send Fuller Details
  - 1300 – Unsatisfactory
    - 1301 – Return for Credit
    - 1302 – Offer to Exchange
    - 1303 – Decline Exchange

- **2000 – Quantity of Goods**
  - 2100 – None Rec'd
    - 2101 – Not Time Yet
    - 2102 – Started Tracer
    - 2103 – Held by Credit Dept.
    - 2104 – Goods Not on Hand
    - 2105 – Order Now Rec'd
  - 2200 – Item Missing
    - 2201 – Shipped at Once
    - 2202 – Credited on Bill
    - 2203 – Back Ordered
    - 2204 – Not Included in Order
  - 2300 – Short Count
    - 2301 – Credit Passed
    - 2302 – Not Allowed
  - 2400 – Overcount
    - 2401 – Return
    - 2402 – Price Concession

- **3000 – Amount of Bill**
  - 3100 – Overcharged
    - 3101 – Being Investigated
    - 3102 – Credit Passed
    - 3103 – Correct
  - 3200 – Undercharged
    - 3201 – Revised Bill
  - 3300 – Terms Wrong
    - 3301 – Corrected Bill
    - 3302 – Explain Misunderstanding
  - 3400 – Freight Charges Excessive
    - 3401 – Wrong Classification
    - 3402 – Wrong Routing
    - 3403 – Refer to Railroad

Panel 238

ORGANIZING WORK

The correspondent who uses this latter plan may keep on his desk a file of form paragraphs worked out just as I have explained in the previous pages. In dictating he may turn to them as he decides on the Big Idea, but instead of merely noting paragraph numbers for his reply, he may *dictate from the copy and put in changes of wording and individual touches* to make the letter sound strictly personal When a whole paragraph may well be used as it stands, he can give his stenographer the number, and then go on dictating.

Now you have *two ways of organizing your work* on a form paragraph system and if your work requires any such organization at all, you may decide which one best suits your own needs, by submitting them to the test outlined on previous pages

But even the best of form paragraph systems will not meet all the demands on some correspondents' time. In some businesses certain types of letters—like letters acknowledging orders, letters straightening out certain kinds of frequently recurring complaints, letters inquiring for certain standard information, and letters answering magazine or newspaper advertising, occur in such volume and are so similar that, to dictate replies, or even to construct "automatic" replies by a form paragraph system would be out of the question.

For that kind of business or department *a form letter system* is advisable.

The form letter system is but an extension of the form paragraph system. The correspondent instead of constructing individual letters by combinations of form paragraphs, works out *complete letters to meet standard needs*. He analyzes the letters that he finds himself handling, classifies them into types and then builds up complete form letters to handle those types. Here again, as in a form paragraph system, the method of indexing is important, as the clearness of the index will determine how quickly the system can be used.

On the opposite page is the index used in the complaint department of a confectionery manufacturer. It shows how

BUSINESS CORRESPONDENCE

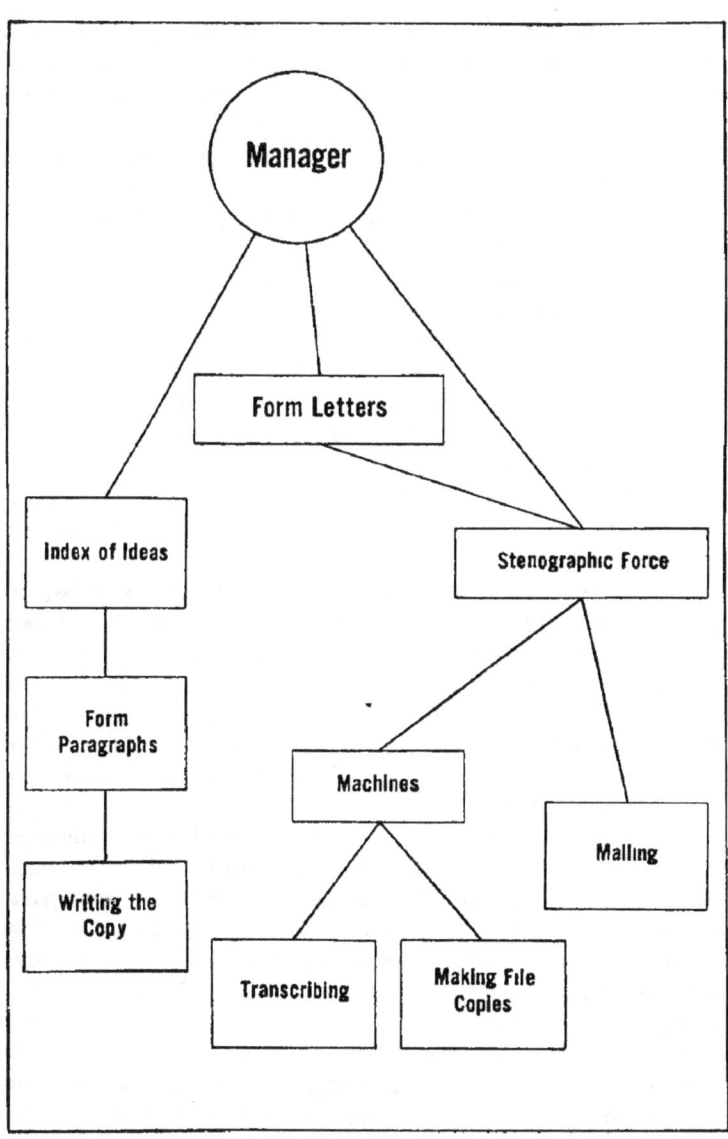

Panel 239

ORGANIZING WORK

the types of form letters needed in a business can be worked out. In this case the bulk of the complaints run to quality of goods, quantity of goods, and amount of bill. Under each of these types the letters vary largely as is shown by the second column. For each of the secondary divisions, a standard treatment or course of action has been decided on, as is shown by the third column of the index and a complete letter has been written to cover it. Blank space for filling in is left whenever specific amounts or names are required.

The complaint manager's work is thus to read each complaint, see what its main type is, what phase of that main type it takes, and then decide on the treatment to accord it. When he has made his decision he has but to write the number of the form letter on the customer's letter and a typist can write the reply complete.

Of course, a few complaints each day go outside this classification and those have to be handled by a form paragraph system or be dictated individually.

The same *system works equally well for collections, sales, inquiries*, and so forth. Where the various forms are being used in sufficient volume, much typing work can be saved by having imitation-typewritten copies made, leaving only the fill-in of names and addresses to be done by typewriter Sometimes such printed copies are made only for a few of the most frequently used forms. Those used less frequently are individually typed

We have now traced the organization of correspondence work up to a point shown by the chart on the opposite page. Such an organization relieves the correspondent or department head or manager, as the case may be, of all the daily work of routine correspondence, and leaves him free to give h s whole attention to those matters requiring individual thought and initiative.

Your business may not require such close organization. It may be handled by an organization involving only a form paragraph system. Or it may be competently served by merely a standard form of conveying your ideas.

BUSINESS CORRESPONDENCE

But you should analyze the needs of your business and see by what degree of organization you can make the most out of your correspondence work with the least loss of time.

The same fundamental principles can be applied to the organization of circular-letter work. If you send out circular letters only occasionally you can easily see the most economical organization (as for the most economical organization for the writing of just one occasional individual letter) is no organization at all. In other words, the most efficient mode of handling circular letters for small concerns is to let the job of printing, addressing, and mailing them to a circular-letter house.

But when the *number and frequency of your circular letters* begin to run the cost into real money, then you should add a typist in your own office to do the filling in, addressing and mailing, and let out only the printing. When the number and frequency of circular letters is great enough to keep one form-letter printing machine busy, then efficiency will demand installing one of your own. If it is enough to keep several machines busy, then you will need to relieve yourself of the details of managing by hiring a foreman or forewoman.

You see, you can chart the kind of organization fitted for your needs, by exactly the same method we charted a general correspondence organization.

When the lists to be circularized are of more than a few hundred names, business efficiency demands that before the whole list is mailed the letter itself and the circular, and the particular proposition if it has special features, should be *tested as to its pulling power.*

For no matter how carefully you try to prepare your copy or how much attention you give to every element in it, you never can tell just how well it is going to pay on any particular list until you have tried it. Some little slip may make prospects doubt, or some little wrong angle to the description will make a wrong impression, some careless influence may chill the action-motive, or some little loopholes left by mistakes may postpone action. Often only actual experience will expose the results.

ORGANIZING WORK

The safe course is to make *a preliminary test on every letter*. The engineer does not choose material for a bridge by building a bridge of the material and waiting to see whether it stands. He first tests the material in the laboratory. That is what the business man must do. We all know that we can learn something of the average height of a body of people by studying the heights in a group of a few thousands of people drawn at random from the larger body. Provided that the smaller group is so selected as to insure that it is typical of the larger body and provided the group is large enough to render the law of averages applicable, we know that when we have determined the average height of the smaller group it will roughly coincide with the average height of the larger group This method of studying can be applied in testing letters to be used in a selling campaign. The number of responses per thousand letters can easily be determined.

For a local letter—as one used by a retailer or real estate man or bank—at least 100 names should be taken off the general list and *the letter keyed and mailed* to that 100 names just as you purpose to mail it to the entire list. On a bigger list not less than 500 names should be selected. Then the results should be carefully watched and recorded. The length of *time between mailing and closing a test varies,* of course, according to the distance letters are sent. As a rule, however, two to three weeks is long enough to wait for returns from a test When time enough has elapsed for the bulk of the orders or inquiries to be in that are going to come, their total should be tabulated and compared with the cost of the mailing.

If the results show sufficient profit, then the whole list can safely be mailed, as your test list is quite likely to be an accurate average. But if the results show a loss, or not enough profit to satisfy you, then you know that the entire mailing would have been a much greater loss. Something is wrong with your proposition or your letter or circular and you should try a revision.

To *reduce these principles to a concrete case* suppose the manufacturer of a food product is planning a campaign to

BUSINESS CORRESPONDENCE

reach, not the consumer, but the grocers of the country. Now the whole body of dealers, large and small, handling groceries, numbers something like 250,000. Let the distributor, after working out a set of ideas and forms of expression which seems to him likely to be effective in arousing the desired demand, test this material by mailing it to say 1,000 grocers. The group selected must be large enough to give typical results and it must be so selected as to be representative in character of the whole body of grocers

Granting these elements, the distributor can determine the number of responses from the 1,000 grocers to whom the communication was sent, and can estimate from that result *the average response per thousand* of communications that would have been obtained if the same ideas in the same form of expression had been conveyed to the whole body of 250,000 dealers in groceries in the country. He can then test by means of direct mailing to another group of 1,000 a varying set of ideas or varying forms of expression And so on with other modifications of the selling material. Thus it will be possible to determine what ideas, in what arrangement and in what form of expression, are most effective to arouse the desired demand

That this is practical is indicated by the results of such an intensive study presented in the table on the opposite page. There are shown the results of tests and the results of complete mailings. The tests covered only one stratum of society, a mailing list of bankers being used The purpose of the selling material mailed was to obtain orders for certain publications. Various forms of copy were tested by mailing, usually to 500 names on the list.

Where the *return on any test* exceeded the minimum standard of 20 orders per thousand letters the material was mailed to the complete list. In only one case did the complete mailing fail to show an average return per thousand substantially the same as that derived from the test mailing. In the case of Test D,[1] the return is clearly out of proportion to the results from the mailing. The same material mailed on the

ORGANIZING WORK

same date, however (Test D²), gives for a similar small group a return much closer to the results obtained from the final mailing. *When a minimum standard as low as 20 is used*, and the test group numbers only 500, there is danger that the average will be disturbed as by one individual sending in several orders. *The larger the test group the more exact an index it will give* as to the results which will be obtained from a complete mailing.

Note, too, that the general principles upon which the "testing" method depends, apply when we seek to study the possibilities of the whole market by the intensive cultivation

BANKERS' TESTS
Minimum Standard -- 20 per M.

Material Mailed	Tests				Mailings			
	Date	Number of pieces mailed	Total orders received	Number per M.	Date	Number of pieces mailed	Total orders received	Number per M.
a^1	3/30	500	3	6				
a^2	3/30	500	5	10				
B^1	8/13	500	6	12				
B^2	9/13	500	3	6				
C^1	9/15	500	4	8				
C^2	9/15	500	3	6				
D^1	9/15	453	6 }	25 {	9/27	19,943	360	18
D^2	9/15	500	18 }					
E	9/16	500	7	14				
F^1	9/21	500	24 }	36 {	11/23	16,511	589	35
F^2	9/21	500	12 }					
G	10/18	1,000	30	30	11/28	21,790	643	29.5
H	11/16	500	11	22 {	1/24	6,554	165 }	24
					1/24	16,039	390 }	
I	4/11	500	12 }	24 {	5/5	6,810	145 }	25
	4/11	500	12 }		5/4	12,154	336 }	

Note — Where the same letter appears with different exponents under "material mailed" it indicates that on the test mailing results were kept separately for the same material mailed to two small groups

Panel 240

of one section of it A localized *selling campaign, narrow in extent, will give relatively exact data* from which the possibilities of a nation-wide campaign of like character may be judged. Obviously, if our law of averages holds good, we may carry over the results obtained in one section to other sections, and hence at small cost guide a widespread campaign.

Not only a letter may be tested in this way, but also the goods, the prices of goods and so on. For instance, when a business man contemplates putting a new product on the market, a serious problem is the price at which it shall be sold. In the introduction of a safety razor, for instance, at what price is it to be sold? In such a case the business man seeks to determine which price will give him the best net return, all things considered Now the method of study developed above will permit the business man to *determine by actual test the effective demand* that can be built up at different price levels in different economic and social strata. Hence he can fix the price on the basis of relatively exact data, rather than on a mere guess.

Again the laboratory method here suggested lends itself to a determination of what elements of quality and service in a given product are deemed most essential by the consumer. The effectiveness of the ideas conveyed in building up a demand reflects the intensity of human wants as to the elements of quality and service. The producer can sound the consumer and can adapt his product to his needs.

Thus *an entire selling campaign* can be directed on the basis of what may be termed laboratory study. The empirical methods of the ordinary business man may be supplemented by the tested scientific methods that have proved efficient in other fields.

If a test on a letter fail, the best way to discover the reason for its failure is to follow the process by which you constructed it. Go back to your size-up chart, study to see if the "load" of the letter and the Big Idea are genuinely conveyed. A study made in the cold light of a poor test, long after the enthusiasm of creating has died away, will often show up the faults that the closest inspection failed to disclose while you were still warm over your work.

After you have reviewed the expression of the "load" and the Big Idea, put each other element through a like cold analysis. If you find one or more elements than you now see could be improved, work them over and make another test—on a new selection of names.

If you can't seem to locate a manifestly weak spot, or *after a second test the* letter still fails to pull, then the only thing to do is to discard it and try another completely new letter, or leaving the letter alone, try a completely new circular.

It is *no disgrace to have a letter fail,* even after you have taken the most painstaking care in writing it. I have never known anyone to grow so expert as to have every letter or every advertisement a winner.

It is a disgrace, however, not to study and profit by your mistakes. No matter how well you like a letter or a circular, put it to the acid test and if it won't pay then discard it. The letter writers and ad writers who are ultimate failures, are those who take a notion or a theory that a certain kind of letter or advertisement is good and then refuse to be jarred out of that notion by failure in results.

In the same class are those who are prejudiced against some type or style of letter and will not test it to see if, after all, it won't pay I know men, for instance, who say a long letter won't pay. They won't test a long letter to see; they won't listen to the results others have got from long letters. They just have the notion and nothing can change them.

Now maybe a long letter won't pay in their business—but wouldn't it be much safer to find out by test?

The matter of 1- or 2- or 3-cent postage and filling in the names on a form letter for each proposition can also be decided by test.

On a big mailing, when the cost is going to run into big figures, it is almost always well *to make four parallel tests* at the same time, one to a test list with names filled in to match the imitation typewriting and under first-class postage;

a second with names filled in but sent unsealed under third-class postage; a third without fill-in but under first-class postage; and a fourth without fill-in and unsealed under third-class postage Key your letters carefully and keep accurate account of your returns. (Ways of keying a letter are discussed in the following problem section).

If the outcome of these tests is that the results are as large from the cheapest as from any of the others, then you would be foolish to pay more postage or the cost of filling in.

Of course, an *accurate analysis must be made.* The cheapest form of mailing might bring in as much net profit as the most expensive because of its lower cost and still not bring in as many individual orders. You might say, at first, that as the cheaper form brought in as much net profit and required less investment and work it paid better. But the number of customers might overbalance that advantage, and make the added investment and added trouble of the more expensive form worth while. All such advantages must be carefully weighed.

You see, in this chapter we have been dealing with affairs on which no arbitrary, hard-and-fast rules can be laid down. They must be *adjusted to fit individual businesses* or departments, or individual circumstances.

No one can say how much of an organization correspondence work in general needs. But, knowing the principles of its organization, we can surely tell by study how much of it our own work requires.

No one can say in advance whether or not a certain letter will make sales or collect accounts. But we can test our letters in a preliminary way and find out.

No one can say definitely whether first-class or third-class postage is best for any certain letter, and whether it should be filled in or not. But we can test both ways for ourselves— and then we will know.

ORGANIZING WORK

SUMMARY

WE have seen in this chapter that in any shop or business, organization of correspondence and the use of form paragraphs and form letters will shorten routine, save time, and reduce materially the cost of doing business by letters.

Perhaps you were ready to agree to that before reading this chapter. If so, you found the secret of efficient organization in the indexes that were suggested. After all, form paragraphs are easy to write and in one sense it is no trick at all to prepare a form letter, but to write form paragraphs so that they will link up closely to one another and convey the personality of a dictated letter, or to prepare form letters which do not carry the imprint "machine made" —that is a trick. By building up a letter system on the Big Idea of letters, however, many of the difficulties surrounding short cuts in the correspondence department disappear and letters carry that friendly, sincere "you and I" attitude so greatly to be desired in all our correspondence.

As for testing letters, that is such a variable undertaking that I could only outline it in this chapter. Testing is simple enough—it is merely sending out a few letters in advance of the general mailing. It is scouting by mail. All that one need do is to keep careful count of returns. The one point in regard to testing that we should remember, however, is that every letter can be tested and that testing to an unprejudiced list of prospects is the real proof of the pudding.

In the next and last chapter we shall have a word on office organization. We shall find out where to look for materials for lessons, for instance, and, in this connection, put to test an invaluable Idea Record. We shall also see how to chart the possibilities in our business for letters and letter campaigns, and, concluding, we shall give our attention to considering mailing lists and their sources and how to use them.

PROBLEM SECTION X

THERE is really just one big, tremendously important principle that runs all through the preceding chapter.

If you have grasped that one principle and have realized the full importance of it, you are ready to cash in on the whole book. That one principle is—Testing.

In the foregoing chapter I showed you how to test the pulling power of copy and how to test the practicability of your way of working.

Hitherto we have considered only what might be called the specifications of a good letter. We have been doing what a young student of painting has to do while learning perspective, proportions, relations, color values, and so on. But now, with the technique mastered, we shall put it into practise. That is, we shall, in the practical work of this problem section, apply a set of standards with which to measure up the accuracy of our work, and also the efficiency of our tools.

To find how much organization—how much system, how much machinery, how much help—your work should have, you should measure it up, mentally, with each separate step traced in the last chapter

First, consider whether your work is small enough to allow you to do it all yourself, transcribing, copying, mailing. If not, is it small enough so the mere assistance of a typewriting machine will enable you to handle it without neglecting other work?

To most of you this may seem a foolish question, but on the other hand see how graphically the ability or inability of

ORGANIZING WORK

a form of organization to handle your work is shown up by asking yourself a question like that—just trying to imagine your work being handled by the organization you plan.

When you see, for instance, that an organization embracing only the use of a typewriter would fall below your requirements, you know that the least you can get along with is the form of organization shown at the bottom of page 506 I take it for granted that you all understand that this chart represents the form and not the dimensions of such an organization. By "stenographer" the chart means a stenographic department—whether that in your business consists of one girl, or twenty girls working under a head stenographer. And "manager" means the executive department, whether that consists only of yourself, or of a big executive staff

I need not trace through again the individual steps by which any man or any business may test out the form and extent of organization best adapted to handle daily correspondence You can easily see how such a process, beginning at the smallest possible measurement and trying on each larger one in turn, will ultimately bring you to just the right one.

Getting the very best pulling sales letters, collection letters, follow-up letters, and so on, is a matter of going through the same sort of testing out process.

First you construct your letter by fundamental principles as closely as you can One might be tempted to say that if every principle of letter writing were correctly followed, the letter must surely pull. But where the human element is involved, the slightest, the almost imperceptible of variations will apparently cause an effect-wave that multiplies upon itself like the wave caused by throwing a pebble in the water, until it reaches proportions big enough to neutralize all the other points in your letter. No one can be certain about human nature. All one can do is keep as true as possible to fundamental principles, and then test.

The value of a test, of course, rests largely on the records kept on it. Accurate records in turn depend on keying.

BUSINESS CORRESPONDENCE

Keying a letter means marking it so that replies to it may be readily identified

The simplest method of keying is the enclosing of an order card, an addressed postcard, or an envelop in which to enclose the reply. If only one test is in progress, then no further identification is needed, but if one or more tests are being made, then varying the color of envelop or cards will do the work

If this plan is impractical, then keying in code is in order. The most familiar use of a code is to change the street address slightly or to request that the reply be marked attention of some member of the organization; if not that, the reply may be directed to some department.

The codes above mentioned are in daily use and are easily recognized by many people. Hence, at times it is well to identify the letter by other means. One plan is to give each set of letters an identifying letter or number. All sales letters may be keyed A for instance. The first test letter becomes A-1 and this code may be written at the bottom of the letter in the space usually reserved for the stenographer's initials. The mailing sent out after successful returns on A-1 may be marked AA and so on. Numberless possibilities of keying suggest themselves.

For instance, some firms key letters by quoting the first letters of the first two or three words in the letter. A letter beginning "We recently referred you to the dealer———" may be keyed WRR and the key written as stenographer's initials. This method makes references to the letter easy by people of the house which sends it.

Frequently, for one reason or another, keys are ignored in the replies to a test or a regular mailing. For this reason it is sometimes necessary to instruct the mail-opener to open all letters carefully and attach the unmutilated envelop to the letter. Some firms make this a rule and require all envelops to be attached to correspondence. Then, if the key is omitted, information regarding the letter may be gathered by comparing the postmark on the reply and referring to the mailing date on the original letter. A fair judgment

ORGANIZING WORK

on the source of the order or inquiry can be made in this way.

After a key which will identify the letter has been prepared, a simple record for entering returns should be made up. This is so simple a task that more than passing mention of it is unnecessary. Rule a blank sheet of paper with columns. Enter the code number of the test at the left, enter the date of mailing in the next column, and then in the remaining columns show by days the number of replies received. A total column at the right is useful and the information may be carried to a permanent record, as illustrated in the panel on page 529 Thirty days is sufficient to complete returns on almost any test. Usually two or three weeks is sufficient.

Not only should the copy for circular letters be tested, but copy for regular form letters, and even to a large extent, copy for form paragraphs The matter is not difficult. Suppose you have just built up a form paragraph for some certain purpose. Have your stenographer keep a record of every letter in which it is used for a few days, or few weeks. No great pains need be taken—just a simple notation of the name and address of the person to whom such letters have been sent. Then every week have the stenographer look up the developments on all those letters—whether or not the letter brought results desired. In two or three weeks, time enough will have elapsed to get a fair judgment on whether or not the form paragraph does its work.

If the letters containing it, in a good percentage of cases get results, then you can depend on the paragraph being right. But if few or none of the letters bring results, then you will know that the paragraph should be rewritten.

In this way your whole system of form paragraphs and form letters can gradually be tested out and strengthened until you have a system of real winners.

Now to turn to the problems of the last problem section. First, I gave you a chart of the letterhead requirements of a retail hardware store, asking you to work out from those

BUSINESS CORRESPONDENCE

requirements the general specifications of the letterhead. In the panel below I am reproducing the letterhead which we are discussing.

Now, how closely do your specifications tally with the finished job?

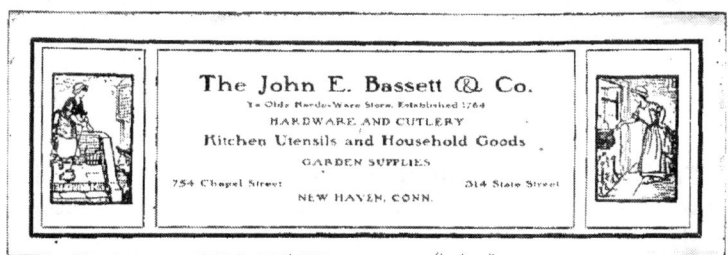

Panel 241

For the first specification, your study of what the letters need—to create confidence and exercise persuasion—coupled with the fact that the business can show a history dating back to 1784, should have indicated to you that the general impression should be of an old, reliable and complete store. You can see that this is the impression given by the original letterhead reproduced above.

For the "matter to appear" my own list ran this way: Firm name subtitle "Ye Old Hardware Store" (this for its effect on confidence); illustration of Colonial Kitchen (this to carry out impression of age); date business was established; list of lines carried; address.

You can easily see how each of these specifications grew out of the list of requirements, and you can also see how they all were actually used in the letterhead itself.

The next problem you had was to chart both requirements and specifications for a bank letterhead which was described to you.

The letterhead I had in mind was that of The Northern Trust Company, reproduced at the top of the opposite page. Now let us run over the facts on the letter so you can compare them with the specifications which you charted.

ORGANIZING WORK

Panel 242

First you see the general impression of solidity and bigness. I don't suppose anyone could have failed to specify that, for on your chart of requirements you must surely have set down a need for reflecting dignity and prestige.

Then there is the capital and surplus—I trust most of you specified that, because it shows that in your chart of requirements you had thought to include something to show "size of business." The illustration of the building is for the same purpose, and the list of directors helps the impression of reliability and prestige.

Panel 243

Your third problem was to work out the complete chart for a letterhead for the Gillette Safety Razor Company. Its letterhead is reproduced in the panel above, so you can check back on yourself just as we did for the bank letterhead.

589

BUSINESS CORRESPONDENCE

In Panel 244, below, is the missionary circular and in Panel 245 is the booklet frontispiece that you were to lay out. The principal thing I wanted you to test yourself on in these two problems was the course provided for the reader's interest to take. How does your work compare with the illustrations below?

In the missionary circular for the haberdasher, the cut should logically come first, if a headline were used it should come second, although in this case the dealer used none. The sample and copy follow in order. The size of the whole affair would not permit much variation except in the order of points.

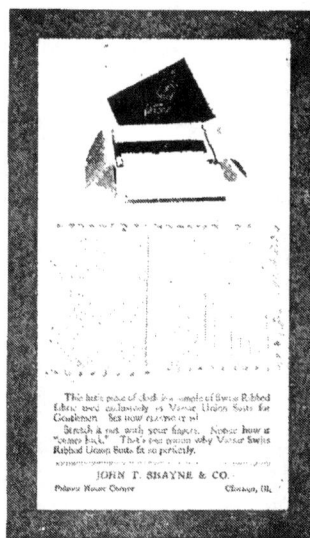

Panel 244

Panel 245

But in the booklet frontispiece the movement of attention from upper left-hand to lower right-hand is very effectively worked out. It is only the general principles of arrangement, however, that I am interested in showing, and I will leave you to go as far into the study of layout details as your personal taste may incline you.

ORGANIZING WORK

This is the final problem section on details. Hereafter we shall consider the letter as a whole. In the next chapter will be traced, step by step, all the points I have outlined in previous chapters and an entire letter will be written from the beginning. The next chapter is one of the most important, for after you have correlated all the points I have brought up, you'll be ready to install my system of letter writing in your own business.

PART XI

MATERIALS FOR LETTERS AND USES FOR THEM

CHAPTER XI

MATERIALS FOR LETTERS AND USES FOR THEM

IF you had a sharp ax and knew how to chop down a tree with it to great profit to yourself, you would soon become dissatisfied with only an occasional job of tree-chopping. You would want to go where more trees were. A machinist who has a fully equipped jobbing shop and who knows how to do jobbing work at a profit, is not long content to do only the jobs that naturally come to him. He begins advertising and soliciting for more jobs. The same holds true for a business man who can either write letters that bring results or who can get them written and mailed with efficiency. He is on the alert for more avenues by which to put his ability to profitable use.

Now we have seen in preceding chapters all the essentials of a good letter for any purpose, and how to incorporate these essentials in our own letters.

But one more step remains. We have a valuable tool in our hands. That tool is the knowledge of how to write a letter which will convey our ideas to another person in such a way that the other person will visualize our idea, believe in it, and act on it if action is desired. And we know how to go about using that tool efficiently on the work that comes to hand. The step which remains, therefore, is to find new uses for our letters and materials for them. And that step is the text of this eleventh and last chapter.

A great deal has been written about finding more and profitable uses for business letters and finding raw materials out of which to build letters, but I think little of it was written by men who had to pay the costs of letters and count

BUSINESS CORRESPONDENCE

the proceeds from them. For the suggestions seem to have been written mostly from the point of view of merely swelling the mails.

To me, developing the uses for letters in any business and gathering the materials out of which to write them is just a simple case of sound merchandising

If you have the right grasp on all that you have read about writing letters you now have this one point firmly in mind: that a letter has as its first purpose the conveying of an idea. With that point in mind, it takes no great reasoning powers to arrive at this conclusion. if you have no idea to convey to a man—or a whole list of men—which will do you or them a benefit, you should not write a letter to him—or them. But the moment you arrive at that conclusion you come face to face with another, and this is: if you have an idea which would benefit you if conveyed to a man or a list of men by letter, then you should by all means write a letter to convey that idea.

Follow me closely in this, because we are getting to the very *corner-stone of efficient mail sales,* mail collections, mail advertising—in fact, of handling any business by mail.

I said handling business by mail was to me a simple case of sound merchandising, and we shall see that it is If you had a store, the prime purpose of which was to purvey shoes, your merchandising plans would always hinge on these conditions: "What shoe stocks can I secure and at what price? How much of them would my trade take at a profitable margin to me?" And when a salesman came along and offered a line of shoes to you, probably you would at once calculate on how your customers would take to them—what price they would probably pay, and how many pairs you could conveniently dispose of.

Now here is one of the rudiments of good merchandising· for the shoe merchant to stock up with a line of shoes unsuited to his trade is bad business; for him to stock up with a line at a price that would put the retail price too high for his trade is also bad business, but to fail to load up to his trade's limit

MATERIALS AND USES FOR LETTERS

with any line that his customers will buy at a good margin to himself—that is just as bad business!

Similar conditions determine the mailing of business letters. If the idea you have for a circular letter to your customers, or to a list of prospects, or to some delinquent debtors, or for a general letter to your salesmen, or for a bulletin to your employees—if the idea for it, on analysis, is not shown to be one that will accomplish some definite benefit greater than its cost, don't mail it. But if there is an idea about your business that would be profitable if conveyed to your customers or your prospects or your debtors or your salesmen or your employees, then it is bad business to neglect mailing a letter to convey it

Now perhaps you may think undue importance has been given to such a simple principle. "I knew that much, all the time," you are saying I have no doubt you did know it, but just the same, I know to a certainty that the average business house and the average business man does not *follow this principle in practise.*

So many times that I can't count them, I have heard business men say: "We aim to get out a letter to our trade once a month," or I have heard advertising men say, "You ought to send a mailing card of some kind to your trade every so often." They say that without a moment's thought as to whether there is an idea that it will pay to convey, to put in each letter or card. And just because so many business men have the foregoing idea and follow that idea up by useless circulars or letters—turning to someone who has a gift for stringing words together and ordering "a letter to be written and mailed out this month" or "a series of mailing cards for this season"—just because that is the way so many business letters are conceived, you hear so many business men say, "Oh, I dump all circular stuff mailed to me straight into the waste-basket."

An alarming percentage of all the trade letters mailed are mailed only because it seems quite the thing "to mail something," and so "something" is prepared. Many sales

BUSINESS CORRESPONDENCE

managers write weekly or monthly letters to all their men simply because they consider it an accepted thing to do, and *not* because they have a Big Idea that, when conveyed to their men, will result in profit.

That is one side of the question. But on the other side are thousands of businesses in which splendid ideas exist. These ideas would mean increased business if conveyed to customers or prospects or salesmen or employees, by letter—but nobody is looking properly for those ideas, recording them, and making use of them.

So you see, some *concrete, simply stated formula* by which to control the use of letters is needed—not only to prevent the use of letters that have no real idea, but also to suggest the use of ideas that would make good letters Therefore, to impress it on you, I shall again state the fundamental of letter writing:

No letter should be given the time for writing or the cost of postage, that does not carry a definite idea, which, when conveyed to those to those addressed, will really pay, either profit or in good will which will bring indirect profit.

Every idea,—sales idea, policy idea, collection idea, informative idea or inspirational idea—that comes up in business and that would make money for the business directly or indirectly, if conveyed to another, should have a letter written and mailed to convey it.

That, as I said before, is the very corner-stone of the only sound policy there is both for finding uses for letters in your business, and finding good material for letters.

A manufacturer in New York, whose name I am not at liberty to give, was spending about $10,000 a year in mailing out form letters, mailing cards, and "broadsides," as he called them, to the trade in his line. He had been doing it for years. He had them prepared for him by an outside writer, to whom he would write, when impulse suggested, "Get us up something to mail out next month and submit copy as soon as you can." He had been doing this for several years and said that

MATERIALS AND USES FOR LETTERS

it paid. But when he was asked for a detailed report on his results he admitted he had none—he just assumed that his policy paid, because, as he said, "We have to do something to keep our name before the trade."

Yet in that man's business there were *dozens of good live ideas cropping up all the time* that would have made business for him, if properly conveyed to the trade, but he never thought of putting them into letters or mailing cards. And the professional letter writer he employed had no opportunity to know of them. One minor item in his line that had never amounted to much, happened to have a point about it of particular war-time interest. By chance a form letter on this item, with a small enclosure and a return order card, was mailed to a list of 3,200 dealers. It brought back over $1,000 worth of orders direct, and before the season was over $6,300 worth had been sold to that list. The whole mailing cost $152.50 complete, including a fee of $100 paid to the letter writer for the copy.

A further study of ideas brought out the fact that the manufacturer always deemed it wise to exchange any numbers a dealer found he could not sell. The policy had been proved a good one and salesmen had made much of it. But it had never been put into a letter. Four different mailing cards and two form letters, each conveying this one idea, were prepared, keyed, and mailed during the year following and brought back several thousand dollars in orders.

Now what had been the trouble with this manufacturer? Such opportunities had always existed. It was simply that he didn't have a set policy to guide him in finding the uses and materials for letters. He was not *properly merchandising the ideas in his business.*

In principle he had been doing no differently than a merchant who has items of merchandise in his store which the trade in his locality would buy if the trade knew of it, but who doesn't think of displaying those goods or of advertising them.

Now to carry this merchandising role a step farther: Every manufacturer and every merchant knows that one of the prime necessities of good merchandising is a stock record. He must know just what stock he has When goods are received they must be entered on the stock record and when they go out they must be deducted from the stock record.

And likewise in merchandising the ideas of a business, the prime necessity is an *Idea Record.* When you think, for instance, of an idea for any department of your business, or when one is suggested to you by an employee, or by a customer's remarks, or by an advertisement, or by a magazine article, or from any other source, it ought to be recorded somewhere, so that it will not be forgotten. Only thus can you prevent good ideas from becoming as much "dead stock" in your business as are the goods a merchant allows to lie on a back shelf until they go out of style or spoil.

Such a record should, and will if used in the way I am going to show you, not only insure new ideas or newly discovered ideas being put to use in letters to customers or prospects, or bulletins to salesmen, or memoranda to house employees; but it will insure their being kept in use, and used to their full capacity.

For instance, a good sales idea after being used is many times shoved out of mind by new ones coming up, when as a matter of fact it might be just as profitably used again the following season and many later seasons, or it might be used several times in the same season. Again, a good idea incorporated in a letter to prospects might be a profitable idea to convey to salesmen, or it might also result in better cooperation in the office if made into a house memorandum.

In short, in organizing or improving the correspondence work of a client I have often found a good live idea being used in one department but unknown in another department which could have used it to equally good advantage.

In other words, ideas will not return half or a quarter or a tenth of their real profit unless they are merchandised, just as a line of goods in a store will not yield its full profit to the merchant unless it is properly merchandised So what we shall build up in this chapter is a merchandising system for

MATERIALS AND USES FOR LETTERS

ideas. And the first step in doing it is study of a graphic Idea Record.

An Idea Record, to be of practical use, must be formed and adapted to the special requirements and opportunities of your own business You must first get a clear, firm grasp on all *the ways in which letters can help your business,* and an equally clear grasp on what sort of materials in your business will make profitable ideas for such letters.

On the next page is a chart showing the whole field of letter activities worked out by SYSTEM from its long experience with the use of letters and its many investigations into the methods of hundreds of businesses.

At first glance this chart looks formidable. But dissect it slowly and you will see that it is really very simple, though very complete. It shows, in the first place, what all letters you may use in your business will do—"Transmit your Ideas." That you already know. In the second place you see "Your Ideas" divided up into seven generic types—"About Your Goods or Services," "About Their Quality, Price, and Utility;" "About Your Materials and Methods," and so on. Analyze those seven types and you will find that, no matter what your particular business is, all the letters you use—we are now considering the routine dictation of a business—fall into one of the seven divisions which have been listed on the chart.

Hence, the thing you should do first in building up an Idea Record is to *study the nature and activities of your own business* and decide which of those seven types of ideas you can use in your business, and cross out from the chart those that do not enter into your sphere. For example, if you have no shop or office or staff of employees, naturally ideas about work standards or discipline will be of no value, so you would cross out that square.

This process of elimination is one that should have careful thought and analysis, as when you are through with it you will have left a chart of the kind of ideas you consider essential to be transmitted to others.

BUSINESS CORRESPONDENCE

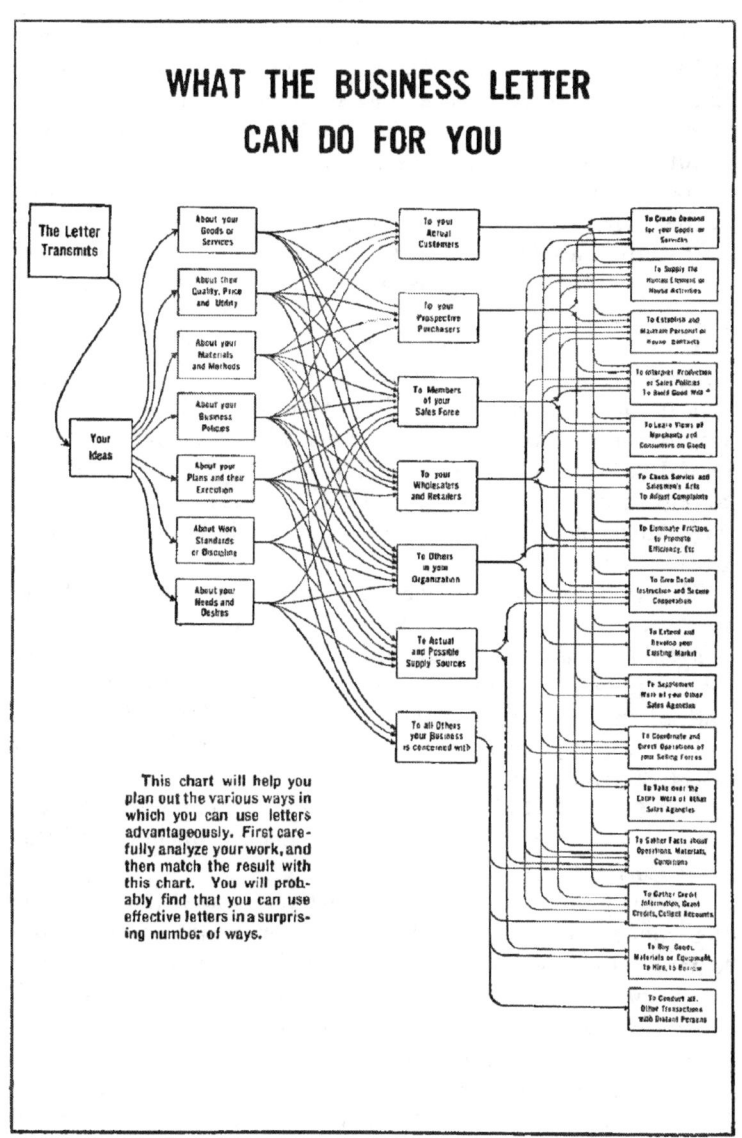

Panel 246

MATERIALS AND USES FOR LETTERS

Next you should trace each of those seven types, or those of them which you have not eliminated, a step further on the chart and then you'll see that each one is again classified according to whom it can be profitable. Thus, your ideas about your goods or services, you will see by following the arrows starting from that square, may with profit be transmitted: first, to your actual customers, second, to your prospective purchasers; third, to members of your sales force; fourth, to your wholesalers and retailers; fifth, to others in your organization.

That is quite simple, isn't it? Now you are ready to analyze the field in your particular business for each separate type of idea and select those that enter into your own business. For example, if you do not come into direct contact with your actual customers, or consumers, scratch out the arrow leading to that field. If you do not deal with wholesalers and retailers, why, then, of course, you may scratch out the arrow leading to that field

You see now what this process of elimination is going to do for you. It is going to provide you with *a graphic chart adapted individually to your own business*, as well as show you all the possible avenues for making profitable use of letters, and all the sources to which to look for profitable ideas.

With the type of ideas and the fields in which to use them selected, from each field you trace the arrows over to the kinds of objects to be attained from that field. Here again, you cross out the fields which you believe do not apply to your business.

Now if you will recopy the chart for yourself, leaving out the squares completely eliminated for your business, and leaving out those arrows connecting the squares that are not applicable to your proposition, you will have a chart that will represent not only *the kinds of ideas to look out for*, but the *avenues on which to use them.*

I have spoken only of the use of such a chart for letters, but if you do other forms of advertising the chart will be of equal service. For instance, while you may not correspond with

Ideas	Home-Office Salesmen		Home-Office Employees		Home-Office Prospects		Dealers		Dealers Lists		Blue Book Lists		Newspapers		Theatre Programs	
	Used	Results	Used	Results	Used	Results	Used	Results	Used	Results	Used	Results	Used	Results	Used	Results
Present price of gasoline and the "Firefly Four's" low fuel consumption	✓				✓ H 11 3/2	Good	✓ O 21 7/2		✓ DL 12 7/2	Good	✓ OBT 3/2	Fair	✓ N 27 3/2 N 28 3/5 N 29 7/11 N 30 3/7 N 42 6/7	Fine Good Good Fair Poor	✓ T15 2/20 T22 6/7	Good Fair
The Firefly's Brake Control and danger of accidents	✓				✓ H-12 7/5	Poor	✓						✓		✓	
Will it be another year for you without that "Firefly Four"?					✓				✓		✓		✓		✓	
"Don't say a customer's car will be ready Saturday unless you're sure it will be ready by Friday!"	✓ 624 4/5	—	✓ 620 4/5	—												

Panel 247

MATERIALS AND USES FOR LETTERS

consumers in your business, if you advertise to them through newspapers or magazines, by leaving them on your chart as a possible field for ideas you can make the chart help you in gathering *ideas for advertising copy* just as much as it would help you in gathering ideas for letters.

At any rate by carrying out my simple little plan you'll get a chart that can be of inestimable value in keeping your mind alert to all the opportunities for merchandising your ideas, through letters, through advertising, or through sales plans.

But now the question is how to put such a chart into practical use. It is a general guide to our idea-merchandising plans, just as a definite knowledge of merchandising values and of buying and selling markets is a general guide to the plans of a merchant. But most of us need something more than a general guide—we need a detailed map, so to speak, on which to trace out specific directions. And this map should be our Idea Record.

The Idea Record that I have been working up to all this time, and the record that our graphic chart lays the foundation for, must be *a permanent record in which we can set down every idea* and every suggestion for an idea that may come to us, and from which we can quickly see not only where and how each idea should be used, but when it was so used.

You probably can understand more quickly what such a record should be, if I at once show you a practical example of one. On the opposite page is an Idea Record kept by an automobile distributor.

This concern has the general distribution of a certain car in a group of eastern states. It acts as the retail agent in its home city, but appoints subdealers in the other cities of its territory. Therefore, the chart illustrated on page 552 would show its "fields" for ideas to be Prospective Purchasers, Members of Sales Force, Dealers, and Others.

Now you will see by consulting the illustration on the opposite page, that in this case the "fields" have been closely specified. Instead of a general type of "prospective purchasers" we find five classifications—those to be reached through the list of home-office prospects, those to be reached through dealers' lists, those to be reached through blue-book lists, those to be reached through newspaper advertising, and those to be reached through theater programs In the same way specific divisions of the general fields indicated on the chart can be with a little ingenuity worked over to suit each particular business.

But the main point to take to heart is that in such an Idea Record you have always at hand *a practical working record* for your big chart.

The automobile distributor keeps his Idea Record in an ordinary trial balance book because the rulings in that book just suited him. Every time he gets the suggestion of an idea, for any purpose, he writes it briefly in pencil in the IDEA column and makes a pencil check in the columns where he thinks it would be of use. It is left that way until he has thought over it enough to determine to try it out. Then he traces over the pencil writing with *red ink*, and in *red ink* he enters the date on which the letter or advertisement or memoranda or circular embodying the idea was used on each of the fields. He also enters the "key number" of the mailing so that he can always quickly find exact copies of any letter or advertisement in which the idea was used. After the results are in, he summarizes them, as the illustration on page 554 shows. One word is a sufficient reminder.

This book, you see, is not the main record of results, but a *sort of manager's private ledger*. The automobile distributor thumbs it and studies it continually, thus keeping every thought that he ever had for a sales or service idea from ever being forgotten When an idea has paid on one field it immediately starts him planning ways of making it pay in other fields. Or if an idea paid last season, then he is reminded to try it again this season.

The entries in the illustration on page 554 are just imaginary ones made to show the workings of the record. The first idea, you can see, was first given a preliminary pencil entry, and then on February 20 was given a test through theater program advertising. The results were good. Therefore, as you may see by the entries on March 2, the *idea was also used on several other fields*, and repeated many times in newspaper advertising.

The second idea was given a test on the list of Home-Office Prospects, but the results did not justify its further use. Its record standing there as a constant reminder will obviate making a like mistake in future.

The third idea has never yet got beyond the stage of a suggestion, but it serves as a reminder and some day just the right angle to it may occur.

The fourth idea, inspection shows, is one purely for the home-office staff.

Do you now see how an Idea Record helps the advertising and mail departments as the stock record of a merchant helps his merchandising plans?

Another point to bear particularly in mind is that an Idea Record book should not be a book designed for one particular season or for any short length of time. It should go on continuously page after page, so that on consulting it you will always be encouraged to look all the way through it. One of its best helps is in the way it *keeps old ideas or old suggestions from being neglected*

In one mail-order business I know of, results for several years had been gradually falling off, until it looked as though the institution's days were done. A new advertising man came into the business and, seeing the condition of things, set about to find the fundamental cause of the decline.

It developed that the firm had changed advertising agents several times and each one had brought in new ideas, until in recent years the whole original character of both advertising and sales letters had been lost. The new advertising man dug out the advertising copy and letters of old days, studied their results, and finally decided to try out some of them again. They brought back as good returns as when the business was young, and by going back to the old ideas altogether, *the business was completely rejuvenated.*

BUSINESS CORRESPONDENCE

That failure was a simple example of what a permanent, carefully kept and constantly studied Idea Record book would have prevented. But just keeping a tabulated record of results of specific letters or advertisements is not enough, for I have never yet seen a business in which tabulated records will be constantly studied. In the interest of watching results from recent letters or advertisements the older ones soon cease to be noticed. But a simple record like the one illustrated keeps the very oldest of records almost as interesting as the very newest ones. More than that, it keeps one alert for uses for ideas instead of specific letters or advertisements. A specific letter may wear out while the Big Idea back of it may be still as potent as ever it was.

Now we have gone two steps forward in making the best use of letters and finding materials for them.

First, from the chart of letter-possibilities on page 552, we can study out the kind of ideas for which to be on the lookout, and all the *possible fields for which each idea can be profitably used.*

From the chart—or rather from the information it discloses—we can then rule up an Idea Record especially adapted to our business, one which will keep before us virtually an inventory of our stock of ideas, while the adjoining columns indicating every possible field on which our letters can be used, will show just how much or how little advantage we have taken of each idea. In other words, such a chart of our letter-possibilities corresponds to the merchant's knowledge of his merchandise and the market for it, while the Idea Record corresponds to his stock record.

Just imagine that you have that much system installed in your own business, so that you can see how it may be put to work for you.

Suppose in the morning's mail you run across a letter from a customer enclosing payment for a bill and expressing appreciation of the goods recently bought. Suppose, in telling how well satisfied he has been, the customer mentions the purpose for which he is using the goods and that purpose is

MATERIALS AND USES FOR LETTERS

one to which you had not given much consideration. But it strikes you that if one customer finds such a use important, others would do likewise.

Hence, in your Idea Record you immediately jot down the idea of this new use for your product. You later decide to try it out in your answers to inquiries from prospective customers. It pays

Now without an Idea Record in which to immediately record that suggestion, do you not see how easily the idea might be forgotten 10 minutes later? Or even if it stuck in your mind long enough to try it out on letters to prospective purchasers, do you not see how it might have gone no farther?

But with your Idea Record ruled according to a chart of all the *possible fields for your ideas,* as soon as one has paid, the mere entering its results in the Idea Record will stimulate you to think of other ways of using it.

Either at once or later you match it up tentatively with other fields represented in your book. Would it pay to get out a letter to regular customers particularly calling their attention to this new use? It might make a much bigger consumption. Would it pay to write a letter on it to dealers? It might help them sell more of your product. Would it pay to send out a memorandum to all office employees calling attention to the new idea? Would it pay to write a special letter to salesmen?

In short, you see how the Idea Record, if based on an accurate chart of your fields for ideas, almost forces you to take a full, 100% advantage of every suggestion

Again, suppose you are a retail merchant and in waiting on a good customer one day she tells you her family didn't like the new kind of coffee you sold her last time. As the coffee was a new brand on which you had the exclusive sale, you inquire if the customer followed directions closely, especially in regard to the directions that not so much coffee was required per cup as with other brands.

You learn that she didn't stop to read the directions and made her coffee the same as usual. You get her to try another pound and she is greatly pleased.

BUSINESS CORRESPONDENCE

Now, with an Idea Record, you, as a merchant, would immediately jot down that point as one to call to particular attention in making coffee sales. You could, and any good merchant would make use of such an idea even without an Idea Record. But the book would immediately suggest the advisability of sending a memorandum to all the clerks. And it might also suggest the profit in sending a circular letter to a list of prospective customers

Hundreds of merchants—not only grocers, but dry goods, drug, hardware, house furnishings, general stores, all other kinds of merchants have told me they like to use circular letters, but *the great problem is what to write about.* Yet in every store, incidents, customers' expressions of satisfaction, customers' complaints, traveling salesmen's selling points, or manufacturers' magazine advertising are constantly revealing suggestions that would make good ideas for letters, but the merchant without an Idea Record does not get them on his books.

Practically all mail delivered to manufacturing, mail-order or wholesale houses, or as far as that goes, to any business, teems with suggestions that can be developed into ideas if somebody will look for them—and record them as they are found. For instance.

In a certain manufacturing city one of the smaller banks which was making strenuous efforts under the leadership of a very aggressive president to get its share of commercial business, had been sending out a monthly circular letter to all rated business houses.

The letters, which were prepared by an out-of-town agency, seemed to be good ones, but the president could never quite say that he saw results from them. One day one of the tellers—a young man in his twenties—came into the president's office and solicited the privilege of submitting copy for some of the bank's letters.

"Why, I've no objection, Dean," said the banker, "but what makes you think you can do such work? It's a specialist's work, in my opinion."

MATERIALS AND USES FOR LETTERS

The young man pulled out a pocket memorandum book. "I've been setting down in this book for a year," he said, "all the *things customers have said to me or asked me*, or strangers have asked, which seemed to me might be good points to make in asking for accounts. I just thought that maybe as these are actual questions which occur to the minds of business men, they might be the questions in which other business men would be interested."

The banker looked them over.

"Good points, by George!" he exclaimed. "But I'm afraid we couldn't write them in letters. Some of my banking friends criticize me for being unethical, as it is."

"I suspect that to a competing bank which has all the business it wants, anything in the way of advertising will seem unethical," replied the teller. "But if these questions are what our customers are asking there can't be anything very wrong about them to prospective customers."

He was given a chance to write a few letters conveying the ideas his note book suggested, and for the first time in the history of the institution that bank's letters began to bring in new accounts

Now that young teller had gone with a sure purpose to the greatest, *most prolific source of letter-ideas that exists*—to the public—in his case to the bank's public. And no matter what your business is, your best source of letter material —idea material—is to be found in what your public thinks and says and writes.

If your business is small you should make it a point to spend a certain portion of your time in meeting and talking not only with your actual customers, but also with the kinds of people from whom customers can be made. If your business is one in which you don't meet your trade personally, then their letters should be studied closely. And every suggestion should be set down religiously in your Idea Record whether it is of assured value or only of doubtful value, because snap judgment on it will not be enough. Get it down where you will come face to face with it every day or every week in the future, and let your mature judgment get a chance at it every once in a while.

In big businesses the policy of employing "Scouts" to travel around and call on customers and prospects—not attempting to sell, but just to gather first-hand suggestions for ideas—has been made to pay big returns for the firms which have tried the plan

Some firms use what are called "Scout Letters"—letters designed to bring back the customer's or prospect's personal point of view. Some use of the firm's product, or general market information, will be put into these letters in the form of a request for the prospect's opinion on it.

On the opposite page you will see a letter of this kind. The manufacturer who wrote it had each of his salesmen get from a few of his best dealers a list of 50 to 100 charge customers who were known to the dealer to be fathers of small children. Between 2,500 and 3,000 names were thus secured and the letter mailed   The replies brought back many suggestions for selling ideas—suggestions that were valuable because they came straight and unaffectedly from the manufacturer's public   While the writers of the letters were trying to answer the points brought up by the manufacturer, most of them either consciously or unconsciously uncovered their personal attitude toward construction toys, and playthings in general, which was what the manufacturer wanted.

Here is another example of the same idea. A New York laundry once sent a letter to all its customers purporting to put to a vote of the customers the advisability of adding a hand-laundering department   The replies uncovered a number of fundamental complaints that had never been given expression before and that not only helped the laundry improve its service, but, when improved, made splendid new ideas for circular letters.

Next, in a search for ideas, after customers and prospects and dealers, *your product itself—or your service or your goods* is probably the best source of material. An analysis of

MATERIALS AND USES FOR LETTERS

the raw materials used; a study into where the raw materials come from; the machinery required, or the watchfulness necessary in its manufacture, the history of the product, and such points, will often put you on the trail of an idea you have missed in the past.

A certain widely advertised tooth paste owes the idea back of its successful advertising to an analysis made by an advertising man of the raw materials. He found one chemical ingredient that he didn't understand, so he went to a library

---

GIGANTO TOY COMPANY
CHICAGO, ILL.

Mr J A Murray,
Milwaukee, Wis.

Dear Sir

    As an American father of an American family would you mind telling me, in the enclosed stamped envelope, your own personal opinion of what the attitude of American fathers towards German made toys is going to be after the war?

    The question is important to me, as I want to know just how far I would be justified in going in enlarging the scope of my toy manufacturing business. Just now, as you probably know — or at least as most fathers know — I specialize only on construction toys. But if I thought Americans would continue to demand only American toys after the war, I might go into the manufacture of general toys.

    Or do you think as a father, that construction toys ought to supplant the more useless toys altogether?

    I have nothing to sell you, as my goods are sold only by dealers, but I would appreciate your honest personal views on the buying of toys by American parents If you don't believe in the cheap German toys, please tell me frankly, and if you don't believe in the more expensive American Construction toys like Giganto and similar toys, please be equally frank

    May I have your opinion?

                           Yours truly,

                           GIGANTO TOY COMPANY

Panel 248

SOURCES OF LETTER MATERIAL
TALKING POINTS

I CUSTOMERS
(1) problems
(2) needs
(3) knowledge of supply to fill their demands
(4) experiences in dealing elsewhere
(5) why they bought your product
(6) their experience with it
(7) their satisfaction
(8) further plans
(9) business
(10) financial standing
(11) accounts and collections
(12) inquiries
(13) complaints
(14) direct correspondence about specific materials

II SALESMEN
(1) daily reports
(2) interviews
(3) field investigations
(4) prize contests for ideas
(5) reports of sales conventions
(6) service bureau for customers
(7) direct correspondence about specific materials

III THE PRODUCT
(1) raw materials used
  —kind
  —quantity
  —quality
  —sources
  —how and by whom obtained
  —dependability
  —cost and terms
(2) manufacturing processes and equipment
  —methods of handling the work
  —skilled and unskilled workmanship
  —appliances for saving labor and money
  —new processes worked out
  —time required in manufacture
  —delays in manufacture
  —how tested
  —accuracy, speed, novelty and complexity of machines and operations
  —inspected systems
  —designing or invention departments

(3) what it has done
(4) what it needs
(5) how you will profit by it
(6) how you can obtain it, price, etc
(7) quantity on hand

IV ADVERTISING
(1) policy
(2) kind
(3) quantity
(4) appropriation
(5) medium
(6) when used
(7) by whom prepared
(8) returns
(9) campaigns
(10) letters, booklets, window displays, catalogs, folders, fixtures, demonstrations, samples testimonials, reports on tests, etc.

V SERVICE
(1) what it includes
(2) when available
(3) how available
(4) where available
(5) delivery
(6) number of orders on hand
(7) facilities for handling orders
(8) what delays in shipment and why
(9) how goods are packed
(10) how goods are shipped, route, date
(11) condition in which they will be received
(12) time to reach the customer
(13) inducements
(14) inside and outside assistance and transportation facilities
(15) general office systems
(16) policies in dealing with customers
(17) terms of sale

VI COMPETITORS
(1) customers

(2) salesmen
(3) product
  —quantity
  —quality
  —difficulty in manufacturing
  —facilities for handling orders
(4) advertising
(5) service
(6) number
(7) size
(8) number of lines
(9) inexperience
(10) terms of sale

VII FIRMS IN SIMILAR LINES
(1) points of contact with your business
(2) advertising
(3) sales campaign
(4) business methods

VIII NON-PURCHASER
(1) why he did not buy your product
(2) what he did
(3) what the results were
(4) what he will do next time

IX MISCELLANEOUS
(1) facts of current issues
(2) human interest stories
(3) news of the day
(4) trade conditions
(5) price fluctuations
(6) droughts, fires, floods.
(7) late or early seasons
(8) changes in tariff or transportation rates
(9) politics
(10) new inventions and discoveries
(11) government tests and trade reports
(12) incidents from history, science, literature, etc.
(13) bumper crops
(14) plays at theaters, pictures, concerts
(15) talks with acquaintances, strangers, friends, relatives

Panel 249

MATERIALS AND USES FOR LETTERS

and studied up on that ingredient. Its chemical reaction on the teeth opened up a new, big idea.

On the opposite page is a composite list of sources for letter and advertising and selling ideas compiled by the editorial staff of System from the methods used in several hundred different businesses. A close study of all the sources utilized by these firms will show you many of a similar kind in your business.

We have now found the way to chart out the possibilities which exist in our various businesses for the use of letters; we have found how to keep all these possibilities before us by a specially ruled Idea Record book, so that every idea we get can be quickly matched up with the possible fields on which to use it; and we have found to what sources to turn for suggestions for ideas

There remains just one point on which some of you may need a little guidance That is how to build up and maintain lists that truly represent the best fields on which you can use letters.

Lists of employees to whom memoranda of house policies, talking points, and so on, should be sent, are easy to compile. Lists of salesmen are always in hand. Lists of prospects from whom inquiries have been received are merely a matter of carding the names and addresses.

It is when one begins to go outside his own business for more theoretical prospects, or for dealers with whom one has never done business, or supply houses from which one never has bought, that care is needed.

There are three general sources of lists outside those created in one's own business.

1. Directories—city, telephone, trade, lodge, society, church and association directories

2. Lists compiled by houses in allied but non-competing lines.

3. Lists sold by regular list houses

The first source of names is open to anyone who will take the trouble to get them.

BUSINESS CORRESPONDENCE

For the local business, there is always the city directory from which names can be taken according to occupation, or according to address; there is the telephone directory from which the names will represent a responsible class, on the average; there is usually a classified telephone directory, classified by trades and professions, there is the rural telephone directory from which the names of farmers in any desired radius can be secured; there is the real estate tax roll giving names of property owners, and the personal property tax roll giving the names of the fairly well to do; there are lists of school teachers, church members, lodge, society and club members

For the business covering all or part of the country there are mercantile reports like Dun's or Bradstreet's, there are directories or lists published for nearly every trade, professional occupation and often various classes to each.

The second source is harder to approach. But many houses that advertise for inquiries or that have compiled special lists are willing to sell the lists after they themselves have worked them When the character of the business is such that the same type of prospect would be a good type for your own business, such lists often can be used with profit. But in purchasing them, care should be taken to see that the names are of comparatively recent origin—if more than a year or two old, the percentage of incorrect addresses is liable to make them useless. Sometimes such lists are offered for sale by list brokers. Or you can pick out for yourself a suitable character of business houses and make direct buying offers to them. The price for such lists varies, according to size and character and sometimes according to the owner's whims, from $2 a thousand up as high, for small highly classified lists, as $20 or $30 a thousand.

The third source—the lists offered for sale or rent by list brokers and addressing houses—represents the main source of supply for business propositions of more than local activity. Almost any sort of list in existence, and almost any quality of such lists desired, can be procured from these list brokers.

MATERIALS AND USES FOR LETTERS

Their catalogs of lists are in themselves a source of inspiration for new uses of selling letters.

In choosing lists from any of these sources, you should first *analyze your field* so as to understand just what sort of lists will cover it. For instance, if you are a real estate man handling home allotments, you should *study the types of people* to whom such homes or lots as you have to sell will appeal. If your property is in an outlying and undeveloped suburb where the principal attraction is price, it is manifest that your analysis would tell you that lists of well-to-do citizens would not be suitable; that lists of workmen who must get quickly back and forth to work, would not be suitable; and that lists of those already owning homes would not do at all.

Therefore, you would know that you could not efficiently use the telephone directory, or the directories of fashionable clubs, and so on. But lists of office employees would probably be a good choice and lists of members of the more modest lodges or poorer churches might be well worth a test letter or two.

You see the first job is to get your type of buyer well in mind, then look over sources of names for lists which represent that type.

The keeping of lists—that is, the physical system of keeping them—whether you keep them on sheets, on cards, or addressing-machine stencils—must depend on the volume of your circularizing and the frequency with which you use your lists. Lists seldom used are probably more economically handled if left merely in sheets, but card lists are so much more easily handled and so much more conveniently checked as to results, that if you are to use a list more than two or three times a year it will pay to put it on cards—one address to each card.

When a list is used with regularity, or when it is of a permanent nature—as lists of customers, dealer lists, and so on—and when, of course, you do your addressing in your own office—an addressing machine operating with cut stencils

BUSINESS CORRESPONDENCE

is efficient. For even very small businesses, these machines have hand-operated types that are economical.

But one mistake you must be sure to avoid! *Do not destroy the identity of individual lists,* by combining them into one general list, that is, if you buy one list of prospects from one broker and another list from another broker, or compile two lists from different directories, don't mix the two, nor your own inquiry list with other lists. If you use an addressing machine, then give each of the individual lists an individual tab, so that it can be readily distinguished

The reason is that different types vary in effectiveness. They vary in the way they deteriorate with age. By keeping each list distinguished in some way, no matter how you acquire it, every letter or mailing card can be keyed with its list name, and you can always tell which lists pay best, or which lists are wearing out.

And each list should be kept up to date. Every change of address should be noted, duplicates carefully weeded out, and every time a piece of mail is returned as undeliverable it should be looked up and, unless an error was made in addressing, the name should be killed. Nothing exasperates a customer quite so much as to get duplicate letters, or to have his letters persistently sent to a wrong address.

Some large users of the mail find it pays to make a "cleanup" mailing once a year to every list by sending either a first-class letter which the post-office will return if undeliverable, or by using third class, but printing a notice to postmasters to request return postage on undeliverable pieces. This *shows up every dead name or changed address* and keeps the list clean.

Another scheme used by shrewd firms is to have a "dummy" name inserted in every list—a name which will bring the letter back to the manager, so he gets a sample of every circular mailed by his house just as his prospects are getting it. He can keep posted in this way on the quality of addressing, fill-in, and printing.

MATERIALS AND USES FOR LETTERS

SUMMARY

AND that is the final suggestion I have to make to you. You have been shown the details of how a letter's work can be sized up—by first deciding the complete "load" it has to carry, then by judging the type of construction necessary to enable it to carry that "load" properly.

You have seen that no letter can carry its "load" properly unless the writer's idea is conveyed to the reader. Below my window as I write is the delivery wagon of a department store. In the wagon is a conglomeration of merchandise. The various items of merchandise constitute the wagon's "load." But you know and I know that that load would not be worth delivering if an idea were not conveyed with it. The driver of the wagon knows, the salesperson who took each order knows, that the delivery of that load of goods would be as nothing to the store if with it there were not conveyed to the customers of that store a Big Idea with each package—the idea of Service.

And so with a letter. Each letter has a "load"—certain opinions of yours, or decisions, or requests, or explanations, or facts. But you wouldn't bother to write them if back of them there weren't an idea in your head that you want the receiver to feel. And it will do you no good to write them if you don't write them in such a way that they not only are read but convey your idea.

So the *"load"* of any letter requires that an idea be incorporated in its construction and *I* have told you how to convey an idea—by visualizing it definitely to yourself, then to pick the important features of it, then to arrange those features in the order most easily grasped by the reader. And then I continued to show you how to convey an imaginary or negative idea. Finally, I discussed with you ways of expressing personality, exercising persuasion, writing the close, and building an artificial Attention-Stopper.

In later chapters you were shown the real principles of letterheads and enclosures and the principles of organizing your work. Lastly in this chapter you were given a means of enlarging the uses for letters in your business, discovering material for them, and extending and keeping your mailing lists.

That is all I can tell you about writing and using business letters I have made it all as plain as I could. I believe if you will practise patiently on the principles laid down you will get better results from your own business letters than you got before.

In the final problem section of this book you will find a brief review of the nine chapters on writing the letter. Follow this review through carefully. It will be of great value to you.

PROBLEM SECTION XI

OUR experience so far in this book has been somewhat like that of a specially picked understudy employed by a big manufacturing plant to learn the business from the bottom up. He probably begins in the drafting room, works there for a couple of months, moves over to the estimating room, works there for a while, changes into the pattern shop, then the foundry, and so on. After several years of detailed, first-hand experience he knows the business, graduates from his apprenticeship, and is promoted to an executive position.

Similarly, this is graduation time, or near it, for the readers of this book on applied business correspondence. In previous problem sections we spent our time on detailed jobs, always having the big work, the finished letter, in view, but never having the satisfaction of trying out at one time *all* that we knew. We learned how to handle that big thought, the "load" of a letter. We studied over the Big Idea, tried our hand at sincerity, tested Mr. Watson's ideas regarding closers and Attention-Stoppers, and progressed steadily to the time when we would write the complete letter.

That time is at hand, and now as our review "quiz" we'll write a letter from start to finish and test all of the nine principles brought out by that novel chart we found in the first chapter.

One point more before we launch on our newest adventure in letter writing. In this problem section we are to work out a sales letter. Now, if you are not a salesman, or if you do not write sales letters, you may feel that there should be also a definite application of Mr. Watson's ideas to a collection letter, to a complaint letter, or to an adjustment letter. In a way the criticism is fair, but when one stops to think about it, every letter is a sales letter. The complaint letter sells satisfaction. The collection letter sells a desire to pay up.

After all, from one way of looking at it, a straight sales letter is really the *simplest* form of business correspondence. Therefore, the principles which it discloses may be turned, with but slight change, to account by collection men, adjustment men, and others. So let's get to work and take for our problem a letter to bankers.

We shall assume that we are the correspondent for a banker's supply company which supplies bankers with everything they need—bronze tablets for the doors, change machines, adding machines, and so on down to a paper of pins. Up to this time, let us say, we have been sending salesmen to meet the trade, but now the territory which can be conveniently handled from the home office has been covered.

There are, however, hundreds of small banks in outlying districts to which it would not pay to send a salesman. These prospects we shall attempt to develop by mail. Our experience with salesmen has been that repeat orders are the rule and that if we sell a banker one product we can sell him others. Consequently, we shall try *to open the new market* with one of our quick-selling leaders, a currency-mending tape which, salesmen tell us, all but sells on sight. The purpose of this letter is to sell, but immediate profit is not the only consideration.

Keep particularly in mind the fact that we are going to sell to *small* banks, banks in which the reader of the letter is probably cashier, purchasing agent, and teller, all rolled into one. For this reason we can use a direct appeal, through the Self-Indulgence Motive, because the buyer will probably use the tape himself, whereas, if we were selling to a big bank we'd probably have to apply the Gain Motive, for in a big bank the buyer would probably *not* use the tape himself but would be influenced by arguments showing how the tape saves time and money and in other ways reflect his ability as a buyer.

MATERIALS AND USES FOR LETTERS

We offer this tape because we have found that bankers and others have considerable difficulty in mending the torn currency, torn checks, and torn documents, which they receive day after day.

We have investigated the market and found that a tough, cheap, gummed tissue paper mender is hard to get. Much of that which is on the market is reported as too narrow, curls when the mucilage is wetted, or is so thick that printed or written words cannot be read through it. We know that our product not only has none of these faults, but also that it is cheaper than others and that it will be a big seller if properly presented.

Therefore, putting ourselves in the expert letter writer's place, we'll try to write the sort of letter that would cost us a fat fee if we turned the job over to an outsider. Probably if we work carefully we'll qualify to save the fee and at the same time make sure that this book on applied business correspondence will much more than pay for itself.

First of all, let us have a look at the chart which is to be found on page 32. (The best way to use the chart, by the way, is to paste it on cardboard or slip it under the glass top of your desk so that reference to it will be easy whenever you have a letter to write.) The first question we should ask ourselves is·

What Is the Complete "Load" My Letter Must Carry?

Exactly what Mr. Watson meant by the "load" of a letter I found a little baffling at first. Perhaps you had the same difficulty. Therefore, before we determine the "load" our letter to bankers is to carry, let us decide on a definition of Mr. Watson's phrase.

The "load" of a letter is what the writer himself thinks about his product, and what the writer must tell his reader in order that the reader will understand the offer and agree with the writer.

In brief, *the "load" of the letter is the writer's point of view.*

BUSINESS CORRESPONDENCE

With that definition in mind it is plain, isn't it, that the "load" of a letter doesn't appear only in the first paragraph, but may—and generally does—appear all through the letter. You may have missed this point and assumed that the first question of the chart dealt with the first paragraph of the letter. Not at all. The "load," being the writer's point of view, is scattered all through it.

Now then, to decide upon the "load" of our letter to bankers. We look over a sample box of mending tape. I have provided a picture of it on the opposite page. If you were to examine it carefully as you should, before writing a selling letter, you would find that the tape is rolled into a neat reel and packed in a pine box with a sliding top. The box has a slot cut in it at the top so that the tape can be drawn out in the length needed and the edge of the slot is sharp so that the tape can be torn easily and evenly. When we inspect the tape we find that it is wider than others on the market. When we consider the price we find that it is one-third the price our nearest competitor asks. When we paste a strip of the tape on a torn check we find that the tape not only holds well, but that we can read through it perfectly.

"Enough! Wait a minute," I hear you say, and ask· "Aren't you giving us the 'features' of the Big Idea?"

No, indeed, I am simply taking *notes on the various selling points*—"pointers," let's call them—of our proposition, so that we can more easily determine the "load" of our letter Of course, it is not necessary to go to such detail for every letter, but this time we want to make the point very clear. As for "features" and the Big Idea, we'll consider them in just a minute.

And then we will notice how the "pointers" of the "load," when examined from another point of view, lead us to the "features" of the Big Idea.

Now the letter we are writing is a sales letter, pure and simple, but if you will reflect a moment you will, I am sure, agree that the facts brought out in our review of the "load" of a letter apply equally well to any kind of letter. If we

MATERIALS AND USES FOR LETTERS

were writing a *collection* letter, for instance, the "load" of the letter might be: "You have held up payment too long and you're heading for trouble." The "pointers" you'd dig up from previous correspondence and other sources would lead you to that conclusion.

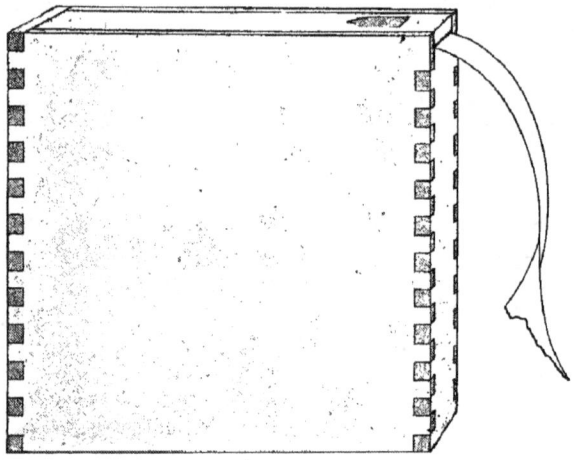

Panel 250

In short, I repeat, the "load" of the letter is the writer's point of view throughout. With that conclusion in mind, we may write on the chart the "load" of our banker's letter as:

"*To make our prospects understand that we have a better, cheaper, handier mending tape.*"

That "load," of course, could be expressed in scores of other ways. The wording of it on the chart is of little consequence. It's just a memorandum. It doesn't make a bit of difference, does it, if your wife ties a red string or ties a blue string around your finger to make sure that you think of an errand? And it doesn't make a bit of difference how you write the "load" of the letter on the chart if you recognize the fact that it's *your point of view* or the point of view of the house behind you. And that brings up another point, which you may think I am disregarding.

BUSINESS CORRESPONDENCE

In previous chapters Mr. Watson hammered continually on the "you and I" element. Remember how he pointed out and cleverly disposed of that "you" fallacy? We agreed then that every really good letter should be written with the reader's point of view in mind. "Visualize your prospect" was suggested over and over again. In this review section, are we going to disregard Mr. Watson's splendid advice?

Decidedly not. But a salesman, whether he writes a good sales letter, a good collection letter, or any other kind of letter (any business letter, remember, is in effect a sales letter) has first to sell himself. That's true, isn't it? In other words, before we can sell a currency mender to anyone else we've got to sell it to ourselves, haven't we? We've got to know our product up and down, backward and forward, believe in it, be ready to fight for it, feel positive, sure, certain, that it can't be beaten. And wouldn't considering the prospect while selling ourselves distract us from the job on hand? It's obvious that it would.

And so, in fixing on the "load" of any letter, *consider yourself first and then consider your prospect.*

Don't try to do both jobs at once. For you to get the prospect's point of view is of the very greatest importance, but not of any greater importance than to establish a definite point of view for yourself. If you are in doubt, if you are undecided, your prospect will feel it, no matter how hard you try to cover up your failing.

How many times have you heard people tell a story in a way that made you say to yourself, "Why, he doesn't believe that himself."

In short, *to sell a man, first sell yourself.* That is the purpose of deciding the "load" of a letter clearly.

That's a fascinating subject, but we must go on.

Having sold ourselves, having written down our conclusions as to the "load" of our letter, henceforth we'll turn all our attention to the prospect and, if we can—and we can—make him feel as we do, and make him do what we want him

MATERIALS AND USES FOR LETTERS

to do. And, therefore, back we go to the chart and to the second question on it:

Will the One to Whom I am Writing Feel a Self-Interest When He Sees a Letter from Me?

We don't have to reflect long to say "no" to that question.

Ours is to be a circular letter to strangers. They'll not be interested in us offhand. But they will be interested in some device that will lessen their work. Our investigations have proved to us and to bankers who have tried our product that our mender will make easier a petty, disagreeable, but necessary job. And with this conclusion we practically answer the chart's second question. We realize that our prospects are not interested in us personally, but, on the other hand, what man or woman isn't glad to make routine work easier? Not one? All right. Then in answer to the question:

In What Is the Reader Interested that I May Gear Up My Proposition in Order to Get His Attention?

We can answer· "*Ways of lightening the routine work of his cage.*" And here we get our first hint that some attention-winning device will probably be necessary. However, that is another point to take up later.

That second question was easy, but now we come to the third, and, in some respects, the most important question on the whole chart.

What Is the Feeling or the Big Idea I Want the Reader to Get?

You may not have grasped at once the difference between the Big Idea and the "load" of a letter. Well, the difference *is* hard to understand at first, but difficulties will disappear, I think, if we keep the following definition in mind.

The Big Idea of any letter is what the writer wants his reader to feel or think when he reads the letter.

See how that ties up with the "you and I" principle. The "load" of your letter is what *you* think about your prospectus. The Big Idea is what you want *your reader* to think about it.

Simple, isn't it? Let's see how it works out. In a selling letter the Big Idea requires the reader to feel a need for your product; in a collection letter, he should feel that he must pay up. When you answer a complaint you want him to feel that you are a good fellow, that the mistake could not be helped and that you are glad to accept an opportunity to make good. It's all so simple and obvious that you may wonder that you didn't get the idea before.

Now that we have the definition of Big Idea clearly in mind, let's apply the principle in our letter to bankers.

Let's see. What do we want the banker to *feel* as he reads the letter? Why, that our tape is so good that he must have some And how shall we try to make him feel that? Why, by considering the facts that sold us and by presenting them so that they will *appeal to his point of view*. If we do that, we'll naturally hit upon a Big Idea something like this:

"This tape will do away with the present nuisance of mending currency and documents and make a disagreeable job quick, simple, and easy "

Of course, making the prospect get this Big Idea isn't simple or easy, but requires careful work along the lines laid down by Mr. Watson in the second chapter. Perhaps, before picking "features," it will be well to consider other questions on the chart. We realize that the flat, abstract statements by which we sold ourselves won't do. Our prospect probably will not believe them, for he doesn't know us or our product. In short, we are at once crowded to the fourth question of the chart, namely:

Will the Reader Be Indifferent or Opposed to Considering My Idea—or Will He Be Open-Minded?

We have just answered that question in our minds. Our prospect has so many unsupported claims brought to his attention by mail, and otherwise, every day, that he is almost sure to discount ours. Therefore, as a reminder, we'll write across the chart in answer to the fourth question:

"Probably indifferent, as he does not know us or our proposition."

Now we can go back to our Big Idea, and, with our analysis well in mind, we can proceed to pick "features" in the way Mr. Watson outlined in the second chapter, so that the Big Idea will get across to the reader and he will take the action we want him to take.

What are "features"? *"Features" are facts about a proposition that will make the prospect feel as you do about it.*

How does one discover "features"? Just as Mr. Watson suggested by means of the Washington Irving quotation and the Delta Land Company letter. For our letter, we must review what we know of bankers and then make careful analysis of our product.

"All right," you say, "Go ahead and analyze—let's see you do it. Your proposition is a new one to me. About all I know of bankers has been gathered from letters telling me my note is due or that my account is overdrawn, or something of the sort "

"There's nothing to it," I answer. "There's no mystery, about this. It's simple. It's easy." You don't have to be brother to a banker to get his point of view.

Just picture yourself in his position and you'll have the key to the selling problem. *Picking "features" is merely an appeal to human nature.* Don't you remember how interestingly Mr. Watson made that plain in the second chapter? And in our letter to bankers what would appeal to us would probably appeal to our prospect.

"Analyzing" and "picking features" sound formidable. The words call up images of hard, bone-racking work. But please don't think that that's the right idea. Merely bear in mind, when you write a sales letter, or any other kind of letter, that picking "features" means putting yourself, as nearly as you can, in the reader's place and thinking of what would appeal to you in the circumstances. Why, it's as easy as getting wet when you fall into water.

When you stop to think of it, you pick "features" every day in your life, only, perhaps, you don't call your work that. Some people call it "putting your best foot foremost." And what is "putting your best foot foremost?" When you stop to think about it, isn't it merely sizing up your man or your proposition and putting yourself or your ideas in their best light? And isn't the "best light" nine times out of ten the prospect's light? In letter writing one can hardly do less The *important* part of the task, however, is to make a note of your mental steps—then you'll be sure to include them all.

Now let's try our hand at picking "features" for our letter To begin: A teller's cage and counter are pretty well packed with files, money, change machines, credit memoranda, debit memoranda, drafts, checks, and so on. The teller has to be neat, orderly, methodical. What is easier, then, than to point out that our box reflects these conditions. And once you do that there are your "features" right at your finger tips. Like this:

The box is neat, small, clean and easy to handle.
The tape doesn't curl when wet
The special glue we use sticks like a nail to a magnet.
The tissue is strong, but so transparent that the finest print beneath it can be read.
It's one-third the price of any other brand

Now wouldn't those "features" make your man think what you want him to think, especially if you had learned that the present brands on the market were unsatisfactory because they lacked the good points that made your product satisfactory? It's safe to say that they would Let us assume that they would, however, and leave the subject, for we still have much to do before we may set pen to paper and make a rough draft of our letter.

When we settled on our Big Idea, we took a look ahead and, you will remember, decided that our reader would be indifferent to our proposition. Consequently we have to overcome that difference. We can hardly find a better way of accomplishing our purpose than by following the methods outlined by Mr. Watson in the third chapter.

That was the chapter which took up the matter of visionary or negative approach which you may have found a little difficult.

Let's clear up any misunderstanding first of all. To boil that chapter down to a sentence we can say: "If a man is indifferent or opposed to your proposition show him the disadvantages of continuing in his present frame of mind."

Nothing hard about that thought, is there? Remember how Ingersoll showed the delegates to the convention the *disadvantages* of not nominating Blaine? And no doubt you will recall the disadvantages portrayed in the Home Laundry letter and others mentioned in the third chapter. That's all there is to *overcoming indifference—show the reader the disadvantages of not doing what you want him to do*

But how are we to do it? In one of two ways. We may either build up a picture of the disadvantages to the reader as Ingersoll did—or we may state the disadvantages and let the reader build up his own picture.

Now that may be done in a number of ways. Some of them Mr Watson suggested in the third chapter. His diagram, however, may lead you to believe that the *disadvantages* of the reader's position should be grouped at the start of the letter and then by means of a *connecting link* the reader should be hooked up to the advantage of doing what you desired. Although this is a very good way of overcoming opposition, and despite the fact that many writers and speakers use it to good effect, we should not assume that it is the *only* way of accomplishing our purpose

No cut and dried rule can be set down If your purpose is better served by putting advantages first, or by scattering advantages among the paragraphs following a recital of disadvantages, *try* your way. *Test* your way. The big, interesting, helpful point—that of showing the prospect the disadvantages of his present position—will, however, always be a powerful factor in making a prospect change to your way of thinking.

But let's go back to the banker's letter. We have to make that letter short and snappy (it's for a business man who hasn't time, we assume, to read a long letter on a simple proposition), and so we'll count on a quick approach. We'll just flash a few disadvantages to the reader who does not use our tape, and let it go at that.

Let's make a note of those disadvantages right now, while we are on the subject, so that we shall not forget them when we write the letter. Here they are:

Papers mended with thick tissue cause eye strain

Competitors' varieties come in small rolls about an inch in diameter. They get lost easily They dry up quickly. They soil. They crumple

Other brands curl and shrivel when drying and hence it is a nuisance to handle them.

And now we are ready to consider arranging "features" so as to make our meaning clear. That brings us to Section 5 on the chart which asks this question

Is the Reader Familiar with the Subject of My Idea or in Sympathy with the Nature of My Feelings?

In other words, must we take pains to make our meaning clear?

For this letter I'd say "no" and I'm sure you'll agree with me. Ours is a simple proposition It is easily understood. We won't have to work hard over the arrangement of our "features." Our readers will not have difficulty in understanding any of them.

I have this thought also to offer in regard to presenting "features." In the fourth chapter, as you will recollect, Mr. Watson suggested that the "features" easiest to understand should be presented first and that others should follow, resting on each other like dishes on a platter. Now some people may

MATERIALS AND USES FOR LETTERS

think that the most important "feature" should always go first. No indeed. A "feature" easy to understand is the "platter"; another "feature" easy to understand goes on top of it, and so on. In other words, why not say that in a letter the "features" should be arranged like a flight of steps? The prospect in reading mounts the first step, a "feature" easiest to understand, then the second, a "feature" a little more difficult, until he reaches the top of the stairs and has the Big Idea of the letter."

With this thought in mind, it's quite easy, I think, to get Mr. Watson's idea. "Features" should be placed in logical sequence. One should not ask a reader to leap to the third step, drop down to the first, jump up to the fifth.

It's hardly necessary to mention, in passing, the importance of keeping in mind that we want to use a banker's style of vocabulary as much as possible. We must know the sort of words he uses. We should use his names for common things.

When it comes to making a reader believe our statements we reach another section of the chart, which asks:

To Make Him Believe, Do I Have to Change Some Accepted Opinion or Disappoint Some Expectation?

For our letter, we can safely answer "yes." Although our article is a good one, one really needed and useful, the reader may be satisfied with his substitute and not willing to make a change. Hence, we make a note of our decision by writing on the chart·

Yes, he probably believes that his present mender is good enough.

That leads us immediately to considering what appeal we shall make to succeed. Shall we appeal to his reason, caution, or business sense, or to his taste, fancy, convenience, or the personal side?

Let us answer from what we have already decided that the appeal is to be made to his convenience and that we'll make buying a personal matter to him. We then cross out the left-hand square at the top of the chart.

BUSINESS CORRESPONDENCE

Now we have to *select the motive* which will appeal to our reader.

Before we turn all our attention to motives, consider whether our reader will believe us. As Mr Watson pointed out, we must make our reader feel the truth and sincerity of our statements, and thereby make it easier for him to accept them. How shall we do that?

Why, by doing what Mr. Watson suggested in the fourth chapter, finding some mutual interest. If our letter were to be a personal letter to a friend or to a person we knew, then we could use our friendship, recall old memories, and so on. But this is a circular letter and personalities, even if we knew them, would be out of place. However, there is one ground sure to be safe. We can *join our knowledge of banking with that of our reader.* We can show him that we are aware of the annoyance and bother he undergoes.

Do you notice that the principles Mr. Watson laid down are really simple when you go about using them? Many people throw up their hands at the talk of meeting prospects on common ground and yet, when you think of it, it can always be done. The collection man can base his letter on a tight money market, thus opening a way to the use of a fair play motive. The complaint letter may dwell on the difficulty of maintaining routine, and the reader out of his experience will generally acknowledge that the best discipline will fail at times. Appeals of that sort can be made in *letters in which personal appeals cannot be used.*

Finding a mutual interest leads us directly to motives, for the two are close allies. In our banker's letter what motive shall we select? Which one will make the best appeal to his convenience? We look over the list of motives Mr. Watson supplied on page 306. Shall we choose Love? Certainly not. Duty? No. Self-Preservation? Hardly.

The Gain Motive makes us pause, but we recollect that the Big Idea of our letter is based on convenience and so we pass on. The Self-Indulgence Motive opens the doors. It can be turned to account by an appeal to the reader's love of ease

MATERIALS AND USES FOR LETTERS

and comfort. The Pride Motive might stir him faintly, but probably not enough to accomplish any perceptible result in this letter. In short, we find but *one* motive, Self-Indulgence, directly available. Perhaps you may ask:

"*How many motives may properly be used in a letter?* Shall we use them all if we can, or shall we use one and work it for all it's worth?"

I believe that we can well take either course, depending upon our propositions. If we feel that a long letter is needed, and particularly if *tests* show that long letters are read by our prospects, then we may wisely make use of several or all of the motives, provided we can do so gracefully. On the other hand, one motive hammered home in quick, hard strokes will do the work most satisfactory at times.

There are so many conditions to be considered in this regard that a positive rule is more than ordinarily difficult to lay down. For instance, in writing, consider whether a letter is one of a series—if it is, it may be well to use one motive in the first letter and another motive in a second letter, and so on.

Our present proposition, however, is one that sells so cheaply that we can't afford to send out a series on it. One letter has to do the work if we are to break even. Hence, we'll stick to the Self-Indulgence Motive and forget the others for the time being.

Before we turn from the chart of motives on page 306, however, let us fix this fact in mind. that chart is merely suggestive. It carries so many ideas that a whole book might be written on its use. As letter writers, our duty is to *study the chart in the light of the suggestions it gives us and to let our imagination work on it.*

Although there are many "liftable" letters scattered through this book, and although there are many ideas that can be copied and turned to use without the expenditure of time and effort upon them, still most of the material which has been supplied is suggestive. The book was written to help you "cook up" ideas and not to supply them "precooked" and

BUSINESS CORRESPONDENCE

"predigested," so to speak. And surely that's the way you'd prefer.

Now for the last two steps in the preparation of our letter. So far we have not written a line We are still *thinking* the letter, and not until we have it all thought out shall we touch pen to paper or ring for the stenographer. And this is the method Mr. Watson follows with every important letter he writes. It is the way the correspondents of the A. W. Shaw Company prepare to write And a dozen other successful men who follow this same plan could be named.

Of course, their thinking is rapid. They don't openly pause to analyze the reason for each step as we have done. Long practise with the principles behind the chart enables them, as it will enable you, to make short cuts. But they do not omit a single step of the chart. Familiarity with it and the train of thought it arouses has merely made it unnecessary for them to write down each step, as I have done. On the other hand, if in beginning the use of the chart you write down the "load." the Big Idea and its "features," and so on, you will quickly train your mind to an accurate method of *thinking the letter*

But we must go on and consider the question of a close for our letter. We have seen in the seventh chapter that a a good close should connect the motive, or motives, to the action desired by some *"little preliminary job" which makes a "connecting path" to action.* Now we may safely assume that at this point we shall have our reader interested. We shall have started him thinking. We shall, therefore, have started a mental action which seeks physical expression. Does this seem far-fetched? Perhaps you think, that this preliminary job idea of Mr Watson's is a little hard to grasp, but tests of the idea have proved it sound over and over again.

It goes back to the simple principle that when a man thinks, he almost always balances his mental effort with a physical reaction He drums on the desk, swings his legs, or taps his teeth with a pencil—the phenomena is common enough. Well, we, as good salesmen, shall take advantage of this and instead

MATERIALS AND USES FOR LETTERS

of letting our prospect make aimless movements, will direct his energy our way. We'll do even more. Since we know that he has an impulse to act we'll make it easy for him; we'll *crystallize his thought and tell him to act our way!*

In studying the currency mender, I found a means for achieving this end. To get a real knowledge of the product, I spent a few hours with a city salesman who was selling a similar article to bankers I heard him make half a dozen sales and mentally noted the "load," the Big Idea, and the "features" of his talk. When we were ready to leave he suggested, "Let's visit one more bank and you try to make a sale."

Well, I stood up to the next banker we met and gave a glowing description of the mender and actually did sell a box. When I left the bank and asked for criticisms, the salesman, who was a friend, and therefore candid, said:

"You did pretty well, but why didn't you hand him the box when he reached for it. Watch your man. If he is interested he'll reach for the box and try its good points for himself. Don't you show him."

And then I remembered that as I explained the virtues of the article I had not gone far before the prospect reached for it. But I did not hand it to him. I went right on and showed him how it worked instead of letting him do the work.

Do you see? That bank teller wanted some easy preliminary job. He wanted to express with his hands the interest he felt.

And so with the letter we are writing, and, as far as that goes, with any letter written to secure action. *Give your prospect, if possible, something to do.* In this case we can't hand him the box of tape but we can do the next thing to it—hand him a sample to test.

Let's jot that point down on our pad and also remind ourselves to include an order card as the "easy connecting path" to the final action we desire. Then we may prepare for the final step, a means of gripping attention

Must we grip attention by some mechanical means in this letter? I'd say "yes"; wouldn't you? For it's to be a cir-

BUSINESS CORRESPONDENCE

cular letter and business men today are flooded with them. Very well, then. What can we do to call attention to our product? How can we write a Stopper that will lead naturally to the Big Idea?

First of all let's recall what Mr Watson said about Attention Stoppers. A man in a pink hat would attract attention, but probably that's all. Attention-winning must be done right if at all. It's a delicate proposition. Therefore, we shall remember to avoid the style of the patent medicine advertisement which starts off with the line, "Saved from Death," and which, in the next breath, tries to prove the efficacy of Old Doc Killem's pills.

From what Mr. Watson has told us, we know the danger of that kind of Attention-Stopper and so our job is to prepare one that will be a part of the letter—one that will lead logically to the Big Idea.

Does that seem difficult? Let's study our proposition and see. We know that the tape is transparent and is a fine material for mending documents. We can easily prove it. All right, let's prove it to our reader by sending him a letter torn and mended by the tape we have to sell.

A torn letter certainly will be something out of the ordinary and will get attention. Then we'll write a first paragraph that will hook the Attention-Getter to the Big Idea, then work up to the order card.

At last we are ready to write. Everything we wish to say has been thought out and written down on the chart reproduced on the following page.

Writing the letter is now comparatively easy. And in this connection let me point out how our system does away with that old bugaboo, "What shall I write?" The man who says that, when he has a letter to write, generally hasn't thought his letter. When we know what we want to say, when we have an idea to convey, when we, as the saying goes, are bursting on account of a desire to talk, then writing is a "copper-riveted cinch." Hence, because of the careful preparation we have made, a letter selling a currency mender

MATERIALS AND USES FOR LETTERS

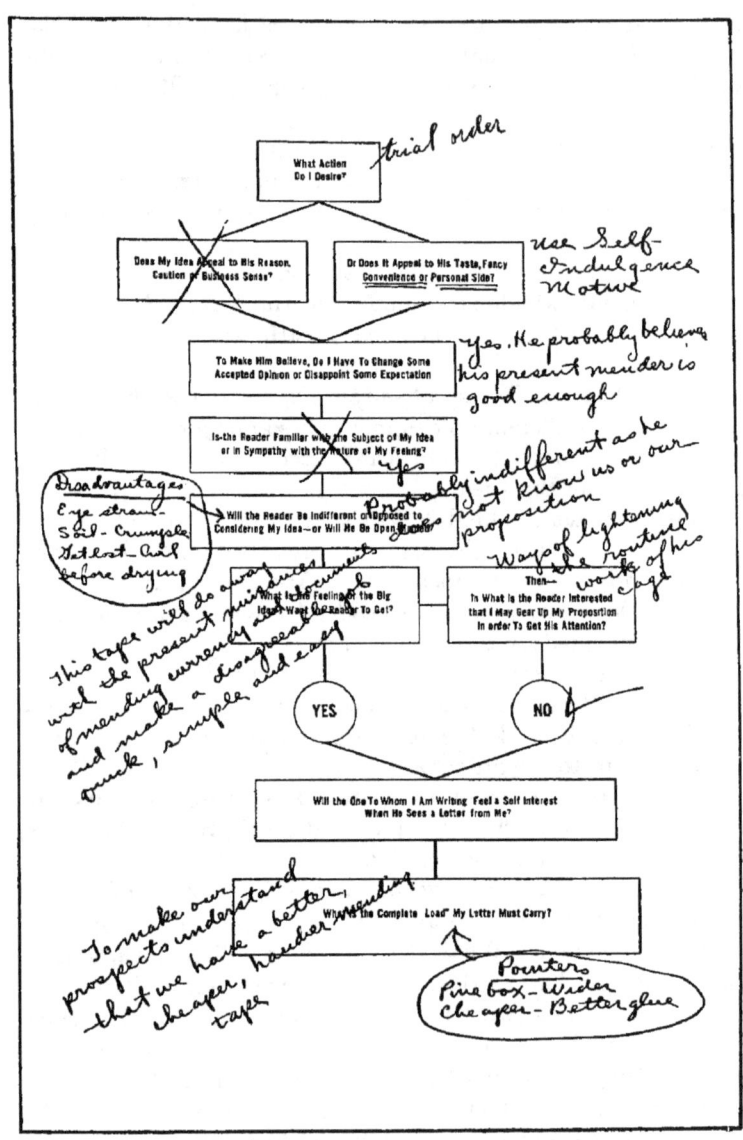

Panel 251

BUSINESS CORRESPONDENCE

now practically writes itself You will find it on the next page. As you read it, note the echo from the letters reproduced in previous chapters. I've dipped into them liberally for ideas

Now, if we pause to consider that letter for a moment, what do we find? First of all that the *thoughts brought out by the chart are scattered through the letter* every which way That will generally be true of letters written according to our chart The mere fact, for instance, that the "load" of the letter is first considered and written down on the chart is no sign that the "load" as written has to be incorporated at the start of the letter or in so many words. *The "load," remember, is what you think about your product* It is merely a memorandum of your point of view. It is never copied from the chart into the letter, but rather appears "between the lines." However, the "pointers" of the "load" are sometimes actually to be found in the letter.

Now as to the Big Idea as it appears on the chart Perhaps you expected to see it actually written in the letter But *the Big Idea, just like the "load," is an intangible something in the letter* It's a memorandum of what you want the reader to feel when he reads the letter, and therefore it, too, is generally to be found "between the lines."

The "features," of course, are more tangibly available You'll generally find them in the letter. Read them in our letter to bankers. Notice, however, that although we put a "feature" easy to grasp near the start of the letter, it was *not* the most important of the lot In fact, it was an unimportant one—one easy to understand

The disadvantages of the reader's present condition are plainly to be read in the letter. Also, notice the quick change to the positive advantages of following the proposed action. The Self-Indulgence Motive and "fuel" for it are also to be found running through the letter. As for the Attention-Stopper and the closer with its easy connecting path, no one can miss them.

Of course, the letter does not even pretend to be the last word on the subject It was not written as a finished, polished,

MATERIALS AND USES FOR LETTERS

BANKERS SUPPLY CO
Chicago

Dear Sir

Mailing a torn and mended letter may seem to be a peculiar thing to do, but I did it purposely. In fact, I tore this letter after it was written, mended it, and then mailed it just to show you a way in which I can make your work easier.

How many times have you strained your eyes trying to read through the thick tissue used to mend torn currency, checks, acceptances, and other paper? How many times have you searched through the drawers of your cage for a piece of tape with which to mend paper only to find a dried up, wrinkled little roll tucked away in some corner? And then, when you tried to use it, it curled -- shriveled as it was drying -- in short, it made you wish that someone, anyone, would provide a tape that would do the work it was intended to do.

Here, then, is what you have been looking for. At the top of this page you'll find a sample of a tape that will end your search, satisfy your want. If you tug at this letter you'll find that the paper will tear before the tough tissue. See how easily words can be read through the tape. Notice how wide this tissue is. And the glue sticks like a nail to a magnet. The neat, wooden box in which each roll is packed can be tucked away in a corner of the counter -- it will never be in the way, but always on hand when wanted. In addition to all these conveniences, this mender is the cheapest on the market.

You buy 100 yards for 100 cents. For others you pay 3 cents a yard and more.

I am so sure this tape is what you have been looking for, that it will save time and make your work easier, I am willing to pay all the expense of your trying it.

Test the sample at the top of this letter and then, when you find that the right kind of mender is at last on the market, simply write your name on the enclosed stamped mailing card and I'll send you a trial box by return mail. If I've missed my guess and the tape isn't exactly what you've wanted for a long time, send it back -- if I'm right, the cent a yard is all you pay for satisfaction.

Isn't this a fair and liberal offer?

Why not get this tape working for you at once by filling out the card today?

Yours very truly,

BANKERS' SUPPLY CO.

Panel 252

selling letter, but merely to help us review our method of writing Perhaps you can improve it. There are many little ways of making the prospect "come across " For instance, more banking terms would count.

One little reminder, please, in conclusion. Now you have had all of the principles in this book placed before you for a final review and if you have read them carefully you are ready to turn them to good account But simple as this book on Applied Business Correspondence is, easy as are the principles it outlines to acquire, the points made and the methods explained cannot possibly be put to the best use without conscientious and continual practise. Reading the book is not enough Every one of the problems to be found in the problem sections should be faithfully worked out and plans for developing a letter tried at every opportunity.

Only in this way can the most be gained from this book This suggestion itself is an adaptation from one of the principles studied. Reading is merely following the "you" idea which we have condemned. But by working out the problems you will follow the "you and I" idea, not only important in letter writing, but powerful in every other line of human activity.

INDEX

Action, stimulating 351–396
ADJUSTMENT LETTER . 48
  the "features" of an 81
ADVERTISEMENT
  an, that is a good example of well-adapted language 210
  four steps in preparing layout for an 492
  Advertisements, the "big idea" back of five well-known . 232

ANALYSIS
  of a letter 53
  of the close of a letter 371–375
  of the first four letters of a collection follow-up series 150

APPLICATION LETTER
  "attention getter" in an 267
  duty motive applied to an . 345
  which won a good job, an . . . 266

ATTENTION
  -gripping, the four principles of 421
  how to grip, before the prospect begins to read 321–433
  how to make letters grip 399–450
  -ray, choosing the right, for the letter 423
Attitude of the reader, the 17
"Automatic letter writer," sample of letter from the 520

B

Banker's experience in getting new depositors through letters, a 560
Banker's letter, with the human touch, a 263
Billy Sunday, the business lesson we can learn from 307
Billy Sunday's sermons, fuel for the motive to be found in one of . . 309
"BIG IDEA"
  back of five well-known advertisements, the 232
  building the 95
  how to connect "features" with the 60
  how to find the 516
  in a circular letter, the 72
  in a collection letter, the 82, 130, 131, 141
  in a follow-up campaign, a diagram of the 149
  in an inquiry letter the 58
  in a purchasing letter, the 358
  in a sales letter, the 95, 114, 116, 118–200
  of Elihu Root's address to the Russian people, the 271

"BIG IDEA" (*Continued*)
  of Ingersoll's speech, the 112, 113
  of Lincoln's Gettysburgh address, the 111, 113
"Burning stamps" 19
Byron, Lord, "words are things, etc." 220

C

Cause of most poor letters, the . 49
Character and personal strength, the backbone of 55
CHART
  analysing the needs of a circular letter 480–482
  for checking results of ideas 554
  for organizing correspondence work 505–510
  for solving letterhead problems 458–460
  size up 32
  showing the whole field of letter activities 552
Charting the "features" of a letter 65–68
CIRCULAR MAIL MATTER
  a fault frequently found in 548
  how to find new uses for your 553
Circular sales letter, size-up of a 71
Circus "barker," how he creates impulse at the critical moment 351–352
Classification of motives, why a, helps to write a letter 319
Clearness, the first essential in any letter 181
"CLOSE"
  diagram for the of a letter 375
  for a very effective follow-up letter 371–373
Code for keying letters . . . 536–537
COLLECTION LETTER
  construction process of a follow-up 149
  follow-up series 130, 131, 155–163, 326, 327
  how a slight change to a, made it yield big returns 362–365
  pride motive applied to a 328
  the "big idea" of a 82, 130, 131, 141
  the "features" of a 314
  the gain motive applied to a 355
  the negative idea in a good 129
  self-preservation applied to a 311, 326, 327, 343
  which builds up a powerful picture, a 201

BUSINESS CORRESPONDENCE

COLLECTION LETTER (*Continued*)
 with a "spineless" ending, a... .. 357
COMPLAINT LETTER
 a typical, and its answer   247–250
 Connecting link, the   133, 172
 Conviction, how to arouse   27
 Copy which pulled 36% returns and the reason behind it   269
CORRESPONDENCE WORK   503
 chart for organizing   505–510
 Coupons and return cards   380–382
 Curiosity motive, how it made two sales letters successful   305

D

Dealer cooperation, a letter unusually successful in securing   376–377
DIAGRAM
 of a follow-up campaign   149
 of "close" of sales letters   373, 375, 390 393–394
 of the negative idea, the positive idea, and the connecting link   132, 133, 136, 143, 175
 of the visionary idea and its "features"   130
 Duty motive applied to an application letter   340

E

Elements of a letter, the ten   38
Enclosure, a manufacturer's and why it pulled orders   383
ENCLOSURES   470–495
 how to figure cost of   434
 how to select the, for your letters   480
 the three types of   471
 what you should keep in mind when you plan   383
 when in a letter will fail in their purpose   479
Envelops   468
Envelop, the window   470
Enthusiasm, the knack of inspiring   29
EXPRESSION
 how to perfect ourselves in   207
 the knack of   13

F

Fear, how mystery adds to   134
Fear motive applied to a collection letter, the   311
"FEATURES"
 charting the, of a letter   65–68
 diagram of the, of a sales letter   166–168
 diagramming the, of a "big idea"   95
 how to arrange the, of a letter   189–205
 how to connect, with the "big idea"   60
 of a collection letter,   314

"FEATURES" (*Continued*)
 of a complaint letter   81
 of a letter refusing a loan   274–275
 of a sales letter   72, 75, 95, 97 101 114, 116, 118, 184, 194, 278
 of Ingersoll's speech   112 113
 of Lincoln's Gettysburg address   111, 113
 picking the, of a good sales letter   64
 selecting the, of a letter   73
 which build up a feeling of satisfaction   83, 82
Feeling or ideas, expressing, in words 53–106
Fifth letter to a debtor the method to use when writing a   325
FOLLOW-UP
 campaign, diagram of a   149
 campaigns, the basis of   143
 collection, series   155–163
 letter, a bad   7
 letter, close for a very effective   371–373
 letters 134, 136, 145, 146, 148, 155, 163
 letters, two, which failed to get across—and why   125
 series, the first four letters of a collection   150
 series, the first four letters of a sales   151–154
Form-letter index used by a complaint department   522
Form letters, the part "openers" play in 517
FORM PARAGRAPHS
 how to index   507–518
 index for, of a complaint department   522–525
Form-paragraph system, how to develop one gradually   507, 509
Formula for controlling use of letters 546–548
Friendliness in a letter, how it may be created   245, 246
Fundamentals of good letter writing, the   548

G

GAIN MOTIVE
 applied to a collection letter, the   355
 applied to a purchasing agent's letter the   342
 applied to sales letters, the   321, 324, 329 353 360, 361
Gettysburg address Lincoln's   111

H

Holman, W C, "Using the proper word"   218–219
Hugo, Victor
 his greatest description   190
 how he would have written a sales letter   195
Human actions and the influences which prompt them   293–296
"Human touch," in a banker's letter, the   263

INDEX

I

"I" point of view, the. 19
Idea, how to convey an . . 15, 69
Idea-expressing paragraphs of a sales letter 182

IDEA RECORD
how an, can be used in any business 550
how an, saved a mail-order business 557

IDEAS
chart for checking results of 554
how to "stack," in a good letter 193
or feeling, the knack of expression 15
where to get, for the letters you write 561-562

IMPULSE
how the circus "barker" creates, at the critical moment 351-352
the part it plays in making people act 351
Inactive accounts, letter to .119, 120

INDEX
a decimal, to help locate "features" of the "big idea" 515
of form paragraphs, an 514
for form paragraphs of a complaint department . . . 522-525

INDIFFERENCE
or opposition, how to overcome 21, 109-177
the line of attack against 132
Ingersoll's speech, nominating J G Blaine 110, 112
Inquiry letter, the "big idea" in an 6, 57, 58
Irving, Washington, his description of the Van Tassel farm 61-64

K

Keying letters, codes for 536-537

KNACK
of creating an imaginary ideal in the reader's mind, the 165
of expression, the 13
of inspiring enthusiasm, the 29
of sincerity, the, and how to cultivate it 281

L

LANGUAGE
how to determine the, to use 213
"of the craft." 224-228
Law of averages, the, as applied to business letters 527
Layout, four steps in preparing, for advertisement 492
Length of a letter, how to determine the 204-206
Legal requirements in order forms, how they can be made simple 379
Letter activities, chart showing the whole field of 552

LETTERHEAD
chart for solving, problems 458
how to chart the work that your, must do 459
point of view from which to study your 457
Letterheads 455, 462, 466
Lincoln's Gettysburg address.. 111

"LOAD"
of a letter, the, what it is . . 5
of a sales letter, the 100
sizing up the, a letter must carry 8
sizing up the, of a sales letter 92-94
Lord Byron, "Words are things, etc.," 220
"Lost idea" the 198
Love motive, how it may be turned to business uses 297

M

MAILING LISTS
how to keep them up to date 568
the sources of, for most businesses 565

MAILING TESTS
"parallel," how they help reduce costs 531
time required to have returns on 537
Meaning, how to make your, clear, 181, 241
Mechanical layout of booklet 485
Mental attitude, fundamental types of 518
Mental effort, how to economize the reader's. . . 75-76

MOTIVES
and ideas, the difference between 296
how to select best, for a letter 331
of human action, the six prime 306
which lead to sales, in what order they are grouped 333-334
Mutual sympathy, source of 246
Mutual understanding, finding a basis of 251
Mystery, how it adds to fear 314

N

NEGATIVE ARGUMENT
a practical test of a 121
letters 116, 119, 120, 122, 126

NEGATIVE IDEA 172
analysing the construction of the 129
diagram of the, the positive idea, and the connecting link
182, 133, 136, 143, 175
in a good collection letter, the 129

O

"One big idea"—best letters based on 49
One way of saving time on letters 507
"OPENER"
the idea behind an, in a very successful sales letter 431-432

OPENER (*Continued*)
the part an, plays in form letters ... 517
Order cards and coupons, the secret of successful ... 382
Order forms, legal requirements in, how they can be made simple ... 379
Originality, a sales letter with ... 192

P

"Parallel" tests of mailings how they help reduce costs ... 531–532
Personal strength and character, the backbone of ... 55
Personality, how to make type and paper reflect ... 211–222
PERSUASION
how to exercise ... 24–25, 293–347
"Philosophy of style, the," by Herbert Spencer ... 186
Poe, Edgar Allen, "The bells" ... 222–223
"Point of contact, finding a with a prospect ... 247
Poor letters, the cause of most ... 49
Positive idea, conveying the ... 129
Power of suggestion, the ... 356
Pride motive applied to a collection letter ... 328
Principles to apply to a sales letter series the ... 327
Psychology, practical ... 362
"Puller" of results, the best ... 29
Pulling power, how to test a letter as to its ... 526–527

PURCHASING LETTER
gain motive applied to a ... 342
how it put its "big idea" across ... 358–359

Q

Quality of letters, what contributes most to improve ... 49

R

Reply blanks, how to make your get best results ... 377
"Restaurant" letter ... 258, 339, 391
Retailer's letter which beams with frankness, a ... 255–256
Return cards and coupons ... 380–382
Right word, how to choose the ... 211–222
Root, Elihu his address to the Russian people ... 271–273

S

Sales follow-up, construction process of a ... 149
SALES LETTER
an unusually good ... 99
appealing to the love motive ... 298
building a ... 64–68
building up a close to a successful ... 369–371

SALES LETTER (*Continued*)
clever, using the thrift motive ... 324
diagram of the "big idea" of a ... 166–168
"features" of a ... 194, 278
gain motive applied to a ... 321, 324, 329, 353, 360–361
idea-expressing paragraphs of a ... 182
picking the "features" of a good ... 64
pleasure motive applied to a ... 304
self-indulgence motive applied to a ... 317
self-preservation motive applied to a ... 332
series the principles to apply to a ... 327–328
size up of a ... 35
that arouses the curiosity motive, a ... 156
that creates mutual understanding and sympathy, a ... 252
that brought the orders rolling in, a ... 423–424
that handles the "you" element tactfully, a ... 255
that is a splendid example of clear expression, a ... 214
that leaves too much mental work to the reader, a ... 202
very successful, with diagram of its "features ... 132
with a good negative approach, a ... 87
with its "features" listed, a ... 97
which lacked punch—why it failed ... 297
which hooks the reader in the first paragraph, a ... 251–252

SALES LETTERS
diagram of close of ... 393
how curiosity as a motive made two, successful ... 305
that gripped attention ... 401–403
Sales manager's letter to a salesman ... 139
Saxon English, superiority of ... 216
"Scout letter," a successful ... 563

SELF-INDULGENCE MOTIVE
applied to a letter soliciting trade ... 337
applied to a sales letter ... 317
how to use it ... 308
Self-interest, how to create ... 11–12

SELF-PRESERVATION MOTIVE
applied to a collection letter ... 311, 326–327, 345
applied to a real estate operator's letter ... 368–369
applied to a sales letter ... 332
Selling campaign, how a local, indicates the trend of the market ... 529–530
Shakespeare, "A word is short and quick, etc.," ... 220

SINCERITY
expressing ... 243–289
the knack of, and how to cultivate it ... 281
Size and shape of letters and envelops— how decided ... 469

INDEX

SIZE UP
chart 32
of a letter from an "oil man" 42
of a letter granting a loan 78
of a letter refusing a loan 37
of a circular letter 71, 100
of a sales letter 85
Sizing up the work your letter must do 1–49
Slow-pay customer, the best method of attacking the 333
Slow pay, first steps in handling a 84
Soliciting trade, letter 215
Sources of letter material talking points, as compiled by SYSTEM 564
Spencer, Herbert 'The philosophy of style' 186
Spencer's essay on style 216

STATIONERY
size and shape of 469

"STOPPER"
how to plan a, for your letter 413–414
linking up a to the big idea of a sales letter 422
picking the, which will attract your prospects 408
that begins its work on the outside of the envelop, a 435–436
which drew the attention of women readers, a 415–416
Suggestion, the power of 356

T

Talking points, sources of letter material, as compiled by SYSTEM 564

Test, of a letter, the 306

TESTING LETTERS
organizing correspondence work and 503–541
"The bells," Edgar Allan Poe 222–223
Trend of the market, how a local selling campaign indicates the 529–530
Trust how to create liking and, in a letter 207
Type and paper how to make, reflect your personality 464

V

VISIONARY APPROACH 117–121, 172
diagram for the 128
Vocabulary, how to adapt your, to the individual 228

W

Window envelop the 420
WORD FILE 225–228
a new use for the 507–509
Words, the choice of 211
Why many letters fail 13

Y

"You and I" talk 270
"YOU ELEMENT
a sales letter that handles the, tactfully 255
putting the, into letters 257–260

CPSIA information can be obtained
at www.ICGtesting.com
Printed in the USA
BVHW042342210421
605537BV00003B/86